This copy of

FUNDAMENTALS OF MARKETING

is from the library of

SIXTH
CANADIAN
EDITION

FUNDAMENTALS OF
MARKETING

SIXTH

CANADIAN

EDITION

FUNDAMENTALS OF
Marketing

Montrose S. Sommers

University of Guelph

James G. Barnes

Memorial University of Newfoundland

William J. Stanton

University of Colorado

Michael J. Etzel

University of Notre Dame

Bruce J. Walker

University of Missouri-Columbia

McGRAW-HILL RYERSON LIMITED

Toronto   Montreal   New York   Auckland   Bogotá
Caracas   Lisbon   London   Madrid   Mexico   Milan
New Delhi   Paris   San Juan   Singapore   Sydney
Tokyo

FUNDAMENTALS OF MARKETING
Sixth Canadian Edition

ISBN: 0-07-551288-2

1 2 3 4 5 6 7 8 9 0   RRD   1 0 9 8 7 6 5 4 3 2

Printed and bound in the United States of America

Care has been taken to trace ownership of copyright material
contained in this text. The Publisher will gladly take any information
that will enable them to rectify any reference or credit in subsequent
editions.

SPONSORING EDITOR: Kelly Smyth
PRODUCTION EDITOR/COPY EDITOR: Wendy Thomas
PROOFREADER: Monica Penner
PERMISSIONS EDITOR: Norma Christensen
COVER AND TEXT DESIGN: Matthews Communications Design
PRINTING AND BINDING: R.R. Donnelley (Canada) Limited

Canadian Cataloguing in Publication Data
  Main entry under title:

  Fundamentals of marketing

  6th Canadian ed.
  Includes index.
  ISBN 0-07-551288-2

  1. Marketing. I. Sommers, Montrose S., 1933–

  HF5415.F85 1992   658.8   C91-095727-4

Dedicated to

Jesse, Annie, and Michael
Jennifer, Stephanie, and
Karen

CONTENTS IN BRIEF

CONTENTS

KEEPING PACE WITH THE DYNAMIC MARKETPLACE

In preparing the sixth edition of our textbook, we have had a number of goals in mind. In the first place, we wanted to make sure that the material was as current as possible, thereby providing students and instructors with up-to-date information on the place of marketing in Canadian organizations. Secondly, we wished to ensure that the content of this book reflects the changes that are currently taking place in marketing in this country. Consequently, you will see a great deal of attention paid to the impact of forces such as international trade, technology, and demographic change, on how marketers will be able to function as we move through the 1990s. Finally, we wanted to produce a practical book. We believe that students and instructors who use this book will find it interesting because it reflects the way marketing is actually practised by Canadian organizations.

To achieve these goals, many changes have been made to reflect the dynamic nature of marketing. New concepts have been introduced, established concepts have been expanded and updated, and current developments have been emphasized. We have added new material and chapters to reflect the way in which marketing is developing.

To achieve our goal of presenting Canadian marketing as it will be practised through the 1990s, we have restructured and revised major sections of the book. This will be most obvious through our move to 22 chapters from 20 and the reorganization of chapters and parts. This edition will provide comprehensive coverage of the essential topics of marketing that have been covered in depth in our previous editions, as well as a thorough discussion of emerging concepts in marketing. It is designed to be a superior learning tool, a pleasure to read and to learn from.

The changes reflected in this sixth edition have been based to a very great extent on feedback that we have received from instructors who have been using our earlier editions in universities and colleges across Canada. We appreciate this feedback and the contribution it has made to our revision.

WHAT'S DIFFERENT ABOUT THIS EDITION?

DESIGN

The sixth edition carries forward the dramatic changes we incorporated into our fifth edition. This edition has been specially designed to be visually appealing, easy to read, and exciting. Through our use of colour photographs and advertisements, and the graphs and illustrations to communicate concepts and information, we have tried to make this a book that is not only easy to read but interesting, and even fun.

ORGANIZATION

While we have continued to integrate current marketing topics throughout the text, we have responded to feedback from instructors and have included separate chapters in this edition dedicated to the important topics of Services Marketing and International Marketing. We have continued to integrate into all of our chapters concepts and illustrations on these topics and on other areas such as business-to-business marketing and nonprofit marketing. This is done for the most part through our use of Marketing at Work Files, which are to be found in increased numbers in all chapters.

NEW AND EXPANDED TOPICS

We have added much new material in this edition, reflecting the expanded application of marketing and its increased importance in many organizations. We have added new chapters on Services Marketing and International Marketing; the first reflects the growing importance being attached by marketers to the area of services, and the second reflects the fact that the global marketplace is undergoing rapid change and Canadian business must pay increasing attention to competition from abroad and to opportunities to export products and services to foreign markets. In addition, we have reinforced the strategic orientation of this text, through the expansion of our coverage of such important strategic concepts as market segmentation and positioning.

CANADIAN APPLICATIONS

We continue in this edition our emphasis on ensuring that the text is completely Canadian in its orientation and content. We have included in this edition new chapter openers and more than 100 Marketing at Work Files, liberally sprinkled throughout the chapters. These vignettes deal with what is happening at this moment in Canadian marketing. Each represents an example of an issue or an interesting situation that is facing a Canadian business or not-for-profit organization. These specific examples, coupled with the hundreds of Canadian companies, products, and brands referenced in the text, make this a book that Canadian students will find especially interesting and relevant to their own situations.

NEW CASES

This edition contains 18 new cases, almost all of which have been written especially for this text. Most deal with actual businesses with which students will be quite familiar. Many of these cases have been written in a two-part format, providing for interesting discussion of a marketing problem and of the action the company took to address it. We have retained from our fifth edition the five-part series of cases on Upper Canada Brewing. This case has been very popular with students and instructors because it gives them an opportunity to follow a company through a series of decisions on each of the elements of the marketing mix.

THE BOOK: ITS BASIC APPROACH

Those familiar with the earlier editions will find that, although some major changes have certainly been made, we have retained the essential features that have made this book an outstanding teaching and learning resource. The writing style continues to make the material interesting and easy to read. The basic organization is appropriate in that it reflects new developments as well as the needs of students and instructors. Material flows logically with a section-heading structure that makes for easier reading and outlining.

PEDAGOGICAL FEATURES

We provide many excellent end-of-chapter discussion questions. Most of these are thought-provoking and involve the application of text material rather than simply its recollection. Each of the 26 cases focuses on a topic covered in the text and provides students with an opportunity to apply concepts, practise analysis, and learn decision making.

We have also retained and updated such teaching and learning features as chapter objectives, chapter summaries, marketing arithmetic appendix, and the glossary. The key terms and concepts are summarized in a list at the end of each chapter with a page reference for the first mention.

"A TOTAL SYSTEM"

The central theme and approach has also been retained from previous editions — that marketing is a total system of business action, rather than a fragmented assortment of functions and institutions. To us, this means that the essential marketing ideas are what matters, not lists of terms and functions or specialized formula approaches. While attention is paid to the role of marketing in our system, the book is written largely from the perspective of marketing personnel in an individual organization. This organization may be a manufacturer, a service provider, or an intermediary in a business or non-business field.

The marketing concept is a philosophy that stresses the need for a marketing orientation compatible with society's long-run interests. This philosophy is evident in the framework of the strategic marketing planning process. A company sets its marketing objectives, taking into consideration the environmental forces that influence its marketing effort. Management next selects target markets. The company then has four strategic elements — its product, price structure, distribution systems, and promotional activities — with which to build a marketing program to reach its markets and achieve its objectives. In all stages of the marketing process, management should use marketing research as a tool for problem solving and decision making.

TOPIC SEQUENCE

This framework for the strategic marketing planning process is reflected generally in the organization of the book's content. The text is divided into seven parts. Part 1 serves as an introduction and includes chapters on the marketing environment and strategic marketing planning. Part 2 is devoted to the analysis and selection of target markets — either consumer or business markets. It includes marketing information systems.

Parts 3 through 6 deal with the development of a marketing program, and each of these parts covers one of the above-mentioned components of the stategic marketing mix. In Part 3 various topics related to the product are discussed, including a separate chapter on services. The company's price structure is the subject of Part 4, and Part 5 covers the distribution system. Part 6 is devoted to the total promotional program, including advertising, personal selling, and sales promotion. Part 7 deals with the implementation and evaluation of the total marketing effort in an individual firm and contains a new chapter on international marketing. It also includes an appraisal of the role of marketing in our society, including the subjects of consumer criticisms and the social responsibility of an organization.

TEACHING AND LEARNING SUPPLEMENTS

This textbook is the central element in a complete package of teaching and learning resources that have been completely revised and considerably expanded for this edition. The package includes the following supplements:

- A *study guide* for students provides chapter outlines, test questions, real-world cases for each chapter, and exercises that involve the students in practical marketing experiences.

- A *book of readings* contains a series of recent real-world marketing articles.
- A *set of video cassettes* highlights well-known companies and provides insights into the firms' marketing strategies. These video segments, which range in length from 10 to 25 minutes, complement and extend the text discussion.
- A set of *Lotus spreadsheet exercises* consists of text-related problems adaptable for use on *IBM and IBM compatible* personal computers.
- A *simulation* is available for use on *IBM and IBM compatible* personal computers. This ''computer game'' is a straightforward one-product simulation calling for a series of marketing decisions.
- An *instructor's manual* provides lecture outlines for each chapter, including many real-world examples not found in the text. This manual also includes commentaries on the end-of-chapter questions, the 26 cases, and the exercises in the student study guide.
- A collection of more than 200 full-colour *transparencies,* most of which are *not* in the text, is available to adopters.
- *Slides* of all transparencies are available to adopters who prefer this alternative to overhead transparencies.
- A *test bank* includes an extensive assortment of multiple-choice, true-false, and short-answer fill-in questions for each chapter. All questions are categorized by difficulty, and the page in the text where the rationale for the correct answer appears is presented for each question. This test bank also is available for IBM compatible computers.
- Our newsletter is designed with instructors in mind. *Sommers and Barnes On Marketing* is published annually to help fill your need for current examples and applications. Suggestions are welcome!
- The Annual Case Update exhibits our commitment to instructors, providing them with additional cases and updates on cases already in the text.
- McGraw-Hill Ryerson and CBC's ''Venture'' have collaborated to provide *a professionally produced marketing video,* which ties segments from the ''Venture'' series to a variety of marketing concepts and applications from the text. It comes with suggestions for classroom use.
- A *video of award-winning television commercials* is available and demonstrates the efforts of and talent behind many Canadian companies cited in the text.

ACKNOWLEDGE-MENTS

Through six editions, many people have made important contributions to the content of this book. These include our students, colleagues, business people, and instructors at many universities and colleges. They have offered their comments and suggestions, which we have incorporated into each new edition.

We wish to acknowledge in particular those research assistants who participated in the preparation of cases and appendices for this edition: Bernita Kiefte, Leanne O'Leary, Robert Power, and Leigh Puddester. We are also indebted to the many business people who cooperated in allowing us to write cases on their companies. They are acknowledged specifically in the notes attached to each case. Their contribution is most important in that they have enabled us to ensure that this book has a real-life orientation.

We would like to express our gratitude to the following Canadian instructors for their thorough and thoughtful reviews of the manuscript in various draft forms.

Henry Klaise, *Durham College*; Neal Beattie, *Sheridan College*; Bill Lucas, *Mohawk College*; Vinay Kanetkar, *University of Toronto*; Gary Dover, *Georgian College*; John McColl, *Humber College*; Pat Kolodziejski, *Mohawk College*; Mary Ann Cipriano, *McGill University*; Douglas Smith, *British Columbia Institute of Technology*; David Chin, *University of Regina*; John Murray, *Humber College*; Ted Brown, *Mt. Royal College*; Gorden Jones, *Sheridan College*; Bill Wellington, *University of Windsor*; Ann Walker, *Ryerson Polytechnical Institute*; Harvey Skolnick, *Sheridan College*; D.W. Greeno, *University of Toronto*; Wayne Carlson, *Southern Alberta Institute of Technology*; and M.L. Huebner, *Seneca College*.

We also thank most sincerely those instructors and students across Canada who have provided helpful suggestions for improvements over almost 20 years since our first edition was published. We would, of course, welcome feedback on this edition as well.

Hundreds of Canadian companies supplied us with photos, videos, advertisements, and other materials that we have incorporated into this book. They are far too numerous to list here, but their input is essential to ensuring that this text is as current, practical and realistic as possible.

Finally, we would like to acknowledge with much appreciation the support and cooperation we receive from the staff of McGraw-Hill Ryerson. In particular, we thank Kelly Smyth, our sponsoring editor, who really ensured that everything came together and tried her best to keep us on schedule. Special thanks also to Wendy Thomas, Susan Calvert, Norma Christensen, Laurie Graham, Betty Tustin, and Sharon Matthews, all of whom did so much to make sure that this edition continues in a tradition of excellence in teaching and learning.

Montrose S. Sommers
James G. Barnes

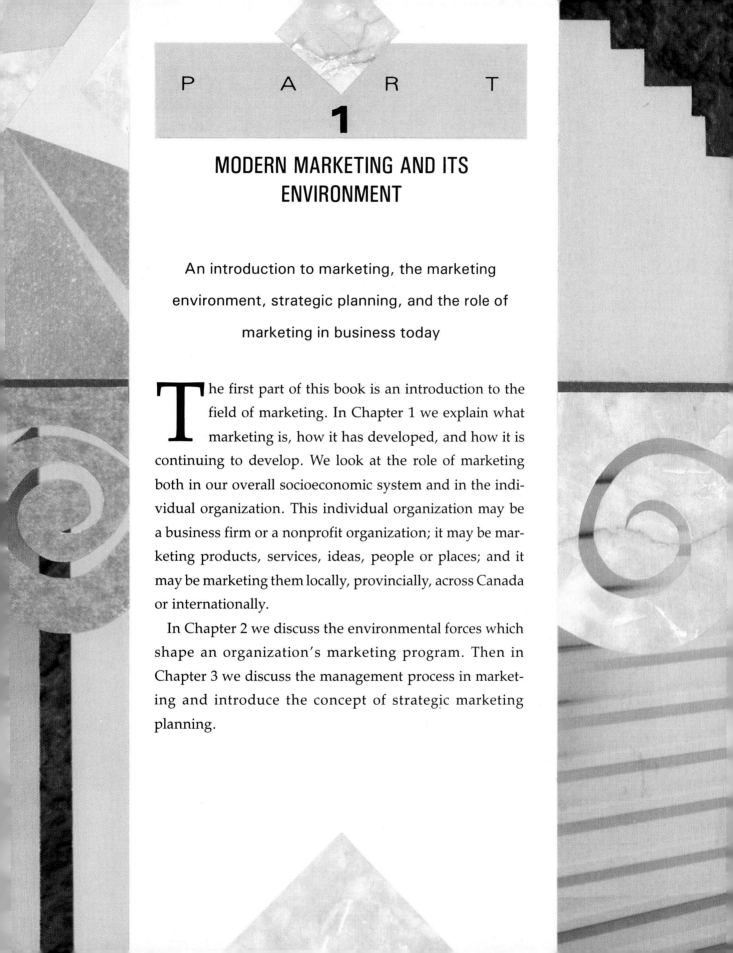

P A R T
1

MODERN MARKETING AND ITS ENVIRONMENT

An introduction to marketing, the marketing environment, strategic planning, and the role of marketing in business today

The first part of this book is an introduction to the field of marketing. In Chapter 1 we explain what marketing is, how it has developed, and how it is continuing to develop. We look at the role of marketing both in our overall socioeconomic system and in the individual organization. This individual organization may be a business firm or a nonprofit organization; it may be marketing products, services, ideas, people or places; and it may be marketing them locally, provincially, across Canada or internationally.

In Chapter 2 we discuss the environmental forces which shape an organization's marketing program. Then in Chapter 3 we discuss the management process in marketing and introduce the concept of strategic marketing planning.

CHAPTER 1 GOALS

''What is marketing?''
Chapter 1 answers this
question—and the answer
may surprise you. After
studying this chapter, you
should be able to explain:

- The meaning of marketing
  —its broad definition and
  business-system
  definition.
- The importance of
  marketing in the global
  economy, in the Canadian
  economy, in an individual
  organization, and to you
  personally.
- The marketing concept.
- The difference between
  selling and marketing.
- The four-stage evolution of
  marketing management.
- The broadened view of the
  marketing concept.

1

The Field of Marketing

The race through the 1990s to the year 2000 is tough, turbulent, and not for the timid — you may feel you are being asked to walk on water. The race is tough because we are dealing with increased levels of competition from other Canadian firms, from American firms newly active in Canada, from Japanese, Korean, Dutch, French, Brazilian, and many others from more and more countries around the world. The race is turbulent because environmental challenges, technological changes, and political shifts are coming at us so fast that if you don't know where to look, your head will spin. Tough and turbulent together mean there is no place to hide, no gains for being timid, no time to be defensive. The 1990s are the most challenging times ever for business. And business needs people who recognize the issues, react to the excitement of the times, and develop themselves and their careers to meet the challenges.

What does it take? Some job placement consultants believe you almost have to be able to walk on water. By this they mean that although it's satisfactory to be a technical genius or a financial whiz, it's better to be both — and more. If you are forward looking, can identify change and adjust to it quickly, and develop a broad range of experience, you are well on your way to developing your career to meet the new challenges. The consultants believe you will need to learn more about business in general and, specifically, more about marketing and finance, the twin pillars of all organizations. And it's important to be able to understand people, think strategically, and communicate well. And where do you get these skills and knowledge? According to the consultants, you can get a lot of what you need to walk on water by having a strong ''customer orientation'' in whatever you do. That is, you have to understand the core of marketing and the core of this book. Those with a background in activities that bring them in close contact with customers — including sales, marketing research, and customer service — are best able to fight and win the battles of this decade. You know by now that the customer orientation experience by itself will not guarantee that you successfully finish the race through the 1990s. But without marketing and its customer orientation, you're not in the race at all.[1]

---

[1]Adapted from Randall Litchfield, ''They Walk on Water,'' *Canadian Business*, September, 1990, pp. 46–49.

NATURE AND SCOPE OF MARKETING

In a business firm, marketing generates the revenues that are managed by the financial people and used by the production people in creating products and services. The challenge of marketing is to generate those revenues by satisfying customers' wants at a profit and in a socially responsible manner.

Broad Dimensions of Marketing

But marketing is not limited to business. Whenever you try to persuade somebody to do something—donate to the Salvation Army, fasten a seat belt, lower a stereo's noise during study hours, vote for your candidate, accept a date with you (or maybe even marry you) — you are using marketing ideas and engaging in a marketing activity. So-called nonbusiness organizations — they really are in business but don't think of themselves as such — also engage in marketing. Their ''product'' may be a vacation place they want you to visit, a social cause or an idea they want you to support, a person they are thrusting

Marketing includes getting new members.

THE FOURTH
PROTOCOL

While etiquette calls for a momentary hush when teeing off from the 4th at King Valley, it certainly permits a triumphant hurrah for the well-placed drive.

From the spectacular elevated tee, one would do well to steer clear of the large pond flanking the left side of the fairway. And it is recommended to follow-up with an exacting iron shot to negotiate the small green nestled between two ponds.

Of course, ultimately the golfer is free to do as he or she wishes. But beware — it's a hole that will only grudgingly yield par, no matter how diplomatically or daringly it is played.

To obtain further information or an appointment and private showing of this exceptional course, located just 30 minutes north of Toronto, contact our Membership Secretary.

(416) 841-9262

M A R K E T I N G   A T   W O R K

FILE 1-1   CARE CANADA DEVELOPS WITH MARKETING

The use of marketing ideas in nonbusiness organizations is illustrated through an advertisement recently placed in national newspapers by CARE Canada. This not-for-profit organization, which directs aid and development funding to Third World countries, advertised for a Fund Raising and Marketing Manager. The successful applicant was to be part of the senior management team and his or her duties would include liaison with the media; the acquisition, retention, renewal, and upgrading of donors; the management of fund-raising programs including direct mail, special events, in memoriam and anniversary giving, gift clubs, sponsorships, memberships and telemarketing; and supporting activities including strategic planning, volunteer and paid personnel motivation, and management, research, and analysis. Why does CARE Canada need a marketing manager? What ''exchanges'' is CARE Canada interested in stimulating? What is its ''product''?

into the spotlight, or a museum or gallery they want you to attend. Whatever the product is, the organization is using marketing ideas and is engaging in marketing.

As you may gather, marketing is a very broad-based activity, and consequently, it calls for a broad definition. **Now the essence of marketing is a transaction—an exchange—intended to satisfy human needs and wants.** That is, marketing occurs any time one social unit (person or organization) strives to exchange something of value with another social unit. Our broad definition then is as follows:

Marketing consists of all activities designed to generate and facilitate any exchange intended to satisfy human needs or wants.[2]

CONCEPT OF EXCHANGE

Now let's examine the concept of **exchange** as this term relates to marketing. Exchange is one of three ways in which a person can satisfy a want. Suppose you want some clothes. You can sew them, knit them, or otherwise produce the clothes yourself. You can borrow them or use some form of coercion to get the clothes. Or you can offer something of value (money, service, other products) to another person who will voluntarily exchange the clothes for what you offer. It is only the third approach that we call an exchange in the sense that marketing is taking place.

Within the context of our definition of marketing, for an exchange to occur the following conditions must exist:

 1. Two or more social units (individuals or organizations) must be involved.

---

[2]In this book the terms *needs* and *wants* are used interchangeably. In a limited physiological sense, we might say that we ''need'' only food, clothing, and shelter. Beyond these requirements we get into the area of ''wants.'' More realistically in our society today, however, many people would say that they ''need'' a telephone or they ''need'' some form of mechanized transportation.

If you are totally self-sufficient in some area, there is no exchange and hence no marketing.

2. The parties must be involved voluntarily, and each must have wants to be satisfied.

3. Each party must have something of value to contribute in the exchange, and each party must believe it will benefit from the exchange.

4. The parties must be able to communicate with each other. Assume that you want a new sweater and a clothing store has sweaters for sale. But if you and the store are not aware of each other—you are not communicating —then there will be no exchange.

Within this broad definition of marketing, then, (1) the marketers, (2) what they are marketing, and (3) their potential markets all assume broad dimensions. The category of **marketers** might include, in addition to business firms, such diverse social units as (a) a political party trying to market its candidate to the public; (b) the director of an art museum providing new exhibits to generate greater attendance and financial support; (c) a labour union marketing its ideas to members and to the company management; and (d) professors trying to make their courses interesting for students.

In addition to the range of items normally considered as products and services, **what is being marketed** might include (a) *ideas*, such as reducing air pollution or contributing to a charity; (b) *people*, such as a new football coach or a political candidate; and (c) *places*, such as industrial plant sites or a place to go for a vacation; and (d) *events*, such as musical, political, or social programs or gatherings.

In a broad sense, **markets** include more than the direct consumers of products, services, and ideas. Thus a college's or university's market includes the legislators who provide funds, the citizens living nearby who may be affected

The not-for-profit market of a telethon.

Watch a miracle happen.

The Hospital For Sick Children Foundation Telethon on CFTO-TV. June 2 & 3.

by student activities, and the alumni. A business firm's market may include government regulatory agencies, environmentalists, and municipal tax assessors.

Business Dimensions of Marketing

Our broad (or macro) definition tells us something about the pervasive role of marketing in our country. But this is a book about the business of marketing in an individual organization. These organizations may be business firms in the conventional sense of the word *business*. Or they may be what is called a nonbusiness or a nonprofit organization—a hospital, university, Big Brothers, church, police department, or museum, for example. Both groups—business and nonbusiness—face essentially the same basic marketing problems and can make use of the same marketing ideas.

Now many executives in those organizations, as well as many household consumers, think they already know a good bit about the business of marketing. After all, churches run newspaper ads and museums sell prints of famous paintings. And people at home watch television commercials that persuade them to buy. These people purchase products on a self-service basis in supermarkets. Some have friends who ''can get it for them wholesale.'' But in each of these examples, we are talking about only one part of the totality of marketing activities. Consequently, we need a micro, business definition of marketing to guide decision makers in business or non-business organizations in the management of their marketing effort.

BUSINESS DEFINITION OF MARKETING

Our micro definition of marketing—applicable in a business or nonbusiness organization—is:

Marketing is a total system of business activities designed to plan, price, promote, and distribute want-satisfying products, services, and ideas to target markets in order to achieve organizational objectives.[3]

Marketing is:	
a system:	for business activities
designed to:	plan, price, promote, and distribute
something of value:	want-satisfying products, services, and ideas
for the benefit of:	the target market—present and potential household consumers or business users
to achieve:	the organization's objectives.

This definition has some significant implications:

- It is a managerial, systems definition.
- The entire system of business activities must be customer-oriented. Customers' wants must be recognized and satisfied effectively.
- The marketing program starts with the germ of a product or service idea

---

[3]This definition is essentially the same as the one used in all previous editions of this book. We modified our original definition slightly to conform generally with a revised American Marketing Association definition. The AMA definition is as follows: ''Marketing is the process of planning and executing the conception, pricing, promotion, and distribution of ideas, goods, and services to create exchanges that satisfy individual and organizational objectives.'' See Peter D. Bennett, ed., *Dictionary of Marketing Terms*, American Marketing Association Chicago, 1988, p. 115.

and does not end until the customer's wants are completely satisfied, which may be some time after the sale is made.

- The definition implies that to be successful, marketing must maximize profitable sales over the *long run*. Thus, customers must be satisfied in order for a company to get the repeat business that ordinarily is so vital to success.

It should be noted that the above definitions, as well as most others commonly used, always include products, services, and ideas in their scope. As a "shorthand," however, products are most frequently referred to and, to a lesser extent, products and services. In fact, the term *product* is now being used in a broader sense than in the past. It stands for various combinations of product, service, and ideas—what could be termed a product/service complex. No longer is it uncommon to hear the term product being used to refer to a "product complex" that consists primarily of services.

From a management perspective, the marketing program comprises four elements known as the organization's marketing mix. The marketing mix consists of (1) an organization's product or service assortment, (2) its pricing structure, (3) the distribution systems used, and (4) the promotional activities. The activities and elements of the marketing mix are continually being reviewed and tested for appropriateness and degree of co-ordination. The marketing mix is expanded upon in Chapter 3 in the discussion of marketing planning.

PRESENT-DAY IMPORTANCE OF MARKETING

Today all nations — regardless of their degree of economic development or their political philosophy — recognize the importance of marketing ideas and activities. Economic growth in developing nations depends greatly upon their ability to develop effective distribution systems to handle their raw materials and their industrial and consumer output. Countries with some major state-owned industries are looking to privatization and modern marketing practices as a way to improve their economic health. The formerly communist countries are vigorously implementing marketing ideas and marketing activities to improve their products and domestic distribution systems and to compete more effectively in international markets. Today, then, there is an explosion in the field of marketing all over the world and many countries contribute to the growth of marketing ideas and improved marketing activities.

Importance in the Canadian Socioeconomic System

In Canada, modern marketing came of age after World War I, when the words *surplus* and *overproduction* became an important part of the economics vocabulary. This is in spite of the fact that the Hudson's Bay Company was incorporated in 1670. Since about 1920, except during World War II and the immediate postwar period, a strong *buyers' market* has existed. That is, the available supply of products and services has far surpassed effective demand. There has been relatively little difficulty in producing most goods. The real problem has been in marketing them. During recession periods, business people soon realize that it is a slowdown in consumption that forces cutbacks in production. It becomes evident that "nothing happens until somebody buys something."

The importance of marketing in the business world might be more easily understood in quantitative terms. *Between one-fourth and one-third of the civilian labour force is engaged in marketing activities.* Furthermore, over the past century, jobs in marketing have increased at a much more rapid rate than jobs in

MARKETING AT WORK

FILE 1-2   **GLOBALIZATION AND MARKETING**

One of the most overused words of today is ''globalization.'' You hear it from everyone all the time. The world is shrinking — compete globally! But what does it mean?

Catherine Johnson, in a study prepared for the Conference Board of Canada, described globalization as the increasing interdependence and inter-connectiveness of national economies, including consumers, suppliers, competitors, and markets in general. This means that for everyday marketing in Canada, more and more attention is being paid to how consumers from different countries respond to various products and services and their supporting price, promotion, and distribution. Knowing these global marketing facts helps you to be successful in Canada.

The other side of the coin, as John Fraser, president and CEO of Winnipeg's Federal Industries Ltd., puts it is that if companies have been successful in their home markets, they have every reason to believe that they can be successful in foreign countries' markets. It's a matter of attitudes. For example, McCain Foods, based on its early Eastern Canadian success, was marketing in Britain before it was marketing in British Columbia.

Adapted from the editorial ''What's Involved in Going Global,'' *Financial Post*, May 7, 1990, p. 18.

---

production. The great increase in the number of marketing workers is a reflection of marketing's expanded role in the economy and the increased demand for marketing services.

Another measure of the importance of marketing is its cost. On the average, about *50 cents of each dollar we spend at the retail level goes to cover marketing costs*. These costs should not be confused with marketing *profits*, however. Nor should it be assumed that products and services would cost less if there were no marketing activities.

AN ECONOMY OF ABUNDANCE AND ITS PROBLEMS

Ours is an economy of abundance in comparison with many economies around the world. This means that as a nation, we produce and consume far beyond our subsistence needs. Although marketing exists in every type of *modern* economy, it is especially important for successful business performance in a highly competitive economy of abundance.

Marketing activity has the task of encouraging the consumption of our output of goods and services at home as well as abroad. Although modern marketing has been successful, its success has also created problems. Many social and economic resources are scarce and are becoming more so. A number of respected students of social, economic, and environmental systems have raised serious questions concerning the influence that marketing has on the allocation of these resources and their environmental effects. The question they raise is whether too much marketing is leading to a misallocation of resources. Is marketing accepting its responsibility to guide our use of resources towards socially desirable goals? We may be so successful in marketing automobiles and fashionable clothing that we overlook more basic values, such as the provision of education and housing, and the elimination of pollution. In other words, are we marketing the wrong things or the wrong way or both?

Importance in the Individual Firm

Responsible marketing should be the most critical factor guiding all short-range and long-range planning in any organization, for two reasons. First, the core of marketing is customer want-satisfaction, and that is the basic social and economic justification for the existence of virtually all organizations. Second, marketing is the revenue-generating activity in any organization—nothing happens until somebody buys something.

Too often, unfortunately, business has been oriented towards production. Products are designed by engineers, manufactured by production people, priced by accountants, and then given to sales managers to sell. That procedure generally won't work with today's intense competition, constant change and environmental concerns. Just *building* a good product will not result in a company's success, nor will it have much bearing on consumer welfare. The product must be *marketed* to consumers in a responsible way before its full value can be realized. The consumer of the nineties demands this.

Today a company must first determine what the nineties' customers want and then build a product and marketing program to satisfy those wants, hopefully at a profit. Many organizational departments in a company are essential to its growth, *but marketing is still the sole revenue-producing activity*. This fact sometimes is overlooked by the production managers who use these revenues and by the financial executives who manage them.

McDonald's Canada brings marketing to Moscow.

MARKETING AT WORK

FILE 1-3   **REAL PRODUCTS ARE FOR REAL USERS**

A production orientation in business and other organizations is illustrated by a disregard for or lack of attention to the customer or other people upon whom the organization must rely if it is to prosper. For example, when most of Canada's food companies develop new products in their test kitchens, they normally go through a very elaborate series of research projects to determine whether the test products are acceptable to target consumers. Failure to do so amounts to producing whatever the plant is able to turn out, without any regard for whether the consumer finds it attractive or wants to buy it. For several years, a small manufacturer of ice-cream snack items asked family members of employees to try new products that the company was considering adding to its product line. The company also occasionally sent samples to local Cub and Brownie groups. They were confident that their product development process was a sound one, because they rarely received any complaints about the new products. Did this ice-cream manufacturer have a marketing orientation?

Importance to You

Okay, so marketing is important globally, in our economy, and in an individual organization. But why should you study marketing? What's in it for you? There are a number of reasons: First, the study of marketing should be interesting and exciting to you because you are participating in marketing in so

Is a tire just a tire?

GIVE YOUR HORSES FREE REIN.

XP2000 Series

GENERAL TIRE
Sooner or later, you'll own Generals.

many of your daily activities. You buy various articles in different stores. You watch television with its advertising commercials, and you read magazines and newspaper ads. As a student, you are part of your school's market and you might complain about the price (tuition) of the service (education) that you are receiving. Truly, marketing occupies a large part of your daily life. If you doubt this, just imagine for a moment where you would be if there were no marketing institutions—no retail stores, no advertising to give you information, etc.

A second reason for your studying marketing is to make you a better-informed consumer. When you buy a product, you'll understand something of the company's pricing or branding strategy. You'll understand the role of promotion and the role of middlemen (retailers and wholesalers) in distribution.

The third reason for studying marketing ties in with your career aspirations. If you plan a career in marketing, then of course you are interested in what we have to say—and particularly in the career section at the end of this chapter. Those of you who plan a career in accounting, finance, or some other business field can learn how marketing affects managerial decision making in your field. Finally, some of you may seek a career in a nonbusiness field. You may work in the field of music, psychology, health care, government, education, social work, etc. It is highly likely that organizations in any of those fields will be involved in marketing.

EVOLUTION OF MARKETING

The foundations of marketing in Canada were laid in pioneer times when French-speaking and then English-speaking settlers traded (exchanged) among themselves and also with the various groups of native peoples. Some settlers even became retailers, wholesalers, and itinerant peddlers. Since then, marketing has evolved through three stages of development. But to understand the *general* evolution of marketing, it is necessary to understand the difference between marketing and selling.

Difference between Marketing and Selling Orientations

Many people, including some executives, still do not understand the difference between a selling orientation and a marketing orientation. In fact, many think they are synonymous. However, as shown below, there are vast differences between the two activities.

Selling Orientation		Marketing Orientation
Emphasis is on the product.	vs.	Emphasis is on customers' wants.
Company first makes the product and then figures out how to sell it.	vs.	Company first determines customers' wants and then figures out how to make and deliver a product to satisfy those wants.
Management is sales-volume-oriented.	vs.	Management is profit-oriented.
Planning is short-run-oriented, in terms of today's products and markets.	vs.	Planning is long-run-oriented, in terms of new products, tomorrow's markets, and future growth.
Stresses needs of seller.	vs.	Stresses needs and wants of buyers.

When a selling orientation is used, a company makes a product and then persuades customers to buy it. In effect, the firm attempts to alter consumer demand to fit the firm's potential supply of the product. When a marketing

FIGURE 1-1
The three stages of marketing evolution.

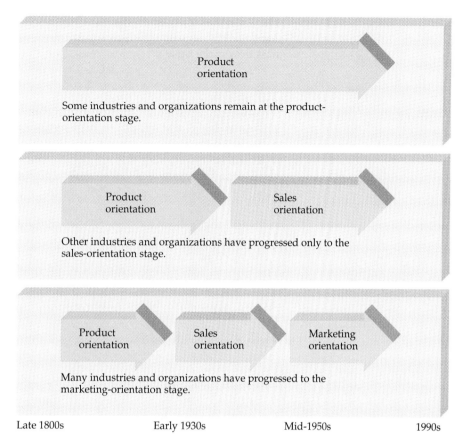

Product orientation

Some industries and organizations remain at the product-orientation stage.

Product orientation   Sales orientation

Other industries and organizations have progressed only to the sales-orientation stage.

Product orientation   Sales orientation   Marketing orientation

Many industries and organizations have progressed to the marketing-orientation stage.

Late 1800s   Early 1930s   Mid-1950s   1990s

orientation is practised, a much different approach is taken. The firm finds out what the customer wants and then develops a product that will satisfy that need and still yield a satisfactory profit. In this case, the company adjusts its supply to the will of consumer demand.

The three stages in the development of marketing are shown in Fig. 1-1.

Production-Orientation Stage

In this first stage, a company typically is production-oriented. Executives in production and engineering shape the firm's planning. The function of the sales department is simply to sell the company's output, at a price set by production and financial executives. This is the "build a better mousetrap" stage. The underlying assumption is that marketing effort is not needed to get people to buy a product that is well made and reasonably priced.

During this stage, the term *marketing* is not yet used. Instead, producers have sales departments headed by executives whose job is to manage a sales force. This stage was dominant until the Great Depression in the early 1930s.

Sales-Orientation Stage

The Depression made it clear that the main problem in the economy no longer was to produce or grow enough but rather was to sell the output. Just making a better product brought no assurance of market success. Firms began to realize that the sale of products required substantial promotional effort. Thus we entered a period when selling activities and sales executives gained new respect and responsibility from company management.

It was also during this period that selling acquired much of its bad reputation.

This was the age of the "hard sell" characterized by the unscrupulous used-car dealer or door-to-door sales person. Even now some organizations believe that they must operate with a hard-sell philosophy to prosper. The sales stage lasted from the early 1930s well into the 1950s, when the marketing era began to emerge.

Marketing-Orientation Stage

By the early 1950s Canada had completed the transition from an economy disrupted by World War II to a peacetime economy. Manufacturing plants were turning out large quantities of consumer goods to satisfy the demand that had built up during the war. As the postwar surge in consumer spending slowed down, many firms found that demand fell short of their production capabilities. Aggressive promotional and sales activities did not resolve the problem. Thus the evolution of marketing continued. Many companies decided they needed to focus on the needs of their customers and carry out a broader range of marketing activities to be successful.

In this third stage, attention is focused on marketing rather than on selling. The top executive responsible for this activity is called a marketing manager or vice president of marketing. Several tasks that traditionally were managed by other executives become the responsibility of the top marketing executive in this stage. For instance, inventory control, warehousing, and some aspects of product planning are turned over to the head of marketing. To be most effective, this executive should be brought in at the beginning, rather than at the end, of a production cycle. Marketing should influence all short-term and long-term company planning.

A key to effective marketing is a favourable attitude towards marketing on the part of a firm's top executives. The following statement reflects an understanding of this point: "Marketing begins with top management. Only top management can provide the climate, the discipline, and the leadership required for a successful marketing program." We are *not* saying that marketing executives should hold the top positions in a company. Nor are we saying that the president of a firm must come up through the marketing department. But it is necessary that the president be *marketing-oriented*.

Many Canadian business firms, as well as some nonprofit organizations, are presently in this third stage in the evolution of marketing. How well these companies have implemented a marketing orientation, however, is questionable. Some firms are using the appropriate titles and other external trappings, but they are still finding it difficult to become truly marketing-oriented.[4]

THE MARKETING CONCEPT

As business people recognized that marketing is vitally important to the success of any organization, a new philosophy of doing business developed. Called the **marketing concept**, it emphasizes customer orientation and coordination of marketing activities to achieve the organization's performance objectives.

Nature and Rationale

The marketing concept is based on three fundamental beliefs:

- All planning and operations should be customer-oriented. That is, the organization and its employees should be focused on determining and satisfying customers' needs.

---

[4]A practical game plan for achieving a marketing orientation is presented in Adrian F. Payne, "Developing a Marketing-Oriented Organization," *Business Horizons*, May–June 1988, pp. 46–53.

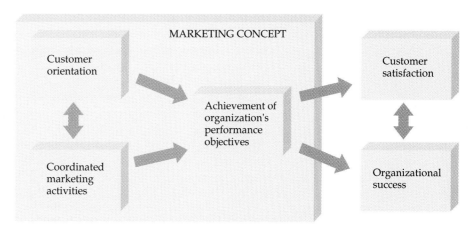

FIGURE 1-2
Components and outcomes of the marketing concept.

- All marketing activities in an organization should be coordinated. In reality this belief means that marketing efforts (such as advertising, product planning, and pricing) should be combined in a coherent and consistent way and that one executive should have overall authority and responsibility for the complete set of marketing activities.
- Customer-oriented, coordinated marketing is essential to achieve the organization's performance objectives.

The marketing concept is equally applicable to businesses and nonprofit organizations. Of course, objectives may be fundamentally different depending on whether the organization is in the business or nonprofit sector. A business firm's objectives, unlike those of a nonprofit organization, ordinarily revolve around profits.

Customer orientation and coordinated marketing activities are the means used to achieve the end that is sought, namely achievement of the organization's performance objectives. Figure 1-2 illustrates this relationship. Sometimes the marketing concept is simply stated as ''The Customer Is King (or Queen)!'' As helpful as it is to stress customer satisfaction, however, this motto must not be allowed to replace achievement of objectives as the fundamental rationale for the marketing concept.

The Societal Marketing Orientation

Off and on for more than 20 years, the marketing concept has come under fire. There have also been calls to make the concept more socially responsible. Its critics charge that, although implementing it may lead to business success, it may encourage actions that in some way conflict with a firm's responsibility to society.

From one point of view, these charges are true. A firm may totally satisfy its customers (in line with the marketing concept), while also adversely affecting society. To illustrate, an Ontario steel producer might be supplying its customers in the U.S. with the right product at a reasonable price, but at the same time be polluting the air and water at home.

Actually the marketing concept and a company's social responsibility can be quite compatible. The key to compatibility lies in extending the *breadth* and *time* dimensions of the marketing concept. With this revision we would have, in effect, a **societal marketing concept**.

When the concept's *breadth* is extended, a company recognizes that a market includes not only the buyers of a firm's products but also other people directly affected by the firm's operations. In our example, the steel mill has several ''customer'' groups to satisfy. Among these are (1) the buyers of the steel, (2) the consumers of the air that contains impurities given off by the mill, and (3) the recreational users of the lake where the mill releases its waste matter.

An extended *time* dimension means that a firm should take a long-term view of customer satisfaction and performance objectives, rather than concentrating only on tomorrow. For a company to prosper in the long run, it must do a good job of satisfying customers' social and economic demands.

Thus the marketing concept and a company's social responsibility are compatible if management strives over the long run to (1) satisfy the wants of its product-buying customers, (2) meet the societal needs of others affected by the firm's activities, and (3) achieve the company's performance objectives.

CAREERS IN MARKETING

At the beginning of this chapter, we noted that about one-quarter to one-third of all jobs are in the field of marketing. These jobs cover a wide range of activities. Furthermore, this variety of jobs also covers a wide range of qualifications and aptitudes. Jobs in personal selling, for example, call for a set of qualifications that are different from those in marketing research. A person likely to be successful in advertising may not be a good prospect in physical distribution. Consequently, the personal qualifications and aptitudes of different individuals make them candidates for different types of marketing jobs.

In this section we shall briefly describe the major jobs in marketing, grouping them by the title of the job or the activity. As you work through the text, you will see the kinds of activities, characteristics, and responsibilities associated with the major marketing jobs, and the context in which they exist.

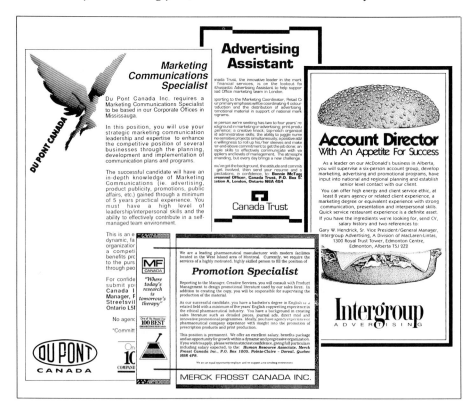

Advertising

Advertising jobs are available in three broad types of organizations. First there are jobs with the *advertisers*. Then there are careers with the various *media* (newspapers, TV stations, magazines, etc.) that carry the ads. And, finally, there are jobs with *advertising agencies*, which specialize in creating and producing individual ads and entire campaigns.

Jobs in advertising encompass a variety of aptitudes and interests—artistic, creative, managerial, research, and sales, for example. There is a real opportunity for the artistic or creative person. Agencies and advertising departments need copywriters, artists, photographers, layout designers, printing and desktop publishing experts, and others to create and produce the ads.

The account executive occupies a key position in advertising agencies. People in this position are the liaison between the agency and its clients (the advertisers). Account executives coordinate the agency's efforts with the clients' marketing programs.

Another group of advertising jobs involves buying and selling the media time and space. Advertisers and agencies also often need people who can conduct consumer behaviour studies and other types of marketing research.

Brand or Product Management

Brand or product managers are responsible for planning and directing the entire marketing program for a given brand, product, or a group of products.

Early on, product managers are concerned with the packaging, labelling, and other aspects of the product itself. They also are responsible for doing the necessary marketing research to identify the market. They plan the advertising, personal selling, and sales promotional programs and also are concerned with the pricing, physical distribution, and legal aspects of the product. All in all, being a product manager is almost like running your own business.

Typically, the job is a staff position in the organization, rather than a line operating position. Thus, the product manager often has much responsibility for a product's performance but must coordinate with line managers to see that his or her directives and plans are put into effect.

Consumer Affairs and Protection

This broad area encompasses several activities that provide job and career opportunities. Many of these jobs are an outgrowth of the consumer movement discussed in Chapter 2. Many companies, for example, have a consumer affairs department to handle consumer complaints. Various federal and provincial agencies are set up to keep watch on business firms and to provide information and assistance to consumers. Grocery products manufacturers and gas and electric companies regularly hire consumer and marketing specialists to aid consumers in product use. Government and private product-testing agencies hire people to test products for safety, durability, and other features.

Distribution

A large number of jobs exist in this field, and the prospects are even brighter as we look ahead in the 1990s. More and more firms are expected to adopt the systems approach in distribution to control the huge expenses involved in materials movement and warehousing.

Manufacturers, retailers, and all other product-handling firms have jobs that involve two stages of distribution. First, the product must be moved to the firm for processing or resale. Then the finished products must be distributed to the markets. These distribution tasks involve jobs in transportation management, warehousing, and inventory control. In addition, the many transportation carriers and warehousing firms also provide a variety of jobs.

Marketing Research

Marketing research jobs cover a broad range of activities. People are hired for marketing research jobs by manufacturers, retailers, service marketers, government agencies, and other types of organizations. There also are a number of specialized marketing research companies. Generally, however, there are fewer jobs in marketing research than in personal selling or in advertising.

Marketing research people are problem solvers. They collect and analyze masses of information. Consequently, they need an aptitude for methodical, analytical types of work. Typically, some quantitative skills are needed. It helps if you understand statistics and feel comfortable using a computer.

Public Relations

The public or community relations department in an organization is the connecting link between that organization and its various publics. The department especially must deal with, or go through, the news media to reach these publics. Public relations people must be especially good at communications.

In essence, the job of public relations is to project the desired company image to the public. More specifically, public relations people are responsible for telling the public about the company—its products, community activities, social programs, environmental improvement activities, labour policies, views regarding controversial issues, and so on.

Purchasing

The opposite of selling is buying, and here there are a lot of good jobs. Every retail organization needs people to buy the merchandise that is to be sold. Frequently the route to the top in retailing is through the buying (also called merchandising) division of the business. Large retailers have many positions for buyers and assistant buyers. Typically, each merchandise department has a buyer.

The purchasing agent is the business market counterpart of the retail-store buyer. Virtually all firms in business or industrial markets have purchasing departments. People in these departments buy for the production, office, and sales departments in their firms.

Retail buyers and purchasing agents need many of the same skills. They must be able to analyze markets, determine merchandise needs, and negotiate with sellers. It also helps if you have some knowledge of credit, finance, and distribution.

Personal Sales

By far, product and service sales jobs are the most numerous of all the jobs in marketing, with telemarketing sales being one of the fastest growing areas of opportunity. These personal selling jobs (1) cover a wide variety of activities, (2) are found in a wide variety of organizations, and (3) carry a wide variety of titles. Consider the following people: a sales clerk in a department store; a sales engineer providing technical assistance in the sales of hydraulic valves; a representative for Canadair selling a fleet of airplanes; a marketing consultant presenting his or her services; a telemarketing representative for local theatre groups. All these people are engaged in personal selling, but each sales job is different from the others.

The sales and service representation job is the most common entry-level position in marketing. Furthermore, a sales job is a widely used stepping-stone to a management position. Many companies recruit people for these jobs with the intention of promoting some or all of them into management positions. Personal selling and sales management jobs are also a good route to the top in a firm. This is so because it is relatively easy to measure a person's performance and productivity in selling. Sales results are highly visible.

Sales Promotion

The main function of sales promotion is to tie together the activities in personal selling and advertising. Effective sales promotion requires imagination and creativity, coupled with a sound foundation in marketing fundamentals.

One group of sales promotion activities involves retail in-store displays and window displays — planning and creating them. Another area of sales promotion jobs involves direct-mail advertising programs. Still another area deals with service demonstrations, trade shows, and other company exhibits. Sales promotion activities also include the development and management of premium giveaways, contests, product sampling, and other types of promotion.

Marketing careers can be pursued in large and small firms, in all parts of Canada as well as abroad in Canadian international marketing activities. Opportunities for marketing careers exist at all levels of the economy, ranging from manufacturing and production organizations through wholesaling, retailing and service provision and marketing. More than ever before, marketing careers exist in nonprofit organizations as well as business.

STRUCTURAL PLAN OF THIS BOOK

The overall plan of this book is to use the managerial-micro approach to study the strategic management of the marketing activities in an individual organization. The book is divided into seven parts consisting of 22 chapters in total.

Part 1 provides us with the global context, background and framework within which we can build our marketing program. The first chapter has covered the nature, importance, and evolution of marketing. In Chapter 2 we see that a company's marketing activity is shaped largely by external, uncontrollable environmental forces, as well as by the environment within the firm. Chapter 3 explains the marketing management process, the marketing mix, and the fundamentals of strategic planning in a marketing organization.

Part 2 — Chapters 4 through 7 — deals with the identification and analysis of a company's target markets. In Chapters 4 and 5, we examine segmentation and positioning in dealing with markets. In Chapter 6 we review the sociological and psychological influences on buying behaviour in consumer and industrial markets. We discuss the topics of marketing information systems and research in Chapter 7.

Parts 3 through 6 — Chapters 8 through 19 — are devoted to designing and developing a strategic marketing mix. A marketing mix is a combination of the four elements that constitute the core of a marketing program. The four are an organization's product or service assortment (Part 3), price structure (Part 4), distribution system (Part 5), and promotional activities (Part 6).

Part 7 deals with the implementation of strategic planning as well as an evaluation of the performance of the organization's marketing program. In Chapter 20 we examine the international dimensions of marketing programs. In Chapter 21, we use a micro approach to evaluate the performance of the marketing effort in an individual firm. In Chapter 22 we use a macro approach as we evaluate the role of marketing in our socioeconomic system.

For additional help and information we have provided two appendices to provide additional information on sources of secondary marketing information as well as financial accounting for marketing.

SUMMARY

In a broad sense, marketing is any exchange activity intended to satisfy human wants. In this context we need to look broadly at (1) who should be classed as marketers, (2) what is being marketed, and (3) who are the target markets. In a business sense, marketing is a system of business action designed to plan, price, promote, and distribute want-satisfying products, services, and ideas to market in order to achieve organizational objectives.

Marketing is practised today in all modern nations around the world, regardless of their political philosophies. One of every three or four people is employed in marketing, and about half of what consumers spend goes to cover the costs of marketing.

The philosophy of the marketing concept holds that a company should (1) be customer-oriented, (2) strive for profitable sales volume, and (3) coordinate all its marketing activities. Marketing management is the vehicle that business uses to activate the marketing concept. Our socioeconomic structure — and marketing management is part of it — has evolved:

- from an agrarian economy in a rural setting,
- through a production-oriented, subsistence-level economy in an urban society,
- and then through a sales-oriented economy,
- into today's customer-oriented economy, featuring a society with a great deal of discretionary purchasing power.

Looking to the future, our attention is shifting to societal relationships:

- to the quality of our life and environment.
- to the conservation and allocation of our scarce resources.
- to a greater concern for people.

These point up the need to broaden the marketing concept to include satisfaction of *all* a company's markets, while generating profits *over the long run*.

KEY TERMS AND CONCEPTS

The numbers refer to the pages on which the terms and concepts are defined. In addition, see the glossary at the back of the book.

Marketing (broad definition) 5	Production-orientation stage 13
Concept of exchange 5	Sales-orientation stage 13
Marketing (micro, business definition) 7	Marketing-orientation stage 13
	Marketing concept 14
Marketing mix 8	Societal-orientation stage 15
Economy of abundance 9	Broadening the marketing concept 15

QUESTIONS AND PROBLEMS

1. Explain the concept of an exchange, including the conditions that must exist for an exchange to occur.
2. In the following marketing exchanges, what is the "something of value" that each party contributes in the exchange?
   a. Your school ←————————→ You as a student.
   b. Fire department ←————————→ People in your hometown.
   c. Flour miller ←————————→ Bakery.
   d. CARE Canada ←————————→ Contributors.
   e. Delta Hotels ←————————→ Publisher's sales meeting.

3. In line with the broader, societal concept of marketing, describe some of the ways in which nonbusiness organizations to which you belong are engaged in marketing activities.

4. For each of the following organizations, describe (1) what is being marketed and (2) who is the target market.
   a. Calgary Stampeders professional football team.
   b. Canadian Auto Workers labour union.
   c. Professor teaching a first-year chemistry course.
   d. Fire department in your city.

5. One writer has stated that any business has only two functions—marketing and innovation. How would you explain this statement to a student majoring in engineering, accounting, finance, or personnel management?

6. One way of explaining the importance of marketing in our economy is to consider how we would live if there were no marketing facilities. Describe some of the ways in which your daily activities would be affected under such circumstances.

7. Explain the three elements that constitute the marketing concept.

8. Explain the difference between marketing and selling.

9. Name some companies that you believe are still in the production or sales stage in the evolution of marketing management. Explain why you chose each of them.

10. The marketing concept does not imply that marketing executives will run the firm. The concept requires only that whoever is in top management be marketing-oriented. Give examples of how a production manager, company treasurer, or personnel manager can be marketing-oriented.

CHAPTER 2 GOALS

A variety of environmental forces have a considerable influence on the way in which an organization conducts its marketing activities.

Some are external to the firm and are therefore largely uncontrollable. Others are internal and are to a greater extent controllable by management.

After studying this chapter, you should have an understanding of:

- How the following macroenvironmental factors can influence a company's marketing system:
  a. Demography.
  b. Economic conditions.
  c. Competition.
  d. Social and cultural forces.
  e. Political and legal forces.
  f. Technology.
- How the external microenvironmental factors of the market, suppliers, and marketing intermediaries all can influence an organization's marketing program.
- How the nonmarketing resources within a company can influence that firm's marketing system.
- The need to coordinate the marketing activities within an organization.

The Marketing Environment

There can be no denying that we live in a world of accelerating change. Everywhere we turn, there are new products, new technology, and emerging competitors. To keep abreast of this change and to gain some insight into the major developments that are likely to occur during the last decade of the twentieth century, many business people turn to the predictions of noted futurists such as John Naisbitt, and Canada's John Kettle and Frank Feather.

The question is ''What is going on out there that will influence how I will have to do business in the future?'' At a speech in Toronto, Naisbitt selected major themes from his best-selling book, *Megatrends 2000*, and observed that the world in the 1990s will be shaped by six major movements:

- a renaissance in the arts, literature, and spirituality;
- a decline in the welfare state and the emergence of free-market socialism;
- the emergence of English as the first truly universal language;
- a decline in the importance of cities and the emergence of a new ''electronic heartland'';
- a move towards worldwide free trade;
- a global economic boom.

The trends predicted by Naisbitt and others may or may not occur, but there is no doubt that change is all around us, and marketing managers must listen to such predictions and to other sources to ensure that they are knowledgeable about what is occurring in their environments. To quote Colin Deane of Ernst & Young, ''Some change happens so slowly that it is almost imperceptible. As population structures change, for example, over time, you need to change your distribution channels or marketing approach to reflect the change in your target markets. A lot of companies miss opportunities because they don't spend enough time dealing with longer-term trends, which sometimes can put a major corporation out of business.''[1]

---

[1]Jim Cormier, ''Trending Upward,'' *En Route*, vol. 18, no. 11, November 1990, pp. 27–50.

The challenge (and the opportunity) that faces marketers, therefore, is to identify developing trends and their implications for marketing strategies. Consider, for example, how Alex Tilley, president of Tilley Endurables, established his successful company to take advantage of the fact that Canadians were expressing an increasing interest in the outdoors and in durable, yet stylish, clothing. This, coupled with the trend to home catalogue shopping, provided Tilley the opportunity to establish retail stores in Toronto, Montreal, and Vancouver, and to launch a successful catalogue operation. He responded to the multiple trends to outdoor recreation, convenience, and quality.

An organization operates within an *external* environment that is continually changing and generally *cannot* be controlled by an individual organization. At the same time, a set of marketing and nonmarketing resources *within* the organization generally *can* be controlled by its executives.

External forces can be divided into two groups:

- *Macro* influences (so called because they affect all firms) include demographics, economic conditions, culture, and laws.
- *Micro* influences (so called because they affect a particular firm) consist of suppliers, marketing intermediaries, and customers. These micro elements, while external, are closely related to a specific company and are part of the company's total marketing system.

Successful marketing depends largely on a company's ability to manage its marketing program within its environmental framework. Thus management must strive to forecast the direction and intensity of changes in the external environment and to respond to these changes through effective utilization of its controllable resources.

EXTERNAL MACROENVIRONMENT

The following six interrelated macroenvironmental forces have a considerable effect on any organization's marketing system. Yet they are largely *not* controllable by management. See Figure 2-1.

- Demography.
- Economic conditions.
- Competition.
- Social and cultural forces.
- Political and legal forces.
- Technology.

FIGURE 2-1
Major forces in a company's macroenvironment.

EXTERNAL MACROENVIRONMENTAL FORCES

| Demography | Economic conditions | Competition | Social and cultural forces | Political and legal forces | Technology |

COMPANY'S MARKETING PROGRAM

Note that we just said that these forces are *largely*, but not *totally*, uncontrollable by management in a firm. That is, a company must be able to manage its external environment to some extent. For example, through company and industry lobbying in Ottawa or provincial capitals, a company may have some influence on the political-legal forces in its environment. Or new-product research and development that is on the technological frontier can influence a firm's competitive position. In fact, it may be *our* company's technology that is the external environmental force of technology that is affecting *other* organizations.

If there is one similarity in these six environmental factors, it is that they are all subject to considerable change—and at different rates. Also, an important point from a marketing perspective is that not all markets or all consumers are affected by these changes in the same way. For example, some consumers cope with difficult economic times better than others do; some people are more adept at using the latest technological innovations; some accept new ideas and new ways of doing things much more readily than others do. The result is an extremely complex marketplace that is influenced by external factors that the marketer cannot influence but must understand and appreciate. In the following section, we will examine each of the six major environmental forces.

Demography   We may define **demography** as the statistical study of human population and its distribution. It is especially important to marketing executives, because people constitute markets. Demography will be discussed in greater detail in the section on markets. At this point we shall mention just a couple of examples of how demographic factors influence marketing systems.

In the mid-1980s, for the first time in history, the number of people 65 and older surpassed the number of teenagers—and this gap will widen considerably as we progress through the 1990s. The marketing implications of this trend are substantial. Many marketers have added to their product lines items that are specifically aimed at customers who are in their fifties and sixties and older. Realizing that Canadians over the age of 55 control more than 70 percent of the country's wealth, banks are establishing special seniors' banking areas in their branches to serve older customers. The Royal Bank of Canada has hired part-time employees who are themselves retired. The role of this group, known as the "Grey Panthers," is to call on other seniors to ensure that they are aware of the bank's products and services.[2]

Mature actors and celebrities promote various products and services in advertising. Shoppers Drug Mart has featured Beatrice Arthur of "The Golden Girls"; Ray Charles has appeared for Diet Pepsi; Bill Cosby promotes Kodak film. Martha Raye is featured in advertising for Polident, and Tommy Hunter has appeared in television commercials for Air Atlantic. Bob Cole of "Hockey Night in Canada" is the advertising spokesman for the General Motors dealers of Atlantic Canada. Movie theatres, bus companies, airlines, and many department stores give discounts to customers aged 65 and older.

Internationally, the growing population of older consumers is having a profound influence on the development of marketing programs. In Great Britain,

---

[2]Heather D. Whyte, "Banking Industry Changes to Focus on Seniors Market," *The Financial Post*, March 25, 1991, p. 8.

MARKETING AT WORK

FILE 2-1   **THE FACTS ARE ALREADY THERE**

Demographics have long been ignored by most segments of the Canadian government, businesses, and economists. However, if studied intently, they could be used as a marketer's crystal ball to enable businesses to foresee and cater to the needs and wants of future target markets years in advance. Through the analysis of demographics, business could prepare for such phenomena as the eventual migration of aging baby boomers from the bright lights of the city to the more peaceful, healthy life of rural regions. They could also foresee the increasing importance of productivity based on technology, not people, as the population of young North Americans dwindles. They could even predict the demise of the local tennis club, because ''people over 25 don't play tennis.'' These conclusions and many more are all ultimately arrived at by this one simple fact: ''Every year you get one year older.''

Source: Adapted from Daniel Stoffman, ''Completely Predictable People,'' *Report on Business Magazine*, November 1990, p. 78–84.

for example, financial institutions have found that people over 55 hold two-thirds of the country's savings. In France, insurance companies have seen that a new market in retirement insurance is booming, as people grow increasingly concerned about the stability of the country's public pension system.[3]

Another significant demographic development is the growing market segment comprising single people. As recently as 1956, less than 8 percent of adult Canadians lived alone. Today, well over 20 percent of Canadian households comprise adults who live alone. A large percentage of these single-person households are made up of older women who have been widowed. Many of these older singles have very active life-styles, enjoying organized activities such as travel tours.

The marketing implications of this demographic force are almost limitless. The frozen-food industry caters to this market with high-quality frozen entrées in a wide variety of menu offerings, many of which involve single servings. Automobile manufacturers and banks recognize the increased buying power of single women and have developed marketing programs and services specifically for this segment. Homebuilders are designing homes, condominium units, and housing developments with older singles in mind, while tour companies regularly offer bus tour vacations and cruises for this increasingly affluent group.

Economic Conditions   People alone do not make a market. They must have money to spend and be willing to spend it. Consequently, the **economic environment** is a significant force that affects the marketing system of just about any organization. A marketing system is affected especially by such economic considerations as the current stage of the business cycle, inflation, and interest rates.

[3]See ''Grappling with the Graying of Europe,'' *Business Week*, March 13, 1989, pp. 54–56.

STAGE OF THE BUSINESS CYCLE

Marketing executives should understand what stage of the business cycle the economy currently is in, because this cycle has such an impact on a company's marketing system. The traditional business cycle goes through four stages—prosperity, recession, depression, and recovery. However, various economic strategies have been adopted by the federal government; these strategies have averted the depression stage in Canada and other developed countries for 60 years. Consequently, today we think of a three-stage cycle—prosperity, recession, recovery—then returning full cycle to prosperity.

Essentially, a company usually operates its marketing system quite differently during each stage. Prosperity is characterized typically as a period of economic growth. During this stage, organizations tend to expand their marketing programs as they add new products and enter new markets. A recession, on the other hand, involves higher rates of unemployment and reduced consumer spending and typically is a period of retrenchment for consumers and businesses. People can become discouraged, scared, and angry. Naturally these feelings affect their buying behaviour, which, in turn, has major implications for the marketing programs in countless firms.

Recovery finds the economy moving from recession to prosperity: the marketers' challenge is determining how quickly prosperity will return and to what level. As the unemployment rate declines and disposable income increases, companies expand their marketing efforts to improve sales and profits.

INFLATION

Inflation is a rise in price levels. When prices rise at a faster rate than personal income, there is a decline in consumer buying power. During the late 1970s and early 1980s, Canada experienced what for us was a high inflation rate of 10 to 15 percent. Although inflation rates declined in recent years to less than 5 percent, with economic growth there is a fear that higher rates may return. Consequently, this spectre continues to influence government policies, consumer psychology, and business marketing programs.

Inflation presents some real challenges in the management of a marketing program—especially in the area of pricing and cost control. Consumers are adversely affected as their buying power declines. At the same time, they may overspend today for fear that prices will be higher tomorrow.

INTEREST RATES

Interest rates are another external economic factor influencing marketing programs. When interest rates are high, for example, consumers tend to hold back on long-term purchases such as housing. Consumer purchases also are affected by whether they think interest rates will increase or decline. Marketers sometimes offer below-market interest rates (a form of price cut) as a promotional device to increase business. Auto manufacturers have used this tactic extensively in recent years, for example.

EMPLOYMENT RATES

One of the most important indicators of the strength of an economy is the percentage of people who are employed and the percentage looking for work. During a strong economic period, unemployment rates are generally lower.

At other times, or in certain parts of Canada, unemployment is higher. This affects greatly the amount of disposable income that consumers have to spend on products and services and is of considerable interest to marketers.

A marketer must pay considerable attention to the condition of the economy in which his or her company is operating. Purchasers of certain products and services may react quickly to changes or expected changes in economic conditions. The marketer must be ready to respond with changes in the marketing program.[4]

Competition

A company's competitive environment obviously is a major influence shaping its marketing system. Any executives worth their salt should be constantly gathering intelligence and otherwise monitoring all aspects of competitors' marketing activities—that is, their products, pricing, distribution systems, and promotional programs. Under expanded trade with other countries, Canadian firms will have to pay greater attention to *foreign competition* and, with the movement towards global free trade, increasingly find opportunities for Canadian products and services in foreign markets. Two aspects of competition that we shall consider briefly here are the types of competition and the competitive market structure in which companies may be operating.

A firm generally faces competition from three sources:

- *Brand competition* from marketers of similar and directly competing products. Air Canada competes with Canadian Airlines International on many domestic routes and with British Airways, KLM, American Airlines, and other airlines for international business. Bauer competes with Micron, Lange, and CCM in the skate business. Cooper competes with overseas companies such as Karhu and Koho for the attention of Canadian hockey stick purchasers. Even charitable organizations such as the Canadian Cancer Society, the Canadian Heart Foundation, and the Salvation Army compete for our donations and for the time of canvassers and volunteers.
- *Substitute products* that satisfy the same basic need. For example, vinyl records have all but disappeared in the face of competition first from tape cassettes and then from compact discs. Local courier companies and Canada Post have seen a portion of their business taken away by business use of facsimile (fax) machines. Many conventional department stores and clothing retailers are realizing that their competition is coming not only from other stores down the street or in the same town, but from catalogue companies such as Sears and Tilley Endurables, some of which, including L. L. Bean and Lands' End, are in other countries.
- In the third type of competition—more general in nature—*every company or organization* is competing for the consumer's limited buying power. In this regard, the competition faced by a marketer of tennis rackets may come from other companies that are marketing slacks or shoes, or from a car repair bill, or a weekend ski holiday.

---

[4]An interesting account of how Canadian consumers responded to the high levels of interest rates and inflation in the early 1980s is presented in James G. Barnes and Lessey Sooklal, ''The Changing Nature of Consumer Behaviour: Monitoring the Impact of Inflation and Recession,'' *The Business Quarterly*, Summer 1983, pp. 58–64.

Brand Competition: it's a jungle.

Social and Cultural Forces

The impact of the sociocultural environment on marketing systems is reflected in several sections of this book. Much of two chapters—2 and 6—is devoted to the topic. To add to the complexity of the task facing marketing executives, cultural patterns—life-styles, social values, beliefs—are changing much faster than they used to. At this point we shall note just a few that have significant marketing implications.

CHANGING VALUES—EMPHASIS ON QUALITY OF LIFE

Our emphasis today is increasingly on the *quality* of life rather than the *quality* of goods. The theme is ''Not more—but better.'' We seek value, durability, comfort, and safety in the products and services we buy. Looking ahead, we will worry more about inflation, health, and the environment, and less about keeping up with the neighbours in autos, dress, and homes. Our growing concern for the environment and our discontent with pollution and resource waste are leading to significant changes in our life-styles. And when our life-styles change, of course marketing is affected.

This change in values among Canadians is evident in a number of areas, as consumers reject the accumulation of assets that characterized the 1980s in favour of a return to products that reflect the values of old. This trend is reflected, for example, in the breakfast cereal industry, where companies began to experience significant increases in sales at the end of the 1980s, after a decade of declining consumption. The sales upturn is being led by traditional hot cereals, such as Cream of Wheat, and the basis upon which these products are being marketed is reflected in the nostalgic approach taken by some brands. A Quaker Oats commercial encourages consumers to eat old-fashioned porridge because it is the right thing to do, and an advertisement for Kellogg's Rice Krispies displays an advertising illustration from the 1930s. Such campaigns would probably not have worked in the 1970s and 1980s.[5]

EMPHASIS ON SERVICE QUALITY

As consumers have become more confident of their rights and the power they wield in the marketplace, they have become increasingly demanding concerning the manner in which they are treated by business. Although companies have long appreciated that they must produce quality products in order to compete effectively for the consumer's loyalty, most are now beginning to realize that quality is equally important in the delivery of service. Increasingly, consumers are making decisions to shop at certain stores or to stay at certain hotels not only on the basis of tangible products or the decor of the room or the quality of food in the restaurant (although these are important) but on the much more intangible factor of the level of service. Customers now regularly tell businesses they want to be treated as if they are important and their business is welcomed and appreciated. The best companies have responded with sophisticated programs to measure the satisfaction of customers and with quality programs designed to deliver a higher level of service quality.

ROLE OF WOMEN

One of the most dramatic occurrences in our society in recent years has been the changing role of women. Especially significant is the breaking away from the traditional and sometimes discriminatory patterns that have stereotyped the male-female roles in families, jobs, recreation, product use, and many other areas. Today, women's growing political power, economic power, and

---

[3]Alanna Mitchell, ''Breakfast Is a Kinder, Gentler Affair,'' *Globe and Mail*, March 23, 1991, p. D3.

The new woman makes a statement.

Make a **S**tatement

The new sporty 2+2 Scoupe from Hyundai makes a serious statement about how much fun you like to have in the car you choose to drive.

Just looking at the inspired design is the start of the love affair. And the suave looks don't lie about the performance promise.

The 1.5 litre engine with overhead cam and multi point electronic fuel injection is all spice. Front wheel drive, rack and pinion steering, and 4-wheel independent suspension create a relationship with the road of subtle seduction.

More car for your money continues with body-contoured front bucket seats, a 60/40 fold-down rear seat that opens to the trunk, and a huge array of standard features.

The Scoupe LS, for example, comes with power windows, power dual remote rearview mirrors, Premium ETR AM/FM stereo cassette with 4 speakers, power steering, power brakes, sunroof, aluminum alloy wheels with P185/60HR14 Michelin All-Season steel-belted tires, and more — all standard.

So spoil yourself. Even show off a little. Start a beautiful relationship, and make a statement that says you've earned the right to get some fun out of life. The Scoupe is at your Hyundai dealer now.

CONFIDENCE IN QUALITY
3 Years / 60,000 km Comprehensive Warranty
5 Years / 100,000 km Powertrain Warranty

1991 **S**COUPE   **HYUNDAI**
Cars that make sense.

new job opportunities have considerably changed their perspectives and those of men as well.

The evolving roles of women have many implications for marketers. Well over one-half of the women in Canada are working outside the home today. This has changed some traditional buying patterns in households. Many men now shop for groceries, while women buy gas and arrange for auto maintenance. Women working outside the home buy different clothing than women working at home. With both spouses working, the demand for microwave ovens and household services, for example, has increased because time-saving and convenience are major factors in buying. Many women with young children work outside the home, increasing the demand for day-care centres and nursery schools.

ATTITUDES TOWARDS PHYSICAL FITNESS AND EATING

In recent years, an increased interest in health and physical fitness seems generally to have cut across most demographic and economic segments of our society. Participation in physical fitness activities from aerobics to yoga (we could not think of any activity beginning with a Z) is on the increase. Stores supplying activity products and service organizations catering to this trend have multiplied. Public facilities (bicycle paths, hiking trails, jogging paths, and playgrounds) have been improved.

Paralleling the physical fitness phenomenon, we are experiencing significant changes in the eating patterns of Canadians. We are becoming more sensitive to the relationship between our diet and major killing diseases such as heart attacks and cancer. Consequently, there is a growing interest in weight-control eating, foods low in salt, additives, and cholesterol, and foods high in vitamins, minerals, and fibre content. Health foods now occupy large sections in many supermarkets. Per capita consumption of red meat, eggs, and canned

Communicating environmental awareness.

NEVER LET IT BE SAID WE DIDN'T SEE THE BIG PICTURE.

We do not want our children, twenty years from now, to accuse us all of being blind to environmental concerns. Sunlight dishwasher detergent is as efficient as ever, yet it now has 50% l phosphate than most other leading brands; in keeping with our vision of a cleaner world.

S U N L I G H T. 5 0 % L E S S P H O S P H A T E.

vegetables has been declining in recent years, as Canadians turn increasingly to fresh fruit and vegetables, poultry products, and fish.

CONCERN FOR THE ENVIRONMENT

Possibly one of the most important forces that will influence Canadian business and marketing in the coming years is Canadians' concern for the physical environment. As we have seen the damage that has been done to the quality of water, air, and the land during this century, there has been a collective outpouring of support for programs and products that allow us to take action to protect the environment.

Consequently, governments have moved to control the emissions of automobiles and factories; food manufacturers package products in less wasteful and more biodegradable packages; and municipalities across the country have established recycling programs in which many householders and most businesses participate. Supermarket chains stock many products labelled "environmentally friendly," meaning that their packages and ingredients are not

MARKETING AT WORK

FILE 2-2 **GOING GREEN**

Canadians are going green and they don't like what they see. A 1990 national survey of 1,500 adults conducted by the Environics Research Group Ltd. found that Canadians were as green as grass with respect to protecting the environment. They want an end to industrial pollution (with severe legal punishment to those who don't comply), and they want to see increased government funds and actions directed towards solving environmental problems. From the same population that so violently opposes the federal Goods and Services Tax, an enormous 73 percent of Canadians would be fully prepared to pay a ''green tax.'' It is clear that people have already made significant changes in the way they lead their lives — 72 percent of Canadians reported changing their purchase decisions because of environmental concerns. In doing so, they may be quietly transforming the consumer marketplace in Canada.

Source: Doug Miller, ''Gung-ho for Green,'' *Globe and Mail*, Tuesday, December 11, 1990, p. 15.

harmful to the environment. The result is a major movement driven by the changing values of consumers. The implications for business will last throughout the remainder of this century.

DESIRE FOR CONVENIENCE

As an outgrowth of the increase in discretionary purchasing power and the importance of time, there has been a continual increase in the consumer's desire for convenience. We want products ready and easy to use, and convenient credit plans to pay for them. We want these products packaged in a variety of sizes, quantities, and forms. We want stores located close by and open at virtually all hours.

Every major phase of a company's marketing program is affected by this craving for convenience. Product planning is influenced by the need for customer convenience in packaging, quantity, and selection. Pricing policies must be established in conformity with the demand for credit and with the costs of providing the various kinds of convenience. Distribution policies must provide for convenient locations and hours of business. As a result, Canada's banks have placed thousands of automated banking machines in various locations in cities and towns across Canada, so that their customers now have access to banking services in off-premise locations and at any time of the day or night. Another example of business responding to the consumer's desire for convenience is the increasing use of catalogues to order products. Even people who live in major cities, who have access to a wide variety of retail stores, find it less time-consuming and more convenient to shop from catalogues. These catalogue retailers make shopping from home as easy as possible through the use of toll-free 1-800 telephone numbers, acceptance of major credit cards, and relatively risk-free shopping through generous exchange and refund policies.

IMPULSE BUYING

Recently there has been a marked increase in impulse buying — purchases made without much advance planning. A shopper may go to the grocery store with a mental note to buy meat and bread. In the store, he may also select some fresh peaches because they look appealing or are priced attractively. Another shopper, seeing cleansing tissues on the shelf, may be reminded that she is running low and so may buy two boxes. These are impulse purchases.

A key point to understand is that some impulse buying is done on a very rational basis. Self-service, open-display selling has brought about a marketing situation wherein planning may be postponed until the buyer reaches the retail outlet. Because of the trend towards impulse buying, emphasis must be placed on promotional programs designed to get people into a store. Displays must be appealing because the manufacturer's package must serve as a silent sales person.

Even the new breed of non-store retailers, those who sell their products through vending machines, catalogues, and home demonstration parties, must be mindful of the phenomenon of impulse shopping. Again they make their offerings as attractive as possible and facilitate the process by offering free delivery, free catalogues, credit, and toll-free telephone numbers.

POLITICAL AND LEGAL FORCES

To an increasing extent, every company's conduct is influenced by the political-legal processes in society. Legislation at all levels exercises more influence on the *marketing* activities of an organization than on any other phase of its operations. The political-legal influences on marketing can be grouped into six categories. In each, the influence stems both from legislation and from policies established by the maze of government agencies. The categories are:

1. *General monetary and fiscal policies*. Marketing systems obviously are affected by the level of government spending, the money supply, and tax legislation.

2. *The new constitution, our legislative framework, codes and policies set by government agencies*. Human rights codes and programs to reduce unemployment fall in this category. Also included is legislation controlling the environment. For example, marketers in the direct mail business are coming under increasing attack for what some consumers feel is the waste involved in flyers and mailing pieces that arrive unsolicited in their mailboxes, much of which ends up in the garbage unread. Legislators are being pressured by environmental groups to pass legislation regulating the sending of such mail. The City of Montreal passed a law in early 1991 that forbids private companies distributing flyers to any residence displaying a special "no-junk-mail" sticker.[6]

3. *Social legislation*. Governments often pass legislation that is intended to protect members of society. A ban on smoking in airplanes, mandatory seat belt use, and the prohibition of cigarette advertising are examples of this type of legislation.

4. *Government relationships with individual industries*. Here we find subsidies in agriculture, shipbuilding, passenger rail transportation, culture, and other industries. Tariffs and import quotas also affect specific industries. In the 1990s, government *deregulation* continues to have a significant effect on financial institutions and on the airline and trucking industries.

---

[6]Marina Strauss, "Junk-mail Marketing Riles Homeowners," *Globe and Mail*, January 25, 1991, p. B6.

5. *Legislation specifically related to marketing*. Marketing executives do not have to be lawyers. But they should know something about these laws, especially the major ones — why they were passed, what are their main provisions, and what are the current ground rules set by the courts and government agencies for administering these laws.

The federal Department of Consumer and Corporate Affairs administers much of the legislation that is included in categories 3 and 4 above. Table 2-1 is a summary of the acts for which the department has responsibility. We shall not continue our discussion of marketing legislation at this point. Instead, we shall cover the relevant legislation in the appropriate places throughout this book.

TABLE 2-1   **Legislation Administered by Consumer and Corporate Affairs Canada**

1. Fully Administered by Department of CCA
   • Bankruptcy Act and Bankruptcy Rules
   • Boards of Trade Act
   • Canada Business Corporations Act
   • Canada Cooperative Association Act
   • Canada Corporations Act
   • Competition Act
   • Consumer Packaging and Labelling Act
   • Copyright Act
   • Department of Consumer and Corporate Affairs Act
   • Electricity and Gas Inspection Act
   • Farmers' Creditors Arrangement Act
   • Gas Inspection Act
   • Government Corporations Operation Act
   • Hazardous Products Act
   • Industrial Design Act
   • Insurance Companies Canadian and British Loan Companies Act
   • Integrated Circuit Topography Act
   • Lobbyists Registration Act
   • National Trade Mark and True Labelling Act
   • Patent Act
   • Pension Fund Societies Act
   • Precious Metals Marketing Act
   • Public Servants Inventions Act
   • Tax Rebate Discounting Act
   • Textile Labelling Act
   • Timber Marketing Act
   • Trade Marks Act
   • Weights and Measures Act
2. Administered Jointly With Other Departments
   • Canada Agricultural Products Standards Act (with Agriculture)
   • Canada Dairy Products Act (with Agriculture)
   • Fish Inspection Act (with Environment)
   • Food and Drugs Act (with Health and Welfare)
   • Maple Products Industry Act (with Agriculture)
   • Shipping Conferences Exemption Act (with Transport)
   • Winding-up Act (with Finance)

6. *The provision of information and the purchase of products.* This sixth area of government influence in marketing is quite different from the other five. Instead of telling marketing executives what they must do or cannot do—instead of the legislation and regulations—the government is clearly helping them. The federal government, through Statistics Canada, is the largest source of secondary marketing information in the country. And the government is the largest single buyer of products and services in the country.

TECHNOLOGY

Technology has a tremendous impact on our lives—our life-styles, our consumption patterns, and our economic well-being. Just think of the effect of major technological developments such as the airplane, plastics, television, computers, antibiotics, and birth control pills. Except perhaps for the airplane, all these technologies reached the large-scale marketing stage only in your lifetime or your parents' lifetime. Think how your life in the future might be affected by cures for the common cold, development of energy sources to replace fossil fuels, low-cost methods for making ocean water drinkable, or even commercial travel to the moon.

Consider for a moment some of the dramatic technological breakthroughs that will expand our horizons in the 1990s. The role of robots undoubtedly will expand considerably. At the heart of a robot's operating mechanism is a miniature electronic computer system, which leads us into another technological breakthrough area—miniature electronic products. It's hard to grasp the fantastic possibilities in this field. Then there is the awesome potential of the superconductor—a means of transmitting electrical energy with virtually no

Using technology to get at the daily problems.

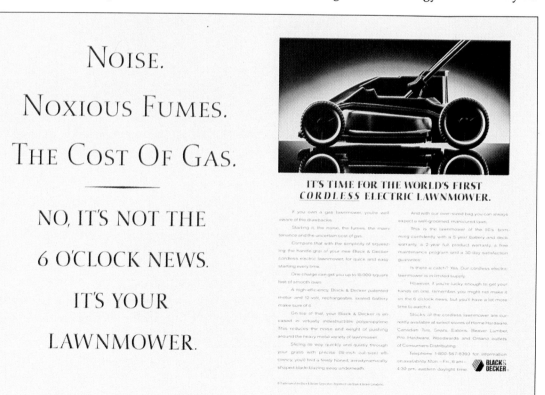

MARKETING AT WORK

FILE 2-3   **CAN YOU SAY IT?**

Canadian legal and governmental restrictions often govern the fashion in which many companies market their products to consumers.

Often these restrictions are said to protect consumers from misleading or deceptive ads, but businesses sometimes find the restrictions frustratingly arbitrary. In 1987, Thomas J. Lipton Inc., the producer of Becel margarine, was charged by the Canadian government because of an ad that Ottawa claimed was an attempt to promote Becel as a prevention for heart disease. The ad boasted that Becel contains a higher proportion of polyunsaturated fats than any other margarine in Canada, "polyunsaturate intake (being) an important factor in the prevention of certain types of heart disease. Eat heart smart and spread a good example, with Becel." Under the federal Food and Drugs Act, however, any attempt to sell products as a prevention or cure for a disease is considered illegal. This screening of all proposed food, cosmetic, and non-prescription drug commercials is a phenomenon not found in the United States, where American companies have been increasingly trying to cash in on the health and fitness craze of recent years.

Source: Adapted from Marina Strauss, "Government Must Restrain Ad-lib Claims," *Globe and Mail*, November 30, 1990, p. 2.

---

resistance. Further developments in fibre optics and high-definition television will open vistas of communication that were not possible even ten years ago. For example, the next generation of automated banking machines (ABMs) will offer customers many additional services, all made possible by advancing technology. While the first ABMs did little more than dispense cash and accept deposits, the new machines dispense stamps and movie tickets, issue travellers' cheques, print account statements, and handle orders for personalized cheques.[7] With more transactions of a diverse nature being handled by ABMs, lines have been getting longer, moving some banks to install cash dispenser machines, the "express lines" of the automated banking business.

Major technological breakthroughs carry a threefold impact on marketing. They are:

- to start entirely new industries, as computers, robots, lasers, and facsimile machines have done;
- to radically alter, or virtually destroy, existing industries. Television had a significant impact on radio and movies when it was introduced in the 1950s. Compact discs and cassette tapes have virtually eliminated the vinyl record business. Facsimile (fax) machines have made major inroads into the conventional business of local courier services and Canada Post, to which the latter has responded with its own courier service and volume electronic mail.[8]

---

[7]Matt Barthel, "U.S. Banking Machines Get New Bells and Whistles," *Globe and Mail Report on Business*, May 20, 1991, p. B6.

[8]Michael Ryval, "Toast to the Post," *Canadian Business*, November 1990, pp. 58–68.

MARKETING AT WORK

FILE 2-4 **"FASTER THAN...?"**

Facsimile, or fax, machines are the most recent superstars to arrive on the technological market. They have transformed many Canadian businesses. In a world that thrives on speed — from instant data to instant breakfasts — fax has become the fast food of communication, led by names such as Canon, Ricoh, and Panafax. Instead of taking days or weeks, today two parties can exchange documents in only a matter of minutes. Since the introduction of fax machines, falling prices and improved quality have kept them in high demand among Canadians. Whereas 1990 saw 133,000 units sold, in 1991 an estimated 147,000 units will be purchased. Fax machines are inundating not only businesses but homes, giving rise to a demand for machines that are priced more accessibly (between $400 and $1,500). If used frequently faxes are cheaper than couriers — and you don't have to worry about postal strikes.

Source: Adapted from Bruce Gates, "Plain-Paper Fax, New Technology Key to Growth," *Financial Post*, January 18, 1991, p. 11.

- to stimulate other markets and industries not related to the new technology. New home appliances and entertainment products have certainly altered the pattern of time use within the home and outside. Cable television, the videocassette recorder (VCR), pay TV, video rentals, and video games have revolutionized the use of television and has led to fragmentation of the television audience.

There is virtually no aspect of our lives that is not being affected in a significant way by new technology. In the home, a majority of Canadian families own a microwave oven and a VCR. With the variety of microwavable foods available, some forecasters are predicting that many families will add a second microwave oven, to allow family members to enjoy a "multiple-choice" meal.[9] Telephone companies have installed voice-activated answering systems that allow the caller to direct his or her calls to the correct department by pressing the appropriate button on a touch-tone telephone. Long-distance operators now "hand off" collect calls to a computerized voice that is able to ask whether the person being called will accept the charges.[10] These computerized "operators" can also respond to questions.

Supermarket chains are experimenting with new computerized systems that will dispense coupons electronically, giving shoppers instant discounts at the point of sale, eliminating paper coupons, the vast majority of which are not redeemed, and making environmentalists a little happier.[11] Banks have been testing the consumer acceptance of a "debit card," which will allow shoppers

---

[9]Marina Strauss, "Get Ready for the Two-microwave Family," *Globe and Mail Report on Business*, May 7, 1991, p. B4.

[10]Mary Gooderham, "Phone Operators Becoming Voice of the Past," *Globe and Mail*, May 7, 1991, pp. A1, A4.

[11]Marina Strauss, "Grocery Coupons on a Card," *Globe and Mail Report on Business*, April 22, 1991, pp. B1, B2.

to pay for items purchased in a retail store by direct debit to their bank accounts, thereby eliminating the writing of cheques and the incurring of the interest charges involved in the use of a credit card.[12]

Despite the advances that have been made, technology is often a mixed blessing. A new technology may improve our lives in one area, while creating environmental and social problems in other areas. The automobile makes life great in some ways, but it also creates traffic jams and air pollution. Television provides built-in baby-sitters, but it also can have an adverse effect on family discussions and on children's reading habits. It is a bit ironic that technology is strongly criticized for creating problems (air pollution, for example), but at the same time is expected to solve these problems.

Monitor the Environment

We have finished our discussion of the major external environmental forces that shape an organization's marketing system. When you stop to think about it, you may realize what a monumental task a marketing executive has in adjusting to these external influences. Obviously, the more executives know about their environment and its future development, the better the job they can do in planning and operating their company's marketing systems. One key to learning about the environment is to monitor it in a systematic, ongoing fashion. In each of the six environmental categories, marketing executives should be alert to trends, new developments, and other changes and future scenarios that may present marketing opportunities or problems for their particular firm.

Management should assign this monitoring responsibility specifically to certain people or departments in the organization. Most of the information probably will be derived from a systematic review of existing sources of information such as periodicals, news releases, and government publications. Personal discussions with particular information sources typically are valuable. In some situations, a company may regularly conduct its own marketing field research to determine some aspect of consumer behaviour or competitor activity.

EXTERNAL MICROENVIRONMENT

Three environmental forces are a part of a company's marketing system, but are external to the company. These are the firm's market, producer-suppliers, and marketing intermediaries. While generally classed as noncontrollable forces, these external elements can be influenced to a greater degree than the macro forces. A marketing organization, for example, may be able to exert some pressure on its suppliers or middlemen. And, through its advertising effort, a firm should have some influence on its present and potential market. (See Fig. 2-2.)

FIGURE 2-2
External microenvironment of a company's marketing program.

[12]Marina Strauss, ''Banks Happy with Debit Card Test,'' *Globe and Mail Report on Business,* May 10, 1991, p. B3.

The Market As both an external force and a key part of every marketing system, the market is really what marketing and this book are all about—how to reach the market and serve it profitably and in a socially responsible manner. The market is (or should be) the focal point of all marketing decisions in an organization. This tremendously important factor is the subject of Part 2 (Chapters 4 to 7), and it crops up frequently throughout the text.

WHAT IS A MARKET?

The word *market* is used in a number of ways. There is a stock *market* and an automobile *market*, a retail *market* for furniture, and a wholesale *market* for furniture. One person may be going to the *market*; another may plan to *market* a product. *What, then, is a market?* Clearly, there are many usages of the term in economic theory, in business in general, and in marketing in particular. A *market* may be defined as a place where buyers and sellers meet, products or services are offered for sale, and transfers of ownership occur. A *market* may also be defined as the demand made by a certain group of potential buyers for a product or service. For example, there is a farm *market* for petroleum products. The terms *market* and *demand* are often used interchangeably, and they may also be used jointly as *market demand*.

These definitions of a market may not be sufficiently precise to be useful to us here. Consequently, in this book a **market** is defined as people or organizations with wants (needs) to satisfy, money to spend, and the willingness to spend it. Thus, in the market demand for any given product or service, there are three factors to consider — people or organizations with wants (needs), their purchasing power, and their buying behaviour.

We shall employ the dictionary definition of *needs*: A need is the lack of anything that is required, desired, or useful. As noted in Chapter 1, we do not limit needs to the narrow physiological requirements of food, clothing, and shelter essential for survival. In effect, in our discussion, the words *needs* and *wants* are used synonymously and interchangeably.

A **market** is people or organizations with ← Needs (or wants) to satisfy / Money to spend / Willingness to spend it

SUPPLIERS

You can't sell a product if you can't first make it or buy it. So it is probably rather obvious that **producer-suppliers** of products and services are critical to the success of any marketing organization. In our economy a buyer's market exists for most products. That is, there is no problem in making or buying a product; the problem is usually how to market it.

Marketers often do not concern themselves enough with the supply side. However, the importance of suppliers in a company's marketing system comes into focus sharply when shortages occur. But shortages only highlight the importance of cooperative relationships with suppliers. Suppliers' prices and services are a significant influence on any company's marketing system. At the same time, these prices and services can very often be influenced by careful planning on the part of the buying organization.

MARKETING INTERMEDIARIES

Marketing intermediaries are independent business organizations that directly aid in the flow of products and services between a marketing organization and its markets. These intermediaries include two types of institutions: (1) resellers — the wholesalers and retailers — or the people we call "middlemen" and (2) various "facilitating" organizations that provide transportation, warehousing, financing, and other supportive services sellers need to complete exchanges between buyers and sellers.

These intermediaries operate between a company and its markets and between a company and its suppliers. Thus they complete what we call "channels of distribution" or "trade channels."

In some situations it may be more efficient for a company to operate on a "do-it-yourself" basis without using marketing intermediaries. That is, a firm can deal *directly* with its suppliers or sell *directly* to its customers and do its own shipping, financing, and so on. But marketing intermediaries do perform a variety of services. They are specialists in their respective fields. Typically, they justify their economic existence by doing a better job at a lower cost than the marketing organization can do by itself.

ORGANIZATION'S INTERNAL ENVIRONMENT

An organization's marketing system is also shaped to some extent by *internal* forces that are largely controllable by management. These internal influences include a firm's production, financial, and personnel capabilities. If Procter & Gamble is considering adding a new brand of soap, for example, it must determine whether existing production facilities and expertise can be used. If the new product requires a new plant or machinery, financial capability enters the picture. Other nonmarketing forces are the company's location, its research and development (R&D) strength as evidenced by the patents it holds, and the overall image the firm projects to the public. Plant location often determines the geographic limits of a company's market, particularly if high transportation costs or perishable products are involved. The R&D factor may determine whether a company will lead or follow in the industry's technology and marketing. (See Fig. 2-3.)

Another environmental consideration here is the necessity of coordinating the marketing and nonmarketing activities in a company. Sometimes this can be difficult because of conflicts in goals and executive personalities. Production people, for example, like to see long production runs of standardized items. However, marketing executives may want a variety of models, sizes, and

FIGURE 2-3
Internal environment of a company's marketing program.

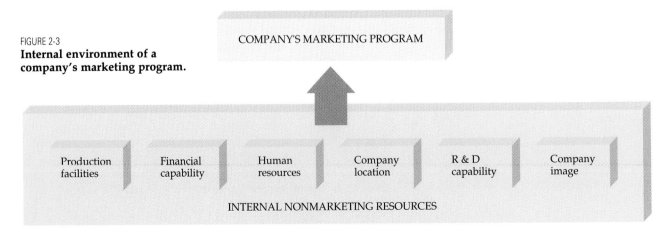

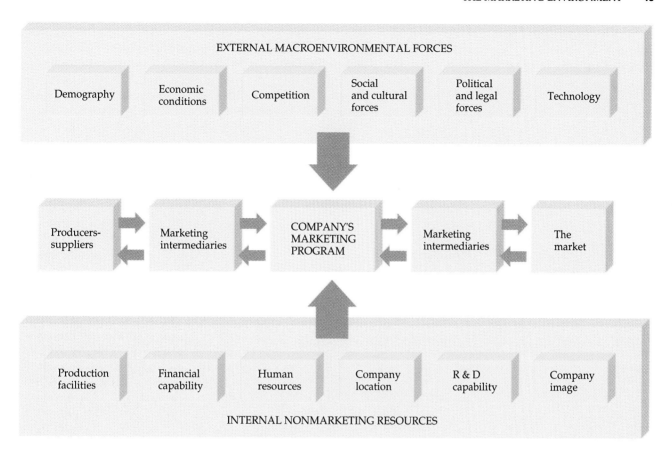

EXTERNAL MACROENVIRONMENTAL FORCES

Demography | Economic conditions | Competition | Social and cultural forces | Political and legal forces | Technology

Producers-suppliers | Marketing intermediaries | COMPANY'S MARKETING PROGRAM | Marketing intermediaries | The market

Production facilities | Financial capability | Human resources | Company location | R & D capability | Company image

INTERNAL NONMARKETING RESOURCES

FIGURE 2-4
A company's marketing environment.

colours to satisfy different market segments. Financial executives typically want tighter credit and expense limits than the marketing people feel are necessary to be competitive.

To wrap up our discussion of the marketing environment, Fig. 2-4 shows the environmental forces that combine to shape an organization's marketing program. Within the framework of these constraints, management should develop a marketing program to provide want-satisfaction to its markets. The next chapter is devoted to an introduction to the basic concepts of marketing planning.

SUMMARY

A company operates its marketing system within a framework of ever-changing forces that constitute the system's environment. Some of the forces are broad, external variables that generally cannot be controlled by the executives in a firm. Demographic conditions are one of these macro influences. Another is economic conditions such as the business cycle, inflation, interest rates, and unemployment. Management must be aware of the various types of competition and the competitive structure within which a given firm operates.

Social and cultural forces, including cultural changes, are another factor with which to contend. Political and legal forces, along with technology, round out the group of external macroenvironmental influences. Management should establish a system for monitoring these external forces.

Another set of environmental factors—producer-suppliers, marketing intermediaries, and the market itself—is also external to the firm. But these elements clearly are part of the firm's marketing system and can be controlled to some extent by the firm. At the same time a set of nonmarketing resources *within* the firm (production facilities, personnel, finances) influences its marketing system. These variables generally are controllable by management.

KEY TERMS AND CONCEPTS

Demography 25
Economic conditions 26
  Business cycle 27
    Inflation 27
    Interest rates 27
    Employment rates 27
  Competition 28
Social and cultural forces 29

Political and legal forces 35
Technology 37
Environmental monitoring 40
Market 41
Suppliers 41
Marketing intermediaries 41

QUESTIONS AND PROBLEMS

1. It is predicted that university and college enrolments will decline during the next several years. What marketing measures should your school take to adjust to this forecast?

2. For each of the following companies, give some examples of how its marketing program is likely to differ during periods of prosperity as contrasted with periods of recession.
   a. McCain's orange juice.
   b. CCM skates.
   c. Adidas athletic shoes.
   d. Sony Walkman.

3. If interest rates are high, how is the situation likely to affect the market for the following products?
   a. Roots sweatshirts.
   b. Building materials.
   c. Videocassette recorders.
   d. Day-care programs.

4. Explain the three types of competition faced by a company. What marketing strategies or programs would you recommend to meet each type?

5. Give some examples of how the changing attitudes of Canadians towards the environment and their changing food consumption patterns have been reflected in the marketing programs of various companies.

6. What are some of the marketing implications of the increasing public interest in health and physical fitness?

7. What should be the role of marketing in treating the following major social problems?
   a. Air pollution.
   b. The depletion of irreplaceable resources.
   c. Seasonal unemployment.

8. Give some examples of the effects of marketing legislation in your own buying, recreation, and other everyday activities. Do you believe these laws are effective? If not, what changes would you recommend?

9. Using examples other than those in this chapter, explain how a firm's marketing system can be influenced by the environmental factor of technology.

10. Explain how each of the following resources within a company might influence that company's marketing program.

11. Specify some internal environmental forces affecting the marketing program of:

a. Shoppers Drug Mart.   c. A local restaurant.

b. Your school.   d. Air Canada.

12. Explain how or under what conditions a company might exert some control over its suppliers and intermediaries in its marketing program.

CHAPTER 3 GOALS

The marketing system must be managed—and its activities must be planned—for effective operation within its environment. After studying this chapter, you should be able to explain:

- The management process as it applies to marketing.
- The meanings of some basic management terms.
- The nature, scope, and importance of planning in marketing.
- Some fundamentals of strategic company planning and strategic marketing planning.
- The concept of the marketing mix.

Strategic Marketing Planning

S trategic marketing planning? At Canada Post? Yes!

It has been called a most surprising turnaround. In the mid-1980s, Canada Post was considered disorganized and unfocused. It had been handed a three-part mandate: (1) to change from a civil-service-run public service organization (as a government department) to a service-oriented corporate organization (as a Crown corporation); (2) to become financially self-sufficient; and (3) to improve labour relations.

At that time Don Lander, the newly appointed president of the corporation, turned his attention to improving delivery service — the basic strategy for achieving two parts of the mandate. A 1985 Postal Services Review Committee Report made 50 recommendations for service improvement and Canada Post implemented the 40 under its jurisdiction. Some of these recommendations became more detailed objectives, others became detailed strategies, still others became tactical moves. All became part of Canada Post's marketing planning process that would produce a customer service system with defined customer categories, established service standards, and objectives that could be communicated to customers and employees. The system then had to be managed and evaluated.

Currently, independent audits prove that Canada Post is meeting its on-time commitments for various forms of customer service better than ever. On a national basis, 98 percent of the mail within the same urban centre is delivered within two business days; 98 percent of the mail between urban centres in the same province is delivered within three days; 98 percent of the mail between urban centres in different provinces is delivered within four days. Reliability is up; productivity is up; employee morale is up, and absenteeism is down. Much of the credit is given to Lander's dedication to customer service. Under Lander, all levels of the organization have a greater sense of accountability to the customer. The marketing plan was detailed and well communicated, and performance was carefully evaluated—Ernst and Young have been conducting independent audits on delivery performance four times a year since the fall of 1987.

The company, of course, has supporters as well as detractors. Its major supporters are the business users who provide more than 80 percent of its revenues. It has a good relationship with the Canadian Direct Marketing Association and its 550 corporate members, as well as with the National Association of Major Mail Users—those firms that send out the bulk of the first class mail volume and make up more than half of total revenues. For the major users, the post office's customer orientation has worked.

But some aspects of the new customer orientation and the aggressive marketing of new services are not appreciated. For members of the Canadian Courier Association, Canada Post's Priority Courier is unwelcome competition. Other voices berate Canada Post for not providing door-to-door mail delivery services. The Canadian Union of Postal Workers would rather the company be a public service organization than a business. Work stoppages and labour problems make it difficult for the company to implement its plan effectively and maintain and improve its service. But the company points to a first-ever $96-million profit in 1988–89; $149 million in 1989–90; and a projected $251 million by 1995–96. There's still a lot to be done, but the marketing planning framework is in place. Can the company manage its human resources so it can deliver as planned?

In the preceding chapter we saw that a company's marketing system is strongly influenced by external environmental forces and also by the firm's internal environment. Those influences are very apparent in the Canada Post story. In this chapter, we consider how a company manages its marketing activities within its environment. Specifically, we shall discuss the management process as it applies to a marketing program, and one major part of this management process—namely, strategic planning. Canada Post provides us with an illustration of strategic planning in action. Our discussion which follows is brief, to the point, and at a level that is appropriate for your first course in marketing.

MANAGING A MARKETING SYSTEM

Within its environment, an organization—whether large or small, business or not-for-profit — must plan, implement, and evaluate its marketing system. That is, the organization must *manage* its marketing effort—and must do this effectively.

The ''marketing'' part of the term *marketing management* was defined in Chapter 1 and the marketing mix was briefly introduced. But what about the ''management'' part? The terms *management* and *administration* are used synonymously here. They may be defined as the process of planning, implementing, and evaluating the efforts of a group of people towards a common goal. Through management, the combined group output surpasses the sum of the individual outputs.

The Management Process

The management process, as applied to marketing, consists basically of (1) planning a marketing program, (2) implementing it, and (3) evaluating its performance. The **planning** stage includes setting the goals and selecting the strategies and tactics to reach these goals. The **implementing** stage includes forming and staffing the marketing organization and directing the actual operation of the organization according to the plan. The **performance-evaluation**

---

[1]Adapted from Michael Ryval, ''Toast to the Post,'' *Canadian Business*, November, 1990, pp. 58–68 and Harvey Enchin, ''Second Class Mail,'' *Globe and Mail*, October 26, 1991, p. D1.

FIGURE 3-1
The management process in marketing systems.
Plans are implemented and performance results are evaluated to provide information used to plan for the future. The process is continuous and allows for adapting to changes in the environment.

Planning	Implementation	Evaluation
Setting goals Selecting strategies and tactics	Organizing Staffing Operating	Comparing performance with goals

Feedback of evaluation, so management can adapt future goals, plans, and their implementation to the changing environment.

stage is a good example of the interrelated, continuing nature of the management process. That is, evaluation is both a look back and a look ahead—a link between past performance and future planning and operations. Management looks back to analyze performance in light of organizational goals. The findings from this evaluation of past performance then are used to look ahead in setting the goals and plans for future periods. (See Fig. 3-1.)

Throughout the past 20 years, a tremendous amount of attention in business has been devoted to the planning phase of the management process. Several planning models were developed, and most of the large companies used one or more of these models. The popular term for this activity—virtually a buzzword in business — is strategic planning. In the next major section of this chapter, we shall briefly discuss strategic planning—especially strategic marketing planning. Business also typically devotes much time and effort to the performance-evaluation activities in the management process.

In Parts 2 through 5 of this book, we shall be discussing the planning and development of a marketing program in an organization. Periodically throughout those chapters, we shall be dealing with the implementation of marketing plans. Then, near the end of the book, we devote an entire chapter (Chapter 21) to the implementation and evaluation stages of the marketing management process.

Some Basic Management Terminology

Several basic terms continually appear in discussions of the management of a marketing system. These terms sometimes are used carelessly, and they may mean different things to different people. Consequently, at this point let's look at the way these terms will be used in this book.

OBJECTIVES AND GOALS

We shall treat these two terms—objectives and goals—as synonymous and to be used interchangeably in all our discussions. An **objective** (or **goal**) is something that is to be attained. Effective planning must begin with a series of objectives that are to be reached by carrying out the plans. The objectives are, in essence, the reasons for the plans. Furthermore, the objectives should be stated in writing, to minimize (1) the possibility of misunderstanding and (2) the risk that managerial decisions and activities will not be in accord with these goals.

To be effective, the goals also should be stated as specifically as possible:

Too vague, too general	More specific
1. Increase our market share.	1. Next year, increase our market share to 25 percent from its present 20 percent level.
2. Improve our profit position.	2. Generate a return on investment of 15 percent next year.

STRATEGIES

A **strategy** is a broad, basic plan of action by which an organization intends to reach its goal. The word *strategy* (from the Greek word *strategia*) originally was related to the science or art of military generalship. A strategy is a grand plan for winning a battle as a step towards achieving the objective of winning the war.

In marketing, the relationship between goals and strategies may be illustrated as follows:

Goals	Possible strategies
1. Reduce marketing costs next year by 15 percent below this year's level.	1a. Reduce warehouse inventories and eliminate slow-moving products.
	1b. Reduce number of sales calls on small accounts.
2. Increase sales next year by 10 percent over this year's figure.	2a. Intensify marketing efforts in domestic markets.
	2b. Expand into foreign markets.

Two companies might have the same goal, but use different strategies to reach that goal. For example, two firms might each aim to increase their market share by 20 percent over the next three years. To reach this goal, one firm's strategy might be to intensify its efforts in the domestic markets. The other company might select the strategy of expanding into foreign markets.

Conversely, two companies might have different goals but select the same strategy to reach them. As an illustration, suppose one company's goal is to increase its sales volume next year by 20 percent over this year's sales. The other company wants to earn a 20 percent return on investment next year. Both companies might decide that their best strategy is to introduce a major new product next year.

TACTICS

A **tactic** is an operational means by which a strategy is to be implemented or activated. A tactic typically is a more specific, detailed course of action than is a strategy. Also, tactics generally cover shorter time periods—are more closely oriented to short-term goals than are strategies.

Let's look at some examples:

Strategies	Tactics
1. Direct our promotion to males, age 25–40.	1a. Advertise in magazines read by this market segment.
	1b. Advertise on television programs watched by these people.
2. Increase sales-force motivation.	2a. Conduct more sales contests.
	2b. Increase incentive features in pay plans.
	2c. Use more personal supervision of sales people.

MARKETING AT WORK

FILE 3-1   SUN ICE PROMOTIONS SHINE

Sun Ice is a Calgary company that designs, manufactures, and markets ski wear, casual outerwear, active sportswear, and leisure wear. It distributes its products throughout all ten provinces and 31 states of the United States. A recent marketing goal of the company has been to expand its markets in Ontario and Quebec and throughout the United States. The marketing strategies used by Sun Ice include offering no discounted or "off-price" goods, assisting retailers in the merchandising of Sun Ice products, and investing heavily in marketing "Canadian manufactured products." Sun Ice also promotes its products through sponsorship of athletic events and through projects such as "Adult Lift Ticket Hang Tags" and the "Junior Learn-to-Ski Program." These promotions give purchasers the right to ski free for a day when they buy a Sun Ice product. Can you contrast these strategies with those used by competing manufacturers of similar clothing products?

To be effective, the tactics selected must parallel or support the strategy. It would be a mistake, for example, to adopt a strategy of increasing our sales to the women's market—and then advertise in men's magazines or use advertising messages that appeal to men.

POLICY

A **policy** is a course of action adopted by management or the owner/operator to routinely guide future decision making in a given situation. Policies typically are used on all levels in an organization—from the presidential suite down to new employees. It may be company *policy*, for example, to have a union leader on the board of directors. Sales managers may follow the *policy* of hiring only college graduates for sales jobs. In the office of a small service business, the *policy* may be that the last person leaving must turn off the lights and lock the door.

A policy typically is an "automatic decision-making mechanism" for some situation. That is, once a course of action is decided upon in a given situation, then that decision becomes the *policy* that we follow every time the same situation arises. For example, to reach the goal of a certain sales volume in our company, suppose we decided on a strategy of offering quantity discounts in pricing. The relevant tactic we selected was a certain detailed discount schedule. Now, once those decisions have been made, we can follow the pricing *policy* of routinely granting a quantity discount according to our predetermined schedule.

CONTROL

Many writers and business executives refer to the management process as consisting of planning, implementation, and *control*. In this book we use the term *performance evaluation* to represent the third activity in the management process. To speak of *control* as only one part of the management process seems to be a misleading and unduly restricted use of the term.

Control is not an isolated managerial function — it permeates virtually all other managerial activities. For example, management *controls* its company operations by virtue of the goals and strategies it selects. The type of organization structure used in the marketing department determines the degree of *control* over marketing operations. Management *controls* its sales force or service providers by means of the compensation plan, the territorial structure, and so on.

Levels of Goals and Strategies

When discussing objectives, strategies, and tactics, it is important to identify the organizational level that we are talking about. Otherwise, we run the risk of creating confusion and misunderstanding, for a very simple reason: What is an *objective* for an executive on one organizational level may be a *strategy* for management on a higher level.

As an illustration, suppose one executive says, ''Our goal is to enter the four-province Western market next year and generate a sales volume of at least $1 million.'' A second executive says, ''No—entering that new market is only a strategy. Our goal is to increase our market share to 15 percent next year.'' A third executive says that the second is wrong. ''Increasing our market share is our strategy,'' is this person's argument. ''Our goal is to earn a 20 percent return on investment.''

Actually, all three executives are correct. They simply are speaking from the perspectives of different organizational levels in their firm. These relationships may be summarized as follows:

- *Company goal:* To earn a 20 percent return on investment next year.
- *Company strategy (and marketing goal):* To increase our share of the market to 15 percent next year.
- *Marketing strategy (and sales-force goal):* To enter the four-province Western market next year and generate a minimum sales volume of $1 million.

And so on down to an individual sales representative. This person's goal may be to exceed quota by 15 percent, and the proposed strategy may be to average three more sales calls per day.

In any case, for a particular *level of objective*, a *strategy* is a plan of action designed to reach that objective. *Tactics* then are the operational details that implement this plan.

NATURE AND SCOPE OF PLANNING

We now are ready to talk about developing a marketing program in an organization. To do an effective job in developing such a program, however, management first should prepare a strategic plan for the total organizational effort. Then this total-company planning should be followed by strategic planning in the organization's various functional divisions, including marketing. The success of a company's marketing effort depends largely upon management's ability to strategically plan a marketing program within the environmental framework discussed earlier in this chapter and then to carry out that plan.

But before we discuss strategic company planning, let's first understand the concept of planning in general.

The Importance of Planning

There's an old saying to the effect that if you don't know where you're going, then any road will take you there. That is, you need a plan. If you don't have a plan, you cannot get anything done—because you don't know what needs to be done or how to do it. In simple English, **planning** is studying the past to decide in the present what to do in the future. Or deciding what we are going to do later, when and how we are going to do it, and who will do it.

The Nature of Planning

In business management, one type of planning that we find very useful is the more formal concept called strategic planning. **Strategic planning** may be defined as the managerial process of matching an organization's resources with its marketing opportunities over the long run. Note (1) that strategic planning is a total-company concept and (2) that it involves a long-run orientation.

The concept of planning is not new. However, market and economic conditions in recent years have led to a better understanding of the need for formal planning. Truly, any success that management has in increasing the profitability of marketing operations depends in large part upon the nature of its marketing planning. Formal planning is one of the most effective management tools available for reducing risks.

Scope of Planning Activities

Planning may cover long or short periods of time. **Long-range planning** (for 3, 5, 10, or even 25 years) usually involves top management and special planning staffs. It deals with broad, company-wide issues such as plant, market, or product expansion. **Short-term planning** typically covers a period of one year or less and is the responsibility of lower- and middle-echelon executives. It involves such issues as planning next year's advertising campaign, making merchandise-buying plans in a store, or setting sales quotas for a sales force.

The planning activities in an organization may be conducted on three or four different levels, depending upon the size of the organization and the diversity of its products or services. These planning levels are as follows:

1. **Strategic company planning.** At this level, management defines the organization's mission, sets the organization's long-range goals, and decides on broad strategies formulated to achieve the goals. These long-range, company-wide goals and strategies then become the framework within which departmental planning is done. This total-company planning takes into consideration an organization's financial requirements, production capabilities, labour needs, research and development effort, and marketing capabilities.
2. **Strategic business unit planning.** In large, diversified organizations, a modification of strategic company-wide planning has emerged in recent years. For more effective planning and operation, the total organization is divided into separate divisions called *strategic business* units (SBUs). Each SBU is, in effect, a separate ''business,'' and each SBU conducts its own strategic ''business-wide'' planning.
3. **Strategic marketing planning.** At this level, management is engaged in setting goals and strategies for the marketing effort in the organization. In smaller or nondiversified organizations, the SBU planning and marketing planning may be combined into one strategic planning activity. Or, in small, single-business organizations, the top three levels of planning (company, SBU, marketing) may be combined into one planning activity.

    Strategic marketing planning includes (1) the selection of target markets and (2) the development of the four major ingredients in a company's marketing program — the product, the distribution system, the pricing structure, and the promotional activities. In Parts 3 to 6 of this book, these four ingredients will be considered individually.

4. **Annual marketing planning.** The annual marketing plan is one part, covering one time segment, of the ongoing strategic marketing planning process. It is a master plan covering a year's marketing operations for a given product line, major product, brand, or market. Thus, this plan serves as a tactical operational guide to the executives in each phase of the marketing effort for the given product or market.

STRATEGIC COMPANY PLANNING

Strategic company planning is the managerial process of matching an organization's resources with its marketing opportunities over the long run. This process consists of (1) defining the organization's mission, (2) setting organizational objectives, (3) evaluating the strategic business units (this is called *business portfolio analysis*), and (4) selecting appropriate strategies so as to achieve the organizational objectives. (See Fig. 3-2.) The strategic planning process will be influenced considerably by the external macroenvironmental forces such as economic conditions, technologies, and competition.[2] It probably is obvious that management's planning also will be influenced by the

FIGURE 3-2
The strategic planning process for the total organization.

Define organizational mission

Determine organizational objectives

Conduct organizational portfolio analysis (SBU planning)

Select organizational strategies for the total organization (in a small, one-product company) or for each SBU (in a larger multiproduct company)

[2]Techniques for identifying and monitoring nontraditional competitors are discussed in William E. Rothschild, "Who Are Your Future Competitors?" *The Journal of Business Strategy*, May/June 1988, pp. 10–14.

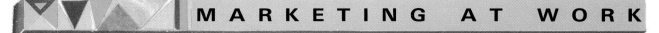

MARKETING AT WORK

FILE 3-2   **MARKETING WITH A MISSION**

Compare and discuss the following mission statements, and explore the implications of each for the marketing progams of the respective companies:

Sun Ice: to market fashion outerwear and leisure wear that performs.

Four Seasons Hotels: to be recognized as the company that operates the finest hotel wherever we locate — and profitably.

A&W: to be an energetic, consumer-driven growth company that builds on earning the trust of all its business partners.

---

organization's internal resources such as its financial condition, production facilities, research and development capabilities, etc.

Define Organizational Mission

The first step in the strategic process, as applied to the organization as a whole, is to clearly define the company's mission. For some firms, this step requires only the review and approval of a previously published mission statement. But, for most firms, whether big or small, this step in formal planning really has never been clearly articulated.

Defining an organization's mission means answering the question, ''What business are we in?'' And further, management may also ask, ''What business *should* we be in?'' Unless the organization's basic purpose is clear to all managers, any efforts at strategic planning are likely to be ineffective.

Tactic: emphasizing fast photography for speedy descriptions.

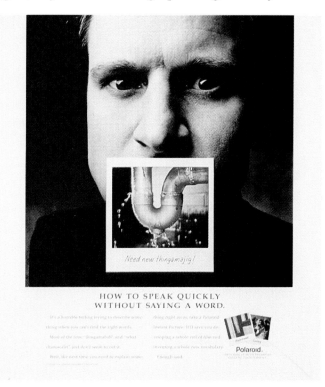

Need new thingamajig!

HOW TO SPEAK QUICKLY
WITHOUT SAYING A WORD.

Polaroid.

An organization's purpose, or mission, should be stated in writing and well publicized. A properly prepared statement of company mission can be an effective public relations tool. The statement should not be too broad or vague —nor should it be too narrow or specific. To say that our mission is "to benefit consumers" is too broad and vague. To say that our business is "to make tennis balls" is too narrow. Neither statement provides sufficient guidance to management.

Traditionally, companies have stated their mission in production-oriented terms: "We make telephones (or furnaces or skis)." Management might say, "We are in the trucking business (or in furniture manufacturing or in the mutual funds business)."

Today, in line with the marketing concept, organizations are urged to be marketing-oriented in their mission statements. Executives should be thinking of the benefits they are marketing and the wants they are satisfying. (See Table 3-1). Thus, instead of saying, "We make telephones," a phone company should define its mission as the marketing of communication services. Instead of "making furnaces," the Lennox Company's mission should be stated as the marketing of home climate control. Not only are these marketing-oriented mission statements more attractive to the public, but also they serve to broaden a company's market and extend the company's life. If your mission is to make furnaces, you will be out of business when furnaces are replaced by heat pumps or solar heating units. But if your mission is to market climate control, then you can discontinue furnace production, switch to alternative energy sources, and continue competing with the new generation of heating and air-conditioning companies.

TABLE 3-1 **What Business Are You In?**

	Production-oriented answer	Marketing-oriented answer
Bell Canada	We operate a phone company.	We market a communications system.
Esso	We produce oil and gasoline products.	We market energy.
Roots Canada	We make sweatshirts.	In wearing apparel, we offer comfort, fashion, and durability.
Xerox Canada	We make copy machines.	We market automated office systems.
Kodak Canada	We make cameras and film.	We market beautiful memories.
Revlon Cosmetics—the president said:	"In the factory we make cosmetics."	"In the drugstore, we sell hope."

Determine Organizational Objectives

The next step in the strategic planning process is for management to decide upon a set of objectives that will guide the organization in accomplishing its mission. These objectives can also serve as guides for managerial planning at lower levels in an organization. And they provide standards for evaluating an organization's performance.

In effect, the definition of what business we are in and a statement of our goals are critically important to the marketing effort in our organization. The

Dofasco's mission is more than selling steel.

WE'RE COOKING

From ranges to roofing, cans to cars, Dofasco people are helping North American manufacturers improve quality and control costs.

Modern product design and manufacturing processes call for very precise matching of steels to specific end uses.

Dofasco design and materials engineers often play an important role in that matching process, which involves selecting from thousands of different types and grades of steel in Dofasco's material 'palette.' Then fine-tuning the chosen steel to precisely match the individual customer's specific needs.

Our customer support teams even propose changes to the customer's design when we spot opportunities to improve quality and cost effectiveness.

We've worked on a variety of projects with customers in various industries. In the appliance industry, for example, we can analyse appliances part-by-part to determine whether parts could be made from more economical grades. In design 'teardowns' such as these, our expertise in steel coatings can be particularly helpful.

We're working more closely with customers to help them achieve their performance and cost objectives.

We believe this kind of teamwork is the natural result of a determination we share with our customers. A determination to win globally.

DOFASCO
Our product is steel. Our strength is people.

mission statement tells us something about the markets to be served, and the objectives give us some direction in determining how we will implement the marketing concept. Together, the statements of mission and objectives should help us to be marketing-oriented rather than production- or sales-oriented.

Objectives should be action-stimulators, because objectives are achieved by actions that carry out plans. To fulfil their purposes, objectives must possess a number of attributes. They should be:

- Clear and specific
- Stated in writing
- Ambitious but realistic

- Consistent with each other
- Quantitatively measurable whenever possible
- Tied to a specific time period

Some examples of objectives that illustrate these criteria are as follows:

Too general: To increase the company's profitability.

More specific: To increase the company's return on investment to 18 percent within two years.

Not measurable: To improve the company's public image.

Measurable: To receive favourable recognition awards next year from at least three consumer or environmental groups.

Conduct Organizational Portfolio Analysis: Strategic Business Unit (SBU) Planning

Many organizations are so diversified that total-company planning cannot serve as an effective guide for the executives who manage the component divisions of the organizations. At Imasco, for example, the mission, objectives, and strategies of the tobacco division are quite different from those of the Shoppers Drug Mart division. Most large and medium-sized companies—and even many small firms — are multiproduct, and even multibusiness, organizations.

Consequently, for more effective planning and operation, the total organization should be divided into major product or market divisions. The divisions are called *strategic business units* (SBUs) — a term coined some years ago by a major consulting firm in its work with General Electric. Each SBU may be a major division in an organization, a group of related products, or even a single major product, or brand.

To be identified as an SBU, a unit should posses these characteristics:

- It is a separately identifiable business.
- It has its own distinct mission.
- It has its own competitors.
- It has its own executives and profit responsibility.
- It may have its own strategic plan.

To illustrate, some possible SBU divisions are as follows:

General Electric: Electrical motors, major appliances, jet engines, medical equipment, lighting equipment, electronic supplies, etc.

A university: Different schools (engineering, business, education, law, etc.) *or* different teaching methods (on-campus courses, television courses, correspondence courses).

Dylex: Retail stores throughout Canada, operated under a variety of different names, including Tip Top Tailors, Harry Rosen, Braemar, Big Steel, Fairweather, L A Express, Suzy Shier, Thrifty's, Diva, Fantasia, Feathers, Bi-Way, and Town and Country.

Sears retail stores: Auto supplies, furniture, large appliances, plumbing and heating equipment, home furnishings, women's apparel, men's apparel, sporting goods, hardware, etc.

The trick here is to set up the proper number of SBUs in an organization. If there are too many, management can get bogged down in the planning, operating, and reporting details. If there are too few SBUs, each unit covers too broad an area to be useful for managerial planning and control.

The total organization may then be viewed as a "portfolio" of these businesses. And a *key step in strategic planning* is an evaluation of the individual businesses in the organization's portfolio. This evaluation is called a **business** (or **product**) **portfolio analysis**. Or we can use the broader term **organizational portfolio** analysis, to imply the use of this planning concept in nonbusiness, nonprofit organizations.

A portfolio analysis is made to identify the present status of each SBU and to determine its future role in the company. This evaluation also provides guidance to management in designing the strategies and tactics for an SBU. Management typically has limited resources to use in supporting its SBUs. Consequently, management needs to know how to allocate these limited resources. Which SBUs should be stimulated to grow, which ones maintained in their present market position, and which ones eliminated? A business portfolio analysis is designed to aid management in this decision making.[3]

Selected Organizational Strategies

By this point in its strategic planning, presumably the organization has determined where it wants to go. The next step in strategic planning is to design the ways to get there. These are the organizational strategies—the broad, basic plans of action by which an organization intends to achieve its goals and fulfil its mission. We are speaking about selecting strategies (1) for the total organization in a small, one-product company or (2) for each SBU in a larger, multiproduct or multibusiness or multinational organization.

Several models have been developed that management can use as guides in its selection of appropriate organizational strategies. To illustrate the possible strategic use of these models, at this point we shall describe very briefly three of them. Any further discussion of these and other planning really is outside the scope of this book.

PORTER'S GENERIC-STRATEGIES MODEL

Professor Michael Porter of the Harvard Business School has developed a model in which he indentifies the following three generic strategies to achieve success in a competitive market.[4]

- *Overall cost leadership:* Produce a standardized product at a low price and then underprice everybody else.
- *Differentiation:* Market at a higher-than-average price something that customers will perceive as being unique in quality, design, brand, or some other feature.
- *Focus:* Concentrate on a small specialty market (particular consumer group, geographic market) or a segment of the product line.

---

[3]Several approaches have been developed for conducting an organizational portfolio analysis. For more on these methods, see William A. Cohen, *The Practice of Marketing Management*, Macmillan Publishing Co., New York, 1988; and David W. Cravens, *Strategic Marketing*, 2nd ed., Richard D. Irwin, Homewood, Ill., 1987.

[4]This discussion is adapted from Walter Kiechel, III, "Three (Or Four, or More) Ways to Win," *Fortune*, Oct. 19, 1981, p. 181; and by same author, "The Decline of the Experience Curve," *Fortune*, Oct. 5, 1981, p. 146. See also Michael E. Porter, *Competitive Strategy: Techniques for Analyzing Industries and Competitors*, The Free Press, New York, 1980.

MARKETING AT WORK

FILE 3-3 **STRATEGIES FOR SUCCESS IN THE GLOBAL MARKETPLACE**

Twenty years ago, Four Seasons Hotels had just two hotels; today it has invaded major markets in the United States and Britain, which are dominated by large chains and prestigious names, and has become the largest luxury hotel operator in the world. Foreseeing a "one-world market," they have focused their energies in the last few years upon expanding into Europe and the Pacific Rim—and they have met with success. This is how.

1. By Having a Sense of Purpose/Vision: Four Seasons' commitment is "to be recognized as the company that operates the finest hotel wherever (they) locate, and to do it profitably." Their purpose — customer satisfaction — emphasizes a strong customer orientation. The company places great importance on making sure that *all* employees are aware of this goal, for it is the lowest-paid, least-motivated dishwashers and bellmen who make or break a luxury hotel's reputation.

2. By Concentrating on Key Markets and Services: To compete globally, Four Seasons has tried to be distinctive from other hotels, with clear notions of what it is selling and to whom. Its customers are top executives, frequent travellers who want the best and will pay for it, customers who are price insensitive. Four Seasons offers them a luxury life-style—aesthetics, comfort, convenience, personal services — and in doing so have tapped a premium quality niche that nobody else has claimed. The advantages of focusing on the luxury market are that it has strong growth potential, is least susceptible to recession, and is the easiest in which to win recognition.

3. By Allocating Resources to Areas of Greatest Strength: In slow economic times, Four Seasons spent a lot of money upgrading hotels, raising quality, and making it consistent while other hotels were cutting staff and maintenance. Over time, this has resulted in a brand name so synonymous with quality that even on its own it generates enormous profits.

4. By Teaming Up with Foreign Companies in Foreign Markets: This is the fastest, cheapest way to build global volume at the lowest possible cost. In teaming up with Fujita Group, a Japanese hospitality group, Four Seasons was able to successfully break into the fastest-growing Japanese market, a feat it could never have done on its own because of Japan's scarce land and political and cultural barriers.

Source: Adapted from John Sharpe, "Making It in the Global Market," *Business Quarterly*, Winter, 1990, pp. 23-27.

Porter's model is shown in Fig. 3-3. Companies in the upper left-hand end of the curve are profitable even with a small market share, because their products and/or markets are specialized and command above-average prices. Firms at the upper right-hand end of the curve also are successful. This is because they differentiate their products or they have a large market share because of low prices and low costs. It is the firms in the middle (low) part of the curve that are in trouble. They have low profits and a modest share because they have nothing going for them.

FIGURE 3-3
Porter's generic-strategies model.

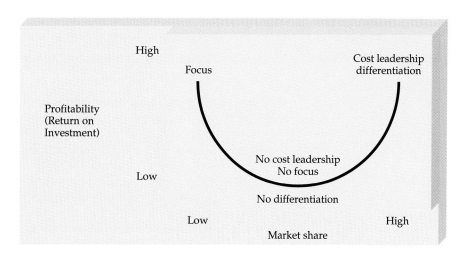

BOSTON CONSULTING GROUP MATRIX

The Boston Consulting Group (BCG), a well-known management consulting firm, has developed a new strategic planning matrix.[5] See Fig. 3-4.

FIGURE 3-4
Boston Consulting Group's strategic planning matrix.

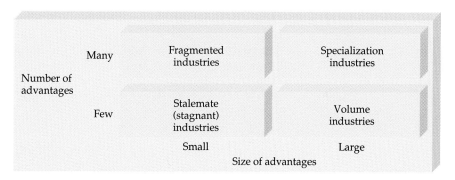

On the vertical axis is plotted the number of ways the company can obtain a marketing advantage, from few to many. On the horizontal axis we plot the size of the advantage, ranging from small to large. The resulting model may be divided into four cells, each identifying a different strategic industrial situation, as follows:

- *Stalemate (stagnant) industries:* Very few advantages, and they are small—steel or uncoated paper, for example.
- *Volume industries:* Very few advantages, but they are big—such as the cost advantage in a large aluminum plant.
- *Fragmented industries:* Many competitive advantages, but each one is limited in size—as in the restaurant industry.
- *Specialization industries:* Many competitive advantages, and they are large—Japanese automobile manufacturers or television manufacturers, for example.

---

[5]This discussion is based on Kiechel, "Three . . . Ways to Win," pp. 184, 188.

M A R K E T I N G   A T   W O R K

FILE 3-4 **NEW CHAPTER AT COLES**

In 1989, Coles Book Stores Ltd., Canada's largest bookseller, ended the year with its worst earnings performance in eight years. For a long time, Coles was characterized by its limited range of books and services, heavy discounting, and a promotional approach that encouraged customers to ''buy books by the pound.'' Now, however, Coles is changing its marketing strategy and tactics — ''We've recognized that to be profitable, you can't continue to focus on discounting'' — and is zeroing in on who and where its customers really are. Coles' research shows that 48 percent of all book purchases are made on impulse, a fact that provoked Coles to discard its warehouse-style stores (which reach only 22 percent of book buyers) and to cater to more discriminating customers by offering them an innovative variety of specialized stores, books, and services. One example of this diversification is The Book Company, an upscale division launched in 1989, that contains a wider selection (20,000 titles compared to fewer than 10,000 at standard Coles stores) and offers ''quiet areas'' with plush chairs that allow customers to sit and read. Another is Active Minds, a six-store unit that sells children's books and games and is advised by a board of educators. Both divisions have already turned profits, proving how business can benefit from innovative product/market expansion strategies.

Source: Adapted from Beppi Crosariol, ''Coles Opens a New Chapter,'' *Financial Times of Canada*, January 21, 1991, p. 6.

PRODUCT/MARKET EXPANSION STRATEGIES

Most statements of mission and objectives reflect an organization's intention to grow — to increase its revenues and profit. In such cases, an organization may take either of two routes in its strategy design. It can continue to do what it is now doing with its products and markets — only do it better. Or the organization can venture into new products and/or new markets. These two routes, when applied to markets and products, result in the following four strategic alternatives.[6] See Fig. 3-5.

- *Market penetration:* A company tries to sell more of its present products to its present markets. Supporting tactics might include an increase in expenditure for advertising or personal selling.
- *Market development:* A company continues to sell its present products, but to a new market. Thus, a manufacturer of power tools now selling to domestic industrial users might decide to sell portable tools to foreign industrial users.
- *Product development:* This strategy calls for a company to develop new products to sell to its existing markets. A stereo records company recently introduced laser discs to its present customers.

---

[6]First proposed by H. Igor Ansoff, ''Strategies for Diversification,'' *Harvard Business Review*, September/October 1957, pp. 113–24. An excellent article stressing that strategy should focus on customer needs, not just on beating competition, is Kenichi Ohmae, ''Getting Back to Strategy,'' *Harvard Business Review*, November/December 1988, pp. 149–56.

FIGURE 3-5
Organizational strategies for product/market expansion.

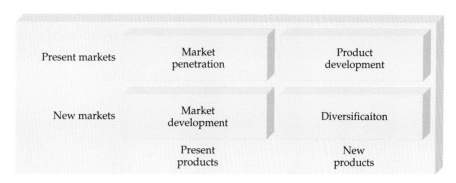

	Present products	New products
Present markets	Market penetration	Product development
New markets	Market development	Diversificaiton

- *Diversification:* A company develops new products to sell to new markets. Sears, for example, diversified into insurance, financial services, and a credit-card program.

STRATEGIC MARKETING PLANNING

After completing the strategic planning for the total organization and for each SBU, management can do the planning for each major functional division, such as marketing or production. The planning for marketing (or for any functional division, for that matter) should be guided by the mission and objectives of the total organization or the SBU.

The Planning Process

The **strategic marketing planning process** consists of these steps: (1) conduct a situation analysis; (2) determine marketing objectives; (3) select target markets and measure the market demand; (4) design a strategic marketing mix; (5) prepare an annual marketing plan. See Fig. 3-6.

A *situation analysis* is a review of the company's existing marketing program. By analyzing where the program has been and where it is now, management can determine where the program should go in the future. A situation analysis normally includes an analysis of the external environmental forces[7] and the nonmarketing resources that surround the organization's marketing program. A situation analysis also includes a detailed review of the company's present marketing mix — its product and pricing situation, its distribution system (including suppliers and middlemen), and its promotional program.

The next step in the marketing planning process is to *determine the marketing objectives*. As with organizational objectives, the marketing goals should be realistic, specific, measurable, and mutually consistent. And they should be clearly stated in writing.

The goals at the marketing level are closely related to the company-wide goals and strategies. In fact, a company strategy often translates into a marketing goal. For example, to reach an organizational objective of a 20 percent return on investment next year, one organizational strategy might be to reduce marketing costs by 15 percent. This organizational strategy would then become a marketing goal.

The *selection of target markets* is obviously a key step in marketing planning. Management should analyze existing markets in detail and identify potential

---

[7]A graphical approach for assessing a firm's strengths and weaknesses in relation to other firms in an industry is presented in Emilio Cvitkovic, ''Profiling Your Competitors,'' *Planning Review*, May/June 1989, pp. 28–30.

FIGURE 3-6
The strategic marketing planning process.

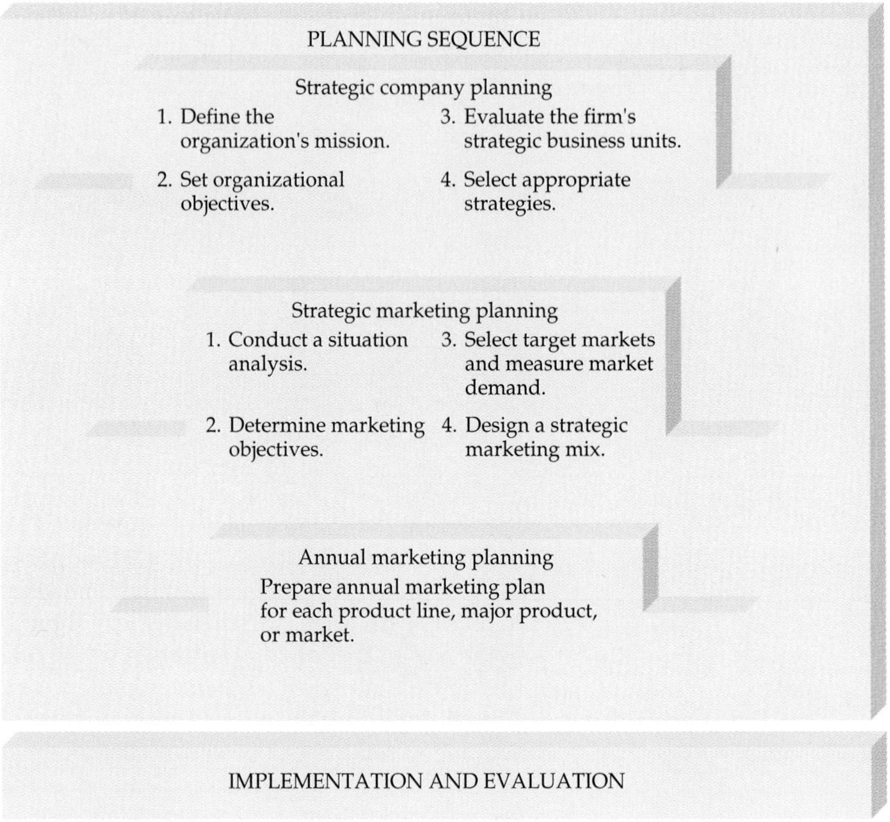

PLANNING SEQUENCE

Strategic company planning

1. Define the organization's mission.

2. Set organizational objectives.

3. Evaluate the firm's strategic business units.

4. Select appropriate strategies.

Strategic marketing planning

1. Conduct a situation analysis.

2. Determine marketing objectives.

3. Select target markets and measure market demand.

4. Design a strategic marketing mix.

Annual marketing planning

Prepare annual marketing plan for each product line, major product, or market.

IMPLEMENTATION AND EVALUATION

markets. At this point, management also should decide to what extent, and in what manner, it wants to segment its market. As part of this step in the planning process, management also should forecast its sales in its various markets.

The Marketing Mix

Management next must *design a strategic marketing mix* that enables the company to satisfy the wants of its target markets and to achieve its marketing goals. The design, and later the operation, of the marketing mix constitutes the bulk of the company's marketing effort.

Marketing mix is the term that is used to describe the combination of the four inputs that constitute the core of an organization's marketing system. These four elements are the product or service offerings, the price structure, the promotional activities, and the distribution system. While the marketing mix is largely controllable by company management, this mix still is constrained by external environmental forces. The mix also is both influenced and supported by a company's internal nonmarketing resources. Figure 3-7 reflects a company's total marketing system as being a combination of these environmental and internal forces.

The four "ingredients" in the marketing mix are interrelated. Again we see the *systems* concept; decisions in one area usually affect actions in the others. Also, each of the four contains countless variables. A company may market one item or several — related or unrelated. They may be distributed through wholesalers or directly to retailers, and so on. Ultimately, from the multitude of variables, management must select the combination that will (1) best adapt

FIGURE 3-7

A company's complete marketing system: a framework of internal resources operating within a set of external forces.

MACROENVIRONMENTAL
FORCES
Demography
Economic conditions
Social and cultural forces
Technology   Competition
Political and legal forces

Suppliers | Marketing intermediaries | COMPANY'S MARKETING MIX
Product planning   Distribution system
Price structure   Promotional activities | Marketing intermediaries | The market

NONMARKETING
RESOURCES IN THE FIRM
Production Financial Location Personnel
Research & Development
Public image

to the environment, (2) satisfy the target markets, and (3) still meet the organizational and marketing goals.

Product   Managing the product ingredient includes planning and developing the right products and/or services to be marketed by the company. Strategies are needed for changing existing products, adding new ones, and taking other actions that affect the assortment of products carried. Strategic decisions are also needed regarding branding, packaging, and various other product features.

Price   In pricing, management must determine the right base price for its products. It must then decide on strategies concerning discounts, freight payments, and many other price-related variables.

Promotion   Promotion is the ingredient used to inform and persuade the market regarding a company's products. Advertising, personal selling, and sales promotion are the major promotional activities.

Distribution   Even though marketing intermediaries are primarily a noncontrollable environmental factor, a marketing executive has considerable latitude when working with them. Management's responsibility is (1) to select and manage the trade channels through which the products will reach the right market at the right time and (2) to develop a distribution system for physically handling and transporting the products through these channels.[8]

---

[8]For a historical perspective on the marketing mix, see G. Ray Funkhouser, ''Technological Antecedents of the Modern Marketing Mix,'' *Journal of Macromarketing*, Spring 1984, pp. 17–28.

MARKETING AT WORK

FILE 3-5   **BACK TO OUR MARKETING ROOTS**

Roots retail stores are operated by Natural Footwear Limited. This company, established in 1973, began by marketing a line of "natural" shoes. Over the years, the company has expanded its product line so that shoes represent a very small portion of total sales. The **product** component of the company's marketing mix now includes a complete line of leisure clothing and accessories, from the well-known Roots sweatshirts, to sweaters, leather goods, and outer clothing. The company's products would be in the medium to upper **price** range; **promotion** is done primarily through advertising in newspapers and through point-of-sale materials (although the company's own sweatshirts, bearing the Roots brand, might themselves be considered a form of advertising); and **distribution** is accomplished through more than 38 company-owned and franchised stores in Canada, 3 in the United States, and new stores in Japan shortly. Compare this marketing mix with the approach taken by other manufacturers of similar product lines.

NONBUSINESS MARKETING MIX

The concept of a marketing mix is also applicable to nonbusiness and/or non-profit organizations. To illustrate, the marketing mix for the Winnipeg Symphony might include:

- *"Product":* Concerts of classical, semiclassical, and even "pop" music that provide product benefits of social uplifting, music appreciation, enjoyment, relaxation, and use of leisure time.
- *Price:* Public donations and admission charges.

Nonbusiness organizations also need a marketing mix.

Pass on the gift of a lifetime

The Salvation Army battles poverty, illness, and hopelessness on many fronts. It is a never-ending struggle.
You can contribute your strength by making The Salvation Army a beneficiary in your will. When you are gone your generosity will help those who still live. Only you possess the power to pass on the gift of a lifetime.

God knows you can make a difference

- *Distribution:* Direct from the orchestra to its market; no intermediaries (middlemen) are used.
- *Promotion:* Advertisements in the media telling about the forthcoming season, or ads for individual concerts; signs outside the concert hall; an advertising campaign to sell season tickets.

Annual Marketing Plans

Periodically, the ongoing strategic marketing planning process in an organization culminates in the preparation of a series of short-term marketing plans. These plans usually cover the period of a year — hence the name ''annual marketing plan.'' However, in some industries it is necessary to prepare these plans for even shorter time periods because of the nature of the product or market. A separate annual plan should be prepared for each product line, major product, brand, or market.

An **annual marketing plan** is the master guide covering a year's marketing activity for the given business unit or product. The plan then becomes the how-to-do-it document that guides executives in each phase of their marketing operations. The plan includes (1) a statement of objectives, (2) the identification of the target markets, (3) the strategies and tactics pertaining to the marketing mix, and (4) information regarding the budgetary support for the marketing activity.[9]

In an annual marketing plan, more attention can be devoted to tactical details than is feasible in longer-range planning. As an example, long-range marketing planning may emphasize the role of personal selling in the promotional mix. The annual plan then might be concerned, for example, with increased college recruiting as a source of sales people.

In conclusion, let's sum up the role of marketing in an individual organization. To fulfil its mission and achieve its goals, a company should start and end its marketing effort with a consideration of its customers and their wants (see Fig. 3-8). Thus, management first should select and analyze its markets.

FIGURE 3-8
Marketing in the firm begins and ends with the customers.

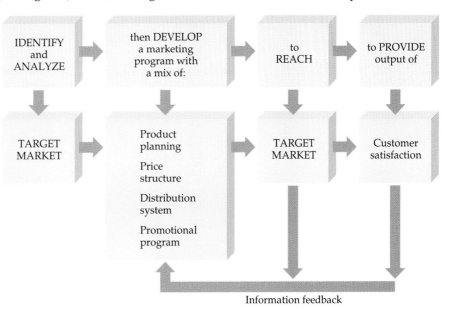

[9]An excellent source of information on how various companies prepare their annual marketing plans is Howard Sutton, *The Marketing Plan*, The Conference Board, New York, 1990.

Then, within a framework of the environmental constraints that face the organization, management should develop a marketing program to provide want-satisfaction to those markets. Permeating the planning and operation of this model is the company's marketing information system—a key marketing subsystem intended to aid management in its decision making. The next section deals with customers — their characteristics and behaviour; gathering customer and market information; and the structure of the marketing information system that supports marketing planning, implementation, and evaluation.

SUMMARY

Within its external and internal environment, a company must develop and operate its marketing system. That is, the organization must *manage* its marketing effort. The management process, as applied to marketing, involves (1) *planning* the company's goals and strategies, (2) *implementing* these plans, and (3) *evaluating* the marketing performance. Executives need to understand the management concepts of objectives, strategies, tactics, and policies.

Strategic planning is a major key to a company's success. With regard to the organizational level on which it is conducted, we find company-wide planning, strategic business unit planning, and strategic marketing planning. Strategic *company* planning is the process of matching an organization's resources with its marketing opportunities over the long run. The organization-wide strategic planning process consists of (1) defining the organization's mission, (2) setting organizational objectives, (3) conducting an organizational portfolio analysis, and (4) designing organizational strategies to achieve the objectives.

Strategic *marketing* planning should be done within the context of the organization's overall strategic planning. The strategic marketing planning process consists of (1) conducting a situation analysis, (2) setting marketing goals, (3) selecting target markets, (4) designing a strategic marketing mix to satisfy those markets and achieve those goals, and (5) preparing an annual marketing plan to guide the tactical operations.

A company's marketing mix is the core of its marketing system. The mix is a combination of the firm's product offerings, price structure, distribution system, and promotional activities.

KEY TERMS AND CONCEPTS

QUESTIONS AND PROBLEMS

1. Which, if any, of the main topics discussed in this chapter are useful to a small manufacturer or retailer?

2. Explain the relationship among the three main stages of the management process.

3. a. Explain the terms *strategy* and *tactic*, using examples.
   b. What is the difference between a strategy and a policy in marketing management?

4. Explain the difference between organizational objectives and marketing objectives in strategic planning. Give some examples of each.

5. Using a marketing approach (benefits provided or wants satisfied), answer the question, ''What business are you in?'' for each of the following companies:
   a. Holiday Inn.
   b. Adidas sports shoes.
   c. Apple computers.
   d. National Sea Products.
   e. Goodyear Tire.
   f. Roots clothing.

6. Using examples, explain the concept of a strategic business unit (SBU).

7. What criteria should an organizational division meet in order to be classified as a strategic business unit?

8. For each of the following Porter generic strategies, give some examples of organizations that might employ the particular strategy.
   a. Cost leadership.
   b. Differentiation.
   c. Focus.

9. For each of the following product/market growth strategies, give some examples (other than those in this chapter) of how a company might employ the particular strategy.
   a. Market penetration.
   b. Market development.
   c. Product development.
   d. Diversification.

10. In the situation-analysis stage of the marketing planning process, what are some points that should be analyzed by a manufacturer of backpack equipment for wilderness camping?

11. Explain how the concept of the marketing mix might be applied to:
   a. The Salvation Army.
   b. An art museum.
   c. Your school.
   d. Your local police force.

CASE 1.1 **Upper Canada Brewing Company (A): Evaluating the Market Opportunity**

Of all possible entrepreneurial endeavours, few can be as daunting as brewing beer. The heavy capital outlay for plant and equipment in a sector dominated by established giants could deter even the most determined of adventurers. But not Frank Heaps! In October 1983, Frank invested in the Granville Island Brewing Company, and, only two months later, he was evaluating the market opportunity of starting a similar cottage brewery in his hometown, Toronto, Ontario. To enable him to make a good decision, he knew he needed reliable information; market research was undertaken for this purpose. He carefully analyzed the information before him to make this important decision — should he put this deal together and start the Upper Canada Brewing Company?

THE MARKET

In Canada in 1983, the brewing industry was dominated by three large brewers that supplied 98 percent of the domestic Canadian market. The big three national brewers — Molson Breweries of Canada Ltd., John Labatt Ltd., and Carling O'Keefe Breweries of Canada Ltd. — all engage in a fierce struggle for a greater share of a large but essentially stable market. To compete, the brewing industry in Canada paid six-figure sums for market research and boosted their combined advertising expenditures from $52.4 million in 1982. Despite these efforts, 1983 sales were still dropping, accompanied by serious declines in profit. (See Exhibit A-1).

The greatest threats to the big brewers are demographic and life-style changes. Many male "baby boomers" drank less as they got older, and there were fewer young men to take their place. As well, some customers were bypassing beer for other types of beverages. The result was a market that was flat, with no anticipated significant rise in consumption in the near future.

Nevertheless, beer is still big business. According to Statistics Canada, in 1983 Canadians spent nearly $7 billion on beer, with 99 percent of that amount going to domestic brewers; sales of imported beer accounted for only $14 million. However, sales of the higher-priced imported beers had been growing in Ontario over the past few years and represented the only segment of the beer market that showed an increase (see Exhibit A-2). This increased demand for premium-priced imports was taken to indicate that tastes were changing in some market segments towards specialty alternatives rather than mass-produced products.

MARKET RESEARCH

The Granville Island Brewing Venture Market research was an important element in the decision to establish Granville Island Brewing, a cottage brewery in downtown Vancouver, British Columbia. This micro brewery, scheduled to open during the spring of 1984, was expected to be the first retail cottage brewery in Canada. The owners' concept was to make beer that would be noticeably different from the mass-produced products dominating the market. The products would be different in taste, like the products of small traditional breweries in Europe; different in quality, being carefully crafted in small quantities with special all-natural ingredients; different in price, where high price would support the perception (and fact) of superior quality; and different in organization, where the new small and independent brewery would be closer to the customer and thus have the advantage of appealing to consumers' desires. Market research supported the perceived need for something different and identified the market opportunity as a relatively small, upscale niche.

Frank Heaps, a management consultant working in Vancouver at the time, liked the concept, decided to invest in the Granville Island Brewing

This case was prepared by Donna M. Stapleton and is intended to stimulate discussion of an actual management problem and not to illustrate either effective or ineffective handling of that problem. The author wishes to acknowledge the support provided by The Upper Canada Brewing Company, and particularly by Frank Heaps, President.

EXHIBIT A-1

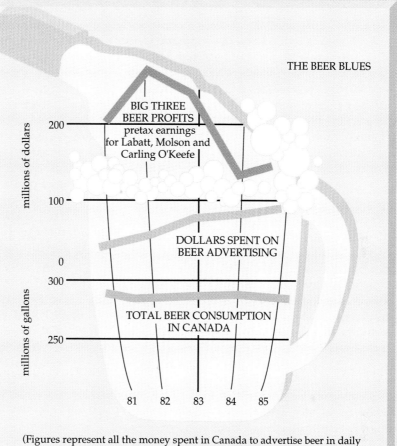

THE BEER BLUES

BIG THREE
BEER PROFITS
pretax earnings
for Labatt, Molson and
Carling O'Keefe

DOLLARS SPENT ON
BEER ADVERTISING

TOTAL BEER CONSUMPTION
IN CANADA

millions of dollars

200

100

0

millions of gallons

300

250

81   82   83   84   85

(Figures represent all the money spent in Canada to advertise beer in daily
newspapers, farm papers, consumer magazines, radio and television.)

Source: Media Measurement Services Inc.

EXHIBIT A-2

Ontario Beer Consumption (Million of Gallons)

Distributors	1981	1982	1983
Brewers' Warehousing	168.3	168.4	164.5
Liquor Control Board of Ontario—Domestic	8.0	7.8	7.8
—Imported*	1.1	1.3	1.4
TOTAL	177.4	177.5	173.7

*Heineken, Lowenbrau, Tuborg, Kronenburg and other European lagers comprising
about 65%.

SOURCE: Liquor Control Board of Ontario (L.C.B.O.)

venture, and immediately began thinking of the feasibility of introducing the concept into his hometown market, Toronto. If the concept could work in Vancouver, why not Toronto? He did not believe there was a significant difference in beer drinkers in the two markets. As an investor in Granville Island, he knew that the principals had conducted extensive market research before reaching their decision to enter the Vancouver market. He felt that the data collected on the attitudes of the general public for the Vancouver market were also relevant to his decision. A copy of the research report showed that the public were:

— increasingly interested in returning to more traditional elements of life-styles, particularly with regards to food and beverage products;

—increasingly supportive of products perceived to be more wholesome;

—part of the "small is beautiful" trend, resulting in significant commercial support for goods that were more handcrafted and of a higher quality than those that were mass produced;

—prepared to give trial support for the products of small local entrepreneurs as an alternative to those of diversified national corporations.

Upper Canada Brewing Venture   Granville Island as the "pioneering venture" served as the precedent for Frank Heaps to evaluate the potential viability of the Upper Canada Brewing proposal. His premise was that "if the Toronto market showed as good a potential as the Vancouver market then the decision would be to go ahead." Research was designed to compare the Toronto and Vancouver markets. The analysis consisted of a comparison of published statistical data on the two markets and the results of 100 group and one-on-one interviews. The interviews were conducted by frequenting taverns and other licensed establishments in the Toronto area and talking with individuals and groups as they enjoyed their beer or ale.

A comparison of published statistical reports showed similarities and differences in the two markets (see Exhibit A-3). There were obvious population differences of persons 20 years of age and older between the Vancouver Census Metropolitan Area (CMA) and the Toronto CMA. As well, a comparison of the population by sex and age revealed that the Toronto marketplace showed significantly greater potential than the Vancouver marketplace, especially with the heavy beer drinkers (males 20–34 years). The large ethnic population in Toronto, especially those of European origin, also indicated greater market potential for the European-style products of the proposed new brewery income levels and current growth rate were comparable for the two markets.

A comparison of the number and concentration of taverns and other licensed establishments in the two markets revealed that there was a significantly larger number in Toronto (concentrated in a typical retail 5 km radius). In addition,

many more licensees were open on Sunday, allowing another day of sale.

The interviews indicated that similar attitudes existed with regard to natural, wholesome, "small batch," and more traditional products. While this attitude appeared more prevalent in Vancouver, other research with retail food outlets suggested that the larger market of Toronto provided more potential. Torontonians also appeared to be willing to try new beer products at least as readily as Vancouverites. This seemed to be as true with tavern and restaurant owners as with the general public. Furthermore, tavern owners, because of the very competitive environment in the Toronto market, were prepared to provide "whatever the customer wanted."

In addition, there existed in Toronto a very large network of Brewers' Retail stores, which were conveniently located with ample parking. These stores, equipped with refrigerated storage and selling capacity, would be very important in the distribution of the product because its "all natural," "non-pasteurized" nature required refrigeration during storage and display. In Vancouver, such cold beer stores were not available and this restricted distribution to the brewery site alone.

From the data, Mr. Heaps concluded that the Toronto market potential was as great as, and probably greater than, that of Vancouver. However, he was also aware of the "brewery wars" so evident in the Toronto market. With the strength and financial resources of the large brewers, Mr. Heaps wondered whether he would be able to compete. With a total Ontario beer market of about 175 million gallons a year, a market share of 0.1 percent in the first year, growing to less than 0.3 percent in five years, was a conservative estimate of the volume of business needed to be viable. Did the Ontario market have the potential for the Upper Canada Brewing venture to achieve this volume? Given the hostile nature of this market, what should he do?

QUESTIONS

1. Do you think the Toronto market represented a "good opportunity" for Mr. Heaps? Why or why not?

EXHIBIT A-3 **Market Related Data (1981 Census)**

	The Toronto Marketplace		The Vancouver Marketplace	
Population				
Sex and age group	City	CMA	City	CMA
Male				
20–24	29,180	140,255	20,435	58,780
25–34	62,225	262,590	41,245	115,180
35–44	38,610	198,115	24,370	83,650
45–54	33,280	174,985	21,215	69,885
55–64	27,040	130,865	20,850	57,525
65–69	10,375	43,190	9,110	22,870
70 years & older	18,335	65,100	16,800	37,955
Female				
20–24	31,645	146,545	22,440	61,005
25–34	63,820	279,690	40,020	117,330
35–44	36,990	200,085	23,385	81,460
45–54	31,690	171,680	22,070	66,665
55–64	30,220	141,595	24,455	65,650
65–69	13,160	52,965	11,640	28,135
70 years & older	32,955	112,180	25,680	56,985
Total Population	599,217	2,998,947	414,281	1,268,183
Current Growth Rate	−0.05%	6.5%	1.1%	8.3%
Income				
Average Family Income	$29,794	$31,238	$30,252	$31,634
Median Family Income	23,608	27,775	25,525	28,292
Mother Tongue				
English		2,136,975		982,465
French		45,455		20,470
Italian		219,925		66,555
Portuguese		78,785		41,315
Chinese		67,910		19,385
German		58,390		18,265
Other		391,505		119,730
Retail Sales (1983 as a percentage above national average)		11%		7%

SOURCE: Statistics Canada

2. What additional information do you think would be required in assessing this market oportunity? How and where would you obtain it?

3. Which market segment(s) would you say have the greatest potential for the Upper Canada Brewing Company? Why?

4. What types of retaliation by competitors should Mr. Heaps expect?

CASE 1.2 **"Smoking, Taxing, and Choice"**

Jesse Saunders, Michael Adam, and Leah Adam, Michael's sister, were mulling over the question of the cigarette industry, federal government action, and emerging social trends. Their firm, JML Canada Ltd., has been in the business of offering marketing and social-trend research services to a number of national clients — some in the private sector, some national citizen organizations, as well as some federal government departments. Jesse, as president of JML, was now being approached by a number of the firm's citizen organization clients for some help in a peculiar situation. These organizations were being lobbied to publicly support either anti-smoking campaigns and the groups involved in them or smoker's rights campaigns and the groups involved in them. Since the topic involved issues that caused many heated arguments in these organizations, the senior people had decided that outside advice from JML and perhaps some concrete information would help them determine how to handle the requests being made of them. Jesse asked Michael and Leah to review the most easily obtainable trend reports on the matter and brief him so that he would be informed sufficiently to continue discussions with his clients.

Michael and Leah began gathering information and immediately found that Canada was one of the leading countries in the world when it came to restricting and combatting cigarette smoking; they found that many countries, particularly those in the European Economic Community, were watching Canadian developments closely with a view to copying some of the government actions.

Their most easily arrived-at conclusion was that most non-smoking Canadians — by 1991, 68 percent of the adult population — accepted that cigarette smoking and exposure to second-hand cigarette smoke was hazardous to health. It was also clear that the industry took the view that the link between smoking and health hazards such as cancer was not proven.

It was also clear from their review that there were interesting differences in attitudes among smokers and recent quitters. The recent quitters had stopped primarily, it was thought by some, as a result of the health hazard information made available by anti-smoking groups and the federal and other levels of government that caused them to change their attitudes. Others, who wanted to stop smoking, found that its addictive nature made voluntary cessation too difficult to achieve regardless of their attitudes. Some smokers did not accept the information on the hazards of smoking and so did not change their attitudes. Another group of smokers, while accepting that smoking was hazardous to their health, maintained the right to make their own decisions about putting themselves at risk. They were supported in this view by some non-smokers.

Michael and Leah could also see that as attitudes against smoking shifted over time, more and more publicly supported restrictions against smoking were put into place. These had the twin effects of continuing the attitude shifts among non-smokers and some smokers and making the continuation of smoking more difficult to accomplish. The federal government, in June of 1988, brought into law the Tobacco Products Control Act, phasing in a ban on tobacco advertising in newspapers, in magazines, and on billboards, as well as placing severe restrictions on sponsorships, promotion, and packaging. The Act provided for much stronger health warnings on cigarette packages than had previously been the case.

Restricting the places where people could smoke was one way of making smoking more difficult to accomplish. Various levels of government and private organizations restricted smoking either to designated areas of public and private work and service spaces or prohibited it completely. Another way of making smoking more difficult to accomplish was by increasing the price of cigarettes. Provincial and federal governments continued to increase cigarette taxes, and while they

SOURCES: Adapted from Barrie McKenna, "Just Another Round in Cigarette Ad Fight," *Globe and Mail*, July 29, 1991, pp. B1, B5; Mark Evans, "Cigarettes Drooping," *Financial Post*, July 18, 1991, p. 3; address by Prof. Richard Pollay, 16th Annual Macro-Marketing Conference, Vancouver, August 14, 1991; Andy Willis, "The Wacky World of Tobacco Taxation," *Financial Times*, August 26, 1991, pp. 1, 5.

were doing this, cigarette manufacturers were also increasing their prices. In New Brunswick, a pack of 20 cigarettes carried a $4.29 tax, the highest in the world. Across the New Brunswick border in Maine, the tax was 70 cents. In Ontario, a carton of cigarettes retailed for about $45, with the tobacco company receiving about $6.35.

The result of all these moves was that in the six years between 1982 and 1988, total tobacco consumption declined by 17.8 percent. In 1989 alone, sales declined by 8 percent; in 1990 by another 6.7 percent; in 1991 by another 10 percent (estimated). Michael and Leah were surprised that in spite of the drop in consumption, the profits of tobacco companies continued to increase, as 32 percent of Canadian adults continued to smoke and pay higher prices. This occurred even with the advent of the Tobacco Products Control Act and the very large tax increases that were implemented at the same time. In 1991, the latest federal cigarette tax increase was 75 cents per package and Ontario's increase was 42 cents two months later. The tobacco industry responded to these large tax increases by appealing to the public. It launched a write-in campaign and asked Canadians to send pre-printed letters (part of the cigarette package and reproduced for broader use) to the prime minister, asking him to stop the unfair taxation of cigarette products. The 25 percent drop in consumption between 1988 and 1991 was the largest decline in any developed country. Some observers felt that most of it was due to price increases and that attitudes had been changed as much as they were ever likely to be.

After the 1988 Tobacco Products Control Act came into effect, the cigarette industry, still lobbying the federal and provincial governments, launched a court challenge against the Act on the grounds that it violated its right to freedom

---

TAX PROTEST
OPPOSITION À LA TAXE

Complete form below and drop in mail.

Remplir le carton ci-dessous et le mettre à la poste.

IMPORTANT
Fold and detach along dotted lines.

I am of voting age.
I want you to stop the unfair taxation of tobacco products in Canada.
What are you going to do about it?
I expect a reply.

My comments
Mes commentaires: _____

Name
Nom: _____

Address
Adresse: _____

_____

Signature: _____

Je suis majeur(e).
Je vous demande de cesser de taxer injustement les produits du tabac au Canada.
Qu'allez-vous faire à ce sujet?
J'attends votre réponse.

Postal Code
Code postal: _____

IMPORTANT
Plier le long de la ligne pointillée et détacher.

Voice your opinion as many times as you wish.

Exprimez votre opinion autant de fois que vous le désirez.

of expression — the right to advertise a legal product—guaranteed under the Canadian Charter of Rights and Freedoms. In July of 1991, at the time that Michael and Leah were reviewing materials, the Quebec Superior Court ruled that the federal ad ban violated the Charter's right to free speech. Within a few weeks, the federal government appealed the ruling; it was expected that the appeal would take two to three years to be heard and decided upon.

Michael and Leah were puzzled. Based on what they had reviewed, what kind of a preliminary report could they make to Jesse? What could they conclude about social trends and support for and against smoking? About government legal action? Federal and provincial tax levels? The attitudes and behaviour of smokers? The behaviour of tobacco companies? The behaviour of anti-smoking groups? Were there other groups, trends, and factors to be considered at this stage? Was the tobacco situation so different from that of the alcohol situation?

CASE 1.3 **Planning Markets in the Fast Food Business: Introducing New Products — How Far To Go?**

Students of North American eating habits blame it on the baby boomers. It seems that everything has either been blamed on them or revolves around them. As the boomers age, begin to thicken around the middle, and consider their mortality, health, and nutrition, but maintaining their attitude of "I want what I want when I want it," new problems are posed for the food industry in general, especially the snack-food and fast-food industries. This means more planning for markets, new missions for companies, new goals and objectives, perhaps new strategies and tactics.

Not only are Canada's demographics different, so are our tastes, preferences, and eating behaviour. There are more "olders" and fewer "youngers"; there's more disposable income for teens as well as greying boomers and seniors. Different behaviours mean more "grazing" as well as eating out at different times of the day; where and what one eats for breakfast, lunch and dinner, and in between those times, is changing. Different preferences mean we want foods if the taste is right (which means they have the fat content we like) and the nutrition is right (which can mean the taste isn't right even if the nutrition is) as well as where and when we like to eat what.

One result is that for the first time in 20 years,

the snack-food industry is developing new products. It is making healthier snacks from grains that are prepared with little or no saturated fats. Pretzels and popcorn, old standards made without oils, are thriving anew and being re-marketed with a vengeance. Frito-Lay, the giant of the snack-food business (with nearly 50 percent market share of the major snack-food categories except nuts), is now making Sun Chips, a nutritious multi-grain chip, after ten years in development and 10,000 taste tests. Also being tested is a durum wheat-based snack. Management at Frito-Lay believes that people do not *need* snack food; thus it is up to the company to entertain and please customers at different places and at different times to maintain attention and interest in the product category. It is a fact of life that about 80 percent of snack food is eaten by 20 percent of all consumers — most of them under 20 years of age.

Many of North America's fast-food marketers are worried about the same kinds of problems as the snack-food industry, only with an additional concern — that after the industry growth of the last decade, consumers are bored with the same old food. An additional problem that exists is that some of North America's fast food companies treat the United States and Canada as one market with some regional variations. This is

SOURCES: Adapted, in part, from David Kilgour, "Number Two KFC Tries Harder," *Marketing*, March 18, 1991, p. 3; Anthony Ramirez, "Developing Junk Food for Discriminating Tastes," *Globe and Mail*, June 3, 1991, p. B12; Deborah Jones, "McLobster Rolls onto Market," *Globe and Mail*, June 18, 1991, p. B1; David Kilgour, "KFC Shifts from Hairy Arm through the Wall Marketing," *Marketing*, March 25, 1991, p. 3.

particularly the case of those U.S. firms that have a smaller share of the Canadian market, such as Burger King, Wendy's, Arby's, and Taco Bell. But even the largest co-ordinate their U.S. and Canadian product launches and promotions very closely.

North America's giant, McDonald's, is reported to be testing more than 100 items ranging from tortellini to chicken fajitas. McDonald's Canada, the market leader with current sales of $1.3 billion, keeps adapting its menu to meet changing consumer tastes and concerns and has successfully offered salads, the new McLean Deluxe burger (launched at the same time as in the United States), low-fat milkshakes and yogurts, low-fat cholesterol-free apple bran muffins and cereals. It has also catered to regional and seasonal tastes with McLobsters in its 50 Atlantic Canada stores and poutine (chips with melted cheese curds) in Quebec outlets. McDonald's Canada has tested pizzas in Kingston and sells pizza at its Toronto SkyDome outlet.

Kentucky Fried Chicken, Canada's second-ranked fast-food restaurant (sales of $545 million), is going through a massive overhaul of its marketing strategy and operations. KFC's major competitors in terms of product type are Swiss Chalet (owned by Cara Operations) and St. Hubert Chicken — mostly Quebec based. While the current KFC format is take-out, Swiss Chalet has eat-in and take-out in non-fast food restaurant formats with more menu selection. Since the word "fried" is not quite as popular and acceptable as in the past, and since Kentucky Fried has frequently been known as KFC, that will be the new name. There will be a new logo to go with KFC and a new format for the 800 Canadian stores. The new approach is to swing away from a stand-in-line take-out store to become a mainstream fast-food place. About 100 stores have been renovated and the others will be complete within five years. KFC studies indicate that the company outperforms all the hamburger food competitors in food quality but that the hamburger competitors, in turn, outperform KFC in facilities and management. KFC research has discovered that consumers want more menu choice and more products that make sense in the nineties.

The KFC plan includes new graphics, new packaging, and a new menu to increase visits by existing customers at different times of the day as well as to bring in new customers. The company is testing, in Western Canada, new chicken variations — Lite 'n' Crispy (skin removed), Extra Tasty Crispy and Hot 'n' Spicy. Its new Hot Wings program appears to have been very successful, and it is also working on salads, biscuits, and yogurt.

Third in size is Harvey's with $280 million in sales and 232 stores across Canada. Harvey's is actually second to McDonald's if KFC, under its present format, is excluded from the fast-food category because of its lack of seating and very narrow menu selection. While Harvey's belongs to Cara Operations Ltd., which runs other food-service businesses (Swiss Chalet and Steak 'n' Burger), it is a domestic firm without the advantages and disadvantages of a U.S. parent operation when it comes to product development, testing, and advertising from U.S. television programs sponsored by its parent. Harvey's is constantly aware of what McDonald's is doing even though Harvey's management believes that they are somewhat differently positioned since McDonald's tends to target children and Harvey's targets adults.

Harvey's is testing and will shortly introduce a low-fat burger to compete against the McLean (8 percent fat compared with the McLean's 9 percent). Harvey's lean burger was tested in 25 stores at $2.59 or 25 cents more than the regular burger. The McLean was priced at $2.79 to $2.99, compared to the Big Mac standard of $2.16. These price differentials are the result of the higher costs of lean meat, as well as a specialty product market differential. Harvey's is testing a low-fat yogurt and has begun to use vegetable shortening instead of a blend with higher fat content. Cara research shows that consumers are interested in greater selection as well as healthier foods and preparation methods.

QUESTIONS

1. Is the snack-food and fast-food industry in competition? With whom does KFC compete?

2. What environmental factors are common to each industry? Are any unique?

3. What kind of a mission statement would you write for each of these three firms?

4. Does the objective of giving current customers more choice and attracting new customers with more choice — and for both at different meal times — mean that these three firms are trying to be all things to all people all of the time? If so, does this seem possible?

5. What is the difference between McDonald's, Harvey's, and KFC's marketing strategies in regard to target market and product development strategies?

6. What strategy differences are represented by price differences between the ''standard'' burgers and the lean versions offered by McDonald's and Harvey's?

P A R T
2

TARGET MARKETS

An analysis of the people and organizations
who buy, why they buy, and how they buy

In Part 1, we stressed the importance of customer orientation in an organization's marketing efforts. We
also defined strategic planning as the process of
matching an organization's resources with its marketing
opportunities. These notions suggest that early in the strategic marketing process, an organization should determine
who its potential customers are. Only then can management develop a marketing mix intended to satisfy the
wants of these customers. Therefore, in Part 2 we discuss
the selection of an organization's intended customers —
that is, its target market.

In Chapter 4, we examine the concept of market segmentation as it relates to the selection of target markets, and
we discuss several approaches to the segmentation of markets. In Chapter 5, we explore the strategic concept of positioning as a means to ensure that a company's offerings
are found appealing by its target segments. We also discuss
the important topic of forecasting. Chapter 6 is devoted to
consumer buying behaviour and the buying process
involved in the purchase of products and services. In Chapter 7, we cover the important topics of marketing research
and information systems, the means whereby marketers
learn about their markets and the consumers who comprise
them.

CHAPTER 4 GOALS

This is the first of four chapters dealing with the marketplace, which is made up of ultimate consumers and industrial or business users. We introduce the concepts of market segmentation and target markets. These are fundamental concepts that underlie the practice of marketing.

This is one of the most important principles of marketing; that all consumers are not the same and cannot be treated as if they are. After studying this chapter, you should understand:

- Fundamentals of target-market selection.
- The concept of market segmentation—its meaning, benefits, limitations, and conditions for use.
- The difference between ultimate consumer markets and business user markets.
- Bases for segmenting consumer markets.
- Segmentation implications in the distribution and composition of population.
- Segmentation implications in consumer income distribution and spending patterns.

Foundations for Market Segmentation

P eople *are* different in different parts of the country, and regional differences *do* exist in product preferences, purchase patterns, product ownership, and brand preferences. In the home baking product category, for example, flour and other baking ingredients sell in much greater volumes and in larger package sizes in rural areas of the country, such as rural Quebec and the Atlantic provinces, where there is still a great deal of home baking done, as compared with large cities, where flour may be used primarily for making gravies and sauces. Coca-Cola is the leading cola soft drink in most provinces, except in Quebec and Newfoundland, where Pepsi outsells Coke by a wide margin. Down-filled clothing sells better in ski regions than it does in small Prairie farm towns.

On the next page is a list of product ownership, household characteristics, and other indicators that illustrate differences that exist across provincial markets. These are all 1989 per-capita expenditure data, collected by Statistics Canada.[1] Each of these indicators represents important information for marketers in particular businesses.

Why do you suppose people in British Columbia spend so much money in restaurants, and why do so many of the households in Newfoundland have home freezers? In addition to obvious regional differences that result from climate and geography, many marketers find that purchase patterns and consumer preferences are influenced by age, ethnic background, cultural influences, and other demographic factors. Food consumption patterns of people who live in Quebec, downtown Toronto, or the Prairie provinces, for example, are greatly influenced by their ethnic backgrounds. (Remember, in Chapter 2, we defined *demography* as the statistical study of human population and its distribution.)

In short, any marketer who hopes to be successful in the changing markets of the 1990s must be fully aware of the changing demographic situation that Canadian companies and other organizations will be facing. It is impossible for a marketer to be on top of the market without an appreciation for demographic trends. It is the demographic characteristics of a market that help shape preferences, determine attitudes, mould values, and ultimately influence purchase decisions. Unless marketers monitor the shifting market and

---

[1]*Market Research Handbook*, Ottawa: Statistics Canada, catalogue No. 63–224 annual, 1991.

interpret the implications of the changes for their companies, they face a very real danger of being left behind.[2]

Marketers have successfully responded to the demographic characteristics of particular markets by developing specific products and services or by orienting advertising and other marketing programs towards certain target groups. Those that have been most successful have kept up to date on the changing nature of the Canadian population and have constantly explored the implications of the changes taking place in the demographic composition of the population. In short, they have segmented the market into components that are defined by their geographic and demographic characteristics. As we shall see later in this chapter, these are but two of the ways in which marketers can segment markets, but they are the most obvious ones and are therefore most often used.

In keeping with a segmentation strategy, we see restaurants and movie theatres offering discounts for seniors; hotel chains offer weekend specials to attract the travelling family market; in Toronto and other large cities, specialty retailers offer a variety of food products to appeal to ethnic markets. Some clothing retailers specialize in clothes for larger people, while others offer a line of ''petites.'' The Canadian Cancer Society and the Canadian Lung Association target their anti-smoking messages to teenagers (to discourage them from starting to smoke), to smokers (to encourage them to quit), and to legislators and municipal governments (to encourage the establishment of smoke-free areas).

Product/Indicator	Most Developed Market	Least Developed Market	Total Canadian Market
Annual per capita expenditures in restaurants, taverns	British Columbia $709	Newfoundland $325 Prince Edward Island	$659
Per capita retail sales	Alberta $7,061	$5,630	$6,684
One-person households	British Columbia 24.8%	Newfoundland 10.2%	21.5%
Homes without mortgages	Newfoundland 55.7%	Quebec 25.7%	32.0%
Homes with home freezers	Newfoundland 74.3%	Quebec 45.4% Prince Edward Island	58.3%
Homes with clothes dryers	New Brunswick 78.9%	63.6%	70.3%
Homes with dishwashers	Alberta 56.0%	Newfoundland 19.8% Prince Edward Island	42.5%
Homes with microwave ovens	Alberta 71.8%	47.7% Prince Edward Island	63.4%
Homes with cable television	British Columbia 84.0%	45.5% Prince Edward Island	70.8%
Homes with video recorders	Alberta 64.0%	50.0%	58.8%
Homes with compact disc players	Ontario 13.5%	New Brunswick 7.0%	11.6%

[2]Three excellent articles on the implications of the changing demographic picture are: Ken Dychtwald and Greg Gable, ''Portrait of a Changing Consumer,'' *Business Horizons*, vol. 33, no. 1, January/February 1990, pp. 62-73; Daniel Stoffman, ''Completely Predictable People,'' *Report on Business Magazine*, November 1990, pp. 78–84; and Gord McLaughlin, ''The New ME Generation,'' *The Financial Post Magazine*, January 1991, pp. 30–35.

The common thread in all of these situations is that each organization adopted a strategy of market segmentation as part of its target market selection. Strategic planning was defined in Chapter 2 as the matching of an organization's resources with its market opportunities. In this chapter we discuss market opportunities, focusing on the selection of target markets and decisions regarding market segmentation. The segmentation discussion will include a consideration of the geographic-demographic and buying-power dimensions of target markets.

SELECTING A TARGET MARKET

In Chapter 1 we defined a *market* as people or organizations with (1) wants (needs) to satisfy, (2) money to spend, and (3) the willingness to spend it. A **target market** is a group of customers (people or firms) at whom the seller specifically aims its marketing efforts. The careful selection and accurate definition (identification) of target markets are essential for the development of an effective marketing program.

Guidelines in Market Selection

Four general guidelines govern the selection of target markets. The first one is that target markets should be compatible with the organization's goals and image. A firm that is marketing high-priced personal computers should not sell through discount chain stores in an effort to reach a mass market.

A second guideline—consistent with our definition of strategic planning—is to match the market opportunity with the company's resources. National Sea Products followed this guideline when it launched its Fastbreak line of microwaveable burgers. Management realized that this product line, even if quite successful, would never account for as large a portion of the company's business as its main seafood products. However, there was also an appreciation that a market segment existed for targeting with a microwaveable product that children and young teens could prepare for themselves after school. Consequently, the company matched its limited research and marketing resources with the intended market segment.

Over the long run, a business must generate a profit if it is to survive. This rather obvious, third guideline translates into what is perhaps an obvious market selection guideline. That is, an organization should consciously seek markets that will generate sufficient sales volume at a low enough cost to result in a profit. Surprisingly, companies often have overlooked the profit factor in their quest for high-volume markets. The goal was sales volume alone, not *profitable* sales volume.

Finally, a company ordinarily should seek a market wherein the number of competitors and their size are minimal. An organization should not enter a market that is already saturated with competition unless it has some overriding competitive advantage that will enable it to take customers from existing firms.

Market Opportunity Analysis

Theoretically a market opportunity exists any time and any place there is a person or an organization with an unfilled need or want. Realistically, of course, a company's market opportunity is much more restricted. Thus selecting a target market requires an appraisal of market opportunities available to the organization. A market opportunity analysis begins with a study of the environmental forces (as discussed in Chapter 2) that affect a firm's marketing program. Then the organization must analyze the three components of a market—people or organizations, their buying power, and their willingness to spend. Analysis of the ''people'' component involves a study of the geographic distribution and demographic composition of the population. The second component is analyzed through the distribution of consumer income and consumer expenditure patterns. Finally, to determine consumers' ''willingness to spend,'' management must study their buying behaviour. Population and buying power are discussed more fully later in this chapter. Buying behaviour is covered in Chapter 6.

Target-Market Strategy: Aggregation or Segmentation

In defining the market or markets it will sell to, an organization has its choice of two approaches. In one, the total market is viewed as a single unit—as one mass, aggregate market. This approach leads to the strategy of *market aggregation*. In the other approach, the total market is seen as many smaller, homogeneous segments. This approach leads to the strategy of *market segmentation*, in which one or more segments is selected as top target market(s). Deciding which of the two strategies to adopt is a key in selecting target markets. We shall discuss market aggregation and segmentation in more detail later in this chapter.

Measuring Selected Markets

When selecting target markets, a company should make quantitative estimates of the potential sales volume of the market for its product or service. This process requires estimating, first, the total industry potential for the company's product in the target market and second, its share of this total market. It is essential that management also prepare a sales forecast, usually for a one-year period. A sales forecast is the foundation of all budgeting and short-term operational planning in all departments—marketing, production, and finance. Sales forecasting will be discussed in more detail in Chapter 5 after we build a better knowledge of market segmentation.

NATURE OF MARKET SEGMENTATION

The total market for most types of products is too varied—too heterogeneous—to be considered a single, uniform entity. To speak of the market for vitamin pills or electric razors or education is to ignore the fact that the total market for each product or service consists of submarkets that differ significantly from one another. This lack of uniformity may be traced to differences in buying habits, in ways in which the product or service is used, in motives for buying, or in other factors. Market segmentation takes these differences into account.

Not all consumers want to wear the same type of clothing, use the same hair shampoo, or participate in the same recreational activities. Nor do all business firms want to buy the same kind of word processors or delivery trucks. At the same time, a marketer usually cannot afford to tailor-make a different good or service for every single customer. Consequently market segmentation is the strategy that most marketers adopt as a compromise between the extremes of one product or service for all and a different one for each customer. A major element in a company's success is its ability to select the most effective location on this segmentation spectrum between the two extremes.[3]

---

[3]For a thoughtful analysis of the meaning and use of market segmentation and an effort to distinguish segmentation from product differentiation, see Peter R. Dickson and James L. Ginter, ''Market Segmentation, Product Differentiation, and Marketing Strategy,'' *Journal of Marketing*, April 1987, pp. 1–10.

What Is Market Segmentation?

Market segmentation is the process of dividing the total heterogeneous market for a product or service into several segments, each of which tends to be homogeneous in all significant aspects. Management selects one or more of these market segments as the organization's target market. A separate marketing mix is developed for each segment or group of segments in this target market.

Market aggregation is the opposite of market segmentation. **Market aggregation** is the strategy whereby an organization treats its total market as a unit —that is, as one mass aggregate market whose parts are considered to be alike in all major respects. The organization then develops a single marketing mix to reach as many customers as possible in this aggregate market.

In the language of economic theory, in market aggregation the seller assumes there is a single demand curve for its product. In effect, the product is assumed to have a broad market appeal. In contrast, in market segmentation the total market is viewed as a series of demand curves. Each one represents a separate market segment calling for a different product, promotional appeal, or other element in the marketing mix. (See Fig. 4-1.) Thus, instead of speaking of one aggregate market for personal computers, this total market can be segmented into several submarkets. We then will have, for example, a college student market segment for personal computers. Other submarkets might consist of segments representing homemakers, professors, travelling executives, travelling sales people, or small businesses. Stated another way, in market segmentation we employ a "rifle" approach (separate programs, pinpointed targets) in marketing activities. In contrast, market aggregation is a "shotgun" approach (one program, broad target).

FIGURE 4-1

Demand curves representing market aggregation and market segmentation.

The object of aggregation is to fit the market to the product. Segmentation is an attempt to fit the product to the market.

Price

AGGREGATION

Quantity

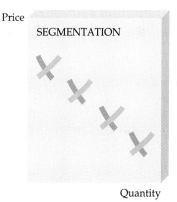

Price

SEGMENTATION

Quantity

Benefits of Market Segmentation

Market segmentation is a customer-oriented philosophy and thus in consistent with the marketing concept. We first identify the needs of customers within a submarket (segment) and then satisfy those needs.

By tailoring marketing programs to individual market segments, management can do a better marketing job and make more efficient use of marketing resources. A small firm with limited resources might compete very effectively in one or two market segments, whereas the same firm would be buried if it aimed for the total market. By employing the strategy of market segmentation, a company can design products that really match market demands. Advertising media can be used more effectively because promotional messages—and the media chosen to present them—can be aimed specifically towards each segment of the market.

Some of the most successful marketers are small or medium-sized firms that have decided to concentrate on a small number of market segments and to gain a strong market position and disproportionate market share in these segments. This relates to the principle of niche marketing, which will be discussed in greater detail in Chapter 5.

Even very large companies with the resources to engage in mass marketing supported by expensive national advertising campaigns are now abandoning mass marketing strategies. Instead these companies are embracing market segmentation as a more effective strategy to reach the fractured fragments that once constituted a mass, homogeneous market. Procter & Gamble's marketing program nicely illustrates these changing conditions. Once the epitome of a mass marketer with innovative but utilitarian products, P&G advertised heavily on network television. But today it's a different ball game. Fewer people are at home to watch daytime television; the cost of advertising on network television is very high; and TV ads are often lost in the clutter of 15-second commercials. Therefore, P&G has developed a variety of marketing campaigns, each designed to target a specific market segment. The company now has five different varieties of its market-leading Tide detergent, each targeted to a different segment of the market. Similarly, different promotional campaigns for Crest toothpaste are directed towards children, parents, dentists, and physicians.[5]

Limitations of Market Segmentation

Although market segmentation can provide a lot of marketing benefits to an organization, this strategy also has some drawbacks with respect to costs and market coverage. In the first place, market segmentation can be an expensive proposition in both the production and marketing of products. In production, it obviously is less expensive to produce mass quantities of one model and one colour than it is to produce a variety of models, colours, and sizes.

Segmentation increases marketing expenses in several ways. Total inventory costs go up because adequate inventories of each style, colour, and the like must be maintained. Advertising costs go up because different ads may be required for each market segment. Or some segments may be too small for the seller to make effective use of television or another advertising medium. Administrative expenses go up when management must plan and implement several different programs.

Conditions for Effective Segmentation

Ideally, management's goal should be to segment markets in such a way that each segment responds in a homogeneous fashion to a given marketing program. Three conditions will help management move towards this goal.

- The basis for segmenting — that is, the characteristics used to categorize customers—must be *measurable*, and the data must be *accessible*. The "desire for ecologically compatible products" may be a characteristic that is useful in segmenting the market for a given product. But data on this characteristic are neither readily accessible nor easily quantified.
- The market segment itself should be *accessible* through existing marketing institutions — distribution channels, advertising media, company sales force—with a minimum of cost and waste. To aid marketers in this regard

---

[4]Stuart Gannes, ''The Riches in Market Niches,'' *Fortune*, April 27, 1987, p. 227.

[5]''Stalking the New Consumer,'' *Business Week*, August 28, 1988, p. 54.

some national magazines, such as *Maclean's* and *Chatelaine*, publish separate geographical editions. This allows an advertiser to run an ad aimed at, say, a Western segment of the market, without having to pay for exposure in other, nonmarket areas.

- Each segment should be *large enough* to be profitable. In concept, management could treat each single customer as a separate segment. (Actually this situation may be normal in business markets, as when Canadair markets passenger airplanes to commercial airlines or when the Royal Bank of Canada makes a loan to a company planning to export to Europe.) But in segmenting a consumer market, a firm must not develop too broad an array of styles, colours, sizes, and prices. Usually the diseconomies of scale in production and inventory will put reasonable limits on this type of oversegmentation.

BASES FOR MARKET SEGMENTATION — ULTIMATE CONSUMERS AND BUSINESS USERS

A company can segment its market in many different ways. And the bases for segmentation vary from one product to another. At the top of the list, however, is the division of the entire potential market into two broad categories: ultimate consumers and business users.

The sole criterion for placement in one of these categories is the customer's *reason for buying*. **Ultimate consumers** buy goods or services for their own personal or household use. They are satisfying strictly nonbusiness wants, and they constitute what is called the ''consumer market.''

Business users are business, industrial, or institutional organizations that buy goods or services to use in their own businesses or to make other products. A manufacturer that buys chemicals with which to make fertilizer is a business user of these chemicals. Farmers who buy the fertilizer to use in commercial farming are business users of the fertilizer. (If homeowners buy fertilizer to use on their yards, they are ultimate consumers because they buy it for personal, nonbusiness use.) Supermarkets, museums, and paper manufacturers that buy the service of a chartered accountant are business users of this service. Business users constitute the ''business market''—discussed in greater detail later in this chapter.

The segmentation of all markets into two groups—consumer and business—is extremely significant from a marketing point of view because the two markets buy differently. Consequently the composition of a seller's marketing mix—products, distribution, pricing, and promotion—will depend on whether it is directed towards the consumer market or the business market.

Business users constitute a major market segment that is quite different from the consumer market.

BASES FOR CONSUMER MARKET SEGMENTATION

Dividing the total market into consumer and business segments is a worthwhile start towards useful segmentation, but it still leaves too broad and heterogeneous a grouping for most products. We need to identify some of the bases commonly used to segment these two markets further.

As shown in Table 4-1, the consumer market may be segmented on the basis of the following characteristics:

- Geographic.
- Demographic.
- Psychographic.
- Behaviour towards product (product-related bases).

TABLE 4-1 **Segmentation Bases for Consumer Markets**

Segmentation basis	Examples of typical market segments
Geographic	
Region	Atlantic provinces; Quebec; Ontario; Prairie provinces; B.C.: census regions.
City or CMA size	Under 25,000; 25,000 to 100,000; 100,000 to 250,000; 250,000 to 500,000; 500,000 to 1,000,000; over 1,000,000.
Urban-rural	Urban; rural; suburban; farm.
Climate and topography	Mountainous; seacoast; rainy; cold and snowy; etc.
Demographic:	
Age	Under 6, 6–12, 13–19, 20–34, 35–49, 50–64, 65 and over.
Gender	Male, female.
Family life cycle	Young single, young married no children, etc.
Education	Grade school only, high school graduate, college graduate.
Occupation	Professional, manager, clerical, skilled worker, sales, student, homemaker, unemployed.
Religion	Protestant, Catholic, Jewish, other.
Ethnic background	White; black; oriental.
	British; French; Chinese; German; Ukrainian; Italian; Indian; etc.
Income	Under $10,000, $10,000–$25,000, $25,000–$35,000, $35,000–$50,000, over $50,000.
Psychographic:	
Social class	Upper class, upper middle, lower middle, upper lower, etc.
Personality	Ambitious, self-confident, aggressive, introverted, extroverted, sociable, etc.
Life-style	Conservative, liberal, health and fitness oriented, ''straight,'' ''swinger,'' adventuresome.
Behaviour towards product (or product-related bases):	
Benefits desired	Examples vary widely depending upon product: appliance: cost, quality, life, repairs toothpaste: no cavities, plaque control, bright teeth, good taste, low price.
Usage rate	Nonuser, light user, heavy user.

Marketing executives should be especially aware of trends in each subcategory of these segments.

In using these bases to segment markets, we should bear in mind two points. First, buying behaviour is rarely traceable to only one segmentation factor. Useful segmentation is developed by including variables from several bases. To illustrate, the market for a product rarely consists of all people living in British Columbia or all people over 65. Instead, the segment is more likely to be described with a few of these variables. Thus a market segment for a financial service might be families living in British Columbia, having young children, and earning above a certain income. As another example, one clothing manufacturer's target market might be affluent young women (income, age, sex).

The other point to observe is the interrelationships among these factors, especially among the demographic factors. For instance, age and life-cycle stage typically are related. Income depends to some degree on age, life-cycle stage, education, and occupation.

We shall discuss the two most commonly used bases for segmentation—geographic and demographic—in this chapter, leaving to Chapter 5 a detailed discussion of the more complex bases of market segmentation.

Geographic Segmentation

Subdivisions in the geographical distribution and demographic composition of the population are widely used bases for segmenting consumer markets. The reason for this is simply that consumers' wants and product usage often are related to one or more of these subcategories. Geographic and demographic groupings also meet the conditions for effective segmentation—that is, they are measureable, accessible, and large enough. Let's consider how the geographic distribution of population may serve as segmentation basis.

Total Population

A logical place to start is with an analysis of total population, and here the existence of a "population explosion" that has fizzled becomes evident. The population of Canada did not reach 10 million until about 1930. However, it took only another 35 years to double, and by 1966 the total population of the country stood at just over 20 million. But then the rapid growth in population that had been experienced during the baby boom years from 1945 to the early 1960s began to slow down and by 1990 the Canadian population had reached only 26.6 million. With the current low birth rate expected to continue, projections are that the total population will not go beyond 31 million by 2011. Unless the federal government relaxes restrictions on immigration, Canada could face a situation of *declining* population early in the twenty-first century. The result of a decline in the birth rate from almost four children per family to 1.7 and reduced immigration levels is a static, aging population.

The total market is so large and so diverse that it must be analyzed in segments. Significant shifts are occurring in regional and urban-rural population distribution patterns. Market differences traceable to differences in age, gender, household arrangements, life-styles, and ethnic backgrounds pose real challenges for marketing executives.

Regional Distribution

Figure 4-2 shows the distribution of Canadian population in 1989 and its projected growth to 2011 by province. The biggest markets and the largest urban areas are located in central Canada, where the provinces of Ontario and Quebec together account for 62 percent of Canadian population. However,

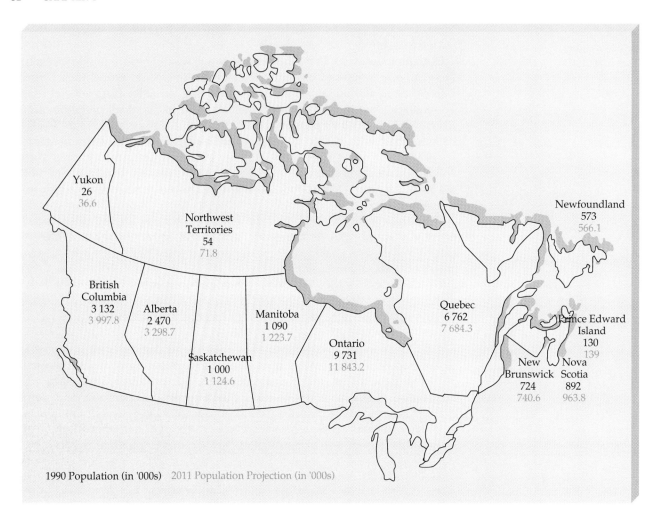

Yukon
26
36.6

Northwest
Territories
54
71.8

Newfoundland
573
566.1

British
Columbia
3 132
3 997.8

Alberta
2 470
3 298.7

Manitoba
1 090
1 223.7

Saskatchewan
1 000
1 124.6

Ontario
9 731
11 843.2

Quebec
6 762
7 684.3

Prince Edward
Island
130
139

New
Brunswick
724
740.6

Nova
Scotia
892
963.8

1990 Population (in '000s)   2011 Population Projection (in '000s)

FIGURE 4-2
**Provincial distribution of
Canadian population, 1990, and
projected growth to 2011.**

Source: Statistics Canada, *Market Research Handbook*, 1991, catalogue no. 63–224, pp. 140, 537.
Note: The projections of provincial population figures to 2011 are based on a series of assumptions.
In this case, it is assumed that the birth rate continues at approximately the level that pertained
at the end of the 1980s, namely, approximately 1.7 births per woman, and that the level of
immigration is approximately 200,000 per year.

the greatest rate of population growth since the early 1980s has occurred in
Ontario and Western Canada, in particular in British Columbia where population increased by 11.3 percent from 1983 to 1990.

The regional distribution of population is important to marketers, because
people within a particular geographic region broadly tend to share the same
values, attitudes, and style preferences. However, significant differences do
exist among the various regions, because of differences in climate, social customs, and other factors. Ontario is a more urbanized province and represents
the greatest concentration of people in Canada, especially in the corridor
between Oshawa and Niagara Falls. This market is attractive to many marketers because of its sheer size and the diversity of consumers living there.
On the other hand, the Atlantic region and the Prairie provinces are characterized by a much more relaxed and rural life-style, which suggests demand

M A R K E T I N G   A T   W O R K

FILE 4-1   **THE GEOGRAPHY OF BEER**

The Canadian beer market is exceptionally geographically segmented. The so-called national market is actually a series of regional markets, often dramatically divergent. Canadians visiting other parts of the country are often surprised to learn that the top brand in their province sells poorly elsewhere—or not at all. British Columbia is a prime example of the industry's strongly regional nature. Kokanee, a brand with a 3 percent provincial share in 1982, has become B.C.'s top selling brew. It evolved from an obscure brand popular in only one small region to a market share "well up in the twenties in a very short time, easily surpassing Labatt's Blue, which now has a share of less than 10 percent, far lower than in most provinces. Although its advertising budget is tiny compared with many national brands, Kokanee has benefited from "goofy" humour, including showing Kokanee bottles swimming upstream like salmon (there is a salmon species in B.C. known as Kokanee).

Source: Adapted from Jim McElgunn, "Kokanee: The Rise and Rise of B.C.'s Brew", *Marketing*, October 1, 1990. p. 1.

Producers of outdoor furniture typically segment their markets by geographic region.

for different types of products and services. People in the West appear to be more relaxed and less formal than Eastern Canadians, and they spend more time outdoors. As this Western Canadian market grows, there will be a growth in demand for products associated with an outdoors life-style.

Urban, Rural, and Suburban Distribution

For many years in Canada there has been both a relative and an absolute decline in the farm population, and this decline in the rural market is expected to continue. The declining farm population has led some people to underestimate the importance of rural markets. However, both as an industrial market for farm machinery and other resource industry equipment and supplies, and as a consumer market with increased buying power and more urban sophistication, the rural market is still a major one. Sociological patterns (such as average family size and local customs) among rural people differ significantly from those of city dwellers. These patterns have considerable influence on buying behaviour. Per capita consumption of cosmetics and other beauty aids, for example, is much lower in farm and rural markets than in city markets.

Census Metropolitan Areas

As the farm population has shrunk, the urban and suburban population has expanded. In recognition of the growing urbanization of the Canadian market, some years ago the federal government established the concept of a Census Metropolitan Area (CMA) as a geographic market-data-measurement unit. A CMA is defined by Statistics Canada as the main labour market of a continuous built-up area having a population of 100,000 or more. Table 4-2 indicates the growth in the population of the 25 CMAs in Canada from 1979 to 1989. By 1989, these 25 areas accounted for more than 60 percent of the total population of Canada, and this percentage is expected to continue to increase. This is especially so as immigration to Canada increases, and as most immigrants settle in urban areas. Obviously, these Census Metropolitan Areas represent attractive, geographically concentrated market targets with considerable sales potential.

In several places in Canada, the metropolitan areas have expanded to the point where there is no rural space between them. This joining of metropolitan

TABLE 4-2 **Census Metropolitan Areas Population, 1979, 1986, and 1989 (in thousands)**

	1979	1986	1989
Calgary, Alberta	530.9	671.3	705.9
Chicoutimi-Jonquière, Quebec	132.3	158.5	157.9
Edmonton, Alberta	608.2	785.5	803.4
Halifax, Nova Scotia	274.1	296.0	306.3
Hamilton, Ontario	537.5	557.0	583.0
Kitchener, Ontario	281.8	311.2	333.9
London, Ontario	279.4	342.3	359.7
Montreal, Quebec	2,799.8	2,921.4	3,021.3
Oshawa, Ontario	149.4	203.5	234.6
Ottawa-Hull, Ontario-Quebec	712.6	819.3	853.2
Quebec, Quebec	562.4	603.3	615.4
Regina, Saskatchewan	159.6	186.5	190.0
St. Catharines-Niagara Falls, Ontario	305.5	343.3	352.5
St. John's, Newfoundland	148.8	161.9	163.3
Saint John, New Brunswick	114.0	121.3	122.9
Saskatoon, Saskatchewan	143.7	200.7	204.3
Sherbrooke, Quebec	—	130.0	133.7
Sudbury, Ontario	151.5	148.9	149.7
Thunder Bay, Ontario	121.8	122.2	123.1
Toronto, Ontario	2,910.0	3,427.2	3,666.5
Trois-Rivières, Quebec	—	128.9	130.9
Vancouver, British Columbia	1,207.6	1,380.7	1,506.0
Victoria, British Columbia	223.5	255.5	272.5
Windsor, Ontario	250.4	254.0	258.1
Winnipeg, Manitoba	583.0	625.3	640.4

SOURCE: Statistics Canada, *Market Research Handbook*, 1991, catalogue no. 63-224.

areas has been called "interurbia." Where two or more city markets once existed, today there is a single market. For example, there is virtually no space between Quebec City and Niagara Falls that is not part of a major urban area.

Suburban Growth

As the metropolitan areas have been growing, something else has been going on *within* them. The central cities are growing very slowly, and in some cases the older established parts of the cities are actually losing population. The real growth is occurring in the fringe areas of the central cities or in the suburbs outside these cities. For the past 40 years, one of the most significant social and economic trends in Canada has been the shift of population to the suburbs. As middle-income families have moved to the suburbs, the ecnomic, racial, and ethnic composition of many central cities (especially core areas) has changed considerably, thus changing the nature of the markets in these areas.

The growth of the suburban population has some striking marketing implications. Since a great percentage of suburban people live in single-family residences, there is a vastly expanded market for lawn mowers, lawn furniture, home furnishings, and home repair supplies and equipment. Suburbanites are more likely to want two cars than are city dwellers. They are inclined to spend more leisure time at home, so there is a bigger market for home entertainment and recreation items.

As we near the end of the century, marketing people are watching two possible counter-trends. One is the movement from the suburbs back to the central cities by older people whose children are grown. Rather than contend with commuting, home maintenance, and other surburban challenges, older people are moving to new apartments located nearer to downtown facilities. And it is not just older people who are returning to the downtown areas. In many Canadian cities, young professional families are locating close to their downtown places of work, preferring to renovate an older home, rather than contend with commuting and other perceived shortcomings of suburban living.

The other reversal is that there has been an increase in the rural population near larger cities. Although the rural population of Canada has increased very little in recent years, most of that growth occurred in close proximity to the large Census Metropolitan Areas. This growth has been brought about, not only because some people wish to live in a more rural setting, but also because of rising real estate prices in and near many Canadian cities.

Demographic Segmentation

The most common basis for segmenting consumer markets is some demographic category such as age, gender, family life-cycle stage, income distribution, education, occupation, or ethnic origin.

Age Groups

Analyzing the consumer market by age groups is a useful exercise in the marketing of many products and services. Age is one of the most fundamental bases for demographically segmenting markets, as we can see from the large number of products and services directed at seniors, children, teens, young adults, and so on. But marketers must be aware of the changing nature of the age mix of the Canadian population. Looking ahead again to the year 2011, we see an aging population and one that is not growing very quickly. In 1986, for example, there were 3.71 million people in Canada aged between 10 and 19. By 1996, this age group will have become slightly smaller at 3.68 million, but by 2011, there will be only 3.53 million Canadians in this age bracket, assuming the birth rate remains at the present level. On the other hand, in 1986, there were only 2.7 million Canadians aged 65 and older. By 1996, this

M A R K E T I N G   A T   W O R K

FILE 4-2   **THE GOLDEN REVOLUTION**

You will never hear the end of it. The boomers are aging and no one but the boomers are surprised. But marketing researchers and strategists are beginning to pay more attention and now see some segmentation in the mature market:

- The New Mature, 50-64-year-olds, who by 2000 will number 4.6 million. They are seen as a new market for home furnishings, travelling, dining, entertainment, and extensive financial services.
- The Early Mature, aged 65–74, 2.1 million in Canada by 2000. They consider ''life facilitation'' as increasingly important and ''life enhancement'' as very meaningful—more attention to clothing sizing, food preparation and ingredients, and noncontact sports.
- The Late Mature, aged 75 and up, consisting of 1.7 million in Canada by 2000. Mostly women, lowest discretionary income, their health and nutrition needs as well as entertainment are of prime concerns.

The revolution means that there are many new opportunities but not for mortgages, teen clothes, disposable diapers, or beers—unless you have sensible mature versions.

Source: Adapted from Jan Drabek, ''The Golden Revolution,'' *Vista*, September, 1989, pp. 73-77.

group will increase in number to 3.58 million and to 4.93 million by 2011.

The *youth* market (roughly aged 5 to 13) carries a three-way market impact. First, these children can influence parental purchases. Second, millions of dollars are spent on this group by their parents. Third, these children themselves make purchases of goods and services for their own personal use and satisfaction, and the volume of these purchases increases as the children get older. Promotional programs are often geared to this market segment. Manufacturers of breakfast cereals, snack foods, and toys often advertise on television programs that are directed at children—except on the CBC television network, which prohibits advertising on children's programs.

The *teenage* market is also recognized as an important one, and yet many companies find it difficult to reach. The mistake might be in attempting to lump all teenagers together. Certainly, the 13-to-16 age group is very different from the 17-to-20 age bracket. Yet marketers must understand the teenage market because of the size of the segment and because its members have a great deal of money to spend. This group has considerable discretionary buying power, because of their part-time jobs and allowances that often come from two income-earning parents. Although the total number of teens has decreased, this group still represents a major market segment for marketers of clothing, cosmetics, fast food, tapes and compact discs, driving lessons, and other products and services.[6]

---

[6]For additional information on the buying power of the teen market, see *Youth in Canada*, Ottawa: Statistics Canada, catalogue No. 89–511, 1989. And, for an interesting discussion on the globalization of the teen market, with the proliferation of international brands, see Jim Cormier, ''Planet Teen,'' *Vista*, vol. 2, no. 7, October 1989, pp. 68–77.

In the 1990s the early *middle-age* population segment (35 to 50) is an especially large and lucrative market. These people are the products of the post-World War II baby boom and were the rebels of the 1960s and 1970s. They also were a very big and profitable teenage and young adult market for many companies during those years. Now, as they move towards middle age in the 1990s, they are reaching their high earning years. Typically, their values and life-styles are far different from those found among the people of the same age category in previous generations. Already, companies are adjusting to these changing demographics. While toothpaste manufacturers like Procter & Gamble and Colgate-Palmolive capitalized on concern about cavity prevention in children's teeth in the 1950s and 1960s, 30 years later they are producing toothpaste to fight tartar—an adult dental problem. This generation, with more dual-income families and fewer children, have more money to spend on themselves. As a result, they are a prime market for products that promise convenience and for home and garden services.[7]

At the older end of the age spectrum are two market segments that should not be overlooked. One is the group of people in their fifties and early sixties. This *mature* market is large and financially well off. Its members are at the peak of their earning power and typically no longer have financial responsibility for their children. Thus, this segment is a good target for marketers of high-priced, high-quality products and services.

The other older age group comprises people over 65 — a segment that is growing both absolutely and as a percentage of the total population. Manufacturers and middlemen alike are beginning to recognize that people in this age group are logical prospects for small, low-cost housing units, cruises and foreign tours, health products, and cosmetics developed especially for older people. Many firms are also developing promotional programs to appeal to this group because their purchasing power is surprisingly high. Also, the shopping behaviour of the over-65 market typically is different from that found in other age segments. On a per capita basis, seniors are increasing their spending faster than average in areas such as health care, entertainment, recreation, gifts, and contributions. In this latter category, seniors give more dollars than the average Canadian, making them an attactive market segment for charities and religious groups.[8]

Companies engaging in international marketing also are paying attention to the older-age market segment. Volkswagen, for instance, has consciously segmented its European markets by age. The company has targeted the older (and wealthier) consumers for its German-made cars, while the company's manufacturing facility in Spain concentrates on producing less expensive cars for younger customers. The Dutch electronics giant, Philips Company, makes products such as VCRs and compact disc players with simpler instructions in large print for the elderly market.[9]

---

[7]For a discussion of the buying power of the aging baby boom-generation, see Kenneth Kidd, "Inheritances: The Boomers' Next Boom," *Globe and Mail Report on Business*, July 2, 1990, pp. B1, B2; and "Those Aging Boomers," *Business Week*, May 20, 1991, pp. 106–112.

[8]The implications of the increasing number of seniors is discussed in Jan Drabek, "The Golden Revolution," *Vista*, vol. 2, no. 6, September 1989, pp. 72–77; and in Mary Anne Burke, "Implications of an Aging Society," *Canadian Social Trends*, Spring 1991, pp. 6–8.

[9]See "Grappling with the Graying of Europe," *Business Week*, March 13, 1989, pp. 54–56.

MARKETING AT WORK

FILE 4-3 **THE FEMALE FINANCIAL OFFICER**

Canadian women (86 percent of them) appear to be confident about handling their finances. They know their bank balances (81 percent), monitor current interest rates (66 percent), and keep an eye on their budget—sort of (51 percent). About 73 percent feel it's important to have their partner involved in all financial decisions—outside of Quebec, that is. In Quebec, only 61 percent feel this way.

Sixty percent of Canadian women feel that the use of credit is unwise unless it is for very large purchases. Quebec women are the most liberal in their credit views (50 percent) while women in Atlantic Canada are most credit averse (66 percent).

While women say they are risk averse (80 percent), 66 percent would like financial advice but only 30 percent are prepared to pay for it.

Women do not believe that, given the way financial institutions currently operate, they get any useful advice; 42 percent say they get none. Only one out of two says that financial institutions generally make women comfortable. Seventy-one percent believe they have more problems obtaining credit than do men. There seems to be a message here that gender segmentation exists in the financial services market.

Source: Adapted from Jeannette Tanguay and Gregory White, ''Money Matters,'' *Playback Strategy*, May 6, 1991, p. 6.

Gender

Gender is an obvious basis for consumer market analysis. Many products are made for use by members of one gender, not both. In many product categories —autos, for example—women and men typically look for different product benefits. Market analysis by gender is also useful because many products have traditionally been purchased by either men only or women only.

However, some of these traditional buying patterns are breaking down, and marketers certainly should be alert to changes involving their products. Not too many years ago, for example, women did most of the grocery shopping, and men bought hardware and products and services needed for automobiles. Today, men are frequent food shoppers, and women buy auto accessories and arrange for repairs and maintenance. Many products and services that were once considered the near-exclusive domain of either men or women are now purchased regularly by both sexes.

The number of women, both married and single, who are employed outside the home is increasing dramatically. By 1989, more than 57 percent of women in Canada were employed outside the home. Women now account for more than 45 percent of the Canadian workforce in the age bracket between 15 and 44. It is expected that the labour force participation rates for men and women will be approximately the same in the age bracket from 25 to 44, as we near the end of the 1990s. These facts are significant for marketers. Not only are the life-style and buying behaviour of women in the labour force quite different from those of women who do not work outside their homes, but many of those women are members of households where their spouses also are employed, thereby producing Canadian households with considerable buying power.[10]

Family Life Cycle

Frequently the main factor accounting for differences in consumption patterns between two people of the same age and sex is that they are in different life-cycle stages. The concept of the family life cycle implies that there are several distinct stages in the life of an ordinary family. The traditional six-stage family cycle is shown in Fig. 4-3, along with three alternative stages that reflect significant changes from traditional patterns. Life-cycle position is a major determinant of buyer behaviour and thus can be a useful basis for segmenting consumer markets.[11]

A young couple with two children (the full-nest stage) has quite different needs from those of a couple in their mid-fifties whose children no longer live at home (the empty-nest stage). A single-parent family (divorced, widowed, or never married) with dependent children faces social and economic problems quite different from those of a two-parent family. Young married couples with no children typically devote large shares of their income to clothing, autos, and recreation. When children start arriving, expenditure patterns shift as many young families buy and furnish a home. Families with teenagers find larger portions of the budget going for food, clothing, and educational needs.

One of the most rapidly growing segments among the Canadian population is the *singles*. In 1961, only 9.3 percent of Canadian households consisted of just one person — a **single**. By 1986, just 25 years later, more than 21 percent of Canadian homes had only a single occupant, although the percentage of people living alone differs considerably from province to province. In British Columbia, for example, 24.8 percent of the households have only a single occupant, while the corresponding percentage at the opposite end of the country in Newfoundland is only 10.2 percent. The total number of one-person households is increasing at a much faster rate than that of family units. Among the reasons for this increase in the number of one-person households are:

- The growing number of working women.
- People marrying at a later age.
- The reduced tendency for single people to live with their parents.
- A rising divorce rate.

The impact that single people of both sexes have on the market is demonstrated by such things as apartments for singles, social clubs for singles, and special tours, cruises, and eating places seeking the patronage of singles. Even in the mundane field of grocery products the growing singles market (including the divorced and widowed) is causing changes by retailers and food manufacturers.

---

[10]For additional perspective on the changing segmentation in the women's market, see *Women in Canada: A Statistical Report*, Ottawa: Statistics Canada, catalogue No. 89–503E, 1989; and Jo-Anne B. Parliament, ''Women Employed Outside the Home,'' *Canadian Social Trends*, Summer 1989, pp. 2–6.

[11]For a view of the family life cycle that reflects the growing number of single adults, with or without dependent children, see Patrick E. Murphy and William A. Staples, ''A Modernized Family Life Cycle,'' *Journal of Consumer Research*, June 1979, pp. 12–22; and *New Trends in the Family: Demographic Facts and Features*, Ottawa: Statistics Canada, catalogue No. 91–535E occasional, 1991.

FIGURE 4-3
The family life cycle.

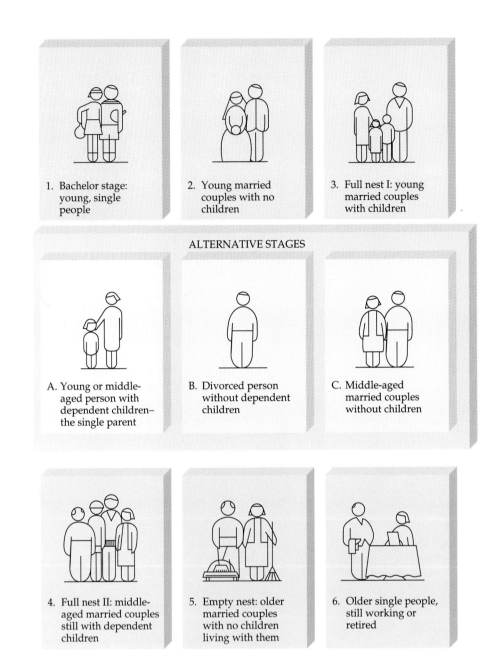

1. Bachelor stage: young, single people

2. Young married couples with no children

3. Full nest I: young married couples with children

ALTERNATIVE STAGES

A. Young or middle-aged person with dependent children–the single parent

B. Divorced person without dependent children

C. Middle-aged married couples without children

4. Full nest II: middle-aged married couples still with dependent children

5. Empty nest: older married couples with no children living with them

6. Older single people, still working or retired

Singles in the 25-to-39 age bracket are especially attractive to marketers because they are such a large group. Compared with the population as a whole, this singles group is:

- More affluent.
- More mobile.
- More experimental and less conventional.
- More fashion- and appearance-conscious.
- More active in leisure pursuits.
- More sensitive to social status.

MARKETING AT WORK

FILE 4-4   **NEW IN CANADA: TRILINGUAL LABELLING**

The growing ethnic population in Canada has created numerous opportunities for marketers. Best Foods, Toronto, has introduced various products for the Chinese community. However, these are not packaged like most other food products as they feature trilingual labels — Chinese, English, and French. A media campaign has also begun to promote Best products. Since the Asian population in Canada now numbers more than 600,000, consideration is being given to targeting other southeast Asian ethnic groups, in their first language — in addition to English and French.

Source: Adapted from *Marketing*, ''Best Foods Campaign Is Trilingual,'' February 11, 1991, p. 18.

Other Demographic Bases for Segmentation

The market for some consumer products is influenced by such factors as education, occupation, religion, or ethnic origin. With an increasing number of people attaining higher levels of **education**, for example, we can expect to see (1) changes in product preferences and (2) buyers with more discriminating taste and higher incomes. **Occupation** may be a more meaningful criterion than income in segmenting some markets. Truck drivers or auto mechanics may earn as much as young retailing executives or college professors. But the buying patterns of the first two are different from those of the second two because of attitudes, interests, and other life-style factors.

For some products, it is useful to analyze the population on the basis of *religion* or *ethnic origin*. The most important distinction in Canada is between the two founding races. French-English differences are fundamental to doing business in Canada and will be dealt with in much greater detail in Chapter 6. Marketers have known for some time that certain products such as instant coffee and tomato juice sell much better in Quebec.

In larger Canadian cities, the cultural diversity of the population creates an increasing marketing opportunity for companies that specialize in products and services that are directed towards a particular ethnic community. In Toronto, for example, almost half the population was born outside Canada. Persons of Italian heritage represent more than 5 percent of the population in Ontario and more than 10 percent in Toronto. Almost 8 percent of the population of Alberta have German roots, as do almost 13 percent of people in Saskatchewan. Almost 8 percent of the population of Manitoba are Ukrainian.

In certain areas of the country, such as the large German population around Kitchener-Waterloo, Ontario, and in many of the larger cities, ethnic groups represent a viable target market segment for certain specialty products and services. The large number of recent immigrants from Hong Kong and other Asian countries has transformed some neighbourhoods in some cities, as did immigrants from Portugal, Italy, and the Caribbean before them. These new Canadians have created a new market segment in certain parts of the country and represent an ethnic market that will continue to grow if the Canadian government relaxes its restrictions on immigration in the face of a declining rate of population growth. This will contribute to an even more diversified ethnic community in Canada. Developing marketing programs to meet the needs of these ethnic market segments can be a very successful initiative for some marketers.[12]

CONSUMER INCOME AND ITS DISTRIBUTION

People alone do not make a market; they must have money to spend. Consequently, income, its distribution, and how it is spent are essential factors in any quantitative market analysis.

Nature and Scope of Income

What is income? There are so many different concepts of income that it is good to review some definitions. The following outline is actually a "word equation" that shows how the several concepts are related.

National income: Total income from all sources, including employee compensation, corporate profits, and other income

Less: Corporate profits, and pension and social program contributions
Plus: Dividends, government transfer payments to persons, and net interest paid by government
Equals:

Personal income: All forms of income received by persons and unincorporated businesses; including wages, salaries, and supplementary labour income; military pay and allowances; net income of nonfarm business including rent; net income of farm operators from farm production; interest, dividends, and miscellaneous investment income; and transfer payment income from government, corporations, and non-residents

Less: All personal federal, provincial, and municipal taxes
Equals:

Personal disposable income: Personal income less personal direct taxes and other current transfers to government from persons; represents the amount available for personal consumption expenditures and savings

Less: (1) Essential expenditures for food, clothing, household utilities, and local transportation and (2) fixed expenditures for rent, house mortgage payments, insurance, and instalment debt payments
Equals:

Discretionary purchasing power: The amount of disposable personal income that is available after fixed commitments (debt repayments, rent) and essential household needs are taken care of. As compared with disposable personal income, discretionary purchasing power is a better (more sensitive) indicator of consumers' ability to spend for *nonessentials*.

In addition, we hear the terms "money income," "real income," and "psychic income." **Money income** is the amount a person receives in actual cash or cheques for wages, salaries, rent, interest, and dividends. **Real income** is what the money income will buy in goods and services; it is purchasing power. If a person's money income rises 5 percent in one year but the cost of purchases increases 8 percent on average, then real income decreases about 3 percent. **Psychic income** is an intangible, but highly important, income factor related to comfortable climate, a satisfying neighbourhood, enjoyment of one's job,

---

[12]A very good overview of the changing demographics is contained in Gordon Priest, "The Demographic Future," *Canadian Social Trends*, Summer 1990, pp. 5–8.

Using discretionary income
with class.

WITH AN EYE TO THE CLASSICS.

JAGUAR SOVEREIGN

The Jaguar Sovereign's pre-eminent elegance and scintillating performance are renowned throughout the world. But, that's hardly surprising, considering Jaguar's over six-decade tradition of automotive excellence.

Its sweeping lines are as aesthetically pleasing and emotionally satisfying at rest, as they are in swift, aerodynamic flight. Warm, handpolished burl walnut and rich hand-sewn leathers are traditional interior appointments. A new, six-speaker Alpine entertainment system, complete with a compact disc player, is an inspirational addition. In three simple words, the Sovereign is: elegance, performance, and value.

All new Jaguars are protected by an exclusive Club Jaguar membership, which includes no-cost scheduled maintenance, 24-hour emergency roadside service, and other valuable benefits for the full three-year or 60,000 km warranty period. At your discretion, you can choose to augment your Club Jaguar Warranty with an additional two-year or 40,000 km warranty programme.

Nothing surpasses the Sovereign's classic elegance. For more information, contact a Jaguar dealer or send your business card to:

Jaguar Canada Inc.,
Communication Services, Indell Lane,
Bramalea, Ontario L6T 4H3.

JAGUAR

A BLENDING OF ART AND MACHINE.

and so on. Some people prefer to take less real income so they can live in a part of the country that features a fine climate—greater psychic income.

As measured by income, the Canadian market has grown dramatically in recent years. Until the economic downturn of the early 1980s, the economy had enjoyed almost uninterrupted growth since the end of the Second World War. Personal disposable income had grown to more than $393 *billion* by 1988. This represents an increase of more than 250 percent in just ten years. Discretionary purchasing power increased at approximately the same rate through the 1980s. Even after allowing for the increases in prices that occurred over that period, the increase in consumer buying power is impressive.

M A R K E T I N G   A T   W O R K

FILE 4-5   **WHAT TO DO WHEN YOU CAN'T TAKE IT WITH YOU**

Canadians over 55 years of age control more than 70 percent of our wealth. The seniors' market, as it is called, is expected to grow to 3.5 million people by the year 2000 — double the size it was in 1971. Currently, liquid personal assets amount to $700 billion and are expected to grow to $1 trillion by 2000. Although every senior will not be rich, the bulk of our wealth will continue to be controlled by those over 55.

Five years ago, the Royal Bank of Canada's Grey Panthers division was the only financial services sales force dedicated to serving seniors. Today, although it is still the leader in the development of products and services, it is but one of a large and growing group of competitors. In the past, it was assumed that once people retired, they began to run down the capital they had saved. Research indicated that these people accumulated money for several years beyond retirement. Every bank is now busily working to innovate new products and services for this market including ''snowbird'' services; special branches; new approaches to mutual funds, annuities, RRSPs, and income funds; private banking; telephone banking; ''smart'' cards; debit cards; new integrated data bases to facilitate counselling; and cross selling of products — and last but not least, a great deal of staff training to create a core of financial advisors for seniors.

Income Distribution

To get full value from an analysis of income, we should study the variations and trends in the distribution of income among regions and among population segments. Regional income data are especially helpful in pinpointing the particular market to which a firm wishes to appeal. Income data on cities and even on areas within cities may indicate the best locations for shopping centres and suburban branches of downtown stores.

There has been a genuine income revolution going on in Canada over the past 30 years or so. During the second half of the twentieth century, the pattern of income distribution has been dramatically altered. (See Table 4-3.) There has been a tremendous growth in the middle-income and upper income segments and a corresponding decrease in the percentage of low-income groups.

The purchasing power of the average Canadian family is expected to continue to increase over the next ten years. We will see the effects of higher personal incomes and higher participation rates in the labour force. It is entirely possible that more than half of all Canadian families will have a total annual income in excess of $50,000 by the year 2000. This anticipated increase in the number of affluent households is the result of several factors. These include (1) the large growth in the number of people in the prime earning years 25 to 45, (2) the increase in dual-income families, and (3) the wider distribution of inherited wealth. We will still have low-income families. However, there will be fewer below the poverty line, even though that level (by government definition) is moving up, in recognition of both inflation and a society that is generally better able to provide its members with a reasonable income.

TABLE 4-3 **Percentage Distribution of Families by Income Groups in Canada Annual Income 1979, 1984, 1989**

Income group	1979	1984	1989
less than $10,000	15.2	6.7	2.4
$10,000 to $14,999	11.5	9.3	4.5
$15,000 to $19,999	14.7	9.5	7.4
$20,000 to $24,999	16.0	9.0	6.4
$25,000 to $29,999	13.4	10.1	7.0
$30,000 to $34,999	10.0	10.1	7.3
$35,000 to $39,999	6.8	9.6	8.1
$40,000 to $44,999	4.2	8.1	7.7
$45,000 to $49,999	2.6	6.5	7.5
$50,000 to $59,999	2.9	9.1	12.6
$60,000 and over	2.5	12.1	29.1

Source: *Income Distribution by Size in Canada 1989*, Ottawa: Statistics Canada, catalogue No. 13–707 annual, 1989, p. 55.

Marketing Significance of Income Data

The declining percentage of families in the poverty bracket, coupled with the sharp increases in the upper-income groups, presages an explosive growth in discretionary purchasing power. And, as discretionary income increases, so too does the demand for items that once were considered luxuries.

The middle-income market is a big market and a growing market, and it has forced many changes in marketing strategy. Many stores that once appealed to low-income groups have traded up to the huge middle-income market. These stores are upgrading the quality of the products they carry and are offering additional services.

In spite of the considerable increase in disposable income in the past 30 years, many households are still in the low-income bracket or find their higher incomes inadequate to fulfil all their wants. Furthermore, many customers are willing to forgo services in order to get lower prices. One consequence of this market feature has been the development of self-service retail outlets, discount houses, and the more recent superstores such as those operated by furniture and appliance retailers like The Brick Warehouse in Ontario and Western Canada and by specialists in electronic sound equipment such as Majestic Electronic Stores, which operate almost 40 stores in Ontario.

Earlier in this chapter we noted the dramatic increase in the number of working women. This demographic factor also has had a tremendous impact on family income levels. The increase in two-income families has significant marketing and sociological implications. Dual incomes generally enable a family to offset the effects of inflation. But more than that, two incomes often enable a family to buy within a short time the things that their parents worked years to acquire.

CONSUMER EXPENDITURE PATTERNS

How consumers' income is spent is a major market determinant for most products and services. Consequently, marketers need to study consumer *spending patterns*, as well as the *distribution* of consumer income. Marketers also should be aware of the significant *shifts* in family spending patterns that have occurred over the past two or three decades. Energy costs, inflation, and heavy consumer debt loads have had a major impact on our spending patterns. As examples, let's consider just a few of the changes in spending patterns that have occurred between the 1960s and the 1990s. Over that time span, families have *increased* the percentage of their total expenditures going for housing, health, and utilities. Spending (as a percentage of total) has *decreased* for food, beverage, clothing, and home expenses (except utilities).

But expenditure patterns are not the same for all families. These patterns vary considerably, depending upon family income, life-cycle stage, and other factors.

Relation to Stage of Family Life Cycle

Consumer expenditure patterns are influenced by the consumer's stage in the life cycle. There are striking contrasts in spending patterns between, say, people in the full-nest stage with very young children and people in the empty-nest stage. Table 4-4 summarizes the behavioural influences and the spending patterns for families in each stage of the cycle. (This table expands the number of stages shown earlier in Fig. 4-3.) Young married couples with no children typically devote large shares of their income to clothing, autos, and recreation. When children start arriving, expenditure patterns shift as many young families buy and furnish a home. Families with teenagers find larger portions of the budget going for food, clothing, and educational needs. Families in the empty-nest stage, especially when the head is still in the labour force, are attactive to marketers. Typically, these families have more discretionary buying power.

Relation to Income Distribution

The pattern of consumer expenditures is influenced significantly by the income level of the household. For example, as we can see in Table 4-5, families with incomes in the range of $15,000 to $19,999 spend an average of 17.3 percent of their expenditures on food. This percentage drops to 14.8 percent for those with annual incomes between $35,000 and $39,999, and to 11.4 percent for those with incomes above $60,000 per annum. These and other findings from the analysis of Statistics Canada data suggest the type of information that marketers might obtain from analyzing spending patterns by income groups. Some additional generalizations from such data are summarized below.

- There is a high degree of uniformity in the expenditure patterns of *middle-class* spending units. As we shall note in Chapter 6, however, social-class structure is often a more meaningful criterion for determining expenditure patterns.
- For each product category, there is a considerable *absolute increase* in dollars spent as income rises (or, more correctly, as we compare one income group with a higher income group). In other words, people in a given income bracket spend significantly more *dollars* in each product category than those in lower brackets. However, the lower-income households devote a larger *percentage* to their total expenditures to some product categories, such as food. Marketers are probably more concerned with the total *dollars* available from each income group than with the *percentage* share of total expenditures.
- In each successively higher income group, the amount spent for food declines as a *percentage* of total expenditures.
- The percentage of expenditures devoted to housing, household operation,

TABLE 4-4 **Behavioural Influences and Buying Patterns, by Family Life-Cycle Stage**

Bachelor stage; young single people not living at home	Newly married couples; young, no children	Full nest I; youngest child under 6	Full nest II; youngest child 6 or over	Full nest III; older married couples with dependent children
Few financial burdens.	Better off financially than they will be in near future.	Home purchasing at peak.	Financial position better.	Financial position still better.
Fashion opinion leader.	Highest purchase rate and highest average purchase of durables.	Liquid assets low.	Many wives work.	Many wives work.
Recreation-oriented.		Some wives work.	Less influenced by advertising.	Some children get jobs.
Buy: Basic kitchen equipment, basic furniture, cars, equipment for the mating game, vacations.	Buy: Cars, refrigerators, stoves, sensible and durable furniture, vacations.	Dissatisfied with financial position and amount of money saved.	Buy larger-sized packages, multiple-unit deals.	Hard to influence with advertising.
		Interested in new products.	Buy: Many foods, cleaning materials, bicycles, music lessons, pianos.	High average purchase of durables.
		Like advertised products.		Buy: New, more tasteful furniture, auto travel, nonnecessary appliances, boats, dental services, magazines.
		Buy: Washers, dryers, TV sets, baby food, chest rubs and cough medicine, vitamins, dolls, wagons, sleds, skates.		

Empty nest I; older married couples, no children living with them, head in labour force	Empty nest II; older married couples, no children living at home, head retired	Solitary survivor, in labour force	Solitary survivor, retired
Home ownership at peak.	Drastic cut in income.	Income still good but likely to sell home.	Same medical and product needs as other retired group; drastic cut in income.
Most satisfied with financial position and money saved.	Keep home.		Special need for attention, affection, and security.
Interested in travel, recreation, self-education.	Buy: Medical appliances, medical care, products which aid health, sleep, and digestion.		
Make gifts and contributions.			
Not interested in new products.			
Buy: Vacations, luxuries, home improvements.			

Source: William D. Wells and George Gubar, ''Life Cycle Concept in Marketing Research,'' *Journal of Marketing Research*, November 1966, p. 362.

TABLE 4-5 **Detailed Family Expenditure by Selected Family Income Categories all families and unattached individuals 1986**

Expenditure Category	Family Income		
	$15,000 – $19,999	$35,000 – $39,999	$60,000 and over
Food	17.3	14.8	11.4
Shelter	21.6	16.4	12.2
Household operation	5.2	4.2	3.8
Household furnishings and equipment	3.9	3.4	3.5
Clothing	5.9	6.0	6.8
Transportation	15.4	13.6	12.7
Health care	2.3	1.9	1.4
Personal care	2.3	2.0	1.6
Recreation	5.0	5.1	5.4
Reading materials and other printed matter	0.7	0.6	0.5
Education	0.8	0.6	1.1
Tobacco products and alcoholic beverages	4.5	3.8	2.3
Miscellaneous	2.5	2.7	2.4
Personal taxes	7.0	17.6	26.6
Security	2.5	4.6	5.0
Gifts and contributions	3.3	2.7	3.2

Source: *Market Research Handbook*, Ottawa: Statistics Canada, 1991, catalogue No. 63-224, pp. 200-201.

and utilities totals approximately 21 percent. This varies from more than 38 percent for the lowest-income consumers to 16 percent for those whose family incomes are more than $60,000 annually.

- Dramatic differences are observed across income groups in their actual dollar expenditures on recreation. Whereas a family in the lower-income bracket may spend as little as $327 annually, the higher-income family will spend as much as $4000.
- The percentage spent on clothing remains fairly constant across income groups, ranging from 5.5 percent to 6.8 percent. Dollar expenditures, however, range from $500 to more than $5,000 annually.
- A major difference between low-income and higher-income Canadian families lies in the percentage of their total income that goes to government in the form of taxes. Whereas a family whose total income is in the top 20 percent in Canada will pay 25 percent or more of total personal income in taxes, lower-income families may pay no tax at all.
- Major differences in expenditure patterns are also found when the Canadian population is examined across geographic regions. This is related in part to income differences, but also is caused to a degree by the differences in the cost of certain items in different areas of the country. For example, the average family in Montreal spends 15 percent of total expenditures on food, while a family in Calgary spends only 12.9 percent. On the other hand, a family in Victoria will spend 18.4 percent of its total expenditures on housing, as compared with only 15.8 percent in Saint John, New Brunswick.

Generalizations such as these provide a broad background against which marketing executives can analyze the market for their particular product or service. People with needs to satisfy and money to spend, however, must be *willing* to spend before we can say a market exists. Consequently, in Chapter 6 we shall look into consumer motivation and buying behaviour — the "willingness-to-buy" factor in our definition of a market.

THE BUSINESS MARKET

The factors affecting the market for business products are the number of potential business users and their purchasing power, buying motives, and buying habits. In the following discussion, we identify several basic *differences* between consumer markets and business markets.

Number and Types of Business Users

TOTAL MARKET

The business market contains relatively few buying units when compared with the consumer market. There are approximately a half million business users, in contrast to about 27 million consumers divided among more than 9 million households. The business market will seem even more limited to most companies, because they sell to only a segment of the total market. A firm selling to meat-processing plants, for example, would have about 45 potential customer plants. If you were interested in providing services to battery manufacturers, you would find about 25 companies as basic prospects. Consequently, marketing executives must try to pinpoint their market carefully by type of industry and geographic location. A firm marketing hard-rock mining equipment is not interested in the total business market, or even in all firms engaged in mining and quarrying.

One very useful source of information is the Standard Industrial Classification system (SIC), which enables a company to identify relatively small segments of its business market. All types of businesses in Canada are divided into 12 groups, as follows:

1. Agriculture.
2. Forestry.
3. Fishing and trapping.
4. Mines, quarries, and oil wells.
5. Manufacturing industries (20 major groups).
6. Construction industry.
7. Transportation, communication, and other utilities.
8. Trade.
9. Finance, insurance, and real estate.
10. Community, business, and personal service industries (8 major groups).
11. Public administration and defence.
12. Industry unspecified or undefined.

A separate number is assigned to each major industry within each of the above groups; then, three- and four-digit classification numbers are used to subdivide each major category into finer segments. To illustrate, in division 5 (manufacturing), major group 4 (leather) contains:

Business targeting small
business.

SIC code	Industrial group
172	Leather tanneries
174	Shoe factories
175	Leather-glove factories
179	Luggage, handbag, and small-leather goods manufacturers

SIZE OF BUSINESS USERS

Although the market may be limited in the total number of buyers, it is large in purchasing power. As one might expect, business users range in size from very small companies with fewer than five employees to firms with staff numbering more than 1,000. A relatively small percentage of firms account for the greatest share of the value added by a given industry. For example, Statistics Canada data on the manufacturing sector in Canada indicate that slightly more than 1 percent of manufacturing firms—those with 500 or more employees—account for approximately 40 percent of the total value added by manufacturing and for more than 30 percent of the total employment in manufacturing. The firms with fewer than 50 employees, while accounting for more than 80 percent of all manufacturing establishments, produce less than 15 percent of the value added by manufacturing.

The marketing significance in these facts is that the buying power in the business market is highly concentrated in relatively few firms. This market concentration has considerable influence on a seller's policies regarding its channels of distribution. Middlemen are not as essential as in the consumer market.

REGIONAL CONCENTRATION OF BUSINESS USERS

There is a substantial regional concentration in many of the major industries and among business users as a whole. A firm selling products usable in oil fields will find the bulk of its market in Alberta, the Northwest Territories, offshore Newfoundland, and the U.S. and abroad. Rubber products manufacturers are located mostly in Ontario, shoes are produced chiefly in Quebec, and most of the nation's garment manufacturers are located in southern Ontario and Quebec. There is a similar regional concentration in the farm market.

Although a large part of a firm's market may be concentrated in limited geographic areas, a good portion may lie outside these areas. Consequently, a distribution policy must be developed that will enable a firm to deal directly with the concentrated market and also to employ middlemen (or a company sales force at great expense) to reach the outlying markets.

IMPORTANCE OF THE SERVICE SECTOR

There is a very real danger, when we refer to the business or industrial sector, to assume that we are discussing only manufacturing companies. In fact, we probably should look for new terminology. Previous editions of this and other marketing textbooks tended to refer to this important market sector as the *industrial* market. We have decided to adopt more current terminology and refer to it as the *business* market. In fact neither term is precisely correct, as this sector includes *all* entities that are not part of the end consumer market. To refer to this market as *industrial* gives the impression that we are concerned only with industry or with manufacturing. In fact, less and less of the total output of Canadian business is being accounted for by manufacturing. When we consider that government, hospitals, universities, schools, retailers, banks, and charities are all part of the nonmanufacturing sector, it should be obvious that the term *industrial* is no longer appropriate. In fact, the *service* sector in this country has grown to the point that it now accounts for more than 60 percent of the Gross Domestic Product and approximately 70 percent of all jobs. The obvious importance to Canadian marketers of the growing market for services is dealt with in greater detail in Chapter 11.

When we consider all those Canadians who are working for various government departments and agencies, for banks and other financial institutions, for retail stores, hotels and restaurants, for universities, colleges and other not-for-profit organizations, it is not difficult to understand how more than nine million Canadians are now working in service sector jobs.

Many service companies are quite small, partly because of the low cost of going into business. There is considerable *ease of entry* for many service firms, especially in the provision of personal services such as child care and home cleaning and in certain professional services such as management consulting. While these service firms do not purchase raw materials for further manufacture, they nevertheless represent a major market for office supplies and furnishings, computer software, and communications equipment. In fact, the dramatic advances that have been made in technology and communications have enabled service companies to locate in fairly remote areas of the country. Toll-free telephone lines, facsimile machines, and computer networks mean that there is no need for airline reservations offices and similar services to be located in major cities.

Buying Power of Business Users

Another determinant of business market demand is the purchasing power of business users. This can be measured, either by the expenditures of business users or by their sales volume. Many times, however, such information is not available or is very difficult to estimate. In such cases, it is more feasible to use an **activity indicator** — that is, some market factor that is related to income generation and expenditures. Sometimes an activity indicator is a combined indicator of purchasing power and the number of business users. Following are examples of activity indicators that might be used to estimate the purchasing power of business users.

MEASURES OF MANUFACTURING ACTIVITY

Firms selling to manufacturers might use as market indicators such factors as the number of employees, the number of plants, or the dollar value added by manufacturing. One firm selling work gloves used the number of employees in manufacturing establishments to determine the relative values of various geographic markets. Another company that sold a product that controls stream pollution used two indicators—(1) the number of firms processing wood products (paper mills, plywood mills, and so forth) and (2) the manufacturing value added by these firms.

MEASURES OF MINING ACTIVITY

The number of mines operating, the volume of their output, and the dollar value of the product as it leaves the mine all may indicate the purchasing power of mines. This information can be used by any firm marketing industrial products to mine operators.

MEASURES OF AGRICULTURAL ACTIVITY

A company marketing fertilizer or agricultural equipment can estimate the buying power of its farm market by studying such indicators as cash farm income, acreage planted, or crop yields. The chemical producer that sells to a fertilizer manufacturer might study the same indices, because the demand for chemicals in this case is derived from the demand for fertilizer.

MEASURES OF CONSTRUCTION ACTIVITY

If a firm is marketing building materials, such as lumber, brick, gypsum products, or builders' hardware, its market is dependent upon construction activity. This may be indicated by the number and value of building permits issued or by the number of construction starts by type of housing (single-family residence, apartment, or commercial).

Buying Patterns of Business Users

Overt buying behaviour in the business market differs significantly from *consumer* behaviour in several ways. These differences obviously stem from the differences in the products, markets, and buyer-seller relationships.

DIRECT PURCHASE

Direct sale from the producer to the ultimate consumer is rare, although increasing through the use of catalogues and other direct marketing vehicles. In the business market, however, direct marketing from the producer to the user is quite common. This is true especially when the order is large and the buyer needs much technical assistance. From a seller's point of view, direct marketing is reasonable, especially when there are relatively few potential buyers, they are big, and they are geographically concentrated.

FREQUENCY OF PURCHASE

In the business market, firms buy certain products very infrequently. Large installations are purchased only once in many years. Smaller parts and materials to be used in the manufacture of a product may be ordered on long-term contracts, so that an actual selling opportunity exists only once every year. Even standardized operating supplies, such as office supplies or cleaning products, may be bought only once a month.

Because of this buying pattern, a great burden is placed on the advertising and personal selling programs of businesses who market to other businesses. Their advertising must keep the company's name constantly before the market. The sales force must call on potential customers often enough to know when a customer is considering a purchase.

SIZE OF ORDER

The average order to a business customer is considerably larger than its counterpart in the consumer market. This fact, coupled with the infrequency of purchase, highlights the importance of each sale in the business market. Losing the sale of a pair of shoes to a consumer is not nearly as devastating as losing the sale of ten airplanes.

LENGTH OF NEGOTIATION PERIOD

The period of negotiation in a business-to-business sale is usually much longer than in a consumer market sale. Some of the reasons for the extended negotiations are (1) several executives are involved in the buying decision; (2) the sale often involves a large amount of money; (3) the product is often made to order; and (4) considerable discussion is involved in establishing the specifications.

DEMAND FOR PRODUCT SERVICING

The user's desire for excellent service is a strong business buying motive that may determine buying patterns. Consequently, many sellers emphasize their service as much as their products. Frequently a firm's only attraction is its service, because the product itself is so standardized that it can be purchased from any number of companies.

Sellers must stand ready to furnish services both before and after the sale. A manufacturer of computers may study a customer firm's accounting operations and suggest more effective systems that involve using the seller's products. The manufacturer will also arrange to retrain the present office staff. After the machines have been installed, other services, such as repairs, may be furnished.

QUALITY AND SUPPLY REQUIREMENTS

Another business buying pattern is the user's insistence upon an adequate quantity of uniform-quality products. Variations in the quality of materials going into finished products can cause considerable trouble for manufacturers. They may be faced with costly disruptions in their production process if the imperfections exceed quality-control limits. Adequate *quantities* are as important as good quality. A work stoppage that is caused by an insufficient supply of material is just as costly as one that is caused by inferior quality of a tangible product. In fact, recent research on the level of satisfaction of business customers has tended to show that business customers are often less satisfied with the ability of their suppliers to deliver on time than they are with the quality of their products. In many product categories, technology and quality control have improved to the point where the actual products rarely fail. In such cases, the ability of a supplier to compete often depends far more on the firm's ability to deliver on time. Thus, its ability to provide service is often at least as important as the product itself.

Adequacy of supply is a problem especially for sellers and users of raw materials such as agricultural products, metal ores, or forest products. Climate conditions may disrupt the normal flow of goods—logging camps or mining operations may become snowbound. Agricultural products fluctuate in quality and quantity from one growing season to another. These "acts of God" create managerial problems for both buyers and sellers with respect to warehousing, standardization, and grading.

LEASING INSTEAD OF BUYING

A growing behavioural pattern among firms in the business and service sector is that of **leasing** products instead of buying them outright. In the past, this practice was limited to large equipment, such as computers and heavy construction equipment. Today, firms are expanding leasing arrangements to include delivery trucks, sales-force automobiles, machine tools, and other items generally less expensive than major installations.

Leasing has several merits for the firm leasing out its equipment. Total net income — after charging off pertinent repair and maintenance expenses — is often higher than it would be if the unit were sold outright. Also, the market may be expanded to include users who could not afford to buy the product, especially large equipment. Leasing offers an effective method of getting distribution for a new product. Potential users may be more willing to rent a product than to buy it. If they are not satisfied, their expenditure is limited to a few monthly payments.

BASES FOR BUSINESS MARKET SEGMENTATION

Several of the bases used to segment the consumer market can also be used to segment the broad business market. For example, we can segment business markets on a geographical basis. Several industries are geographically concentrated, so any firm selling to these industries could nicely use this segmentation basis. Sellers also can segment on product-related bases such as usage rate or benefits desired.[13]

Let's look at three of the bases that are used solely for segmenting business markets—type of customer, size of customer, and type of buying situation.[14]

TYPE OF CUSTOMER

Any firm that sells to customers in a variety of business markets may want to segment this market on the basis of customer types. In Chapter 4 we discussed the Standard Industrial Classification (SIC) code as a very useful tool for identifying business and institutional target markets. A firm selling display cases or store fixtures to the retail market, for example, might start out with potential customers included in the two-digit code number 61 for shoe, apparel, fabric and yarn industries—retail. Then the three-digit code 612 identifies potential customers in the retail clothing business. Finally, the four-digit code number 6121 pinpoints men's clothing specialty stores.

A firm selling janitorial supplies or small electric motors would have a broad potential market among many different industries. Management in this firm could segment its market by type of customer and then perhaps decide to sell to firms in only a limited number of these segments.

SIZE OF CUSTOMER

In this situation, size can be measured by such factors as sales volume, number of production facilities, or number of sales offices. Many business-to-business marketers divide their potential market into large and small accounts, using separate distribution channels to reach each segment. The large-volume accounts, for example, may be sold to directly by the company's sales force. But to reach the smaller accounts, the seller will use a manufacturers' agent or some other form of middleman.

TYPE OF BUYING SITUATION

In Chapter 6, we will discuss three types of buying classes—new buy, modified rebuy, and straight rebuy. We also recognize in that discussion that a new buy is significantly different from a straight rebuy in several important respects. Consequently, a business seller might well segment its market into these three

---

[13]For examples of benefit segmentation as used in the business market, see Mark L. Bennion, Jr., "Segmentation and Positioning in a Basic Industry," *Industrial Marketing Management*, February 1987, pp. 9–18; Susan A. Lynn, "Segmenting a Business Market for a Professional Service," *Industrial Marketing Management*, February 1986, pp. 13–21; Rowland T. Moriarty and David J. Reibstein, "Benefit Segmentation in Industrial Markets," *Journal of Business Research*, December 1986, pp. 483–86; and Cornelis A. de Kluyver and David B. Whitlark, "Benefit Segmentation for Industrial Products," *Industrial Marketing Management*, November 1986, pp. 273–86.

[14]For some additional approaches to business marketing segmentation, see Benson P. Shapiro and Thomas V. Bonoma, "How to Segment Industrial Markets," *Harvard Business Review*, May/June 1984, pp. 104–110. See also James G. Barnes and Ronald McTavish, "Segmenting Industrial Markets by Buyer Sophistication," *European Journal of Marketing*, vol. 17, no. 6, 1983, pp. 16–33.

buy-class categories. Or the seller could at least set up two segments by combining new buy and modified rebuy into one segment. Then different marketing programs would be developed to reach each of these two or three segments.[15]

SUMMARY   A sound marketing program starts with the identification and analysis of target markets for whatever it is that an organization is selling. A market consists of people or organizations with needs or wants, money to spend, and the willingness to spend it. There are some general guidelines to follow when selecting target markets.

Some form of market segmentation is the strategy that most marketers adopt as a compromise between the extremes of an aggregate, undifferentiated market and a different product tailor-made for each customer. Market segmentation is the process of dividing the total heterogeneous market into several homogeneous segments. A separate marketing mix is developed for each segment that the seller selects as a target market. Market segmentation is a customer-oriented philosophy that is consistent with the marketing concept.

Market segmentation enables a company to make more efficient use of its marketing resources. Also, this strategy allows a small company to compete effectively in one or two segments. The main drawback of market segmentation is that it requires higher production and marketing costs than does a one-product, mass-market strategy. The requirements for effective segmentation are that (1) the bases for segmentation be measurable with accessible data; (2) the segments themselves be accessible to existing marketing institutions; and (3) the segments be large enough to be potentially profitable.

The total market may be divided into two broad segments — ultimate consumers and business users. The four major bases that may be used for further segmenting the consumer market are: (1) geographic—the distribution of population; (2) demographic—the composition of population such as age, gender, and income distribution; (3) psychographic—personality traits and life-styles; and (4) product-related—product benefits desired and product usage rates.

In the consumer market, the makeup of the population—its distribution and composition—has a major effect on target-market selection. For some products it is useful to analyze population on a regional basis. Another useful division is by urban, suburban, and rural segments. In this context, the bulk of the population is concentrated in metropolitan areas. Moreover, these areas are expanding and joining together in several parts of the country.

The major age groups of the population make up another significant basis for market analysis — young adults, teenagers, the over-65 group, and so on. The stage of the family life cycle influences the market for many products. Other demographic bases for market analysis include education, occupation, religion, and ethnic origin.

---

[15]For an excellent review of the literature on industrial market segmentation — some 30 articles spanning 20 years—see Richard E. Plank, "A Critical Review of Industrial Market Segmentation," *Industrial Marketing Management*, May 1985, pp. 79–91. Also, a detailed coverage of the topic is contained in Thomas V. Bonoma and Benson P. Shapiro, *Segmenting the Industrial Market*, Lexington, MA: Lexington Books, 1983.

Consumer income—especially disposable income and discretionary income—is a meaningful measure of buying power and market potential. The distribution of income affects the markets for many products. Income distribution has shifted considerably during the past 25 years. Today, a much greater percentage of families are in the over $60,000 bracket and a much smaller percentage earn under $10,000. A family's income level and life cycle are, in part, determinants of its spending patterns.

We can also examine the ''demographic'' characteristics of the business market by reviewing the number, size, and location of companies and other organizations that make up this important market sector. The business-to-business market has been growing, particularly in the area of services, which now account for more than 60 percent of Canada's Gross Domestic Product. We can segment the business market in much the same way as we approach the consumer market, primarily on the basis of the type of company we are dealing with, whether it is a small business or a large company or organization, and the type of buying situation, whether a new purchase or a rebuy.

KEY TERMS AND CONCEPTS

Market 85
Target market 85
Target market strategy 86
Market segmentation 86
Conditions for effective segmentation 88
Ultimate consumers 89
Business users 89
Bases for segmenting consumer market 90
Regional distribution of population 91
Urban-suburban-rural distribution 93
Census Metropolitan Areas (CMA) 94
Demographic segmentation 95

Market segmentation by gender 98
Family life cycle 99
Consumer income 102
Personal disposable income 102
Discretionary purchasing power 102
Income distribution 104
Expenditure patterns 105
Business market 109
Standard Industrial Classification System (SIC) 109
Buying power of business users 112
Bases for segmenting business market 115

QUESTIONS AND PROBLEMS

1. Distinguish between market aggregation and market segmentation.
2. What benefits can a company expect to gain from segmenting its market?
3. Cite some regional differences in product preferences caused by factors other than climate.
4. Give several examples of products whose market demand would be particularly affected by each of the following population factors:
   a. Regional distribution.
   b. Marital status.
   c. Gender.

    d. Age.

    e. Urban-rural-suburban distribution.

5. List three of the major population trends noted in this chapter (for instance, a growing segment of the population is over 65 years of age). Then carefully explain how *each* of the following types of retail stores might be affected by *each* of the trends.

    a. Supermarket.

    b. Sporting goods store.

    c. Drugstore.

    d. Restaurant.

6. In which stage of the life cycle are families likely to be the best prospects for each of the following products or services?

    a. Braces on teeth.

    b. Suntan lotion.

    c. Second car in the family.

    d. Vitamin pills.

    e. Refrigerators.

    f. Life insurance.

    g. Jogging suits.

    h. Fourteen-day Caribbean cruise.

7. In what ways has the rise in disposable personal income since 1960 influenced the marketing programs of a typical department store? A supermarket?

8. Give examples of products whose demand is substantially influenced by changes in discretionary purchasing power.

9. Using the demographic and income segmentation bases discussed in this chapter, describe the segment likely to be the best market for:

    a. Skis.

    b. Good French wines.

    c. Power hand tools.

    d. Birthday cards.

    e. Outdoor barbecue grills.

10. Describe what you believe to be the demographic characteristics of heavy users of:

    a. Dog food.

    b. Ready-to-eat cereal.

    c. Videocassette recorders.

    d. Pocket calculators.

11. Suppose you are marketing automobiles. How is your marketing mix likely to differ when marketing to each of the following market segments?

    a. High school students.

    b. Husbands.

    c. Blue-collar workers.

    d. Homemakers.

    e. Young single adults.

12. Why should a marketer of children's clothing be interested in expenditure patterns on this product category across income levels and across provinces and cities? Consult Statistics Canada data to identify whether major differences exist in expenditures on children's clothing by these categories of consumers.

13. How would you segment the market for photocopying machines such as those sold by Xerox, Canon, and Toshiba?

14. How can the principles of demographic segmentation be applied in the business market as they are in segmenting consumer markets?

CHAPTER 5 GOALS

In this chapter, we continue our discussion of market segmentation and introduce the important strategic concept of positioning. Positioning involves occupying a gap that has been ignored or vacated by other brands.

We conclude the chapter with a detailed discussion of forecasting, the last stage in the marketer's quest for target markets. To do an effective job of targeting, the marketer must not only know the characteristics of the segments, but also must be aware of their buying potential. After studying the chapter, you should understand:

- How to approach the segmentation of markets from a life-style or product-related perspective.
- How to deal with a number of different segments.
- The importance of positioning a brand or company so as to appeal to target market segments.
- Niche marketing and other positioning strategies to appeal to different consumers or segments.
- The importance of being able to forecast market demand and the market potential of each target segment.

Segmentation, Positioning, and Forecasting

*E*ven the largest of companies must from time to time rethink their position in the marketplace and undertake a new strategy that will have greater appeal to the target segments of the market that management wishes to attract. Such was the case at General Motors of Canada as that company faced increasing competition from foreign imports and a customer base that was becoming increasingly fragmented. General Motors revised its entire marketing effort to ensure that it was in a position to compete effectively throughout the 1990s.

The general director of marketing at General Motors of Canada, Peter Bagnall, observed that "the small-car market and the impact that offshore manufacturers are having on the business is causing the industry to sit up and take note." General Motors moved to strengthen its position in the economy- and compact-car markets by targeting segments such as first-time car buyers, realizing that 60 percent of Canadian car sales are accounted for by smaller models. At the heart of the re-emphasis on smaller cars is the launch of General Motors' new compact Geo line, which will join established GM makes at a renamed Chevrolet-Geo-Oldsmobile dealer network. Meanwhile, the new GM Saturn is sold through the former Passport dealerships, under the new name Saturn-Saab-Isuzu.[1]

Over at the Pontiac-Buick-GMC division, new things have also been happening with the addition of a number of new models, including a fuel-efficient Pontiac LeMans and a sporty two-door coupe from Isuzu in Japan, and a virtual relaunch of the Buick line. Management of Buick found through research that over the years Buick had lost its distinctiveness by trying to appeal to too wide a range of customers. A strategic decision was made to concentrate on the strengths that Buick had enjoyed in the North American car market. Based upon consumer research, it was decided that all Buicks were to be positioned as premium cars, whose characteristics would be described as substantial, distinctive, powerful, and mature. Models that did not fit this new theme were dropped.[2]

---

[1]Randy Scotland, "Geo at the Heart of GM Repositioning," *Marketing*, June 3, 1991. p. 1.

[2]Alex Taylor III, "How Buick Is Bouncing Back," *Fortune*, May 6, 1991, pp. 83–88.

The new Buick line from General Motors is positioned to appeal to members of a growing, older, well-off market segment, who want to drive a solid automobile. Research conducted in the United States during the 1990 model year confirmed that the repositioning strategy had worked as the median age of Buick buyers that year was 61, and their average income $42,700.

This example reflects the principal topics of Chapter 5. We see how General Motors has decided to segment the Canadian automobile market, not only on demographics, but also on the life-style or psychographic characteristics of car buyers. The result was a new positioning of certain General Motors cars to appeal to particular segments of the market and the repositioning of others so that they would hold greater appeal for growing segments whose buying power has increased.

Psychographic Segmentation

As consumers, our buying behaviour and life-styles are influenced considerably by sociological and psychological forces. Sociological influences include our culture, social class, and reference groups, whereas psychological characteristics include our learning experience, personality, attitudes, and beliefs. (These sociological and psychological determinants of buying behaviour are discussed in more depth in the next chapter.) The term *psychographics* is used today by many researchers as a collective classification for these forces. Many companies segment their consumer markets using psychographic bases such as personality characteristics, life-styles, or social class.

PERSONALITY CHARACTERISTICS

Theoretically, personality characteristics should form a good basis for segmenting markets. Compulsive people buy differently than cautious consumers. Quiet introverts presumably do not make the same product choices as gregarious, outgoing people. *Realistically*, however, personality characteristics pose problems that limit their usefulness in practical market segmentation. These characteristics often are virtually impossible to measure accurately in a quantitative sense. Many studies have been made of consumer attitudes and personality traits in relation to product and brand preferences in a wide variety of product categories. But the results generally have been too limited or inconclusive to be of much practical value.

Nevertheless, many firms tailor their advertising to appeal to consumers who have certain personality traits. Even though the given market segment is immeasurable, the seller knows that it does exist and hopes to attract its members. Thus we see a brand advertised to consumers who "are on the way up," or who are "persons of distinction," or who "don't want their family left helpless."

LIFE-STYLES

The term *life-style* is a broad concept that sometimes overlaps personality characteristics. Being cautious, sceptical, ambitious, a workaholic, a copycat — are these personality or life-style traits? Life-styles relate to your activities, interests, and opinions. They reflect how you spend your time and what your beliefs are on various social, economic, and political issues.

There is no commonly accepted terminology of life-style categories for segmenting markets. Nevertheless, people's life-styles undoubtedly affect their

For the do-it-yourself life-style of the '90s.

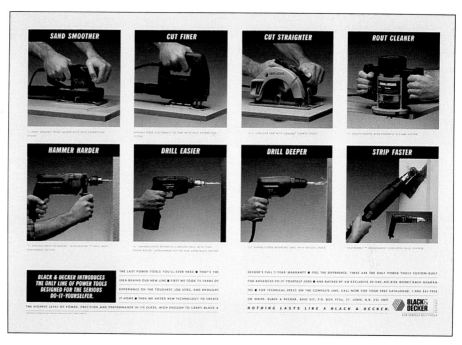

choice of products and their brand preferences. Marketers are well aware of this and often attempt to segment their markets on a life-style basis.

As consumer tastes and life-styles have changed in recent years, most companies have had to make adjustments in their products and services to ensure that they remained attractive to their target customers. The snack-food industry, for example, has responded to consumers' growing concerns about health and nutrition by introducing new products made from grains and prepared with little or no saturated fat. Old stand-bys such as popcorn and pretzels are making a comeback.[3] Busy parents who want to spend as much quality time as possible with their children are increasingly taking them on business trips, causing the travel industry to respond to an emerging market segment, the young seasoned traveller.[4] Firms in many different industries have had to develop creative marketing strategies to deal with the "tough" customers of the 1990s, those who insist on quality, check food labels for additives, buy environmentally friendly products, and complain when they receive poor service.[5]

Although it is a valuable marketing tool, life-style segmentation has some of the same serious limitations ascribed to segmentation based on personality characteristics. It is very difficult to accurately measure the size of life-style segments in a quantitative manner. Another problem is that a given life-style segment simply might not be accessible at a reasonable cost through a firm's usual distribution system or promotional program.

---

[3]Anthony Ramirez, "Developing Junk Food for Discriminating Tastes," *Globe and Mail Report on Business*, June 3, 1991, p. B12.

[4]Miriam Cu-Uy-Gam, "Firms Pull out Red Carpet for Tiny Travellers," *The Financial Post*, April 29, 1991, p. 35.

[5]Faye Rice, "How to Deal with Tougher Customers," *Fortune*, December 3, 1990, pp. 39–48.

SOCIAL CLASS

As we will see in the next chapter, a person's social class — be it upper class, white-collar middle class, or blue-collar working class — has a considerable influence on that person's choice in many product categories. Consequently, many companies select one or two social classes as target markets and then develop a product and marketing mix to reach those segments.

Product-Related Segmentation

Some marketers regularly attempt to segment their markets on the basis of a consumer behavioural characteristic related to the product. In this section we briefly consider two of these product-related segmentation bases — benefits desired and product usage rate.

BENEFITS DESIRED

Conceptually it is very logical to segment a market on the basis of the different benefits customers want from the product. Certainly benefit segmentation is consistent with the idea that a company should be marketing product benefits and not simply the physical or chemical characteristics of a product. From the consumers' point of view, they really are buying product *benefits* and not the product itself. After all, a customer wants a smooth surface (the benefit), not sandpaper (the product).

For benefit segmentation to be effective, two tasks must be accomplished. First, a company must identify the various benefits that people seek in the good or service. To illustrate, in segmenting the market for its ocean cruises, the Viking Steamship Line might pinpoint such benefits as (1) the opportunity to meet people, (2) recreation, (3) education, and (4) rest and relaxation. A classic study that gave rise to the concept of benefit segmentation identified the following benefit segments for toothpaste and the benefits sought by these segments: (1) sensories — flavour and appearance; (2) sociables — brightness of teeth; (3) worriers—decay prevention; (4) independents—low price. Today "tartar control" might qualify as a fifth benefit segment.[6]

Panasonic segments on specific user benefits.

Now moving your buns is a piece of cake.
Because Panasonic's Restaurant Management System can help you move them faster and more efficiently than you ever thought possible. With features like retained cheque and detailed video display for kitchen and bar, our P.O.S. system makes it simple to ring up and control tabs. And to give management more control, it tracks profits, shrinkage and waste, prevents invalid voids and provides 5 levels of security access. Our P.O.S. systems can even interface with PC's. And each can work on its own. Or within a network of up to 20 stations. So if you want to make more dough, just let Panasonic help you move your buns. For your nearest dealer, call 1-800-387-8686.

Panasonic The Perfectionists

We've made it easier to move your buns.

[6]See Russell, J. Haley, "Benefit Segmentation: A Decision Oriented Research Tool," *Journal of Marketing*, July 1968, pp. 30–35. For an update on this classic article and the concept of benefit segmentation, see Haley, "Benefit Segmentation—20 Years Later," *The Journal of Consumer Marketing*, vol. 1, no. 2, 1983, pp. 5–13.

M A R K E T I N G   A T   W O R K

FILE 5-1   **NOT ANY FAN—JUST THE AVID ONE**

The avid sports fan (sometimes known as the heavy user) may be paying a lot of money to watch prime sporting events in the future. Pay-per-view is a phenomenon expected to appear in Canada in the future. This format, where viewers pay to watch programs unavailable on regular cable TV such as Wrestlemania, blockbuster boxing matches, and first-rate movies, has been available in the U.S. for several years. So far, pay-per-view is only in the experimental stage in Canada with tests occurring in parts of Western Canada and Quebec. During a recent championship boxing match in the U.S., viewers paid an average of $34.95 a home to watch. This potential revenue from pay-per-view during just one night is so great that it will undoubtedly be available for Canadians in the years to come.

Source: Adapted from Martin Mehr, ''In This Corner, Pay-Per-View,'' *Marketing*, January 28, 1991, p. 7.

Once these separate benefits are known, the second task is to describe the demographic and psychographic characteristics of the people in each segment. Then the seller is in a position to launch a product and marketing program to reach a selected target segment.

USAGE RATE

Another product-related basis for market segmentation is the rate at which people use or consume a product. Thus we can have categories for nonusers, light users, medium users, and heavy users. Normally a company is most interested in the heavy users of its product. The 50 percent of the people who are the ''heavy half'' of the users of a product typically account for 80 to 90 percent of the total purchases of a given product. The remarkable feature of these usage patterns is that they seem to remain reasonably constant over time. Thus this segmentation base becomes an effective predictor of future buying behaviour. Comparable studies in the 1960s and 1980s showed similar patterns in the percentage of total purchases accounted for by the heavy-user half in several product categories. Some sample products and percentages of the total market accounted for by the heavy half in 1962 and 1982 were as follows: shampoo, 81 and 79 percent; cake mixes, 85 and 83 percent; beer, 88 and 87 percent; soaps and detergents, 80 and 75 percent.[7]

Sometimes the target market is the nonuser or light user, and the objective is to woo these customers into a higher use category. Or light users may constitute an attractive niche for a seller simply because they are being ignored by other firms that are targeting heavy users. Once the characteristics of these light users have been identified, management can go to them directly with an introductory low-price offer. Or a seller might increase usage rates by pro-

[7]Victor J. Cook, Jr., and William A. Mindak, ''A Search for Constants: The 'Heavy User' Revisited,'' *The Journal of Consumer Marketing*, vol. 1, no. 4, 1984, pp. 79–81.

moting (1) new uses for a product (baking soda as a deodorant); (2) new times for uses (off-season vacations); or (3) multiple packaging (a 12-pack of soft drinks).

TARGET-MARKET STRATEGIES

Let's assume that a company is aware of the opportunities for segmenting its market, having analyzed different segmentation bases in relation to its product. Now management is in a position to select one or more segments as its target markets. The company can follow one of three broad strategies in this selection process. The three alternatives are market aggregation, single-segment concentration, and multiple-segment segmentation, as illustrated in Fig. 5-1. Companies engaging in international marketing also need to consider the strategic use of market aggregation and segmentation, something to think about when we deal with international marketing in Chapter 20.

FIGURE 5-1
Alternative target-market strategies.

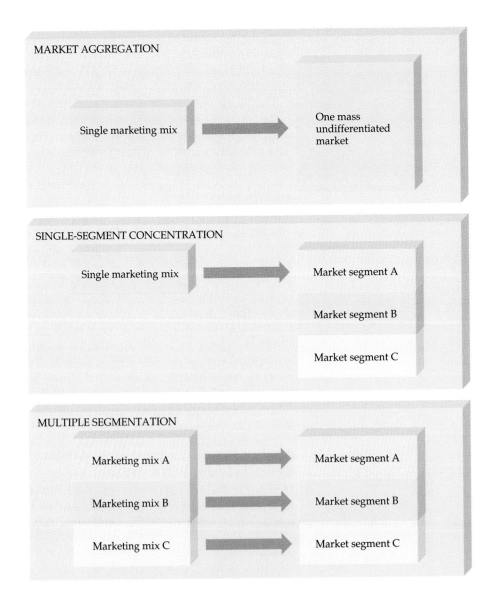

Market Aggregation

By adopting a strategy of *market aggregation* — also known as a *mass-market* or an *undifferentiated-market* strategy — an organization treats its total market as a single unit. This unit is one mass, aggregate market whose parts are considered to be alike in all major respects. Management then develops a single marketing mix to reach as many customers as possible in this aggregate market. That is, the company develops a single product for this mass audience; it develops one pricing structure and one distribution system for its product; and it uses a single promotional program that is aimed at the entire market.

When is an organization likely to adopt the strategy of market aggregation? Generally when a large group of customers in the total market tends to have the same perception of the product's want-satisfying benefits. This strategy often is adopted by firms that are marketing a nondifferentiated, staple product such as gasoline, salt, or sugar. In the eyes of many people, cane sugar is cane sugar, regardless of the brand. All brands of table salt are pretty much alike, and one unleaded gasoline is about the same as another.

Basically, market aggregation is a production-oriented strategy. It enables a company to maximize its economies of scale in production, physical distribution, and promotion. Producing and marketing one product for one market means longer production runs at lower unit costs. Inventory costs are minimized when there is no (or a very limited) variety of colours and sizes of products. Warehousing and transportation efforts are most efficient when one product is going to one market.

Market aggregation will work only as long as the seller's single marketing mix continues to satisfy enough customers to meet the company's sales and profit expectations. The strategy of market aggregation typically is accompanied by the strategy of product differentiation in a company's marketing program. **Product differentiation** is the strategy by which one firm attempts to distinguish its product from competitive brands offered to the same aggregate market. By differentiating its product, an organization hopes to create the impression that its product is better than the competitors' brands. The seller also hopes to engage in nonprice competition and thus avoid or minimize the threat of price competition.

A seller implements this strategy either (1) by changing some superficial feature of the product — the package or colour, for example — or (2) by using a promotional appeal that features a differentiating benefit. Crest says that its toothpaste now fights tartar formation on teeth. Scotian Gold puts its apple juice in aseptic packages that keep fresh without refrigeration. Lever Brothers uses a cuddly bear named Snuggle to promote its fabric softener of the same name, while Downy stresses its "April fresh smell." Dry Idea is differentiated from other roll-on deodorants by the fact that is has "almost no water."

Single-Segment Concentration Strategy

A strategy of **single-segment concentration** involves selecting as the target market one homogeneous segment from within the total market. One marketing mix is then developed to reach this single segment. A small company may want to concentrate on a single market segment, rather than to take on many competitors in a broad market. For example, an Alberta guest ranch got started by appealing only to guest horseback riders who also enjoyed square dancing. A large cruise-ship company, offering a round-the-world luxury cruise, targets its marketing effort at one market segment — older, affluent people who also have time to travel.

M A R K E T I N G   A T   W O R K

FILE 5-2 **CHANGING TARGETS AND APPROACHES**

Today's trends towards consumer convenience have enticed more and more companies to enter the direct marketing industry. One of the latest to enter is the Toronto-based Beaver Canoe retail chain with its first catalogue. This is part of a major repositioning program for the company. The 18-store chain used to aim at the 18- to 25-year olds—the "sweats and tees" crowd—but is now focusing on consumers over 25 with a higher household income. The chain is being positioned as a place where you can buy casual outdoor urban clothing and features the Beaver Canoe label as well as items from Patagonia and Boston Trader. The 12-page catalogue is printed on recycled paper and is being distributed in two formats. One version has been dropped without an order form to more than 300,000 homes and its role is to create awareness and build in-store traffic. The mail-order version with the order form has been sent to a test sample of 10,000 homes and a data base is being developed for the catalogue from in-store shoppers.

Source: Adapted from Martin Mehr, "Beaver Canoe Tests Waters with Catalogue," *Marketing*, October 15, 1990, p. 2.

When manufacturers of foreign automobiles first entered the North American market, they typically targeted a single market segment. The Volkswagen Beetle was intended for the low-priced, small-car market. Honda originally sold only lower-powered motorcycles, and Mercedes-Benz targeted the high-income market. Today, of course, most of the original foreign car marketers have moved into a multisegment strategy. Only a few, such as Jaguar and Ferrari, continue with a concentration strategy.

This strategy enables a company to penetrate one small market in depth and to acquire a reputation as a specialist or an expert in this limited market. A company can enter such a market with limited resources. And as long as the single segment remains a small market, large competitors are likely to leave the single-segment specialist alone. However, if the small market should show signs of becoming a large market, then bigger companies may well jump in. This is exactly what happened in the market for herbal and specialty teas. Prior to the 1980s, rose-hip, camomile, Earl Grey, and similar specialty teas were sold primarily in health-food stores and specialty shops and were available from only a small number of manufacturers and importers. With changing consumer tastes and preferences during the past ten years or so, specialty teas have become more popular. The growth of the herbal and specialty segment was such that new tea companies entered this expanding corner of the market, including some major competitors such as Tetley and Lipton.

The big risk and limitation to a single-segment strategy is that the seller has all its eggs in one basket. If that single segment declines in market potential, the seller can suffer considerably. Also, a seller with a strong name and reputation in one segment may find it difficult to expand into another segment. The Hudson's Bay Company realized the difficulty of competing in a number of different retail segments when it decided to close its Simpsons stores in

On what basis is Michelin positioning its tires?

Ontario in 1991. The company had already successfully positioned its Zellers operation to cater to the discount end of the market and had both The Bay and Simpsons serving the major department-store segment. Management decided to convert many of the Simpsons stores to The Bay outlets and sold others to the rival Sears Canada chain. Clearly, Hudson's Bay Company executives felt that The Bay and Sears were targeting different segments of the retail market and argued that having a Sears outlet occupying a former Simpsons store in the same shopping centre where a Bay store was already operating would not be directly competing, because Sears and The Bay carry a large number of non-competing lines. The Bay executives argued that Sears, with its greater strength in furniture and major household appliances, would actually draw more shoppers to these shopping centres, thereby benefiting both chains.

The strategy of not concentrating the entire marketing effort on a single segment is also reflected in other industries. Both Volkswagen and Honda have traded their lines up to compete with the higher-priced models of BMW and Mercedes: VW with its Audi line, and Honda with its Acura. Nestlé has successfully marketed its instant coffees Nescafé and Taster's Choice for many years and is now challenging the ground coffee segment with its Taster's Choice ground.

Multiple-Segment Strategy

In the strategy of **multiple-segment target markets**, two or more different groups of potential customers are identified. Then a separate marketing mix is developed to reach each segment. A marketer of personal computers, for instance, might identify three separate market segments — college students, small businesses, and homemakers — and then design a different marketing mix to reach each segment. In segmenting the passenger automobile market, General Motors develops separate marketing programs built around its five brands — Chevrolet, Pontiac, Buick, Oldsmobile, and Cadillac. General Motors, in effect, tries to reach the total market for autos, but does so on a segmented basis.

As part of the strategy of multiple segmentation, a company frequently will develop a different variety of the basic product for each segment. However, market segmentation can also be accomplished with no change in the product, but rather with separate marketing programs, each tailored to a given market segment. A producer of cosmetics, for instance, can market the same physical product to the teenage market and to the 25-to-30 age segment. But the packaging and promotional programs for the two markets will differ.

A multiple-segment strategy normally results in a greater sales volume than a single-segment approach. Multiple segmentation also is useful for a company facing a seasonal demand for its product. In England during the summer, several universities market their empty dormitory space to tourists — another market segment. A firm with excess production capacity may well seek additional market segments to absorb this capacity. Probably the biggest drawback to the multiple-segment strategy is that unit costs of production and marketing increase when multiple segments are targeted.

POSITIONING

The concept of market *positioning* is closely related to segmentation; a marketer must determine how the company's brands or stores or image are perceived by the public in general and more particularly by the segment of the market that has been selected as the principal target. As part of a company's marketing strategy, decisions must be made concerning how the company and its brands are to be portrayed to convey the correct image to the target segment. Positioning, therefore, relates to the use of various marketing techniques and marketing-mix variables to create the image or perception that will best fit with what the company wishes to be known for.

A company may develop a positioning strategy for a particular brand or group of brands, for a retail store or chain, or for the company itself. The process involves answering questions such as the following: Who are the target-market segments for this brand or store or company? On what basis do we wish to appeal to this segment? What do we want people to think of when they hear our name? How do we wish to be seen to be different from our competitors or from other brands or companies in the market? In dealing with questions such as these, the company is really asking: what *position* do we wish to occupy in this market?

The company's positioning strategy may be applied at the brand level, at the level of a retail store, or for entire companies. For example, Everfresh, a brand of mineral water with fruit juice added, has been positioned as a product for thoughtful people — for consumers who have a sense of social responsibility, who are concerned about the wellbeing of family and themselves, and who lead a balanced life-style. Through appropriate advertising, the brand

M A R K E T I N G   A T   W O R K

FILE 5-3   **POSITIONING THE RIDERS OFF THE FIELD**

The Canadian Football League has had its share of problems in recent years. A number of teams have come close to bankruptcy only to be saved by last-ditch efforts. Jo-Anne Polak, general manager of the Ottawa Rough Riders, joined the team when they had a terrible losing record and dwindling fan support. However, she determined that an ad campaign was not good enough. What was needed was careful, co-ordinated positioning of the team in the minds of fans. Once the right positioning has been decided, everything else has to reinforce that. Polak decided to raise the profile of the Rough Riders with a player-fan identification theme. In 1988, she promoted quarterback Damon Allen and some other notable players. They made over 400 community appearances in five months. Polak feels the CFL should go after young people aged 12-15, and identification with the players is an ideal way to do it. This apparently has worked, as the team drew many more fans and even made the play-offs in 1990. The addition of American college star Raghib "Rocket" Ismail to the CFL before the 1991 season should help boost attendance even more as a result of the same kind of positioning.

Source: Adapted from David Chilton, "Positioning 'Crucial to Success'," *Playback Strategy*, February 25, 1991, p. 3.

---

has been effectively positioned against other cold beverages, soft drinks, and juices.[8]

Air Canada's enRoute credit card does not go head-to-head with Visa and MasterCard, but has been positioned as the country's leading corporate travel card.[9] Fishery Products International has chosen not to take on National Sea Products in direct competition in the supermarkets of Canada. Instead, it has positioned itself as a leader in the restaurant and food-service sector of the seafood market and in manufacturing quality products under the private labels of large retailers such as Loblaws, Marks & Spencer, and Provigo.[10] In the hotel business Four Seasons has carved out a position at the top of the luxury end of the market where they can charge premium rates and give quality service. In the competitive Ontario consumer electronics market, companies such as Bay Bloor Radio occupy the premium end of the market, while deep discounters, such as Future Shops and Majestic Superstores occupy the discount end of the market. At the corporate level, Dofasco is a company that has positioned itself as a caring employer through its corporate advertising, which features the corporate slogan, "Our product is steel, our strength is people."

Positioning, therefore, is a strategy for locating a brand or store in the consumer's mind, with respect to its rating on certain dimensions or attributes that the consumer considers important. It involves staking out a place in the col-

---

[8]Laura Medcalf, "A 'Thoughtful' Approach," *Marketing*, vol. 95, no. 41, October 8, 1990, p. 4.

[9]Ian Allaby, "enRoute's Corporate Card War," *Canadian Business*, October 1990, pp. 80–86.

[10]See introduction to Chapter 8.

lective perception of consumers in which the brand or store or company can establish an image that will be appropriate for certain segments of the market. This image is created through effective use of marketing-mix variables, including advertising, product design, pricing, packaging, store decor, and sales promotions.

The creation of the appropriate image may be approached in a combination of ways. In the first place, a firm may wish to occupy a position in a market *in relation to that occupied by competitors*. It may choose a position that is distinct from that occupied by a competitor or may choose to challenge a competitor directly, thereby trying to occupy roughly the same position.

On the other hand, the positioning strategy may be developed so as to position the brand or store through the creation of an image tailored to the characteristics, preferences, attitudes, and feelings of a *particular segment of the market*. This approach is dependent upon the company having selected certain target segments. The image of the product, brand, or store is then tailored to appeal to those segments.

Finally, a brand or store may be positioned on the basis of its *inherent characteristics*. In other words, the marketing staff of the company would have to decide what the brand or retailer is to be known for and set about creating the appropriate image. Such an approach deals implicitly with positioning against competition and meeting the needs of particular segments, but is often undertaken in response to the identification of a market gap, where no company has established a dominant position.

POSITIONING MAPS

One of the easiest ways to get a feel for the concept of positioning is to examine products, brands, or stores as they are arrayed on a *positioning map*. Such maps are developed through marketing research, which explores the image that consumers have of the various brands or stores in the market and rates each competing brand or store on a series of attributes. In such research, consumers are typically asked to identify the elements of the purchase situation and the product or store attributes that are important in influencing the purchase decision. Once these attributes and elements have been identified, research is undertaken to determine which are most important in influencing the consumer to select one brand over another. Finally, consumers are asked to rate the competing brands or stores in the market on each of the important dimensions or attributes. Such research data allow the researcher to present the brands or stores of interest in a map similar to that shown in Fig. 5-2.

Positioning maps allow the marketer to see where his or her brand is perceived to lie in the market in comparison with competing brands, how it is rated on various attributes, and where it lies in relation to the various segments that have been identified. Typically, a number of brands that are perceived to have similar characteristics are clustered together in close proximity to those large segments of the market that have considerable buying power. Other brands occupy positions in the market where they are seen to appeal to different segments and to display different characteristics.

One benefit of examining perceptual market maps is that the marketer can identify how his or her brand or store is perceived by consumers in comparison with competitors. Such examination often leads to a decision to reposition a brand, a topic that we will cover later in this chapter. Also, examination of market maps may lead to the identification of market gaps—positions in the

FIGURE 5-2
Perceptual Map Based on Data in Table 5-1.

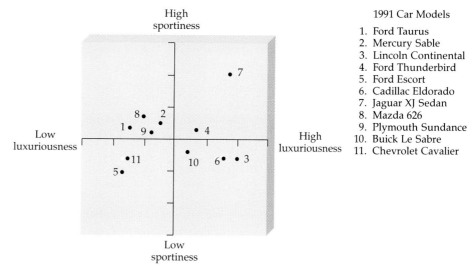

1991 Car Models

1. Ford Taurus
2. Mercury Sable
3. Lincoln Continental
4. Ford Thunderbird
5. Ford Escort
6. Cadillac Eldorado
7. Jaguar XJ Sedan
8. Mazda 626
9. Plymouth Sundance
10. Buick Le Sabre
11. Chevrolet Cavalier

TABLE 5-1 **Rank Order of Similarities Between Pairs of Car Models**

Stimuli	1	2	3	4	5	6	7	8	9	10	11
1	—	8	50	31	12	48	36	2	5	39	10
2		—	38	9	33	37	22	6	4	14	32
3			—	11	55	1	23	46	41	17	52
4				—	44	13	16	19	25	18	42
5					—	54	53	30	28	45	7
6						—	26	47	40	24	51
7							—	29	35	34	49
8								—	3	27	15
9									—	20	21
10										—	43
11											—

The rank number ''1'' represents the most similar pair.

Source: Paul E. Green and Frank J. Carmone, *Multidimensional Scaling and Related Techniques in Marketing Analysis.* Copyright © 1970 by Allyn and Bacon. Reprinted with permission.

market that are not now filled by existing brands or stores and where untapped market demand may be said to exist. In the department store business in Ontario, Bretton's has been successful in occupying a position as a junior department store, lying between the large established department stores, such as The Bay and Eatons, and the discounters, such as Woolco and Zellers. One response to the identification of such market gaps is to become a niche marketer.

NICHE MARKETING[11]

Some marketers may choose to stake out ''niche'' positions for their brands; they create an image that is quite distinct and intended to appeal to a fairly narrow segment of the market. Within the Canadian beer market, for example, brands such as Black Label and O'Keefe's Extra Old Stock are considered to be ''niche'' brands, while mainstream brands such as Molson Canadian and

[11]An excellent review of the concept of niche marketing, with numerous examples, was published by Federal Industries Limited with the company's 1986 Annual Report. The company's address is Suite 2400, One Lombard Place, Winnipeg, Manitoba R3B 0X3

M A R K E T I N G   A T   W O R K

FILE 5-4   "NICHEMANSHIP" IN THE FEDERAL INDUSTRIES TRANSPORT GROUP

Both the strengths and the dangers inherent in niche strategies are illustrated by the history of Federal Industries' Transport Group.

The White Pass and Yukon Railroad was originally built at the turn of the century to serve a very narrowly defined niche in Canada's transportation market—moving gold from the Yukon Territory to Alaska's tidewater. But by the time the rail line was completed, the gold rush was just about over. So the next 85 years were a constant struggle to find ways to make that highly specialized asset profitable. Clearly, there is a risk involved in committing large asset investments to narrowly defined market niches.

White Pass has learned that lesson well, and has emerged as a very successful diversified business and the clear leader in a variety of related niche markets. Now the leading petroleum distributor in Yukon and southeast Alaska, White Pass is also the major force in several transportation markets in its area. Its vitality is no longer threatened by any single customer or event.

White Pass Systems is carving out an important niche in drill rig moving in the Canadian oil patch, by providing dependable and innovative services that customers can count on.

Motorways Direct is an example of geographical nichemanship maturing into leadership in a fairly broad market segment — Less-Than-Truckload (LTL) freight. From an LTL niche in Yukon, White Pass acquired Motorways and attained a position as a major Western Canadian carrier. With the acquisition of Direct, the company has now reached a point where it serves more LTL branch terminals than most other Canadian trucking companies.

Thunder Bay Terminals is the largest and most efficient bulk terminal at Thunder Bay—undisputed leader in a well defined niche. Recognizing the dangers inherent in capital intensive niche markets, the company has a long-term contract that covers the risk, and a diversification plan that is well underway.

Source: Federal Industries 1986 Annual Report.

Labatt's Blue are positioned to appeal to much larger segments. Niche brands generally are not positioned to take on the major competitors head-on, but rather to be a leader in a very narrow area of the market. Smaller companies often successfully "carve out a niche" for themselves. To continue with our beer examples, successful microbrewers such as Upper Canada Brewing and Granville Island Brewery are really niche marketers; they are satisfied with occupying a relatively small position in a very large market by catering to the tastes and preferences of consumers who want something different.

Niche marketing, therefore, is generally a successful strategy for smaller companies that do not have the financial and other resources generally available to large companies. In the travel business, for example, many travel agencies are seeking ways to set themselves apart from their competitors by specializing in narrow parts of the market. As travel has become more complex and travellers more demanding, some travel agencies have found it impossible to serve all segments equally well. Consequently, some become niche players, specializing in cruises, business travel, the ethnic market, or theme travel—

tours organized around a theme such as a murder mystery or a spring-training boat cruise for baseball fans.[12]

To be successful in positioning itself as a niche player in the market, a company or the managers of a niche brand must have identified a segment of the market that is not now being served adequately by the brands and companies which are in the market; that segment must have sufficient potential buying power to warrant the development of a marketing program; it must be sufficiently small that larger companies are unlikely to retaliate if the niche brand is successful; and the niche marketer must have detailed knowledge of the characteristics of the members of the segment and their needs and preferences.

One author has suggested that a company should follow four steps in implementing a successful niche marketing stragegy.[13]

1. *Identify an appropriate niche* through marketing research that will identify segments of the market not now being well served by existing brands.
2. *Exploit the niche* by determining the likelihood of competitive retaliation and the length of time the company will enjoy a competitive advantage.
3. *Expand the niche* by meeting changing needs of the market segment, expanding the customer base, and making more effective use of marketing variables.
4. *Defend the niche* by continuing to meet the needs of segment members through improving the product and offering better service or lower prices.

POSITIONING STRATEGIES

Once a company has determined its market segmentation objectives and has identified the segments towards which its brands are to be targeted, it may adopt a number of positioning strategies to accomplish its objectives.

1. Take on the competition head-on: By deciding to challenge the market leader or to target large segments of the market with a broad appeal, a marketer is saying, "Our brand is as good as or better than the leader." Such a strategy is exemplified in the so-called "cola wars" in which Pepsi-Cola and Coca-Cola have been fighting for market leadership by attempting to create the widest appeal to attract as many consumers as possible.
2. Occupy a gap in the market: A number of companies have moved to fill a gap in a market by positioning a brand to appeal to a certain segment of consumers or to take advantage of the disappearance of a competitor. For example, Blyth and Company moved to establish a luxury railway tour between Vancouver and Calgary to take advantage of demand from tourists when the existing Canadian National passenger service on that route closed. Michelin tries to differentiate its tires from those of competitors by emphasizing safety.
3. Set a brand apart from the competition: Often a company will decide to employ a strategy that says, "Our brand is not like all the others; this is

---

[12]Bruce Gates, "Travel industry moves into specialty markets", *The Financial Post*, February 25, 1991, p. 34.

[13]Allan J. Magrath, "Niche Marketing: Finding a Safe, Warm Cave," *Sales and Marketing Management in Canada*, May 1987, p. 40.

why you should buy ours." This involves positioning a brand or store so as to avoid head-to-head competition with market leaders or with brands that have an established image or reputation and a secure market share.

4. Occupy position of leadership: Some companies that are clearly market leaders are not particularly interested in positioning against the competition, but rather are likely to stake out a position as clear market leader, known to be ahead of the pack and leader in such areas as product quality, service to customers, profitability, innovations, or technology. Companies such as Loblaws, Northern Telecom, and the Royal Bank of Canada tend to be regarded by many consumers as market leaders whose market franchise is so large and well established that competitors often try to emulate them and to position against them.

5. Position to appeal to life-style segments: Often a company will position its brands or retail stores to appeal to certain segments of the market that are defined not only by demographic characteristics but also by their life-styles. For example, Save-On Foods, a Vancouver-based supermarket chain, launched a campaign to position the company to appeal to "value-conscious" customers. Faced with competition from Real Canadian Superstores, which entered the Lower Mainland market with a strong price message, Save-On management decided to develop a new image for the chain, one that would appeal to the more sophisticated customer of the 1990s who "worries less about price and more about service, quality, selection and value."[14]

REPOSITIONING

Repositioning is a variation of a positioning strategy that involves changing the market position of a brand or store in response to changes taking place in the broader market environment. The need to reposition a brand or retail store may result from one of three market conditions. First, management may identify a gap in the market that may be filled by altering the image of the store or brand—that is, changing the position it occupies in the minds of consumers. For example, a retailer in a local market may realize that the average age of its customer base is increasing and may decide to reposition the store to have greater appeal to a younger market segment.

Second, repositioning may be required by an increase in competitive activity. For example, the change of image of Save-On Foods discussed above was brought about partially by the entry into the market of price-based competitors. Save-On's change in emphasis represents a repositioning from the chain's original position as a price leader to one where it is known for value, quality, and service, thereby leaving the competition to fight it out for the price-conscious consumer.

Third, it may be necessary to reposition a brand or store in response to a change in the demographic characteristics or attitudes and values of the consumer market. General Motors repositioned its Buick line to appeal to older, more traditional customers. Auto manufacturers in general have tended to emphasize the safety features of their cars in response to the growing number

---

[14]Bob Mackin, Jr., "New Strategy for Save-On," *Marketing*, June 10, 1991, p. 16.

M A R K E T I N G   A T   W O R K

FILE 5-5   **MOVING FROM QUALITY AND UNIQUENESS TO VALUE**

Advertising a no-name product seems to defeat its whole purpose, but Dave Nichol of Loblaws took to TV to tell consumers they could save money by buying Loblaws' no-name products. Loblaw Companies, Toronto, spent about half of its media dollars for corporate brands to promote its 1,900 no-name products. During hard times, Nichol feels the primary concern of the customer is value and the way to really talk about value is with no-name. He appears to be right as no-name products accounted for approximately 22 percent of Loblaws' sales. How successful was this Loblaw marketing plan? In 1990, net profit increased over 35 percent.

Source: Adapted from Ken Riddell, ''The Man With No Name—He's Back,'' *Marketing*, February 25, 1991, p. 1.

---

of young baby-boomer parents whose safety concerns have been increased by parenthood.[15]

FORECASTING MARKET DEMAND

As the final step in selecting its target markets, a company should forecast the market demand for its product or service. Forecasting market demands means to estimate the sales-volume size of a company's total market and the sales volume expected in each market segment. This step involves estimating the total industry potential for the company's product in the target market. (This industry figure is called the *market potential* for the product.) Then the seller should estimate its share of this total market. (This company figure is called the *sales potential*.)

The key requirement in demand forecasting is the preparation of a sales forecast, usually for a one-year period. A sales forecast is the foundation of all budgeting and operational planning in all departments of a company — marketing, production, and finance.

Definition of Some Basic Terms

Before we discuss forecasting methods, we need to define several terms, because they often are used loosely in business.

MARKET FACTOR AND MARKET INDEX

A **market factor** is an item or element that (1) exists in a market, (2) may be measured quantitatively, and (3) is related to the demand for a product or service. To illustrate, the ''number of cars three years old and older'' is a market factor underlying the demand for replacement tires. That is, this element affects the number of replacement tires that can be sold. A **market index** is simply a market factor expressed as a percentage, or in some other quantitative form, relative to some base figure. To illustrate, one market factor is ''households owning appliance X''; in 1992, the market index for this factor

[15]Paul C. Judge, ''Car Ads Reflecting Buyers' Concern for Auto Safety,'' *Globe and Mail Report on Business*, March 16, 1990, p. B2.

was 132 (relative to 1980 equals 100). An index may also be composed of multiple market factors, such as the number of cars three years old and older, population, and disposable personal income.

MARKET POTENTIAL AND SALES POTENTIAL

The **market potential** for a product is the total expected sales of that product by all sellers during a stated period of time in a stated market. **Sales potential** (synonymous with **market share**) is the share of a market potential that an individual company expects to achieve.

Thus we may speak of the "market potential" for automatic washing machines, but the "sales potential" (or market share) for one company's brand of machine. In the case of either market potential or sales potential, the market may encompass the entire country, or even the world. Or it may be a smaller market segmented by income, by geographic area, or on some other basis. For example, we may speak of the *market potential* for washing machines in the Atlantic provinces, or the *sales potential* for Whirlpool washers in homes with incomes of $25,000 to $35,000. The market potential and sales potential are the same when a firm has a monopoly in its market, as in the case of some public utilities.

SALES FORECAST

A **sales forecast** may be defined as an estimate of sales (in dollars or product units) during some specific future period of time and under a predetermined marketing plan in the firm. A sales forecast can ordinarily be made more intelligently if the company first determines its market and/or sales potential. However, many firms start their forecasting directly with the sales forecast. See Fig. 5-3.

The sales forecast and the marketing plan   The marketing goals and broad strategies—the core of a marketing plan—must be established before a sales forecast is made. That is, the sales forecast depends upon these predetermined

FIGURE 5-3
Business application of some of our definitions.

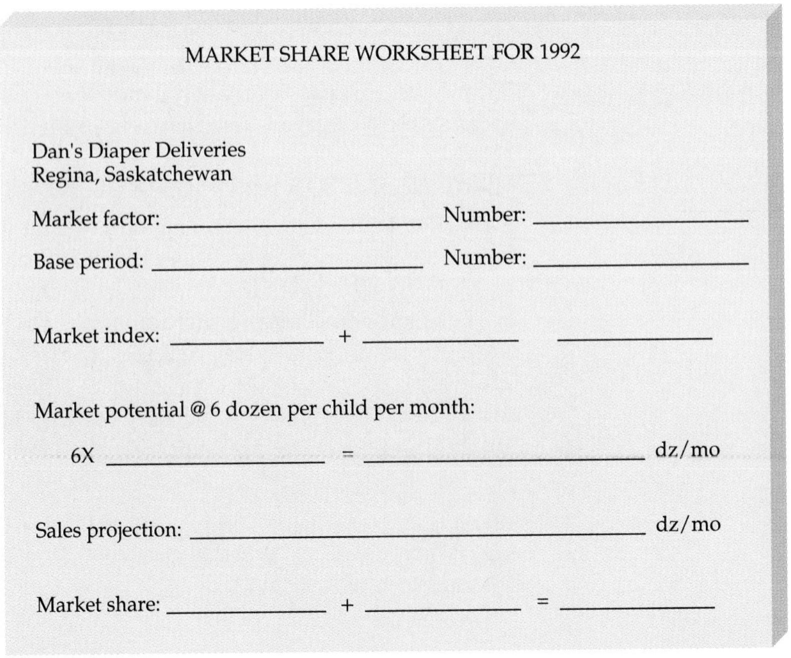

MARKET SHARE WORKSHEET FOR 1992

Dan's Diaper Deliveries
Regina, Saskatchewan

Market factor: _____   Number: _____

Base period: _____   Number: _____

Market index: _____   +   _____   _____

Market potential @ 6 dozen per child per month:

6X _____   =   _____ dz/mo

Sales projection: _____ dz/mo

Market share: _____   +   _____   =   _____

goals and strategies. Certainly, different sales forecasts will result, depending upon whether the marketing goal is (1) to liquidate an excess inventory of product A or (2) to expand the firm's market share by aggressive advertising.

However, once the sales forecast is prepared, it does become the key controlling factor in all *operational* planning throughout the company. The forecast is the basis of sound budgeting. Financial planning for working-capital requirements, plant utilization, and other needs is based on anticipated sales. The scheduling of all production resources and facilities, such as setting labour needs and purchasing supplies and materials, depends upon the sales forecast.

Sales-forecasting periods   The most widely used period for sales forecasting is one year, although many firms will review annual forecasts on a monthly or quarterly basis. Annual sales forecasts tie in with annual financial planning and reporting and are often based on estimates of the coming year's general economic conditions.

Forecasts for less than a year may be desirable when activity in the firm's industry is so volatile that it is not feasible to look ahead for a full year. As a case in point, many firms engaged in fashion merchandising—producers and retailers alike—prepare a forecast that covers only one fashion season.

Methods of Forecasting Demand

A company can forecast its sales by using either of two basic procedures—the "top-down" or the "buildup" approach.[16]

Using the **top-down** (or **breakdown**) approach, management generally would:

1. *start with a forecast of general economic conditions*, as the basis to
2. *determine the industry's total market potential for a product or service*; then
3. *measure the share of this market the firm is getting*; the measurements in items 2 and 3 form the basis to
4. *forecast the sale of the product or service*.

In the **buildup** technique, management would generate estimates of future demand in segments of the market or from organizational units (sales people or branches) in the company. Then management would simply add the individual estimates to get one total forecast.

Predictions of future market demand — whether they are sales forecasts or estimates of market potential — may be based on techniques ranging from uninformed guesses to sophisticated statistical methods. Marketing executives do not need to know how to do the statistical computations. However, they should understand enough about a given technique to appreciate its merits and limitations. They should also know when each method is best used, and they should be able to ask intelligent questions regarding the assumptions underlying the method.

Here are some of the commonly used methods of predicting demand.

MARKET-FACTOR ANALYSIS

This method is based on the assumption that the future demand for a product is related to the behaviour of certain market factors. If we can determine what

---

[16]For a detailed review of various methods of estimating and forecasting market demand, see James G. Barnes, *Research for Marketing Decision Making*, Toronto: McGraw-Hill Ryerson Limited, 1991, Chapter 5, pp. 83–99.

these factors are and can measure their relationship to sales activity, we can forecast future sales simply by studying the behaviour of the factors.

The key to the successful use of this method lies in the selection of the appropriate market factors. It is also important to minimize the number of market factors used. The greater the number of factors, the greater the chance of erroneous estimates and the more difficult it is to tell how much each factor influences the demand. The two procedures used to translate market-factor behaviour into an estimate of future sales are the direct-derivation method and the correlation-analysis technique.

Direct derivation   Let's illustrate the use of this method to estimate *market potential*. Suppose that a manufacturer of automobile tires wants to know the market potential for replacement tires in Canada in 1993. The primary market factor is the number of automobiles on the road. The first step is to estimate how many cars are likely prospects for new tires. Assume (1) that the seller's studies show that the average car is driven about 16,000 km a year and (2) that the average driver gets about 45,000 km from a set of four tires. This means that all cars that become three years old during 1993 can be considered a part of the potential market for replacement tires during that year. The seller can obtain a reasonably accurate count of the number of cars sold in 1990. (These are the cars that will become three years old in 1993.) The information sources are provincial vehicle licensing offices or private organizations. In addition, the seller can determine how many cars will become 6, 9, or 12 years old in 1993. (These ages are multiples of three. That is, in 1993, a six-year-old car presumably would be ready for its second set of replacement tires.) The number of cars in these age brackets times four (tires per car) should give a fair approximation of the market potential for replacement tires in 1993. We are, of course, dealing in averages. Not all drivers will get 45,000 km from a set of tires, and not all cars will be driven exactly 16,000 km per year.

The direct-derivation method has much to recommend it. It is relatively simple and inexpensive to use, and it requires little statistical analysis. It is reasonably easy to understand, so that executives who are not statistics-oriented can follow the method and interpret the results.

Correlation analysis   This technique is a mathematical refinement of the direct-derivation method. When correlation analysis is used, the degree of association between potential sales of the product and the market factor is taken into account. In effect, a correlation analysis measures, on a scale of 0 to 1, the variations between two series of data. Consequently, this method can be used only when a lengthy sales history of the industry or firm is available, as well as a history of the market factor.

Correlation analysis gives a more exact estimate of market demand, provided that the method is applied correctly. In direct derivation, the correlation measure is implicitly assumed to be 1.00. But rarely does this perfect association exist between a market factor and the sales of a product. Correlation analysis therefore takes the past history into account in predicting the future. It also allows a researcher to incorporate more than one factor into the formula.

There are at least two major limitations to this method. First, as suggested above, a lengthy sales history must be available. To do a really good job, researchers need about 20 periods of sales records. Also, they must assume that approximately the same relationship has existed between the sales and the market factors during this entire period. And, furthermore, they must assume that this relationship will continue in the next sales period. These can be highly unrealistic assumptions. The other major drawback is that not all marketing people understand correlation analysis and can actually do the necessary computations. Thus support of statistical staff may be necessary.

SURVEY OF BUYER INTENTIONS

Another commonly used method of forecasting is to survey a sample of potential customers. These people are asked how much of the stated product or service they would buy or use at a given price during a specified future time period. Some firms maintain consumer panels on a continuing basis to act as a sounding board for new-product ideas, prices, and other features.

A major problem is that of selecting the sample of potential buyers. For many consumer products, a very large, and thus very costly, sample would be needed. Aside from the extremely high cost and large amount of time that this method often entails, there is another very serious limitation. It is one thing for consumers to *intend to buy* a product, but quite another for them to *actually buy* it. Surveys of buying intentions inevitably show an inflated measure of market potential.

Surveys of buying intentions are probably most effective when (1) there are relatively few buyers; (2) these buyers are willing to express their buying intentions; and (3) their past record shows that their follow-up actions are consistent with their stated intentions.

TEST MARKETING

In using this technique, a firm markets its product in a limited geographic area. Then, from this sample, management projects the company's sales potential (market share) over a larger area. Test marketing is frequently used in deciding whether sufficient sales potential exists for a new product. The technique also serves as a basis for evaluating various product features and alternative marketing strategies. The outstanding benefit of test marketing is that it can tell management how many people *actually buy* the product, instead of only how many *say they intend* to buy. If a company can afford the time and money for this method, and can run a valid test, this is the best way of measuring the potential for its product.

These are big ''ifs,'' however. Test marketing is expensive in time and money. Great care is needed to control the test-marketing experiment. A competitor, learning you are test marketing, is usually adept at ''jamming'' your experiment. That is, by unusual promotional or other marketing effort, a competitor can create an artificial situation that distorts your test results. To avoid such test-market ''wars,'' some companies are using simulations of test markets. In effect, these marketers are conducting a test market in a laboratory, rather than in the field.[17]

PAST SALES AND TREND ANALYSIS

A favourite method of forecasting is to base the estimate *entirely* on past sales. This technique is used frequently by retailers whose main goal is to ''beat last

---

[17]For more detail on the use of test markets and simulated test markets, see James G. Barnes, *Research for Marketing Decision Making*, Toronto: McGraw-Hill Ryerson Limited, 1991, pp. 516–522.

year's figures.'' The method consists simply of applying a flat percentage increase to the volume achieved last year or to the average volume of the past few years.

This technique is simple, inexpensive, and easy to apply. For a firm operating in a stable market, where its market share has remained constant for a period of years, past sales alone might be used to predict future volume. On balance, however, the method is highly unreliable.

Trend analysis is a variation of forecasting based on past sales, but it is a bit more complicated. It involves either (1) a long-run projection of the sales trend, usually computed by statistical techniques, or (2) a short-run projection (forecasting for only a few months ahead) based upon a seasonal index of sales. The statistical sophistication of long-run trend analysis does not really remove the inherent weakness of basing future estimates only on past sales activity. Short-run trend analysis may be acceptable if the firm's sales follow a reliable seasonal pattern. For example, assume that sales reach 10,000 units in the first quarter (January-March) and, historically, the second quarter is always about 50 percent better. Then we can reasonably forecast sales of 15,000 units in the April-June period.

SALES-FORCE COMPOSITE

This is a buildup method that may be used to forecast sales or to estimate market potential. As used in sales forecasting, it consists of collecting from all sales people and middlemen an estimate of sales in their territories during the forecasting period. The total (the composite) of these separate estimates is the company's sales forecast. This method can be used advantageously if the firm has competent high-calibre sales people. The method is also useful for firms selling to a market composed of relatively few, but large, customers. Thus, this method would be more applicable to sales of large electrical generators than small general-use motors.

The sales-force composite method takes advantage of the sales people's specialized knowledge of their own market. Also, it should make them more willing to accept their assigned sales quotas. On the other hand, the sales force usually does not have the time or the experience to do the research needed in forecasting future sales.

EXECUTIVE JUDGEMENT

This method covers a wide range of possibilities. Basically, it consists of obtaining opinions regarding future sales volume from one or more executives. If these are really informed opinions, based on valid measures such as market-factor analysis, then the executive judgement is useful and desirable. Certainly all the previously discussed forecasting methods should be tempered with sound executive judgement. On the other hand, forecasting by executive opinion alone is risky. In some instances, such opinions are simply intuition or guesswork.

SUMMARY One of the most important lessons to be learned concerning the use of market segmentation as a marketing strategy is to get beyond the rather simplistic geographic and demographic bases for segmenting a market. Many marketers today are successful in segmenting markets on psychographic and product-usage bases, which involve targeting products and services at groups of consumers based upon their personality and life-style characteristics and upon why they select a product, how much of it they use, or how often they buy it.

There are three alternative segmentation strategies that a marketer can choose from when selecting a target market. The three are market aggregation, single-segment concentration, or multiple segmentation. Market aggregation involves using one marketing mix to reach a mass, undifferentiated market. In single-segment concentration, a company still uses only one marketing mix, but it is directed at only one segment of the total market. The third alternative involves selecting two or more segments and then developing a separate marketing mix to reach each one.

The concept of market positioning involves developing a position for a product, brand, retail store, or company in the minds of the members of the target segment or even in the minds of the general public. In essence, it involves management asking what they want the brand or store to be known for, as compared with the customer's image of the competition; what do they want consumers to think of when they hear the brand or store name? The task of creating the right position or image for a brand or store is accomplished through strategic use of the marketing mix variables.

One of the most effective ways to determine the current position that a brand or store occupies in the consumer's mind is to develop a positioning map based on research into consumer perceptions of the various competitors in the market. Such maps may be used to identify gaps in the market, to determine whether there exists a niche towards which a brand may be directed, and to identify a need to reposition a brand for some other reason.

A company may take a number of approaches to position a brand, a retail store, or the company itself in the minds of target consumers: (1) it may decide to take on competitors head-on; (2) it may reposition a brand to occupy a gap in the market; (3) it may decide to distance a brand from its main competitors; (4) it may stake out a position as the market leader; or (5) it may position it to appeal to certain life-style segments. Often a decision is made to reposition a brand or store because of changes that have taken place within the market environment. Decisions to reposition may result from the identification of a market gap, an increase in competitive activity, or a decision to respond to changing consumer demographics, attitudes, and values.

Before deciding on a target market, the company should forecast the demand in the total market and in each segment under consideration. Demand forecasting involves measuring the industry's market potential, then determining the company's sales potential (market share), and finally preparing a sales forecast. The sales forecast is the foundation of all budgeting and operational planning in all major departments of a company. There are several major methods available for forecasting market demand.

KEY TERMS AND CONCEPTS

QUESTIONS AND PROBLEMS

1. Consult back issues of your local newspaper and a number of consumer magazines and identify examples of companies that are positioning their brands to appeal to target life-style segments of the consumer market. Identify examples of other brands that are targeted at consumers on the basis of product usage.

2. Explain the similarities and differences between a single-segment and a multiple-segment target-market strategy.

3. How might the following organizations implement the strategy of market segmentation?
   a. Manufacturer of personal computers.
   b. Canadian Red Cross.
   c. CBC.
   d. Producer of laser-disc style of stereo records.

4. Assume that a company has developed a new type of portable headphone-type cassette player in the general product category of a Sony Walkman. Which of the three target-market strategies should this company adopt?

5. What positioning strategy has each of the following marketers chosen?
   a. Zellers
   b. Birks
   c. ABC detergent
   d. Canadian Imperial Bank of Commerce
   e. Coffee Crisp chocolate bar
   f. Journey's End hotels

6. Identify a number of brands, retailers, or restaurants with which you are familiar and that have chosen to occupy a niche in the market. How would you describe the niche each occupies? Why do you feel each has chosen this niche?

7. Why would a company decide that one of its brands needs to be repositioned? What market conditions are likely to lead to a decision to reposition

a brand or store? Can you think of any brands or stores with which you are familiar that have recently been repositioned? What were their original positions? How would you describe the new positions each occupies in the market? How was the repositioning accomplished in each case?

8. Carefully distinguish between market potential and a sales forecast, using examples of consumer or industrial products.

9. What are some logical market factors that you might use in estimating the market potential for each of the following products?

a. Central home air conditioners.
b. Electric milking machines.
c. Golf clubs.
d. Sterling flatware.
e. Safety goggles.

10. How would you determine the market potential for a textbook written for the introductory course in marketing?

11. Explain the direct-derivation method of sales forecasting, using a product example other than automobile tires. How does this forecasting method differ from the correlation-analysis method?

12. What are some of the problems a researcher faces when using the test-market method for determining market potential or sales potential?

CHAPTER 6 GOALS

In Chapters 4 and 5, our discussions of market segmentation, positioning, and forecasting focused on target market. In this chapter, we consider the consumer's *willingness to buy* as determined by information sources, social environment, psychological forces, and situational factors. After studying this chapter, you should be able to explain:

- The process consumers go through in making purchase decisions.
- The importance of commercial and social information sources in buying decisions.
- The influence of culture, subcultures, and social class characteristics on buying behaviour.
- The direct impact of reference groups on buying behaviour.
- Family and household buying behaviour.
- The roles of motivation, perception, learning, personality, and attitudes in shaping consumer behaviour.
- The importance of situational factors in buying.

today's new
GRANDPARENT

Written especially
for today's new
grandparents

GRACIOUS
GRANDPARENTING
When do your opinions count?

Top toys for your grandchild

How to stay close from far away

50 instant home proofing tips

Social and Psychological Influences on Buyer Behaviour

Fisher-Price has been in business for more than 60 years. It sees itself as the premier children's products company of the 1990s with one of the most trusted brand names and loyal customer groups in this market. It also knows that 60 percent of the purchase decisions for children's products are made right in the stores. To be successful in the 1990s means dealing with the consumers of the 1990s. And this is no small task, since they are better educated, more experienced, and more demanding than ever before. Just look at today's parents—the baby boomers of the fifties and sixties. And look at today's children—their echoes. And look at the echoes' grandparents —today's sophisticated and relatively affluent seniors.

If you are marketing to parents and grandparents and children, you have to deal with the values that are important to them; how those values will be taught and learned; what kinds of self-concepts the families believe in; what social roles they think are the right ones for males, females, mothers, fathers, grandparents; how all this comes together in product design, product line development and communication and distribution strategy and program design. Because of the obvious role of parents and grandparents, Fisher-Price promotes, supports, and provides child-care and product information for (and, of course, advertises extensively in) *Today's Parent*, Canada's national parenting magazine, and in *Today's New Grandparent*, an annual distributed in Canada to expectant mothers for passing along to their parents. Knowing human and consumer behaviour and their development provides the foundation for Fisher-Price's continued success in the marketplace.

Marketing to consumers has become more complicated. The reason is simple. Domestic and international competition has increased and our understanding of consumer buying behaviour is constantly improving, allowing marketers to refine their efforts. But there is much more to learn. And because marketing success largely depends on the ability to anticipate what buyers will do, in this chapter we examine the challenging topic of consumer buying behaviour. First we develop an overview with a description of the buying-decision process. Next we consider the sources of information used by consumers — without information there are no decisions. We then describe the various social and group forces in society that influence decision making and the psychological characteristics of the individual that affect the decision process in buying. In the final section, our focus shifts to the role in buying played by situational factors.

Figure 6-1 brings all of these dimensions of buying behaviour together in a model that provides the structure for our discussion. The model features a six-stage **buying-decision process** influenced by four primary forces.

DECISION MAKING AS PROBLEM SOLVING

To deal with the marketing environment and make purchases, consumers engage in a decision process. The process, which divides nicely into six stages, can be thought of as a problem-solving approach. When faced with a buying problem (''I'm bored. How do I satisfy my need for entertainment?''), the consumer goes through a series of logical stages to arrive at a decision.

As shown in the centre of Fig. 6-1, the stages are:

1. *Need recognition:* The consumer is moved to action by a need.
2. *Choice of an involvement level:* The consumer decides how much time and effort to invest in the remaining stages.
3. *Identification of alternatives:* The consumer collects information about products and brands.
4. *Evaluation of alternatives:* The consumer weighs the pros and cons of the alternatives identified.
5. *Decision:* The consumer decides to buy or not to buy.

FIGURE 6-1

The consumer buying-decision process and the factors that influence it.

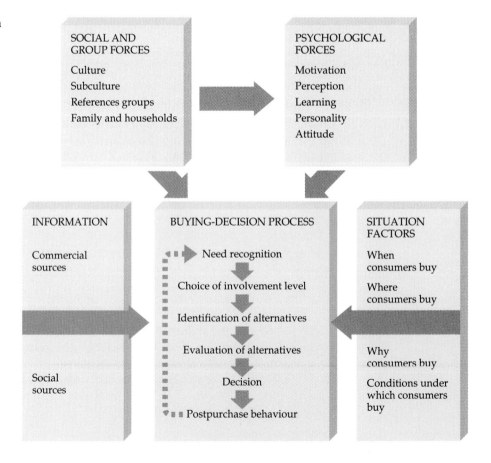

6. *Postpurchase behaviour:* The consumer attempts to resolve anxieties about the choice made.

Though this model is a useful starting point for examining purchase decisions, the process is not always as straightforward as it may appear. First, the potential buyer can withdraw at any stage prior to the actual purchase. If, for example, the strength of the need diminishes or no satisfactory alternatives are available, the process will come to an abrupt end. Second, it is not uncommon for some stages to be skipped. All six stages are likely to be used only in certain buying situations — for instance, when buying high-priced, infrequently purchased items. However, for many products purchasing is a routine affair in which the aroused need is satisfied by repurchasing a familiar brand and thus the third and fourth stages are bypassed. Third, the stages are not necessarily of the same length. In the purchase of a new car, the need might be recognized the moment a mechanic tells you that your car's engine needs an overhaul, but the evaluation of alternatives may go on for weeks. Finally, some stages may be performed consciously in certain purchase situations and subconsciously in others. We do not calculate for every purchase the amount of time and effort we will put forth. Yet the fact that we spend more time on some purchases and less on others indicates that choice of involvement level is part of the process.

In the following discussion, we assume that these stages generally characterize the buying-decision process. However, keep in mind that the model may have to be adapted to fit the circumstances of a particular purchase situation.

1. Recognition of an Unsatisfied Need

The process begins when an unsatisfied need creates tension or discomfort. This condition may arise internally (for example, a person feels hungry). Or the need may be dormant until it is aroused by an external stimulus, such as an ad or the sight of a product. Another possible source of tension is dissatisfaction with a product currently being used.

Once the need has been recognized, consumers often become aware of conflicting or competing uses for their scarce resources of time and money. Let's say a student wants to purchase a personal computer for school, but for the same amount of money she could buy a nice stereo on sale. Or she is concerned that if she buys the computer her friends will think she is becoming ''too studious.'' She must resolve these conflicts before proceeding. Otherwise the buying process stops.

2. Choice of an Involvement Level

Very early in the process the consumer consciously or subconsciously decides how much effort to exert in satisfying a need. Sometimes when a need arises, a consumer is dissatisfied with the quantity or quality of information about the purchase situation and decides to actively collect and evaluate more. These are *high-involvement* purchases that entail all six stages of the buying-decision process. If, on the other hand, a consumer is comfortable with the information and alternatives readily available, the purchase situation is viewed as *low involvement.* In such a case, the buyer will likely skip directly from need recognition to purchase, ignoring the stages in between.

Some of the major differences in consumer behaviour in high- and low-involvement situations are:

Behaviour	High involvement	Low involvement
Time invested	Large amount	Small amount
Information search	Active	Little or none
Response to information	Critically evaluate	Passively accept
Brand judgements	Clear and distinct	Vague and general
Likelihood of brand loyalty developing	Strong	Weak

Though it is somewhat risky to generalize since all consumers are different, involvement tends to be greater under any of the following conditions:

- The consumer lacks information about the purchase.
- The product is viewed as important.
- The risk of making a bad decision is perceived as high.
- The product has considerable social importance.
- The product is seen as having a potential for providing significant benefits.

Since they rarely meet any of these conditions, most buying decisions for relatively low-priced products that have close substitutes would be low involvement. Typical examples are the majority of items sold in supermarkets; variety stores, and hardware stores. However, for a wealthy person the purchase of a car could be low-involving, while for a person with a high need for social acceptance, toothpaste might be highly involving. Thus it is important to remember that involvement must be viewed from the perspective of the consumer, not the product.

Impulse buying, or purchasing with little or no advance planning, is an important form of low-involvement decision making. A shopper who goes to the grocery store with the intention of buying meat and bread and on noticing a display of peaches at an attractive price decides to buy some engages in impulse buying.

Self-service, open-display retailing has conditioned shoppers to postpone planning and engage in more impulse buying. Because of the growth of this type of low-involvement purchasing, greater emphasis must be placed on promotional programs to get shoppers into a store. Also, displays and packages must be made appealing since they serve as silent sales people.

3. Identification of Alternatives

Once a need has been recognized and the consumer has decided how much effort to exert, both product and brand alternatives must be identified. This may involve a simple memory scan or an extensive search. Suppose a family decides to have an already prepared item for their evening meal. They could defrost frozen entrees, have a pizza delivered, or go out for fast food. After one of the alternatives is selected, they must choose a specific brand or fast-food outlet. The search for alternatives is influenced by (1) how much information the consumer already has from past experiences and other sources; (2) the consumer's confidence in that information; and (3) what the time and money costs would be to collect more information.

4. Evaluation of Alternatives

Once all the reasonable alternatives have been identified, the consumer must evaluate each one before making a decision. The evaluation process involves establishing some criteria against which each alternative is compared. The consumer may have a single criterion (''How quickly can we get the meal on

Shopping list,
courtesy of Road & Track.

Nissan offers the first four
alternatives.

the table?'') or several criteria (speed, taste, nutrition, and price). When multiple criteria are involved, they typically do not carry equal weight. Thus taste might be more important than nutrition.

The criteria that consumers use in the evaluation result from past experience and feelings towards various brands. Consumers also consider the opinions of family members and friends in their deliberations.

5. Purchase Decision

There are several possible outcomes of the buying-decision process. After searching and evaluating, the consumer must decide whether to buy. Thus the first outcome is the decision to purchase or not to purchase. If the decision is to buy, a series of related decisions must be made regarding features, where and when to make the actual transaction, how to take delivery or possession, the method of payment, and other issues. So the decision to make a purchase is not the end of the process. It is, in fact, the beginning of an entirely new series of decisions that may be as time-consuming and difficult as the initial one.

One of the most important decisions is selecting a store. The reasons a consumer chooses to shop at a certain store are called **patronage buying motives.** People want to feel comfortable when they shop. They want to be around people like themselves and in an environment that reflects their values. There are consumers, for example, who would feel uncomfortable shopping in an upscale store like Holt Renfrew. Some patronage motives and situational factors are:

- Location convenience.
- Service speed.
- Merchandise accessibility.
- Crowding.
- Prices.

- Merchandise assortment.
- Services offered.
- Store appearance.
- Sales personnel.
- Mix of other shoppers.

Marketers also must recognize that the person at the end of the process is not the same person who began it. Having gathered information, evaluated alternatives, and arrived at a decision, the consumer has acquired additional knowledge about the product and the various brands. Futhermore, new opinions and beliefs have been formed and old ones have been changed. This is

Unique Body Shop products provide the patronage motive.

indicated by a feedback arrow in the buying-decision process model. Consumer behaviour is a continuing process, involving repeat purchases, so discovering what consumers know and how they feel after the purchase decision is made will help the marketer improve the marketing mix.

The marketing concept emphasizes customer satisfaction, yet it is only in the last few years that a serious effort has been made to understand how a state of satisfaction is reached. Consumers form expectations based on past experience, information from social sources, and sales presentations and advertising. When using the product, they compare these *expectations* with their *experience* to arrive at a perceived level of satisfaction. The ideal outcome is for experience to equal or exceed expectations; the result is satisfaction. Alternatively, if experience falls short of expectation, dissatisfaction occurs. The marketer can influence expectations through advertising claims and sales presentations and the consumer's experience through the quality of the product. Clearly establishing and maintaining a balance between expectations and experience is a tricky task.

6. Postpurchase Behaviour

A buyer's feelings after the sale can influence repeat sales and what the buyer tells others about the product. Buyers often experience some postpurchase anxieties in all but routine purchases. This state of anxiety is explained by the theory of **cognitive dissonance.** People strive for internal harmony and consistency among their cognitions (knowledge, attitudes, beliefs, and values) and any inconsistency in these cognitions causes cognitive dissonance.

Postpurchase cognitive dissonance occurs because each of the alternatives considered by the consumer usually has both advantages and limitations. Thus when the purchase decision is finally made, the selected product has certain drawbacks, while the rejected alternatives each possess some attractive features. Negative aspects of the item selected, along with positive qualities of the rejected products, create cognitive dissonance in the consumer.

Dissonance typically increases as (1) the dollar value of the purchase increases; (2) the degree of similarity between items selected and items rejected increases; and (3) the relative importance of the decision increases (buying a house or car creates more dissonance than buying a candy bar).

To restore internal harmony and minimize discomfort, people try to reduce their postpurchase anxieties. Thus they are likely to avoid information (such as ads for the rejected products) that is likely to increase dissonance. At the same time, they seek out ads for the selected product (even after the purchase) in search of reinforcement. Prior to making the purchase, they may shop around quite a bit, especially for high-priced, infrequently purchased articles, to minimize postpurchase dissonance by spending more time in predecision evaluations.

Some useful generalizations can be developed from the theory of cognitive dissonance. For example, anything sellers can do in their advertising or personal selling to reassure buyers — say, by stressing the number of satisfied owners — will reduce dissonance. This reinforces the consumer and increases the likelihood of repeat purchases. Also, the quality of a seller's postsale service program can be a significant factor in reducing dissonance.

With this background on the buying-decision process, we can examine in detail the forces that influence behaviour. Our discussion begins with the sources and types of information used by consumers.

INFORMATION AND PURCHASE DECISIONS

Consumers must find out what products and brands are available, what features and benefits they offer, who sells them at what prices, and where they can be purchased. Without this market information there wouldn't be a decision process because there wouldn't be any decisions to make.

What are some of the sources and types of information that exist in the buying environment? As shown in Fig. 6-1 two information sources, the commercial environment and the social environment, influence the buying-decision process. The **commercial environment** consists of all marketing organizations and individuals who attempt to communicate with consumers. It includes manufacturers, retailers, advertisers, and sales people whenever any of them are engaged in efforts to inform or persuade. The other source is the **social environment** made up of family, friends, and acquaintances who directly or indirectly provide information about products. If you think for a moment about how often your conversation with friends or family deals with purchases you are considering or those you have made, you will begin to appreciate the marketing significance of these social sources.

Advertising is the most common type of commercial information. Other commercial sources are direct sales efforts by store clerks, telemarketing, and direct mail to consumers' homes, as well as consumers' physical involvement with products (examining packages, trial product use, and sampling).

The normal kind of social information is word-of-mouth communication, in which two or more people simply have a conversation about a product. Other social sources include the observations of others using products and exposure to products in the homes of others.

When all the different types of information are taken into consideration, it becomes apparent that there is enormous competition for the consumer's attention. Coincidentally, the consumer's mind has to be a marvellously efficient machine to sort and process this barrage of information. To understand how the consumer functions, we will begin by examining the social and group forces that influence the individual's psychological makeup and also play a role in specific buying decisions.

SOCIAL AND GROUP FORCES

The way we think, believe, and act is determined to a great extent by social forces and groups. In addition, our individual buying decisions—including the needs we experience, the alternatives we consider, and the way in which we evaluate them—are affected by the social forces that surround us. To reflect this dual impact, the arrows in Fig. 6-1 extend from the social and group forces in two directions—to the psychological makeup of the individual and to the buying-decision process. Our description begins with culture, the force with the most *indirect* impact, and moves to the force with the most *direct* impact, the household.

Definition of Culture and Cultural Influence

A **culture** is the complex of symbols and artifacts created by a given society and handed down from generation to generation as determinants and regulators of human behaviour. The symbols may be intangible (attitudes, beliefs, values, languages, religions) or tangible (tools, housing, products, works of art). A culture implies a totally learned and ''handed-down'' way of life. It does *not* include instinctive acts. However, standards for performing instinctive biological acts (eating, eliminating body wastes, and sexual relationships) can be culturally established. Thus everybody gets hungry, but what people eat and how they act to satisfy the hunger drive will vary among cultures.

Actually, much of our behaviour is culturally determined. Our sociocultural

MARKETING AT WORK

FILE 6-1 THE NINETIES' CULTURE: FROM ACTIVE TO PASSIVE

The average Canadian consumer in the 1990s will be an "aging homebody whose idea of a good time is penny-pinching and lying on the couch." In the 1990s Canadians will:

Eat at home, not at restaurants. To please their travel- and restaurant-inspired tastes, however, they will be exchanging Thai rice dishes for boring Uncle Ben's and making use of ethnic convenience stores.

Drink "lite" booze, such as Alberta Distillers' diet rum and Seagram's diet whisky.

Wear clothes without designer labels and with "environmental" looks.

Travel for shorter times, but more frequently. Popular will be cruises (no longer aimed at affluent elders) and "ecotours" (wherein adventurers pay money to go to Peru and clean up other tourists' trash).

Exercise much less rigorously, moving from hard-drive fitness regimens to "easy on the knees 'life-style' recreation." Golf, walking, and gardening will replace 10K "fun runs."

Source: Adapted from Jared Mitchell, "The Snoring '90's," *Report on Business Magazine*, January 1991, p. 36-37.

---

institutions (family, schools, churches, and languages) provide behavioural guidelines. Years ago, Kluckhohn observed: "Culture . . . regulates our lives at every turn. From the moment we are born until we die there is constant conscious and unconscious pressure upon us to follow certain types of behaviour that other men have created for us."[1] People living in a culture share a whole set of similarities — and these can be different from those in or from another culture.

Cultural Change Cultural influences do change over time, as old patterns gradually give way to the new. During the past 10 to 25 years, cultural changes—that is, life-style changes—of far-reaching magnitude have been occurring. Marketing executives must be alert to these changing life-styles so that they can adjust their planning to be in step with, or even a little ahead of, the times. In Chapter 2 we mentioned some of these cultural changes when we discussed social and cultural forces as an environmental factor influencing a company's marketing system. Now at this point we shall simply summarize a few of the sociocultural changes that significantly affect consumer buying behaviour.

- From a husband-dominated family towards equality in husband-wife roles; or, in a broader context, the changing role of women.
- From emphasis on *quantity* of goods to emphasis on *quality* of life.
- From postponed gratification to immediate gratification.
- More concern about the pollution of our natural environment.
- A concern for more safety in our products and in our occupations.
- A concern for the conservation of irreplaceable resources.

---

[1]Clyde Kluckhohn, "The Concept of Culture," in Richard Kluckhohn (ed.), *Culture and Behaviour*, The Free Press, New York, 1962, p. 26.

Subcultures Given the multicultural nature of Canadian society, marketers should understand the concept of subcultures and analyze them as potentially profitable market segments. Any time there is a culture as heterogeneous as ours, there are bound to be significant subcultures based upon factors such as race, nationality, religion, geographic location, age, and urban-rural distribution. Some of these were recognized in Chapter 4, when we analyzed the demographic market factors. Ethnicity, for example, is a cultural factor that has significant marketing implications. Concentrations of Middle or Eastern Europeans in the Prairies provide a market for some products that would go unnoticed in Italian or Chinese sections of Toronto.

The cultural diversity of the Canadian market has taken on increased importance for some companies in recent years. Twenty years ago, most companies ignored the ethnic market, but the 1986 Census showed that almost 40 percent of Canada's population had origins other than British, French, or native. Almost four million Canadians claimed a mother tongue other than English or French.

The most obvious efforts to reach ethnic market segments are, of course, found in major urban markets such as Toronto and Vancouver. In Toronto, for example, a multicultural televison channel, MTV, carries European soccer and other programming directed to ethnic markets. These and similar media represent attractive advertising outlets for companies who wish to reach this growing market segment.

The sharpest subcultural differences are portrayed in behavioural differences between English- and French-Canadian communities on a country-wide basis, although to the urban dweller in Toronto or Montreal the acceptance (or ritual avoidance) of the obvious differences between a diversity of ethnic minorities is now a matter of course. As indicated in Chapter 4, marketing to French Canada involves considerably more than cursory acknowledgement of ethnic differences.

''Coming Home to Dempster's'' is communicated to Greek-speaking customers.

Ελάτε στο σπίτι με ψωμί Dempster's.

The Changing Nature of the French-Canadian Market

French Canada, as a subculture, has undergone a revolution during the past 25 years. This has had a profound effect on the nature of the French-Canadian market.

French Canadians have taken major steps to preserve their cultural identity in the English-dominated North American society and to prevent the assimilation of French Canada into this society. They developed programs to preserve the French language, improved health and education programs, and renewed interest in French-Canadian crafts and culture. The roles of religion, the family, and women have changed dramatically during this revolutionary period. No longer do the traditional professions of the priesthood, law, and medicine dominate the cultural hierarchy. A new middle class has developed in French Canada that is less traditional in its outlook and is more attuned to youth and business. The Quebec business scene is vibrant and entrepreneurial. New, exciting opportunities are developing for Quebec-owned businesses and hundreds of new businesses have been established in the province in recent years. Quebec now accounts for more than one-third of all business graduates from Canadian universities.

Differences in Consumption Behaviour

Cultural differences lead to differences in consumption behaviour between English- and French-Canadians. Certain products sell in much larger quantities in Quebec than in other provinces, while other products that sell well in English Canada are rarely purchased by French Canadians. Some examples of differences in product preferences and buying behaviour follow.[2]

- There is a better acceptance in Quebec of premium-priced products such as premium-grade gasoline and expensive liquors.
- French Canadians spend more per capita on clothing, personal care items, tobacco, and alcoholic beverages.
- The French Canadian consumes more soft drinks, maple sugar, molasses, and candy per capita than does the English Canadian.
- French Canadians have much higher consumption rates for instant and decaffeinated coffee.
- French Canadians watch more television and listen to radio more than do English Canadians.
- Premiums and coupons are more popular in Quebec.
- French Canadians buy more headache and cold remedies than do English Canadians.
- In many Quebec homes a full meal is served both at noon and in the evening.
- French-Canadian consumers may experience higher levels of dissatisfaction

---

[2]See Nariman K. Dhalla, *These Canadians: A Sourcebook of Marketing and Socioeconomic Facts*, McGraw-Hill, Toronto, 1966, pp. 287-300; Frederick Elkin and Mary B. Hill, "Bicultural and Bilingual Adaptation in French Canada: The Example of Retail Advertising," *Canadian Review of Sociology and Anthropology*, August 1965, pp. 132-148; M. Brisebois, "Marketing in Quebec," in W. H. Mahatoo (ed.), *Marketing Research in Canada*, Thomas Nelson and Sons, Toronto, 1968, pp. 88-90; Bruce Mallen, "The Present State of Knowledge and Research in Marketing to the French-Canadian Marketing," in Donald N. Thompson and David S. R. Leighton (eds.), *Canadian Marketing: Problems and Prospects*, Wiley Publishers of Canada Limited, Toronto, 1973, pp. 100-101; and Jean-Charles Chebat and Georges Hénault, "The Cultural Behavior of Canadian Consumers," in Vishnu H. Kirpalani and Ronald H. Rotenberg (eds.), *Cases and Readings in Marketing*, Holt, Rinehart and Winston of Canada Limited, Toronto, 1974, pp. 178-180.

with repairs and general consumer services and with professional and personal services than is the case for English-speaking Canadians.[3]

Factors Influencing French-English Consumption Differences

Although it is relatively easy to determine where actual differences in consumption behaviour exist between French and English Canadians, it is somewhat more difficult to identify reasons for the existence of such differences. And yet, it is important for marketers to have some understanding of the factors that contribute to these differences if they are to market effectively to both market segments.

In the past, authors have pointed out that French Canadians have a lower per capita income than do English Canadians, that they have lower average education levels, and that they are a much more rural population. These differences along income and other demographic lines might suggest that the differences in product purchase rates and shopping behaviour between French Canadians and English Canadians may be attributable simply to demographic differences and that the consumption behaviour of French Canadians is really no different from that of English Canadians with similar demographic characteristics. At least two studies have refuted this argument.

An early one indicated that consumption behaviour was significantly different between Quebec and Ontario households when households of *similar size and income levels were compared*.[4] A second study found significant differences in household expenditure levels between English-Canadian and French-Canadian households for eight consumption expenditure categories after certain noncultural differences (such as the rural-urban breakdown of the groups and stage of the family life cycle) between the two groups were controlled.[5] Such findings suggest that the consumption behaviour differences between French and English Canadians are not attributable solely to demographic differences but, rather, are more likely explained by cultural differences.

Certain characteristics of the French-Canadian culture and directions in which that culture appears to have changed were discussed earlier. The important message for the marketer is that French Canada is culturally distinctive from English Canada and that certain products and other elements of the marketing mix are perceived quite differently by the French Canadian than they are by the English Canadian. As has been suggested, the *function and meaning* of products sold to French Canada must be perceived by the French-Canadian culture as consistent with that culture.

The Impact of Cultural Differences on Marketing

The fact that French Canada represents a distinctively different culture from that found in English Canada requires that marketers who wish to be successful in the French-Canadian market develop unique marketing programs for this segment. There must be an appreciation of the fact that certain products

---

[3]S. B. Ash, Carole P. Duhaime, and John A. Quelch, ''Consumer Satisfaction: A Comparison of English- and French-Speaking Canadians,'' in Vernon J. Jones (ed.), *Marketing*, vol. 1, part 3, *Proceedings* of the Administrative Sciences Association of Canada, Marketing Division, Montreal, 1980, pp. 11-20.

[4]Kristian S. Palda, ''A Comparison of Consumer Expenditures in Quebec and Ontario,'' *Canadian Journal of Economics and Political Science*, February 1967, p. 26.

[5]Dwight R. Thomas, ''Culture and Consumption Behavior in English and French Canada,'' in Bent Stidsen (ed.), *Marketing in the 1970s and Beyond*, Canadian Association of Adminstrative Sciences, Marketing Division, Edmonton, 1975, pp. 255-261.

- As-tu brisé   - Non,
  la glace   il est pas
  avec le   vite sur
  beau Serge ?   ses patins !

Venez faire le tour du monde
sur la patinoire du coin.
Entre deux coups de patins,
on s'y raconte les derniers potins.

À vous de jouer.

PARTICIPACTION

The logic of Participaction for francophones.

will not be successful in French Canada simply because they are not appropriate to the French-Canadian culture and life-style. In other cases, products that are successful in English Canada must be marketed differently in French Canada because the French Canadian has a different perception of these products and the way in which they are used. It may be necessary for companies to develop new products or appropriate variations of existing products specifically for the French-Canadian market. Similarly, the retail buying behaviour of French-Canadians may necessitate the use of different channels of distribution in Quebec.

In the area of advertising, many national companies have encountered problems in reaching the French-Canadian market. In the past, much of the national advertising in Canada was prepared by English-Canadian advertising agencies (usually based in Toronto) that developed advertisements for use in both English and French Canada. These agencies generally employed translators whose responsibility it was to translate the advertisements, which had been developed by English Canadians for the English culture, so that they might be used in the Quebec market. In many cases, literal translations were demanded and the end results were inappropriate for the French market.

The challenges of advertising in French Canada go far beyond those of translating English to French. Even where the translation is a good one and English expressions and slang are converted into expressions that are meaningful to French Canadians, the problem still remains that the basic approach to the advertisement is based in English-Canadian or even American culture. Many advertisements contain illustrations, themes, and representations of life-styles that are quite appropriate in English Canada but quite inappropriate in Quebec. What is needed is that advertising that is to be directed to the French-Canadian market be planned from "scratch" with that market in mind. The advertising content must be consistent with the culture of the market, and this requires that it be developed and written by French Canadians. Many national advertisers now place their English-language advertising with an English-Canadian agency, but use a Montreal-based French-language agency to develop advertising for the Quebec market.[6]

In the packaging and labelling of consumer products there have also been recent developments that are important for marketing in French Canada. For many years, Canadian companies made no special effort to prepare product labels for use in French Canada, with the result that most of the products on the shelves of Quebec retail stores bore English labels. Since 1967, however, it has been a requirement of the Quebec government that all labels on food products sold in that province give at least equal prominence to the French language. Similarly, the federal government's Consumer Packaging and Labelling Act and its regulations require that all label information on consumer products produced in Canada or imported into this country be conveyed in both English and French.

---

[6]For a discussion of the evolution of advertising agencies in Quebec, see Madeleine Saint-Jacques and Bruce Mallen, "The French-Canadian Market," in Peter T. Zarry and Robert D. Wilson (eds.), *Advertising in Canada: Its Theory and Practice*, McGraw-Hill Ryerson Limited, Toronto, 1981, pp. 349-368; and Robert MacGregor, "The Impact of the Neo-Nationalist Movement on the Changing Structure and Composition of the Quebec Advertising Industry," in the *Proceedings* of the Administrative Sciences Association of Canada, Marketing Division, 1980, p. 237.

REFERENCE GROUP INFLUENCES

Consumers' perceptions and buying behaviour are also influenced by the reference groups to which they belong. These groups include the large social classes and smaller reference groups. The smallest, yet usually the strongest, social-group influence is a person's family.

Influence of Social Class

People's buying behaviour is often influenced by the class to which they belong, or to which they aspire, simply because they have values, beliefs and life-styles that are characteristic of a social class. This occurs whether they are conscious of class notions or not. The idea of a social-class structure and the terms *upper*, *middle*, and *lower* class may be repugnant to many Canadians. However, it does represent a useful way to look at a market. We can consider social class as another useful basis for segmenting consumer markets.[7]

A social-class structure currently useful to marketing managers is one developed by Richard Coleman and Lee Rainwater, two respected researchers in social-class theory. The placement of people in this structure is determined primarily by such variables as *education, occupation,* and *type of neighbourhood of residence.*[8]

Note that "amount of income" is *not* one of the placement criteria. There may be a general relationship between amount of income and social class — people in the upper classes usually have higher incomes than people in the lower classes. But *within* each social class there typically is a wide range of incomes. Also, the same amount of income may be earned by families in different social classes.

For purposes of marketing planning and analysis, marketing executives and researchers often divide the total consumer market into five social classes. These classes and their characteristics, as adapted from Warner and the Coleman structure previously noted, are summarized below. The percentages are only approximations and may vary from one city or region to another.

SOCIAL CLASSES AND THEIR CHARACTERISTICS

The **upper class,** about 2 percent of the population, includes two groups: (1) the socially prominent "old families" of inherited wealth and (2) the "new rich" of the corporate executives, owners of large businesses, and wealthy professionals. They live in large homes in the best neighbourhoods and display a sense of social responsibility. They buy expensive products and services, but they do not conspicuously display their purchases. They patronize exclusive shops.

The **upper-middle class,** about 12 percent of the population, is composed of moderately successful business and professional people and owners of medium-sized companies. They are well educated, have a strong drive for success, and want their children to do well. Their purchases are more conspicuous than those in the upper class. This class buys status symbols that show their success, yet are socially acceptable. They live well, belong to private clubs, and support the arts and various social causes.

---

[7]D. W. Greeno and W. F. Bennett, "Social Class and Income as Complementary Segmentation Bases: A Canadian Perspective," in *Proceedings* of the Marketing Division, Administrative Sciences Association of Canada, 1983, pp. 113-122.

[8]W. Lloyd Warner and Paul Lunt, *The Social Life of a Modern Community,* Yale University Press, New Haven, Conn., 1941; and W. Lloyd Warner, Marchia Meeker, and Kenneth Eells, *Social Class in America,* Science Research Associates, Inc., Chicago, 1949.

The **lower-middle class,** about 32 percent of the population, consists of the white-collar workers — office workers, most sales people, teachers, technicians, and small-business owners. The **upper-lower class,** about 38 percent of the population, is the blue-collar ''working class'' of factory workers, semiskilled workers, and service people. Because these two groups together represent the mass market and thus are so important to most marketers, the attitudes, beliefs, and life-styles they exhibit are the focus for much marketing research.

The **lower-lower class,** about 16 percent of the population, is composed of unskilled workers, the chronically unemployed, unassimilated immigrants, and people frequently on welfare. They typically are poorly educated, with low incomes, and live in substandard houses and neighbourhoods. They tend to live for the present and often do not purchase wisely. The public tends to differentiate (within this class) between the ''working poor'' and the ''welfare poor.''

MARKETING SIGNIFICANCE OF SOCIAL CLASSES

Now let's summarize the basic conclusions from social-class research that are highly significant for marketing:

- A social-class system can be observed whether people are aware of it or not. There are substantial differences between classes regarding their buying behaviour.
- Differences in beliefs, attitudes, and orientations exist among the classes. Thus the classes respond differently to a seller's marketing program.
- For many products, class membership is a better predictor of buyer behaviour than is income.

This last point — the relative importance of income versus social class — has generated considerable controversy. There is an old saying that ''a rich man is just a poor man with money — and that, given the same amount of money, a poor man would behave exactly like a rich man.'' Studies of social-class structure have proved that this statement simply is not true. Two people, each earning the same income but belonging to different social classes, will have quite different buying patterns. They will shop at different stores, expect different treatment from sales people, and buy different products and even different brands. Also, when a family's income increases because more family members get a job, this increase almost never results in a change in the family's social class.

Influence of Small Reference Groups

Small-group influence on buyer behaviour introduces to marketing the concept of reference-group theory, which we borrow from sociology. A **reference group** may be defined as a group of people who influence a person's attitudes, values, and behaviour. Each group develops its own standards of behaviour that then serve as guides, or ''frames of reference,'' for the individual members. The members share these values and are expected to conform to the group's normative behavioural patterns. It is likely that a person's reference groups are to be found in their own social class category.

Consumer behaviour is influenced by the small groups to which consumers belong or aspire to belong. These groups may include family, social organizations, labour unions, church groups, athletic teams, or a circle of close friends or neighbours. Studies have shown that personal advice in face-to-

M A R K E T I N G   A T   W O R K

FILE 6-2   "FORTYSOMETHING" REFERENCE GROUP?

They all grow up in the same era and had similar experiences and values. More than 400,000 Canadian baby boomers turned 40 in 1991, joining the other 10 million members of the "fortysomething" crowd and pushing up the average age of the Canadian population. This "greying" of Canada will undoubtedly have a great impact on businesses that have spent the last generation catering to the boomers' seemingly insatiable desires. Boomers who once considered themselves the inventors of sex, Sunday brunch, and natural fibre clothing have now invented something new—middle age. However, marketers will have to be careful, for Canadian "fortysomething"ers show no intention of winding down their lives. Fuelled by talent and experience they've acquired over the years, they're far more likely to strike out and make bold changes. As a popular T-shirt says, "I may be growing older, but I refuse to grow up." The 1990s will be interesting as marketers try to adapt to a nation dominated by Peter Pans.

Source: Adapted from Murray Campbell, "From thirtysomething to fortysomething", *Globe and Mail*, February 3, 1990, p. 1.

face groups is much more effective as a behavioural determinant than advertising in newspapers, television, or other mass media. That is, in selecting products or changing brands, we are more likely to be influenced by word-of-mouth advertising from satisfied customers in our reference group. This is true especially when the speaker is considered to be knowledgeable regarding the particular product.

A person may agree with all the ideas of the group or only some of them. Also, a person does not have to belong to a group to be influenced by it. Young people frequently pattern their dress and other behaviour after that of an older group that the younger ones aspire to join.

Another useful finding pertains to the flow of information between and within groups. For years marketers operated in conformity with the "snob appeal" theory. This is the idea that if you can get social leaders and high-income groups to use your products, the mass market will also buy them. The assumption has been that influence follows a *vertical* path, starting at levels of high status and moving downward through successive levels of groups. Contrary to this popular assumption, studies by Katz and Lazarsfeld and by others have emphasized the *horizontal* nature of opinion leadership. Influence emerges on each *level* of the socioeconomic scale, moving from the opinion leaders to their peers.[9]

The proven role of small groups as behaviour determinants, plus the concept of horizontal information flow, suggests that a marketer is faced with two key problems. The first is to identify the relevant reference group likely to be used by consumers in a given buying situation. The second is to identify and com-

[9]See Elihu Katz and Paul Lazarsfeld, *Personal Influence*, Free Press, New York, 1955, especially p. 325.

municate with two key people in the group—the innovator (early buyer) and the influential person (opinion leader). Every group has a leader — a taste-maker, or **opinion leader** — who influences the decision making of others in the group. The key is for marketers to convince that person of the value of their products or services. The opinion *leader* in one group may be an opinion *follower* in another. Married women with children may be influential in matters concerning food, whereas unmarried women are more likely to influence fashions in clothing and makeup.

Family and Household Influence

A **family** is a group of two or more people related by blood, marriage, or adoption living together in a household. During their lives many people will belong to at least two families—the one into which they are born and the one they form at marriage. The birth family primarily determines core values and attitudes. The marriage family, in contrast, has a more direct influence on specific purchases. For example, family size is important in the purchase of a car.

A **household** is a broader concept than a family. It consists of a single person, a family, or any group of unrelated persons who occupy a housing unit. Thus an unmarried homeowner, college students sharing an off-campus apartment, and cohabiting couples are examples of households.

This distinction between family and household stems from relatively recent changes in the "typical" household. At one time, marketers could safely assume that a household consisted of a married couple and their children. As discussed in previous chapters, this is no longer the case.

Sensitivity to household structure is important in designing marketing strategy. It affects such dimensions as product size (How large should refrigerators be?) and the design of advertising (Is it appropriate to depict a traditional family in a TV ad?).

In addition to the direct, immediate impact households have on the purchase behaviour of members, it is also interesting to consider the buying behaviour of the household as a unit. Who does the buying for a household? Marketers should treat this question as four separate ones because each may call for different strategies:

- Who influences the buying decision?
- Who makes the buying decision?
- Who makes the actual purchase?
- Who uses the product?

Different people may assume these various roles, or one individual may play several roles in a particular purchase. In families, for many years the female household head did most of the day-to-day buying. However, this behaviour has changed as more women have entered the work force and men have assumed greater household responsibility. Night and Sunday business hours in stores in suburban shopping centres in some provinces also encourage men to play a bigger role in family purchasing.

In recent years, teenagers and young children have become decision makers in family buying, as well as actual shoppers. Canadian teenagers could represent a $10 billion market by the year 2000, up from $6 billion today.[10] This

---

[10]Kenneth Kidd, "Teen Pockets Run Deep," *Globe and Mail*, March 3, 1991, pp. B1-B2.

certainly is enough to warrant the attention of many manufacturers. Even very young children influence buying decisions today because they watch TV advertising and ask for products when they shop with their parents. Purchasing decisions are often made jointly by husband and wife. Young couples are much more likely to make buying decisions on a joint basis than older couples are. Apparently the longer a couple lives together, the more they feel they can trust each other's judgement.

Knowing which family member is likely to make the purchase decision will influence a firm's entire marketing mix. If children are the key decision makers, as is often the case with breakfast cereals, then a manufacturer will produce something that tastes good to children, design the package with youngsters in mind, and advertise on Saturday morning cartoon shows. This would be done regardless of who actually makes the purchase and who else (besides the children) in the household might eat cereal.

PSYCHOLOGICAL FACTORS

In discussing the psychological component of consumer behaviour, we will continue to use the model presented in Fig. 6-1. One or more motives within a person activate goal-oriented behaviour. One such behaviour is perception, that is, the collection and processing of information. Other important psychological activities are learning and attitude formation. We then consider the roles that personality and self-concept play in buying decisions. These psychological variables help to shape a person's life-style and values. The term psychographics is being used by many researchers as a synonym for those variables and life-style values.

Motivation — The Starting Point

To understand why consumers behave as they do, we must first ask why a person acts at all. The answer is, "Because he or she experiences a need." All behaviour starts with a recognized need. A **motive** is a need sufficiently stimulated that an individual is moved to seek satisfaction. Security and prestige are examples of needs that may become motives.

A need must be aroused or stimulated before it becomes a motive. We have many dormant needs that do not activate behaviour because they are not sufficiently intense. Thus hunger that is strong enough that we search for food and fear great enough that we seek security are examples of aroused needs that become motives for behaviour.

Explanations for behaviour can range from simple to unexplainable. To illustrate, buying motives may be grouped on three different levels depending on consumers' awareness of them and their willingness to divulge them. At one level, buyers recognize, and are quite willing to talk about, their motives for buying certain products. At a second level, they are aware of their reasons for buying but will not admit them to others. A man may buy a luxury car because he feels it adds to his social position in the neighbourhood. Or a woman may buy a leather coat to keep up with her peer group. But when questioned about their motives, they offer other reasons that they think will be more socially acceptable. The most difficult motives to uncover are those at the third level, where even the buyers themselves cannot explain the real factors motivating their buying actions.

To further complicate our understanding, a purchase is often the result of multiple motives. Moreover, various motives may conflict with one another. In buying a new dress, a young woman may want to (1) please herself, (2) please her boyfriend, (3) be considered a fashion leader by other young women in her social circle, and (4) strive for economy. To accomplish all of these objectives in one purchase is truly a difficult assignment. Also a person's buying behaviour changes because of changes in income, life-style, and other factors. Finally, identical behaviour by several people may result from quite different motives, and different behaviour by the same person at various times may result from the same motive.

CLASSIFICATION OF MOTIVES

Psychologists generally agree that motives can be grouped in two broad categories: (1) needs aroused from *physiological states* of tension (such as the need for sleep) and (2) needs aroused from *psychological states* of tension (such as the needs for affection and self-respect).

The psychologist Abraham Maslow formulated a theory of motivation based on needs. He identified a hierarchy of five levels of needs, arrayed in the order in which people seek to gratify them.[11] This hierarchy is shown in Fig. 6-2. Maslow recognized that a normal person is most likely to be working towards need satisfaction on several levels at the same time and that rarely are all needs on a given level fully satisfied. However, the hierarchy indicates that the majority of needs on a particular level must be reasonably well satisfied before a person is motivated at the next higher level.

In their attempts to market products or communicate with particular segments, marketers often must go beyond a general classification like Maslow's to understand the specific motives underlying behaviour. For example, to observe that a consumer on a shopping trip may be satisfying physiological and social needs because he or she purchases food and talks to friends in the store may be correct, but it is not very useful. Addressing this issue, Edward Tauber described 13 specific motives reported by shoppers including recrea-

FIGURE 6-2
Maslow's hierarchy of needs.

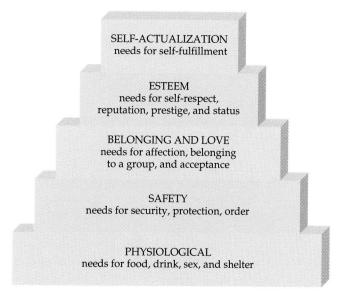

---

[11]A. H. Maslow, *Motivation and Personality*, Harper & Row, New York, 1954, pp. 80-106.

tion, self-gratification, sensory stimulation, peer group attraction, and status.[12] Using these motives, marketers are better prepared to design appealing products and stores. Much more needs to be done, however, to identify marketing-specific motives and to measure their strengths.

Perception   A motive is an aroused need. It, in turn, activates behaviour intended to satisfy the aroused need. One form that behaviour takes is collecting and processing information from the environment, a process known as **perception.** We constantly receive, organize, and assign meaning to stimuli detected by our five senses. In this way, we interpret or give meaning to the world around us. Perception plays a major role in the alternative identification stage of the buying-decision process.

What we perceive—the meaning we give something sensed—depends on the object and our experiences. In an instant, the mind is capable of receiving information, comparing it to a huge store of images in memory, and providing an interpretation.

Every day we come in contact with an enormous number of marketing stimuli. However, a process of selectivity limits our perceptions. As an illustration, consider that:

- We pay attention by exception. That is, of all the marketing stimuli our senses are exposed to, only those with the power to capture and hold our attention have the potential of being perceived. This phenomenon is called **selective attention.**
- We may alter information that is inconsistent with our beliefs and attitudes. thus someone may say, ''Despite the evidence, I don't believe smoking will be hazardous to my health.'' This is **selective distortion.**
- We retain only part of what we have selectively perceived. We may read an ad but later forget it. This is known as **selective retention.**

There are many communications implications in this selectivity process. For years advertisers in magazines have felt that the upper-left corner of a page gets more attention since we read from left to right and top to bottom. In a study for Bombay gin, researchers found that an ad got 28 percent more attention when it appeared above a magazine article rather than below it.

To gain attention, a stimulus must be sufficiently different from what the consumer expects or is used to. For example, Benetton ran ads for its Sisley clothing line upside down in *Rolling Stone.* In another bid for attention, an ad for Libby's canned meats had the product protruding outside the normal rectangular space into the editorial copy.[13] You have probably noticed headlines that run off the page and print ads that are mostly white space are more likely to get your attention than are traditional layouts.

As part of perception, new information is compared with a person's existing store of knowledge, or frame of reference. If an inconsistency is discovered, the new information will be distorted to conform to the established beliefs. Thus if a consumer believes foreign-made cars are better built than domestic ones, a claim of superior quality by Ford will be viewed as an exaggeration or an attempt at deception rather than as fact.

[12]Edward M. Tauber, ''Why Do People Shop?'' *Journal of Marketing,* October 1972, pp. 46-49.

[13]These examples are from Ronald Alsop, ''Advertisers See Big Gains in Odd Layouts,'' *The Wall Street Journal,* June 29, 1988, p. 25.

M A R K E T I N G   A T   W O R K

FILE 6-3 **PERCEIVING THE OFF-PRICE**

The off-price has always been popular with American retailers whose warehouse-type stores sell end-of-line shirts, sweaters left over from bankruptcies, or trousers that were never shipped by suppliers due to credit problems. However in Canada, from time to time, entrepreneurs who have attempted to start such off-price outlets have met with great resistance—mostly due to a national psychology of scepticism and caution. "There's too much resistance from the customer who's scared there might be something wrong," says Harold Weisfeld, owner of four off-price stores called Ends. Weisfeld has been lucky enough to carve out a profitable niche for himself selling discount clothing, but has found it difficult initially to attract Canadian consumers. Sometimes, although prices are 25 to 65 percent below the orignal retail prices suggested by manufacturers, stores' price tags sometimes understate the original selling price—for the sake of credibility. "If we tell the truth, sometimes we look like liars."

Source: Adapted from Kenneth Kidd, "Off-Price Outlets Put Canadians On Guard," *Globe and Mail*, November 28, 1990, p. 4.

To reduce distortion, advertisers strive for meaningful, strong messages that will be believed. A major factor influencing the believability of a message is the credibility of the source. Advertisers use recognized experts to endorse their products—Michael Jordan for Nike shoes and Wayne Gretzky for Zurich Canada insurance to add credibility to their messages.

Even messages received undistorted are still subject to selective retention. Consequently ads are repeated many times. The hope is that numerous exposures will etch the message into the recipient's memory.

Learning   **Learning** may be defined as changes in behaviour resulting from previous experiences. Thus it excludes behaviour that is attributable to instinct such as breathing or temporary states such as hunger or fatigue. The ability to interpret and predict the consumer's learning process enhances our understanding of buying behaviour since learning plays a role at every stage of the buying-decision process. No simple learning theory has emerged as universally workable and acceptable. However, the one with the most direct application to marketing strategy is the stimulus-response theory.[14]

Stimulus-response theory holds that learning occurs as a person (1) responds to some stimulus and (2) is rewarded with need satisfaction for a correct response or penalized for an incorrect one. When the same correct response is repeated in reaction to the same stimulus, a behaviour pattern or learning is established.

Research has shown that attitudes and other factors also influence a consumer's response to a given stimulus. Thus a learned response does not necessarily occur every time a stimulus appears.

---

[14]Other schools of thought on learning, principally the cognitive approach and gestalt learning, are discussed in books on consumer behaviour. See David Loudon and Albert J. Della Bitta, *Consumer Behaviour*, 3rd ed., McGraw-Hill, New York, 1988.

Four factors are fundamental to the process:

- **Drives,** or motives, are strong stimuli that require the person to respond in some way.
- **Cues** are signals from the environment that determine the pattern of response.
- **Responses** are behavioural reactions to the drive and cues.
- **Reinforcement** results when the response is rewarding.

If the response is rewarding, a connection among the drive, cues, and response will be established. Learning, then, emerges from reinforcement, and repeated reinforcement leads to a habit or brand loyalty. For example, a person motivated to shop *(drive)* who has found bargains *(reinforcement)* when going into stores *(response)* that have ''sale'' signs in their windows *(cues)* will respond *(learn)* by going into other stores with ''sale'' signs.

Once a habitual behaviour pattern has been established, it replaces conscious, willful behaviour. In terms of our model, this means that the consumer would go directly from the recognized need to purchase, skipping the steps in between. The stronger the habit (the more it has been reinforced), the more difficult it is for a competitive product to break in. On the other hand, if the learned response is not rewarding, the consumer's mind is open to another set of cues leading to another response. The consumer will try a substitute product or switch to another brand.

Personality   The study of human personality has given rise to many, sometimes widely divergent, schools of psychological thought. As a result, attempts to inventory and classify personality traits have produced a variety of different structures. In this discussion, **personality** is defined broadly as an individual's pattern of traits that influence behavioural responses. We speak of people as being self-confident, aggressive, shy, domineering, dynamic, secure, introverted, flexible, or friendly and as being influenced (but not controlled) by these personality traits in their responses to situations.

It is generally agreed that personality traits do influence consumers' perceptions and buying behaviour. However, there is considerable disagreement as to the nature of this relationship; that is, *how* personality influences behaviour. Although we know that people's personalities often are reflected in the clothes they wear, the cars they drive (or whether they use a bike or motorcycle instead of a car), and the restaurants they eat in, we have not been successful in predicting behaviour from particular personality traits. The reason is simple: many things besides personality enter into the consumer buying-decision process.

THE SELF-CONCEPT

Your **self-concept,** or self-image, is the way you see yourself. At the same time it is the picture you think others have of you. Psychologists distinguish between (1) the **actual** self-concept (the way you really see yourself) and (2) the **ideal** self-concept (the way you want to be seen or would like to see yourself). To some extent, the self-concept theory is a reflection of other psychological and sociological dimensions already discussed. A person's self-concept is influenced, for instance, by innate and learned physiological and psychological needs. It is conditioned also by economic factors, demographic factors, and social-group influences.

M A R K E T I N G   A T   W O R K

FILE 6-4   **THE FACE IN THE NINETIES' MIRROR**

A few hundred years ago, women with large bodies were considered ''voluptuous.'' In North America today, such women are simply considered fat. In the health-crazed 1980s and 1990s, more than ever before the cultural values of youth and appearance seem to be turning into an obsession, especially with women. Women's desires to conform provoke requests for Elizabeth Taylor's eyes, Isabella Rossellini's lips, and Kim Basinger's breasts, while more men are having work done on their noses, chins, and stomachs than ever before. Surgeons and social observers say mass media push the idea that only those who look young and beautiful can be successful, popular, or loved. This notion, when combined with medical technology, increased disposable income, and the age of the population, has led to a recent explosion in cosmetic surgery. In 1988, more than 40,000 operations were performed in Canada by over 300 surgeons. Even Santa Claus got in on the act. During Christmas of 1990, dozens of trendy teens in urban centres asked for and received Yuletide gifts of plastic surgery — girls getting liposuction to sculpt their cheeks and boys getting new noses.

Source: Adapted from Vivian Smith, ''Tens of Thousands Seek Beauty under the Knife,'' *Globe and Mail*, January 13, 1991, p. 1.

This hosiery ad relies on the ideal self-concept for its impact.

An extension

of the ego.

Ultra Silk.
In 17
couture
colors.

THE LADY PREFERS
Hanes

Levi's speaks to a well-defined segment's self-concept.

Be cool. It's strange out there.

Studies of purchases show that people generally prefer brands and products that are compatible with their self-concept. There are mixed reports concerning the degree of influence of the actual and ideal self-concepts on brand and product preferences. Some psychologists contend that consumption preferences correspond to a person's *actual* self-concept. Others hold that the *ideal* self-concept is dominant in consumers' choices.

Perhaps there is no consensus here because in real life we often switch back and forth between our actual and our ideal self-concepts. A middle-aged man may buy some comfortable, but not fashionable, clothing to wear at home on a weekend where he is reflecting his actual self-concept. Then later he buys some expensive, high-fashion exercise clothing, envisioning himself (ideal self-concept) as a young, active, upwardly mobile guy. This same fellow may drive a beat-up pickup truck for his weekend errands (actual self-concept). But he'll drive his new foreign sports car to work where he wants to project a different (ideal) self-concept.[15]

Attitudes

A classic definition of **attitude** is: a learned predisposition to respond to an object or class of objects in a consistently favorable or unfavorable way.[16] In our model of the buying-decision process, attitudes play a major role in the evaluation of alternatives. Numerous studies have reported a relationship between consumers' attitudes and their buying behaviour regarding both types of products selected and brands chosen. Surely, then, it is in a marketer's best interest to understand how attitudes are formed, the functions they perform, and how they can be changed.

All attitudes have the following characteristics in common:

- Attitudes are *learned*. The information individuals acquire through their direct experiences with a product or an idea, indirect experiences (such as reading about a product in *The Canadian Consumer*), and interactions with

[15]For an analytical review of self-concept studies, the research problems connected with these studies, and a comprehensive bibliography, see M. Joseph Sirgy, "Self-Concept in Consumer Behaviour: A Critical Review," *Journal of Consumer Research*, December 1982, pp. 287-300.

[16]Gordon W. Allport, "Attitudes," in C. A. Murchinson (ed.), *A Handbook of Social Psychology*, Clark University Press, Worcester, Mass., 1935, pp. 798–844.

M A R K E T I N G   A T   W O R K

FILE 6-5   GREGG ON ATTITUDES

The predictions of Allan Gregg are some of the most sought-after words in Canadian business. Gregg is the founder of polling firm Decima Research and in "one of the bitchiest, ego-driven industries anywhere" has achieved fame for his marketing analyses. Gregg sees a significant shift in Canadians' attitudes in the 1990s as the things "Canadians have held dear and believed to be true are increasingly falling by the wayside." Satiated with the quest for material goods and status symbols, consumers of all incomes will turn to systems such as education and health care and demand that they be improved —a dramatic shift from emphasis on quantity to quality of life. As Canadians' faith in national and public institutions falters, individuals will be demanding greater involvement in government and demanding greater attention from businesses, who will discover the profit-making sense of industrial and workplace reform: from on-site day care to environmental concerns. Business leaders will have to link good marketing with good morals.

Source: Adapted from Jennifer Wells, "The Big Think," *Financial Times of Canada*, December 31, 1990, p. 10-11.

---

their social groups all contribute to the formation of attitudes. For example, the opinions expressed by a good friend about garage sales plus the consumer's favourable or unfavourable experience as a result of going to garage sales will contribute to an attitude towards garage sales in general.

- Attitudes have an *object*. By definition, we can hold attitudes only towards something. The object can be general (professional sports) or specific (Toronto Blue Jays); it can be abstract (campus life) or concrete (the computer centre). In attempting to determine consumers' attitudes it is very important to carefully define the object of the attitude since a person might have a favourable attitude towards the general concept (health food) but a negative attitude towards a specific dimension (broccoli).
- Attitudes have *direction* and *intensity*. Our attitudes are either favourable or unfavourable toward the object. They cannot be neutral. In addition, they have a strength. For example, you may mildly like this text or you may like it very much (we hope!). This factor is important for marketers since both strongly held favourable and stongly held unfavourable attitudes are difficult to change.
- Finally, attitudes are arranged in structures that tend to be *stable* and generalizable. Once formed, attitudes usually endure, and the longer they are held, the more resistant to change they become. People also have a tendency to generalize attitudes. For instance, if a person is treated nicely by a sales clerk in a particular store, there is a tendency to form a favourable attitude towards the entire store.

A consumer's attitudes do not always predict purchase behaviour. A person may hold very favourable attitudes towards a product but not buy it because of some inhibiting factor. Typical inhibitors are not having enough money or discovering your preferred product or brand is not available when the purchase must be made. Under such circumstances, purchase behaviour may even contradict attitudes.

As the preceding discussion suggests, it is extremely difficult to change strongly held attitudes. Consequently when the marketer is faced with negative or unfavourable attitudes, there are two options. The first is to try to change the attitude to be compatible with the product. The second is to determine what the consumers' attitudes are and then change the product to match those attitudes. Ordinarily it is much easier to change the product than it is to change consumers' attitudes.

Nevertheless, in some situations, attitudes have been changed. Consider how negative attitudes have changed in favour of small cars, yellow tennis balls, off-season vacations, and coed dorms in universities.

Values and Life-styles

One of the most valuable ways of looking at a market and its potential involves consideration of consumer life-styles and values. Marketers now develop marketing programs based not only on how old their customers are or where they live, but also on how they spend their leisure time, what type of movies they like to watch, and what things they consider important in their lives. This is an integral part of the concept of market segmentation, which we discussed in Chapters 4 and 5. Essentially, the Canadian market is made up of many different types of people. Once we can identify how these various groups think and live, we can do a better job of developing products, services, advertising, and other marketing techniques to appeal to them.

Budget facilitates the getaway part of life-style.

CANADIANS AS LIFE-STYLE SEGMENTS

Trying to get a fix on the real you? According to the first Canada Lifestyle study, English Canadians over the age of 18 can be neatly divided into the following 14 "lifestyle segments":

Diana, "The Working Mother" (20%): Not a "mother who works" but a "worker with kids." Aggressively social, active, mobile and practical.

Sue, "The Social Single" (17%): A remnant of the "Me Generation." Well educated and a voracious cultural consumer but incapable of making commitments and fearful of marriage, family, and romance.

Liz, "The Upscale Pacesetter" (15%): An affluent, sophisticated homemaker who runs her home as if it were a business. Cultured, well educated, well informed, and confident.

Sara, "The Traditionalist" (12%): A middle-aged, middle-class housewife who lives according to the values she was brought up on. Thoughtful and articulate, she is constantly looking for ways to improve herself.

Brenda, "Blue Jeans Mother" (10%): A young, lower-income homemaker trying to cope with the transition from being a carefree single to the responsibilities of family life. Depends on a "strong leader"—either husband or father—and exercises thrift in her spending.

Fran, "The Happy Homemaker" (9%): Her interests are the family, home, and church, and she pours most of her energy into the home. Traditional, security conscious, and sceptical of women's lib.

Gran, (9%): Old-fashioned and traditional, she lives morally in the nineteenth century. More family oriented than any other segment.

Edna, "The Malcontent" (8%): Emotionally and intellectually negative, she is a homebody who hides within the fortress of her family. She sees only deterioration in the world around her.

Steve, "The Hardhat" (21%): Usually employed in a skilled trade, he is well paid but depressed by the routine of the working day. Conservative and materialistic, he admires strong leaders and can be prone to violence.

Ross, "The Urban Businessman" (20%): Well educated and status conscious, he is probably in a professional or executive position. Although he observes some traditions, he is progressive and modern in his thinking. He enjoys competition but lives in constant fear of failure.

Dave, "The Playboy" (17%): Extremely social, a swinger and a sportsman. Sensitive about his self-image, he avoids personal commitment but is determined to succeed professionally.

Henry, "The Old Guard" (16%): A gentleman, a churchman, and a traditionalist. Ultraconservative, he is disillusioned by the decline of morals in the contemporary world but is content with his own achievements.

Bert, "The Egotist" (13%): Chauvinistic and macho, he is obsessed with his masculinity. Most likely to work at a job that requires more strength than skill, he harbours fantasies about becoming a person of great strength who defies danger and wins the day.

Roy, "The Homespun Handyman" (13%): Canada's cowboy, fisherman, farmer, or artisan. Dedicated to his trade and his family, he has no illusions about social status and is happy with the old-fashioned way he has chosen to live.

Reprinted with permission from Ian Pearson, "Social Studies," *Canadian Business,* December 1985, p. 73.

The field of psychographic research was developed in the 1960s and initially examined consumer activities, interests, and opinions. A more recent development has been the use of a program known as VALS (Values, Attitudes, and Life-style), which was developed in the United States at the Stanford Research Institute. VALS research involves the study of thousands of consumers and measures their opinions, interests, attitudes, values, beliefs, and activities in a variety of different areas. Using sophisticated computer-based data analysis techniques, the developers of VALS have identified nine different segments or clusters of consumers in the U.S. population. In Canada, a similar study has revealed 14 different "life-style segments," eight female and six male (see box). The company that developed this way of looking at the market in Canada has given each segment a name and can describe personal attributes of its members.

SITUATIONAL INFLUENCE

These life-style or psychographic definitions of market segments are much more interesting and useful to the marketer than are segments based only on demographic characteristics such as age, income levels, and marital status. For example, groups for which convenience is of considerable importance represent target segments for home cleaning services and automatic teller machines. Often the situations in which we find ourselves play a large part in determining how we behave. Students, for example, act differently in a classroom than they do when they are in a stadium watching a football game. The same holds true of buying behaviour. You might get your hair cut because of an upcoming job interview. On vacation you might buy a souvenir that seems very strange when you get home. For a close friend's wedding gift, you might buy a fancier brand of small appliance than you would buy for yourself. These are all examples of **situational influences**, temporary forces associated with the immediate purchase environment that affect behaviour. Situational influence tends to be less significant when the consumer is very loyal to a brand and when the consumer is highly involved in the purchase. However, it often plays a major role in buying decisions. The five categories of situational influences are explained next.

When Consumers Buy— The Time Dimension

Marketers should be able to answer at least two time-related questions about consumer buying: Is it influenced by the season, week, day, or hour? What impact do past and present events have on the purchase decision?

The time dimension of buying has implications for promotion scheduling. Promotional messages must reach consumers when they are in a decision-making frame of mind. Marketers also adjust prices in an attempt to even out demand. For instance, supermarkets may offer double coupons on Wednesdays, usually a slow business day. If seasonal buying patterns exist, marketers can sometimes extend the buying season. There is obviously little opportunity to extend the buying season for Easter Bunnies or Christmas ornaments. But the season for vacations has been shifted to such an extent that winter and other "off-season" or "shoulder-season" vacations are now quite popular.

The second question concerns the impact of past or future events. For example, the length of time since you last went out to dinner at a nice restaurant may influence a decision on where to go tonight. Or the significance of an upcoming event, such as a vacation trip to a resort area, could result in a greater than normal amount of clothing purchases. Marketers need to know enough about the targeted consumers to anticipate the effects of these past and future events.

Where Consumers Buy — The Physical and Social Surroundings

Physical surroundings are the features of a situation that are apparent to the senses, such as lighting, smells, weather, and sounds. Think of the importance of atmosphere in a restaurant or the sense of excitement and action created by the sights and sounds in a gambling casino. Music can be an important element in a store's strategy.

The social surroundings are the number, mix, and actions of other people at the purchase site. You probably would not go into a strange restaurant with an empty parking lot. And in a crowded store with other customers waiting, you will probably ask the clerk fewer questions and spend less time comparing products.

How Consumers Buy — The Terms and Conditions of the Purchase

How consumers buy refers to the terms and conditions of sale as well as the transaction-related activities that buyers are willing to perform. Many more retailers sell on credit today than just a few years ago. Not only do consumers use credit for instalment purchases (to buy things today with future income), but many now use credit for convenience. The ability to use Visa or MasterCard to make a wide variety of purchases while not carrying cash is an attractive option to many consumers. Another recent development is the increase in purchases made by mail and phone. The growth of catalogue distribution and telephone shopping services has enabled consumers to buy everything from jewellery to food without setting foot in a store. Finally, the trend towards one-stop shopping has encouraged retailers to add even unrelated items to their basic mix of products. Consider, for example, the wide variety of goods found in what we call a drugstore.

Marketers have also experimented with transferring functions or activities to consumers. For instance, consumers have shown a willingness to assemble products, pack their own groceries, and buy in case quantities—all in exchange for lower prices.

Why Consumers Buy — The Objective of the Purchase

The intent or reason for a purchase affects the choices made. We are likely to behave very differently if we are buying a product for a gift as opposed to buying the same product for our personal use. When purchasing a wristwatch, a consumer may be most interested in one that will provide accurate time at a reasonable price. However, the appearance of a watch bought as a graduation present can be very important.

A marketer must understand the consumer's objective in buying the product in order to design an effective marketing mix. For example, the failure by most watchmakers to appeal to the functional, nongift watch market is what allowed Timex to be so successful with its reasonably priced product.

Conditions under Which Consumers Buy — States and Moods

Sometimes consumers are in a temporary state that influences their buying decisions. When you are ill or rushed, you may be unwilling to wait in line or you do not take the time or care that a particular purchase deserves. Moods can also influence purchases. Feelings such as anger or excitement can result in purchases that otherwise would not have been made. In the exciting atmosphere of a rock concert, for example, you might pay more for a commemorative T-shirt than you would under normal circumstances. Sales people must be trained to recognize consumers' moods and adjust their presentations accordingly.

Marketers have noticed the impact of a variety of situational influences, some easy to interpret and others somewhat baffling. For instance, the sale of lip balm can be explained by a combination of temperature, humidity, and wind. And a McCann-Erickson researcher noted that people are more susceptible to food ads on the day they shop for groceries, but food commercials on TV are not advisable too soon after the dinner hour. On the other hand, how do you explain why soft drink consumption goes up with wind velocity? When a particular situational influence becomes widely accepted and strongly embedded (such as the notion that orange juice is for morning consumption), overcoming it can be difficult. The marketer may have to carry out an extensive campaign utilizing various techniques with no guarantee of success.

Buying Motives of Business and Industrial Users

In general terms, everything we have said about the factors that influence the buying behaviour of consumers applies to business users. The difference is the importance of some factors in the buying process. These differences make business and industrial buying like a very organized form of family influenced buying. The person responsible for buying equipment, materials, supplies, and services for others to use in service agencies, manufacturing or retailing organizations is truly a family purchasing agent.

Business buying behaviour, like consumer buying behaviour, is initiated when an aroused need (a motive) is recognized. This leads to goal-oriented activity designed to satisfy the need. Once again, marketing practitioners must try to determine what motivates the buyer.

Business buying motives, for the most part, are presumed to be rational, and a business purchase normally is a methodical, objective undertaking. Business buyers are motivated primarily by a desire to satisfy the various users or ''specifiers'' within the organization (family) and, at the same time, to maximize their firms' profits. More specifically, their buying goal is to achieve the optimal combination of price, quality, and service in the products they buy for others. On the other hand, sales people would maintain that some business buyers seem to be motivated more towards personal goals that are in conflict with their employers' goals.

Actually, such buyers have two goals — to improve or secure their positions in their firms (self-interest) and to further their company's position (in profits, in acceptance by society). Sometimes these goals are mutually consistent, and sometimes they are in conflict. Obviously, the greater the degree of consistency, the better for both the organization and the individual. When very little mutuality of goals exists, the situation is poor. Probably the more usual situation is to find some overlap of interests, but also a significant area where the buyer's goals do not coincide with those of the firm. In these cases, a seller might appeal to the buyer both on a rational, ''what's-good-for-the-firm'' basis and on an ego-building basis. Promotional efforts attuned to the buyer's self-concept are particularly useful when two or more competing sellers are offering essentially the same products, prices, and services.

The Business Buying Process

Competition and the complexity of business marketing have encouraged companies to focus attention on the *total* buying process. Buying is treated as an ongoing relationship of mutual interest to both buyer and seller. As one example of this approach, researchers in a Marketing Science Institute study developed a framework to explain different types of business buying situations.[17]

---

[17]Patrick J. Robinson, Charles W. Faris, and Yoram Wind, *Industrial Buying and Creative Marketing*, Allyn and Bacon, Boston, 1967. For a different perspective on the buy-grid concept, see Joseph A. Belizzi and Phillip McVey, ''How Valid Is the Buy-Grid Model?'' *Industrial Marketing Management*, February 1983, pp. 57-62.

The model for this framework—called a **buy-grid**—is illustrated in Table 6-1. The model reflects two major aspects of the buying process: (1) the classes of typical buying situations and (2) the sequential steps in the buying process.

TABLE 6-1   **The Buy-Grid Framework**

Stages in the business buying process (buy phases) in relation to buying situations (buy classes)

Buy phases (stages in buying-decision process)	Buy classes		
	New class	Modified rebuy	Straight rebuy
1. Recognize the problem.	Yes	Maybe	No
2. Determine product needs.	Yes	Maybe	No
3. Describe product specifications.	Yes	Yes	Yes
4. Search for suppliers.	Yes	Maybe	No
5. Acquire supplier proposals.	Yes	Maybe	No
6. Select suppliers.	Yes	Maybe	No
7. Select an order routine.	Yes	Maybe	No
8. Evaluate product performance.	Yes	Yes	Yes

SOURCE: Adapted from Patrick J. Robinson, Charles W. Faris, and Yoram Wind, *Industrial Buying and Creative Marketing,* Allyn and Bacon, Inc., Boston, 1967, p. 14.

Three typical buying situations (called **buy classes**) were identified as follows: new tasks, modified rebuys, and straight rebuys. The **new task** is the most difficult and complex of the three. More people influence the new-task buying-decison process than influence the other two types. The problem is that new-information needs are high, and the evaluation of alternatives is critical. Sellers are given their best opportunity to be heard and to display their creative ability in satisfying the buyer's needs. Note the similarity in approach to the high-involvement consumer.

Straight rebuys—routine purchases with minimal information need no real consideration of alternatives—are at the other extreme. Buying decisions are made in the purchasing department, usually from a list of acceptable suppliers. Suppliers, especially those from new firms not on the list, have difficulty getting an audience with the buyer (the low-involvement consumer?). **Modified rebuys** are somewhere between the other two in time required, information needed, alternatives considered, and other characteristics. It is not too hard to see these three buy classes in the context of family-influenced buying behaviour.

The other major element in the buy-grid reflects the idea that the business buying process is a sequence of eight stages, called **buy phases.** The process starts with the recognition of a problem. It ranges through the determination and description of product specifications, the search for an evaluation of alternatives, and the buying act. It ends with postpurchase feedback and evaluation. This surely is reminiscent of the consumer's buying-decision process previously outlined in this chapter.

Multiple Buying Influences—The Buying Centre

One of the biggest problems in marketing to a business user is determining who in the organization buys the product. That is, who influences the buying decision, who determines the product specifications, who makes the buying decision, and who does the actual buying (places the order). These activities

MARKETING AT WORK

FILE 6-6 **DECISION MAKERS DON'T KNOW EVERYTHING**

When we think of advertising, we generally think of producers advertising to consumers, but before this occurs there is another stage of advertising—the business-to-business kind. The producers must decide which medium to use. In order to entice prospective advertisers, some media advertise exclusively for this purpose. Recently, TSN, the 24-hour sports cable TV network, launched a campaign to convince media decision makers that its predominantly male viewers buy more than beer and razor blades. TSN has undertaken campaigns like this in some marketing magazines but this effort is designed primarily to reach CEOs and other senior executives with client companies who don't read those publications. The campaign, which has been run on a weekly basis in the *Globe and Mail*'s Report on Business section, features photos of sweaty men in sports equipment juxtaposed with copy that reveals unexpected things about TSN's audience. One execution, for example, shows a muddy footballer with the headline "This man runs a 4.7 forty, bench presses 350 pounds, and sells flowers."

Source: Adapted from *Marketing*, "TSN Ads Make Their Daily Debut," October 15, 1990, p. 13.

typically involve several people—there is a **multiple or family type buying influence**—particularly in medium-sized and large firms. Even in small companies where the owner-managers make all major decisions, they usually consult with knowledgeable employees before making some purchases.

Understanding the concept of a buying centre is helpful in identifying the multiple buying influences and understanding the buying process in industrial organizations. A **buying centre** may be defined as all the individuals or groups who are involved in the purchasing decision-making process. Thus a buying centre includes the people who play any of the following roles.[18]

- **Users:** The people who actually use the product—perhaps a secretary, a production-line worker, or a truck driver.
- **Influencers:** The people who set the specifications and aspects of buying decisions because of their technical expertise, their financial position, or maybe even their political power in the organization.
- **Deciders:** The people who make the actual buying decision regarding the product and the supplier. A purchasing agent may be the decider in a straight rebuy situation. But someone in top management may make the decision regarding whether to buy an expensive computer.
- **Gatekeepers:** The people who control the flow of purchasing information within the organization and between the buying firm and potential vendors. These people may be purchasing agents, secretaries, receptionists, or technical personnel.

[18]Frederick E. Webster, Jr., and Yoram Wind, "A General Model for Understanding Organizational Buying Behavior," *Journal of Marketing*, April 1972, pp. 12-19. Also see Webster and Wind, *Organizational Buying Behaviour*, Prentice-Hall, Englewood Cliffs, N.J., 1972, especially pp. 75-87; and Thomas V. Bonoma, "Major Sales: Who *Really* Does the Buying," *Harvard Business Review*, May/June 1982, pp. 111-119.

- **Buyers:** The people who select the suppliers, arrange the terms of sale, and process the actual purchase orders. Typically, this is the purchasing department's role. But again, if the purchase is an expensive, complex new buy, the buyer's role may be filled by someone in top management.

Several people in an organization may play the same role — for example, there may be several users of the product. Or the same person may occupy more than one role. A secretary may be a user, an influencer, and a gatekeeper in the purchase of an office machine.

The size and composition of a buying centre will vary among business organizations. Also, within a given organization, the size and makeup of the buying centre will vary depending on the product's expense, complexity, and length of life. The buying center for a straight rebuy of office supplies will be quite different from the centre handling the purchase of a building or a fleet of trucks.

It is probably obvious that the variety of people involved in any business buying situation, plus the differences among companies, present some real challenges to sales people. As they try to determine "who's on first" — that is, determine who does what in a buying situation — the sales reps often will call on the wrong executives. Even knowing who the decision makers are is not enough — these people may be very difficult to reach.

SUMMARY

The focus of this chapter is ultimate consumers and business firms that also purchase goods and services. The consumer discussion is built around a five-part model — the buying-decision process, information, social and group forces, psychological forces, and situational factors.

The buying-decision process is composed of six stages consumers go through in making purchases. The stages are need recognition, choice of an involvement level, identification of alternatives, evaluation of alternatives, decision, and postpurchase behaviour.

Information is the fuel that drives the buying-decision process. Without it there would be no decisions. There are two information sources — the commercial environment and the social environment. Commercial sources include advertising, personal selling, telemarketing, and personal involvement with a product. Word of mouth, observation, and experience with a product owned by someone else are social sources.

Social and group forces are composed by culture, subculture, social class, reference groups, family, and households. Culture has the broadest and most general influence, while household has the most immediate impact. Social and group forces have a direct impact on the individual purchase decisions and on the psychological makeup of an individual.

Psychological forces that affect buying decisions are motivation, perception, learning, personality, and attitudes. All behaviour is motivated by some aroused need. Perception is the way we interpret the world around us and is subject to three types of selectivity: attention, distortion, and retention. Learning is a change in behaviour as a result of experience. Stimulus-response learning involves drives, cues, responses, and reinforcement. Continued reinforcement leads to habitual buying and brand loyalty.

Personality is the sum of an individual's traits that influence behavioural responses. The self-concept, or the way we see ourselves and the way we think others see us, is related to personality. Because purchasing and consumption are very expressive actions, they allow us to communicate to the world our ideal self-concepts.

Attitudes are learned predispositions to respond to an object or class of objects in a consistent fashion. Besides being learned, all attitudes are directed towards an object, have direction and intensity, and tend to be stable and generalizable. Strongly held attitudes are difficult to change. Values and lifestyles provide rich psychologically and social-group-based descriptions of consumers and their behaviour.

Situational influences deal with when, where, how, and why consumers buy, and the consumer's personal condition at the time of purchase. Situational influences are often so powerful that they can override all of the other forces in the buying-decision process.

The business and industrial market differs from the consumer market in a number of important ways. Business buying is more like family decision making in the consumer market. The buy-grid framework indicates the business buying-decision process for each of the buy classes: new, modified rebuy, straight rebuy. The buying centre concept helps in identifying the influences commonly brought to bear on the buying decision. The logical five-stage process the consumer goes through in making a buying decision is very similar to the eight stages in the business buying process.

Marketers must be aware that while business users are more deliberate in their buying than are many consumers, they are also human and influenced by their work, family, recreational, and other large and small reference groups. Thus, in general terms, the factors that influence consumer perceptions also influence those of business buyers. While there are important differences in detail, the same general principles of buyer behaviour apply to both consumer and business markets.

KEY TERMS AND CONCEPTS

QUESTIONS AND PROBLEMS

1. Which needs in Maslow's hierarchy might be satisfied by each of the following products or services?
   a. Home burglary alarm system.
   b. Pepsi-Cola.
   c. *World Book Encyclopedia.*
   d. Body lotion.
   e. Chartered accountant.
   f. Starting your own business.

2. Explain what is meant by the selectivity process in perception.

3. Discuss the concept of a small reference group, explaining the meaning of the concept and its use in marketing.

4. Explain how factors of *when* and *where* people buy might affect the marketing program for each of the following products:
   a. House paint.
   b. High-quality sunglasses.
   c. Outboard motors.
   d. Room air conditioners.

5. Distinguish between *drives* and *cues* in the learning process.

6. Describe the differences you would expect to find in the self-concepts of an insurance sales person and an assembly-line worker in an automobile plant. Give some examples of resultant buying behaviour. (Assume that both have the same income.)

7. Following is a series of headlines or slogans taken from advertisements of various retailers. To what patronage motive does each appeal?
   a. ''Factory-trained mechanics at your service.''
   b. ''We never close.''
   c. ''One dollar down, no payments until the strike is over.''
   d. ''We treat you like a somebody.''
   e. ''We won't be undersold.''

8. What causes cognitive dissonance to increase in a buying situation? What can a seller do to decrease the level of dissonance in a given purchase of the seller's product?

9. Select four of the buy phases in the industrial buying process and explain how the relative importance of each one changes, depending upon whether the buying situation is a new task or a straight rebuy.

10. What suggestions do you have for business sellers to help them determine who influences the buying decision among business users?

11. In the buying centre in an industrial organization, discuss briefly the role of each of the following:
    a. Influencers.
    b. Buyers
    c. Gatekeepers.

12. Explain how business buying is like family-influenced buying of consumer goods.

CHAPTER 7 GOALS

A marketing system runs on current, accurate information—about the market, the macroenvironment, and internal and external operations. This chapter is concerned with the sources and uses of such information. After studying this chapter, you should understand:

- Marketing information systems—what they are, why they are needed, and how they are used.
- The relationship between a marketing information system and marketing research.
- The role of marketing research.
- The procedure in marketing research investigations.
- The current status of marketing research.

Marketing Information Systems and Marketing Research

*D*espite extremely high satisfaction levels reported by owners of Honda lawnmowers, a research study revealed a very low level of awareness of the lawnmower line among non-owners. Honda Power Equipment decided to trade upon the excellent reputation of Honda cars and motorcycles by running a series of television and outdoor advertisements with the headline: "We also make fine automobiles."

- Research conducted for Canada Post showed that only 4.4 percent of Canadians collect stamps and that 50 percent of philatelists are aged 35 and older. In an effort to encourage more young people to take up stamp collecting, Canada Post entered into marketing arrangements with corporate sponsors such as McDonald's and Petro-Canada to promote interest in stamps.

- A study conducted for Participaction has shown that 25 to 30 percent of Canadians are actively engaged in fitness or exercise, and that 15 percent do not exercise and probably never will. As a result, Participaction has targeted the remaining 55 percent who are aware of Participaction and its objectives, but do not now exercise regularly.

- While 38 percent of female respondents in a survey said that they "enjoy shopping a lot," the corresponding figure for men was only 13 percent. In fact, many men seem to feel so uncomfortable shopping in retail stores that they willingly allow their spouses and partners to buy clothing for them. Another study showed that 58 percent of men's underwear and 76 percent of men's bathrobes and pyjamas are bought by women.

- Research conducted for Everfresh, a line of mineral water with pure fruit juice, identified an emerging set of priorities among Canadian adults — a desire for a more balanced life-style and for diversity of experience, a heightened sense of social responsibility, and an increased concern for family and self.

- A series of focus group interviews was conducted for Beaver Lumber, prior to the development of an advertising campaign. In those groups containing only men, participants confessed that they suffered from a humiliating sense of ignorance about tools, they regularly make mistakes in their attempts at repairs and renovations, and they live in fear of embarrassing themselves doing fix-it jobs around the home.

The above companies and organizations all had one thing in common. They needed information to aid them in decision making regarding their stated problems. Some years ago, Marion Harper, Jr., then president of a large advertising agency, said, ''To manage a business well is to manage its future; and to manage the future is to manage information.'' That statement applies today in any organization—business or nonbusiness, profit or nonprofit, domestic or international.

Management in any organization needs information—and lots of it—about potential markets and environmental forces. In fact, *one essential requirement for success in strategic marketing planning is information — effectively managed.* Today a mass of information is available both from external sources and from within a firm. The problem, however, is to sort it out and use it effectively— to manage it. This is the role of a marketing information system. The use of this tool should permeate every phase of a company's marketing program. For this reason, we discuss information management after we have introduced the marketing environment, market demographics and buying power, and consumer and industrial buying behaviour. It is the effective use of marketing information that makes possible market segmentation strategy—Chapter 4— and programming the marketing mix elements—Parts 3, 4, 5, and 6, which follow.

WHAT IS A MARKETING INFORMATION SYSTEM?

With the popularization of computers as business tools in the late 1950s and early 1960s, expanded data manipulation and storage capability became important aids in marketing decision making. What quickly developed was the **marketing information system (MkIS)**—a concept that is still evolving today. An MkIS is an ongoing, organized set of procedures and methods designed to generate, analyze, disseminate, store, and retrieve information for use in making marketing decisions. The ideal MkIS has the ability to:

- Generate regular reports and ad hoc studies as needed.
- Integrate old and new data to provide information updates and identify trends.
- Analyze data using mathematical models that represent the real world.
- Allow managers to get answers to ''what if'' questions. (For example, ''What if we increase our TV advertising in Western Canada 20 percent and add 10 percent to inventories?'')

The increased use of personal computers, ''user friendly'' software, and the ability to link computer systems at different locations (networking) have greatly enhanced the potential of MkIS.

The value and, ultimately, the success of an MkIS depends on three factors:

- The nature and quality of the data available to it, much of which is produced from marketing research.
- The accuracy and realism of the models and analytic techniques applied to the data.
- The working relationship between the operators of the MkIS and the managers who use the output.

The availability of more sophisticated computer hardware and software has led to the development, particularly in larger companies, of the most current form of MkIS, labelled a **Marketing Decision-Support System** (MDSS). Such a system utilizes data bases of information that are compiled from a variety of sources and that then may be accessed and manipulated by the marketing

MARKETING AT WORK

FILE 7-1   **FREE TRADE MEANS MORE RESEARCH**

As the global economy evolves into strategic north-south trading blocks, Canada's trading importance with the United States will be further enhanced. From a U.S. perspective, knowledge of Canadian business customers lags greatly behind that of U.S. business customers. This is a problem for business marketers in Canada as they have had to rely extensively on existing U.S. marketing data and field intelligence from their Canadian sales people. The lack of sound business and industrial research has been a chronic problem for marketers in Canada. Much of it stems from the fact that Canadian business marketers are very sales-driven and not market-driven, as in the U.S. However, the strong trend towards customer service in recent years has provided incentives to conduct research into business consumer attitudes as this is one area where competitors can provide meaningful differences. The Canada-U.S. free trade pact will lead to additional market research from both Canadian and U.S.-based companies in the years to come.

Source: Adapted from Jon Arnold, "Biz-to-biz Research is Rare in Canada, but Situation Changing," *Marketing News*, March 4, 1991, vol. 25, p. 10.

---

decision maker, using appropriate computers and software. The benefits associated with an MDSS, which are not present in less sophisticated information systems, relate to the interactive nature of the system. Data are collected and continuously added to the system, from a variety of internal and external sources. These data may then be accessed by managers, combined with data from other sources, and presented in a form that addresses a marketing problem and in a manner that should be of interest to other departments of the company as well.[1]

Need for a Marketing Information System

Today many environmental forces dictate that every firm manage its marketing information as effectively as possible. Let's consider some of these factors and their relationship to information management:

- Executives have less time for decision making. Companies are being forced to develop and market new products more quickly than ever before.
- Marketing activity is becoming increasingly complex and broader in scope. Companies are expanding their markets, and many operate in both domestic and foreign markets.
- Energy, labour, and other raw materials are becoming more costly. Firms must make more efficient use of resources and labour in order to compete.
- Customer expectations are growing. The lack of timely, adequate information about a problem with some aspect of an organization's marketing program can result in lost business.
- The quantity of information is expanding. Computer technology has made

---

[1]See James G. Barnes, *Research for Marketing Decision Making*, Toronto: McGraw-Hill Ryerson Limited, 1991, pp. 15–16; and Louis A. Wallis, *Decision-Support Systems for Marketing*, Conference Board Research Report No. 923. New York: The Conference Board, Inc., 1989.

so much information available that the challenge often is to figure out what to do with it.

A marketing information system can help marketers cope with each of these dynamic forces.

Benefits of an MkIS

An organization generates and gathers much information in its day-to-day operations, and much more is available to it. But unless the company has some system to retrieve and process these data, it is unlikely that it is using its marketing information effectively.

A well-designed MkIS can provide a fast and more complete information flow for management decision making. The storage and retrieval capability of an MkIS allows a wider variety of data to be collected and used. Management can continually monitor the performance of products, markets, sales people, and other marketing units in detail.

A marketing information system is of obvious value in a large company where information is likely to get lost or distorted as it becomes widely dispersed. However, experience shows that integrated information systems can also upgrade management's performance in small and medium-sized firms.

The broad array of types and prices of computer hardware and software currently available brings MkIS capability to almost any organization. Figure 7-1 illustrates the characteristics and operation of an MkIS.

FIGURE 7-1
The structure of a marketing information system.

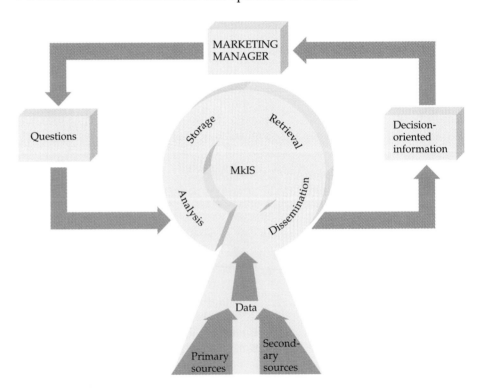

Relationship between MkIS and Marketing Research

The relationship between marketing information systems and marketing research is perceived quite differently by different people. Some see an MkIS as a logical, computer-based extension of marketing research. Others see the two as distinctly different activities, related only to the extent that they both deal with the management of information.

When this latter approach is accepted, marketing research tends to be conducted on a project-by-project basis, with each project having a starting and ending point. Projects often tackle unrelated problems on an intermittent, almost as-needed basis. Marketing research focuses on past events and their consequences to solve current problems.

This project orientation is reflected in the definition endorsed until recently by the American Marketing Association (AMA): Marketing research is the ''systematic gathering, recording, and analyzing of data relating to the marketing of goods and services.''[2] By this definition marketing research is a small part of the MkIS. Its function is simply to provide and process data. But researchers have taken issue with this limited role, suggesting that it excludes involvement with problems, ideas, actions, and decisions from marketing research.[3] According to the definition, a researcher would not generate hypotheses, test theories, or participate in setting strategy.

Thus, the AMA has adopted a new definition, which is intended to reflect marketing research in the 1990s. This definition states that **marketing research** links the consumer, customer, and public to the marketer through information — information used to identify and define marketing opportunities and problems; generate, refine, and evaluate marketing actions; monitor marketing performance; and improve understanding of marketing as a process. Marketing research specifies the information required to address these issues; designs the methods for collecting information; manages and implements the data collection process; analyzes the results; and communicates the findings and their implications.[4]

This rather lengthy definition differs from its predecessor in two major ways. First, it emphasizes the researcher's responsibility to develop managerially useful *information* rather than simply generate data. Second, the new definition proposes greater *involvement* for researchers in the decision-making process. If it is widely accepted and implemented, the definition will resolve the debate.

Marketing research as it is conventionally known, consisting of both qualitative and quantitative forms of research, represents one of the principal sources, but not the sole source, of information that flows into the marketing information system. The data that represent the input may come from either primary or secondary sources, and may be either internal or external to the firm. Reports generated from internal data, reports on competitors' activities, market projections by trade associations and economists, data from secondary sources such as governments and universities, as well as the firm's own marketing research activities, all represent important inputs into the marketing information system.

At this point, we will turn to the subject of marketing research. We will discuss (1) its scope within companies and organizations; (2) typical procedures in a marketing research study; (3) organizational structures for conducting research; and (4) the current status of the marketing research field.

---

[2]''Report of the Definitions Committee of the American Marketing Association,'' American Marketing Association, Chicago, 1961.

[3]Lawrence D. Gibson, ''What Is Marketing Research?'' Vol. 1, No. 1, *Marketing Research*, March 1989, pp. 2–3.

[4]''New Marketing Research Definition Approved,'' *Marketing News*, Vol. 21, No. 1, Jan. 2, 1987, p. 1.

SCOPE OF MARKETING RESEARCH ACTIVITIES

The scope of marketing research activities that are typically practised by larger companies in particular is reflected in Table 7-1. These results from a recent Canadian study indicate the percentage of companies that currently engage in each of these types of research.[5] Some of the results are particularly interesting and reflect the activities and interests of businesses in the 1990s. For example, approximately 90 percent of companies indicated that they monitor market share and market trends, and close to 80 percent analyze profits and costs and perform market and sales forecasts. The relatively small percentage engaged in plant location studies and channel performance research probably reflects the fact that many companies are not engaged in the manufacture and distribution of physical products. It is encouraging to see that a very large percentage of the companies who responded to the study indicated that they are carrying out research in the areas of service quality and customer satisfaction. Possibly surprising is the fact that only 20.9 percent of respondents indicated that they are conducting export or international research.

Using marketing research to communicate benefits.

It took Fisher-Price and 2,043 mothers to design a high chair like this.

For example: you told us that you have only two hands and one of them is juggling the baby.

So we designed our high chair tray to slide in or out with one hand. And to clip onto the side, freeing *both* hands. (It's also sloped a bit, to keep spills away from the spiller.)

Then we eliminated cereal-catching crannies. And both the seat cushion and safety belt come off to make this the easiest-to-clean high chair ever.

There's a handy rack in back to hang up bibs and a towel. And as sturdy and stable as it is, our chair folds flat in one easy motion.

So, if you love this high chair, and we think you will, it's all because Fisher-Price® listens to experts like you.

Traditional wood chair with same wraparound tray.

---

[5]James G. Barnes and Eva Kiess-Moser, *Managing Marketing Information for Strategic Advantage*, Ottawa: The Conference Board of Canada, 1991.

TABLE 7-1 **Selected marketing research activities of larger Canadian companies**

Subject areas examined	% doing
Business/economic and corporate research:	
Industry/market characteristics and trends	91.5
Market share analyses	89.7
Corporate image research	72.3
Quality/satisfaction research:	
Customer satisfaction research	81.6
Customer profiling and segmentation research	74.1
Service quality research	70.9
Product quality research	68.4
Pricing Research:	
Profit analysis	80.9
Demand analysis research:	
Market potential	77.0
Sales potential	74.5
Sales forecasts	77.0
Cost analysis	76.2
Product Research:	
Concept development/testing	66.3
Competitive product studies	52.5
Testing existing products	50.0
Test marketing	45.4
Distribution Research:	
Plant/warehouse location studies	38.7
Channel performance studies	31.6
Advertising and Promotion Research:	
Copy testing	52.5
Sales force compensation studies	51.4
Media research	48.9
Public image studies	47.9
Advertising post-testing	42.9
Buyer Behaviour Research:	
Market segmentation research	56.4
Brand awareness research	48.2
Brand image/attitudes	47.5
Purchase intentions research	46.5

SOURCE: James G. Barnes and Eva Kiess-Moser, *Managing Marketing Information for Strategic Advantage*, Ottawa: The Conference Board of Canada, 1991.

Much of the marketing research conducted by Canadian business tends to be done on behalf of larger companies. Among companies with annual sales in excess of $5 million, 50 percent have an organized marketing research department and an additional 28 percent have at least one person with responsibility for marketing research. Typically in these companies, marketing research departments are quite small, averaging 3.8 employees, including researchers and support staff. The small size reflects the fact that most com-

MARKETING AT WORK

FILE 7-2 **LET YOUR FACE SAY IT**

Emotional response is the latest technique being used to develop commercials. Canada Life has recently launched a new TV and print ad campaign developed using Emotional Measurement System (EMS) research. With EMS, people are shown a commercial and then look at pictures of 53 different facial expressions. They are asked to pick the expressions that reflect how they felt after seeing the commercial. Canada Life chose to use a picnic scene in its ads because the research found people reacted in an ''Interested/Hopeful'' way. This corresponded well to the copy written under the picture saying, ''The single most enduring product we can offer our clients is financial peace of mind.''

Source: Adapted from *Marketing*, ''Ad Campaign Rated Using Picture Test,'' October 8, 1990, p. 11.

panies have the actual marketing research studies conducted on their behalf by outside marketing research specialists. The staff of the marketing research departments in most cases carry out studies of the economy and industry trends and will supervise the purchase of specialized research services from outside suppliers.

PROCEDURE USED IN MARKETING RESEARCH

The general procedure illustrated in Fig. 7-2 is applicable to most marketing research projects. Some of the steps are not needed in every project, however. The numbers in the following section headings correspond to the steps in Fig. 7-2.

1. Define the Objective

Researchers should have a clear idea of what they are trying to accomplish in a research project—that is, the goal of the project. Usually the objective is to solve a problem, but this is not always so. Often the purpose is to *define* the problem, or to determine whether the firm even *has* a problem. To illustrate, a manufacturer of commercial air-conditioning equipment has been enjoying a steady increase in sales volume over a period of years. Management decided to do a sales analysis. This research project uncovered the fact that, although the company's volume had been increasing, its share of the market had declined. In this instance, marketing research uncovered a problem that management did not know existed.

The following case history illustrates the first three steps in a marketing research project—namely, problem definition, situation analysis, and informal investigation. A small manufacturer of camera accessories developed a compact, 2 kg rechargeable power cell for use in professional flash photography. The general problem, as presented to an outside marketing research firm, was to determine whether the company should add this product to its line. A breakdown of the problem into parts that could be handled by research resulted in the following specific questions:

- What is the market demand for such a product?
- What additional features are desired, if any?
- What channels of distribution should be used for such a product?
- What will technology be like in the next five years?
- What will the competition be like in the next five years?

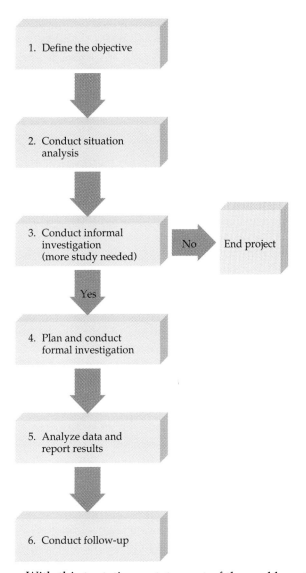

FIGURE 7-2
Marketing research procedure.

1. Define the objective

2. Conduct situation analysis

3. Conduct informal investigation (more study needed)

No → End project

Yes

4. Plan and conduct formal investigation

5. Analyze data and report results

6. Conduct follow-up

With this tentative restatement of the problem, the researchers were ready for the next procedural step, the situation analysis.

2. Conduct Situation Analysis

The **situation analysis** involves obtaining information about the company and its business environment by means of library research and extensive interviewing of company officials. The researchers try to get a "feel" for the situation surrounding the problem. They analyze the company, its market, its competition, and the industry in general.

In the situation analysis, researchers also try to refine the problem definition and develop hypotheses for further testing. A research **hypothesis** is a tentative supposition or a possible solution to a problem. A well-run project generates information to support or reject each hypothesis.

In the camera accessory case the situation analysis suggested the following hypotheses:

- There is adequate demand for the product.
- To reach the professional market, full-line camera stores should be emphasized in distributing the product.

- Advances in technology will not quickly make the product obsolete.
- Competition is not a serious threat to the product's success.

3. Conduct an Informal Investigation

Having gotten a feel for the problem, the researchers are now ready to collect some preliminary data from the marketplace. This **informal investigation** consists of gathering information from people outside the company—middlemen, competitors, advertising agencies, and consumers.

The researchers in the camera accessory case talked with many people outside the company. From telephone conversations with officials of trade associations representing photographers and photo equipment manufacturers, the researchers developed an estimate of the potential market for the product. This estimate suggested that the market was large enough to warrant further investigation. Fifteen photographers in three cities were then asked to evaluate the product itself as well as photographic practices in general. All liked the product, but they did suggest some product modifications.

To investigate channels of distribution, the researchers talked by telephone with several photo retailers across the country. The consensus was that the retailers would not stock this new product. The researchers then visited the annual Photo Marketing Trade Show to talk with more retailers and to get a line on the competition. Again, the retailers' reaction was negative. The researchers also learned that three major competitors soon would introduce rechargeable batteries that would compete directly with the new product. Furthermore, there was a rumour that a Japanese company soon would be entering the market.

The informal investigation is a critical step in a research project because it will determine whether further study is necessary. Decisions on the main problem can often be made with information gathered in the informal investigation. In fact, at this point the camera accessory company decided not to market its portable power cell.

4. Plan and Conduct the Formal Investigation

If the project warrants continued investigation, management and the researcher must determine what additional information is needed. The next step for the researcher is to plan where and how to get the desired data and then to gather them.

SELECT SOURCES OF INFORMATION

Primary data, secondary data, or both can be used in an investigation. **Primary data** are original data gathered specifically for the project at hand. **Secondary data** have already been gathered for some other purpose. For example, when researchers stand in a supermarket and observe whether people use shopping lists, they are collecting primary data. When they get information from Statistics Canada, they are using a secondary source.

One of the biggest mistakes made in marketing research is to collect primary data before exhausting the information available in secondary sources. Ordinarily, secondary information can be gathered much faster and at far less expense than primary data.

Syndicated data represent a third source of information that is a hybrid between primary and secondary data. Syndicated data are collected by a research supplier and may be purchased from that supplier by a number of clients, some of whom may be in direct competition with each other. The most common form of syndicated data involves the collection of data on a regular basis from an established sample or panel of consumers or retail stores. Clients subscribe to the reports, which are produced by the research company and essentially share the cost of collecting the data from the large sample. Although syndicated research does not provide privileged information to a single company, it does allow companies to obtain information on a shared-cost basis.

Sources of Secondary and Syndicated Data Several excellent sources of secondary information and syndicated data are available to marketers and marketing researchers in Canada. The following represents a summary of such sources; a much more detailed review of the main sources of secondary and syndicated data in this country may be found in Appendix A.

1. *Internal company records.* Information that the company already has in its files may be considered secondary data in the sense that it already exists. Companies regularly maintain orderly records of the reports of sales personnel, customer complaints, and sales by territory, product, and type of customer. When a problem must be addressed, the first place a company should go for information is its own files.

2. *Parent company records.* Many Canadian companies are subsidiaries of larger multinational companies. The parents and affiliates of these companies can often provide useful data on worldwide market conditions and on their experiences in foreign markets.

3. *Federal government.* The Government of Canada can furnish more marketing data than any other single source. Because of its legal powers to collect data, it has access to information that cannot be collected by private companies. Statistics Canada, as the statistical arm of government, collects much of the available information on behalf of government. Annual catalogues list the many publications of Statistics Canada and other departments and agencies of government.

4. *Provincial governments.* The provincial and territorial governments regularly produce reports and statistical summaries of broad economic interest. Many operate their own statistical offices, which produce reports of provincial statistics.

5. *Trade, professional, and business organizations.* Associations are excellent sources of information for their members. They often publish reports on surveys of members, and supply data of interest to outside groups. Some groups, such as the Conference Board of Canada and the Canadian Chamber of Commerce, which represent members with a wide variety of interests, will produce reports on an appropriately wide variety of topics. Others, such as the Canadian Bankers' Association, produce studies and reports specific to their industry.

6. *Advertising media.* Many magazines, newspapers, radio and television networks and stations, and outdoor advertising companies publish information that marketing researchers find useful. Such information usually relates to circulation data, station reach and coverage maps, and statistics on trading areas.

7. *University research organizations.* Some universities operate research units and publish research results that are of interest to business.

8. *Foundations.* Nonprofit research foundations and related groups carry out many research projects of interest to business. Such groups include the Conference Board of Canada, the C. D. Howe Institute, and the Institute for Research in Public Policy.

9. *Government-sponsored commissions*. Many government royal commissions, at both the federal and provincial levels, produce reports relating to business. Other permanent commissions, such as the Economic Council of Canada, publish annual reports and occasional studies on topics relating to the economy.

10. *Libraries*. For the marketing researcher and the student of marketing, a good library is probably the best, single, all-around source of secondary information. It will contain publications from practically all the sources listed above and from many others.

11. *Private research companies*. Private marketing research companies, advertising agencies, and other firms may be able to provide data needed by a marketer and represent the most important source of syndicated data. Companies such as A. C. Nielsen Company of Canada, Canadian Facts, and Market Facts of Canada conduct various kinds of marketing research and sell the results to clients who subscribe to their various services. Such syndicated data services are described in greater detail in Appendix A.

The risk with secondary data is that the user has no control over how, when, or why it was collected. As a result, the information may be inaccurate or dated. Or the definitions may not meet the user's needs. For example, a secondary source may define the "youth market" in terms of school grade but the user may need information by age. Thus researchers should check the source, motivation for the study, and key definitions before relying on secondary data.

Sources of primary data After exhausting all reasonable secondary sources of information, researchers may still lack sufficient data. Then they will turn to primary sources and gather the information themselves. In a company research project, for instance, a researcher may interview that firm's sales people, middlemen, or customers to obtain the pertinent market information.

DETERMINE METHODS FOR GATHERING PRIMARY DATA

There are three widely used methods of gathering primary data: survey, observation, and experimentation. A growth area in marketing research, which may be considered a branch of survey research, involves the collection of qualitative data. Normally all are not used on one project. The choice of method will be influenced by the availability of time, money, personnel, and facilities.

Survey Method A **survey** consists of gathering data by interviewing people. The advantage of a survey is that information is firsthand. In fact, it may be the only way to determine the opinions or buying intentions of a group.

Inherent in the survey method are certain limitations. There are opportunities for error in the construction of the survey questionnaire and in the interviewing process. Moreover, surveys can be very expensive, and they are time-consuming. Other weaknesses are that potential respondents sometimes refuse to participate and the ones who do respond often cannot or will not give true answers.

Survey interviews may be done by the researcher in person, by telephone, or by mail. **Personal interviews** are more flexible than the other two types because interviewers can probe more deeply if an answer is incomplete. Ordinarily it is possible to obtain more information by personal interview than by telephone or mail. Also the interviewer, by observation, can obtain data regarding the respondents' socioeconomic status — their home, neighbourhood, and apparent standard of living.

With mall intercept interviewing, the researcher knows that the respondents are actual shoppers.

Rising costs and other problems associated with door-to-door interviewing have prompted many marketing researchers to survey people in central locations, typically regional shopping centres. This technique is called the **shopping mall intercept** method of interviewing. By interviewing people as they pass through a shopping mall, the interviewer is better able to encounter large numbers of people, as the urban mall has essentially become the "main street" of North America. Although data collection is made somewhat easier by this method, the researcher is less confident that he or she is obtaining a representative sample of the population of interest. In such a situation, the ability to access large numbers of people at relatively low cost outweighs concerns about the representativeness of the sample.[6]

In a **telephone survey**, the respondent is approached by telephone, and the interview is completed at that time. Telephone surveys can usually be conducted more rapidly and at less cost than either personal or mail surveys. Since a few interviewers can make any number of calls from a few central points, this method is quite easy to administer. Computer-assisted techniques have broadened the scope of telephone interviewing. These techniques involve automated random-number dialling and a facility for the interviewer to record the respondent's answers directly into the computer as they are received. This technology speeds up the entry and processing of data and the production of reports.

A telephone survey can be timely. For instance, people may be asked whether they are watching television at the moment and, if so, the name of the program and the advertiser. One limitation of the telephone survey is that interviews cannot be too long, although telephone interviews that take 20 to 30 minutes to complete are not uncommon. In fact, one of the myths of telephone interviewing is that the questionnaire must be very short, because participants will not be willing to stay on the line for more than a minute or so. This is simply not so, as many Canadians appear quite co-operative in participating in surveys that take five to ten minutes to complete. What *is* making it more difficult to conduct telephone survey research is that progressively fewer people are at home, and those that are at home are becoming more difficult to reach. Although there appears to be no dramatic increase in the frequency of unlisted numbers, more and more people are installing telephone answering machines and are using them to screen incoming calls. The result is that telephone interviewers are unable to reach an increasing percentage of the population, thereby making telephone interviewing more costly and resulting in more biased samples.

Telephone surveys have been used successfully with executives at work. When preceded by a letter introducing the study and a short call to make an appointment for the actual interview, these surveys can elicit a very high co-operation rate.

Interviewing by mail involves mailing a questionnaire to potential respondents and having them return the completed form by mail. Since no interviewers are used, this type of survey is not hampered by interviewer bias or

---

[6]For discussion of the issue of the representativeness of the sample in mall-intercept surveys, as compared with other approaches to data collection, see Alan J. Bush and A. Parasuraman, "Mall Intercept versus Telephone-Interviewing Environment," *Journal of Advertising Research*, vol. 25, no. 2, April/May, 1985, pp. 36–43; and Thomas D. Dupont, "Do Frequent Mall Shoppers Distort Mall-Intercept Survey Results?" *Journal of Advertising Research*, vol. 27, August/September 1987, pp. 45–51.

MARKETING AT WORK

FILE 7-3 FROM CHANNEL HOPPING TO QUESTION HOPPING

Convenient ways to conduct marketing research has been a key problem for marketers. However, new technology may help lessen this problem. The Federal Communications Commission in the U.S. has proposed establishing a special TV broadcast frequency that could benefit marketers and marketing researchers. The frequency would allow TV viewers to interact with on-screen programs. Viewers could order products and services, respond to polls, and take college courses. In tests, a remote-control device and transmitter were placed in selected homes. The transmitter sent digitally encoded information, such as viewer responses to commercial or news polls, to a cell site that subsequently transmitted it by satellite to a mainframe computer for processing. So instead of dialing an 800 number, consumers just pressed a button to purchase goods. If the tests prove successful, interactive TV could be a trend of the future.

Source: Adapted from Cyndee Miller, ''FCC Proposes Frequency for Interactive TV,'' *Marketing News*, March 18, 1991, vol. 25 no. 6, p. 1.

---

problems connected with the management of interviewers. Mailed questionnaires are more economical than personal interviews and are particularly useful in national surveys. If the respondents remain anonymous, they are more likely to give true answers because they are not biased by the presence of an interviewer.

A major problem with mail questionnaires is the compilation of a good mailing list, especially for a *broad-scale* survey. If the sample can be drawn from a *limited* list, such as property taxpayers in certain counties, regions, or municipalities or subscribers to a certain magazine, the list presents no problem. Another significant limitation concerns the reliability of the questionnaire returns. The researchers have no control over who actually completes the questionnaire or how it is done. For example, a survey may be addressed to the male head of the household but because he is unavailable or not interested, his teenage daughter ''helps out'' by completing it. In addition, because there is no personal contact with the respondents, it is impossible to judge how much care and thought went into providing the answers.

Still another limitation is that there is usually a low response rate to a mail survey. It is not uncommon to receive completed replies from only 10 to 30 percent of those contacted. This is particularly important because if the respondents have characteristics that differentiate them from nonrespondents on certain dimensions of the survey, the results will be invalid. Techniques for improving mail response rates have been the subject of hundreds of experiments.[7]

---

[7]See, for example, Srinivasan Ratneshwar and David W. Stewart, ''Nonresponse in Mail Surveys: An Integrative Review,'' *Applied Marketing Research*, Summer 1989, pp. 37–46; Bruce J. Walker, Wayne Kirchmann, and Jeffery S. Conant, ''A Method to Improve Response to Industrial Mail Surveys,'' *Industrial Marketing Management*, November 1987, pp. 305–14.

Qualitative Research   While a survey is generally intended to collect numeric data, so that a researcher can say that a certain percentage of respondents preferred a certain brand or regularly watch a certain television program, qualitative research is intended to probe more deeply into the opinions and attitudes of people interviewed. To do so, the researcher must use different techniques. Consequently, qualitative research usually employs much smaller samples and interviews people in greater depth and for as long as 90 minutes or two hours. The two most widely used qualitative research techniques are the individual depth interview and the focus group interview.[8]

The **individual depth interview** is used in situations where the marketing researcher wishes to probe into the consumer's thoughts concerning his or her purchase and use of a certain product or service. It is conducted in an individual rather than a group format often because the topics to be discussed are sensitive ones or because the people are difficult to reach and would be unlikely to attend a focus group session. For example, the individual depth interview is often used to interview business executives and professionals. Such interviews often take one hour or more to complete and range over a number of different topics. The interviewer generally conducts the interview from a prepared interview guide or questionnaire.

In the case of the **focus group interview**, approximately eight to ten people are ''recruited'' to participate. They are usually selected to meet certain criteria relating to demographic characteristics, the use of a particular brand, frequent visits to certain vacation destinations, or similar criteria of interest to the researcher and client. The focus group interviewer or moderator orchestrates the discussion using a fairly unstructured interview guide, rather than the more structured questionnaire of the typical one-on-one interview. Many interesting and enlightening findings are revealed through focus group interviews, which have become one of the most widely used techniques in marketing research.[9]

Because these are qualitative marketing research techniques, their results are completely non-quantifiable. They do produce valuable insights into how consumers feel about certain concepts and why they make decisions as they do. The principal use of the focus group interview, for example, is to allow the marketer to really understand why customers are buying one brand over another, what they like and dislike about each, how they feel about the various brands in the marketplace, and what would have to happen for them to switch brands. Occasionally, marketing researchers will use the focus group technique to learn more about how consumers think about certain product categories or approach certain purchase decisions. They are then in a better position to design larger research surveys that may involve several hundred interviews with consumers.

Observational method   In the **observational method**, the data are collected by observing some action of the respondent. No interviews are involved,

[8]For additional detail on the use of the individual depth interview and the focus group interview, see James G. Barnes, *Research for Marketing Decision Making*, Toronto: McGraw-Hill Ryerson Limited, 1991, Chapter 12.

[9]For two interesting articles on the use of focus group interviews by Canadian firms, see Suanne Kelman, ''Consumers on the Couch,'' *Report on Business Magazine*, February 1991, pp. 50–53; and Jared Mitchell, ''The Truth Is Not for the Squeamish,'' *Report on Business Magazine*, March 1987, pp. 75–76.

although an interview may be used as a follow-up to get additional information. For example, if customers are observed buying beer in cans instead of bottles, they may be asked why they prefer that one form of packaging to the other.

Information may be gathered by personal or mechanical observation. In one form of personal observation, the researcher poses as a customer in a store. This technique is useful in getting information about the calibre of the sales people or in determining what brands they promote. Mechanical observation is illustrated by an electric cord stretched across a highway to count the number of cars that pass during a certain time period.

The observation method has several merits. It can be highly accurate. Often it removes all doubt about what the consumer does in a given situation. The consumers are usually unaware that they are being observed, so presumably they act in their usual fashion.

The observation technique reduces interview bias. However, the technique is limited in its application. Observation tells *what* happened, but it cannot tell *why*. It cannot delve into motives, attitudes, or opinions.

To overcome the biases inherent in the survey method, some firms are using sophisticated observational techniques that involve a combination of cable TV, electronic scanners in supermarkets, and computers. For example, some marketing research companies in Canada and the United States have established ''scanner panels.'' Selected households are invited to participate in a program that involves recording electronically every TV commercial watched in participants' homes; every purchase the participants make in supermarkets that are equipped with checkout scanners is electronically recorded. With this observational method, researchers can measure which products members of the households are buying and determine which TV commercials they have seen. It provides an improved link between advertising and purchase that allows for more accurate measurement of which advertising works and which does not.

The A.C. Nielsen Company and the BBM Bureau of Measurement have installed ''people meters'' in more than 2000 Canadian homes. These devices record electronically the channels to which TV sets are tuned and who is watching the programs. Computers are already programmed with data on each member of the households that participate in the panel. Data are recorded continuously and fed to a central computer each night, providing the TV networks and advertisers with detailed, timely, and accurate information concerning program audiences and the exposure of TV commercials.

Experimental method   An **experiment** is a method of gathering primary data in which the researcher is able to observe the result of changing one variable in a situation while holding all others constant. Experiments are conducted in laboratory settings and in the field. In marketing research, the word *laboratory* is used to describe an environment over which the researcher has complete control during the experiment.

Consider this example. A small group of consumers is assembled and presented with a brief product description and proposed package for a new breakfast cereal. After examining the package, the people are asked whether they would buy the product and their responses are recorded. Next a similar group of consumers is brought together and presented with the identical package and product information, except that a nutritional claim is printed on

Test your market with a taste test.

the package. This group is also asked if it would buy the product. Because the researcher had complete control over the test environment and the only thing changed was the nutritional claim on the package, any difference in buying intentions can be attributed to the claim.

Laboratory experiments can be used to test virtually any component of marketing strategy. However, it is important to recognize that the setting is unnatural and consumers' responses may be biased by the situation.

An experiment in the *field* is called test marketing. It is similar to a laboratory experiment but is conducted under more realistic conditions. The researcher therefore has less control. In **test marketing** the researcher duplicates real market conditions in a small geographic area to measure consumers' responses to a strategy before committing to a major marketing effort. Test marketing may be undertaken to forecast sales or to evaluate different marketing mixes.

The advantage of field experiments over laboratory experiments is their realism. However, there are several disadvantages. Test marketing is expensive ($500,000 is not uncommon), time-consuming (9 to 12 months is normal), and impossible to keep secret from competitors (who may intentionally disrupt the test by temporarily changing their marketing mixes). Another problem is the researcher's inability to control the situation. For example, a company that is test marketing a new product may encounter a certain amount of publicity while the product is in the test market, simply because of the innovativeness of the product. Although such publicity would normally be considered a good thing, when faced with it in a test market situation, the marketer is not sure to what extent it has distorted the sales results. In other words, what volume of sales resulted from the product and the regular marketing efforts of the company (what was actually being tested?), and what resulted from the publicity that was generated?

Because of its inherent limitations, the use of traditional test marketing declined as faster, less expensive alternatives were developed. One of these alternatives is the **simulated test market**, in which a sample of consumers is shown ads for the product being tested as well as for other products. The subjects are then allowed to ''shop'' in a test store that resembles a small grocery store. Follow-up interviews may be conducted immediately and also after the products have been used to better understand the consumers' behaviour. The entire set of data goes into a statistical model and sales for the product are forecast.

The potential benefits of simulated test marketing include:

- Lower costs than a traditional test market.
- Results in as little as eight weeks.
- A test can be kept secret.

The drawbacks are:

- Questionable accuracy for unique, new products.
- Application limited to traditional packaged goods.
- Inability to predict the response of competitors or retailers.
- Inability to test changes in marketing variables like packaging or distribution due to the simulation's short duration.[10]

---

[10]Howard Schlossberg, ''Simulated Vs. Traditional Test Marketing,'' *Marketing News*, October 23, 1989, pp. 1–2, 11.

Simulated test marketing has not replaced traditional test markets because of these limitations. In fact, the two methods are often used together, with the simulation results used to make marketing mix modifications before beginning the traditional test market.[11]

PREPARE DATA-GATHERING FORMS

When the interviewing or observation method is used, the researcher must prepare standard forms to record the information. However, the importance of the questionnaire in the survey method and the difficulty of designing it cannot be overemphasized. In fact, most of the problems in data collection, whether it is done by personal interview, mail, or telehone survey, centre on the preparation of the questionnaire. Extreme care and skill are needed in designing questionnaires to minimize bias, misunderstanding, and respondent anger.

SOME TYPICAL ERRORS IN QUESTIONNAIRE DESIGN

- The respondent feels the information requested is none of your business: What is your family's income? How old are you? What percentage of your home mortgage remains to be paid?
- Questions lack a standard of reference: Do you like a large kitchen? (What is meant by ''large''?) Do you attend church regularly?
- The respondent does not know the answer: What is your spouse's favourite brand of ice cream?
- The respondent cannot remember and, therefore, guesses: How many calls did you (as a sales rep) make on office supply houses during the past year?
- Questions are asked in improper sequence. Save the tough, embarrassing ones for late in the interview. By then, some rapport ordinarily has been established with the respondent. A ''none-of-your-business'' question asked too early may destroy the entire interview.

PRETEST THE QUESTIONNAIRE OR OTHER FORMS

No matter how good a researcher thinks the questionnaire is, it still should be pretested. This process is similar to field-testing a product. In pretesting, a questionnaire is simply tried out on a small number of people similar to those who will be interviewed. Their responses should tell the researcher whether there are any problems with the questionnaire.

PLAN THE SAMPLE

Normally, it is unnecessary to survey every person who could shed light on a given research problem. It is sufficient to survey only some of these people, if their reactions are representative of the entire group. However, before the data can be gathered, the researchers must determine whom they are going to survey. That is, they must plan or establish a sample. Sampling is no stranger to us because we employ it frequently in our everyday activities. We

---

[11]A useful comparison of various test marketing techniques is found in Patricia Greenwald and Marshall Ottenfeld, ''New Product Testing: A Review of Techniques,'' *Applied Marketing Research*, Summer 1989, pp. 17–24.

often base our opinion of a person on only one or two conversations with that person. We often take a bite of food before ordering a larger quantity.

The fundamental idea underlying the concept of **sampling** is as follows: If a small number of items (the sample) is selected at random from a larger number of items (called a "universe"), then the sample will have the same characteristics, and in about the same proportion, as the universe. In marketing research, sampling is another procedural step whose importance is difficult to overestimate. Improper sampling is a source of errors in many survey results. A survey of New Brunswick residents that was conducted only in English created a very biased picture of public opinion. By not surveying the French-speaking population of the province, the researchers had tapped a biased (unrepresentative) sample.

One of the first questions asked regarding sampling is: How large should the sample be? To be statistically reliable, a sample must be large enough to be truly representative of the universe or population.

To be statistically reliable, a sample must also be proportionate. That is, all types of units found in the universe must be represented in the sample. Also, these units must appear in the sample in approximately the same proportion as they are found in the universe. Assume that a manufacturer of power lawnmowers wants to know what percentage of families in a certain metropolitan area own this product. Further, assume that one-half of the families in the market live in the central city, and the other half in the suburbs. Relatively more families in the suburbs have power mowers than do families in the city. If 80 percent of the sample is made up of suburban dwellers, the percentage of families owning power mowers will be overstated because the sample lacks proportionality.

Several sampling techniques can be used in marketing research. Some of these are quite similar, and some are hardly ever used. For a basic understanding of sampling, we shall consider three types: (1) simple random samples, (2) area samples, and (3) quota samples. The first two are probability (random) samples, and the third is a nonrandom sample. A random sample is one that is selected in such a way that every unit in the predetermined universe has a known chance of being selected.

In a **simple random sample**, each unit in the sample is chosen directly from the universe. Suppose we wished to use a simple random sample to determine department store preferences among people in Ottawa, Ontario. We would need an accurate and complete listing of all people within the city limits. This would be our universe. Then in some random fashion we would select our sample from this universe.

A widely used variation of the simple random sample is the **area sample**. An area sample may be used where it is not economically feasible to obtain a full list of the universe. In the Ottawa department store study, for example, one way to conduct an area sample would be first to list all the blocks in the city. Then select a random sample of the blocks. Then every household or every other household in the sample blocks could be interviewed.

A **quota sample** is both nonrandom and stratified (or layered). Randomness is lost because the sample is "forced" to be proportional in some characteristic. Every element in the universe does *not* have an equal chance of being selected. To select a quota sample, the researchers first must decide which characteristic will serve as the basis of the quota. Then they determine in what proportion this characteristic occurs in the universe. The researchers then choose a sample with the same characteristic in the same proportion.

As an example, let us consider a research study of tourists who visit Nova Scotia during the summer of 1992. Interviewers might be stationed at airports, ferry terminals, and tourist information centres. The research company conducting the survey could decide to use a quota sample based on the tourists' place of residence. If we assume that the Nova Scotia Department of Tourism has secondary information — probably from earlier studies — that approximately 25 percent of the tourists who visit Nova Scotia are from Ontario, 15 percent from Quebec, 20 percent from other Atlantic provinces, 10 percent from Western provinces, and 30 percent from the United States, the researcher might then select a sample of vacationers in which 25 percent of the sample is from Ontario, 15 percent from Quebec, and so on. The sample is constructed on a nonrandom basis according to the place of residence of the tourist. That is, every tourist to Nova Scotia during the summer of 1992 does not have an equal chance of being included in the survey.

Random sampling has one big advantage. Its accuracy can be measured with mathematical exactness. In quota sampling, much reliance is placed on the judgement of those designing and selecting the samples. There is no mathematical way of measuring the accuracy of the results.

COLLECT THE DATA

The actual collection of primary data in the field — by interviewing, observation, or both — normally is the weakest link in the entire research process. Ordinarily, in all other steps, reasonably well-qualified people are working carefully to ensure the accuracy of the results. The fruits of these labours may be lost if the fieldworkers (data gatherers) are inadequately trained and supervised. The management of fieldworkers is a difficult task because they usually are part-time workers with little job motivation. Also, their work is done where it cannot be observed, often at many widely separated locations.

A myriad of errors may creep into a research project at this point, and poor interviewers only increase this possibility. Bias may be introduced because people in the sample are not at home or refuse to answer. In some instances, fieldworkers are unable to establish rapport with respondents. Or the interviewers revise the wording of a question and thus obtain untrue responses. Finally, some interviewers just plain cheat in one way or another.

5. Analyze the Data and Present a Report

The value of research is determined by the results. And since data cannot speak for themselves, analysis and interpretation are key components of any project. Computers have made it possible for researchers to tabulate and process masses of data quickly and inexpensively. This tool can be abused, however. Managers have little use for reams of computer printouts. The researcher's ability to identify pivotal relationships, spot trends, and find patterns is what transforms data into useful information.

The end product of the investigation is the researcher's conclusions and recommendations. Most projects require a written report, often accompanied by an oral presentation to management.

6. Conduct Follow-up

Researchers should follow up their studies to determine whether their recommendations are being used. For several reasons, management may choose not to use a study's findings. The original problem may have been misdefined, become less urgent, or even disappeared. Or the project may have been completed too late to be useful. Without a follow-up, the researcher has no way of knowing if the project was on target and met managements's needs or if it fell short. Thus an important source of information for improving research performance in the future would be ignored.

WHO DOES MARKETING RESEARCH?

Marketing research can be done by a firm's own personnel or by an outside organization.

Within the Company

Separate marketing research departments exist primarily in larger companies and are usually quite small. The marketing research department may consist of only a single manager or may be as large as four or five professionals in large consumer products companies. In most such situations, the marketing research department rarely conducts research utilizing its own staff, but rather contracts the work out to suppliers outside the company. The primary role of the marketing research department, therefore, is to organize, monitor, and coordinate marketing research, which may be done by a number of different suppliers throughout the country. The manager of the marketing research department reports either to the chief marketing executive or directly to top management. The researchers who staff this department must be well versed in company procedures and know what information is already available within the company. They must also be familiar with the relative strengths and weaknesses of potential marketing research suppliers.

Outside the Company

A sign of maturity in marketing research is the fact that it has already developed many institutions from which a company may seek help in marketing research problems. There exist in Canada today well over 100 companies that operate in the field of marketing research. When a marketing manager requires information on Canadian marketing research suppliers, a number of sources exist that may be consulted in order to obtain a list of potential suppliers. One listing of such suppliers is the *Directory of Canadian Marketing Research Organizations*, produced by the Professional Marketing Research Society. This directory provides detailed information on those companies that operate in Canada in marketing research and related fields.

There are more than 30 full-service marketing research companies in Canada. These companies include such firms as the Creative Research Group, Canadian Facts, Market Facts of Canada, and Thompson Lightstone. They provide a full range of marketing research services, from the design of a research study to the submission of a final report. In addition to the full-service marketing research companies, there are in Canada dozens of smaller firms that operate in various specialized areas of marketing research. These companies are usually small and may specialize by geographic region, by industry, or by service performed. Some concentrate in either consumer or industrial research or carry out studies that involve the application of specialized techniques. Other companies provide specialized marketing research services, such as the analysis of survey data. Some marketing research is also conducted in Canada by advertising agencies and by management consulting firms.

Status of Marketing Research

Canadian business is just beginning to realize the potential of marketing research. Significant advances have been made in both quantitative and qualitative research methodology, to the point where researchers are making effective use of the behavioural sciences and mathematics. Still, however, far too many companies are spending dollars on manufacturing research, but only pennies to determine the market opportunities for their products.

Several factors account for this less-than-universal acceptance of marketing research. Unlike the results of a chemical experiment, the results of marketing research cannot always be measured quantitatively. The research director or brand manager cannot conduct a research project and then point to x percent increase in sales as a result of that project. Also, if management is not convinced of the value of marketing research, it will not spend the amount of money necessary to do a good job. Good research costs money. Executives may not realize that it is a false economy to spend less money: half the amount of money spent will usually result in a job that's less than half as good.

Marketing research cannot predict future market behaviour accurately in many cases, yet often that is what is expected of it. In fact, when dealing with consumer behaviour, the research is hard-pressed to get the truth regarding *present* attitudes or motives, much less those of next year.

Possibly a more fundamental reason for the relatively modest status of marketing research in some companies has been the failure of researchers to communicate adequately with management. Admittedly, there are poor researchers and poor research. Moreover, sometimes the mentality of the quick-acting, pragmatic executive may be at odds with the cautious, complex, hedging-all-bets mentality of some marketing researchers. However, researchers, like many manufacturers, are often product-oriented when they should be market-oriented. They concentrate on research methods and techniques, rather than on showing management how these methods can aid in making better marketing decisions. Executives are willing to invest heavily in technical research because they are convinced there is a payoff in this activity. Management is often not similarly convinced of a return on investment in marketing research.

Another basic problem is the apparent reluctance of management (1) to treat marketing research as a continuing process and (2) to relate marketing research and decision making in a more systematic fashion. Too often, marketing research is viewed in a fragmented, one-project-at-a-time manner. It is used only when management realizes it has a marketing problem. One way to avoid such a view is to incorporate marketing research as one part of a marketing information system — a system that provides a continuous flow of data concerning the changing marketing environment.[12]

Looking to the future, however, we think the prospects for marketing research are encouraging. As more top marketing executives embrace the concept of strategic marketing planning, we should see a growing respect for marketing research and marketing information systems. The strategic planning process requires the generation and careful analysis of information. Marketing researchers have the particular training, capabilities, and systems techniques that are needed for effective information management.

SUMMARY

For a company to operate successfully today, management must develop an orderly method for gathering and analyzing relevant information. A valuable tool for doing this is a marketing information system — ongoing procedures

---

[12]A series of articles on the use of information systems in business is included in the March 1991 issue of *Canadian Business*, beginning on page 75. See also Harvey Gellman, ''Information Systems for Marketing and Selling,'' *Inside Guide*, April/May 1991, pp. 26–28.

and methods designed to generate, analyze, disseminate, store, and retrieve information for use in making marketing decisions. The traditional view of marketing research positioned it as the data gathering and analyzing component of a marketing information system. However, a new broader definition of marketing research includes information management.

In a marketing research study, the problem to be solved is first identified. Then a researcher conducts a situation analysis and an informal investigation. If a formal investigation is needed, the researcher decides which secondary and primary sources of information to use. To gather primary data, a survey, observation, or the experimental method may be used. The project is completed when data are analyzed and the results reported. Follow-up provides information for improving research.

Marketing research has not yet achieved its potential within organizations because researchers have not effectively communicated with management and because research is used in a fragmented manner.

KEY TERMS AND CONCEPTS

Marketing information system 184
Marketing decision support system 184
Marketing research 186
Situation analysis 191
Hypothesis 191
Informal investigation 192
Primary data 192
Secondary data 192
Syndicated data 192
Survey method 194
Personal interview 194

Shopping mall intercept 195
Telephone survey 195
Mail questionnaire 197
Individual depth interview 197
Focus group interview 197
Observational method 197
Experimental method 198
Test marketing 199
Simulated test market 199
Random sample 201
Area sample 201
Quota sample 201

QUESTIONS AND PROBLEMS

1. Why does a company need a marketing information system?

2. Compare the definition of a marketing information system with the latest definition of marketing research presented in the chapter.

3. Do you think marketing researchers should be involved in setting strategy for their organizations? Why or why not?

4. A group of wealthy business executives regularly spends some time each winter at a popular ski resort—Whistler, British Columbia; Banff, Alberta; or Grey Rocks, Quebec. They were intrigued with the possibility of forming a corporation to develop and operate a large ski resort in the B.C. Rockies near the Alberta border. This would be a totally new venture and would be on federal park land. It would be a complete resort with facilities appealing to middle- and upper-income markets. What types of information might they want to have before deciding whether to go ahead with the venture? What sources of information would be used?

5. The manufacturers of a furniture polish competitive with Pledge want to determine the amount of the product that they can expect to sell throughout the country. To help them in this project, prepare a report that shows the following information for your province and, if possible, your home city or municipality. Carefully identify the source you use for this information, and state other sources that provide this information.

    a. Number of households or families.

    b. Income or buying power per family or per household.

    c. Total retail sales in the most recent year for which you can find reliable data.

    d. Total annual sales of food stores, hardware stores, and drugstores.

    e. Total number of food stores.

6. Explain, with examples, the concepts of a situation analysis and an informal investigation in a marketing research project.

7. Evaluate surveys, observation, and experimentation as methods of gathering primary data in the following projects:

    a. A sporting goods retailer wants to determine college students' brand preferences for skis and tennis racquets.

    b. A supermarket chain wants to determine shoppers' preferences for the physical layout of fixtures and traffic patterns, particularly around checkout stands.

    c. A manufacturer of conveyor belts wants to know who makes buying decisions for the product among present and prospective users.

8. Carefully evaluate the relative merits of personal, telephone, and mail surveys on the basis of flexibility, amount of information obtained, accuracy, speed, cost, and ease of administration.

9. Explain and differentiate among a random sample, an area sample, and a quota sample.

10. What kind of sample would you use in each of the research projects designed to answer the following questions?

    a. What brand of shoes is most popular among the students on your campus?

    b. Should the department stores in or near your hometown be open all day on Sundays?

    c. What percentage of the business firms in the large city nearest your campus have automatic sprinkler systems?

11. Would it be appropriate to interview 200 students as they left your college hockey arena about their feelings towards funding for athletics and then generalize the results to the student body? Why or why not?

12. If you were the research manager, what suggestions would you have for your management if they proposed that you conduct a consumer study to determine the feasibility of introducing a new laundry detergent in several Asian countries?

Sources of Secondary and Syndicated Data

"Secondary data" refers to information that has been collected by other organizations, such as governments, foundations, trade and industry associations, and similar bodies, for their own use and for publication and use by the general public. There are two generic sources of secondary data: **original sources** and **acquired sources**. An acquired source is one that obtained the data from the original source. For example, demographic data appearing in *Canadian Markets*, published by *The Financial Post*, represents publication by an acquired source, as the data were initially obtained from Statistics Canada, the original source.

When using secondary data, it is sometimes preferable to gather it from original sources rather than from acquired sources. Acquired sources may omit important statements, footnotes, and other information that could influence the perceived accuracy of the data reported. In addition, original sources tend to provide more details and citations than do acquired sources, both of which may be important to researchers. This does not mean that acquired sources are unimportant to researchers; the publishers of an acquired source, for example *The Financial Post*, in the case of its annual publication, *Canadian Markets*, provide a valuable service in compiling secondary data into a single volume, thereby saving the user considerable time and effort.

Often, the organizations that collected the data (whether collected from original or acquired sources) will have done so for purposes that may differ significantly from those of the company investigating the sources. Caution must be used in interpreting and relying upon such data, as they may be biased or unsuitable for the intended use. Despite these drawbacks, secondary data are typically readily available, relatively inexpensive, and in many cases allow a marketer to gain valuable insights into a problem area.

In addition to secondary data, there often exist suitable **"syndicated sources"** for data that can be applied to the solution of a marketing problem. The most common form of syndicated research involves the collection of data on a regular basis from a predetermined sample or panel of consumers or retail stores. Syndicated data are made available by a research supplier and may be purchased by several clients, some of whom may be in competition with each other. Clients subscribe to the reports from such a service and, by so doing, essentially share the cost of collecting data from a very large sample. These services allow the clients to monitor changes taking place in their markets in terms of such critical indicators as market share, consumer attitudes, and the acceptance of new brands.

SECONDARY SOURCES OF RESEARCH INFORMATION

Numerous secondary sources of data useful for marketing managers exist within Canada and internationally. A description of the most important of these sources follows.

Internal Data

Internal data are considered a secondary source as the data have already been collected. Most businesses, whether independent retailers or large international organizations, collect some kind of internal data as part of their daily operation. The exact type of data collected will vary by the nature of the business; in small companies, it may be limited to basic accounting reports, whereas in large international organizations, the data collected may cover the entire range of operations. Some large businesses even have information departments whose sole purpose is to gather and disseminate information about the company, its competitors, its markets, etc. Becoming familiar with the various types of information that are available internally, including where to find them, is an important requirement of any marketing manager. Examples of internal data that are typically available in many companies are cost and sales figures, advertising and promotion data, mail order records, credit and charge account data, subscription and donor lists, manufacturing reports, inventory records, production schedules, research and development reports, and annual reports.

Although primarily collected for accounting purposes, cost and sales information can be used by marketing managers to determine levels and trends, broken down by types of customer, sales territories, and even specific products. By using such data in conjunction with advertising and promotional information, measures of marketing effectiveness can be obtained. Retailers can use credit and charge account data and mail order records to identify just who their customers are and the brands or products they purchase most often. This information can then be used, for example, to target promotional material at specific sub-groups of customers or to determine what other types of products customers may be interested in. Not-for-profit organizations and publishing companies can review their subscription and donor lists to identify potential locations and population segments from which to obtain new customers or donors.

Researchers can often find a great deal of useful information on companies in their annual reports, although these are usually available only for publicly owned companies listed on stock exchanges. Annual reports typically contain sections on operations, financial aspects of the company, information on products and services provided by the company, together with shareholder information and lists of directors, principal officers, and subsidiaries. By analyzing annual reports over a five- to ten-year period, a researcher can prepare a profile of a company and its performance over time. This information could be useful for forecasting industry trends.

For industrial marketers, valuable information can be obtained by combining manufacturing reports, production schedules, inventory control data, and research and development material. When utilized in conjunction with cost and sales data, such information can offer important insights into new product and process possibilities, pricing flexibility, etc.

In addition, internal data can often be collected from parent or affiliated companies. Many Canadian companies are subsidiaries of larger multinational companies. The parent companies can sometimes provide useful data on market conditions in other countries as well as their experiences in foreign markets and with relevant products. Canadian companies may also be affiliated with one or more other businesses (either in Canada or abroad) as a result of joint ventures, minority ownership of shares, or simply through friendly agreements to share resources. The companies may then be able to share internal data that will assist all parties involved.

The foregoing are just a few of the types of internal data that are usually accessible and that marketing researchers should not overlook. It is especially important to consider internal data during the initial stages of a research project if information is required in order to design a questionnaire or carry out a survey about a company's customers. By using internal data sources, time and money can be saved and reliable, relevant baseline data obtained.

Federal Government Publications

The Canadian government is the largest source of valuable secondary information in Canada. It gathers, analyzes, and publishes a vast quantity of information, mainly through Statistics Canada, the national statistical agency. Statistics Canada maintains regional offices across the country in St. John's, Halifax, Montreal, Ottawa, Toronto, Winnipeg, Regina, Edmonton, and Vancouver. Each reference centre is equipped with a library, microcomputer diskettes, microfiche, census maps, and the facilities to access and retrieve information from two computerized systems, CANSIM and Telichart. For communities where there is no Statistics Canada office, a toll-free telephone number can be used to gain access to the many services the agency provides. These services include providing statistical information to users in person, by mail or by telephone; assisting users with statistical needs and data problems; providing information and training on how to find and use the data held by Statistics Canada; and arranging for the design and management of surveys and statistical research projects on behalf of the Canadian government, institutions, and private agencies.

In addition to the regional offices, there are more than 50 libraries across Canada that carry all Statistics Canada publications. These full depository libraries automatically receive all federal publications not designated as confidential and provide public access to these documents and materials.

The agency publishes a broad spectrum of material of interest to marketing managers:

The *Statistics Canada Current Publications Index (Catalogue #11-204)* is an annual index referencing all numbered publications released by Statistics Canada during the year. (Statistics Canada publications are given a *catalogue number* to facilitate finding and using them.) The Current Publications Index is divided into two sections; the first section gives a listing of publications by catalogue number and subject, and the second lists publications by title and subject.

The *Census of Population* is the most important source of information collected by Statistics Canada. The census is conducted on the whole of the Canadian population once every five years; the latest census was conducted in 1991. Statistics Canada publishes an impressive array of reports based upon the census. For example, a series of *census profiles* based upon the census allows a marketing manager to collect detailed data on the population of every geographic area of Canada, from urban neighbourhoods of approximately 200 households to the 295 federal electoral districts. An entrepreneur who is considering opening a pet store and grooming service can put together a profile of the population of a specific area of a city by obtaining data on more than 200 characteristics of the population of that area.

Market Research Handbook (Catalogue #63-224) is an annual handbook containing a wide variety of Canadian marketing information derived from a number of Statistics Canada sources, including the census, other federal government agencies, and international organizations. The handbook covers a number of topics of interest to marketers including:

- economic indicators
- government finances and employment
- socio-economic characteristics of the population
- personal income and expenditure
- housing and household facilities and equipment
- international trade
- merchandising and service industries data
- small area data, including Census Metropolitan Areas (CMAs) and Census Agglomerations (CAs)

Statistics Canada has also published a descriptive series entitled the *Focus on Canada Series* based upon census data. It includes such titles as:

Canada's Population from Ocean to Ocean (Catalogue #98-120)
Canada's Seniors (Catalogue #98-121)
Canada's Youth (Catalogue #98-124)
Families in Canada (Catalogue #98-127)
Ethnic Diversity in Canada (Catalogue #98-132)
Canada's Farm Population (Catalogue #98-133)

Each publication includes data presented in easy-to-read tables and charts, together with a description of the main characteristics and trends observed. Many contain comparative data from previous censuses.

Other publications of interest to marketing researchers include:

The Daily (Catalogue #11-001) — contains news summaries and announcements of reports, reference papers, and other releases, together with a list of titles of the publications released.

Infomat (Catalogue #11-002) — a weekly digest that highlights major Statistics Canada reports and other material, containing charts and other summary statistics.

Canada Year Book (Catalogue #11-402) — a biennial reference work providing textual and tabular information on Canada, including demography, social and economic conditions, transportation, and communications.

Canada: A Portrait (Catalogue #11-403) — a biennial publication that provides a synopsis of life in Canada, covering such topics as government, technology, arts, and culture.

Finally, Statistics Canada publishes the *Listing of Supplementary Documents*, which covers works that are usually tentative or speculative in nature, such as discussion and working papers published by government departments.

The publications listed above are just a small sample of those available through Statistics Canada. For a complete listing, the reader should consult the Current Publications index.

In addition to publications, another method of gaining access to Statistics Canada data is through the agency's computerized data bank and information retrieval service called the *Canadian Socio-Economic Information Management System* (CANSIM). CANSIM provides public access, in a number of formats, to current and historical statistics, together with specialized data manipulation and analysis packages, graphics facilities, and a bibliographic search service.

The CANSIM system comprises three data bases:

1. *Time Series data base:* consists primarily of economic and business statistics,

allowing the user to examine how certain indicators or variables have changed over time. Some of the information covered includes:

- prices and price indexes
- primary industries
- merchandising and services
- finance
- transportation
- health and welfare
- labour
- external trade

2. *Cross-Classified data base:* contains multi-dimensional tables of social and economic data gathered from the Agriculture, Health, Justice, Education, Science, and Culture divisions of Statistics Canada. This data permits the examination of interaction among several factors, such as income levels across regions or by sex or age groups.

3. *Census Summary Data Service:* contains summary data from each census since 1961, permitting the user to examine the characteristics of various cities and towns across Canada.

Researchers can gain on-line access to the CANSIM data bases through Statistics Canada regional offices, privately owned computer service bureaus across the country, or through national data transmission networks that are accessed by private terminals or microcomputers equipped with modems. Users of the CANSIM data bases can access a main data base (Main Base) of more than 400,000 entries, or a Mini Base of 25,000 of the more popular time series, both of which are updated daily. Data can be retrieved on paper, tape, or diskette. Time series data can also be produced in graphic form, on paper or slides, through the Telichart interactive colour graphic display service, which produces colour prints on paper, overhead transparencies, 35mm slides, or diskettes.

The vast coverage and level of detail of the data collected by Statistics Canada makes it one of the most valuable secondary data sources in Canada. The information that a researcher can gather from Statistics Canada publications, especially when combined with other complementary sources of data, can usually provide some insights into most marketing problems dealing with the Canadian public or business sector. For example, direct mail marketers often find it quite effective to combine small area data from Statistics Canada with information from Canada Post on where their customers or prospective customers live. For relatively low cost, these direct marketers can determine the characteristics of various postal areas, including the larger Forward Sortation Areas (those areas identified by the first three digits of the postal code) or smaller ''postal walks'' (each postal walk contains 200 to 300 households). By obtaining from Statistics Canada the demographic characteristics of those postal areas in which they are interested, these marketers can direct advertising campaigns and telemarketing programs only to those areas determined to hold the greatest potential for sales.

In addition to Statistics Canada publications, the Government of Canada also publishes thousands of other documents through its many departments and agencies. One valuable source to assist researchers in sorting through these many publications is the Publishing Centre of the Canada Communications Group, which operates under Supply and Services Canada in Ottawa.

The Canada Communications Group is responsible for a number of activities relating to government publications, including:

- providing warehousing and distribution services for federal government publications;
- processing orders for government publications by mail, telex, fax and telephone;
- co-ordinating all publishing activities with the author departments;
- helping design and implement marketing plans and strategies that promote its publications;
- offering Canadian publishers the opportunity to share in the promotion of the federal government's best works (Co-publishing Program);
- assisting individuals and organizations to obtain access to Crown copyright material and granting permission to reproduce these texts.

Provincial Government Publications

While Statistics Canada is the major publisher of statistical data on Canadian society, each of the provinces also operates a statistical office that produces regular reports on trends and economic indicators. Statistics Canada reports generally deal with national and regional data and allow the user of the information to make comparisons across regions and provinces. On the other hand, in many cases, the provincial governments produce data that will allow a more detailed examination of specific aspects of the economy or of business in a particular province.

In addition, provincial governments also publish a tremendous amount of information through the various governmental departments. Subjects typically covered in provincial government publications include:

- agriculture
- education
- environment
- energy
- health
- lands
- mines
- social services
- tourism

Additional information is available through the Queen's Printer, which publishes most provincial works, and through the general guide *Canadiana*, which includes a regular listing of provincial and municipal government publications.

Newspapers and Magazines

Newspapers and magazines can provide a wealth of general business and marketing information. The two newspapers that provide the widest ''business'' coverage in Canada are the *Financial Post* and the *Globe and Mail*, both published daily. Both of these newspapers provide information on business, including advertising and marketing information, issues and trends. The *Globe and Mail* Report on Business is published daily as a section of the newspaper and contains a comprehensive review of business matters, including a weekly section devoted to marketing topics. Both of these newspapers also periodically publish Special Report supplements on areas such as transportation, communications, technology, banking and business finance, small business, and computers. A third newspaper, the *Financial Times of Canada*, is published weekly and also provides a good source of information on more general financial aspects of business in Canada.

The Report on Business Magazine is a monthly publication distributed with the *Globe and Mail*. It contains full-length articles on Canadian business topics. *The Financial Post Magazine*, a monthly business magazine available to subscribers of the parent newspaper, is also of value on a wide range of business topics. Two other general business magazines of interest are *Canadian Business* and *Profit*.

Trade, Professional, and Business Publications:

There are numerous trade, professional, and business magazines and journals that cover a wide range of topics dealing with business in Canada. These include:

- *Au Courant*, published by the Information Section of the Economic Council of Canada on a quarterly basis, presents reports that reflect the viewpoint of the Economic Council and covers research studies, discussion papers, and other background papers prepared for the council by staff members and others.
- *Canadian Social Trends*, published quarterly by Statistics Canada (Catalogue #11-008), provides an interesting interpretation of statistical trends in Canadian society.
- *The Business Quarterly*, published by the School of Business Administration, the University of Western Ontario, contains articles of interest to a business audience, written by practising managers and by university business school professors.
- *The Canadian Banker* is the journal of the Canadian Bankers' Association. Published six times annually, this journal contains articles of particular interest to bankers.
- *The Canadian Journal of Economics*, published quarterly by the University of Toronto Press, discusses Canadian economic developments.
- The quarterly, *Canadian Public Administration*, covers a variety of topics dealing with administration, politics, and public policy.

Publications by such organizations as chambers of commerce and boards of trade can also be useful. These organizations usually have access to and publish economic demographic governmental, and other information on a municipal level. Examples of such publications include the *Metropolitan Business Journal*, published by the Board of Trade of Metropolitan Toronto, and *News and Views*, published by the St. John's Board of Trade in Newfoundland.

Regional Publications

There are a number of regional publications that report on activities within the regions covered, for example, the Atlantic Provinces Economic Council publishes a variety of useful material on the Atlantic provinces; *Business Life in Western Canada* reports on the Western business climate; and *Alberta Report* reports on business and commerce in the Province of Alberta.

Foundations

A number of research foundations and ''think tanks'' regularly publish reports on topics of interest to marketers that are of assistance in understanding markets and how they are changing. These include the Institute for Research in Public Policy, the Economic Council of Canada, the C.D. Howe Institute, the Hudson Institute of Canada, the Atlantic Provinces Economic Council, and the Fraser Institute. Publications by these groups include *Policy Options*, the bimonthly publication of the Institute for Research on Public Policy, which provides a forum for diverse views on public policy and related areas, and *Canadian Business Review*, published quarterly by the Conference Board of Canada, which contains articles of general business interest.

The Conference Board of Canada also produces a number of other publications. The *Handbook of Canadian Consumer Markets* contains data on consumer markets gathered from numerous government, trade, and Conference Board sources. The main topics of the handbook include population, labour and employment, income and expenditures, production and retail trade, and price indices. *Canadian Outlook: Economic Forecast* and *Provincial Outlook: Economic Forecast* are quarterly publications that provide forecasts of a number of economic indicators including prices, costs, employment, and housing. The Canadian version provides the information for the country as a whole, whereas the provincial version has separate sections for each province. The Conference Board also offers a marketing data base that contains time-series and cross-sectional data. This data base is part of the AERIC System, the board's on-line analysis and forecasting system. The AERIC System allows immediate access to, and manipulation of, data base information. Available software permits the user to perform immediate and straightforward data manipulation, for example, percentage change, plotting, correlations, and regression.

Advertising Media

For researchers looking for information directly pertaining to advertising in Canada, there are a number of publications that may be of assistance:

Canadian Advertising Rates and Data, published monthly by Maclean Hunter Limited, is the most comprehensive source of data on the advertising industry in Canada, containing advertising rates, circulation data, mechanical requirements, addresses, personnel, and ownership information on virtually all advertising media in Canada.

The National List of Advertisers, an annual publication of Maclean Hunter Limited, contains detailed information on more than 3000 national advertisers, their brand names, advertising agencies and their accounts, advertising budgets, media used, and companies that provide direct marketing and advertising services.

Maclean Hunter also publishes the annual *Report on Advertising Revenues in Canada*, which contains total expenditures on advertising in Canada, broken down by the various media. Billings for major advertising agencies are also presented.

Finally, the company also publishes the *Media Editorial Profile* once a year. This publication provides abbreviated information on the subject matter and editorial focus of more than 700 Canadian consumer, farm, and business magazines.

The Canadian Marketing Goldbook, published annually by Roger E. Murray, contains more than 20,000 listings covering all aspects of the Canadian marketing industry, including sections on media, services and supplies, event facilities, design, advertising, direct response, and photography.

Marketing Publications

One of the leading sources of information and publications on marketing in general is the American Marketing Association (AMA). The association publishes a number of marketing periodicals, some of which are more technical in nature than others.

The *Journal of Marketing* is published quarterly by the AMA. This journal contains a regular feature entitled "Marketing Abstracts," in which articles from a variety of periodicals are listed under major subject headings and subheadings. Researchers will appreciate the abstracts that accompany each article as they can substantially reduce the amount of time spent searching for the listed publications.

The American Marketing Association also publishes the *Journal of Marketing Research*, which deals with quantitative aspects of marketing research; the *Journal of Health Care Marketing*, which covers the health care field and related topics; *Marketing News*, a biweekly newspaper that deals with marketing topics; and a quarterly journal entitled *Marketing Research*.

Most AMA publications can be found in university libraries, or through the association's Canadian chapters, which are located in Quebec City, Montreal, Ottawa, Toronto, and Vancouver.

Other marketing-related publications include the Canadian weekly, *Marketing*, published by Maclean Hunter, which deals with the marketing and advertising industries. *Strategy* (formerly called *Playback Strategy*) is a biweekly newspaper devoted to marketing topics, published by Brunico Publishing of Toronto. American publications that also contain articles relating to the marketing and advertising industries and that occasionally present Canadian material, include *Sales and Marketing Management, Advertising Age*, and *Applied Marketing Research*, the latter published by the Marketing Research Association.

Indexing Services and Data Bases

The publications and secondary sources of information listed above obviously constitute only a fraction of those available. With this huge number of sources, how is a marketer to quickly and easily find the sources of most value to the problem being studied? Fortunately, the work is greatly simplified by the use of published indexes and commercial data bases.

Published indexes contain listings of references to articles and studies that have been published on particular topics. Such indexes are available in most public and corporate libraries.

The Canadian Business Index (formerly the *Canadian Business Periodicals Index*) is a reference guide to Canadian periodicals and reports in business, industry, economics, and related areas. It is published monthly along with an annual cumulative index published at the end of each year. The index covers more than 45,000 articles a year from more than 160 Canadian business publications, including the *Globe and Mail*, the *Financial Post* and the *Financial Times of Canada*, as well as from many very specialized periodicals.

In addition, researchers can save themselves hours of work in libraries by accessing commercial data bases to search for information pertinent to a marketing problem. There are more than 500 on-line services in existence offering more than 4000 data bases on a variety of topics. All that is needed to gain access to these data bases is a personal computer equipped with a telephone hook-up. In addition, most major university and public libraries offer data base search services.

Computerized data bases are searched for information on a subject by entering one or more keywords or terms that describe the topic of interest. The computer then searches for data that are related to the keywords and provides a listing of citations for the user. The listings can vary in format, but most contain at minimum a basic bibliographical citation consisting of author, title, publication name, date, and page numbers.

While there are literally thousands of different data bases covering almost every topic imaginable, there are four main categories:

1. Bibliographic. These data bases offer on-line bibliographies or indexes, as well as abstracts of books, journals, reports, and other such information. One such data base of specific interest to marketers and researchers is the Canadian Business and Current Affairs (CBCA) data base, an on-line version of three indexes (*Canadian Business Index, Canadian News Index,* and *Canadian Magazine Index*). It contains bibliographic reference to articles on business and management subjects that may be printed in any of the major Canadian business newspapers and periodicals. The CBCA is published by Micromedia Limited and is available on that company's DIALOG service.

Another bibliographic data base is the PTS Marketing and Advertising Reference Service (PTS MARS), offered by Predicasts Inc. This data base contains abstracts on information relating to the advertising and marketing of consumer goods and services.

2. Full text. These data bases contain the entire text of articles, reports, and other secondary source data. The PTS New Product Announcements (PTA NPA) data base, also published by Predicasts Inc., is an example of a full-text data base of interest to marketers and researchers. The PTA NPA contains the full text of company press releases dealing with the introduction of new products.

3. Directory. Directory data bases provide on-line lists of names, services, companies, publications, and other sources. The National Standards Assocation provides a directory data base entitled FINDEX Reports and Studies, available through the DIALOG on-line service. FINDEX provides a listing of more than 10,000 published, commercially available business and market research reports, studies, and surveys from more than 300 international publishers, including a number in Canada. FINDEX is published annually with a mid-year supplement.

4. Statistical. Statistical data bases provide numerical data, including financial statistics, in preformatted or raw form. The CANSIM system of Statistics Canada described earlier is an example of a statistical data base.

A number of companies have been established in recent years to serve the growing market for on-line data base information. Three of the largest in Canada are Micromedia Limited, Info Globe, and Infomart Online.

Micromedia Limited is a business information supplier established in the early 1970s to supply data bases, on-line services, and publications. Micromedia is the Canadian entity in the SVP International network and is also the official agent for DIALOG Information Services Inc., the Ontario Securities Commission, University Microfilms International, and Statistics Canada, among others. The data bases available through Micromedia include Canadian Business and Current Affairs, the Canadian Corporations Database, the Directory of Associations in Canada, and Microlog, a Canadian research index that provides access to more than 7,000 Canadian government and institutional reports.

Many national publishers now offer ''on-line'' versions of their publications that are accessible by any researcher who has access to a microcomputer and modem. Such publications may be ''searched'' electronically for articles of interest to marketers and marketing researchers. These include Info Globe, the electronic publishing division of the *Globe and Mail*. In addition to providing an on-line version of the daily newspaper, Info Globe publishes the *Canadian Periodicals Index* and acts as marketing agent for a number of other on-line services, including the Dow Jones News/Retrieval and Profile data bases.

Infomart Online, a division of Southam, Inc., provides access to numerous business and news information sources in Canada and the United States, by offering on-line versions of many daily newspapers and news wire services.

The Financial Post Information Service offers FP OnLine Electronic Editions, which feature the full text of such publications as the *Financial Post, Maclean's,* the *Directory of Directors,* the *Survey of Industrials,* and the *Survey of Mines and Energy Resources.*

Bibliographies

Bibliographies, especially those that offer annotated descriptions of entries, are another source of data that can save researchers a considerable amount of time. Bibliographies offer information on a number of topics; one bibliography of particular interest to marketing researchers is the *Bibliography of Marketing Research Methods* compiled by John R. Dickinson of the University of Windsor. Other bibliographies provide information about recent Canadian publications, such as *Books in Canada*, issued ten times a year, and *Canadian Studies*, an annual publication of the Canadian Book Publishers' Council. *Canadian Books in Print* is published annually by the University of Toronto Press and lists by subject all books published in Canada.

Directories

Directories are an often overlooked source of information, especially when a marketing manager is interested in identifying individuals or companies who could be of assistance or offer market potential. The Yellow Pages of telephone directories can be a valuable source of information, and city directories are also useful. For example, R. L. Polk and Company Limited publishes annual city directories for most of the larger urban centres in Canada. These directories include four main sections: a buyer's guide; an alphabetical list of names of residents and business and professional concerns; a directory of householders, including street and avenue guide; and a numerical telephone guide.

Numerous trade directories are published and may be classified into three categories: (1) general trade directories, such as the *Canadian Trade Index*; (2) specific industry directories, such as the *Pulp and Paper Directory*; and (3) regional trade directories, such as *Scott's Directories: Atlantic Manufacturers*. Financial directories, such as the *Financial Post Survey of Industrials, Survey of Mines & Energy Resources,* and *Survey of Investment Funds*, provide information on an annual basis about companies involved in these industries.

Other general directories such as *Who's Who in Canada*, the *Financial Post Directory of Directors*, and *Canadian Who's Who* provide information on prominent Canadians. Canadian almanacs can be useful sources of data as well. The only exclusively Canadian almanac is the *Canadian World Almanac*, published annually by Global Press.

Canadian Markets, published annually by the *Financial Post*, is a handbook of marketing data and facts gleaned mainly from Statistics Canada sources. It also includes Buying Power Indices, which are indicators of the relative strength of consumer markets across Canada, and a Focus on Industrial Development section, which includes the names and addresses of industrial contacts for more than 250 cities and towns across Canada. As well, there are comparative rankings of major metropolitan markets and comprehensive listings of media by market area.

Sales and Marketing Management publishes two issues each year that are devoted to its "Survey of Buying Power." These issues contain a considerable volume of data on the U.S. market, but the publisher offers similar Canadian data to readers who may write and order a Canadian report. The Canadian "Survey of Buying Power" contains information on retail sales, population, effective buying income, and buying power indexes for provincial and metropolitan markets.

The Industrial Marketing and Research Association of Canada (IMRAC) publishes the *Canadian Guide to Industrial Marketing Information*, a comprehensive directory of sources of information about business-to-business marketing in Canada.

The *Financial Post* and *Canadian Business* publish a ranking of Canada's top 500 companies in May and June each year. *Report on Business Magazine* publishes a ranking of the top 1,000 companies in Canada in July, and together these provide a wealth of information on corporate performance in Canada.

As well as these secondary sources, there are numerous private research organizations that undertake a large variety of research and data collection projects. The section on syndicated data that follows deals with a number of such organizations and describes the manner in which they collect syndicated data.

International Sources

The sources described so far have concentrated mainly on Canada, however many of the same types of sources are also available in other countries. Some information can be provided by foreign governments; census data similar to those collected in Canada are also available in the United States and most other nations with statistical agencies. A number of international organizations also offer sources of data. The United Nations publishes the *Statistical Yearbook*, which contains data on international trade, broken down by imports and exports for individual countries. The Work Bank publishes the *World Atlas*, which provides general data on population, growth, trends, and economic conditions. It also publishes the *World Tables*, which are a series of tables giving economic, demographic, and social data for a large number of countries.

Private publishers may also provide data on foreign countries. For example, Predicasts Inc. offers *World Studies*, which provides information on markets, product prices, trends, capital, producers, trend forecasts, and geo-political data on a number of countries. Euromonitor publishes *International Marketing Data and Statistics*, which provides marketing related statistics for more than 100 countries around the world. It also publishes *European Marketing Data and Statistics*, which covers European countries in more detail than the international edition. As well, Gower Publishing offers a *World Index of Economic Forecasts*, which provides information on a large number of organizations that make economic forecasts of countries around the world.

Trade associations in other countries, such as foreign chambers of commerce, can often provide information similar to that of their Canadian counterparts. In general, most Canadian sources of data can also be found for foreign countries, although the exact nature and detail of these sources will obviously vary.

Other Secondary Sources

University research departments, royal commissions, private institutions, review boards, and the like also provide considerable information that can be of use to marketing departments and researchers. The intention has not been to provide in this section an exhaustive list of secondary data sources, but rather an illustrative one. As can be seen, there are many such sources in Canada.

SYNDICATED SOURCE DATA

"Syndicated data" refers to data that is gathered from samples on a subject of interest and made available to clients who share the cost of the project. Typically, a private supplier of syndicated data, such as a marketing research firm, will develop and conduct a syndicated study and sell the results to organizations interested in the results. Long-term agreements for such studies will often be arranged as they benefit both the supplier and subscriber; such agreements allow the supplier to cover the typically high fixed and overhead costs of the study and ensure the subscriber receives continuous information that is important for monitoring and valuative purposes. Often, the supplier will allow the subscribing organizations to include private questions in the study for an additional fee. The results of these private questions are then analyzed and reported only to the client who paid for them. Subscribers may also be given the exclusive rights to certain portions of the study, again for an extra fee.

Data collection methods used in conducting syndicated research vary with the syndicated suppliers, depending upon the sample size, type of data required by the clients, and the geographic regions to be included. Some studies use telephone surveys or mailed questionnaires sent to a recruited panel of consumers or to a random sample. Other studies are more technically complex and involve the use of technical measurement equipment to monitor television viewing, magazine readership, purchase behaviour, etc. The specific methods used will also depend on what the study is measuring. Syndicated studies are typically used for tracking, performance monitoring, and for market penetration, brand share, and brand awareness.

The principal advantage of syndicated data to subscribers is that they often allow companies to receive valuable information at a lower cost and more quickly than if the study was conducted for just one subscriber. The drawbacks to such data are that the results are usually shared by a number of companies, thus preventing any one company from gaining an informational advantage, and that the data may not specifically meet the needs of the subscriber. The study may use secondary data which in turn could be out of date or inaccurate, or the study may not cover the exact markets or products and services of interest to the user.

There are a number of syndicated services that serve the Canadian market. For purposes of description, these can be classified into syndicated services that provide either general data, specialized data, retail data, or media and audience measurement data.

General Data Services

Canadian Facts is a full-service research company based in Toronto that operates the *C.F. Monitor*, a continuous, shared-cost survey that supplies information on large representative samples. Each month, a personal survey of 2,000 individuals aged 15 years and over is conducted throughout all of Canada except for the Northwest Territories and Yukon. The survey provides representative coverage of the country as a whole as well as for five, more focused regions: British Columbia, the Prairies, Ontario, Quebec, and the Atlantic provinces.

Contemporary Research Centre operates the *CRC Omnibus,* a bi-monthly, shared-cost survey of representative samples of 2,000 respondents 15 years of age and older across Canada. All the interviews are conducted in-home with a family member being selected at random. *Criterion Research Corporation* also conducts a quarterly omnibus survey that covers social and public affairs issues in Manitoba.

Gallup Canada Inc. carries out periodic syndicated studies that are either market-based or population-based, the former focusing on the market for specific products and the latter designed to examine sub-populations, such as farmers. For instance, the *Gallup National Omnibus* is a personal in-home omnibus survey conducted weekly with a different sample of 1,000 Canadian adults. Subscribers to the Omnibus provide questions to be included in the survey and receive the resulting tabulated data on a confidential and exclusive basis. For clients who need information only on a provincial or regional basis, Gallup also periodically conducts the *Regional Omnibus Program* in British Columbia, Alberta, Saskatchewan, Ontario, Quebec, and the Atlantic region.

Market Facts of Canada Limited conducts the quarterly *CMP National Omnibus* among proportionate samples of all Canadian households, either nationally or regionally. Sample sizes range from 1,000 to 10,000. The company also offers a syndicated telephone survey called *Telenation,* which surveys 1,000 different adults twice each month.

Omnifacts Research Limited, with offices in St. John's, Dartmouth and Fredericton, offers the *Omnifacts Atlantic Report,* a syndicated, semi-annual survey of social, economic, and political issues conducted with more than 1,500 households throughout the four Atlantic provinces. For an additional fee, clients can submit specialized questions of interest and receive an exclusive analysis and report of the findings.

Omnitel is a monthly omnibus offered by *Thompson Lightstone & Company Limited.* From a network of central telephone facilities in a number of urban centres, this omnibus surveys random national samples of 2,000 Canadians 18 years of age and older on issues of interest to subscribers.

Specialized Data Services

There are also a number of syndicated services that offer data on more specialized subjects:

For the agriculture sector, *Criterion Research Corporation* offers *Agwatch,* an omnibus survey of farm operators in the Prairies, Ontario, and Quebec. A typical Agwatch study would sample 1,000 farm operators; 300 in Ontario, 200 each in Alberta, Saskatchewan, and Manitoba, and 100 in Quebec.

ISL International Surveys Ltd. provides specialized, syndicated services for the medical and health-care markets, computing and home electronics, together with a *National Omnibus Survey* that is conducted five times a year with a probability sample of 2,000 adults. *Schema Research Ltd.* provides a service called *Contact,* which allows access to a national sample of physicians five times a year, as well as several other health-care market monitors.

In addition to its general omnibus, *Market Facts of Canada* also conducts a number of specialized studies:

- The *Household Equipment Audit* provides market information on more than 70 home appliance and electronic products for 8,000 households at the end of each year;
- *Infostudy* measures eating-out behaviour based on a sample of 1,000 households per quarter;

- The quarterly *Household Flow of Funds and Customer Service Survey* measures ownership and dollar value of all major savings and investments, based on a sample of 1,200 households;
- The *Canadian Eating Habits Study* consists of a population-based sample of 4,000 Canadians who report consumption data throughout one year;
- The *Health Care Monitor* provides information on more than 60 ailments and illnesses, with 30,000 Canadians reporting annually on chronic illness and 8,000 reporting at six-month intervals on common ailments;
- Market Facts of Canada also operates a *farm panel*, a *baby panel*, and a *microwave oven owner panel*.

Compusearch Market and Social Research Limited offers clients a different form of syndicated research reports. Compusearch compiles data from Statistics Canada and other secondary sources and repackages the information in a form that is useful to the client. The company presents detailed demographic and other relevant data by neighbourhoods, trading areas, sales territories, or any other geographic areas of interest to purchasers of the data. Data can be provided by neighbourhoods as small as 200 households and can be used by clients to identify the characteristics of target markets, to determine where new branches or stores should be located, and to target the most promising consumer groups.

Retail Data Services

A.C. Nielsen Company of Canada Limited offers a number of retail indices such as the Food Index, the Drug Index, the Confectionery/Tobacco Index and the Mass Merchandiser Index, collectively known as Neilsen's *Retail Index Services*. In developing these indices, a disproportionate sample of retail chains, voluntary group associations, and unaffiliated independent retailers are audited by *A.C. Nielsen*. Every two months, auditors enter the stores and take in-store inventory counts and review store purchase invoices. They may also collect observable information such as prices, sales, display space, and point of purchase promotions. By collecting this information, the company can determine such measures as what products and brands are being bought, general trends for specific products and product groups, and market share data.

For example, the grocery industry is served by the Food Index. This index is based on a sample of 475 grocery stores across Canada, measuring more than 200 product categories. The reports are tailored to clients' needs and contain quantitative results of market size and direction, brand/size sales volume and share, plus a host of "reasons why" data.

Also serving the grocery industry is Nielsen's *Warehouse Shipment Service*, which provides a measurement of grocery shipments from chain/wholesale warehouses to individual retail stores. More than 500 categories are covered in regions from Newfoundland to British Columbia, with reports based on four-week intervals covering all items shipped through the warehouse. The major advantage of data collected from warehouses is that it permits companies to monitor the effectiveness of promotions by comparing movement of products before, during and after promotions are offered.

Media and Audience Measurement Data Services

Media and audience-measurement data represent another important segment of syndicated data. A number of services exist to provide users with data on print media readership and radio and television audiences.

PRINT MEDIA MEASUREMENT

Most publishers of print media are interested in determining who is reading their publications, as are companies trying to plan and evaluate their print advertising programs. The Print Measurement Bureau (PMB) is a non-profit, tri-partite industry association that offers standardized readership information on the publications of its member companies. Samples of Canadian residents 12 years of age and older are interviewed regularly and the results of the last two years' worth of data are compiled into an annual report made available exclusively to PMB members. The role of the Print Measurement Bureau has also been expanded to include the collection of data on the exposure of consumers to other media, their lifestyles, and product usage.

To provide information on print advertising, there is a syndicated readership service called the *Starch Readership Studies*, produced by *Starch Research Services Inc.* This service examines receivers and readers of print media and the extent to which they read specific editorials, articles, and advertisements. On a continuing basis, the Starch Readership Studies cover more than 10,000 advertisements in more than 50 Canadian publications, although almost any issue of any publication can be Starch measured, including magazines, newspapers, and the business press.

Starch also offers a readership study for advertising on posters, superboards, backlights, mall posters, car cards, bus boards, and bus shelter posters. In-home interviews with 400 to 500 people are used to compile information on the awareness and penetration of advertisements in these locations. Syndicated readership studies for specialized print media are also offered by the company. For example, to measure penetration and readership of medical journals among Canadian physicians, Starch offers a continuous research program called the Canadian Medical Media Study.

RADIO AUDIENCES

One of the best known organizations involved in determining audience estimates for radio stations and programs in Canada is the BBM Bureau of Measurement, an independent, non-profit organization with approximately 1,000 members and associates from the broadcasting industry. BBM conducts surveys of radio audiences up to four times a year, depending on the size and competitive nature of the areas surveyed. The first step BBM takes in conducting a survey is to select a random sample of telephone listings from more than 346 sampling ''cells'' across Canada that are consistent with Statistics Canada market definitions. Once demographic data from the telephoned households are collected and verified to be representative of the Canadian population in size, location, and demographics, BBM recruits entire households to take part in the survey. In exchange for a small cash token of appreciation, each member of a recruited household agrees to record the listening done over a seven-day period. From this sample, radio audiences for more than 150 markets are developed and published in syndicated reports that are made available to members as part of their membership entitlement.

TELEVISION AUDIENCES

The BBM Bureau of Measurement also undertakes television surveys up to ten times a year, using the same sampling approach and seven-day period as with radio surveys. Household members record in their diaries when they watch television, for how long, and on which sets. The results are published in ''market'' and ''reach'' report books, consisting of ratings and audiences.

The A.C. Nielsen Company of Canada also surveys Canadian television households and until 1989 also used a television diary. However, these diaries have now been phased out by Nielsen, in favour of a new technological approach to the recording of television viewing. A small device known as a people meter is connected to the television set in the home of each participant, and this device is connected to a microprocessor installed inside the television. The computer measures when the set is on and in what format, that is, local television channels, cable, VCR, pay TV, and so on. All individuals in the household are assigned numbers that they use to enter data into the people meter to indicate when they and any others are watching television.

The people meter was a technological breakthrough that opened the door for a new concept in research, that of "single-source data." Single-source data gathering involves the measurement of television viewing, and product/service purchases. This concept allows a more accurate and detailed analysis of the links between television viewership and products purchased in stores; it encompasses a number of areas including product/service tracking, television audience measurement, casual data collection, data processing on a large scale, and the production of action-oriented reports for clients.

Under the single-source system, A.C. Nielsen monitors a national panel of households in major cities. Households agree to have their television viewing monitored using a people meter and to have their purchases recorded whenever they buy products at retail stores equipped with scanners. Each member of the panel is assigned a number that is used to record purchases at the retail stores and to register television viewing patterns through the people meter. Information from the retail scanners is transmitted via telephone lines to a central computer for analysis. Advertisements watched on television by the same consumer panel are charted by viewers entering appropriate information into the people meter through a hand-held device similar to a television remote-control unit. Again this information is transmitted daily to a central computer. Single-source data represent a tool for planning, purchasing, and evaluating television advertising, based on actual customer purchase behaviour.

Another company involved in the single-source data area, but which uses slightly different techniques, is PEAC Media Research Inc. of Toronto. This company has developed a customized, microcomputer-based diagnostic and valuative system called the Program Evaluation Analysis Computer (PEAC) system. It is used for testing advertising and television programs in a group setting. Use of the PEAC system involves a two-stage group meeting. In the first stage, a target group is exposed to advertisements or television programs, and the PEAC system collects the group's reaction to the advertising individually, spontaneously, and anonymously. In the second stage, these results are put in a graphical form and synchronized with the test material to see reactions to specific sections of the advertisement or program. Using these results, the group moderator can solicit further group discussions about the viewing session, probing for reasons to explain the observations.

PEAC Media Research also offers a technological system used for electronic test marketing and electronic single source systems. For example, the Viewfacts division of the company offers a single-source measurement service for the Toronto market. This service records program audiences and actual purchase or service usage which is obtained by equipping all households in a consumer panel with a hand-held scanning device. Viewing information is recorded using a proprietary "on-screen prompt" people meter.

C A S E S   F O R   P A R T   2

CASE 2.1   ## The Atlantic Bank of Canada: Development of a Regional Marketing Plan

Bill Owens drove slowly, rehearsing street names and committing to memory his impressions of Dartmouth and its suburbs. The people appeared friendly—he had observed many stopping to chat as they passed one another on the sidewalks. One thing was for certain; the hustle and bustle obvious in Toronto's business community, from which he had just been transferred, was not commonplace here.

May was drawing to a close at a comfortable 23°. Bill had immediately noticed the fresh, ocean air when he had arrived in Dartmouth two days earlier. This freshness, coupled with the warm temperatures Nova Scotia had enjoyed for a week now, had eased his anxiety over his big move. In fact, he was feeling very much relieved to have escaped the anticipated mugginess of Toronto's summer season.

DARTMOUTH, NOVA SCOTIA

Dartmouth, located on the eastern side of Halifax Harbour in Nova Scotia, together with Halifax, makes up the largest population centre in Atlantic Canada. Incorporated in 1961, Dartmouth has become known for excellence in medical, educational, recreational, and shopping facilities. The city is located near several of the largest naval operations in Canada, a number of oil refineries, and the world-renowned Bedford Institute of Oceanography. The 25 lakes located within the city have led to it being called the City of Lakes. The MacDonald and Mackay bridges across Halifax Harbour provide Dartmouth's link to Halifax, the province's capital city and the commercial centre of Atlantic Canada.

The city of Dartmouth has two regional shopping malls, eight other smaller shopping centres,

33 churches, two large provincial health care units and a general hospital, 34 schools, and approximately 56 community organizations. Bill had already developed the feeling that Dartmouth represented a growing market area, which meant considerable potential for the bank. He was looking forward to the challenge.

NEW RESPONSIBILITIES

The move from Toronto to Dartmouth was initiated when Bill had accepted an opportunity with which he had been presented last fall. He had worked in a commercial capacity with the Atlantic Bank of Canada, a Schedule I bank, since graduating from York University's Bachelor of Business Administration program six years ago. During the past year or so, the bank had begun to implement a number of structural changes. Commercial and residential responsibilities at the local level were in the future to be divided between two senior managers across a cluster of three to five branches, unlike the former system where area managers had responsibility for 16 or 17 branches.

Bill's new position as senior residential banking manager for Dartmouth was to begin June 1, 1991. He would be situated in the Woodlawn Mall branch and would report to Ian Brown, vice-president for Nova Scotia. This position included responsibility for the development of a Dartmouth Community Marketing Game Plan from a residential perspective. Bill was particularly interested in developing a competitive strategy for the Woodlawn Mall branch, which was being renovated. The road leading to the mall had been undergoing reconstruction for several weeks. This hampered access to the mall, which

Copyright 1990. This case has been prepared by James G. Barnes and Bernita Kiefte of Memorial University of Newfoundland. It has been written to stimulate discussion of an actual marketing situation, and not to indicate either effective or ineffective handling of that situation. The authors wish to thank Gordon MacAskill and Darryl Kay of the Bank of Montreal, for providing advice on the nature of the Dartmouth market; and Dr. John Leyes, Director of the Small Area and Administrative Data Division of Statistics Canada. The preparation of this case was made possible through a grant from Statistics Canada.

had not attracted its regular volume of clientele since construction began.

Bill, as well as being senior residential banking manager, would hold the position of manager of the Woodlawn Mall branch. He knew that he would have to make the branch grow quickly in order that it not be regarded unfavourably in comparison to some of the larger, faster-growing branches. Posing an additional challenge was the mall's landlord, who was being somewhat inflexible in accommodating some of the changes the bank wished to make.

As a product of the Community Plan, a District Bank Plan was to be developed for the entire province. The District Marketing Plan was to be much more detailed than the Community Plans and would constitute a portion of the plan for Atlantic Canada. Bill had only three weeks to complete his community project and had access to previous reports, as well as to Statistics Canada data on the Dartmouth area. Following the completion of the various plans, Bill was to oversee the creation and execution of a residential marketing strategy for the four branches in the Dartmouth region, and to ensure that the bank's products matched specific customer needs. All projects were expected to be finalized well before the next fiscal year commencing November 1, 1991.

THE DARTMOUTH BRANCHES

1. Main Office — opened in 1955. This is the bank's parent branch for the community of Dartmouth. The branch is a full-service, five-day-a-week branch located on Portland Street in the downtown area. Expansion is foreseen in the future as the present facilities are barely adequate to cope with the number of customers.

2. Mic Mac Mall—opened in 1973. A large, six-day-a-week retail operation, this branch has two full-service automated banking machines available during the mall hours of 6:00 a.m. to 10:00 p.m. Monday to Saturday. Additional space will be required in future as growth trends have caused the bank to outgrow its present facilities.

3. Woodlawn Mall — opened in 1972. This medium-sized, six-day-a-week, full-service branch is in the centre of the community, near a substantial suburban commercial core. Available 24 hours per day are an automated banking machine and a cash dispenser. Recent renovations, conducted to conform to a strip mall concept, have created some havoc for the branch.

4. Cole Harbour—opened in 1977. A medium-sized, six-day-a-week operation, this branch is the fastest growing of the four branches and is located in a rapidly expanding residential area. One automated banking machine is available at all times.

THE MARKETING PLAN

The format that has been adopted by the Atlantic Bank of Canada for the preparation of marketing plans, which are to be developed at the branch, region, and provincial levels, comprises eight distinct sections as follows:
- definition of the market;
- analysis of the economy;
- analysis of demographics;
- analysis of industrial/commercial sectors;
- analysis of the competition;
- objectives;
- priorities;
- strategies.

DATA COMPILATION

Although Bill's expertise was developed in a commercial market, he was excited by the challenge offered by the Dartmouth area. Prior to leaving Toronto, he had contacted the bank's research department and asked the staff to compile Statistics Canada data with reference to the province of Nova Scotia, the Halifax Census Metropolitan Area (CMA), the city of Dartmouth, and the immediate areas in which each of the four branches is located.

The research staff in Toronto had explained that the data from Statistics Canada for the more specific areas around each of the branches is organized in accordance with Canada Post's FSAs (Forward Sortation Areas). The FSA code refers to the first three characters of the postal code, within which various postal walks are located. The research people had suggested that data from each FSA could be used to develop appropriate strategies that effectively target the branches' most profitable clientele.

WOODLAWN MALL

Bill looked at data on the FSAs in Dartmouth and, through discussions with senior personnel in the bank's regional office in Halifax, had determined that he should first examine the data pertaining to the FSA labelled B2W, as these data would be the most accurate indicator of the Woodlawn Mall branch customer base. Bill felt that, although little emphasis had been placed on statistical data by the bank in the past, a heavier utilization should be made of such information in the development of regional reports. Therefore, Bill wanted to take a closer look at this geographic area with a view to planning expansion of branch operations in the future.

It had been determined that the Woodlawn Mall branch market area could be divided into three distinct areas. One of the areas is well established with older homes, many apartment buildings, and a number of schools and churches. The majority of people living in this area would be in the middle-income category, although the range is probably fairly broad. The second area is a newer residential growth area and represents primarily single-family dwellings with middle to upper incomes. The third area is the business sector. Main Street and Portland Street are very retail-oriented, lined with food and other outlets, auto dealers, and the beginnings of the three new mini malls.

FACTORS FOR BILL TO CONSIDER

Five other Schedule I banks operate several branches within the Dartmouth area, providing a source of competition that must be factored into any strategies recommended by Bill in the marketing plans. One Schedule II bank, a credit union, and two trust companies are also located in the city, all of which had been identified on the map supplied to him by the regional office. There are many branches of these same banks in Halifax, just over the bridges, where many residents of Dartmouth travel every day to work.

The majority of the bank's advertising and promotion information literature is developed on a centralized basis at head office. However, local marketing initiatives, such as telemarketing, can be undertaken to promote particular services that are deemed appropriate for the area. Word-of-mouth, both from bank employees and customers, is also considered an extremely useful tool, based on past experience. However, Bill felt that reliance on this vehicle entirely could prove detrimental. Other means of communicating the factors considered important by customers in dealing with banks is critical. Several such factors requiring consideration include convenience, security, confidentiality, and expertise.

One issue Bill knew he must settle immediately related to which side of the billboard pylon the bank's signage should face at the Woodlawn Mall branch location. The pylon faced both the main artery and the residential district, so a decision was necessary. Bill was already wondering how he could possibly begin to prepare brand and region plans within the next three weeks when he had to deal with details such as this as well.

To start the planning project, Bill thought it best to tour Dartmouth both by car and on foot, in an effort to gain an appreciation for the city's flavour. Bill foresaw that such efforts would enable him to approach the marketing plans in a more realistic and expert fashion. Although he understood that operations in a residential capacity compared to a commercial one mean differences in such factors as hours of operation and automated teller machine usage, Bill felt that he must assess the compiled statistics to appreciate fully the needs of the branches' present and potential clientele.

QUESTIONS

1. Given the statistics on the market area and on the province of Nova Scotia, as provided by Statistics Canada, how would you define the financial services market of Dartmouth?
2. Which demographic segments should Bill recommend that the Woodlawn branch target? What services are most aptly suited for such a market? How would you rank these services? What strategies should be implemented and through which media vehicles?
3. Are there any specific needs that may potentially differ in the B2W postal area, as compared to the Dartmouth area as a whole? Is there any evidence of major differences across the four data areas provided?
4. How would you formalize the objectives of this marketing plan?

5. Would data requirements differ if Bill had been responsible for the development of Commercial Marketing Plans? Given that there is presently a small commercial pres-ence at the Woodlawn Mall branch, what implications would the introduction of a commercial lender to this branch have on Bill's marketing strategies?

EXHIBIT 1   **1986 Census Data**

	B2W-FSA	%	DARTMTH.	%	HALIFAX CMA	%	N.S.	%
OCCUPIED PRIVATE DWELLINGS	9,185		23,400		103,835		295,780	
Owned	7,670	84%	11,815	50%	60,500	58%	211,645	72%
Rented	1,510	16%	11,585	50%	43,330	42%	82,995	28%
Other	5	—	—	—	5	—	1,140	—
PRIVATE HOUSEHOLDS	9,190		23,390		103,830		295,785	
1 person	640	7%	4,295	18%	20,220	20%	54,895	18%
2 persons	2,015	22%	7,480	32%	31,335	30%	85,625	29%
3 persons	2,010	22%	4,855	21%	20,175	19%	56,180	19%
4–5 persons	3,925	43%	6,085	26%	28,505	28%	84,825	29%
5–9 persons	585	6%	670	3%	3,520	3%	13,940	5%
10 + persons	15	—	5	—	75	—	320	—
Average	3.4		2.7		2.8		2.9	
CENSUS FAMILIES IN HOUSEHOLD	8,480		18,035		77,930		230,495	
2 persons	2,310	27%	7,480	42%	30,680	39%	88,015	38%
3 persons	2,100	25%	4,595	25%	18,785	24%	53,665	23%
4 persons	2,685	32%	4,150	23%	19,605	25%	56,485	25%
5 + persons	1,385	16%	1,810	10%	8,860	12%	32,330	14%
HUSBAND/WIFE FAMILIES	7,585		15,295		67,435		200,185	
No child home	1,865	25%	5,870	38%	24,610	36%	70,825	35%
Children home	5,730	75%	9,425	62%	42,825	64%	129,360	65%
1 child home	1,785	31%	3,795	40%	15,650	37%	44,835	35%
2 children	2,615	46%	3,890	41%	18,615	43%	53,470	41%
3 + children	1,330	23%	1,740	19%	8,560	20%	31,055	24%
CHILDREN AT HOME	12,980		21,550		97,790		307,010	
Under 6 years	2,990	23%	5,305	25%	23,685	24%	68,950	23%
6–14 years	4,485	35%	7,040	33%	34,690	35%	111,885	36%
15–17 years	1,705	13%	2,680	12%	12,220	13%	40,340	13%
18–24 years	3,090	24%	5,120	24%	20,740	21%	63,640	21%
25 + years	710	5%	1,405	6%	6,455	7%	22,195	7%
Children/family	1.5		1.2		1.3		1.3	

SOURCE: Statistics Canada

(continued overleaf)

EXHIBIT 1 *(continued)*

	B2W-FSA	%	DARTMTH.	%	HALIFAX CMA	%	N.S.	%
HIGHEST LEVEL								
OF SCHOOLING								
Pop. 15 + years	23,885		52,085		232,925		676,880	
< Grade 9	2,220	9%	5,025	10%	24,715	11%	116,045	17%
Grades 9–13								
Without cert.	7,010	29%	14,780	28%	64,845	28%	221,775	33%
With cert.	2,320	10%	4,685	9%	20,145	9%	54,280	8%
Trades cert./dip.	685	3%	1,570	3%	6,345	3%	20,540	3%
Nonuniv. education								
Without cert.	1,295	6%	2,855	6%	11,565	5%	29,475	4%
With cert.	4,855	20%	10,505	20%	42,820	18%	111,035	16%
University								
Without degree	3,060	13%	6,330	12%	29,235	13%	64,855	10%
With degree	2,440	10%	6,335	12%	33,255	14%	58,875	9%

EXHIBIT 2 **1987 Statistics**

	B2W-FSA	DARTMTH.	HALIFAX
RRSP'S			
Taxfilers, No. of	19,350	58,050	86,025
RRSP Contrib., No. of	3,875	11,075	17,275
RRSP Contrib. $			
(000's)	11,260	34,530	55,007
INVESTMENTS			
Taxfilers, No. of	19,350	58,050	86,025
Invest. Income, No. declaring	7,325	21,800	37,675
Invest. Income $			
(000's)	10,646	44,110	155,762

SOURCE: Statistics Canada

EXHIBIT 3 **1988 Statistics**

	B2W-FSA	%	DARTMTH.	%	HALIFAX	%	N.S.	%
TAXFILERS								
Total taxfilers	17,525		59,650		89,200		565,950	
Male	9,075	52%	30,350	51%	43,675	49%	293,350	52%
Female	8,450	48%	29,300	49%	45,525	51%	272,600	48%
MARITAL STATUS								
Single	4,475	26%	17,950	30%	33,450	37%	161,450	29%
Married	11,250	64%	33,575	56%	41,200	46%	323,250	57%
Sep./Divorced	1,250	7%	5,525	9%	8,525	10%	45,825	8%
Widow/Widower	550	3%	2,625	5%	6,025	7%	35,400	6%
AGE DISTRIBUTION								
Under 25	3,100	18%	11,175	19%	16,150	18%	97,850	17%
25–34	5,125	29%	17,725	30%	25,175	28%	148,925	26%
35–49	5,525	32%	17,425	29%	22,275	25%	162,250	29%
50–64	2,875	16%	8,800	15%	13,450	15%	89,200	16%
65 +	875	5%	4,500	7%	12,175	14%	67,700	12%
INCOME EARNERS								
Wages/Salaries/								
Commissions	14,650		47,900		67,375		407,825	
Dividends	1,125		4,050		9,525		35,025	
Interest	7,125		23,125		39,375		211,825	
U.I.	2,575		9,275		13,175		127,275	
Pensions	2,475		9,575		18,725		113,125	
INCOME $	374.6M		1,228.6M		1,842M		9,743M	
Wages/Salaries/								
Commissions	325.6M	87%	1,037.9M	84%	1,419.8M	77%	7,583.2M	78%
Dividends	2.0M	1%	10.3M	1%	45.8M	3%	129.7M	1%
Interest	9.6M	2%	41.9M	3%	123.9M	7%	471.2M	5%
U.I.	8.5M	2%	30.6M	3%	43.5M	2%	495.4M	5%
Pensions	28.9M	8%	107.9M	9%	209.0M	11%	1,063.5M	11%
TAXFILERS IN								
LABOUR FORCE								
With Employmt.								
Income	15,100		49,450		70,250		434,525	
Male	8,325	55%	27,075	55%	37,000	53%	246,800	57%
Female	6,775	45%	22,375	45%	33,250	47%	187,725	43%
With U.I. Income	2,575		9,275		13,175		127,275	
Male	1,150	45%	4,350	47%	6,825	52%	72,300	57%
Female	1,425	55%	4,925	53%	6,350	48%	54,975	43%
MEDIAN TOTAL								
INCOME								
Both sexes	$19,500		$18,200		$18,000		$15,000	
Male	$29,500		$27,000		$22,600		$21,100	
Female	$12,600		$12,200		$14,400		$9,700	
Cdn. Index	113		106		105		87	
Prov. Index	130		121		120		100	

(Note: The indices refer to the medians for both sexes.)

(continued overleaf)

EXHIBIT 3 *(continued)*

	B2W-FSA	%	DARTMTH.	%	HALIFAX	%	N.S.	%
TOTAL INCOME	17,500		59,500		89,025		564,675	
Under $15,000	6,950	40%	25,125	42%	37,550	42%	282,825	50%
Male	2,150	31%	8,100	32%	14,000	37%	101,950	36%
Female	4,800	69%	17,025	68%	23,550	63%	180,875	64%
$15,000–24,999	3,725	21%	13,100	22%	21,700	24%	124,850	22%
Male	1,550	42%	5,875	45%	9,950	46%	70,475	56%
Female	2,175	58%	7,225	55%	11,750	54%	54,375	44%
$25,000–34,999	3,000	17%	9,650	16%	13,950	16%	79,050	14%
Male	2,075	69%	6,575	68%	8,125	58%	57,000	72%
Female	925	31%	3,075	32%	5,825	42%	22,050	28%
$35,000–49,999	2,625	15%	7,675	13%	9,650	11%	53,900	9%
Male	2,200	84%	6,150	80%	6,525	68%	42,450	79%
Female	425	16%	1,525	20%	3,125	32%	11,450	21%
$50,000–74,999	1,000	6%	3,150	5%	4,025	5%	17,670	53%
Male	925	93%	2,875	91%	3,200	80%	15,450	87%
Female	75	7%	275	9%	825	20%	2,225	13%
$75,000–$99,999	125	1%	500	1%	1,050	1%	3,325	1%
Male	125	100	450	90%	875	83%	2,900	87%
Female	—	—	50	10%	175	17%	425	13%
$100,000 +	75	—	300	1%	1,100	1%	3,050	1%
Male	75	100	275	92%	950	86%	2,750	90%
Female	—	—	—	—	150	14%	300	10%

AVERAGE HOUSEHOLD EXPENDITURE (1988/89)
in dollars

	B2W-FSA	%	DARTMTH.	%	HALIFAX	%		
Food	5,951	14%	5,797	15%	5,819	16%		
Shelter	7,182	18%	7,312	18%	6,260	17%		
Clothing	2,498	6%	2,493	6%	2,242	6%		
Transportation	4,815	12%	4,496	11%	4,705	13%		
Health & Personal Care	1,538	4%	1,494	4%	1,391	4%		
Recreation, Reading & Education	2,476	6%	2,461	6%	2,031	5%		
Taxes & Securities	9,639	24%	9,405	23%	7,534	21%		
Other	6,640	16%	6,804	17%	6,498	18%		
Total Expenditures	40,739		40,262		36,480			

SOURCE: Statistics Canada

EXHIBIT 4 **Dartmouth, N.S. Delivery area and forward sortation areas**

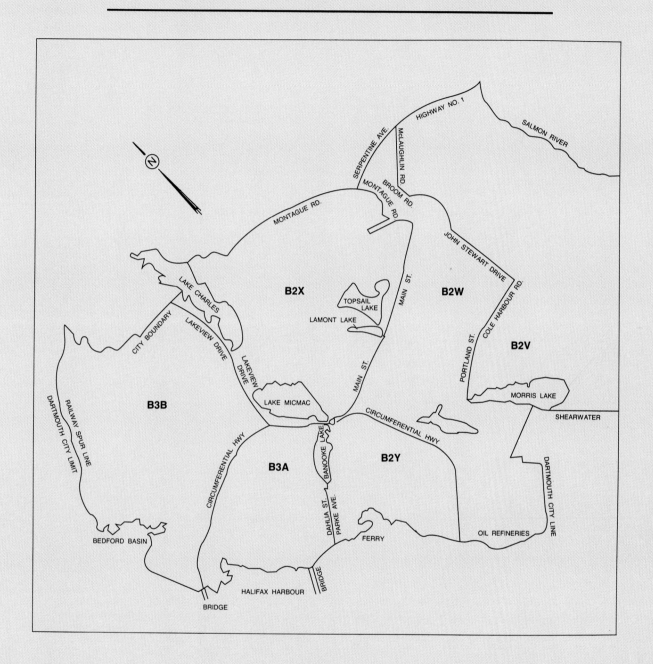

EXHIBIT 5

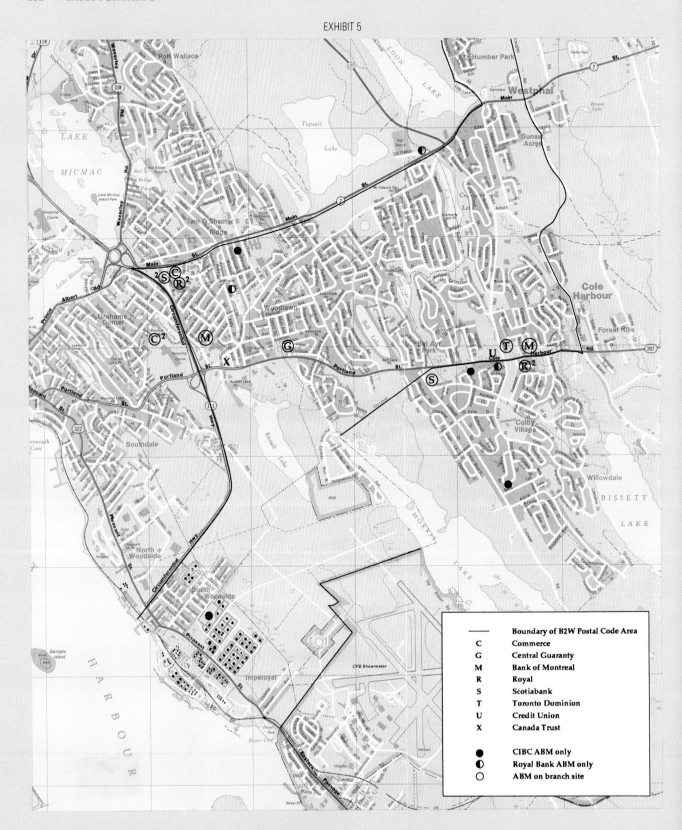

——	**Boundary of B2W Postal Code Area**
C	**Commerce**
G	**Central Guaranty**
M	**Bank of Montreal**
R	**Royal**
S	**Scotiabank**
T	**Toronto Dominion**
U	**Credit Union**
X	**Canada Trust**
●	**CIBC ABM only**
◐	**Royal Bank ABM only**
○	**ABM on branch site**

CASE 2.2   # Peter Taylor Buys Running Shoes

April was drawing to a close and the signs of spring were evident throughout the nation's capital. Peter Taylor was in the process of writing the final set of examinations for his Master's Degree in Business Administration at the University of Ottawa. As a marketing major and sports enthusiast, his primary job-search objective was to find a position in sports marketing, preferably in Toronto. Peter knew that Canada's largest city contained an established base of sports and fitness organizations that could be targeted as employment prospects. In addition, Toronto contained the head offices of many large corporations that are involved in sports sponsorship. He had already made tentative plans to be in Toronto by June 1.

Peter had been involved in sports and athletics for as long as he could remember. His father, also an athlete and a soccer coach, encouraged Peter's initial involvement in hockey and baseball from the time Peter was five or six years old. Up to high school, Peter's active involvement in the local minor hockey program was maintained throughout the fall and winter, and he was active in baseball during the spring and summer seasons. The high school hockey schedule demanded early morning and evening practices, which eventually led him to decrease his hockey participation to a recreational level.

As a natural athlete, Peter enjoyed the competition offered by court sports. He became an avid competitor throughout the school year — soccer in the fall, volleyball until Christmas, basketball in the new year until Easter, and then track and field in the spring.

Peter has always felt that a physically active life-style enhanced his academic performance and general wellbeing. His parents were very outdoors-oriented and concerned about health and diet. These factors contributed to Peter's performance and drive in all his athletic endeavours. After he completed high school in Peter-

borough and began his undergraduate program at Trent University, a heavy course schedule prevented him from participating in team sports as actively as he had previously. For recreation and to keep the old gang together, Peter and a group of his high school friends arranged for free gym time in their old school. Every couple of weeks they would round up players for an afternoon or evening of basketball or volleyball.

Peter was also an active intramural competitor. Twenty or so of Peter's friends in his Business Administration class were athletically inclined. They competed in a variety of intramural sports as the nucleus of the Business Administration teams throughout their four years at Trent. The team performed reasonably well, although the Arts and Physical Education teams were very competitive.

When Peter went on after graduation to the University of Ottawa for his MBA, few of his friends were surprised. They had expected for some time that Peter would try to combine his interest in marketing with his love for sports. During the often-gruelling two-year MBA program, Peter found less and less time for organized team sports. He rarely played hockey and did not compete in intramural sports. He did find time each week to swim in the university pool and he cycled to the university regularly from his apartment in the Glebe area of the city. He also took squash more seriously, playing at least twice a week, although he had played only a little at Trent. This was a sport he felt he could continue to play after graduation.

Now that Peter was nearing the end of his MBA program, he realized that an active involvement in team sports would become difficult. He intended to continue playing squash, as he required only one partner to play. However, he wished to pursue an alternative form of exercise to balance and enhance his overall fitness. He considered weight training, but preferred more active sports. Having done quite well in middle-distance track and field competitions during high school, Peter decided to take running more seriously. During his two years in Ottawa, he had done a little jogging from time to time along the Rideau Canal, which runs near the university, but the cold Ottawa winters discouraged him from maintaining a year-round schedule. He realized, however, that running was one physical activity he could do according to his own schedule. He felt he might even consider competing in some of the middle and longer distance runs that he knew were held on a regular basis in and around Toronto.

Although Peter considered himself quite knowledgeable about most sports, he also felt that there was probably more to running than just putting on a pair of sneakers and going out for a jog. He decided that he should take advantage of the fact that the head office of Athletics Canada was located in Ottawa to obtain some technical information on the sport. Intuition told him that he should expand his common-sense list of "do's" and "don'ts." By placing a telephone call to the office of Athletics Canada, he was able to obtain the address of the Ontario Track and Field Association, which he was advised could provide him with a list of track and roadrunning clubs he might wish to join in the Toronto area.

As he walked through the Rideau Centre on a Saturday afternoon, following the exam in his Marketing Strategy course, he stopped into W. H. Smith, a bookstore that carried a wide range of magazines. He was particularly interested in buying a running magazine that might tell him something more about the right equipment for the sport. He found two such magazines in the sports and fitness section of the magazine rack, *Runner's World* and *Running Times*. He was not familiar with either magazine, but as he thumbed through them he was surprised by the number of advertisements for running shoes, and by the "high-tech" descriptions of many of the shoes. He selected *Running Times*, primarily because of the section labelled "Annual Running Shoe Guide," which seemed to be just what he needed.

Of particular concern to Peter was the financial investment he would need to make if he was to take running seriously. Although he owned an ample supply of basic sportswear such as shorts, sweatshirts, and T-shirts, he knew that top-of-the-line running shoes and a rainsuit were two necessities that together might cost him $300 or more. Peter did not yet have a salary, but he was never one to scrimp on sports equipment. He rationalized that the time he invested in such activities deserved a comparable monetary investment. His father had always taught him the value of good equipment as insurance against accidents and injuries.

Peter decided that he would wait until he moved to Toronto to join a running club and to learn more about the technique of the sport. Right now, he determined that he needed to get back to exercising regularly again, following the past few months of the MBA program, which had left him little time to work out. The more he thought about running, and stimulated by the articles in *Running Times*, the more anxious he was to begin running regularly as soon as his exams were over. He realized that he needed to know what running shoes to purchase and how best to prevent running injuries.

He was also beginning to realize that he knew very little about the engineering and technology of running shoes. Although he had bought other athletic footwear during the past few years, he had not appreciated the diversity of styles and models available. Advertisements in *Running Times* stressed materials such as Hexalite and Dynalite, cushioning based on air, fluids, gel, and foam, and glitzy colours and styles. Peter was unaware of the benefits that each system offered. He read terms such as "rearfoot control," "heel counter," and "shock distribution," but felt ignorant about what shoe he should buy.

The wide variety of running shoes displayed in retail stores and featured in running magazines and the range of prices, colours, and styles made the decision even more complex. Rapidly changing technology, eye-catching innovations, and clever marketing tended to sway Peter from brand to brand without his knowing if the shoe matched his own needs and requirements. Running-shoe purchases, as Peter had learned through consumer behaviour textbooks, seemed to be determined by how the buyer wishes to be perceived, whether to be trendy or athletic. Running-shoe buyers often appeared to Peter to be very fickle, depending on what appealed to them or caught their eye at the point of purchase. He knew that serious runners often buy two or three different pairs, rotating them from day to day. He concluded that, as advanced engineering has transformed running shoes into technical and fashionable articles, their purchase had become a conspicuous activity and their wearing a "fashion statement."

Peter wanted to make sure that he bought the right brand of running shoe. As he mulled over his decision, he identified criteria he felt he should consider in the selection process. Despite the wide price range of the shoes advertised in the magazine, high price was not a deterrent to Peter's purchase decision. Although he expected to pay more than $100 for a pair of quality running shoes, he preferred to keep the expense close to that level if at all possible. Comfort, availability, and protection against injury were critical to Peter. Colour was not at all important, although some shoes seemed a little too flashy. He was tending towards a lighter-weight shoe, which seemed to be preferred for longer distances, to protect against tiring. Peter felt that if each of these criteria was satisfied, he could run at his optimal capability.

To ensure that he was on the right track, he arranged a meeting with Sheila Cambridge at Athletics Canada. Sheila was a consultant with the association and held the provincial record for the 10-km distance. Peter had met Sheila at a campus party several weeks ago and knew that she was held in high regard in the local athletic community. She would also be well versed in the technical aspects of running-shoe construction, as she had graduated from the University of Ottawa a year earlier having specialized in kinesiology. Peter felt confident that she would be able to provide the expert advice he needed to pick the *right* pair of running shoes. "Besides," thought Peter as he walked along the canal towards Sheila's office, "it will be nice to see Sheila again."

Peter enjoyed the meeting with Sheila, as they discussed mutual friends and Sheila's training for the summer roadracing season. Peter learned that she had been training for the past four months in preparation for her first attempt at the marathon distance, to take place in mid-May in Ottawa's National Capital Marathon. Peter began to feel a little ill at ease, as he realized that

Sheila was obviously far more knowledgeable about running than he was. He wondered whether he would ever reach the same level of training that she had achieved and felt a little uncomfortable at the thought of asking very basic questions about what shoes he should buy. He wondered whether he shouldn't just end the conversation.

It was too late when Sheila said, "Enough about my running. You wanted to talk about running shoes, didn't you? How much running are you planning to do?" Peter explained that he had participated in track and field in high school, but at distances from 400 to 1500 m. He now wanted to try running some longer distances, primarily to get back in shape. He also thought he might like to run some road races and even try a little cross-country. With that, Sheila pulled from a pile of magazines and books on her desk a back issue of *Running Times*. She turned to a page that contained a diagram of the various components of a running shoe (Exhibit 1). She explained to Peter those components to which he should pay particular attention. "In selecting a running shoe," she explained, "the factor that I consider most important is fit. If the shoe doesn't fit well, you are likely to encounter problems down the road."

Sheila further suggested that one of the main criteria that Peter must satisfy in his purchase of running shoes was protection against injury and overload. Research into the causes of injury have pointed to the type of running surface as one of the possible causes. She explained that common running injuries and ailments include leg fractures, muscle pulls and tears, heel spurs, shin splints, and knee injuries.

Although Peter felt he would prefer cross-country training through wooded and grassy areas, he observed that access to scenic trails would likely be limited once he moved to Toronto. "In that case," explained Sheila, "your running shoe must provide stability and protection against the high impact of pounding on the pavement. Not only do the interior components of the shoe have to protect your feet, but the exterior components such as the outsole will be important in cushioning against impact."

Other factors Sheila mentioned as contributing to injury were the type of movement, the training distance per week, and the intensity of train-

EXHIBIT 1

Glossary of Terms

Shoe Part	Term	Explanation
	Rearfoot Stability	Prevents excessive lateral wobble or sag, and is important to severe pronators (see opposite page).
	Achilles Notch	Soft, padded material above heel counter cushions Achilles tendon and is sometimes notched to prevent irritation of the tendon.
	Heel Counter	Rigid cup holds heel firmly in place to prevent lateral motion.
	Heel Counter Collar	Reinforces heel counter.
	Dual-density midsole	Higher density on medial (inner) side of shoe resists compression and makes it harder for the foot to pronate (roll or sag sideways toward the inward side).
Rear Foot	**Forefoot stability strap**	Helps to keep the upper material (usually a light nylon fabric or mesh) from sagging or bursting out; also helps to prevent excessive lateral motion of the forefoot.
	Toe Box	Should be roomy enough to let toes wiggle freely, with at least a thumb's width of space between toe and front wall of box. Foot should be snug around the heel, roomy around the toes.
	Midsole	Cushions the foot. Simplest midsoles are pieces of EVA foam. A more durable material is lightweight polyurethane (PU).
	Air Sac and Fluid Sac Midsole Components (Nike Air, Etonic StableAir, Brooks Hydroflow, Asics Gel, Reebok ERS, Hi-Tec AirBall, etc.)	Cushions impact of heel on the road, lengthens life of the shoe by preventing squashing of midsole (units are usually contained in strong PU casings) and may help stabilize ride by distributing impact.
Upper & Midsole	**Flexible Plate Midsole Components** (Nike Footbridge, Avia ARC, Etonic graphite plate, etc.)	Cushions impact by distributing impact over a wider area, and ARC combines this cushioning with a trampoline effect for greater energy return or "bounce."
	Heel Plug	Carbon/rubber resists abrasion, prevents wearing through prematurely at outside corner of the heel.
	Horseshoe Outsole (Nike Center-of-Pressure, Avia Cantilever)	Distributes weight to perimeter to maximize stability, while allowing center of rearfoot outsole to be scooped out (see Exposed Midsole, below).
	Exposed (Recessed) Midsole	Often in the center of the rearfoot bottom, and sometimes across the midfoot bottom, sections of dense outsole are scooped out in areas where foot contact with the ground isn't needed. This cuts down on the weight of the shoe, helps to keep the heel centered (by allowing it to sink down more in the center than on either side), and allows the foot to trampoline for better energy return.
	Filled-in Medial Arch	Resists pronation by preventing sag at instep. Similarly, **straight-lasted** shoe has straight shape suitable for stabilizing motion for hard heel-hitters and severe pronators. **Curved-lasted** models facilitate natural motion for forefoot-strikers and faster-paced runners.
Outsole	**Outsole Studs or Lugs**	Provide traction, especially important in the forefoot area, for both heel-strikers and forefoot-strikers. Tread patterns vary widely, but generally the smoother patterns are more effective for roads, the toothier patterns better in snow or mud or off-road.

Reprinted with permission of *Running Times* magazine.

ing. She went on to explain that protection against overloading is also important. ''Load is the external force acting upon a body. It results both from dynamic factors such as the type of movement, the velocity of limbs, posture, muscular activity, and the number of repetitions, and also from boundary conditions such as the shoe surface, obstacles, anthropometric factors, and individual situation,'' she explained.

Peter found himself listening less intently as the information that Sheila was offering began to sound much more technical than he had expected. He really just wanted her to recommend a pair of running shoes and was not interested in all the technical jargon. When Sheila suggested that he attend a running clinic to check out what some of the local runners were wearing, Peter asked her what she would buy if she was in his position.

Sheila said that she really couldn't recommend a brand or model that would be best for him, as there were many acceptable shoes available. She did say that she ran in Nike shoes and that Nike is, in her opinion, the leading running shoe in the market. She suggested that he probably wouldn't be disappointed if he bought a Nike shoe, possibly an Air Stab or an Air Span. Peter wondered if her opinion might be biased by her personal choice. He thanked her, but felt a little disappointed to have left without knowing why Nike would be a good choice.

Heading home the next day, following his final exam in marketing research, Peter decided to visit Sports Experts, a sporting goods store in the Rideau Centre, to look at the selection of running shoes and to price the various brands and styles that he had seen in a recent advertising flyer from the store. He had often found the sales clerks in sporting goods stores to be knowledgeable and hoped that he might get some advice concerning running shoes. Although he was familiar with a number of sporting goods stores in the Ottawa area, Peter decided to visit only three of them, all located within the downtown area. Over the next day or two, he would check the variety and prices at Sports Experts, Elgin Sports, and Sports-4.

Sports Experts had a reputation for a wide selection and good service. Generally, Peter did not appreciate being hounded by sales clerks in stores. He had never found the sales clerks in this particular store to be pushy, but rather genuinely helpful and friendly. Many seemed to be students who were working in the store part-time. After he had been given a few minutes to scan the huge wall display of running, court, squash, tennis, aerobic, basketball, cross-training, volleyball, sprinting, cycling, and windsurfing shoes, a sales clerk approached him and offered her assistance.

Peter had been looking closely at several Nike and Brooks styles, as he had worn both brands in the court and cross-training styles in the past and had been very satisfied with them. He asked the sales clerk which of the brands was considered best and what benefits each had to offer.

The Sports Expert sales clerk, Donna Williams, proceeded to explain that neither was necessarily the best brand. She suggested that Peter's decision should be based on comfort and ensuring that the width was neither too narrow nor so wide that the foot shifted from side to side. She felt that price was generally a good measure of the quality of the shoe, but not necessarily of the brand. She recommended that Peter try one style of each of the major brands, so that he could determine the fit of each of the shoes, and whether the cushioning felt right.

Donna went on to suggest that sturdiness could be tested by bending the shoe from right to left, and by ensuring that the heel components of the shoe felt firm. The lightness of the various shoes could be compared easily. Once the most comfortable brand of shoe was identified, price could be used along with a visual test of features to determine which shoe fulfilled his need. Donna suggested that generally the higher the price, the more stability and features were associated with the running shoe. She felt that gimmicks, such as endorsements by personalities, Velcro closures, and fluorescent colours, would probably inflate the price, but did not necessarily enhance the shoe's quality. So the quality-conscious consumer, as compared to the socially conscious one, would need to search beyond superficial features. Donna Williams indicated that it was often very difficult to tell, having been influenced by advertising and other marketing strategies, which features were truly beneficial for a runner such as Peter and which had merely been promoted to make a shoe stand out from the competition. She felt that the consumer did not necessarily need to be a technical expert or sports engineer to perceive the difference, but should be educated as to what was most necessary given his or her running style, training schedule, desired features, and price range.

Peter proceeded to try one Nike, one Brooks, one Reebok, and one Asics running shoe, all within the same price range. Donna Williams suggested that he walk and jog down the mall corridor outside the store for a more realistic indication of comfort and stability. This comparison would give him a better basis for comparing what features were offered by each brand. Peter declined the offer to jog in the mall. Instead, he tried on each pair of shoes and walked around the store. He decided that he felt most comfortable with the Nike shoes, as the air cushioning and light weight seemed to offer more spring, and he felt would diminish some of the impact he would experience running on hard surfaces.

Peter remembered Sheila Cambridge's recommendation. Although Peter was sold on the Nike brand, the particular style he had tried, the Air Max, felt a little wide on his narrow foot. Donna Williams explained that the only shoe manufacturer who offered shoes in a full range of widths was New Balance, and asked whether he would like to try a pair. Peter explained that he really liked the feel of the Nike shoe, but he wanted to find one that felt a little less wide. Donna suggested another Nike shoe, the Air Stab, which Peter proceeded to try. Feeling satisfied with the shoe, he jogged on the spot as a test of this new style. He felt that he had finally found what he had been looking for.

Peter asked Donna to hold the shoes for him until closing that night. This would provide ample time for him to ensure that the other stores were not offering the Nike Air Stab at a lower price than $129.99. Peter thanked Donna Williams for her help and left Sports Experts to see what the other stores had to offer. As he walked towards the mall exit on Laurier Street, he passed another sporting goods store and was attracted by a large wall display of athletic shoes. Athlete's World was offering the Nike Air Stab at the same price he had found at Sports Experts, so Peter left the store quickly, feeling that Sports Experts deserved the sale, considering that Donna Williams had invested considerable time helping him.

Peter decided to head for Bank Street, where he could see the offerings at Elgin Sports and Sports-4. Elgin Sports was an established Ottawa sporting goods store, with its original outlet on Elgin Street. A couple of years ago, the company had opened a second store on Bank Street, which offered a wide variety of sports clothing and shoes. Sports-4 was a newer store, having opened just two or three years ago. Peter felt that the Sports-4 outlet was much more of a running specialty store, as a display near the door contained notices of forthcoming road races and triathlons.

The Elgin Sports store on Bank Street also had the Air Stabs priced at $129.99, which left Peter wondering if he was needlessly running around the city when he could have purchased the pair of shoes he had seen at Sports Experts. Upon entering Sports-4, Peter was pleasantly surprised, as the Nike Air Stab was on a special promotion for $99.99. Peter was thrilled with this $30 savings and asked if he could try on a size 9, feeling he really couldn't buy a pair of shoes without trying them on. The sales clerk disappeared into the storage room for a few minutes only to walk out empty-handed. He looked at Peter apologetically and informed him that unfortunately a 9 1/2 was the smallest size they had in stock.

Peter decided to try them on anyway. Perhaps the extra half-size wouldn't make much difference to the fit. After all, he would be saving $30 in the process. However, the extra space in the toe was quite noticeable, even with the thick socks the clerk had handed him to try with the shoes. Peter wondered how this difference might affect his running performance. His past experience with athletic footwear suggested that the shoe would stretch a little with wear, especially if exposed to wet conditions. Disappointed, Peter felt he would have to forfeit the $30 savings and be satisfied with the fact that he was still fairly close to this initial price range.

Geoff Wallace, the clerk at Sports-4, suggested that he measure Peter's foot to make sure that he did indeed require a size 9. Having confirmed that this was Peter's correct size, he advised strongly against buying a half-size larger, indicating it was his opinion that fit is of critical importance when selecting a pair of running shoes. He then asked Peter to walk up and down in front of the shoe display so that he might examine how his feet struck the floor as he walked.

Geoff observed that Peter tended to strike the floor first with the outer edge of his foot, a tendency referred to as supination, and suggested that Peter might like to try a pair of Brooks GFS-105 shoes, explaining that this was a shoe that offered excellent fit and the Hydroflow cushioning system. He also explained that the GFS-105 featured a curved last, which was recommended for people who tended to supinate. Peter was impressed at the time Geoff was taking to help him select the right shoe and with the fact that the Brooks GFS-105 shoe was on sale at a special price of $109. Peter declined Geoff's suggestion politely, explaining that he had decided on the Nike Air Stab.

Peter was wondering, as he left Sports-4, if he might be able to strike a deal at Sports Experts, considering he should probably think about buying a rainsuit anyway. After dinner, he walked back to the Rideau Centre, wandered into Sports Experts, and was met by Donna Williams, who had been so helpful earlier in the day. Peter requested the running shoes that he had asked her to hold for him, but expressed his dismay over the better deal offered by Sports-4. Peter asked if he might speak with the manager about the possibility of matching the Sports-4 price.

While Donna disappeared to get the manager, Peter spotted a Nike rainsuit that appealed to him and had been marked down in price. As he took the rainsuit off the display rack, he was greeted by the manager who had been directed to Peter by Donna Williams. Peter explained his dilemma and asked if Sports-4's sale price on the Nike Air Stab might be matched, provided that he purchase the rainsuit he had selected. The manager was eager for business and goodwill, especially since he considered Sports-4 to be Sports Experts' main competitor for running and triathlon equipment in the city. He nodded and offered to ring in the sale for him, all the while making conversation about running in Ottawa. Peter appreciated the concession that Sports Experts had made and thanked the manager and Donna Williams, telling them that he would be sure to shop at Sports Experts stores in Toronto on a regular basis.

While running slowly along the Rideau Canal later that evening, Peter met Sheila Cambridge, who had just finished a 10-km run. The clean white of Peter's new shoes caught her eye and she commented that he had made an excellent choice. Peter continued on his run towards his apartment on the other side of the canal, feeling satisfied with his purchase. He could sense that he was going to enjoy running, and he was already thinking about entering his first road race later that summer.

QUESTIONS

1. Identify the various factors that influenced Peter Taylor's behaviour in selecting a pair of running shoes. Why did he select the Nike brand?

2. What objectives do you feel Peter was trying to accomplish in the selection of running shoes? What motivated his final selection?

3. Why did he buy his shoes at Sports Experts? What could Geoff Wallace have done to persuade Peter to buy the Brooks shoe (or any other) at Sports-4?

CASE 2.3 **Atlantic Lottery Corporation**

In 1989, recognizing the steady increase of consumer dollars spent on government lotteries in Canada, Rafael Candela, Manager — Research and Development for the Atlantic Lottery Corporation, decided that the corporation required detailed information on their customers if they were to develop this market further. Mr. Candela's objective in requesting this research was to determine the buying behaviour of lottery ticket purchasers in Atlantic Canada.

LOTTERIES IN CANADA

The Atlantic Lottery Corporation was formed in 1976 with the signing of an interprovincial agreement by the four Atlantic provinces and the creation of a Crown corporation for the management and operative functions of the lottery. This grouping of the provinces followed a general movement across Canada, since the legalization of lotteries in 1969, towards the formation of regional lottery corporations. In 1976, the four regional corporations joined to form the Interprovincial Lottery Corporation. Several Canada-wide lotteries developed from this — The Provincial in 1976, Super Loto in 1980, and Lotto 6/49 in 1982. The Interprovincial Lottery Corporation presently comprises five regional marketing organizations — the Atlantic Lottery Corporation, Loto Quebec, the Ontario Lottery Corporation, the Western Canada Lottery Corporation, and the British Columbia Lottery Corporation.

The legalization of Canadian lotteries and the increasing opportunities to participate have prompted regular ticket purchases. Since 1976, the amount spent on government lotteries has increased dramatically to a level of $2.7 billion in 1985.

In Canada, as in other countries, mixed feelings exist towards state-sponsored lotteries. Some proponents argue that lotteries act to discourage the flow of funds into illegal gambling and provide a safe outlet for the disposal of funds that might otherwise be used for alcohol or drug consumption. These supporters of the concept view lotteries as harmless entertainment that assists in funding government programs and services, through a vehicle that is socially more acceptable than higher taxation. Opponents, on the other hand, argue that lotteries encourage excessive and compulsive gambling, weaken moral fibre, discourage the "work ethic," and diminish the equality of the economy's income distribution.

INSTANT GAMES

Instant games are of two varieties: "Scratch-and-win" or "Break-Open" (Nevada). Scratch-and-win tickets cost the purchaser either $1 or $2, whereas Nevada tickets are usually priced at 50¢. The outcome of playing the game is known to the purchaser at the point of purchase. This feature differentiates instant games from non-instant games. The retailer reimburses the player with any winnings (within a range) to which the player is entitled. Maximum winnings for $1 tickets are usually $1,000, and for $2 tickets, $10,000.

There are a variety of instant games available from most government-sponsored lotteries, including sports games, card/dice games, seasonal games, match games, and add-up games. Rafael Candela knew tht consumer preferences for these games vary and are not only dependent on the type of game, but also on perceptions about a number of factors, including game newness, prize levels, and "personal decision rules."

Approximately 3,500 retailers throughout Atlantic Canada sell and promote the Atlantic Lottery Corporation's products and games, and they are paid a commission for every ticket sold. Although ticket commissions make up the most

Copyright 1991. This case has been written by Leanne O'Leary and James G. Barnes of Memorial University of Newfoundland, with the co-operation of the Atlantic Lottery Corporation, and is intended to illustrate various aspects of marketing and not to indicate the correct or incorrect handling of marketing activities. The authors acknowledge the co-operation and support of Rafael Candela, Manager of Research and Development, Atlantic Lottery Corporation, and Craig Wight, Executive Vice-President, Omnifacts Research Limited, in the preparation of this case.

significant portion of retailer remuneration, seller's prizes and fees for cashing winning tickets have contributed increasingly to total retailer compensation. Fees are paid to retailers for every cash prize paid to holders of winning tickets.

Tickets are distributed through a variety of outlets. Ticket booths, convenience stores, supermarkets, mall kiosks, and local bars are popular spots for purchasing both instant and non-instant lottery games. Although the instant-ticket player segment includes a wide range of people, qualitative research has been successful in identifying the purchase patterns of these buyers. Research conducted for the Atlantic Lottery Corporation had shown that the purchase of scratch-and-win tickets in a shopping mall setting generally follows the purchase of another kind of ticket. However, some instant-win players make special trips to buy scratch-and-win tickets. These tickets are often purchased with food items in smaller retail locations. The research concluded that generally, in all locations, instant tickets are an impulse purchase.

MARKETING RESEARCH

After evaluating the resources within the Atlantic Lottery Corporation, Rafael Candela realized that the nature of the additional research to be conducted would require the services of an external marketing research company. A review of several regional and national marketing research firms resulted in the choice of Omnifacts Research Limited, a regional marketing research company with offices in Halifax, Nova Scotia; St. John's, Newfoundland; and Fredericton, New Brunswick. Mr. Candela discussed the objectives that Atlantic Lottery had established for the research project with Craig Wight, executive vice-president of Omnifacts and account manager for the Atlantic Lottery project. The goals established for the project were: to examine the purchase habits of instant-ticket buyers; to discuss retailer influence; to determine and rank the reasons for game purchase; to determine the factors that influence the purchase of instant-game tickets; to examine new games and the various changes in a game's features that would constitute a new game by lottery ticket buyers; and to examine wins and the use of winnings.

In designing the marketing research project, and in particular the collection of data, Craig Wight proposed using a combination of focus groups and in-mall testing. Focus groups that addressed consumer and retailer opinions appeared to be the best method to gather the necessary information.

CONSUMER FOCUS GROUPS

Six consumer focus group interviews were conducted in Dartmouth, Nova Scotia; St. John's, Newfoundland; and Saint John, New Brunswick. The composition of the groups was determined after screening on the basis of occupation and prior participation in focus groups. Those qualifying as participants were instant-game players who spent $3 or more on scratch-and-win lottery games every week. The participants were grouped by sex and age in four groups: younger male (19-35 years), younger female (19-35 years), older male (36-65 years), older female (36-65 years). There were two mixed groups.

A questionnaire, administered at the beginning of each focus group session, asked players to indicate which instant games they played. This short questionnaire listed all the instant games that have been available in Atlantic Canada, as well as two fictitious games. Results indicated that participants had played an average of approximately 10 out of the 23 games listed, suggesting that the groups comprised long-term, involved instant game players.

From the focus group discussions, it was discovered that tickets are usually bought if the game is perceived to be new or the newest because these games have a novelty and excitement appeal and are felt to have a fresh prize pool. Old tickets are difficult to sell because they are perceived as leftovers, having few remaining winners. These tickets become attractive only if players are aware of remaining unclaimed prizes. Knowledge of previous wins from a particular game (for either that person or another individual) increases the appeal of that game.

Focus group participants were also asked to rate the importance of several factors in their game evaluation process; the results of this procedure are contained in Exhibit 1. The use of quantitative techniques such as ranking with a ten-point scale was included in the qualitative

EXHIBIT 1 **Importance of Game Factors**

	Group 2	Group 3	Group 4	Group 6
Familiar/Habit			8.0	7.8
New	7.3	8.0	8.4	7.5
Prize Levels				6.4
Previous Wins	7.4			
Design	7.1			
Different			8.1	
Simple			8.5	

focus group to pinpoint respondents' feelings. The data provided from this exercise were not interpreted literally but were used as a guideline to generate group discussion.

Game appeals include newness, themes such as cards, sports, or seasonal (attraction to males predominantly), colours (females predominantly), add-up games, and match games. Add-up games require that the player add several scores to match or beat a score; for example, in a baseball game the player would attempt to add innings and home runs to beat a given number of home runs.

Variety was also found to be critical to the success of instant games. Exhibit 2 provides the results of participant ratings of the various types of instant game styles. The focus groups revealed that ticket selection is a process based primarily on personal decision rules. Such rules, as admitted by the participants, may be: "If they are all neat and one is crooked, I'll buy that one"; "I always pick from the same spot on the board"; and "If the guy doesn't pick one ticket, I'll make sure I get that one." Some players will purchase tickets from the newest game, believing it to have the largest number of prizes remaining. It appears that the use of such decision rules for selecting tickets depends entirely on the individual.

The level of winnings was infrequently mentioned during the focus group discussion. Prize levels over $1,000 are not seen to be important to the instant-game purchase as players expect to win only the small prizes. Smaller winnings are often used to justify the purchase of more tickets. Self-choice of tickets is a major part of instant-ticket purchase and focus groups participants indicated that locations where this choice is unavailable are often avoided.

Consumers purchasing $2 instant games rather than the $1 games do so because of the higher prize level and two play areas, each offering the opportunity to win. The $2 games are played less frequently than $1 games because consumers find it more difficult to part with the larger amount of money.

The focus group participants stated that there was limited retailer influence on the instant-ticket purchase decision.

RETAILER FOCUS GROUPS

Four retailer focus groups were conducted, with five to seven participants per group, selected in conjunction with Atlantic Lottery Corporation. Topics discussed were similar to those covered in the consumer focus groups sessions. Two

EXHIBIT 2 **Ratings of Game Styles**

GAME	Group 2	Group 3	Group 4	Group 5	Group 6
Card Game	5.3	7.2	8.5	8.3	7.9
Match Game	9.0	8.3	8.6	7.5	7.2
Add-Up	6.1	5.4	7.1	6.5	7.3
Sports	3.0	4.7	6.4	4.9	5.7
Dice		7.6	8.5		
Seasonal				5.3	6.0

additional topics of discussion included an analysis of items that increase and decrease sales, and a look at visits of Atlantic Lotto sales personnel to the retailer outlets. Two focus groups were conducted in Dartmouth, one in St. John's, and one in Saint John. The first Dartmouth group comprised mainly large mall accounts; the second contained primarily smaller accounts. The other two groups contained a mixture of large and small accounts.

The discussions with retailers revealed that some retailers use suggestive selling techniques (special occasions, clever use of change, etc.) to encourage instant-ticket purchases. This influence is minimal and inconsistent, however, as a number of retailers, especially those in smaller operations, merely display tickets and wait for customer requests. Retailers were also found to be reluctant to sell a large number of games in their stores because of the difficulty of managing many different games. Evidence revealing ineffective use of sales materials and displays, and inactive selling roles, indicated that the Atlantic Lottery sales force could take more initiative to encourage greater retailer participation. However, most retailers indicated that they were well informed by the Atlantic Lottery sales force.

Retailers described heavy instant players as older, less well-off, office and mall workers, who they perceived to play for "time-killing" purposes or as activities during breaks from work. Factors considered important as instant-game selection criteria by retailers paralleled those discussed in the consumer focus groups.

IN-MALL TEST

To quantify the variables that were identified throughout the focus groups, Craig Wight at Omnifacts developed a creative data-collection methodology. For the Atlantic Lottery project, Mr. Wight employed an in-mall consumer test. This testing methodology draws on the principles of mall intercept, experimental, and survey techniques. The in-mall test, utilizing these varied principles of research, provides a novel quantitative methodology for lottery research in Canada. Conducted in St. John's, the test consisted of four interview stations and was administered to 200 people. Each station isolated one or two key variables for testing with participants, all of whom were regular instant-game players spending at least $3 weekly on instant games.

At the first interview station, participants rated six types of instant games by circling a number from 1 to 10 (10 being an excellent game type). Each game type received a high rating from approximately the same number of people, leading Mr. Wight to conclude that different people prefer different types of games and that no game has universal appeal.

The second station tested the prize level at which participants would play. The results supported the focus group findings that many instant players do not really expect to win large prizes and would opt for smaller prizes with better odds. Exhibit 3 contains results from the testing at the second station.

Station 3 presented participants with the opportunity to select two tickets from a pool of eleven different tickets. Upon selection, the participant was asked to quantify the reasons for his or her choice and the importance of the varied prize levels. The results obtained from this test, as detailed in Exhibit 4, parallel the focus group discussions.

At the final station, participants were offered a selection of two $1 tickets or one $2 ticket. After the selection process was complete, the participants were questioned concerning the reasons

EXHIBIT 3 **Prize Level**

Level Chosen	n	%
Total Sample	201	100
$5	19	9
$25	20	10
$100	40	20
$1,000	122	61

EXHIBIT 4 **Reasons for Game Choice 1**

	Triple Play	Loto Hockey	Jokers Wild	Lucky Dice	Holiday Cash	Holiday Bonus	7-11-21	Tic-Tac-Toe	Zodiac	Match 3
	%	%	%	%	%	%	%	%	%	%
Total Sample	100	100	100	100	100	100	100	100	100	100
Prize level	37	0	34	11	21	0	0	0	0	11
Game theme	11	67	9	5	31	25	15	21	57	0
Style of play	15	22	13	25	7	25	23	21	14	11
Has won before	11	0	22	18	28	50	15	7	14	0
Colour	4	0	0	2	0	0	0	0	0	22
Graphics	11	0	0	4	3	0	8	0	0	0
Familiar with game	4	0	0	11	3	0	8	7	14	0
You can win more	4	11	19	19	3	0	23	14	0	33
Easy to understand/play	0	0	0	4	3	0	0	14	0	22
Don't know	4	0	3	4	0	0	8	14	0	0

Reasons for Game Choice 2

	Triple Play	Loto Hockey	Jokers Wild	Lucky Dice	Holiday Cash	Holiday Bonus	7-11-21	Tic-Tac-Toe	Cold Cash	Zodiac	Match 3
	%	%	%	%	%	%	%	%	%	%	%
Total Sample	100	100	100	100	100	100	100	100	100	100	100
Prize level	20	0	15	17	26	14	16	13	0	7	0
Game theme	20	54	28	21	17	14	5	23	0	43	0
Style of play	33	15	21	10	9	0	16	19	0	14	11
Has won before	7	8	10	7	13	0	11	0	0	29	0
Colour	7	0	0	0	9	43	0	3	50	0	11
Graphics	0	8	3	0	0	0	0	0	50	7	33
Familiar with game	0	0	3	3	0	14	11	13	0	0	11
You can win more	0	15	15	21	22	14	42	16	0	0	33
Easy to understand/play	0	0	3	3	0	0	0	6	0	0	0
Don't know	13	0	3	17	4	0	0	6	0	0	0

for their choices. The results at this final step supported the focus-group findings in that prize level and more chances to win were mentioned more often as reasons for choice. The choice of $1 tickets generally centred on perceptions regarding the chances of winning (more prizes), prize level, and game style, whereas $2 tickets were chosen most often because of higher prize levels and two playing areas (the perception of more chances to win).

RESEARCH RECOMMENDATIONS

Upon completion of the data collection and data analysis, Omnifacts Research presented Atlantic Lottery Corporation with a formal research report. The report prepared for Rafael Candela and the Atlantic Lottery management team included recommendations based on the research results.

Consumer Oriented

- Sell four to six $1 instant games at any given time (e.g., a card game, a sports game, an appropriate seasonal game, a matching game, and an add-up game).
- Discontinue the unnecessary rotation of games every three or four months. Initiate long runs in two- to three-month rotations as

new games signify new prize pools for players. Very subtle changes in the games, such as colour or design, may be perceived as new games for the player, although not by the Lottery Corporation.

- Consider a $500 maximum prize for $1 tickets and eliminate game prize levels over $1,000 for this ticket prize.
- Sell two or three $2 instant games at any given time, following a colour pulsing strategy.
- Reduce the $2 instant game maximum jackpot to $10,000, providing for more intermediate winners.
- Launch one or two "totally new" instant games annually with colour pulsing to replace one of the available games.
- For "mature" ticket games on the market, communicate unclaimed prizes to ticket buyers to prevent games from being avoided because of the misconception that no prizes remain to be won.

Retailer Oriented

- Encourage ticket displays that allow consumers to choose their own tickets.
- Educate retailers concerning effective merchandising and selling techniques, providing

financial support to expand or improve the area where lottery tickets are sold.
- Treat suggestion implementation as a case study in order that results are documented and used as an incentive to other retailers.

QUESTIONS

1. Evaluate the research methodology and results obtained from the marketing research conducted for Rafael Candela.

2. What additional information does Mr. Candela need to prepare a strategy for the marketing of instant-win lottery games? How should this information be obtained?

3. What research might the Atlantic Lottery Corporation and other lottery corporations conduct to allow them to do a better job of marketing other lottery products such as Lotto 6/49? How would this research be different from that which has been described in this case?

4. What differences can you identify between research on lottery products and research that might be conducted for marketing managers who deal with other products and services?

CASE 2.4   **Bookends, Limited***

PLANNING A MARKETING RESEARCH PROJECT

Late one August morning, Katie Martin, co-owner of Bookends, Limited, sat at her desk near the back wall of her cluttered office. With some irritation, she had just concluded that the calculator on her desk could help no more. "What we still need," she thought, "are estimates of demand and market share . . . but at least we have two weeks to get them."

Martin's office was located at the rear of Bookends, a 200-square-metre bookstore specializing in quality paperbacks. The store carried over

10,000 titles and had sold more than $600,000 worth of books in 1988. Titles were stocked in 18 categories ranging from art, biography, and cooking to religion, sports, and travel.

Bookends was located in a small strip shopping centre, across the street from the main entrance of Prairie University (PU). The university had a student population of approximately 10,000 students, enrolled in arts and science programs and in a number of professional schools (including Business, Engineering, Social Work, and Education). Despite downward trends in enrolment in many Canadian universities, the

---

*This case was adapted by James G. Barnes from a case originally developed by James E. Nelson. Used with permission

PU admissions office had predicted that the number of students entering first year would grow at about 1 percent a year until the mid 1990s. The city in which PU was located, with a population of approximately 150,000, was expected to grow at about twice that rate.

Bookends carried no textbooks, even though many of its customers were PU students. Both Martin and her partner, Susan Campbell, felt that the PU campus bookstore had too firm a grip on the textbook market because of price, location, and reputation to allow Bookends to make any inroads into that market. Bookends also carried no classical records. They had been part of the regular stock of the store until two months earlier, when that area of the store was converted to an expanded fitness and nutrition section. Martin recalled with some discomfort the $15,000 or so they had lost on classical records. "Another mistake like that and the bank will end up running Bookends," she thought. "And, despite what Susan thinks, the photocopy service could just be that final mistake."

The idea for a photocopy service had come from Susan Campbell. She had seen the candy store next door to Bookends go out of business in July. She had immediately asked the owner of the shopping centre, Angus Anderson, about the future of the 80-square-metre space. Upon learning it was available, she had met with Martin to discuss her idea for the photocopy service. She had spoken excitedly about the opportunity: "It can't help but make money. I could work there part-time and the rest of the time we could hire students. We could call it 'Copycats' and even use a sign with the same type of letters as we do in 'Bookends.' I'm sure we could get Angus to knock out the wall between the two stores, if you think it would be a good idea. Probably we could rent most of the copying equipment, so there's not much risk."

Martin was not so sure. A conversation yesterday with Anderson had disclosed his preference for a five-year lease (with an option to renew) at $1,000 per month. He had promised to hold the offer open for two weeks before attempting to lease the space to anyone else. Representatives from copying equipment suppliers had estimated that charges would run between $200 and $2,000 per month, depending on equipment, service, and whether the equipment was bought or leased. The photocopy service would also incur other fixed costs — utility expenses, interest, and insurance. Further, Bookends would have to invest a sizeable sum in fixtures and inventory (and possibly equipment). Martin concluded that the service would begin to make a profit at about 20,000 copies per month under best-case assumptions, and at about 60,000 copies per month under the worst-case scenario.

Further formal investigation had identified two major competitors. One was the copy centre located in the university library on the west side of the campus, about a kilometre away. The other was a private firm, Goodland's Stationery, located on the northern boundary of the campus, also about a kilometre from Bookends. Both offered service "while you wait," on several copying machines. The library's price was about $1/2$ cent per copy higher than Goodland's. Both offered collating, binding, colour copying, and other services. The library copying centre was open seven days a week; Goodland's was closed on Sundays.

Actually, Martin had discovered in talking with a number of students and faculty members that a third major "competitor" consisted of the photocopying machines scattered throughout the university's various departments and faculties. Most faculty and administrative copying was done on these machines, but students were also allowed the use of some, at cost. In addition, at least 20 self-service coin-operated copying machines were located on campus in the library, the student centre, and several other buildings.

Moving aside a stack of books on her desk, Katie Martin picked up the telephone and dialled her partner. When Campbell answered, Martin asked, "Susan, do you know how many copies a student might make in a semester? I mean, according to my figures, we would break even somewhere between 20,000 and 60,000 copies per month. I don't know if this is half the market or what."

"You know, I have no idea," Campbell answered. "I suppose when I was going to university I probably made 10 copies a month — for articles, class notes, old exams, and so on."

"Same here," Martin said. "But some of the graduate students I knew made at least that many copies each week. I think we ought to do some marketing research before we go much farther with this. What do you think?''

''Sure. But we can't afford to spend much time or money on it. What do you have in mind, Katie?''

''Well, we could easily interview our customers as they leave the store and ask them how many copies they have made in the past week or so. Of course, we would have to make sure they were students.''

''What about a telephone survey?'' Campbell asked. ''That way we can have a random sample. We would still ask about the number of copies, but now we would know for sure that they were students.''

''Or, what about interviewing students in the cafeteria in the student centre? There's always a large crowd there at lunchtime, and that would be even quicker.''

''I just don't know,'' Campbell replied. ''Why don't I come in this afternoon? We can talk about it some more.''

''Good idea,'' Martin responded. ''Between the two of us, we should be able to come up with something.''

QUESTIONS

1. What sources of information should Martin and Campbell use?
2. How should Martin and Campbell collect the information they need?
3. What questions should they ask?
4. How should they select a sample of people to interview?

P A R T

3

PRODUCTS
AND
SERVICES

The planning, development, and management
of the want-satisfying goods and services that
are a company's products

Part 2 focuses on the selection and identification of
target markets in accordance with the firm's marketing goals. The next step in the strategic marketing planning process is to develop a marketing mix that
will achieve these goals in the selected target markets. The
marketing mix is a strategic combination of four variables
— the organization's product, pricing structure, distribution system, and promotional program. Each of these
is closely interrelated with the other three variables in the
mix.

Part 3, consisting of four chapters, is devoted to the
product phase of the marketing mix. In Chapter 8 we
define the term *product*, consider the importance of
product planning and innovation, and discuss the new-
product development process. Chapter 9 deals mainly
with product-mix strategies, the management of the
product life cycle, and a consideration of style and
fashion. Chapter 10 is concerned with branding,
packaging, labelling, and other product features. Chapter
11 introduces the nature of service creation and its
delivery to consumers.

CHAPTER 8 GOALS

This chapter will show you why "building a better mousetrap" is *not* enough to ensure success. After studying this chapter, you should be able to explain:

- The meaning of the word *product* in its fullest sense.
- What a "new" product is.
- The classification of consumer and business products.
- The relevance of these product classifications to marketing strategy.
- The nature and characteristics of services.
- The importance of product innovation.
- The steps in the product-development process.
- The criteria for adding a product to a company's line.
- The new-product adoption and diffusion processes.
- Organizational structures for new-product planning and development.

BLAZIN' REDFISH™

NEW

The Hottest Fish In The Sea.

If you've been fishing around for a hot new menu item, you've just found it. Blazin' Redfish™ from Fishery Products International. The hottest fish in the sea. These all-natural Newfoundland Redfish fillets are fully prepared, portion controlled and economically priced. Serve them as an appetizer or light entree. Your patrons will love them for several reasons. They're not messy; they're meaty; and they're a great change of taste. Serve them with the dipping sauce suggestion on the back of this sheet, and watch the feeding frenzy begin.

FPI

FISHERY PRODUCTS INTERNATIONAL

BLAZIN' REDFISH™

C H A P T E R   8

Product Planning and Development

During the last three years, the Atlantic coast fishery has been having more than its usual cyclical problems. The health of the northern cod stock has been a major issue and the federal government has put in place a reduced quota system so that fish supplies will be drastically reduced and constrained well into the 1990s. For a company whose main resource was northern cod, Fishery Products International (FPI) had to make some innovative moves in product development and marketing strategy to continue to grow and maintain its competitive viability against foreign competition.

FPI is not a household name, but it is firmly entrenched as a dominant brand in the food-service industry—particularly in the United States, its major market. It has long been a supplier of cod, flounder, scallops, and shrimp to such customers as Red Lobster, Shoney's, and the Marriott Corporation. The FPI processed product line has appealed to every major segment of the food-service industry from fast-food chains such as Hardee's, Sizzler's, and Denny's to the first-class cabins of British Airways and KLM. Another important branch of the business has been product development and processing for the private labels of such firms as Loblaws (President's Choice), Marks and Spencer, and Provigo in Canada and the United States and Migros in Switzerland.

With supply problems mounting, FPI made a strategic marketing shift from being an Atlantic-based groundfish company to a more broadly based international seafood company. This was achieved by acquiring Clouston Foods, increasing product-development efforts and developing stronger ties with the retail market. The acquisition of Clouston Foods expanded the FPI product line to include such popular products as black tiger shrimp from Thailand, king crab from Alaska, farmed salmon from British Columbia, swordfish from Chili, and scampi from Iceland. Not only did this move assure a whole new assortment of products to deal with the resource challenge, but also it provided FPI with the foundation for extensive new product-development efforts.

Every new seafood species added to the fresh product assortment provides the opportunity to innovate in higher value-added processed products. This means that product research and development focusing on product form, coatings, flavourings, portions, preparation style, or combinations of these-provides for the further development of markets in Canada, the United States,

Japan, and Europe. FPI keeps a close watch on the low-cholesterol, low-fat, health-conscious consumers in these markets in order to continue to manage its brands and add new products to its portfolio.

THE MEANING OF PRODUCT

In a very *narrow* sense, a product is a set of tangible physical attributes assembled in an identifiable form. Each product carries a commonly understood descriptive (or generic) name, such as apples, steel, or baseball bats. Product attributes appealing to consumer motivation or buying patterns play no part in this narrow definition. A Cuisinart and a La Machine are one and the same product—a food processor.

This definition is far too limited to convey the breadth of the product concept. In marketing we need a definition that communicates the idea that consumers want to buy not products, but solutions to problems. Thus we don't want sandpaper; we want a smooth surface. To develop a sufficiently broad definition, we start by setting up "product" as an umbrella term that includes tangible goods, services, places, persons, and ideas. Throughout this book when we speak of *products*, we are using this broad meaning.

Notice that a product that provides benefits may not be a tangible article at all. The Holiday Inn product is a *service* that provides the benefit of a comfortable night's rest at a reasonable price. The Vancouver Visitors Bureau product is a *place* that provides the sea, sun and sand, relaxation, and other benefits. In a political campaign, the New Democratic or Conservative party's product is a *person* (candidate) that the party wants you to buy (vote for). The Canadian Cancer Society is selling the *idea* and the benefits of not smoking. In Chapter 11 we discuss in more detail the marketing of intangible products such as services and ideas.

A new package—the bottle—creates a new product.

To further expand our definition, we treat each *brand* as a separate product. In this sense, Kodak Kodacolor film and Fujicolor film are two different products. Lantic sugar and St. Lawrence sugar are also separate products, even though their only tangible difference may be the brand name on the package. But the brand name suggests a product difference to the consumer, and this brings the concept of consumer want-satisfaction into the definition.

Any change in a feature (design, colour, size, packaging), however minor it may be, creates another product. Each such change provides the seller with an opportunity to use a new set of appeals to reach what essentially may be a new market. Pain relievers (Tylenol, Anacin) in capsule form are a different product from the same brand in tablet form, even though the chemical contents of the tablet and the capsule are identical.

We can broaden this interpretation still further. A Sony television set bought in a discount store on a cash-and-carry basis is a different product from the identical model purchased in a department store. In the department store, the customer may pay a higher price for the TV set. But he buys it on credit, has it delivered free of charge, and receives other store services. Our concept of a product now includes services accompanying the sale, and we are ready for a definition that is useful to marketers.

Our definition is as follows: A **product** is a set of tangible and intangible attributes, including packaging, colour, price, quality, and brand, plus the services and reputation of the seller. A product may be a tangible good, service, place, person, or idea. (See Fig. 8-1.) In essence, then, consumers are buying more than a set of physical attributes. They are buying want-satisfaction in the form of product benefits.

FIGURE 8-1

A product is more than just a product.

MARKETING AT WORK

FILE 8-1   **USERS THINK BENEFITS, PRODUCERS THINK FEATURES, MARKETERS THINK BOTH**

A product is more than its tangible, obvious features. It is, in fact, a means to an end. When we buy sandpaper, we don't want sandpaper; we want a smooth surface. We don't want a 1/4-inch drill; we want a 1/4-inch hole. We don't buy a car, we buy a means of transportation, which also offers many other benefits.

So the challenge to the marketer is to tell us what the product can do for us —what the end benefits are.

- Calvin Klein, Lee, and GWG jeans are not items of clothing. They are a sex symbol and a fashion status symbol.
- Labatt's Blue beer isn't a beer. It's a blue-collar macho symbol.
- Visa and American Express cards are not credit cards that let you charge what you buy. They are a security blanket.
- Canada's Wonderland is not simply an amusement park with rides and shows. It is an escape from reality.
- West Edmonton Mall is not a shopping centre. It is a multi-faceted experience.
- Birks is not a chain of jewellery stores. It is a place that takes the risk out of buying diamonds and lets you buy with confidence.
- Dinner at a fine local restaurant isn't just a meal. It's . . .

CLASSIFICATION OF PRODUCTS

Just as it is necessary to segment markets to improve the marketing programs in many firms, so also it is helpful to separate *products* into homogeneous classifications. First we shall divide all products into two groups—consumer products and business products—in a classification that parallels our segmentation of the market. Then we shall divide each of these two product categories still further. In a separate chapter that follows, we will highlight the unique characteristics of services.

Consumer Products and Business Products

Consumer products are intended for use by ultimate household consumers for nonbusiness purposes. **Business products** are intended to be sold primarily for use in producing other goods or for rendering services in a business. The fundamental basis for distinguishing between the two groups is the *ultimate use* for which the product is intended in its present form.

Particular stages in a product's distribution have no effect upon its classification. Cornflakes and children's shoes are classed as consumer products, even if they are in the manufacturer's warehouse or on retailer's shelves, *if ultimately they will be used in their present form by household consumers*. Cornflakes sold to restaurants and other institutions, however, are classed as business products.

Often it is not possible to place a product only in one class or the other. A personal computer may be considered a consumer good if it is purchased by a student or a homemaker for nonbusiness use. But if the computer is bought by a travelling sales representative for business use, it is classed as a business product. The computer manufacturer recognizes that the product falls into both categories and therefore develops separate marketing programs for the two markets.

The two-way product classification is a useful framework for the strategic planning of marketing operations. Each major class of products ultimately goes to a different type of market and thus requires different marketing methods.

Classification of Consumer Products

The marketing differences between consumer and business products make this two-part classification valuable. Yet, the range of consumer goods is still too broad for a single class. Consequently, consumer products are further classified as convenience goods, shopping goods, specialty goods, and unsought goods. (See Table 8-1.) This subdivision is based on *consumer behaviour* rather than on *types of products*.

TABLE 8-1 **Consumer Products: Characteristics and Some Marketing Considerations**

Characteristics and marketing considerations	Type of product*		
	Convenience	**Shopping**	**Specialty**
Characteristics:			
1. Time and effort devoted by consumer to shopping	Very little	Considerable	Cannot generalize; consumer may go to nearby store and buy with minimum effort or may have to go to distant store and spend much time and effort
2. Time spent planning and purchase	Very little	Considerable	Considerable
3. How soon want is satisfied after it arises	Immediately	Relatively long time	Relatively long time
4. Are price and quality compared?	No	Yes	No
5. Price	Low	High	High
6. Frequency of purchase	Usually frequent	Infrequent	Infrequent
7. Importance	Unimportant	Often very important	Cannot generalize
Marketing considerations:			
1. Length of channel	Long	Short	Short to very short
2. Importance of retailer	Any single store is relatively unimportant	Important	Very important
3. Number of outlets	As many as possible	Few	Few; often only one in a market
4. Stock turnover	High	Lower	Lower
5. Gross margin	Low	High	High
6. Responsibility for advertising	Manufacturer's	Retailer's	Joint responsibility
7. Importance of point-of-purchase display	Very important	Less important	Less important
8. Advertising used	Manufacturer's	Retailer's	Both
9. Brand or store name important	Brand name	Store name	Both
10. Importance of packaging	Very important	Less important	Less important

*Unsought products are not included. See text explanation.

CONVENIENCE GOODS

The significant characteristics of convenience goods are (1) that the consumer has complete knowledge of the particular product wanted *before* going out to buy it and (2) that the product is purchased with a minimum of effort. Normally, the gain resulting from shopping around to compare price and quality is not considered worth the extra time and effort required. A consumer is willing to accept any of several brands and thus will buy the one that is most accessible. For most buyers, this subclass of goods includes groceries, inexpensive candy, drug sundries, such as toothpaste, and staple hardware items such as light bulbs and batteries.

Convenience goods typically have a low unit price, are not bulky, and are not greatly affected by fad and fashion. They usually are purchased frequently, although this is not a necessary characteristic. Items such as Christmas-tree lights or Mother's Day cards are convenience goods for most people, even though they may be bought only once a year.

Marketing considerations   A convenience good must be readily accessible when the consumer demand arises so the manufacturer must secure wide distribution. But, since most retail stores sell only a small volume of the manufacturer's output, it is not economical to sell directly to all retail outlets. Instead, the producer relies on wholesalers to reach part of the retail market.

The promotional strategies of both the manufacturer and the retailer are involved here. Retailers typically carry several brands of a convenience item, so they are not able to promote any single brand. They are not interested in doing much advertising of these articles because many other stores carry them. Thus, any advertising by one retailer may help its competitors. As a result, virtually the entire advertising burden is shifted to the manufacturer.

SHOPPING GOODS

Shopping goods are products for which customers usually wish to compare quality, price, and style in several stores before purchasing. This search continues only as long as the customer believes that the gain from comparing products offsets the additional time and effort required. Examples of shopping goods include most clothing items, furniture, major appliances, and most used automobiles.

Marketing considerations   The buying habits that consumers demonstrate in the purchase of shopping goods affect the distribution and promotional strategy of both manufacturers and middlemen. Manufacturers of shopping goods require fewer retail outlets because consumers are willing to look around a bit for what they want. To increase the convenience of comparison shopping, manufacturers try to place their products in stores located near other stores carrying competing items. Similarly, department stores and other retailers who carry primarily shopping goods like to be bunched together.

Manufacturers usually work closely with retailers in the marketing of shopping goods. Since manufacturers use fewer retail outlets, they are more dependent upon those they do select. Retail stores typically buy shopping goods in large quantities. Thus, distribution direct from manufacturer to retailer is common. Store names often are more important to buyers of shopping goods than are manufacturers' names.

Many people like to shop around for shoes.

The Spirit of Spring

SPECIALTY GOODS

Specialty goods are those products for which consumers have a *strong* brand preference and are willing to expend special time and effort in purchasing them. The consumer is willing to forgo more accessible substitutes in order to obtain the wanted brand, even though this may require a significant expenditure of time and effort. Examples of products usually classified as specialty goods include expensive suits and other fashion clothing, stereo sound equipment, health foods, photographic equipment, and, for many people, new automobiles and certain home appliances.

Marketing considerations   Since consumers *insist* on a particular brand and are willing to expend considerable effort to find it, manufacturers can afford to use fewer outlets. Ordinarily, the manufacturer deals directly with these retailers. The retailers are extremely important, particularly if the manufacturer uses only one in each area. And, where the franchise to handle the product is a valuable one, the retailer may become quite dependent upon the producer. Thus, they are interdependent; the success of one is closely tied to the success of the other.

Because brand is important and because only a few outlets are used, both the manufacturer and the retailer advertise the product extensively. Often the manufacturer pays some portion of the retailer's advertising costs, and the retailer's name frequently appears in the manufacturer's advertisements.

UNSOUGHT GOODS

The very title of this category suggests a somewhat unusual type of product that does not parallel the three categories already discussed. For this reason we did not try to include unsought goods in Table 8-1.

There are two types of unsought products: (1) new products that the consumer is not yet aware of and (2) products that right now the consumer does not want. For some people, products in the first group might include computers that speak, or video telephones. Examples of the second type of product might include prepaid burial insurance or gravestones. Some people believe that tobacco products are moving into this category. The title of this product category also suggests that a seller faces a monumental advertising and personal selling job when trying to market these products.

Classification of Business Goods

As was the case with consumer products, the general category of business products is too broad to use in developing a marketing program. The practices used in marketing such goods are just too different. Consequently, we separate business products into five categories: raw materials, fabricating materials and parts, installations, accessory equipment, and operating supplies. (See Table 8-2.) This classification is based on the broad *uses* of the product.

TABLE 8-2 **Classes of Business Goods: Characteristics and Marketing Considerations**

Characteristics and marketing considerations	Type of product				
	Raw materials	**Fabricating parts and materials**	**Installations**	**Accessory equipment**	**Operating supplies**
Example:	Iron ore	Engine blocks	Blast furnaces	Storage racks	Paper clips
Characteristics:					
1. Unit price	Very low	Low	Very high	Medium	Low
2. Length of life	Very short	Depends on final product	Very long	Long	Short
3. Quantities purchased	Large	Large	Very small	Small	Small
4. Frequency of purchase	Frequent delivery; long-term purchase contract	Infrequent purchase, but frequent delivery	Very infrequent	Medium frequency	Frequent
5. Standardization of competitive products	Very much; grading is important	Very much	Very little; custom-made	Little	Much
6. Limits of supply	Limited; supply can be increased slowly or not at all	Usually no problem	No problem	Usually no problem	Usually no problem
Marketing considerations:					
1. Nature of channel	Short; no middlemen	Short; middlemen only for small buyers	Short; no middlemen	Middlemen used	Middlemen used
2. Negotiation period	Hard to generalize	Medium	Long	Medium	Short
3. Price competition	Important	Important	Not important	Not main factor	Important
4. Presale/postsale service	Not important	Important	Very important	Important	Very little
5. Demand stimulation	Very little	Moderate	Sales people very important	Important	Not too important
6. Brand preference	None	Generally low	High	High	Low
7. Advance buying contract	Important; long-term contracts used	Important; long-term contracts used	Not usually used	Not usually used	Not usually used

RAW MATERIALS

Raw materials are business goods that will become part of another physical product. They have not been processed in any way, except as necessary for economy or protection during physical handling. Raw materials include (1) goods found in their natural state, such as minerals, land, and products of the forests and seas; and (2) agricultural products, such as wheat, potatoes, fruits, vegetables, livestock, and animal products — eggs and raw milk. These two groups of raw materials are marketed quite differently.

Marketing considerations   The marketing of raw materials in their natural state is influenced by several factors. The supply of these products is limited and cannot be substantially increased. Usually only a few large producers are involved. The products must be carefully graded and, consequently, are highly standardized. Because of their great bulk, their low unit value, and the long distance between producer and business user, transportation is an important consideration.

These factors necessitate short channels of distribution and a minimum of physical handling. Frequently, raw materials are marketed directly from producer to user. At most, one intermediary may be used. The limited supply forces users to assure themselves of adequate quantities. Often this is done either (1) by contracting in advance to buy a season's supply of the product or (2) by owning the source of supply. Advertising and other forms of demand stimulation are rarely used. There is very little branding or other product differentiation. Competition is built around price and the assurance that a producer can deliver the product as specified.

Agricultural products used as business raw materials are supplied by many small producers located some distance from the markets. The supply is largely controllable by producers—frequently through marketing boards—but it cannot be increased or decreased rapidly. The product is perishable and is not produced at a uniform rate throughout the year.

Close attention must be given to transportation and warehousing. Transportation costs are high relative to unit value, and standardization and grading are very important. Because producers are small and numerous, many producer co-operatives, middlemen, and long channels of distribution are needed. Promotional activity is usually carried out by marketing boards.

FABRICATING MATERIALS AND PARTS

Fabricating materials and parts are business goods that become an actual part of the finished product. They have already been processed to some extent (in contrast to raw materials). Fabricating **materials** will undergo further processing. Examples include yarn being woven into cloth and flour becoming part of bread. Fabricating **parts** will be assembled with no further change in form. They include such products as windows in houses and semiconductor chips in computers.

Marketing considerations   Fabricating materials and parts are usually purchased in large quantities. To ensure an adequate, timely supply, a buyer may place an order a year or more in advance. Because of such buying habits, most fabricating products are marketed on a direct sale basis from producer to user.

Middlemen are used most often where the buyers are small or where they place small fill-in orders for a rapid delivery. Normally, buying decisions are

These windows are classed as fabricating parts.

based on the price and the service provided by the seller. Branding is generally unimportant. However, some firms have made successful attempts to pull their products out of obscurity by identifying them with a brand. Pella windows and the NutraSweet brand of sweetener are notable examples.

INSTALLATIONS

Installations are manufactured business products—the long-lived, expensive, major equipment of an industrial user. Examples include large generators in a dam, a factory building, diesel engines for a railroad, blast furnaces for a steel mill, and jet airplanes for an airline. The *differentiating characteristic of installations is that they directly affect the scale of operations in a firm.* Adding 12 new microcomputers will not affect the scale of operations of Canadian Airlines International, but adding 12 new jet airplanes certainly will. Therefore, the airplanes are classed as installations, but the microcomputers are not.

Marketing considerations The marketing of installations presents a real challenge to management because every single sale is important. Usually no middlemen are involved; sales are made directly from producer to industrial user. Typically, the unit sale is large, and often the product is made to the buyer's detailed specifications. Much presale and postsale servicing is required. A high-calibre sales force is needed to market installations, and often sales engineers are used. Promotional emphasis is on personal representation and service rather than advertising, although some advertising is used.

This GEAC mainframe computer is classed as accessory equipment.

ACCESSORY EQUIPMENT

Accessory equipment is used in the production operations of a business firm, but it does not have a significant influence on its scale of operations. Accessory equipment does not become an actual part of the finished product. The life of accessory equipment is shorter than that of installations and longer than that of operating supplies. Examples include cash registers in a retail store, small power tools, forklift trucks, and the microcomputers mentioned above.

Marketing considerations   It is difficult to generalize about the distribution policies of firms that market equipment. In some cases, direct sale is used. This is true particularly where the order is for several units of the product or where the product is of relatively high unit value. A firm that manufactures forklift trucks may sell directly because the price of a single unit is large enough to make this distribution policy profitable. In the main, however, manufacturers of accessory equipment use middlemen. They do so because (1) the market is geographically dispersed, (2) there are many different types of potential users, and (3) individual orders may be relatively small.

OPERATING SUPPLIES

Operating supplies are the "convenience goods" of the business field. They are short-lived, low-priced items usually purchased with a minimum of effort. They aid in a firm's operations but do not become a part of the finished product. Examples are lubricating oils, pencils and stationery, registration supplies in a university, heating fuel, and washroom supplies.

Marketing considerations   Like consumer convenience products, industrial operating supplies must be distributed widely. The producing firm makes extensive use of wholesale middlemen. This is done because the product is low in unit value, is bought in small quantities, and goes to many users. Price competition is heavy because competitive products are quite standardized and there is little brand insistence.

IMPORTANCE OF PRODUCT INNOVATION

The social and economic justification for the existence of a business is its ability to satisfy its customers while making a profit. A company meets this basic responsibility to society through its products. Effective new-product planning and development are vital to a company today. Good executive judgement elsewhere cannot offset weaknesses in product planning. A company simply cannot successfully sell a bad product over the long run.

Requirement for Growth

A watchword for management is "innovate or die." For many companies, large or small, a substantial portion of sales volume and net profit this year wil come from products that did not exist five to ten years ago. Because products, like people, go through a life cycle, new products are essential for sustaining a company's expected rate of profit. They grow (in sales), then decline, and eventually are replaced.

The concept of the product life cycle is discussed in more detail in Chapter 9 but we mention it here because it has two significant implications for product innovation. First, every company's present products will eventually become obsolete as a result of changes in customer needs and domestic and global increases in competition. Therefore, their sales volume, market share, and profitability decline. The introduction of a new product at the proper time generally will help maintain a company's desired profit level.

Increased Consumer Selectivity

In recent years, consumers have become more selective in their choice of products. As consumers' disposable income has increased, and as an abundance of products has become available, consumers have fulfilled many of their wants. The large middle-income group is reasonably well fed, clothed, housed, transported, and equipped. If market satiation—in terms of quantity—does exist to some extent, it follows that consumers may be more critical in their appraisal of new products. While the consumer has become increasingly selective, the market has been deluged with products that are imitations or that offer only marginal competitive advantages. This may lead to "product indigestion." The cure is to develop *truly* new products—to *innovate* and not just *imitate*.

Resources and Environment Considerations

We are finally realizing that the supply of many of our natural resources is limited and irreplaceable. These two conditions clearly demonstrate the importance of careful new-product planning. Increasingly, environmental factors will influence product decisions, because we simply cannot afford to continue wasting our natural resources and polluting our environment. Both K mart and McDonald's, for example, have publicly stated a commitment to carry merchandise and use packaging that are better for the environment in their use and disposal.

DEVELOPMENT OF PRODUCTS

It has been said that nothing happens until somebody sells something. This is not entirely true. First there must be something to sell—a product, a service, or an idea—something that is in some way new. And that "something" must be developed.

What Is a "New" Product?

Just what is a "new" product? Are the new models that auto manufacturers introduce each autumn new products? If a firm adds a wrinkle-remover cream to its assortment of women's cosmetics, is this a new product? Or must an item be totally new in concept before we can class it as a *new* product?

MARKETING AT WORK

FILE 8-2 FISH FOOD FOR YOUR LAWN

Consumer environmental awareness and the desire to diversify product lines, as well as corporate interests in effective resource utilization, have given National Sea Products a new product opportunity. The company has introduced its first nonfood product — a fish-based organic lawn and plant food called Seagreen. Seagreen is deodorized fertilizer that contains fish bone and bone meal blended with fish emulsion and potash. Fish bones are a by-product of the company's food operations and, since they are organic, neatly address environmental issues. National Sea invested $250,000 in product development and expects to earn that back within two years. Seagreen is designed to be used by recreational gardeners; packaged in recyclable bags of 5, 8, and 16 kilograms.

Source: Adapted from Sandra Porteous, "Fish-Based Fertilizer New from NSP," *Marketing*, April 15, 1991, p. 4.

New packaging to meet new environmental standards.

Here, we need not seek a very limited definition. Instead, we can recognize several possible categories of new products. What is important, however, is that each separate category may require a quite different marketing program to ensure a reasonable probability of success.

Three recognizable categories of *new products* are as follows:

- Products that are *really* innovative — truly unique. Examples would be a hair restorer or a cancer cure—products for which there is a real need but for which no existing substitutes are considered satisfactory. In this category we can also include products that are quite different from existing products but satisfy the same needs. Thus, microwave ovens compete with conventional ovens and solar power competes with other energy sources.
- Replacements for existing products that are *significantly* different from the existing goods. For many people instant coffee replaced ground coffee and coffee beans; then freeze-dried instant replaced instant coffee. Compact-disc players are replacing tape cassettes, which in turn replaced conventional stereo records and players. Automatic 35 mm cameras and cordless telephones are replacing some traditional models. In some years, annual model changes in autos and new fashions in clothing are different enough to fit into this category.
- Imitative products that are new to a particular company but not new to the market. The company simply wants to capture part of an existing market with a "me-too" product. Thus, Polaroid introduced conventional film in addition to its instant lines, in order to compete with Kodak and Fuji.

Perhaps the key criterion as to whether a given product or service is new is how the intended market perceives it. If buyers perceive that a given item or service is significantly different (from what is being replaced) in some characteristic or benefit (appearance, performance), then it is a new product or service.

The development process for new products should begin with the selection of an explicit new-product strategy. This strategy then can serve as a meaningful guideline throughout the step-by-step development process used for each individual new product.

Selection of New-Product Strategy

The purpose of an effective overall new-product strategy is to identify the strategic role that new products are to play in helping the company achieve its corporate and marketing goals. For example, a new product might be designed to defend a market-share position or to maintain the company's position as a product innovator. In other situations, the product's role might be to meet a specific return-on-investment goal or to establish a position in a new market.

A new product's intended role also will influence the *type* of product to be developed. To illustrate:

Company goal	Product strategy
1. To defend a market-share position.	1. Introduce an addition to an existing product line, or revise an existing product.
2. To further the company's position as an innovator.	2. Introduce a *really* new product—not just an extension of an existing one.

MARKETING AT WORK

FILE 8-3 **SOMETIMES BENEFITS JUST AREN'T**

Marketers are sometimes faced with ethical considerations about certain products in their product lines. Fast-food restaurants have become concerned about the environmental impact of disposable food trays and some, such as McDonald's, have eliminated many moulded polyurethane products that have been linked to a deterioration of the ozone layer around the earth. Should restaurants switch to biodegradable trays, packages, and cups?

A major Canadian brewer was testing consumer reaction to several packaging innovations, one of which was a new "rip cap" that allowed the consumer to open a bottle of beer with a pull on a ring tab, similar to those used to open cans of soft drinks. The company discontinued testing of the cap when a number of people interviewed expressed concerns about safety implications of walking on discarded rip caps on beaches and in other public places.

Possibly the most controversial of all consumer products continues to be cigarettes. Although it is perfectly legal to sell these products, public concern about the health hazards of cigarette use has led to increasing bans on smoking in public work places and in airplanes, and to legislation to restrict advertising and promotion of the products. A growing number of retailers now refuse to sell cigarettes in their stores. This is a particularly contentious point for drugstores, whose product lines generally are associated with health. Should drugstores sell cigarettes? Should cigarettes be banned?

Only in recent years have many companies consciously identified new-product strategies as a separate and explicit activity in the development process. Since then, however, there has been a dramatic increase in the efficiency of the development process. To illustrate, a survey by the Booz, Allen & Hamilton management consulting firm reported that in 1968 there were 58 new-product ideas considered for every successful new product introduced. In 1981, only seven new-product ideas were required to generate one successful new product — truly a dramatic improvement in the mortality rate for new-product ideas.[1]

Steps in the Development Process

With the company's new-product strategy as a guide, the development of a new product can proceed through a series of six steps (or stages). (See Fig. 8-2.) During each stage, management must decide whether to move on to the next stage, abandon the product, or seek additional information.

The first two steps — generating new-product ideas and evaluating them — are tied especially to the overall new-product strategy. This strategy can provide (1) a focus for generating new-product ideas and (2) a criterion for screening and evaluating these ideas.

---

[1]See *New Products Management for the 1980s*, Booz, Allen & Hamilton, New York, 1982, pp. 10-11. Also see Earl L. Bailey (ed.), *Product-Line Strategies*. The Conference Board, New York, report no. 816, 1982, pp. 6-23.

FIGURE 8-2
Major stages in new-product development process.

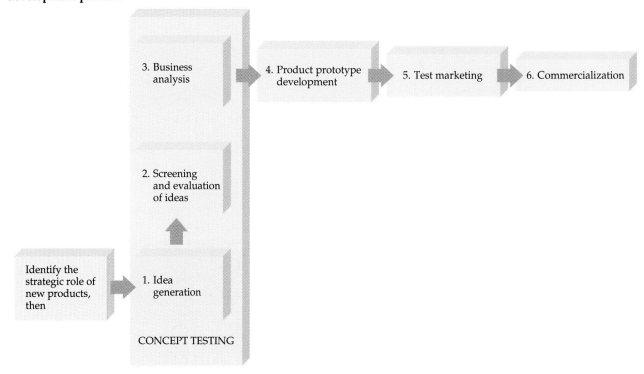

1. **Generation of new-product ideas.** New-product development starts with an idea. The particular source of ideas is not nearly so important as the company's system for stimulating new ideas and then acknowledging and reviewing them promptly.
2. **Screening and evaluation of ideas.** In this stage new-product ideas are evaluated to determine which ones warrant further study.
3. **Business Analysis.** A new-product idea that survives to this stage is expanded into a concrete business proposal. Management (a) identifies product features, (b) estimates market demand and the product's profitability, (c) establishes a program to develop the product, and (d) assigns responsibility for further study of the product's feasibility.

    These first three steps are together referred to as *concept testing.* This is pretesting the product *idea,* as contrasted to later pretesting of the product itself and its market.
4. **Product development.** The idea-on-paper is converted into a physical product. Pilot models or small quantities are manufactured to designated specifications. Laboratory tests and other necessary technical evaluations are made to determine the product feasibility of the article.
5. **Test marketing.** Market tests, in-use tests, and other commercial experiments in limited geographic areas are conducted to ascertain the feasibility of a full-scale marketing program. In this stage, design and production variables may have to be adjusted as a result of test findings. At this point, management must make a final decision regarding whether or not to market the product commercially.

M A R K E T I N G   A T   W O R K

FILE 8-4   **CANADIANS WIN THE SCREENING GAME**

Many people fantasize about inventing their own board game, marketing it, and becoming rich. However, according to The Games Gang (the third-biggest game company after Parker Brothers and Milton Bradley), chances of the idea making it into the stores are very slim. In 1988, The Games Gang received 2,100 ideas for games, found 12 worth considering, and ended up developing none of them. However would-be-millionaires should not be too discouraged. After all, Monopoly (which has sold 125 million copies since its 1935 debut) was initially criticized for having "52 fundamental errors," Scrabble (100 million copies since 1952) was considered too highbrow, and Trivial Pursuit (which tripled the size of the games market in the mid-1980s) was deemed too expensive; but each game appeared during an economic downturn and defied the industry's conventions. And until 1986 with the invention of the charades-on-paper game, Pictionary—which has become the no. 1 board game with sales of $350 million—The Games Gang itself was only a tiny operation. The success of Pictionary, Trivial Pursuit, and other games such as Balderdash have crowned Canada the world leader in producing board games.

Source: Adapted from "Toying with Board Games Can Be a Costly Business," *Financial Times of Canada*, January 7, 1991, p. 25.

---

6. *Commercialization.* Full-scale production and marketing programs are planned, and then the product is launched. Up to this point in the development process, management has virtually complete control over the product. Once the product is "born" and enters its life cycle, however, the external competitive environment becomes a major determinant of its destiny.

In this six-step evolution, the first three—the idea, or concept, stages—are the critical ones. Not only are they least expensive—each stage becomes progressively more costly in dollars and scarce human resources. But more important, many products fail because either the idea or the timing is wrong—and those three stages are designed to identify such situations.

Producer's Criteria for New Products

When should a proposed new product be added to a company's existing product assortment? Here are some guidelines that some producers use in answering that question:

- There should be an *adequate market demand*. This is by far the most important criterion to apply to a proposed product. Too often, management begins with a question such as, "Can we use our present sales force?" or "Will the new item fit into our production system?" The basic question is, "Do enough people really want our product?"
- The product must be compatible with current *environmental and social standards*. Do the manufacturing processes heavily pollute air or water (as steel or paper mills do)? Will the use of the finished product be harmful to the environment (as automobiles are)? After being used, is the product harmful to the environment (as some detergents are)? Does the product have recycling potential?

Reebock believed that there was a strong market demand for the pump feature of its new athletic shoes.

- The product should fit into the company's present *marketing* structure. The general marketing experience of the company is important here. Alfred Sung probably would find it easy to add designer sheets and towels to his clothing line, whereas paint manufacturers would find it quite difficult to add margarine to theirs. More specific questions may also be asked regarding the marketing fit of new products: Can the existing sales force be used? Can the present channels of distribution be used?
- A new-product idea will be more favourably received by management if the item fits in with existing *production* facilities, labour power, and management capabilities.
- The product should fit from a *financial* standpoint. At least three questions should be asked: Is adequate financing available? Will the new item increase seasonal and cyclical stability in the firm? Are the profit possibilities worthwhile?
- There must be no *legal* objections. Patents must be applied for, labelling and packaging must meet existing regulations, and so on.
- *Management* in the company must have the time and the ability to deal with the new product.
- The product should be in keeping with the the *company's image* and objectives. A firm stressing low-priced, high-turnover products normally should not add an item that suggests prestige or status.

Middlemen's Criteria for New Products

When retailers or wholesalers are considering whether to take on a new product, they should use all the above criteria except those related to production. In addition, a middleman should consider:

M A R K E T I N G   A T   W O R K

FILE 8-5   **THE NEW TURKEY: MEETING NEW CRITERIA**

In 1950, when Mac Cuddy went into business selling turkeys, they were only sold and eaten at Thanksgiving and Christmas. Back then, the birds weighed only 2 kg, had black feathers, and were considered dry and tasteless. Thirty years later, Cuddy has changed all this and made the turkey more useful for more people. Using artificial light, he convinced turkeys that they could breed at any time of the year, freeing himself (and consumers) from the notion of turkey as holiday fare. To stimulate demand, Cuddy made the turkeys more appealing, changing their feather colour to white through cross-breeding. He then bred a line of 7 kg birds that were ideally suited for a wide range of turkey-related products — which is where Cuddy has achieved his greatest success. Cuddy's London, Ontario-based private company makes imitation ham, roasts, hot dogs, bratwurst, schnitzel, cutlets, fingers, and nuggets — all from turkey. These products are sold to restaurants and cafeterias as a lower-cost alternative to pork and to hospitals and nursing homes because of turkey's lower fat and cholesterol levels. They provide McDonald's with their McNuggets, Loblaws President's Choice label with their chicken, an increasing number of European and Asian countries with a low-cost source of animal protein, and Cuddy itself with a sales increase of 20 percent over the past three years. In doing so, Cuddy has proved that turkey isn't just for Christmas any more.

Source: Adapted from Oliver Bertin, "A Turkey in Every Pot . . . or Was That Ham?" *Globe and Mail*, December 13, 1990, p. 1-2.

- *The relationship with the producer*: The producer's reputation, the possibility of getting exclusive sales rights in a given geographic territory, and the type of promotional and financial help given by the manufacturer.
- *In-store policies and practice*: What type of selling effort is required for the new product? How does the proposed product fit with store policies regarding repair service, alterations (for clothing), credit, and delivery?

NEW-PRODUCT ADOPTION AND DIFFUSION PROCESSES

The opportunity to market a new product successfully is increased if management understands the adoption and the diffusion processes for that product. The **adoption process** is the decision-making activity of *an individual* through which the new product — the innovation — is accepted. The **diffusion** of the new product is the process by which the innovation is spread through a *social system* over time.[2]

Stages in Adoption Process

A prospective user goes through the following six stages during the process of deciding whether to adopt something new:

---

[2]For some foundations of diffusion theory, a review of landmark studies on diffusion of innovation, and extensive bibliographical references, see Everett M. Rogers, *Diffusion of Innovations*, 3d ed. The Free Press, New York, 1983.

Stage	Activity in That Stage
Awareness	Individual is exposed to the innovation; becomes a prospect.
↓	
Interest	Prospect is interested enough to seek information.
↓	
Evaluation	Prospect mentally measures relative merits.
↓	
Trial	Prospect adopts the innovation on a limited basis. A consumer buys a small sample; for example, if for some reason (cost or size) an innovation cannot be sampled, the chances of its being adopted will decrease.
↓	
Adoption	Prospect decides whether to use the innovation on a full-scale basis.
↓	
Postadoption confirmation	The innovation is adopted; then the user continues to seek assurance that the right decision was made.

Adopter Categories in the Diffusion Process

Some people will adopt an innovation quickly, others will delay, and still others may never adopt it. Researchers have identified five categories of individuals, based on the relative time when they adopted a given innovation. Figure 8-3 illustrates the proportion of adopters in each category. The categories are somewhat arbitrarily positioned to represent standard deviations from average time of adoption.

INNOVATORS

Innovators, a *venturesome* group, constitute about 2.5 percent of the market and are the first to adopt an innovation. In relation to later adopters, the innovators are likely to be younger, have a higher social status, and be in a better financial position. Innovators also tend to have broader, more cosmopolitan social relationships. They are likely to rely more on impersonal sources of information, rather than on sales people or other word-of-mouth sources.

EARLY ADOPTERS

Early adopters — about 12.5 percent of the market — tend to be a more integrated part of a local social system. That is, whereas innovators are cosmop-

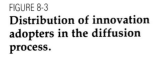

FIGURE 8-3
Distribution of innovation adopters in the diffusion process.

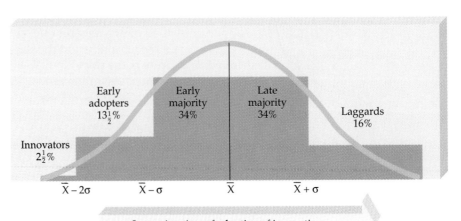

Innovators $2\frac{1}{2}$%

Early adopters $13\frac{1}{2}$%

Early majority 34%

Late majority 34%

Laggards 16%

$\overline{X} - 2\sigma$ $\overline{X} - \sigma$ $\overline{X}$ $\overline{X} + \sigma$

Increasing time of adoption of innovations

olites, early adopters are localites. Thus the early-adopter category includes more opinion leaders than any other adopter group. Early adopters are greatly *respected* in their social system. An "agent of change" is a person who is seeking to speed up the diffusion of a given innovation. This change agent will often try to work through the early adopters because they are not too far ahead of others in their peer group. As information sources, sales people are probably used more by the early adopters than by any other category.

EARLY MAJORITY

The more *deliberate* group, the early majority, represents about 34 percent of the market. This group tends to accept an innovation just before the "average" adopter in a social system. This group is a bit above average in social and economic terms. Its members rely quite a bit on advertisements, sales people, and contact with early adopters.

LATE MAJORITY

Representing about another 34 percent of the market, the late majority is a *sceptical* group. Usually its members adopt an innovation in response to an economic necessity or to social pressure from their peers. They rely on their peers — late or early majority — as sources of information. Advertising and personal selling are less effective with this group than is word-of-mouth.

LAGGARDS

This *tradition-bound* group—16 percent of the market—includes those who are the last to adopt an innovation. Laggards are suspicious of innovations and innovators. By the time laggards adopt something new, it may already have been discarded by the innovator group in favour of a newer idea. Laggards are older and are at the low end of the social and economic scales.

   At this point we might recall that we are discussing only *adopters* (early or late) of an innovation. For most innovations, there are still many people who are *not* included in our percentages. These are the people who *never do* adopt the innovation—the nonadopters.

Innovation Characteristics Affecting Adoption Rate

The following five characteristics of an innovation, as perceived by individuals, seem to influence the adoption rate:[3]

- *Relative advantage.* The degree to which an innovation is superior to preceding ideas. Relative advantage may be reflected in lower cost, higher profitability, or some other measure.
- *Compatibility.* The degree to which an innovation is consistent with the cultural values and experiences of the adopters.
- *Complexity.* The more complex an innovation is, the less quickly it will be adopted.
- *Trialability.* The degree to which the new idea may be sampled on some limited basis. For instance, a central home air-conditioning system is likely to have a slower adoption rate than a new seed or fertilizer, which may be tried on a small plot of ground.
- *Observability.* The more an innovation can be seen to work, the more likely

[3]Rogers, op. cit.

it is to be adopted. A weed killer that works on existing weeds will be accepted sooner than a pre-emergent weed killer. The reason is that the latter — even though it may be a superior product — produces no dead weeds to show to prospective buyers.

ORGANIZING FOR PRODUCT INNOVATION

For new-product programs to be successful, *they must be supported by a strong and continuing commitment from top management over the long term.* Furthermore, this commitment must be maintained even in the face of the failures that are sure to occur in some individual new-product efforts. To effectively implement this commitment to innovation, new-product programs must be soundly organized.

Types of Organization

There is no "one best" organizational structure for new-product planning and development. Many companies use more than one structure to manage these activities. Some widely used organizational structures for planning and developing new products are:

- *Product-planning committee.* Members usually include the company president and executives from major departments — marketing, production, finance, engineering, and research.
- *New-product department.* Generally these units are small, consisting of four or five or even fewer people, and the department head reports to the president.
- *Venture team.* A venture team is a small, multidisciplinary group, organizationally segregated from the rest of the firm. It is composed of representatives of engineering, production, finance, and marketing research. The team operates in an entrepreneurial environment, in effect being a separate small business. Typically the group reports directly to top management.[4]
- *Product manager.* We discuss this concept later in this section.

Upon the completion of the development process, responsibility for marketing a new product usually is shifted to another organizational unit. This unit may be an existing department, or a new department established just for this new product. In some cases, the team that developed the product may continue as the management nucleus of a newly established division in the company.

Which of these particular organizational structures is chosen is not the critical point here — each has its strengths and weaknesses. The key point is to make sure that some person or group has the specific organizational responsibilities for new-product development — and is backed by top management. Product innovation is too important an activity to let it be handled in an unorganized, nonchalant fashion, figuring that somehow the job will get done.

At least two risks are involved in the course of organizationally integrating new products into departments now marketing established, mature products. First, the executives involved with ongoing products may have a short-term outlook as they deal with day-to-day problems of existing products. Consequently, they tend to put the new products on the back burner, so to speak.

---

[4]See Frank G. Bingham and Charles J. Quigley, Jr., "Venture Team Application to New Product Development," *Journal of Business and Industrial Marketing,* Winter/Spring 1989, pp. 49-59.

Second, managers of successful existing products often are reluctant to assume the risks involved in marketing new products.[5]

PRODUCT MANAGER

In many companies a product manager—sometimes called a brand manager or a merchandise manager—is the executive responsible for planning related to *new* products as well as to *established* ones. A large company may have several product managers, who report to a top marketing executive. The wealth of discussion in business regarding the product manager's function is some indication of management's interest in this organizational structure.

In many large firms—Procter & Gamble, Maple Leaf Foods, and General Foods, for example—the product manager's job is quite broad. This executive is responsible for *planning the complete marketing program* for a brand or group of products. Thus, he or she may be concerned with new-product development as well as the improvement of established products. Responsibilities include setting marketing goals, preparing budgets, and developing plans for advertising and field selling activities. At the other extreme, some companies limit product managers' activities essentially to the areas of selling and sales promotion.

Probably the biggest problem in the product-manager system is that a company will saddle these executives with great responsibility, yet it will *not* give them the corresponding authority. They must develop the field selling plan, but they have no line authority over the sales force. Product managers do not select advertising agencies, yet they are responsible for developing advertising plans. They have a profit responsibility for their brands, yet they are often denied any control over product cost, prices, or advertising budgets. Their effectiveness depends largely on their ability to influence other executives to co-operate with their plans.

Interestingly enough, there are some indications that the product-manager system may change considerably in the 1990s. The system was widely adopted and thrived particularly during the period of economic growth and market expansion in the 1950s to 1970s. In the 1980s, however, many industries experienced slow economic growth in maturing markets, coupled with a trend towards strategic planning that stressed centralized managerial control. Because of these environmental forces, one careful study concluded that the product-manager system will be greatly modified in many companies and eventually abolished in some firms.

WHY NEW PRODUCTS FAIL OR SUCCEED

Why do some products fail while others succeed? In the various research studies regarding this question, we find some consistently recurring themes. The key reasons typically cited for the failure of new products are as follows.[6]

- *Poor marketing research*: Misjudging what products the market wanted; overestimating potential sales of the new product; and lack of knowledge of buying motives and habits.

---

[5]For more of this problem, see Roger C. Bennett and Robert G. Cooper, "The Product Life Cycle Trap," *Business Horizons*, September-October 1984, pp. 7-16.

[6]See David S. Hopkins, *New-Product Winners and Losers*, The Conference Board, New York, report no. 773, 1980, pp. 12-20. Also see Valerie S. Folkes and Barbara Kotsos, "Buyers' and Sellers' Explanations for Product Failure: Who Done It?" *Journal of Marketing*, April 1986, pp. 74-80.

- *Technical problems in the new product's design or in its production*: Poor product quality and performance; products that were too complicated; and especially products that did not offer any significant advantage over competing items already on the market.
- *Poor timing in product introduction*: Delays in bringing the product to the market, or, conversely, rushing the product too quickly to the market.
- *Other poor management practices*: Lack of a well-defined new-product strategy; lack of a strong, long-term commitment by top management to new-product development; ineffective organization for new-product development.

Now let's look at the good news. Corrective actions to remedy these deficiencies have increased the systemization and effectiveness of the new-product development process. Specifically, we can attribute new-product success to these product factors and management characteristics.

- The product satisfies one or more market needs.
- The product is technologically superior, and it enjoys a competitive cost advantage.
- The product is compatible with the company's internal strengths in key functional areas such as selling, distribution, and production.
- Top management makes a long-term commitment to new-product development. The experience thus gained enables management to improve its performance in introducing new products over a period of years.
- Strategies for new products are clearly defined. They enable a company to generate and select new products that specifically meet internal strategic needs and external market needs.
- There are effective organization and a good management style. The organization structure is consciously established to promote new-product development. The management style encourages new-product development and can adjust to changing new-product opportunities.

One authority on new products observed that in the history of every successful product he studied, he always found at least one of three advantages — a product advantage, a marketing advantage, or a creative advertising advantage. Without at least one of these three, it appeared there simply was no chance for success. Here are some examples of these features as developed by companies you'll probably recognize.

Product advantage. NutraSweet artificial sweetener (tastes more like sugar without the fattening and cavity-causing effects); facsimile machine (sends printed messages instantaneously over the telephone lines); *Financial Post* (a proven business newspaper, now delivered daily); Pizza Experts restaurant (pizza cooked to your order and delivered to your home in 35 minutes or you get it free).

Marketing advantage: Tupperware and Regal Stationery (products are distributed to customers in their own homes); Sears Canada (offers the convenience of catalogue shopping as well as large department stores); Royal LePage Real Estate (nationwide computer listings of homes for sale).

Creative advertising advantage. Harvey's Restaurants ("makes a hamburger a beautiful thing"); Panasonic ("just slightly ahead of our time"); Ford of Canada ("At Ford, Quality is Job 1"). These companies developed attention-getting advertising that assisted in differentiating them from the competition and in repositioning them in their respective markets.

SUMMARY

If the first commandment in marketing is "Know thy customer," then the second is "Know thy product." A firm can fulfil its socioeconomic responsibility to satisfy its customers by producing and marketing truly want-satisfying products or services. In light of a scarcity of resources and a growing concern for our environment, socially responsible product innovation becomes even more important. The new products or services marketed by a firm are a prime determinant of that company's growth rate, profits, and total marketing program.

To manage their product assortments and services effectively, marketers should understand the full meaning of the term *product* and the different concepts of what a *new product* is. Products can be classified into two broad categories — consumer products and business products. Then each of these two major groups should be further subdivided, because a different marketing program is required for each subgroup.

There are seven steps in the development process for new products, starting with a clear statement of the intended new-product strategy. The early stages in this process are important. If a firm can make an early (and proper) decision to drop a product, a lot of money and labour can be saved. In its decision regarding whether to accept or reject a new product, there are several criteria for a manufacturer or a middleman to consider. The product should fit in with marketing, production, and financial resources. But the key point is that there *must* be an adequate market demand for the product. Management should understand the adoption and diffusion processes for a new product. Adopters of a new product can be divided into five categories, depending upon how quickly they adopt a given innovation. In addition, there usually is a group of nonadopters.

Organizational relationships are typically reported as a major problem in new-product planning and development. Top management must be deeply committed to product innovation and must support this activity in a creative fashion. Most firms that report reasonable success in product innovation seem to use one of these four organizational structures for new-product development: product-planning committee, new-product department, venture team, or product-manager system. Successful products typically have an advantage in at least one of three areas—as a want-satisfying product, in their marketing program, or their advertising.

KEY TERMS AND CONCEPTS

1. In what respects are the products different in each of the following cases?
   a. An Inglis dishwasher sold at an appliance store and a similar dishwasher sold by Sears under its Kenmore brand name. Assume Inglis makes both dishwashers.
   b. A Sunbeam Mixmaster sold by a leading department store and the same model sold by a discount house.

2. a. Explain the various interpretations of the term *new product*.
   b. Give some examples, other than those stated in this chapter, of products in each of the three new-product categories.

3. ''As brand preferences are established with regard to women's ready-to-wear, these items, which traditionally have been considered shopping products, will move into the specialty-products category. At the same time, women's clothing is moving into supermarkets and variety stores, thus indicating that some articles are convenience products.'' Explain the reasons involved in these statements. Do you agree that women's clothing is shifting away from the shopping-products classification? Explain.

4. In what way is the responsibility for advertising a convenience product distributed between the manufacturer and the retailers? A shopping product? A specialty product?

5. Compare the elements of a manufacturer's marketing mix for a convenience product with those of the mix for a specialty product.

6. In which of the five subclassifications of industrial products should each of the following be included? Which products may belong in more than one category?
   a. Trucks.
   b. Medical x-ray equipment.
   c. Typing paper.
   d. Copper wires.
   e. Printing presses.
   f. Nuts and bolts.
   g. Paper clips.
   h. Land.

7. What are some of the marketing implications in the fact that services possess the characteristic of intangibility?

8. Services are highly perishable and are often subject to fluctuations in demand. In marketing its services, how can a company offset these factors?

9. Cite some examples of service marketers that seem to be customer-oriented, and describe what these firms have done in this vein.

10. Present a brief analysis of the market for each of the following service firms. Make use of the components of a market as discussed in Chapters 4 to 6.
    a. Laundry and dry-cleaning firm located in a shopping centre close to your campus.
    b. Four-bedroom house for rent at a major seashore resort.
    c. Bowling alley.
    d. Nursing home.

11. What are some of the ways in which each of the following services firms might expand its line?
    a. Advertising agency.
    b. Telephone company.
    c. Automobile repair garage.

12. What factors account for the growing importance of product planning?

13. In planning and developing new products, how can a firm make sure that it is being socially responsible in regard to scarce resources and our environment?

14. What are some of the questions that management is likely to want answered during the business-analysis stage of new-product development?

15. Assume that the following organizations are considering the following additions to their product lines. In each case, should the proposed product be added?
    a. McDonald's—lasagna.
    b. Safeway supermarkets—automobile tires.
    c. Petro-Canada—personal computers.
    d. Bank of Montreal—life insurance.
    e. General Motors—outboard boat motors.

16. In the "trial" stage of deciding whether to adopt an innovation, the likelihood of adoption is reduced if the product cannot be sampled because of its cost or size. What are some products that might have these drawbacks? How might these drawbacks be overcome?

17. What are some of the problems typically connected with the product-manager organizational structure?

18. Why do so many new products turn out to be failures in the market?

CHAPTER 9 GOALS

At any given time, a firm may be marketing some new products and some older products, while others are being planned and developed. This chapter is concerned with the managing of the entire range of products. After studying this chapter, you should be able to explain:

- The difference between product mix and product line.
- The major product-mix strategies, such as:
  a. Expansion.
  b. Contraction.
  c. Alterations.
  d. Positioning.
  e. Trading up and trading down.
- A product's life cycle and its management.
- Planning obsolescence:
  a. Style and fashion.
  b. The fashion-adoption process.

9

Product-Mix Strategies

*A*di Dassler was once a shoemaker. Today his business is Adidas, with the stated goal of being the equipment manager to the world's athletes and teams and the athletically inclined of the world. Of course, there are many competitors in many countries — LA Gear, Reebok, Pony, Nike . . . the list is almost endless. All have managed their product lines in a variety of ways — changing the line, expanding, contracting, re-focusing. To meet the tough competition of this rapidly evolving industry, Adidas has decided to get back to basics and has defined a series of product or Equipment lines for each sport and its special needs. For running, each major running need was defined by Adidas. The running Equipment product line has been expanded so that a separate product exists to satisfy a runner's major athletic need whether it be cushion, support, foot guidance, or racing.

In addition to the four-product running Equipment line, Adidas offers tennis Equipment with two products; basketball Equipment with two products; soccer with two products; adventure with three; and squash, volleyball, and training each with one product.

Athletic needs are thus the basis of product-line development and management as well as the positioning of the lines to retailers and consumers. For athletic Equipment retailers and consumers, Adidas marketing emphasizes breadth and depth in athletic needs and how each product provides performance, protection, comfort, and quality rather than being a "promotional gimmick" — not quite the same as the product-mix strategies of some of Adidas's major competitors.

PRODUCT MIX AND PRODUCT LINE

A broad group of products, intended for essentially similar uses and possessing reasonably similar physical characteristics, constitutes a **product line**. Wearing apparel is one example of a product line. But in a different context, say, in a small specialty shop, men's furnishings (shirts, ties, and underwear) and men's ready-to-wear (suits, sport jackets, topcoats, and slacks) would each constitute a line. In another context, men's apparel is one line, as contrasted with women's apparel, furniture, or sporting goods. (See Fig. 9-1.)

The **product mix** is the full list of all products offered for sale by a company. The structure of the product mix has dimensions of both breadth and depth. Its *breadth* is measured by the *number* of product lines carried; its *depth*, by the variety of sizes, colours, and models offered *within* each product line.

FIGURE 9-1
Product mix—breadth and depth.
Part of the product mix in a lawn and garden store.

	Breadth (different lines)		
	Lawn mowers	Gardening tools	Lawn furniture
Depth (assortment within a line)	Power rotary	Rakes	Chairs
	Power reel-type	Hoes	Chaise longues
	Hand-powered	Pruning shears	Benches
	-------	Shovels	------------
	Each in various sizes and prices	-------	Various sizes and prices in redwood or aluminum with plastic webbing
		Each in various sizes and prices	

MAJOR PRODUCT-MIX STRATEGIES

Several major strategies used by manufacturers and middlemen in managing their product mix are discussed below. A discussion of planned obsolescence as a product strategy, and of fashion as an influence on the product mix, is deferred until later in the chapter.

Product Positioning

Management's ability to position a product appropriately in the market is a major determinant of company profit. A product's **position** is the image that the product projects in the minds of consumers compared to competitive products and to other products marketed by the same company.

Marketing executives can choose from a variety of positioning strategies, in order to create the most useful meaning in the minds of consumers:[1]

- *Positioning in relation to a competitor.* For some products (Coca-Cola and Pepsi-Cola, for example), the best position is directly against the competition. For other products, head-to-head positioning is exactly what *not* to do, especially when a competitor has a strong market position. Canon's desk-top copier avoids competing against the Xerox floor models, but Midas Muffler went head-to-head with Speedy Muffler King, terming its mechanics the ''top guns.''

---

[1]Adapted from David A. Aaker and J. Gary Shansby, ''Positioning Your Product,'' *Business Horizons*, May/June 1982, pp. 56-58.

MARKETING AT WORK

FILE 9-1   **REACHING FOR THE "QUALITY POSITION"**

Hennessy, maker of France's best-selling cognac, has a simple strategy for success in the 1990s—offer the highest cost quality brandy in the world. And at a time when liquor sales are falling due to the general health trend (especially in North America), the company's sales have increased by more than 70 percent over the last decade and they have captured 36 percent of the booming Asian cognac market. Today, one out of every three bottles of quality French brandy sold in the world is marked Hennessy. And despite consumers' shift away from hard liquor, the company is not worried. "People are drinking less, but they are drinking better."

Source: Adapted from Reuter-Paris, "Hennessy Banks on 'Most Expensive' Cognac," *Globe and Mail*, February 15, 1990, p. 5.

- *Positioning in relation to a target market.* In the face of a declining birth rate, Johnson & Johnson repositioned its mild baby shampoo for use by mothers, fathers, and people who must wash their hair frequently. Air Canada and Canadian Airlines International aim their frequent flyer programs at regular business travellers in an attempt to build "brand" loyalty. When Labatt Breweries introduced the first light beer in the Canadian market, its Labatt's Lite appealed primarily to diet-conscious consumers who drank relatively little beer. Molson Light was introduced as light beer with the taste of a regular beer — a beer with "heart." Miller Lite was positioned as a beer with a great taste, but less filling.
- *Positioning in relation to a product class.* Sometimes a company's positioning strategy involves associating its product with (or disassociating it from) a common class of product. The soft drink 7-Up was positioned as an uncola with no caffeine, to set it apart from Coca-Cola and the other cola drinks. Libby's, Del Monte, Campbell Soups, Kellogg's cereals, and other food processors introduced product lines with one common denominator — no salt (or very little) was added. Thus these items were positioned against the food products that are packed with the conventional (larger) amounts of salt.
- *Positioning by price and quality.* Some retail stores are known for their high-quality merchandise and high prices (Harry Rosen, Birks). Positioned at the other end of the price and quality scale are discount stores such as K mart and Zellers.

Trying to reposition a company on the price and quality spectrum can be a tricky proposition. In the 1970s, Woolco and other discount department stores tried to upgrade their fashion and quality image by adding lines of brand-name fashion clothing, while at the same time trying to retain their image for low price and "good value for the money." The move met with varying degrees of success, serving in some cases to blur the corporate image and to confuse some customers. Zellers, similarly, has been working on trading up its image towards becoming a family department store, rather than a discount store.

MARKETING AT WORK

FILE 9-2   **McDIFFERENT IN THE NINETIES**

Traditionally, McDonald's fast food has excelled at offering customers standardized meals and settings in which to eat them. (For example, hamburger buns should be all 9 cm wide and preparation of a burger, fries, and shake should take 50 seconds).

Its success has led to 11,200 restaurants in 52 countries. But the 1990s will see McDonald's ready for more and faster changes that include:

- an outlet in New York's financial district featuring a doorman, a pianist, candlelight, and reservations
- introduction of 20 to 30 new food products such as the 91-percent-fat-free burger and the Lean Deluxe sandwich, which contains only 10 grams of fat
- small-town, sit-down outlets designed with the nostalgic ambiance of 1950s' diners
- a move into hospital food (like rivals Wendy's and Burger King) where they are experimenting with carrot and celery sticks
- more regional menu promotions such as poutain in Quebec and McLobster in Atlantic Canada.

Source: Adapted from Michael Kesterton, ''Social Studies,'' *Globe and Mail,* January 10, 1991, p. 18.

Positioning by quality.

Zellers has added designer-label clothing lines to the store's own labels and has introduced well-known brand names in a new cosmetics section.[2]

Expansion of Product Mix

A firm may elect to expand its present product mix by increasing the number of lines and/or the depth within a line. New lines may be related or unrelated to the present products.

The *Globe and Mail,* expanding into the information business from the publishing business not only began to publish *Report on Business Magazine,* but also began to market various kinds of data bases (Info Globe being one). Labatt's launched Blue Light as an extension to its popular Labatt's Blue brand. Campbell's moved a little away from soup with its Belgian-made Godiva chocolates. Pillsbury launched a number of premium frozen vegetable mixes under its Green Giant label.

Expanding into somewhat unrelated lines, Bata moved into kids' clothing, Coca-Cola bought Columbia Pictures, and General Mills owns Eddie Bauer, the retailer of outdoor gear. McCain's, a major food manufacturer, branched into transportation and courier services.

Contraction of Product Mix

Another product strategy is to thin out the product mix, either by eliminating an entire line or by simplifying the assortment within a line. The shift from fat and long lines to thin and short lines is designed to eliminate low-profit products and to get more profit from fewer products. A few years ago, IBM discontinued the PC*jr* when it did not meet volume expectations in the personal computer market. After a six-year stint in the wine business, Coca-Cola sold its wine brands when the products did not meet profit expectation. RJR Nabisco decided to get out of the ocean-shipping and energy-generating businesses and concentrate on cigarettes, food products (Del Monte, Oreo, Ritz, Kentucky Fried Chicken), and drinks (Canada Dry, liqueurs and wines). A number of brokerage firms decided to abandon the consumer or retail accounts and pursue only business accounts.

Sears is using specialty departments to position its large stores against competition from specialty retailers.

[2]For a step-by-step procedure to follow in selecting a positioning strategy, see Aaker and Shansby, op. cit., pp. 58-62; and William D. Neal, ''Strategic Product Positioning: A Step-by-Step Guide,'' *Business,* May-June 1980, pp. 34-42. See also Kenneth G. Hardy, ''The Power of Positioning Your Product Lines,'' *Business Quarterly,* vol. 51, no. 3, November 1986, pp. 90-92.

The practice of slimming the product mix has long been recognized as an important product strategy. However, during the past decade it has been used extensively to cope with economic and competitive conditions as well as to retrench from the highly expansionary strategies of earlier years.

Alteration of Existing Products

As an alternative to developing a completely new product, management should take a fresh look at the company's existing products. Often, improving an established product can be more profitable and less risky than developing a completely new one. Most of you are probably familiar with the story of how Coca-Cola altered its existing product when the company came out with New Coke. Not only did New Coke find a market, but consumer demand caused Coca-Cola to re-introduce their original product as Coke Classic. The Coke move demonstrates both the hazards and advantages of altering existing products. The substitution of aspartame for saccharin in diet soft drinks (Diet Coke, Pepsi, 7-Up, and others) clearly was a successful alteration.

For some products, *redesigning* is the key to their renaissance. Gillette reformulated and relaunched Silkience Shampoo and Conditioner. *Packaging* has been a popular area for product alteration, especially for consumer products. Even something as mundane as bread, glue, or cheesecloth can be made more attractive by means of creative packaging and display.

A common strategy is resizing an existing product.

Trading Up and Trading Down

As product strategies, trading up and trading down involve, essentially, an expansion of the product line and a change in product positioning. **Trading up** means adding a high-priced, prestige product to a line in the hope of increasing the sales of existing lower-priced products. In the automobile industry some years ago, Ford introduced the Thunderbird, Chevrolet the Corvette. Then along came the Toyota Cressida and the Honda Prelude, all positioned in such a way that the lower-priced cars produced by these companies could

MARKETING AT WORK

FILE 9-3 **KEEPING THEM YOUNG ON THE FARM**

Although they are not new, Canadian farm animals have changed considerably in the last 20 years in order to escape obsolescence and the hazards of maturity. Reasons have to do with consumers' demand for leaner meat and the modernization of meat packers' plants into highly efficient, semi-automated "disassembly lines" that will no longer accept the variety of meat sizes and shapes that came down the chute in the 1960s. But a third reason has to do with fashion. To some it appears that farmers are fashion-conscious . . . . White cows popular five years ago, but black cows coming back now. In the 1960s, consumers wanted thick, juicy steaks, so farmers provided them with a short, fat, black animal raised on corn — the Aberdeen Angus. But the health craze of the 1980s dampened the demand for the tender, fattier meat and Angus went out of style. Farmers instead turned to Hereford cattle — red and white animals that are skinny and tall and produce a beef that is lean. Herefords were bred to be so lean, however, that they also gained the side effect of being tough and tasteless. In the 1990s, therefore, farmers see the Angus coming back into style. However, the Angus of the nineties are taller and leaner than their predecessors. They have to be if they are going to remain fashionable.

Source: Adapted from Oliver Bertin, "Farmers Kowtowing to Leaner Tastes," *Globe and Mail*, October 24, 1990, pp. 1–2.

---

benefit from the reflected image of the higher-priced models. This has been continued by Toyota with the introduction of the luxury Lexus.

When a company embarks upon a policy of trading up, at least two avenues are open with respect to promotional emphasis: (1) the seller may continue to depend upon the older, lower-priced product for the bulk of the sales volume and promote it heavily, or (2) the seller may gradually shift promotional emphasis to the new product and expect it to produce the major share of sales volume. In fact, the lower-priced line may be dropped altogether after a transition period.

A company is said to be **trading down** when it adds a lower-priced item to its line of prestige products. The company expects that people who cannot afford the original product will want to buy the new one because it carries some of the status of the higher-priced good. In line with this strategy, major manufacturers of 35 mm single lens reflex (SLR) cameras, such as Pentax, Canon, and Minolta, have introduced smaller, simplified cameras for photography buffs who want to be seen to be using the major brands but who do not want to be bothered with the intricacies of 35 mm photography. Mont Blanc, the West German manufacturer of the "world's most famous fountain pen," introduced a lower-priced ballpoint pen, thereby allowing its purchasers to own a Mont Blanc without having to pay more than $300 for the top-of-the-line fountain pen.

Trading up and trading down are perilous strategies because the new product may simply confuse buyers, so that the net gain is negligible. Nor is any useful purpose served if sales of the new item are generated at the expense of the older products. When *trading down* is used, the new article may permanently hurt the firm's reputation and that of its established high-quality product.

In *trading up*, on the other hand, the seller's major problem is to change the firm's image enough so that new customers will accept the higher-priced product. At the same time, the seller does not want to lose its present customers. The real risk is that the company will lose *both* customer groups through this change in its product positioning: The former customers may become confused because the company has clouded its image; and the new target market may not believe that the company is marketing high-quality merchandise.

THE PRODUCT LIFE CYCLE

Products have life cycles that can have a direct bearing on a company's survival. The life cycle of a product can be divided into four stages: introduction, growth, maturity, and decline. It is essential to note that the product life-cycle concept applies to a generic category of product (microwave ovens, for example) and not to specific brands (such as General Electric). A product life cycle consists of the aggregate demand for all brands comprising a generic product category. A company's marketing success can be affected considerably by its ability to understand and manage the life cycles of its products. The product life cycle can be illustrated with the sales volume and profit curves, as shown in Fig. 9-2. The *shapes* of these curves will vary from product to product. However, the basic shapes and the relationship between the two curves are usually as illustrated.

The profit curve for most new products is negative through most of the introductory stage. Also, in the latter part of the growth stage, the profit curve starts to decline while the sales volume is still ascending. This occurs because a company usually must increase its advertising and selling effort or cut its prices (or do both) to continue its sales growth during the maturity stage in the face of intensifying competition. Introducing a new product at the proper time will help maintain the company's desired level of profit.

FIGURE 9-2
Typical life cycle of a product— sales and profit curves.
Profit usually starts to decline while a product's sales volume is still increasing. How does the relationship between these curves influence the time at which additional new products should be introduced?

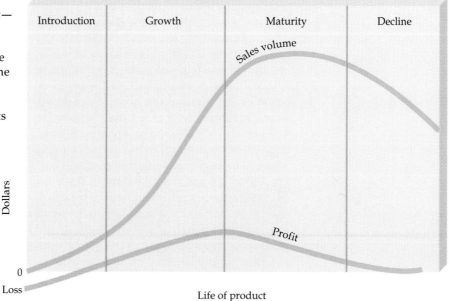

Characteristics of Each Stage

Management must recognize what part of the life cycle its product is in at any given time. The competitive environment and resultant marketing strategies ordinarily will differ depending on the stage.

INTRODUCTION

During the first stage of a product's life cycle, it is launched into the market in a full-scale promotion and marketing program. It has gone through the embryonic stages of idea evaluation, pilot models, and test marketing. The entire product may be new, like a machine that cleans clothes electronically without using any water. Or the basic product may be well known but have a new feature or accessory that is in the introductory stage — a gas turbine engine in an automobile, for example.

There is a high percentage of product failures in this period. Operations in the introductory period are characterized by high costs, low sales volume, net losses, and limited distribution. In many respects, the pioneering stage is the most risky and expensive one. However, for really new products, there is very little direct competition. The promotional program is designed to stimulate *primary,* rather than *secondary,* demand. That is the *type of product,* rather than the *seller's brand,* is emphasized.

GROWTH

In the growth, or market-acceptance, stage, both sales and profits rise, often at a rapid rate. Competitors enter the market—in large numbers if the profit outlook is particularly attractive. Sellers shift to a ''buy-my-brand'' rather than a ''try-this-product'' promotional strategy. The number of distribution outlets increases, economies of scale are introduced, and prices may come down a bit. Typically profits start to decline near the end of the growth stage.

MATURITY

During the first part of this period, sales continue to increase, but at a decreasing rate. While sales are levelling off, the profits of both the manufacturer and the retailers are declining. Marginal producers are forced to drop out of the market. Price competition becomes increasingly severe. The producer assumes a greater share of the total promotional effort in the fight to retain dealers and the shelf space in their stores. New models are introduced as manufacturers broaden their lines, and trade-in sales become significant.

DECLINE AND POSSIBLE ABANDONMENT

For virtually all products, obsolescence sets in inevitably as new products start their own life cycles and replace the old ones. Cost control becomes increasingly important as demand drops. Advertising declines, and a number of competitors withdraw from the market. Whether the product has to be abandoned, or whether the surviving sellers can continue on a profitable basis, often depends upon management's abilities.

For some markets this product is already in the growth stage; for others it is in the introductory stage.

Length of Product Life Cycle

The length of the life cycle varies among products. It will range from a few weeks or a short season (for a fad or a clothing fashion) to several decades (for, say, autos or telephones). In general, however, product life cycles are getting shorter as the years go by. Rapid changes in technology can make a product obsolete. Or, if competitors can quickly introduce a ''me-too'' version

M A R K E T I N G   A T   W O R K

FILE 9-4 **WHAT TO DO WHEN IT'S NEW**

Cellular phone companies have been astonished by the growth of business in Canada—over 600,000 people are users, ranking Canadians among the highest per capita subscribers in the world. However, for increasing numbers of non-subscribers, this era of personal communications is becoming a little too impersonal as users bring their phones and their conversations into public places. Warnings to switch off cellular phones are becoming common in restaurants and in theatre programs. Phone companies have responded to nonuser backlash. While Cantel Inc., under the guise of Ms. Mobile Manners, warned customers to use the phones responsibly and unobtrusively, Motorola Cellular, Canada's largest manufacturer of cellular phones, has set out guidelines on safety and good manners for users that include turning off the phone while dining or attending theatre or sporting events, and speaking softly (although most people raise their voices in business conversations, the phones have sensitive microphones). Because it's a relatively new tool, people sometimes use it inappropriately.

Source: Adapted from Mary Gooderham, "Portable Phones Mean New Rules of Etiquette," *Globe and Mail*, January 17, 1991, p. 5.

---

of a popular product, this product may move quickly into the maturity stage.

Although Fig. 9-2 suggests that the life-cycle stages cover nearly equal periods of time, that is *not* the case. The stages in any given product's life cycle usually last for *different* periods of time. Also, the duration of each stage will vary among products. Some products take years to pass through the introductory stage, while others are accepted in a few weeks. Moreover, not all products go through all the stages. Some may fail in the introductory stage, and others may not be introduced until the market is in the growth or maturity stage. In virtually all cases, however, decline and possible abandonment are inevitable. This is because (1) the need for the product disappears (as when frozen orange juice generally eliminated the market for juice squeezers); (2) a better or less expensive product is developed to fill the same need (electronic microchips made possible many replacement products); or (3) the people simply grow tired of a product (a clothing style, for example), so it disappears from the market.

Life Cycle Is Related to a Market

When we say a product is in its growth stage or some other stage, implicitly we are referring to a specific market. A product may be well accepted (growth or maturity stage) in a number of markets but be in the introductory stage in other markets. To illustrate, Ortho Pharmaceutical's Retin-A was introduced as a treatment for teenage acne. In the late 1980s this product was in the maturity stage in the teenage market. Having proven to be a wrinkle-remover, however, in the late 1980s Retin-A entered the introductory stage in the market of middle-aged and older people.

In terms of international markets a product may be in its maturity stage in one country and in the introductory stage or perhaps even unknown in another country. Sink-installed garbage disposals, for example, are well known and widespread in North America. Yet they are very rare in Japan and virtually unknown in many parts of Italy. Steel-belted radial auto tires were in their maturity stage in Western Europe well before they were introduced broadly in Canada. Soccer (called football in the rest of the world) is in its maturity stage as a spectator sport and recreational activity in most countries, but in parts of Canada and the United States, it is still in the introductory or growth stage.

Management of the Product Life Cycle

The shape of a product's sales and profit curves is not predetermined. To a surprising extent, the shape can be controlled. Successful life-cycle management strategies are (1) to predict the shape of the proposed product's cycle even before it is introduced and (2) at each stage to anticipate the marketing requirements of the following stage. The introductory period, for instance, may be shortened by broadening the distribution or by increasing the promotional effort.[3]

STRATEGY FOR ENTRY STAGE

In the management of a product's life cycle, a crucial question concerns the timing of entry into the new market. Should we enter during the introductory stage? Or should we wait and plunge in during the early part of the growth stage, after innovating companies have proved that there is a viable market?

New styles and brands help to rejuvenate an established product.

The strategy of entering during the introductory stage is based on the idea of building a dominant market position and thus lessening the effectiveness of competition. This was the tactic pursued by Sony Walkman, Litton in microwave ovens, Perrier in bottled sparkling water, and Nike in running shoes. Marketing executives and published research generally support this strategy.

TRANSFORMING THE WAY WE RELAX

GENUINE
LA-Z-BOY

[3]For an excellent discussion of strategies that can be employed in managing a product's life cycle, see Sak Onkvisit and John J. Shaw, "Competition and Management: Can the Product Life Cycle Help?" *Business Horizons*, July-August 1986, pp. 51-62.

The hurdles may be insurmountable when you enter with a "me-too" product and try to play catch-up.

At the same time, there are compelling reasons for delaying entry until the market is proven. Pioneering requires a large investment, and the risks are great—as demonstrated by the high failure rate among new products. Later-entry success stories usually come out of large companies with the marketing resources to overwhelm smaller innovating firms. In one such case, Diet Rite Cola, an early pioneer, was later surpassed by Tab, Diet Coke, and Diet Pepsi. And after Apple proved there was a viable market, IBM successfully entered the personal computer field.

There is no clear-cut answer as to which is the better timing strategy. Perhaps the best answer is that old reliable in marketing—it all depends. Each strategy has its advantages and limitations, its successes and failures. Certainly sound executive judgement is critical, whatever decision is made.[4]

MANAGING DURING MATURITY STAGE

A product's line may be extended during the maturity stage of its life cycle by making product modifications, designing new promotion, or devising new uses. We find one example of this in the refrigerator industry—an industry considered dull and mature even by some people in it. Admiral rejuvenated this staid product by adding features that enable the user to make ice cream, cold soup, and slush drinks. The company also built in a wine rack and microwave storage trays. Campbell's have low-sodium and calorie-reduced soup. To boost the image of a tired brand, GWG brought out a line of 1911's jeans made of heavier denim and with a distinctive leather patch GWG logo.[5]

In 1988 Du Pont's Teflon celebrated its fiftieth birthday. But management continues to keep this mature product very much alive and growing by devising new uses for it. For instance, Teflon was packaged in a spray can to be used (among other purposes): on walls to protect against fingerprints; on neckties to repel food stains; and on ski clothes to keep them dry in snow.[6] Even Aspirin—certainly the epitome of a mature product—found a new market among people who have survived one heart attack. Aspirin was proven to reduce considerably the chances of a second attack. In the early 1990s, Fiberglas Canada created an attention-getting and humourous series of commercials using pink flamingos to re-vitalize brand awareness for insulation material.

MANAGING DURING SALES-DECLINE STAGE

Perhaps it is in the sales-decline stage that a company finds its greatest challenges in life-cycle management. At some point in the product's life, management may have to consider whether to abandon the product. The cost of carrying profitless products go beyond the expenses that show up on financial statements. The real burdens are the insidious costs accruing from managerial

---

[4]For more on this subject, see Steven P. Schnaars, "When Entering Growth Markets, Are Pioneers Better than Poachers?" *Business Horizons*, March-April 1986, pp. 27-36.

[5]Wayne Mouland, "How to Promote Sales of Mature Brands," *Marketing*, November 17, 1986, p. CP and 14.

[6]Laurie Hays, "Teflon Is 50 Years Old, but Du Pont Is Still Finding New Uses for Invention," *The Wall Street Journal*, April 7, 1988, p. 30.

TEN WAYS TO DREAM UP NEW PRODUCTS AND REVITALIZE OLDER ONES

Originally, some of these ideas were intended to stimulate new-product development and others were for revitalizing older products. Whatever the case may be, they can create additional sales for a company.

- *Take something out of the product.* Removing caffeine and sugar from soft drinks and some of the sodium from various processed foods resulted in new products.
- *Add something to the product.* Extra-large chocolate chips boosted sales of some brands of chocolate chip cookies. Periodically, soap and detergent makers add something new to a basic product—bleach, softener, lemon scent, or an antistatic agent.
- *Listen to consumers' complaints.* "The smell of my antiperspirant clashes with my perfume." "Why is the fruit in my yogurt always at the bottom?" Listening to these gripes resulted in an odorless antiperspirant and a yogurt with fruit dispersed throughout.
- *Transfer success from one product category to another.* Pump dispensers proved popular with mustard, ketchup, and skin lotion, so this form of packaging was used for toothpaste.
- *Make the task easier.* Combining shampoo with hair conditioner eliminates one task. And microwaving is a lot easier than traditional methods of cooking many foods, and the results are just as tasty.
- *Dream up new uses.* Chex cereals are the key ingredint in a line of party snacks. Sales of Cow Brand baking soda increased considerably after the product was advertised as a refrigerator deodorant.
- *Add new distribution channels.* Woolite, a soap for woollen items, for years was sold only in department stores. When the company made this product available in supermarkets, sales tripled the first year.
- *Add a dramatic guarantee.* Spray 'n' Wash sales were declining as competitive products were introduced. The company then made this guarantee: "If Spray 'n' Wash doesn't remove a stain from a shirt—any shirt—we'll buy you a new shirt." This guarantee boosted sales considerably, and only a few people requested a new shirt.
- *Don't stymie creativity.* A Sony executive walking through a laboratory saw a miniature tape recorder project and a headphone project. Creative thinking combined the two projects, resulting in the Walkman.
- *Look overseas for inspiration.* Europe gave us mineral water, hair mousse, aseptic packaging, and soft-batch cookies.

SOURCE: Adapted from Calvin L. Hodock, "Nine Surefire Ways to Cook Up New Ideas," *Sales & Marketing Management*, August 1988, p. 40, and Gerald Schoenfeld, "Treat Old Products Like New," *Marketing News*, July 31, 1989, p. 15.

time and effort that are diverted to sick products. Management often seems reluctant to discard a product, however.

When sales are declining, management has the following alternatives, some of which are reflected in the box above.

- Improve the product in a functional sense or revitalize it in some manner.
- Make sure that the marketing and production programs are as efficient as possible.

- Streamline the product assortment by pruning out unprofitable sizes and models. Frequently, this tactic will *decrease* sales and *increase* profits.
- "Run out" the product; that is, cut all costs to the bare-minimum level that will optimize profitability over the limited remaining life of the product.

In the final analysis the only reasonable alternative may be simply to abandon the product. Knowing when and how to abandon products successfully may be as important as knowing when and how to introduce new ones. Certainly management should develop a systematic procedure for phasing out its weak products.[7]

PLANNED OBSOLESCENCE AND FASHION

The North American consumer seems to be on a constant quest for the "new" but not "*too* new." The market wants newness — new products, new styles, new colours. However, people want to be moved gently out of their habitual patterns, not shocked out of them. This has led many manufacturers to develop the product strategy of planned obsolescence. Its objective is to make an existing product out of date and thus to increase the market for replacement products.

Nature of Planned Obsolescence

The term **planned obsolescence** may be used in two ways:

- *Technological or functional obsolescence.* Significant technical improvements result in a more effective product. For instance, pocket calculators made slide rules technologically obsolete. This type of obsolescence is generally considered to be socially and economically desirable.
- *Style obsolescence.* This is sometimes called "psychological" or "fashion" obsolescence. Superficial characteristics of the product are altered so that the new model is easily differentiated from the previous model. The intent is to make people feel out of date if they continue to use old models.

When people criticize planned obsolescence, they are usually referring to the second interpretation — style obsolescence. In our discussion, planned obsolescence will mean only style obsolescence, unless otherwise stated.

Nature of Style and Fashion

Although the word *style* and *fashion* are often used interchangeably, there is a clear distinction between the two. A **style** is defined as a distinctive manner of construction or presentation in any art, product, or endeavour (singing, playing, behaving). Thus we have styles in automobiles (sedans, station wagons), in bathing suits (one-piece, bikinis), in furniture (Early American, French Provincial), and in dancing (waltz, rumba).

A **fashion** is any style that is popularly accepted and purchased by several successive groups of people over a reasonably long period of time. Not every style becomes a fashion. To be rated as a fashion, or to be called "fashionable," a style must become popularly accepted.

A **fad** normally does not remain popular as long as a fashion, and it is based on some novelty feature.

Basic styles never change, but fashion is always changing. Fashions are found in all societies, including primitive groups, the great Oriental cultures, and the societies of ancient and medieval Europe.

---

[7]For suggestions on how to recognize the technological limits of an existing product — in effect, knowing when to get off the curve for an existing product and to jump on the curve for the next product — see Richard Foster, "When to Make Your Move to the Latest Innovation," *Across the Board*, October 1986, pp. 44-50.

Origin of Fashion

Fashion is rooted in sociological and psychological factors. Basically, people are conformists. At the same time, they yearn to look, act, and be a *little* different from others. They are not in revolt against custom; they simply wish to be a bit different and still not be accused of bad taste or insensitivity to the code. Fashion discreetly furnishes them the opportunity for self-expression.

Stanley Marcus, the president of Nieman-Marcus, the high fashion department store in Dallas, Texas, once observed:[8]

> If, for example, a dictator decreed feminine clothes to be illegal and that all women should wear barrels, it would not result in an era of uniformity, in my opinion. Very shortly, I think you'd find that one ingenious woman would color her barrel with a lipstick, another would pin paper lace doilies on the front of hers, and still another would decorate hers with thumbtacks. *This is a strange human urge toward conformity, but a dislike for complete uniformity.*

Fashion-Adoption Process

The fashion-adoption process reflects the concepts of (1) large group and small group influences on consumer buying behaviour and (2) the diffusion of innovation, as discussed in Chapters 6 and 8. People usually try to imitate others in the same social stratum or those on the next higher level. They do so by purchasing the fashionable product. This shows up as a wave of buying in that particular social stratum. The **fashion-adoption process** then, is a series of buying waves that arise as the given style is popularly accepted in one group, then another and another, until it finally falls out of fashion. This wavelike movement, representing the introduction, rise, popular culmination, and decline of the market's acceptance of a style, is referred to as the **fashion cycle.**

Three theories of fashion adoption are recognized (see Fig. 9-3):

- **Trickle-down,** where a given fashion cycle flows *downward* through several socioeconomic classes.
- **Trickle-across,** where the cycle moves *horizontally* and *simultaneously within* several social classes.
- **Trickle-up,** where the cycle is initiated in lower socioeconomic classes, then later the style becomes popular among higher-income and social groups.

Traditionally, the trickle-down theory has been used as the basic model to explain the fashion-adoption process. As an example, designers of women's apparel first introduce a style to the leaders—the tastemakers who usually are the social leaders in the upper-income brackets. If they accept the style, it quickly appears in leading fashion stores. Soon the middle-income and then the lower-income markets want to emulate the leaders, and the style is mass-marketed. As its popularity wanes, the style appears in bargain-price stores and finally is no longer considered fashionable.

To illustrate the trickle-across process, let us again use the example of women's apparel. Within a few weeks at the most, at the beginning of the fall season, the same style of dresses appears (1) in small, exclusive dress shops appealing to the upper social class, (2) in large department stores appealing to the middle social class, and (3) in discount houses and low-priced women's ready-to-wear chain stores, where the appeal is to the upper-lower social class.

---

[8]Stanley Marcus, ''Fashion Merchandising,'' a Tobé lecture on retail distribution, Harvard Business School, March 10, 1959, pp. 4-5.

FIGURE 9-3
Fashion-adoption processes.

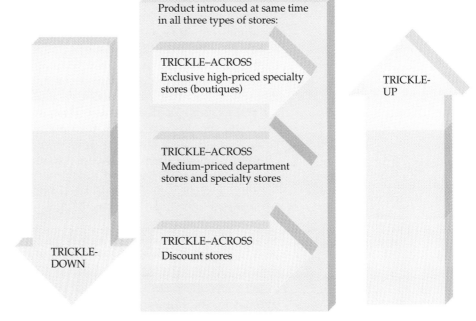

Price and quality mark the differences in the dresses sold on the three levels
—*but the style is basically the same. Within each class* the dresses are purchased
early in the season by the opinion leaders — the innovators. If the style is
accepted, its sales curve rises as it becomes popular with the early adopters,
and then with the late adopters. Evenually, sales decline as the style ceases to
be popular. This cycle, or flow, is a horizontal movement occuring virtually
simultaneously within each of several social strata.

Today the trickle-across concept best reflects the adoption process for most
fashions. Granted, there is some flow downward, and obviously there is an
upward influence. But market conditions today seem to foster a horizontal
flow. By means of modern production, communication, and transportation
methods, we can disseminate style information and products so rapidly that
all social strata can be reached at about the same time. In the apparel field
particularly, manufacturing and marketing programs tend to foster the horizontal movement of fashions. Manufacturers produce a wide *variety* of essentially one style. They also produce various *qualities* of the same basic style so
as to appeal to different income groups simultaneously. When an entire cycle
may last only one season, sellers cannot afford to wait for style acceptance to

THE "TRICKLE-UP" PROCESS

Blue jeans, denim jackets, T-shirts, and outdoor wear in the 1990s. Years earlier
there were popular styles of music we call jazz and the blues. These all have one
thing in common. They are styles that *trickled up* in popularity; that is, they were
popular first with lower socioeconomic groups. Later, their popularity trickled up
as these styles gained wide acceptance among the higher-income markets. T-shirts
—once the domain of beer-drinking blue-collar workers and radicals—have moved
up considerably in social respectability and price. Now they are designed by Yves
Saint Laurent, Calvin Klein, Alfred Sung, Ralph Lauren, and others.

M A R K E T I N G   A T   W O R K

FILE 9-5   **CLOSING THE FASHION GAP**

While most fashion retailers have been suffering from a dwindling market, San Francisco-based Gap Inc. has been expanding all over—with 24 stores in Canada and plans for 10 to 15 more in the next few years (there are already 1,072 Gap stores in Canada, Britain, and the United States). The Gap owes its success to two factors. The first is its ability to successfully maintain its image as a purveyor of hip and trendy colourful clothes, while providing basic natural-fibre casual wear for the 15-to-35-year-old market. As a customer says, "It's just good basic stuff you can kick around in. A Ralph Lauren shirt would cost me double." Within this image it has been able to broaden and successfully cater to the children of its original 1960s customers, opening up GapKids in 1985 and babyGap stores in 1989. It also introduces six new clothing lines each year to keep up with consistently changing fashions. The second reason for The Gap's success is the close control it maintains over all of its operations: product design, distribution, and advertising. Not only does this create increased focus and communication within the company, but it cuts down on operating costs since there is no middleman to pay—The Gap is both wholesaler and retailer.

Source: Adapted from Adele Weder, "A Survivor for the Recession," *Financial Times of Canada,* December 17, 1990, p. 5.

trickle down. They must introduce it into many social levels as soon as possible.

Marketing Considerations in Fashion

When a firm's products are subject to the fashion cycle, management must know what style the cycle is in at all times. Managers must decide at what point to get into the cycle, and when they should get out.

Accurate forecasting is of inestimable value in achieving success in fashion merchandising. This is an extremely difficult task, however, because the forecaster is often dealing with complex sociological and psychological factors. Frequently a retailer or a manufacturer operates largely on intuition and inspiration, tempered by considerable experience.

The executives also must know what market they are aiming for. Ordinarily, a retailer cannot successfully participate in all stages of the fashion cycle at the same time. A high-grade specialty store selling apparel — whose stocks are displayed in limited numbers without price tags—should get in at the start of a fashion trend. A department store appealing to the middle-income market should plan to enter the cycle in time to mass-market the style as it is climbing to its peak of popularity.

Some styles remain in fashion for a long time.

ANOTHER "LAW OF FASHION"

The same dress is indecent 10 years before its time, daring 1 year before its time, chic in its time, dowdy 3 years after its time, hideous 20 years after its time, amusing 30 years after its time, romantic 100 years after its time, and beautiful 150 years after its time.

SOURCE: James Laver, British costume historian, in *Today's Health,* October 1973, p. 69.

SUMMARY

To make the product-planning phase of a company's marketing program most effective, it is imperative that management select appropriate strategies for the company's product mix. One strategy is simply to expand the product mix by increasing the number of lines and/or the depth within a line. An alternative is to prune out the product mix by eliminating an entire line or by simplifying the assortment within a line. Another strategy is to alter the design, packaging, or other features of existing products. Still another is appropriate "positioning" of the product, relative to competing products or to other products sold by the firm. In other strategies, management may elect to trade up or trade down, relative to its existing products.

Managers need to understand the concept of a product's life cycle and the characteristics of each stage in the cycle. The task of managing a product as it moves through its life cycle presents both challenges and opportunities — perhaps most frequently in the sales-decline stage.

An especially controversial product strategy is that of planned obsolescence, built around the concepts of style, fashion, and the fashion cycle. Fashion — essentially a sociological and psychological phenomenon — follows a reasonably predictable pattern. With advances in communications and production, the fashion-adoption process has moved away from the traditional trickle-down pattern. Today the process is better described as trickle-across. There also are some noteworthy examples of fashions trickling up. Style obsolescence, in spite of its critics, is based on consumer psychology.

KEY TERMS AND CONCEPTS

Product line 280
Product mix 280
Product-mix breadth and
  depth 280
Product positioning 280
Expansion of product mix 283
Contraction of product mix 283
Product alteration 284
Trading up/trading down 284
Product life cycle 286

Planned obsolescence 292
Fashion (style) obsolescence 292
Style 292
Fashion 292
Fad 292
Fashion-adoption process 293
Fashion cycle 293
Trickle-down 293
Trickle-across 293
Trickle-up 293

QUESTIONS AND PROBLEMS

1. "It is inconsistent for management to follow concurrently the product-line strategies of *expanding* its product mix and *contracting* its product mix." Discuss.

2. "Trading up and trading down are product strategies closely related to the business cycle. Firms trade up during periods of prosperity and trade down during depressions or recessions." Do you agree? Why?

3. Name some products that you believe are in the introductory stage of their life cycles. Identify the market that considers your examples to be new products.

4. Give examples of products that are in the stage of market decline. In each case, point out whether you think the decline is permanent. What recommendations do you have for rejuvenating the demand for the product?

5. How might a company's pricing strategies differ, depending upon whether its product is in the introductory stage or maturity stage of is life cycle?

6. What advertising strategies are likely to be used when a product is in the growth stage?

7. What products, other than wearing apparel and automobiles, stress fashion and style in marketing? Do styles exist among industrial products?

8. Select a product and trace its marketing as it moves through a complete fashion cycle. Particularly note and explain the changes in the distribution, pricing, and promotion of the product in the various stages of the cycle.

9. Is the trickle-down theory applicable in describing the fashion-adoption process in product lines other than women's apparel? Explain, using examples.

10. Planned obsolescence is criticized as a social and economic waste because we are urged to buy things we do not like and do not need. What is your opinion in this matter? If you object to planned obsolescence, what are your recommendations for correcting the situation?

11. What effects might a recession have on:
a. Product life cycles?
b. Planned obsolescence?

What marketing strategies might a firm employ to counter (or take advantage of) these effects?

CHAPTER 10 GOALS

The title of this chapter could be "Product Presentation"—because the way in which a physical product is presented to potential customers is very much a part of the product itself. After studying this chapter, you should understand:

- The nature and importance of brands, including the characteristics of a good brand and the problem of generic brand names.
- Brand strategies of manufacturers and middlemen.
- The "battle of the brands."
- The nature and importance of packaging.
- Major packaging strategies.
- Types of labelling.
- The marketing implications in some other product features—design, colour, quality, warranty, and servicing.

CHAPTER 10

Brands, Packaging, and Other Product Features

Would you buy a used Miata or a second-hand Miele? Today it is extremely difficult to come up with a good brand name for a new product. If customers cannot pronounce the name, they are not as likely to ask for the brand in a store. The challenge of selecting a brand name is doubly difficult in Canada where brand names have to be acceptable to both French-speaking and English-speaking consumers. With this in mind, would you consider the choice of some of the following brands to be a little risky?

Acura (automobile)

Jhirmack (shampoo)

Miele (bicycle)

Infiniti (automobile)

Häagen-Dazs (ice cream)

Antiphlogistine Rub A535
   (analgesic rub)

Benetton (clothing)

Orville Redenbacher (popcorn)

Unisys (computers and
   information systems)

Bain de Soleil (suntan lotion)

Xylocaine (anaesthetic)

Vaudreuil (dairy products)

Uhu (glue stick)

Leica (cameras)

Kronenbourg (beer)

Miata (automobile)

Nike (athletic shoes and clothing)

How does a company come up with a good brand name? What makes a good brand? Why do some attact a loyal consumer following and others die as quickly as they are introduced? Why do some brands convey clear images to consumers, while others seem confused and less well defined? It is true that some brands are successful at communicating a strong quality image to a majority of consumers. Recent research showed that the brands that were perceived by consumers to stand for high quality were (in order) Mercedes-Benz automobiles, Kodak film, Fisher-Price toys, Hallmark cards, Levi's jeans, IBM computers, Hershey's chocolate, Lego toys, Michelin tires, and Campbell's soups.[1]

---

[1]Marina Strauss, ''A High Profile Isn't Everything, Survey of Brand Names Reveals,'' *Globe and Mail Report on Business*, January 18, 1990, p. B22.

Other brands have remained market leaders for more than half a century. Brands that were market leaders in Canada in 1925 and that remain the market leaders in their product categories today include Nabisco biscuits, Kellogg's cereals, Wrigley chewing gum, Kodak film, Gillette razors, Crisco shortening, Lipton tea, and Campbell's soup.[2] Why have some brands remained market leaders for more than 65 years? Is it that some of these leading brands also appear on the perceived high-quality list? This clearly has something to do with their success, but it may not explain it entirely. What is obvious is that major brands that continue to please consumers have succeeded in creating an image the consumers find attractive and one that encourages them to buy those brands again and again.

Given the vast number of products that appear on the shelves of retail stores today, the difficulty of choosing a brand name for a new product is enormous. And yet the success of that new product will depend to a very great degree on the image that is communicated by the brand name. Otherwise, how do you account for some people wanting Bayer Aspirin and others preferring a private label ASA brand, when both are physically and chemically the identical product? Some people buy Esso motor oil, while others choose the Petro-Canada brand. Yet many people contend that there are no significant differences among the well-known brands of motor oils.

Why do some people use certain brands and not others? The buyer's choice may be affected by the package, warranty, colour, design, or some other feature of the product. In packaging, for example, dairy products companies such as the makers of Yoplait yogurt use a multiple-unit packaging strategy to encourage shoppers to buy four containers rather than just one. Colgate, Maclean's, and Crest toothpaste increased sales when they marketed this product in a pump-dispenser package. Holiday Inn found that by offering a money-back guarantee, the company gained a second chance with unhappy customers and also improved its own service. The effective use of product quality as a marketing tool by Panasonic, Sony, and other Japanese manufacturers is known worldwide. All these product characteristics combined project an image to prospective customers. Consequently, because these product features are such important elements in a company's marketing program, we devote this chapter to them.

BRANDS

The word *brand* is a comprehensive term, and it includes other, narrower terms. A **brand** is a name, term, symbol, or special design, or some combination of these elements, that is intended to identify the goods or services of one seller or a group of sellers. A brand differentiates one seller's products or services from those of competitors. A brand **name** consists of words, letters, and/or numbers that can be *vocalized*. A brand **mark** is the part of the brand that appears in the form of a symbol, design, or distinctive colouring or lettering. It is recognized by sight but may not be expressed when a person pronounces the brand name. Ski-Doo, du Maurier, Gillette, and Robin Hood are brand names. Brand marks are illustrated by the picture of Robin Hood on the flour package, the distinctive CN logo of Canadian National, and the Root Bear character who promotes A&W. These marks, logos, or designs are usually registered and may be used only by the company that owns the mark.

[2]Larry Black, ''What's in a Name?'' *Report on Business Magazine*, November 1989, pp. 98–110.

Izod is a brand name, and the alligator is a brand mark. Together they are a brand.

IZOD. LACOSTE.

THE ORIGINAL SINCE 1933

A company with a well-known trademark must defend itself.

XEROX

You can't Xerox a Xerox on a Xerox.

But we don't mind at all if you copy a copy on a Xerox copier.

In fact, we prefer it. Because the Xerox trademark should only identify products made by us. Like Xerox copiers and Xerox printing systems.

As a trademark, the term Xerox should always be used as an adjective, followed by a noun. And it is never used as a verb. Of course, helping us protect our trademark also helps you.

Because you'll continue to get what you're actually asking for.

And not an inferior copy.

 XEROX **The Document Company**

A **trademark** is defined as a brand that is given legal protection because, under the law, it has been appropriated by one seller. Thus *trademark* is essentially a legal term. All trademarks are brands and thus include the words, letters, or numbers that can be pronounced. They may also include a pictorial design (brand mark). Some people erroneously believe that the trademark is only the pictorial part of the brand.

One major method of classifying brands is on the basis of who owns them —producers or retailers. Major brands such as Sony, Zenith, Arrow, Sunlight, GWG, and Kellogg are producers' brands, while Motomaster, President's Choice, Birkdale, Viking, Kenmore, Body Shop, and Life are all brands that are owned by retailers.

The term *national* has been used for many years to describe producer-brand ownership, while brands owned by retailers are generally referred to as *private* brands or private labels. However, more acceptable terminology for many marketers would be the terms *producer* and *retailer* brands. To say that a brand of a small manufacturer of poultry feed in British Columbia, who markets in only two or three Western provinces, is a *national brand*, while those of Canadian Tire, Shoppers Drug, Eaton's, Loblaws, and Sears are private brands, seems to be misusing these terms to some extent. Nevertheless, the brands of retailers continue to be referred to as *private labels*.

WHAT'S IN A NAME?

A history of brand marketing will tell us that once a brand establishes a position of brand leadership in a product category, this position is often maintained over a very long period of time. Many of the leading brands that we buy today were purchased regularly by our parents and even our grandparents. Brands that continue to dominate their consumer product categories include Kodak, General Electric, Kellogg's, Levi's, Kraft, Nabisco, Tide, and Campbell's.

The development and protection of brand names has become a very important element of marketing management and one that demands increased attention all the time. Companies such as Colgate-Palmolive have made conscious decisions to manage their brand names in such a way as to dominate a product category. For example, this company has made a commitment to position Colgate as an all-purpose supplier of oral-health products. The importance of the Colgate name is summed up in a comment from Patrick Knight, former vice-president of marketing for Colgate-Palmolive: "We now consider the most valuable assets we have to be our trademarks."[3]

Such an attitude towards successful brands has led major companies to ensure that their brand names are assigned a value and shown as assets on their balance sheets. Many of the leading brands have been the major targets in corporate takeovers as the purchasing companies have realized that the equity represented in successful brands is considerably more valuable than factories and distribution systems.[4]

Equally important is the value of established brands in allowing their owners to apply the brands to new products. As the cost of acquiring established brands increases, as does the cost and risk of introducing new products, many

---

[3]Derek Suchard, "How the Pros Build Brands," *Canadian Business*, January 1991, p. 70.

[4]Larry Black, "What's in a Name?" *Report on Business Magazine*, November 1989, pp. 98–110.

MARKETING AT WORK

FILE 10-1   **WHAT'S A BRAND REALLY WORTH?**

Coopers & Lybrand, one of Canada's major consulting and accounting firms, suggests a number of different approaches to determining what a brand can be worth. By using them all and cross-checking the results, it is possible to develop a realistic evaluation.

Comparable Market Transaction: What has someone recently paid for a similar brand? Is this a market price?

Replacement Cost: What would be the cost of bringing a similar successful brand to the market?

Royalty Payment Relief: What would you have to pay in royalties to a brand owner compared with the cost of owning it yourself?

Excess Profit: How much more profitable is your company because of the brands it has compared with competitors in your industry?

Gross Profit Differences: How much more do you earn from your branded product compared with what you would earn if it were a comparable generic or unbranded product?

We said it was possible; we didn't say it would be easy.

Source: Adapted from Derek Suchard, ''How the Pros Build Brands,'' *Canadian Business*, January 1991, p. 72.

companies have been turning in recent years to the launching of *brand extensions* as a way of trading on the success of established brands and reducing the risk of new product failure. Procter & Gamble now offers five varieties of Tide laundry detergent. Nabisco has launched several varieties of the original Oreo cookie, and Oreo ice cream is also available. And the Mars chocolate bar is now sold in a white chocolate version, as well as a frozen ice-cream product.

By stretching the original successful brand name to cover a number of brand extension products, the marketer is trading on the success of the original brand, but is running some risk at the same time. Clearly, there may be some new products to which the original brand should not be applied. This raises the question of how far the successful brand can be ''extended'' before the marketer is stretching the credibility of the link between the brand and the product. Colgate can with confidence launch a line of toothbrushes, dental floss, and mouthwash, but would consumers buy Colgate sunglasses or suntan lotion?[5]

Brands make it easy for consumers to identify goods or services. Brands also help assure purchasers that they are getting comparable quality when they reorder. For sellers, brands can be advertised and recognized when displayed on shelves in a store. Branding also helps sellers control their market because buyers will not confuse one branded product with another. Branding reduces

---

[5]For an interesting review of the value of brand names and the risks associated with brand extensions, the reader is referred to: ''Brand-stretching can be fun—and dangerous,'' *The Economist*, May 5, 1990, pp. 77–80.

price comparisons because it is hard to compare prices on two items with different brands. Finally, for sellers branding can add a measure of prestige to otherwise ordinary commodities (Sunkist oranges, Sifto salt, Lantic sugar, Highliner fish, Chiquita bananas).

Reasons for Not Branding

The two major responsibilities inherent in brand ownership are (1) to promote the brand and (2) to maintain a consistent quality of output. Many firms do not brand their products because they are unable or unwilling to assume those responsibilities.

Some items are not branded because of the difficulty of differentiating the products of one firm from those of another. Clothespins, nails, and industrial raw materials (coal, cotton, wheat) are examples of goods for which product differentiation (including branding) is generally unknown. The physical nature of some items, such as fresh fruits and vegetables, may discourage branding. However, now that these products are often packaged in typically purchased quantities, brands are being applied to the packages.

Producers frequently do not brand that part of their output that is below their usual quality. Products graded as seconds or imperfects are sold at a cut price and are often distributed through channels different from those used for usual-quality goods.

Selecting a Good Brand Name

Selecting a good brand name is not an easy task. In spite of the acknowledged importance of a brand, it is surprising how few really good brand names there are. In a study made many years ago, it was found that only 12 percent of the names helped sell the product; 36 percent actually hurt sales. The other 52 percent were "nonentities — contributing nothing to the sales appeal of the product." There is no reason to believe that the situation has improved materially since that study was made.

CHARACTERISTICS OF A GOOD BRAND

A good brand should possess as many of the following characteristics as possible. It is extremely difficult, however, to find a brand that has all of them. A brand should:

- Suggest something about the product's characteristics — its benefits, use, or action. Some names that suggest desirable benefits include Beautyrest, Cold-spot, Motomaster, and La-Z-Boy. Product use and action are suggested by Minute Rice, Dustbuster, Spic and Span, Gleem, and Easy-Off.
- Be easy to pronounce, spell, and remember. Simple, short, one-syllable names such as Tide, Ban, Aim, and Raid are helpful.
- Be distinctive. Brands with names like National, Star, Ideal, or Standard fail on this point.
- Be adaptable to new products that may be added to the product line. An innocuous name such as Kellogg, Lipton, or Jelinek may serve the purpose better than a highly distinctive name suggestive of product benefits. Frigidaire is an excellent name for a refrigerator and other cold-image products. But when the producer expanded its line of home appliances and added Frigidaire kitchen ranges, the name lost some of its sales appeal.
- Be capable of being registered and legally protected under the Trade Marks Act and other statutory or common laws.

MARKETING AT WORK

FILE 10-2   **FOR THE NINETIES, HIGH-DEFINITION BRANDS**

According to Madeleine Saint-Jacques, president of advertising agency Young and Rubicam's Montreal office, individualistic or "high-definition" brands are the answer to the extreme competition of the 1990s. The age of mass marketing is over for many products and there is a great deal of activity in market targeting, segmentation, and niche marketing. But the danger Ms. Saint-Jacques sees is that too many firms are simply mass marketing to smaller masses.

Creating brands with individuality or high-definition means searching for elements of a product or service that are not necessarily practical or functional but that really sets the item apart—"the accidental, the irrelevant, the soul." The United Colors of Benetton, showing children of different races and nationalities wearing Benetton clothes, is an example of successfully moving from the mass to the individual and establishing a unique brand meaning. Appealing to the individuality of the members of the segment—not their communality—is the key to creative branding.

Source: Adapted from Susan Tolusso, "Marketers Urged to Pursue 'High-definition' Brands," *Playback Strategy*, May 21, 1990, p. 9.

GENERIC USAGE OF BRAND NAMES

Over a period of years, some brands become so well accepted that the brand name is sustituted for the **generic** name of the particular product. Examples of brand names that legally have become generic are linoleum, celluloid, cellophane, kerosene, shredded wheat, and nylon. Originally, these were trademarks limited to use by the owner.

A brand name can become generic in several ways. Sometimes the patent on a product expires. There is no simple generic name available and so the public continues to use the brand name as a generic name. This happened with shredded wheat, nylon, and cellophane. Sometimes a firm just does too good an advertising and selling job with an outstanding brand name. While not yet legally generic, names such as Xerox, Band-Aid, Scotch Tape, Ski-Doo, and Kleenex are on the borderline. They are outstanding brand names for the original product and have been promoted so well that many people use them generically.

It is the responsibility of the trademark owner to assert the company's rights in order to prevent the loss of the distinctive character of the trademark. A number of strategies are employed to prevent the brand name from falling into generic usage. The most common strategy is to ensure that the words "trade mark" or the letters "TM"/® appear adjacent to the brand name wherever it appears.

A second strategy is to use two names—the brand name together with either the company's name or the generic name of the product. An example of this is the name "Thermos Vacuum Bottle," which is designed to suggest to the public that "Thermos" is but one brand of vacuum bottle and that the name "Thermos" should not be applied to all products in that product category.

A third strategy for protecting a trademark involves the incorporation into the trademark of a distinctive signature or logo. Many companies have adopted distinctive ways of presenting the brand name of their products so that the consumer is able to identify their products whenever they encounter the particular brand written as a certain script or type face.

Finally, the owner of a registered trademark must be willing to prosecute any other companies attempting to market products under a brand name that is identical to or similar to the registered brand name. By prosecuting such infrigements of the trademark protection, the company is demonstrating to the courts that it is actively protecting its right to use of the brand and is guarding against the brand falling into generic usage. If the owner company fails to prosecute infringements, even if it decides to prosecute at a later date after other companies have adopted the brand, the distinctive character of the trademark will be lost and the courts are likely to rule that the original owner no longer has exclusive right to use of the brand name, as it is in the public domain. Some companies seek to show competitors or others who wish to make use of registered trademarks that they are willing to take legal action to protect their trademarks. An example of advertising that is designed to achieve this purpose is presented on page 301.

Brand Strategies

Producers and middlemen alike have to make strategic decisions regarding the branding of their goods or services.

PRODUCERS' STRATEGIES

Producers must decide whether to brand their products and whether to sell any or all of their output under middlemen's brands.

Marketing entire output under producers' own brands   Companies that market their entire output under their own brands usually are very large, well financed, and well-managed. Polaroid, Maytag, and IBM are examples. They have broad product lines, well-established distribution systems, and large shares of the market. Only a small percentage of manufacturers follow this policy, and their number seems to be decreasing.

Some reasons for adopting this policy have already been covered in the section on the importance of branding to the seller. In addition, middlemen often prefer to handle producers' brands, especially when the brands have high consumer acceptance.

Branding of fabricating parts and materials   Some producers of industrial fabricating materials and parts (products used in the further manufacturing of other goods) will brand their products. This strategy is used in the marketing of Fiberglas insulation, Pella windows, Acrilan fabrics, and many automotive parts—spark plugs, batteries, oil filters, and so on.

Underlying this strategy is the seller's desire to develop a market preference for its branded part of material. For instance, G.D. Searle wants to build a market situation in which customers will insist on food products sweetened with NutraSweet. In addition, the parts manufacturer wants to persuade the producer of the finished item that using the branded materials will help sell the end product. In our example, the Searle Company hopes to convince food manufacturers that their sales will be increased if their products contain NutraSweet.

Certain product characteristics lend themselves to the effective use of this

Promoting brand loyalty to an ingredient in other companies' products.

strategy. First, it helps if the product is also a consumer good that is bought for replacement purposes. This factor encourages the branding of Champion spark plugs, Atlas batteries, and Fram oil filters, for example. Second, the seller's situation is improved if the item is a major part of the finished product —a television picture tube, for example.

Marketing under middlemen's brands   A widespread strategy is for producers to brand part of all of their output with the brands of their middlemen customers. For the manufacturer, this middlemen's-brand business generates additional sales volume and profit dollars. Orders typically are large, payment is prompt, and a producer's working-capital position is improved. Also, manufacturers may utilize their production resources more effectively, including their plant capacities. Furthermore, refusing to sell under a retailer's or wholesaler's brand will not eliminate competition from this source. Many middlemen want to market under their own brands, so if one manufacturer refuses their business, they will simply go to another.

Probably the most serious limitation to marketing under middlemen's brands is that a producer may be at the mercy of the middlemen. This problem grows as the proportion of that producer's output going to middlemen's brands increases.

MIDDLEMEN'S STRATEGIES

The question of whether or not to brand must also be answered by middlemen. There are two usual strategies, as follows:

Carry only producers' brands   Most retailers and wholesalers follow this policy because they are not able to take on the dual burdens of promoting a brand and maintaining its quality.

Carry middlemen's brands alone or with producers' brands   Many large retailers and some large wholesalers have their own brands. Middlemen may find it advantageous to market their own brands for several reasons. First, this strategy increases their control over their market. If customers prefer a given retailer's brand, they can get it only from that retailer's store. Furthermore, middlemen can usually sell their brands at prices below those of producers' brands and still earn higher gross margins. This is possible because middlemen can buy at lower costs. The costs may be lower because (1) manufacturers' advertising and selling costs are not included in their prices, or (2) producers are anxious to get the extra business to keep their plants running in slack seasons.

Middlemen have more freedom in pricing products sold under their own labels. Products carrying a retailer's brand become differentiated products, and this hinders price comparisons that might be unfavourable to that retailer. Also, prices on manufacturer's brands can be cut drastically by competing retail stores. This last point is what has been happening in recent years in the marketing of clothing with designer labels such as Calvin Klein, Simon Chang, Ralph Lauren, and Alfred Sung. Some of the large retailers in their upper-priced clothing departments have increased their stocks of apparel carrying the store's own brand. These stores (Eaton's, Hugo Boss, The Bay, Harry Rosen, for example), have cut back on products with designer brands such as Calvin Klein and others. The reason for this brand-switching is that some designer-labelled products are now available at much lower prices in stores such as K mart, Zellers, and other ''off-price retailers.''

STRATEGIES COMMON TO PRODUCERS AND MIDDLEMEN

Producers and middlemen alike must adopt some strategy with respect to branding their product mix and branding for market saturation.

Branding a line of products   At least four different strategies are widely used by firms that sell more than one product.

- The same ''family'' or ''blanket'' brand may be placed on all products. This policy is followed by Heinz, Catelli, Campbell's, McCain's, and others in the food field, as well as by Proctor-Silex and Black & Decker.
- A separate name may be used for each product. This strategy is employed by Procter & Gamble and Lever Brothers.
- A separate family brand may be applied to each grade of product or to each group of similar products. Sears groups its major home appliances under the Kenmore name, its paints and home furnishings under Harmony House, and its insurance under Allstate.
- The company trade name may be combined with an individual name for the product. Thus there is Johnson's Pledge, Kellogg's Rice Krispies, Molson Golden, and Ford Mustang.

When used wisely, a family-brand strategy has considerable merit. This

Beatrice offers a light family of products.

strategy makes it much simpler and less expensive to introduce new related products to a line. Also, the general prestige of a brand can be spread more easily if it appears on several products rather than on only one. A family brand is best suited for a marketing situation where the products are related in quality, in use, or in some other manner. When Black & Decker, a manufacturer of power tools, purchased General Electric's line of small appliances, the Black & Decker brand was put on those appliances, *but* not immediately. Because of the perceived differences between kitchen products and workroom products, Black & Decker realized it was a risky proposition to switch brands. Consequently, the company mounted a year-long brand-transition campaign before making the change. Also, during those years, Black & Decker introduced several other houseware products, and this helped in the General Electric-Black & Decker brand transition.

On the other hand, the use of family brands places a greater burden on the brand owner to maintain consistent quality among all products. One bad item can reflect unfavourably, and even disastrously, on all other products carrying the same brand.

Branding for market saturation   Frequently, to increase its degree of market saturation, a firm will employ a mutliple-brand strategy. Suppose, for example, that a company has built one type of sales appeal around a given brand. To reach other segments of the market, the company can use other appeals with other brands. For example, Procter & Gamble markets a line of detergents that includes Tide, Bold, Cheer, Oxydol, and Ivory Snow. There may be some consumers who feel that Tide, even with its many varieties (phosphate-free, with bleach, unscented, liquid, and "regular"), is not suitable for washing lingerie and other delicate clothing. For these people, Procter & Gamble offers Ivory Snow, a detergent whose image is gentler that that of Tide and one that

M A R K E T I N G   A T   W O R K

FILE 10-3 **STRATEGIC BRANDING FOR INTERNATIONAL MARKETING**

Should a company use one brand worldwide for a product or should a different brand be used in each foreign country? Several successful marketers have adopted a one-brand global strategy. Coca-Cola, Pepsi-Cola, Exxon, and Levi's jeans are single brands used worldwide. Colgate toothpaste is sold in 53 countries and Palmolive soap in 43. American Express, VISA, the Red Cross, and Holiday Inn each uses its one brand around the world.

On the other hand, the Henkel Company employs the strategy of separate brands of the same product in different countries. (Henkel is a giant manufacturer of detergents in West Germany and a major rival of Procter & Gamble in Europe.) Examples of Henkel's brand varieties by country are presented below.

We cannot generalize as to which is the better course of action — a global brand or a country-specific name. It is convenient for a company to have one brand name worldwide with a standardized advertising campaign and the ability to add goods or services under that brand. If, on the other hand, the global name means nothing in a local language or even carries a negative connotation, then obviously a country-specific name is better.

	West Germany	Austria	Belgium	Switzerland	Spain	France
Laundry detergent	Liz	Liz	LeChat	Liz	Sil	LeChat
Dishwashing detergent	Dixi	*	*	*	Misol	Rex
Household cleaner	Der General	Sherift	Clien	*	Tenn	Maxinet

*No Henkel brand in that country.

Source: Adapted, in part, from Marina Specht, ''Henkel Thinks Pan-Europe,'' *Advertising Age*, January 30, 1989, p. 44.

---

trades on its assocation with the purity and gentleness of Ivory soap. With this brand line-up, Procter & Gamble is assured of having a brand or a brand variation to appeal to literally every segment of the detergent market.

The Battle of the Brands

Middlemen's brands have proved to be eminently successful in competing with producers' brands. However, neither group has demonstrated a convincing competitive superiority over the other in the marketplace. Consequently, the ''battle of the brands'' shows every indication of continuing and becoming more intense.

About 15 years ago, several supermarket chains introduced products sold under their generic names. That is, the products were simply labelled as pork and beans, peanut butter, cottage cheese, paper towels, and so on. These unbranded products generally sell for 30 to 40 percent less than producers' brands and 20 percent less than retailers' brands. While they are the nutritional equivalent of branded products, the generics (graded ''standard'' in industry terms) may not have the colour, size, and appearance of the branded items (graded "fancy"). Most of the chains sell these products completely unbranded — referring to them as "generic" or "generic products" in the store's advertising. In effect, "generic" becomes an unofficial brand name in that it is the identifying name used by the stores and consumers.

Generic products now account for a large enough share of total sales in some product lines to be a major factor in the battle of the brands. In the late 1980s, the generics' market share levelled off, and even declined, in some product lines. Apparently the low inflation rate had dulled consumers' price sensitivity, and also producers fought back with extensive use of coupons for their brands. Nevertheless, in the early 1990s, generics still are a strong force.

Several factors account for the success of middlemen's brands and generic products. The thin profit margins on producers' brands have encouraged retailers to establish their own labels. The improved quality of retailers' brands has boosted their sales. Consumers have become more sophisticated in their buying and their brand loyalty has declined, so they do consider alternative brands. It is generally known that retailers' brands usually are produced by large, well-known manufacturers. Generic products, with their low-price, no-frills approach, appeal to price-conscious consumers.

Manufacturers do have some effective responses to combat generic labels and retailers' brands. Producers can, for example, devote top priority to product innovation and packaging, an area in which retailers are not as strong. Manufacturers' research and development capacity also enables them to enter the market in the early stages of a product's life cycle, whereas retailer brands typically enter after a product is well established.[6]

Trademark Licensing

An effective branding strategy that has grown by leaps and bounds in recent years is brand (or trademark) licensing. Under this strategy, the owner of a trademark grants permission (a licence) to other firms to use the owner's brand name, logotype (distinctive lettering and colouring), and/or character on the licensee's products. To illustrate, Coca-Cola has allowed (licensed) Murjani International to use the Coca-Cola name and distinctive lettering on a line of clothing (blue jeans, sweaters, shirts, jackets). The owner of the trademark characters in the "Peanuts" cartoon strip (Snoopy, Charlie Brown, Lucy, etc.) has licensed the use of these characters on many different products and services. Sears has introduced McKids, a line of children's clothing featuring McDonald's characters. The licensee typically pays a royalty of about 5 percent on the wholesale price of the product that carries the licensed trademark. However, this figure can vary depending upon the perceived strength of the licensor's brand.

Strategy decisions must be made by both parties — the licensor and the licensee. Alfred Sung (a licensor) must ask, "Should we allow other firms to use our designer label?" A manufacturer of eyeglasses (a licensee) must ask, "Do we want to put out a line of high-fashion eyeglasses under the Alfred Sung name?"

Owners of well-known brands are interested in licensing their trademarks for various reasons. First, it can be very profitable since there is no expense

---

[6]For a review of manufacturer and retailer strategies in the past regarding generic products, and suggestions for future strategies now that generics have reached maturity in many product categories, see Brian F. Harris and Roger A. Strang, "Marketing Strategies in the Age of Generics," *Journal of Marketing*, Fall 1985, pp. 70–81.

involved on the part of the licensor. Second, there is a promotional benefit, because the licensor's name gets wider circulation far beyond the original trademarked article. Third, licensing can help protect the trademark. If Coca-Cola licenses its brand for use in a variety of product categories, it can block any other company from using that brand legally in those product categories.

For the company receiving the licence—the licensee—the strategy is a quick way to gain market recognition and to penetrate a new market. Today there is a high financial cost involved in establishing a new brand name. Even then there is no guarantee of success. It is a lot easier for an unknown firm to gain consumer acceptance of its product if that item carries a well-known brand.

Strategic Branding of Services

Earlier in this chapter, we discussed the competitive edge that a well-selected brand can give to a product. These advantages are equally applicable to tangible goods and intangible services. Furthermore, the marketers of services have to make many of the same strategic branding decisions as do the marketers of tangible products. Perhaps the first of these decisions is to select a good brand name for the service.[7] In services marketing, more so than in the marketing of tangible goods, the company name typically serves as the brand name.

The characteristics of an effective service brand are much the same as for tangible goods. Thus, a service brand should be:

- *Relevant to the service or its benefits*. Ticketron, the sales agency that sells tickets to sporting events, concerts, and other major attractions, conveys the nature of the service and the electronic speed with which it is delivered. VISA suggests an international activity and is relevant for a global financial service. Instant Teller is a good name for the automatic banking machines of the CIBC. Budget implies the best price for people who rent cars from that company. Four Seasons suggests a hotel chain that has something to offer year-round.
- *Distinctive*. This characteristic is difficult to communicate. The point is that companies should avoid branding their service with names that literally anyone could use. Thus, names like National, Canadian, and Royal should probably be avoided because, standing alone, they tell us nothing about the service or its benefits. When names such as these are used, the company will usually add words that tell us what service is being offered, such as Canadian *Airlines International*, Royal *Trust*, and National *Life Insurance*.

  Some service marketers differentiate themselves from the competition by using a symbol (usually referred to as a *logo*) or a distinctive colour. We are all familiar with the golden arches of McDonald's, the lion of the Royal Bank of Canada, and Air Canada's maple leaf in the circle. For colour, we see the green of the Toronto Dominion Bank, the red of Scotiabank, and the blue of the Bank of Montreal. The use of a person's name such as Harvey's, Eaton's, and Tilden, or a coined word, such as Avis, Re/Max, and AMEX, also offers distinctiveness, but it tells us little about the service being offered. This is the case until the name has been firmly established

---

[7]For a good discussion of this topic, see Leonard L. Berry, Edwin F. Lefkowith, and Terry Clark, ''In Services, What's in a Name?'' *Harvard Business Review*, September/October 1988, pp. 38–30. Some of the examples in this section are drawn from this source.

and it comes to mean something to the consumer. Certainly, many such names have become very well established in the marketplace.

- *Easy to pronounce and remember*. Simple, short names, such as Delta and A&W usually meet this criterion. Others, such as Aetna and Overwaitea, pose pronunciation problems for some people. Sometimes, unusual spelling aids in having the consumer remember the name — the reverse R in Toys ''Я'' Us, for example.
- *Adaptable to additional services or regions*. Companies that change their mix of services and their geographical locations over time should be flexible enough to adapt to these extensions of their operations. One Canadian bank, the Canadian Imperial Bank of Commerce, has shortened its name to CIBC in anticipation of expanding its range of financial services beyond banking. Many successful companies (Montreal Trust, London Life, Great-West Life) have been able to establish national reputations despite the fact that their names suggest a regional association, although it may be easier for companies with names like Canada Life and Canada Trust to do so. When companies have names with geographic connotations, such as Canadian Pacific, they are often abbreviated when expansion takes place, as in CP Hotels. Airlines with names like Air BC and Air Atlantic are obviously regional carriers, while one named Air Nova may find it easier to expand beyond its original market area.

Another decision is whether to use family branding. Insurance companies and financial services firms often use the same brand name for the variety of services offered. On the other hand, the Canadian chartered banks generally operate their brokerage arms as separate entities. The Dylex Group operates its many different retail chains under a variety of names — Fairweather, Big Steel, Tip Top, Harry Rosen, and Braemar.

Whether to get into trademark licensing is a strategic branding decision for many services firms. Companies, entertainers, and many professional sports teams, such as the Montreal Canadiens, Edmonton Oilers, and Toronto Blue Jays, license their names for use on many different products.

PACKAGING

Packaging may be defined as all the activities of designing and producing the container or wrapper for a product. There are three reasons for packaging:

- Packaging serves several *safety and utilitarian purposes*. It protects a product on its route from the producer to the final customer, and in some cases even while it is being used by the customer. Effective packaging can help prevent ill-intentioned persons from tampering with products. Some protection is provided by ''child-proof'' closures on containers of medicines and other products that are potentially harmful to children. Also, compared with bulk items, packaged goods generally are more convenient, cleaner, and less susceptible to losses from evaporation, spilling, and spoilage.
- Packaging may be a *part of a company's marketing program*. Packaging helps identify a product and thus may prevent substitution of competitive products. At the point of purchase, the package can serve as a silent sales person. Furthermore, the advertising copy on the package will last as long as the product is used in its packaged form. A package may be the only significant way in which a firm can differentiate its product. In the case of convenience goods or business operating supplies, for example, most buyers feel that one well-known brand is about as good as another.

Some feature of the package may add sales appeal — a no-drip spout, a reusable jar, or a self-applicator (a bottle of shoe polish or glue with an applicator top, for example). By packaging their toothpaste in a pump dispenser — a product long used in Europe — Colgate and Close-Up brands increased their sales considerably. Crest and Aim later adopted the same type of packaging.

- A firm can package its product in a way that *increases profit and sales volume*. A package that is easy to handle or minimizes damage losses will cut marketing costs, thus boosting profit. On the sales side, packaged goods typically are more attractive and therefore better than items sold in bulk. Many companies have increased the sales volume of an article simply by redesigning its package. A little later we'll speak more about the strategy of changing packages.

Importance of Packaging in Marketing

Historically, packaging was a production-oriented activity in most companies, performed mainly to obtain the benefits of protection and convenience. Today, however, the marketing significance of packaging is fully recognized, and packaging is truly a major competitive force in the struggle for markets. The widespread use of self-service selling and automatic vending means that the package must do the selling job at the point of purchase. Shelf space is often at a premium, and it is no simple task for manufacturers even to get their products displayed in a retail outlet. Most retailers are inclined to cater to producers that have used effective packaging.

In addition, the increased use of branding and the public's rising standards in health and sanitation have contributed to a greater awareness of packaging. Safety in packaging has become a prominent marketing and social issue in recent years. Extensive consumer use of microwave ovens has had a significant impact on packaging. Many food products are now packaged so that they may go straight from the shelf or freezer into a microwave oven.

New developments in packaging, occurring rapidly and in a seemingly endless flow, require management's constant attention. We see new packaging materials replacing traditional ones, new shapes, new closures, and other new features (measured portions, metered flow). These all increase convenience for consumers and selling points for marketers. One relatively new development in packaging that will be particularly interesting to watch in the coming years is the use of aseptic containers — the well-known "drinking boxes" made of laminations of paper, aluminum foil, and polyethylene. The air-tight features of this container allow beverages and other products to be kept fresh for as long as five months without refrigeration, and it costs only about half as much as cans and 30 percent as much as bottles. It has been used widely in Canada to package juice and other drink products and is widely regarded as extremely convenient. We are likely to see its uses expand in the future, provided that issues related to its environmental impact are resolved.

Packaging is an important marketing tool for companies that operate in international markets. Most countries have regulations governing the packaging of products and the wording that must appear on labels. A company that wishes to export its product to another country must, therefore, be aware of the packaging laws of that country. For example, companies in other countries that export to Canada and the Canadian importers that represent them

Multi-packing for convenience and portion control.

have to be aware of Canadian packaging regulations pertaining to metric package sizes, bilingual labelling, and the standard sizes of packages used in some industries. In addition to regulations, exporters must understand that packages that work in one country may not be accepted in another, because of design, illustration, or colour.

Packaging Strategies

CHANGING THE PACKAGE

In general, management has two reasons for considering a package change—to combat a decrease in sales and to expand a market by attracting new groups of customers. More specifically, a firm may want to correct a poor feature in the existing container, or a company may want to take advantage of new materials. Some companies change their containers to aid in promotional programs. A new package may be used as a major appeal in advertising copy, or because the old container may not show up well in advertisements.

PACKAGING THE PRODUCT LINE

A company must decide whether to develop a family resemblance in the packaging of its several products. **Family packaging** involves the use of identical packages for all products or the use of packaging with some common feature. Campbell's Soup, for example, uses virtually identical packaging on its condensed soup products. Management's philosophy concerning family packaging generally parallels its feelings about family branding. When new products are added to a line, promotional values associated with old products extend to the new ones. On the other hand, family packaging should be used only when the products are related in use and are of similar quality.

REUSE PACKAGING

Another strategy to be considered is reuse packaging. Should the company design and promote a package that can serve other purposes after the original contents have been consumed? Glasses containing cheese can later be used to serve fruit juice. Baby-food jars make great containers for small parts such as nuts, bolts, and screws. Reuse packaging also should stimulate repeat purchases as the consumer attempts to acquire a matching set of containers.

MULTIPLE PACKAGING

For many years there has been a trend towards multiple packaging, or the practice of placing several units in one container. Dehydrated soups, motor oil, beer, golf balls, building hardware, candy bars, towels, and countless other products are packaged in multiple units. Test after test has proved that multiple packaging increases total sales of a product.[8]

Criticisms of Packaging

Packaging is in the forefront today because of its relationship to environmental pollution issues. Perhaps the biggest challenges facing packagers is how to dispose of used containers, which are a major contributor to the solid-waste disposal problem. Consumers' desire for convenience (in the form of throw-away containers) conflicts with their desire for a clean environment.

In many ways, the debate over the environmental impact of packaging often appears impossible to resolve, as the issue of the disposability of packaging is weighed against that of the use of energy and other effects associated with manufacturing it. This debate is best illustrated with the controversy that has been raging over the packaging used by the major fast-food chains, some of whom have moved from using polystyrene packages for their hamburgers, fish filets, and chicken burgers to using paper and cardboard. McDonald's Restaurants, for example, which serves more than 1.5 million meals a day from its 625 outlets in Canada, abandoned polystyrene foam containers in favour of waxed paper in response to protests from customers that the foam boxes were harming the environment.[9]

But the issue is far from a simple one. As is illustrated in Marketing at Work File 10-4, while environmentalists argue that companies should abandon foam

Often packaging is marketed as environmentally friendly.

---

[8]For a further discussion of package design strategies that can boost sales and profit, see Sue Bassin, ''Innovative Packaging Strategies,'' *Journal of Business Strategy*, January/February 1988, pp. 38–42.

[9]John Fox, ''Big Mac Wrap Stirs Hot Debate,'' *The Financial Post*, December 29–31, 1990, p. 1.

MARKETING AT WORK

FILE 10-4 **NO CLEAR ANSWERS TO PACKAGING PROBLEMS!**

A clear answer is nowhere in sight. Despite several years of experience with dwindling landfill sites, household recycling, municipal incineration, and other waste management strategies, very little is known about the environmental costs of making, using and getting rid of packages.

The McDonald's decision illustrates the dilemma. Plastic foam containers satisfied health regulations and did a good job of keeping food warm, but they are made from nonrenewable fossil fuels, are rarely recycled, and usually end up in garbage dumps where they remain intact for generations.

Paper wrappers appear better at first glance because they are made from renewable forest resources and are theoretically decomposable, moving back into the natural cycle.

However, paper is made in an energy-intensive industry notorious for releasing toxic chemicals, such as dioxin, into the environment. Moreover, the burger wrappers are not recycled and end up in the same trash heap as the plastic, where the physical environment prevents them from breaking down much faster than the foam boxes.

Environmentalists have called for McDonald's to use washable plates and cutlery instead of throwaways, but this too has environmental costs. Dishwashers are among the most energy-consuming appliances in a restaurant. Water also has to be heated and a cleaning agent, such as chlorine or ammonia, added.

Source: Excerpted from John Fox, "Big Mac Wrap Stirs Hot Debate," *The Financial Post*, December 29-31, 1990, p. 1.

---

containers, cups, and other disposable products, the alternatives are often fraught with problems in that they require considerable use of energy. The controversy over the impact of packaging on the environment can be expected to rage for some time to come, as scientists and governments try to resolve the question of what types of packaging are most harmful. Clearly some companies and industries are more affected than others, but there are implications for practically all businesses.

Soft drink and beer companies are pressured to move towards a completely refillable packaging strategy, involving the exclusive use of glass bottles. The makers of the convenient aseptic containers are under pressure from environmentalists because the juice boxes are not recyclable and end up in municipal garbage dumps. Companies that have for years been supplying the restaurant industry and providing Canadians with convenient disposable products have been greatly affected by the environmental movement and have had to adopt strategies aimed at developing products that are less harmful to the environment.[10] Major corporations are doing their part to address this global issue by moving to the use of less packaging, refillable containers, and recyclable mate-

---

[10]See Helen Kohl, "Whistling Dixie at Lily Cups," *Canadian Business*, October 1990, pp. 90-94; and Virginia Galt, "Casualties of the Environmental Wars," *Globe and Mail*, February 23, 1991, p. D2.

rials. The support of consumers for such actions is obvious and will guarantee that recycling will represent one of the major growth areas in this country well into the future.

Other criticisms of packaging are:

- Packaging depletes our natural resources. This criticism is offset to some extent as packagers increasingly make use of recycled materials. Another offsetting point is that effective packaging reduces spoilage (another form of resource waste).
- Packaging is excessively expensive. Cosmetic packaging is often cited as an example here. But even in seemingly simple packaging—beer, for example —as much as half the production cost goes for the container. On the other hand, effective packaging reduces transportation costs and losses from product spoilage.
- Health hazards occur from some forms of plastic packaging and some aerosol cans. Government regulations have banned the use of several of these suspect packaging materials.
- Packaging is deceptive. Government regulation plus improvements in business practices regarding packaging have reduced the intensity of this criticism, although it is heard on occasion.

Truly, marketing executives face some real challenges in satisfying these complaints while at the same time retaining the marketing-effectiveness, consumer-convenience, and product-protection features of packaging.

LABELLING

Labelling is another product feature that requires managerial attention. The **label** is part of a product that carries verbal information about the product or the seller. A label may be part of a package, or it may be a tag attached directly to the product. Obviously there is a close relationship among labelling, packaging, and branding.

Types of Labels

Typically, labels are classified as brand, grade, or descriptive. A **brand label** is simply the brand alone applied to the product or to the package. Thus, some oranges are brand-labelled (stamped) Sunkist or Jaffa, and some clothes carry the brand label Sanforized. A **grade label** identifies the quality with a letter, number, or word. Canadian beef is grade-labelled A, B, or C and each grade is subdivided by number from 1 to 4 indicating an increasing fat content. **Descriptive labels** give objective information about the use, construction, care, performance, or other features of the product. On a descriptive label for a can of corn, there will be statements concerning the type of corn (golden sweet), the style (creamed or in niblet kernels), and the can size, number of servings, other ingredients, and nutritional contents.

RELATIVE MERITS

Brand labelling creates very little stir among critics. While it is an acceptable form of labelling, its severe limitation is that it does not supply sufficient information to a buyer. The real fight centres on grade versus descriptive labelling and on whether grade labelling should be made mandatory.

The proponents of grade labelling argue that it is simple, definite, and easy to use. They also point out that if grade labels were used, prices would be more closely related to quality, although grade labelling would not stifle competition. In fact, they believe that grade labelling might increase competition, because consumers would be able to judge products on the basis of both price and known quality.

Those who object to grade labelling point out that a very low score on one grading characteristic can be offset by very high scores on other factors. Companies selling products that score high *within* a given grade would be hurt by grade labelling. These companies could not justify a higher price than that charged for a product that scored very low in the same grade. And some people feel that grades are an inaccurate guide for consumer buying. It is not possible to grade the differences in flavour and taste, or in style and fashion, yet these are the factors that often influence consumer purchases.

Statutory Labelling Requirements

The importance of packaging and labelling in its potential for influencing the consumer's purchasing decision is reflected in the large number of federal and provincial laws that exist to regulate this marketing activity. At the federal level, the Competition Act regulates the area of misleading advertising and a number of companies have been convicted of misleading advertising for the false or deceptive statements that have appeared on their packages. In this case, the information that appears on a package or label has been considered to constitute an advertisement.

The Hazardous Products Act gives the federal government the power to regulate the sale, distribution, advertising, and labelling of certain consumer products that are considered dangerous. A number of products have been banned from sale under this Act and all hazardous products, such as cleaning substances, chemicals, and aerosol products, must carry on their labels a series of symbols that indicate the danger associated with the product and the precautions that should be taken with its use. The symbols illustrate that the product is poisonous, inflammable, explosive, or corrosive in nature.

Similarly the federal Food and Drugs Act regulates the sale of food, drugs, cosmetics, and medical devices. Under this Act, regulations deal with the manufacture, sale, advertising, packaging, and labelling of such products. Certain misleading and deceptive packaging and labelling practices are specifically prohibited.

The Textile Labelling Act requires that manufacturers label their products, including wearing apparel, yard goods, and household textiles, according to the fibre content of the product. In the past, more than 700 fabric names have appeared on products, but most of these were brand names of individual companies. For example, the fibre known generically as polyester has been labelled as Terylene, Trevira, Dacron, Kodel, Fortrel, Tergal, Tetoron, and Crimplene, all of which are manufacturers' brand names for polyester. In order to reduce confusion among the buying public, products now have to be labelled according to the generic fibre content, with the percentage of each fibre in excess of 5 percent listed.

There also exist in Canada two government-sponsored consumer product labelling schemes that are informative in nature. These programs are the Canada Standard Size program and the Textile Care Labelling program. The Textile Care Labelling program involves the labelling of all textile products with symbols that indicate instructions for washing and dry cleaning the product.

The Consumer Packaging and Labelling Act regulates all aspects of the packaging and labelling of consumer products in this country. The regulations that have been passed under this Act require that most products sold in Canada bear bilingual labels. The net quantity of the product must appear on the label

MARKETING AT WORK

FILE 10-5   THE LABEL SAYS IT ALL—OR DOES IT?

Canadian food companies are allowed to list basic nutrient ingredients on their packages but are not allowed to make the nutrient information more meaningful by linking it to health. In the United States, firms are allowed to make health-oriented claims—some would say they hype health unfairly. Consumers face a tough information-processing task in both countries.

According to David Nichol of Loblaw supermarkets, food shoppers are now spending twice as much time in supermarkets as they used to because they are standing around in the aisles reading labels—translating nutritional information into personal health-related information. Environics Research reports that we Canadians rely on ourselves, rather than experts, government or other sources in figuring out what is good. And it seems that we are woefully ignorant; we don't buy aerosol cans in the mistaken belief that the cans in Canada contain CFCs. On the other hand, we don't seem to be very concerned that cardboard milk cartons and coffee-filter papers are said to contain dioxin traces. We are beginning to understand that "light" foods aren't and that "no cholesterol" by itself may not mean much. But confusion reigns supreme and it means that in Canada, governments, trade associations, and consumers have to find a way to understand and learn about nutrition and health that is better than what we now do and different from what Americans do.

Source: Adapted from Marina Strauss, "Food Labels in Need of a Healthy Dose of Information," *Globe and Mail*, January 25, 1990, p. B13.

---

in both metric and imperial units. If the quantity of a food product is expressed in terms of a certain number of servings, the size of the servings must also be stated. Where artificial flavourings are used in the manufacture of a food product, the label must contain the information that the flavour is imitation or simulated. The Act makes provision for the standardization of container sizes. The first set of regulations to be passed under the Act set down the standard package sizes for toothpaste, shampoo, and skin cream products and it is in contravention of the regulations to manufacture these products in other than the package sizes approved.

The Consumer Packaging and Labelling Act requires that manufacturers of consumer products, especially in the food industry, incorporate the bilingual and metric requirements into the design of their labels.

The provinces have also moved into the field of regulating packaging and labelling. A number of provinces have passed legislation regarding misleading advertising and any information that appears on a package or label is considered an advertisement. In Quebec, that province's Official Language Act requires that all labels be written in French or in French and another language. If both English and French appear on the label, at least equal prominence must be given to the French.

Largely in response to complaints from people who suffer from allergies, the federal government moved in 1990 to require the listing of all ingredients on the labels of cosmetics products. Regulations under the Food and Drugs

Meeting market and labelling requirements.

Act cover approximately 4,000 ingredients commonly found in shampoos, soaps, deodorants, and makeup. We can expect to see further changes in the labels required on food and grocery items in the future as consumers demand more information about the products they are consuming and using. The most likely changes relate to the listing of nutritional information on food products, brought about by the increasing interest of consumers in their health and nutrition.

OTHER IMAGE-BUILDING FEATURES

A well-rounded program for product planning and development will include a company policy on several additional product attributes: product design, colour, quality, warranty, and servicing.

Product Design and Colour

One way to satisfy customers and gain a competitive advantage is through skilful **product design**. In fact, a distinctive design may be the only feature that significantly differentiates a product. Many firms feel that there is considerable glamour and general promotional appeal in product design and the designer's name. In the field of business products, *engineering* design has long been recognized as extremely important. Today there is a realization of the marketing value of *appearance* design as well. Office machines and office furniture are examples of business products that reflect recent conscious attention to product design, often with good sales results. The marketing significance of design has been recognized for years in the field of consumer products, from big items like automobiles and refrigerators to small products like fountain pens and apparel.

Good design can improve the marketability of a product by making it easier to operate, upgrading its quality, improving its appearance, and/or reducing manufacturing costs. Recognizing the strategic importance of design, many companies have elevated the design function in the corporate hierarchy. In a number of firms, the director of design (sometimes called the director of human factors) participates in strategic planning and reports directly to top management.[11]

Colour often is the determining factor in a customer's acceptance or rejection of a product, whether that product is a dress, a table, or an automobile. Colour by itself, however, is no selling advantage because many competing firms offer colour. The marketing advantages comes in knowing the right colour and in knowing when to change colours. If a garment manufacturer or a retail store's fashion co-ordinator guesses wrong on what will be the fashionable colour in this season's clothing, disaster may ensue.

Product Quality

The quality of a product is extremely significant, but it is probably the most difficult of all the image-building features to define. Users frequently disagree on what constitutes quality in a product, whether it be a cut of meat or a work of art or music. Personal tastes are deeply involved. One guideline in managing

Being serious about quality.

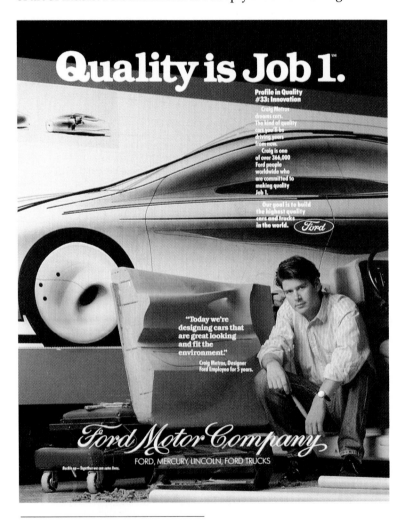

---

[11]See ''Smart Design: Quality Is the New Style,'' *Business Week*, April 11, 1988, p. 102; and ''How Do We Confuse Thee? Let Us Count the Ways,'' *Forbes*, March 1988 p. 156.

product quality is that the quality level should be compatible with the intended use of a product; the level need not be any higher. In fact, *good* and *poor* sometimes are misleading terms for quality. *Correct* and *incorrect* or *right* and *wrong* may be more appropriate. If a person is making a peach cobbler, grade B or C peaches are the correct quality. They are not necessarily the best quality, but they are right for the intended use. It is not necessary to pay grade-A prices for large, well-formed peaches when these features are destroyed in making the cobbler. Another key to the successful management of quality is to maintain *consistency* of product output at the desired quality level.

In recent years, North American manufacturers have been increasingly concerned about the quality of their products. And well they should be! For many years, consumers have complained about the poor quality of some products — both materials and workmanship. Foreign products — Japanese cars, for example — made serious inroads into the market because these products are perceived as being of better quality than their North American counterparts.

Quality of output also is a primary consideration in the production and marketing of services. The quality of its service can determine whether a firm will be successful. Yet it is virtually impossible for a firm to standardize performance quality among its units of service output. We frequently experience differences in performance quality from the same organization in appliance repairs, haircuts, medical exams, football games, or marketing courses. Consequently, it is essential that management do all it can to ensure consistency of quality at or above the level expected by the firm's present and potential customers.[12]

To aid in determining and maintaining the desired level of quality in its goods and services, a company should establish a quality-improvement program. This should be an ongoing group effort of the design, production, marketing, and customer-service departments. Such a program is in sharp contrast to a simple inspection of finished goods or parts on a production line — what some firms call quality control. A total-quality-management program should also include provisions for communicating to the market its commitment to quality. A firm may then justifiably claim in its advertising that its product quality has improved. The problem is getting consumers to believe this fact.[13]

Product Warranty and Product Liability

The general purpose of a warranty is to give buyers some assurance that they will be compensated in case the product does not perform up to reasonable expectations. In years past, courts seemed generally to recognize only **express warranties**—those stated in written or spoken words. Usually these were quite

---

[12]For more on service quality, see Leonard L. Berry, A. Parasuraman, and Valarie A. Zeithaml, "The Service-Quality Puzzle," *Business Horizons*, September-October 1988, pp. 35–43. Service quality is also discussed further in Chapter 11.

[13]For more on quality-improvement programs, see David W. Cravens, Charles W. Holland, Charles W. Lamb, Jr., and William C. Moncrief III, "Marketing's Role in Product and Service Quality," *Industrial Marketing Management*, November 1988, pp. 285–304; Valarie A. Zeithaml, Leonard L. Berry, and A. Parasuraman, "Communication and Control Process in the Delivery of Service Quality," *Journal of Marketing*, April 1988, pp. 35–48; and Stephen B. Castleberry and Anna V. A. Resurrecion, "Communicating Quality to Consumers," *Journal of Consumer Marketing*, Summer 1989, pp. 21–28.

limited in what they covered and seemed mainly to protect the seller from buyers' claims.

But times have changed! Consumer complaints have led to a governmental campaign to protect the consumer in many areas, one of which is product liability. Today, courts and government agencies are broadening the scope of warranty coverage by recognizing the concept of **implied warranty**. This is the idea that a warranty was *intended* by the seller, although not actually stated. Manufacturers are being held responsible, even when the sales contract is between the retailer and the consumer. Warranties are considered to "run with the product." Manufacturers are held liable for product-caused injury, whether or not they are to blame for negligence in manufacturing. It all adds up to "Let the seller beware."

In recent years manufacturers have responded to legislation and consumer complaints by broadening and simplifying their warranties. Many sellers are using their warranties as promotional devices to stimulate purchase by reducing consumers' risks. The effective handling of consumers' complaints related to warranties can be a significant factor in strengthening a company's marketing program.

The Hazardous Products Act indicates how the law has changed regarding product liability and injurious products. This law prohibits the sale of certain dangerous products and requires that other products which may be potentially dangerous carry an indication on their labels of the dangers inherent in their use. As further indication of the growing interest on the part of consumer groups and governments in the protection that existing forms of warranties offer the consumer, the Ontario Law Reform Commission in 1972 issued its Report on Consumer Warranties and Guarantees in the Sale of Goods. This report recommended broad and sweeping changes in the law respecting warranties and guarantees, which would provide the consumer with greater protection. Since the mid-1970s, two provinces, Saskatchewan and New Brunswick, have passed Consumer Products Warranty Acts. The Saskatchewan Act provides for statutory warranties that are deemed to be given by the retailer to the original purchaser and to subsequent owners. It also prescribes the form that written warranties must take.

Product Servicing

A problem related to product liability is that of providing adequate postsale services such as maintenance and repairs. Product servicing becomes essential as products become more complex and consumers grow increasingly disatisfied and vocal. To cope with these problems, management can consider several courses of action. For instance, a producer can establish several geographically dispersed factory service centres, staff them with well-trained company employees, and strive to make servicing a separate profit-generating activity. Or the producer can shift the main burden to middlemen, compensate them for their efforts, and possibly even train their service people.

Today the provision of adequate product servicing should be high on the list of topics calling for managerial action. A perennial major consumer complaint is that manufacturers and retailers do *not* provide adequate repair service for the products they sell. Often the situation is simply that the consumers wish to be *heard*. That is, they simply want someone to listen to them regarding their complaints. In respose to this situation, a number of producers have established toll-free telephone lines to their customer service departments.

SUMMARY   The management of the various features of a product—its brand, package, labelling, design, colour, quality, warranty, and servicing—is an integral part of effective product planning. A *brand* is a means of identifying and differentiating the products or services of an organization. Branding aids sellers in managing their promotional and pricing activities. Brand ownership carries the dual responsibilities of promoting the brand and maintaining a consistent level of quality. Selecting a good brand name—and there are relatively few really good ones—is a difficult task. A good name should suggest a product's benefits, be easy to pronounce and remember, lend itself to product-line additions, and be eligible for legal registration and protection.

Manufactures must decide whether to brand their products and whether to sell under a middleman's brand. Middlemen must decide whether to carry manufacturers' brands alone or whether to establish their own brands as well. Both groups of sellers must set policies regarding branding of groups of products and branding for market saturation. Customer acceptance of private-labelled and generic-labelled products has heated up the ''battle of the brands.'' Another branding strategy is trademark licensing, which is being employed to an increasing extent by owners of well-known brands. The owner allows the use of (licenses) its name or trademarked character to another firm that is looking for a quick, relatively low-cost way of penetrating a market.

Packaging is becoming increasingly important as sellers recognize the problems, as well as the marketing opportunities, involved in packaging, particularly related to the environment. *Labelling* is a related activity. Marketers should understand the merits and problems of grade labelling and of descriptive labelling. Many consumer criticisms of marketing have involved packaging and labelling, and there are federal laws regulating these marketing activities.

Companies are now recognizing the marketing value of product *design*—especially apearance design. Two related factors are product *colour* and product *quality*. Selecting the right colour is a marketing advantage. Projecting the appropriate quality image is essential. In addition, *warranties* and *servicing* require considerable management attention these days because of consumer complaints and governmental regulations in these areas.

KEY TERMS AND
CONCEPTS

QUESTIONS AND PROBLEMS

1. List five brand names that you think are good ones and five that you consider poor. Explain the reasoning behind your choices.

2. Evaluate each of the following brand names in light of the characteristics of a good brand, indicating the strong and weak points of each name.
   a. Xerox (office copiers).
   b. Kodak (cameras).
   c. Bauer (skates).
   d. Dack's (shoes).
   e. A-1 (steak sauce).
   f. Far West (clothing).

3. Suggest some brands that are on the verge of becoming generic. What course of action should a company take to protect the separate identity of its brands?

4. What are brand extensions? Why would a company launch a new product as a brand extension rather than as a completely new brand? What are the risks associated with such a strategy?

5. In which of the following cases should the company adopt the strategy of family branding?
   a. A manufacturer of men's underwear introduces essentially the same products for women.
   b. A manufacturer of women's cosmetics adds a line of men's cosmetics to its product assortment.
   c. A manufacturer of hair-care products introduces a line of portable electric hair dryers.

6. Suppose you are employed by the manufacturer of a well-known brand of skis. Your company is planning to add skates and water skis to its product line. It has no previous experience with either of these two new products. You are given the assignment of selecting a brand name for the skates and water skis. Your main problem is in deciding whether to adopt a family-brand policy. That is, should you use the snow-ski brand for either or both of the new products? Or should you develop separate names for each of the new items? You note that Campbell's (soups) and McCain (french fries) use family brands. You also note that Sears and Procter & Gamble generally do the opposite. They use different names for each *group of products* (Sears) or each *separate product* (P&G). What course of action would you recommend? Why?

7. A manufacturer of a well-known brand of ski boots acquired a division of a company that marketed a well-known brand of skis. What brand strategy should the new organization adopt? Should all products (skis and boots) now carry the boot brand? Should they carry the ski brand? Is there still some other alternative that you feel would be better?

8. Why do some firms sell an identical product under more than one of their own brands?

9. Assume that a large department-store chain proposed to Black & Decker that the latter company supply the chain with a line of power tools carrying the store's own label. What factors should Black & Decker management consider in making such a decision? Would the situation be any different if a supermarket chain had approached Kraft General Foods with a request to supply a private-label jelly dessert similar to Jell-O?

10. A Canadian manufacturer of camping equipment (stoves, lanterns, tents, sleeping bags) plans to introduce its line into several Eastern European countries. Should management select the same brand name for all countries or market under the name that is used in Canada? Should they consider using a different name in each country? What factors should influence this decision?

11. What changes would you recommend in the typical packaging of these products?
   a. Soft drinks.
   b. Hairspray
   c. Potato chips.
   d. Toothpaste.

12. If grade labelling is adopted, what factors should be used as bases for grading the following products?
   a. Lipstick.
   b. Woollen sweaters.
   c. Diet-food products.

13. Give examples of products for which the careful use of the colour of the product has increased sales. Can you cite examples to show that poor use of colour may hurt a company's marketing program?

14. Explain the relationship between a product warranty on small electric appliances and the manufacturer's distribution system for these products.

15. How would the warranty policies set by a manufacturer of skis differ from those adopted by an automobile manufacturer?

CHAPTER 11 GOALS

The special nature of services—especially their intangibility—leads to special marketing problems. After studying this chapter, you should be able to explain:

- What services are and are not.
- The importance of services in our economy.
- The characteristics of services, and the marketing implications of these characteristics.
- The marketing concept in services marketing.
- A program for the marketing of services.
- The future outlook in services marketing.

Marketing and Delivery of Services

The financial services industry will never be the same again. It has gone through a transformation in the 1980s that has led to a variety of new services, new suppliers, and a great deal more competition than existed in the past. Gone is the restricted industry characterized by the "four pillars" — banking, trust services, insurance, and securities brokerage — each limited to the services that it has traditionally provided. The 1980s ushered in the era of one-stop financial services retailing. The leading Canadian banks have established their own brokerage operations or have bought brokerage firms; some are moving into auto insurance; trust companies are now among the biggest sellers of Registered Retirement Savings Plans (RRSPs) and offer financial planning services; insurance companies issue Guaranteed Investment Certificates (GICs), RRSPs, and mutual funds; and credit unions have begun to issue their own credit cards.

These changes have been brought about in part by consumers' desire for greater convenience and better service. Financial services shoppers of the 1990s want to be able to conduct their banking and financial business in a convenient location and at a time that is convenient for them, and they want access to a wide variety of financial products and services. Consequently, gone are "banker's hours," as customers can now meet a banker or financial advisor six days a week and on most evenings. If that is not convenient enough, the banker will come to their homes or places of work or they can do their banking by telephone or by computer link to the bank or financial institution.

In short, the financial services industry has become extremely competitive, marketing oriented, and customer driven. This has led bankers and their competitors into fields into which they had not ventured in the past. New services have been offered, creating a variety of financial "products" that customers often find confusing. The financial services industry is targeting specific market segments with personal banking for the upscale consumer and home banking and banking by telephone for those whose schedules will not permit a visit to the branch. A number of financial institutions have combined to launch a debit card service that will allow customers to pay for their purchases at retail stores by direct debit from their bank accounts, bypassing the writing of a cheque or the use of a credit card.

All the major financial institutions have moved to make their services as conveniently accessible to their customers as possible through their automated teller machine (ATM) networks. The ATM has brought financial services to the consumer at numerous off-site locations at times that are convenient to them. Instead of having to go to the bank, the bank has come to the campus, the hotel, the airport, and the supermarket. Most consumers now use the ATM to withdraw cash, make deposits, pay utility bills, and transfer funds from one account to another. Machines in selected locations allow customers to transact business in a number of different languages and to convert foreign currencies. The next generation of ATMs will allow them to get a loan or buy mutual funds, insurance, postage stamps, and even theatre tickets.

Competition in the financial services industry is not only coming from the members of the established financial community, but also from offshore. During the 1980s, the government of Canada relaxed regulations governing the issuance of bank charters and allowed foreign-owned banks to compete in this country for the first time. The result is that many "Schedule II" banks have opened Canadian offices, the largest of which is the Hongkong Bank of Canada, which has grown through mergers with the Bank of British Columbia and the Continental Bank of Canada.

One of the most formidable competitors in the revamped Canadian financial services industry is American Express, operating as Amex Bank of Canada, a Schedule II bank. Amex does not operate as a regular bank, preferring not to open retail branches, but does compete with VISA and MasterCard for the lucrative charge card business, offering its "members" a variety of cards and access to services that appeal to the upscale adult of the 1990s, including preferred access to theatre and concert tickets through its "Front of the Line" service, and a targeted mail-order business that selects products to be featured on the basis of the expenditure patterns of the cardholder.

There can be little doubt that the established players in the financial services industry will be facing a rapidly changing and increasingly competitive marketplace through the 1990s. We will see continued movement toward a "cashless" society, as credit cards, debit cards, charge cards, and ATMs make it less necessary to carry cash. What will also be obvious is that the consumer will be facing an expansion in the array of products and services available in the financial market. As the range of services becomes more and more complex, the companies participating in the industry will find it more difficult to compete on the basis of product differentiation. Increasingly, the ability to compete for customers will depend not on who can offer the best interest rate or the lowest fees, but on how well the customer is treated.[1]

Financial institutions are typical of many service industries that previously had not been familiar with marketing and simply did not understand what marketing is. In the 1990s, however, it is increasingly evident that many service organizations must become more marketing-oriented if they hope to survive. This chapter will focus on significant differences between marketing services and marketing tangible goods, as well as the current growth and importance of services in our economy.

---

[1] Material for this introduction has been selected from the following articles: Monica Townson, "Rush to Provide Financial 'Shops'," *The Financial Post*, April 29, 1990, p. 26; Bruce Gates, "Bank Machines Now Can Even Sell Mutual Funds," *The Financial Post*, March 11, 1991, p. 15; Marina Strauss, "Banks Happy with Debit Card Test," *The Globe and Mail Report on Business*, May 10, 1991; and Daniel Stoffman, "Class for the Mass," *Report on Business Magazine*, February 1990, pp. 42-48.

NATURE AND IMPORTANCE OF SERVICES

In concept, goods marketing and services marketing are essentially the same. In each case the marketer must select and analyze target markets. Then a marketing program must be built around the parts of the marketing mix—the product or service, the price structure, the distribution system, and the promotional program. In practice, there often are substantial similarities as well. However, the basic characteristics that differentiate services from tangible products typically lead to a quite different marketing program. The strategies and tactics used in conventional product marketing frequently are inappropriate for services marketing.

Definition and Scope of Services

We are talking about the marketing of services, but what do we mean by ''services''? The term is difficult to define, because invariably services are marketed in conjunction with tangible products. Services require supporting products (you need an airplane to provide air transportation services), and products require supporting services (to sell even a shirt or can of beans calls at least for a cashier's service). Furthermore, a company may sell a combination of goods and services. Thus, along with repair service for your car, you might buy spark plugs or an oil filter. It may be helpful to think of every product as a mix of goods and services located on a continuum ranging from pure goods to pure services, as shown in Fig. 11-1.

FIGURE 11-1
A goods–services continuum.

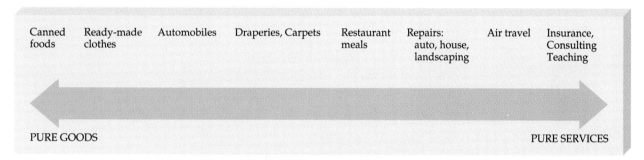

| Canned foods | Ready-made clothes | Automobiles | Draperies, Carpets | Restaurant meals | Repairs: auto, house, landscaping | Air travel | Insurance, Consulting Teaching |

PURE GOODS   PURE SERVICES

To move closer to a useful definition, we identify two classes of services. In the first group are services that are the *main purpose or object of a transaction*. As an example, suppose you want to rent a car from Avis. Avis needs a car (tangible good) to provide the rental service. But you are buying the rental use of the car, not the car itself. The second group consists of *supplementary* services that support or facilitate the sale of a tangible good or another service. Thus, when you buy a compact disc player, you may want technical information service from a sales person and the opportunity to pay with a credit-card service.

Consequently, our definition of services in this chapter is as follows: **Services** are identifiable, intangible activities that are the main object of a transaction designed to provide want-satisfaction to customers. By this definition we exclude supplementary services that support the sale of tangible goods or other services. Although we are interested primarily in the marketing of services that are the principal objective of a transaction, as in financial services, air travel, hotel accommodations, and car rentals, we must not overlook the very important services associated with the marketing of literally every product, whether tangible or intangible. Increasingly, marketers are realizing that one of the most effective ways to compete and to differentiate one's company from the competition is to offer excellent service. Thus, even to a company selling industrial supplies, there is a challenge to deliver the product on time and in good condition and to ensure that the customer is billed correctly and called on regularly.

We are concerned here primarily with the services marketed by business or professional firms with profit-making motives — commerical services. This is in contrast to services of nonprofit organizations, such as churches, universities, colleges, and the government. A useful classification of commercial services by industry is as follows:

- Housing (includes rental of hotels, motels, apartments, houses, and farms).
- Household operations (includes utilities, house repairs, repairs of equipment in the house, landscaping, and household cleaning).
- Recreation and entertainment (includes rental and repair of equipment used to participate in recreation and entertainment activities; also admission to all entertainment, recreation, and amusement events).
- Personal care (includes laundry, dry cleaning, beauty care).
- Medical and other health care (includes all medical services, dental, nursing, hospitalization, optometry, and other health care).
- Private education.
- Business and other professional services (includes legal, accounting, management consulting, and computer services).
- Insurance, banking, and other financial services (includes personal and business insurance, credit and loan service, investment counselling, and tax services).
- Transportation (includes freight and passenger service on common carriers, automobile repairs and rentals).
- Communications (includes telephone, facsimile, computer, and specialized business communication services).

Note that no attempt was made to separate the above groups into consumer and business services, as we did with tangible products. In fact, most are purchased by both market groups.

Importance of Services

North America has genuinely become a service economy. More than 70 percent of all jobs in Canada are now accounted for by the service sector, and over 60 percent of the country's gross domestic product is accounted for by services. Also, service jobs typically hold up better during a recession than do jobs in industries that produce tangible products. Canadians have become more dependent on the service sector for their jobs. Much of that employment, particularly in retail organizations, is now on a part-time basis.

Close to one-half of all consumer expenditures are for the purchase of services. During the 1950s and 1960s, much of the employment growth in services involved jobs in government and other public sector organizations, such as education and health. Since the 1970s, most of the growth has been in the provision of business and personal services. We have seen dramatic growth through the 1980s, for example, in the business services sector, including accounting, engineering, legal and management consulting, and in the provision of personal services, including accommodation and food, amusement, and recreation. The number of people employed in each of these industries rose more than 20 percent through the 1980s.[2]

---

[2]Colin Lindsay, ''The Service Sector in the 1980s,'' *Canadian Social Trends*, Spring 1989, pp. 20-23.

International business services are enjoying substantial growth in the 1990s.

Volume Leader.

Cast moves
more cargo, more frequently,
than other vessel fleets on
the North Atlantic.

CAST

The Blue Box System of Container Shipping

The growth in the market for *personal services* is at least partially explained by the relative prosperity that Canadians have enjoyed during the past 40 years. As consumers became better able to satisfy their demand for tangible items, they turned to services either to provide things that they could not afford before or to do things for them that they no longer wished to do for themselves.

The growth of *business services* may be attributed to the fact that business has become increasingly complex, specialized, and competitive. As a consequence, management has been forced to call in experts to provide services in research, taxation, advertising, labour relations, and a host of other areas.

The rate of growth has not been uniform for all categories of consumer services. As disposable personal incomes have increased and life-styles have changed, the demand for some services has grown relatively faster than for others. Projections through the 1990s suggest that high growth rates in jobs and spending will occur especially in temporary employment, auto repairs, banking and finance fields, leisure-time industries, and home shopping.

Characteristics of Services

The special nature of services stems from a number of distinctive characteristics. These features create special marketing challenges and opportunities. As a result, service firms often require strategic marketing programs that are substantially different from those found in the marketing of tangible goods.

INTANGIBILITY

Because services are intangible, it is impossible for customers to sample — taste, feel, see, hear, or smell — a service before they buy it. Consequently, a company's promotional program must portray the *benefits* to be derived from the service, rather than emphasizing the service itself. Four promotional strategies that may be used to suggest service benefits are as follows.[3]

- *Visualization.* For example, Carnival Cruise Lines depicts the benefits of its cruises with ads that show people dancing, dining, playing deck games, and visiting exotic places.
- *Association.* Connect the service with a tangible good, person, object, or place. The Australian airline, Qantas, uses a cuddly koala bear in its advertising to project a warm, friendly image of Australia. Prudential Insurance suggests stability and security with its Rock of Gibraltar. CIBC features its employees in its advertising to add a personal touch to financial services.
- *Physical representation.* American Express uses colour — green, gold, or platinum — for its credit-card services to symbolize wealth and prestige. Fast-food chains, telephone companies, and many other firms dress their service representatives in clean, distinctive uniforms to stress visibility, cleanliness, and dependability.
- *Documentation.* Air Canada and other airlines cite facts and figures in their ads to support claims of dependability, performance, care for passengers, and safety.

INSEPARABILITY

Services typically cannot be separated from the creator-seller of the service. Moreover, many services are created, dispensed, and consumed simultaneously. For example, dentists create and dispense almost all their services at the same time, *and* they require the presence of the consumer for the services to be performed. Because of this inseparability feature, many people are involved concurrently in the production operations and the marketing effort in services firms. And the customers receive and consume the services at the production site — in the firm's "factory," so to speak. Consequently, customers' opinions regarding a service frequently are formed through contacts with the production-marketing personnel and impressions of the physical surroundings in the "factory." Too often, contact personnel think of themselves as producers-creators of the service rather than as marketers.

From a marketing standpoint, inseparability frequently means that direct sale is the only possible channel of distribution, and a seller's services cannot be sold in very many markets. This characteristic limits the scale of operation in a firm. One person can repair only so many autos in a day or treat only so many medical patients.

As an exception to the inseparability feature, services may be sold by a person who is representing the creator-seller. A travel agent, insurance broker, or rental agent, for instance, may represent and help promote services that will be sold by the institutions producing them. Another way in which services

---

[3]Leonard L. Berry and Terry Clark, "Four Ways to Make Services More Tangible," *Business,* October/December 1986, p. 53. Also see Betsy D. Gelb, "How Marketers of Intangibles Can Raise the Odds for Consumer Satisfaction," *Journal of Services Marketing,* Summer 1987, pp. 11–17.

are delivered by intermediaries is through franchising. Companies such as Swiss Chalet and Tilden Rent-a-Car are in the service business, but their head offices deal with customers through franchise holders in various cities.

The inseparability of a service from the people providing it has important implications for companies that are operating in service-oriented businesses. This includes not only those companies in true "service" industries, such as financial services, entertainment, hotels, and restaurants, but also those who must pay particular attention to the services that support the marketing of their tangible products. For example, although Eastern Bakeries is technically a manufacturer of bakery products such as breads and cakes, it is also in the business of making sure that its products are delivered on time and in the quantity and condition the customer ordered.

For the most part, it is employees of a company who have the greatest influence on the level of service provided to its customers. Eastern Bakeries may bake the most wholesome bread in eastern Canada, but if employees cannot get it to the retail stores in time for consumers to buy it, then any product advantage Eastern may have had will be lost.

In fact, in many industries, particularly those where the products or services are technologically advanced or difficult for the consumer to understand, or where the customer cannot see important differences among the offerings of the various competitors, the ability to compete comes down to whether a company can deliver superior service. Most progressive companies have come to realize that their employees are extremely important in providing a level of service that will keep their customers happy.

This applies to employees who come into direct contact with the customer — sales staff, repair technicians, and flight attendants — as well as to support personnel who can damage a company's relationship with its customers even though they may never meet them directly. A clerk in the accounting department who fails to credit a customer's account correctly, or a baggage handler who sends a passenger's suitcase to Halifax when the passenger was travelling to Calgary, is just as responsible for service and customer relations as those staff members who meet and talk with customers.

HETEROGENEITY

It is impossible for a service industry, or even an individual seller of services, to standardize output. Each "unit" of the service is somewhat different from other "units" of the same service. For example, an airline does not give the same quality of service on each trip. All repair jobs a mechanic does on automobiles are not of equal quality. An added complication is the fact that it is often difficult to judge the quality of a service. (Of course, we can say the same for some goods.) It is particularly difficult to forecast quality in advance of buying a service. A person pays to see a ball game without knowing whether it will be an exciting one (well worth the price of admission) or a dull performance.

The heterogeneity of services is of concern to service providers, but the ability to deliver customer satisfaction is further complicated by the fact that customer expectations are not at all consistent. Although a student on a short lunch break may spend only 15 minutes grabbing a quick meal at a restaurant near campus, the same student may take more than an hour to enjoy a pizza with a friend after a Saturday-night movie. In the first case, the customer wants to be served as quickly as possible; in the second, he or she is prepared to wait a little longer for service. Because service expectations differ across customers and even over time for the same customers, it is very difficult for service businesses to standardize their level of service.

In recent years, some service companies have turned to technology in an attempt to standardize the type and quality of service provided, but at the expense of losing personal contact and the ability to respond to customers' questions or concerns. Nevertheless, some services, such as those provided by automated banking machines, can be standardized and are accepted by a large number of customers. Bell Canada and other telephone companies across Canada are handling certain telephone calls by installing technology that allows callers to interact with voice mail systems and digitally recorded voices, rather than with real "live" operators.[4]

Service companies should therefore pay special attention to the product-planning stage of their marketing programs. From the beginning, management must do all it can to ensure consistency of quality and to maintain high levels of quality control. This important issue of service quality will be discussed in a later section of this chapter.

PERISHABILITY AND FLUCTUATING DEMAND

Services are highly perishable, and they cannot be stored. Unused telephone time, empty seats in a stadium, and idle mechanics in a garage all represent business that is lost forever. Furthermore, the market for services fluctuates considerably by season, by day of the week, and by hour of the day. Most ski lifts lie idle all summer, whereas golf courses go unused in the winter. The use of city buses fluctuates greatly during the day.

There are notable exceptions to this generalization regarding the perishability and storage of services. In health and life insurance, for example, the service is purchased by a person or a company. Then it is held by the insurance company (the seller) until needed by the buyer or the beneficiary. This holding constitutes a type of storage.

The combination of perishability and fluctuating demand offers product-planning, pricing, and promotion challenges to services executives. Some organizations have developed new uses for idle plant capacity during off-seasons. Thus, during the summer, several ski resorts operate their ski lifts for hikers and sightseers who want access to higher elevations. Advertising and creative pricing are also used to stimulate demand during slack periods. Hotels offer lower prices and family packages on weekends. Telephone companies offer lower rates at nights and weekends.

THE MARKETING CONCEPT AND SERVICES MARKETING

The growth in services has generally *not* been a result of marketing developments in service industries, but rather to the maturation of our economy and our rising standard of living. Traditionally, executives in services companies have not been marketing-oriented. They have lagged behind sellers of tangible products in accepting the marketing concept and have generally been slow in adopting marketing techniques. Marketing management in service firms has not been especially creative. Innovations in services marketing have usually come from companies in the consumer-products industries.

---

[4]Mary Gooderham, "Phone Operators Becoming Voice of the Past," *Globe and Mail*, May 7, 1991, pp. A1, A4.

We can identify some reasons for this lack of marketing orientation. No doubt the intangibility of services creates more difficult marketing challenges for sellers of services than for sellers of goods. In many service industries — particularly professional services—the sellers think of themselves as producers or creators, and not as marketers, of the service. Proud of their abilities to represent a client in court, diagnose an illness, or give a good haircut, they often do not consider themselves business people.

The all-encompassing reason, however, is that top management in many cases does not understand (1) what marketing is or (2) its importance to a company's success. Service executives often seem to equate marketing with selling, and they fail to consider other parts of a marketing system. Many service firms also lack an executive whose sole responsibility is marketing — the counterpart of the vice-president of marketing in a goods-producing company.

In defence of firms in certain service industries, however, we note that external influences have contributed to the neglect of marketing. Up until the 1980s, several significant service industries were heavily regulated by governments or professional associations. Banking and all major forms of transportation services, for example, were severely restricted in marketing practices such as pricing, distribution, market expansion, and product expansion. In the fields of law, accounting, and health care, various laws and professional association regulations have prevented the providers from engaging in advertising, price competition, and other marketing activities. During the past 10 to 15 years, though, consumer protests and relaxing of regulations have removed many of these restrictions — thus creating genuine competition and a growing awarness of marketing in these industries.

There are, of course, exceptions to these negative generalizations. The success of such organizations as Four Seasons, American Express, Avis, and Federal Express is due in large part to their marketing orientation. In many services industries, the organizational concept of franchising (discussed in Chapter 16) has been applied successfully. Examples of franchising in services fields include equipment rentals, beauty salons, tax services, printing, lawn care services, and of course, restaurants. Under the umbrella philosophy of a marketing orientation, franchising organizations have used attributes such as good locations, training, and capital investment to meet services marketing challenges of intangibility, labour intensity, and quality control.[5]

The hotel industry provides an interesting example of a service industry that was not particularly marketing-oriented in the past, but that has more recently become extremely competitive and service oriented. As more and more people began to travel on business and vacations during the past 20 years, the hospitality industry in general has responded with promotions and marketing programs to attract various segments of the travelling market.

Some hotel chains, such as Four Seasons and Hyatt, have positioned themselves to appeal to the high end of the business travel market, offering superior service and amenities.[6] Others, including CP Hotels, Sheraton, Hilton, Radisson, Delta, and Westin, are firmly in the business travel and convention business, while others, such as Ramada Inn and Journey's End, are marketing

---

[5]James C. Cross and Bruce J. Walker, "Service Marketing and Franchising: A Practical Business Marriage," *Business Horizons*, November/December 1987, pp. 50-58.

[6]Paul King, "Building a Team the Sharp Way," *Canadian Business*, November 1990, pp. 96–102.

Providing superior service to
the high-end market.

CHRISTIAN IS A MASTER OF
TIME AND MOTION. HE CAN DISPATCH
3-MINUTE EGGS IN 2½ MINUTES.

He has stricken the word "impossible" from his vocabulary. Which is why he can have champagne and caviar brought to you in moments, magically fulfill requests for dishes not listed on the menu, and remember to dispatch the ice cream after the entrée, not a minute before. For like all our employees, Christian realizes everything about your room must be perfect. Including, of course, what is brought into it.

Four Seasons
Hotels·Resorts

aggressively at a more budget-minded market segment, including the economy-minded business traveller. This latter segment is also being targeted by a relatively new entrant into the hotel business, the all-suite hotels now being opened across Canada by companies such as Cambridge Suites and Journey's End Suites. Still other hotel chains, including some of the CP Hotels, are in the resort business, catering largely to conventions and vacationers.

The hotel industry also is beginning to understand how to make effective use of two other powerful marketing tools — creative pricing and skilful promotion. Several chains now offer lower rates for weekend nights, and charge nothing for children accompanying their parents. Realizing that their long-term success lies in being able to attract business travellers to make return visits, many chains are now paying particular attention to regular customers. Some have established ''frequent-guest'' programs, modelled after the airlines' frequent-flyer programs, which reward regular guests with points for each visit. Members of the Westin Premier of Hilton Honors programs, for example, can redeem their points for free nights at Westin and Hilton hotels around the world. This ''membership'' in an exclusive club, coupled with superior service for program members, is intended to create a feeling among regular customers that their business is welcomed and appreciated.

STRATEGIC PLANNING FOR SERVICES MARKETING

Because of the characteristics of services (notably intangibility), the development of a total marketing program in a service industry is often uniquely challenging. However, as in the marketing of goods, management first should define its marketing goals and select its target markets. Then management must design and implement marketing-mix strategies to reach its markets and fulfil its marketing goals.

Target-Market Analysis

The task of analyzing a firm's target markets is essentially the same, whether the firm is selling a tangible product or a service. Marketers of services should understand the components of population and income — the demographic factors—as they affect the market for the services. In addition, marketers must try to determine for each market segment why customers buy the given service. That is, what are their buying *motives*? Sellers must determine buying patterns for their services — when, where, and how do customers buy, who does the buying, and who makes the buying decisions? The psychological determinants of buying behaviour—attitudes, perceptions, and personality— become even more important when marketing services rather than goods, because typically we cannot touch, smell, or taste a service offering. In like manner, the sociological factors of social-class structure and small-group influences are market determinants for services. The fundamentals of the adoption and diffusion of innovation are also relevant in the marketing of services.

Some of the trends noted in Chapters 4 to 6 are particularly worth watching because they carry considerable influence in the marketing of services. As an example, increases in disposable income and discretionary buying power mean a growing market for health care services, insurance, and transportation services. Shorter working hours result in increased leisure time. More leisure time plus greater income means larger markets for recreation and entertainment services.

Market segmentation strategies also can be adopted by services marketers. We find apartment rental complexes for students, for single people, and for the over-65 crowd. Some car repair shops target owners of foreign cars. Limited-service motel chains cater to the economy-minded market segment, while all-suite hotels seek to attract families and business travellers.

Planning of Services

New services are just as important to a service company as new products are to a goods-marketing firm. Similarly, the improvement of existing services and elimination of unwanted, unprofitable services are also key goals.

Product planning and development has its counterpart in the marketing program of a service organization. Management must select appropriate strategies based on answers to these questions:

- What services will be offered?
- What will be the breadth and depth of the service mix?
- How will the services be positioned?
- What attributes, such as branding, packaging, and service quality, will the service have?[7]

---

[7]For a model of new-service development, see Eberhard E. Scheuing and Eugene M. Johnson, "A Proposed Model for New Service Development," *The Journal of Services Marketing*, Spring 1989, pp. 25–34. Also see G. Lynn Shostack, "Service Positioning through Structural Change," *Journal of Marketing*, January 1987, pp. 34–43.

MARKETING AT WORK

FILE 11-1   **TARGETING THE CANADIAN CULTURE MARKET: A MAJOR FIRST STEP**

Some say it's the most sophisticated cultural marketing tool ever developed in Canada. Others say it's a threat to artistic integrity, resulting in art being sold like soap. Nevertheless, the Canadian Arts Consumer Profile is going ahead. The project, expected to cost $955,000, is supported by the federal Department of Communications, ten provincial governments, and the municipalities of Vancouver, Toronto, and Montreal. Arts patrons in such fields as theatre, dance, and music have already participated in the first phase of the three-phase study, which will provide the first comprehensive demographic and psychographic profile of arts consumers. Knowing this information, cultural organizations are hoping to be better able to target their audiences, determine what kinds of cultural service marketing strategies are appropriate, and have the detailed ammunition to execute targeted and tailored promotional programs.

But the marketing of culture and the arts is very controversial. The as-yet unanswered question is: Will arts group managers, many of them representing nonprofit organizations, be willing to use services marketing ideas as opposed to demanding more public funding to be creative in their own terms?

Source: Adapted from Isabel Vincent, ''Making the Perfect Pitch,'' *Globe and Mail*, February 16, 1991, p. C1.

The high perishability, fluctuating demand, and inability to store services make product planning critically important to services marketers. A service organization can expand or contract its product mix, alter existing services, and trade up or down. Insurance firms that formerly specialized in fire–casualty–auto policies have added the more profitable line of life insurance policies. Some services firms have expanded their mix by working jointly with companies selling related services. For instance, automobile-rental firms have arrangements with airlines and hotels so that when customers fly to their destinations, a reserved rental car and hotel room are waiting. For the same reasons, car rental and hotel companies have become affiliated with airline frequent-flyer programs, so that frequent customers of Air Canada will likely rent a car from Avis or Budget and will stay at Westin or Hilton, all of whom give Aeroplan points to their customers and guests.

In some respects product planning is easier for services than for goods. Packaging, colour, and labelling are virtually nonexistent in services marketing. However, in other respects — branding and management of quality, for instance — service industries have greater challenges.

Services branding is a problem because maintaining consistent quality (a responsibility of brand ownership) is difficult. Also, a brand cannot be physically attached to a label or to the service itself. Remember, we can't see, touch, or smell the service, so the brand carries a major marketing burden. A services marketer's goal should be to create an effective brand image. To reach this goal, a key strategy is to develop a total brand theme that includes more than just a brand name. To implement this strategy, the following tactics (besides getting a good brand name) may be employed:

M A R K E T I N G   A T   W O R K

FILE 11-2   GOVERNMENT SERVICES—DO THEY EXIST?

The concept of service quality has reached into the most protected service arena in Canada—provincial government services to taxpayers. The proof is that a number of provincial governments have established either task forces or actual operating units dedicated to determining what services are needed and how to improve those available.

In 1990, the British Columbia government established a unit called Service Quality B.C. The unit has since made recommendations for staff training, hours of operation that are convenient to service users rather than employees, express lanes for the issuing of licences, permits, and associated paper documents, as well as the use of plain language in official publications.

In Ontario, the government created a Customer Service Task Force, which has sent out questionnaires to 10,000 Ontario residents to find out what they like and dislike about the quality of service the government now provides. In addition, 8,000 questionnaires have been sent to civil servants to find out how they think they might do their jobs better.

There are two reasons for the heightened government sensitivity about service. One is the public cry for increased value for increased taxes. The other is the effect of improved services in the private sector and the comparisons vocally expressed by citizens standing in line at provincial government offices.

Source: Adapted from Gene Allen, "Ontario Waiting for Service Tips," *Globe and Mail*, July 4, 1991, pp. 1–2.

- *Include a tangible good as part of the brand image*—like the umbrella of Travelers Insurance, Prudential's Rock of Gibraltar, or the koala bear of Qantas.
- *Tie in a slogan with the brand*—for instance, "You're in good hands with Allstate" or "Membership has its privileges" (American Express).
- *Use a distinctive colour scheme*—such as Avis's red or the green of the Toronto Dominion Bank.[8]

MANAGEMENT OF SERVICE QUALITY

In our brief discussion of product quality in Chapter 10, we noted the elusiveness of this important product feature. Quality is difficult to define, measure, control, and communicate. Yet in services marketing, the quality of the service is critical to a firm's success. Two airlines each fly a Boeing 747 for the same fare; two auto repair shops each use Ford or Chrysler parts and charge the same price; and two banks each offer the same investment accounts at identical interest rates. Assuming similar times and locations, quality of service is the only factor that differentiates the offerings in each of these paired situations.

However difficult it may be to define the concept of service quality, management must understand one thing: *Quality is defined by the consumer and not by the producer-seller of a service.* Your hairstylist may be delighted with the job

---

[8]Leonard L. Berry, Edwin F. Lefkowith, and Terry Clark, "In Services, What's in a Name?" *Harvard Business Review*, September–October 1988, pp. 28–30. Also see Sak Onkvisit and John J. Shaw, "Service Marketing: Image, Branding, and Competition," *Business Horizons*, January/February 1989, pp. 13–18.

she did on your hair. But if you think your hair looks terrible, then the service quality was poor. What counts is what consumers think about a service. Service quality that does not meet customer expectations can result in lost sales from present customers and a failure to attract new customers. Consequently, it is imperative that management strives to maintain *consistent* service quality at or above the level of consumer expectations. Yet it is sometimes virtually impossible to standardize service quality—that is, to maintain consistency in service output. Performance quality typically varies even within the same organization. This is true in such diverse fields as opera, legal services, landscaping, baseball, health care, and marketing courses.[9]

As part of managing service quality, an organization should design and operate an ongoing quality-improvement program that will monitor the level and consistency of service quality. A related, but also difficult, task is to evaluate service quality by measuring customer satisfaction—that is, customers' perceptions of the quality of an organization's services.[10]

Most successful marketers of services and those responsible for the services associated with tangible products have begun to introduce programs that will allow them to measure the quality of the service they provide, as perceived by their customers. Many businesses have existed for years under the assumption that management *knew* what the customer wanted and how he or she wished to be treated. The most successful have now abandoned that way of thinking and have subscribed to the maxim that "good service is whatever the customer says it is." Thus, a program to measure the perceived quality of a business's service must start by defining the aspects of the contact with the company the customer considers to be most important.[11]

Research with a number of Canadian and foreign companies in various industries has confirmed that consumers consider three components of service to be important; (1) the nature of the *service itself* or of services required to ensure that a product performs to expectations; (2) the *process* by which the product or service is delivered; and (3) interaction with the *people* who deliver the service.

For example, customers of Bell Canada and other telephone companies are interested in ensuring that their telephone systems work properly, that calls go through, and that reception is clear (the "product" aspects of the service). In fact, as technology has improved in the telecommunications industry, customers do not expect their telephone systems ever to fail. The next component of service relates to the processes the telephone company has in place to provide and support the service—the accuracy of telephone bills, the speed with which new lines are installed, and how often sales people call to explain new services. Finally, the quality of service as perceived by customers is related to the way in which employees of the company treat their customers—whether

---

[9]For a good summary of service quality, see Leonard L. Berry, A. Parasuraman, and Valarie A. Zeithaml, "The Service-Quality Puzzle," *Business Horizons*, September/October 1988, pp. 35–43.

[10]For more on the measurement of customers' perceptions of service quality, see A. Parasuraman, Valarie A. Zeithaml, and Leonard L. Berry, "SERVQUAL: A Multiple-Item Scale for Measuring Consumer Perceptions of Service Quality," *Journal of Retailing*, Spring 1988, pp. 12–40; Stephen W. Brown and Teresa A. Swartz, "A Gap Analysis of Professional Service Quality," *Journal of Marketing*, April 1989, pp. 92–98; and Kate Bertrand, "In Service, Perception Counts," *Business Marketing*, April 1989, p. 44.

[11]Patricia Sellers, "What Customers Really Want," *Fortune*, June 4, 1990, pp. 58–68.

MARKETING AT WORK

FILE 11-3 **HOW EMPLOYMENT AND INTERNAL MARKETING INCREASE SERVICE PRODUCTIVITY**

CP Express, part of Canadian Pacific Ltd., has found a vital key to increased customer satisfaction as well as increased profitability — employee commitment to service quality. Teams of drivers were involved in selecting new equipment (trucks), inspecting the purchases (by going to France), and operating the truck terminals themselves rather than having them being run by managers. Management decided that giving power to service employees resulted in deeper understanding of the nature of the business and commitment to making it work. And in the freight business, the driver is the key to quality service. As a result of extensive and genuine internal communication, CP Express was able to turn around at a time when de-regulation of trucking resulted in many companies closing their doors.

Now, after the company spent $3 million in training, 34 of its 65 cross-Canada truck terminals are employee operated; employees have detailed information on the costs of keeping trucks on the road and generate ideas to cut costs and increase productivity; drivers discuss problems directly with customers and go out of their way to see that customers' needs are satisfied; drivers supply the sales and marketing staff with customer leads as well as innovative ideas for providing service. And the 14,500-member transport union is more than happy with the outcome as well.

Source: Adapted from Wilfred List, "On the Road to Profit," *Globe and Mail*, July 10, 1991, pp. B1–2.

operators are courteous and polite, whether sales people know the technology, and how complaints are resolved.

One author has suggested that as the nature of service moves farther away from the actual product or service, and more towards the "people" aspects of service, the less control management has over the delivery, and therefore the quality, of the service offered.[12] For example, an airline company can control the actual flight from Toronto to Vancouver (the basic service, getting passengers from one city to another). Barring unforeseen circumstances management can control, to a greater or lesser extent, the services that support that basic product: the frequency of flights, departure and arrival times, the number of ticket agents at the counter, baggage-handling systems, and type of meals served.

Management loses much more control over the details of the service provided at the interface between customer and employee—how the ticket agent greets the customer at the check-in counter, whether the baggage handler puts the suitcase on the right plane, whether the flight attendants are pleasant and helpful. In fact, it is in this latter component of service that many companies feel their greatest potential lies to differentiate themselves from the competi-

---

[12]James G. Barnes, "The Role of Internal Marketing: If the Staff Won't Buy It, Why Should the Customer?" *Irish Marketing Review*, vol. 4, no. 2, 1989, pp. 11–21.

Without international
marketing, Singapore Airlines
can't be the talk of the industry.

FIGURE 11-2
**The domain of customer
service**

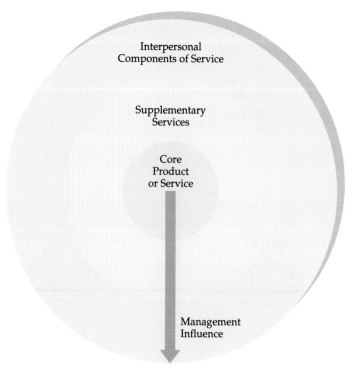

tion. Among international airlines, Air Canada, Singapore Airlines, and Cathay Pacific try to feature superior service and ''cabin comfort'' in their advertising.

It is this realization that employees have the potential to make or break a relationship with a customer that has led many companies to introduce programs of *internal marketing*. These are programs which are intended to ensure that employees ''buy in'' to the concept of customer service and appreciate that every satisfied customer means a returning customer. Again, the more progressive companies, and those which are most committed to exceptional levels of customer service, have developed elaborate training and motivation programs which emphasize excellence in treating the customer and reward those employees who treat customers well.[13]

Pricing of Services

In the marketing of services, nowhere is there a greater need for managerial creativity and skill than in the area of pricing. Earlier we noted that services are extremely perishable, they usually cannot be stored, and demand for them often fluctuates considerably. All these features carry significant pricing implications. To further complicate the situation, customers may perform some services themselves (auto and household repairs, for example).

These considerations suggest that the elasticity of demand for a service should influence the price set by the seller. Interestingly enough, sellers often do recognize inelastic demand. They then charge higher prices. But they fail to act in opposite fashion when faced with an elastic demand—even though a lower price would increase unit sales, total revenue, utilization of facilities, and probably net profit.

Certainly, perfect competition does not apply to any great extent, if at all, in the pricing of services. Because of the heterogeneity and difficulty of standardizing quality, most services are highly differentiated. Also, it is virtually impossible to have complete market information. As an example, consider how difficult it is to get reliable, detailed information on accountants' or lawyers' fees. In any given market, such as a neighbourhood, often there are geographic limits within which a buyer will seek a service. Consequently, there are not a large number of sellers. The heavy capital investment required to produce certain services (transportation, broadcasting, communications) often limits considerably the freedom of entry.

Nevertheless, in recent years price competition in many service areas has increased considerably, going through three identifiable phases:

- In the first phase, price is barely mentioned in the organization's advertising. For example, the Royal Bank of Canada, in advertising its V.I.P. Service, will emphasize the various aspects of the service and how to contact an Account Manager, but will not mention price.
- In the second phase, the seller uses a market segmentation strategy to target a given market at a specific price. To illustrate, the Royal Bank of Canada may advertise its Royal Certified Service and may also mention that this enhanced package of banking services may be had for a certain low monthly charge.
- The third phase involves out-and-out price competition as firms stress comparative prices in their advertising. As banking has become more and

---

[13]''Have a Nice Day,'' *The Economist*, March 2, 1991, p. 64.

Emphasizing service and leaving price for the personal contact.

more competitive, we have seen advertising for the Royal Bank and others stressing their mortgage rates and the interest rates being paid on deposit accounts.

Many of the pricing strategies discussed in Chapter 13 are applicable to services marketing. Quantity discounts, for instance, are used by car-rental agencies. Daily rates are lower if you agree to rent the car for a week or a month at a time. Cash discounts are offered when insurance premiums are paid annually instead of quarterly. Accountants and management consultants can use a variable-price policy. Geographic pricing policies may apply, although the variable here is time, not freight charges. Mechanics will charge more if they must travel out of town, and engineers will usually command higher fees for work in foreign countries.

Channels of Distribution for Services

Traditionally, most services have been sold directly from producer to consumer or business user. No middlemen are used when the service cannot be separated from the seller or when the service is created and marketed simultaneously. For example, public utilities, medical care, and repair services are typically sold without middlemen. Not using middlemen does limit the geographic markets that services sellers can reach. But it also enables sellers to personalize their services and get quick, detailed customer feedback.

The only other frequently used channel includes one agent middleman. Some type of agent or broker is often used in the marketing of securities, travel arrangements, entertainment, and housing rentals. Sometimes dealers are trained in the production of the service and then are franchised to sell it. This is the case with Sanitone dry cleaning, Midas Muffler shops, Computerland, and similar franchises.

In recent years, some firms have realized that the characteristic of inseparability is not an insurmountable limitation to a seller's distribution system. With a little imagination, a services marketer can broaden distribution considerably. Let's look at some examples, starting with location.

The service seller or seller's agent should be conveniently located for customers, because many services cannot be delivered. Many motels and restaurants have gone out of business when a new highway bypassed their locations, thereby drawing away customer traffic. On the other hand, banks have increased business by installing 24-hour automated teller machines and by setting up tellers' windows for drive-in customers. Dental centres, small medical centres, chiropractors, and optometrists have opened offices in shopping-centre malls. Retail-store locations have been especially successful for dental centres, and the idea is spreading to all sections of the country. They offer convenience of location, extended hours, and parking.

The use of intermediaries is another way to expand distribution. Some banks have arranged for companies to deposit employees' pay cheques directly into their bank accounts. The employer thus becomes an intermediary in distributing the bank's service. Insurance firms have broadened distribution by setting up vending machines in airports.

The characteristic of intangibility essentially eliminates physical distribution problems for most service producers. For example, other than supportive supplies, accountants have no physical inventory to store or handle. However, not all service producers are free from physical distribution headaches. A chain of equipment-rental stores, for example, would certainly have to contend with inventory problems.

Promoting a Service   Several forms of promotion are used extensively in services marketing, but personal selling plays the dominant role. Whether or not they realize it, any employee of a service firm who comes in contact with a customer is, in effect, part of that firm's sales force. In addition to a regular sales force, customer contact personnel might include airline counter attendants, law-office receptionists, Federal Express delivery people, bank tellers, and ticket-takers and ushers at ballparks or theatres. We use the term **service encounter** to describe a customer's interaction with any service employee or with any tangible element such as a service's physical surroundings (bank, ballpark, legal office). Customers often form opinions of a company and its service on the basis of service encounters. Consequently, it is essential that management recognizes the strategic importance of service encounters and prepares contact personnel and physical surroundings accordingly. A key step in preparing to sell a service is to provide sales training and service information for contact personnel, impressing on them the importance of their role.[14]

---

[14]For further discussion of personal selling and service encounters, see William R. George, Patrick Kelly, and Claudia E. Marshall, ''The Selling of Services: A Comprehensive Model,'' *Journal of Personal Selling & Sales Management*, August 1986, pp. 29–37; Mary Jo Bitner, Bernard H. Booms, and Mary Stanfield Tetreault, ''The Service Encounter: Diagnosing Favorable and Unfavorable Incidents,'' *Journal of Marketing*, January 1990, pp. 71–84; and Mary Jo Bitner, ''Evaluating Service Encounters: The Effects of Physical Surroundings and Employee Responses,'' *Journal of Marketing*, April 1990, pp. 69–82.

Life insurance companies stress professional teamwork in the delivery of their services.

For years, of course, *advertising* has been used extensively in many service fields — hotels, transportation, recreation, and insurance, for example. What *is* new is the use of advertising by professional-services firms, including legal, accounting, and health services such as physiotherapists and chiropractors. Previously, professional associations in such fields prohibited advertising on the grounds that it was unethical. While some associations still control the type of advertising that may be done, the promotion of professional services is much more open and accepted than ever before.

In *sales promotion*, while point-of-purchase displays of services offered are often impossible, displays of the *results* of using a service can be effective. Many service firms, especially in the recreation and entertainment fields, benefit considerably from free *publicity*. Sports coverage by newspapers, radio, and television provides publicity, as do newspaper reviews of movies, plays, and concerts. Travel sections in newspapers have helped sell transportation, accommodation, and other services related to the travel industry.

As an *indirect type of promotion*, engineers, accountants, lawyers, and insurance agents may participate actively in community affairs as a means of getting their names before the public. Service firms (banks, public utilities, lawyers) may advertise to attract new industry to the community. They know that anything that helps the community grow will automatically mean an expanded market for their services.

THE FUTURE OF SERVICES MARKETING

The boom in the service economy in recent years has been accompanied by a significant increase in competition in many service industries. This competition has been stimulated by several factors. One is the reduction in government regulation in some industries — airlines, trucking, and banking, for example. Relaxed regulations by professional organizations now permit advertising in

M A R K E T I N G   A T   W O R K

FILE 11-4 **DOCTORS HEIGHTEN AWARENESS**

The Supreme Court of Canada has recently struck down a rule in Ontario not allowing dentists to advertise. Because of this ruling, the Ontario College of Physicians has dramatically loosened its tough controls on advertising by doctors. In the past, doctors were allowed to list only their name, address, and phone number in the white pages of the telephone book. However, under the new rules, they can now use any medium to advertise their specialties, hours, and other details of their practices. There are still some restrictions, including:

- Advertised information must be true, verifiable, and relevant to someone choosing a doctor or specialist.
- Doctors can't compare themselves to other doctors.
- The medium used must be open to everyone. (For example, a doctor could not be an exclusive corporate sponsor of the SkyDome.)
- There can be no direct solicitation of patients. (A cosmetic surgeon, for example, would not be allowed to obtain a list of Weight Watcher clients and contact them with an offer of liposuction services.)
- Doctors can't associate themselves with a product or service.

Source: Adapted from Stan Sutter, ''Advertising: It's Just What the Doctor Ordered,'' *Marketing*, October 1, 1990, p. 1.

the medical, legal, and other professions. New techniques have opened new service fields—in solar energy and information processing, for instance. Technological advances have also brought automation and other ''industrial'' features to formerly all-hand-labour service industries. Service chains and franchise systems are replacing the small-scale independent in many fields, including take-out food, auto repairs, beauty shops, and real estate brokerage.

Need for Increased Productivity

The boom has also brought about deterioration in the quality of many services. In general, service industries are often plagued by poor management, inefficiency, and low productivity. This inefficiency—and the need to increase productivity — is probably the biggest problem facing service industries. Low productivity also has significant implications for the health of the total economy. Service industries are very labour-intensive compared with manufacturing. Thus wage increases in the service sector of the economy have a major impact on price levels and inflation. Furthermore, the forecast for the remainder of the 1990s is for continued growth in the service sector, but a decrease in the labour pool for these industries. This projected labour shortage is likely to result in fundamental changes as service industries seek ways to improve productivity rates.

Services firms are employing various strategies to improve productivity. One is to invest in education and training programs, not just to teach basic skills but also to improve workers' efficiency. Another strategy is to bring in new technology and adopt methods used in manufacturing. Machines have enhanced or even replaced hand labour in a wide range of service industries. The most widely adopted technology has been some form of computer-based information system. Computers have increased the efficiency of operations in countless service firms. But the flip side is that computers (or computer users) many times have fallen short of their potential. Sometimes the users are not properly trained, or existing systems are not adapted to make the most effective use of new technologies. A third productivity improvement strategy is to restructure jobs so that each employee can accomplish a lot more in the same amount of time. Thus, auto repair shops have employees who specialize in brakes, transmissions, or mufflers. The introduction of assembly-line techniques at Burger King, Harvey's, and McDonald's has increased output per employee.

Prospects for Growth

There is every reason to believe that services will continue to take an increasing share of the consumer dollar, just as they have done generally over the past 40 years. This forecast seems reasonable even for periods of economic decline. History shows that the demand for services is less sensitive to economic fluctuations than the demand for goods. The demand for *business* services should also continue to expand as business becomes more complex and as management further recognizes its need for business-service specialists. In *professional* services especially, the use of marketing programs is expected to increase considerably during the coming decade. This expansion will occur as engineers, lawyers, and other professionals come to understand and appreciate the social and economic benefits they can derive from an effective marketing program.

Even manufacturers are taking an increasing interest in services as a basis for growth. Most tangible goods can be quickly and easily imitated. Consequently, manufacturers see their accompanying services as a key factor in giving a company a competitive advantage. The idea is to bundle services with goods to respond to a full range of customers' wants.[15]

SUMMARY

Most product offerings are a mix of tangible goods and intangible services, located on a spectrum ranging from pure goods to pure services. Services are separately identifiable, intangible activities that are the main object of a transaction designed to provide want-satisfaction for customers. Conceptually, goods marketing and services marketing are essentially the same. In reality, however, the characteristics that differentiate services from goods usually call for quite different marketing programs.

The scope of services marketing is enormous. About half of what we spend goes for services, and about two-thirds of nongovernmental jobs are in service industries. Not only are services of considerable significance in our economy today, but it is predicted that the services sector will continue to grow faster than the goods sector of the economy. Services generally are intangible, inseparable from the seller, heterogeneous, and highly perishable, and they have a widely fluctuating demand. Each of these distinctive characteristics has several marketing implications.

---

[15]For a further discussion of developing manufacturers' services, with several company examples, see Richard B. Chase and David A. Garvin, "The Service Factory," *Harvard Business Review*, July/August 1989, pp. 61–69.

The growth in services has not been matched by service management's understanding or acceptance of the marketing concept. Service organizations have been slow to adopt marketing programs and techniques that, in goods marketing, have brought satisfaction to consumers and profits to producers.

The development of a program for the marketing of services parallels that for goods, but takes into account the special characteristics of services. Management first identifies its target market and then designs a marketing mix to provide want-satisfaction for that market. In the product-planning stage, the element of service quality is critical to a company's success. Similar pricing strategies are used by services and goods producers. In distribution, middlemen are used very sparingly, and location of the service marketer in relation to the market is important. Personal selling is the dominant promotional method used in services marketing.

As we move through the 1990s, the service environment will continue to change. Probably the biggest challenge for service industries today is to develop ways to improve productivity. Productivity increases in importance as services account for a growing share of the gross national product and consumer expenditures. And this growth pattern is expected to continue at least through the remainder of this century.

KEY TERMS AND CONCEPTS

Services 331
Personal services 333
Business services 333
Intangibility 334
Inseparability 334
Heterogeneity 335
Perishability 336

Fluctuating demand 336
"Membership" programs 338
Service quality 341
Internal marketing 345
Services franchising 347
Service encounter 347

QUESTIONS AND PROBLEMS

1. How do you explain the substantial increase in expenditures for services relative to expenditures for goods in the last 40 years?
2. What are some marketing implications in the fact that services possess the characteristic of intangibility?
3. Why are middlemen rarely used in the marketing programs of service firms?
4. Services are highly perishable and are often subject to fluctuations in demand. In marketing its services, how can a company offset these factors?
5. Cite some examples of services marketers that seem to be customer-oriented, and describe what these firms have done in this vein.
6. "Traditionally, marketers of services have *not* been marketing-oriented." Do you agree? If so, how do you account for this deficiency?
7. Present a brief analysis of the market for each of the following service firms. Make use of the components of a market discussed in Chapters 4 to 7.
   a. Canadian Airlines International.
   b. Hotel near large airport.
   c. Indoor tennis club.
   d. Credit union.

8. What are some of the ways in which each of the following service firms might expand its line?
   a. Chartered Accountant.
   b. Hairstyling salon.
   c. Bank.

9. Explain the importance of demand elasticity in the pricing of services.

10. ''Personal selling should be the main ingredient in the promotional mix for a marketer of services.'' Do you agree? Discuss.

11. Present in brief form a marketing program for each of the following services. Your presentation should start with a description of the target market you have selected for the service. Then explain how you would plan, price, promote, and distribute the service.
   a. A disc jockey for private parties in the community.
   b. Your electric company.
   c. Household cleaning.

C A S E S   F O R   P A R T   3

CASE 3.1   ## Upper Canada Brewing Company (B): Developing a Product Strategy

The deal was finally together! Frank Heaps, founder and president of the Upper Canada Brewing Company, Toronto, had by June 1984 put the management team in place and by December 1984 completed the major task of raising the $3.5 million in start-up capital. He was now ready to begin the challenge of putting together his marketing plan. The major task facing him at present was to plan and develop the actual product itself and to finalize the various product strategies. These decisions had to be made immediately if he was to have the products on the market by the targeted date, June 1985. Given the cyclical nature of this industry, where summer peak sales must compensate for winter lows, this target date was critical to ensuring financial viability.

BACKGROUND

The marketing strategy of the Upper Canada Brewing Company was to make beer pure and simple. Mr. Heaps wanted to carve a market niche for his firm based on the product itself, not advertising and marketing gimmickry. It was his perception that most Canadian beers were made the "same." In fact, he believed, as did others, that most beer drinkers often could not identify their favourite brands in blind taste tests. As well, he felt that a segment of the beer market wanted more than these bland alternatives — they wanted beer that was truly different. He proposed developing a product that would cater to this changing market demand.

The Upper Canada Brewing Company did not endeavour to compete with the major producers for the mass market. Instead it was intended to build market appeal and support within a specialized segment. The target market for the Upper Canada Brewing Company was viewed as a combination of the import and domestic beer markets. The market segment included knowledgeable beer drinkers, yuppies, ethnic groups, natural food enthusiasts, and college/university groups. Mr. Heaps also had an objective to expand the market abroad by exporting the product to countries like the United States, Germany, and maybe even Japan.

The competitive strength of the new company lay in its form — being a small cottage brewery. Its commitment was to a more traditional and natural brewing method that produced a superior quality product, different from the "hi-tech" brews of the major breweries. Cottage breweries also strived to portray a "feeling" for the brewery craft that the major breweries could not impart. The Upper Canada Brewing Company was the first cottage brewery to open in Toronto but was one of several which had re-appeared in Canada after being absent for some 20 years.

THE PRODUCT DECISIONS

The Product Mix   The first major product strategy decision facing Mr. Heaps was to determine what type of beer product(s) to produce. He knew that the beer had to be different, but not too different. He also knew that the product(s) had to be of consistently high quality to be accepted by the consumer. Beer, being a very perishable food product, had to be brewed under strict guidelines to achieve these results.

The strictest of all brewing legislation — the Bavarian Purity Act of 1516 — was adopted to ensure product excellence. Under this code, only the finest barley malt, hops, yeast, and water can be used in beer production. No "adjuncts" (corn, rice, or other grains) or chemical additives can be used to assist fermentation. The Act also forbids the common practice of adding sugar or corn syrup to artificially speed up the brewing

This case was prepared by Donna M. Stapleton and is intended to stimulate discussion of an actual management problem and not to illustrate either effective or ineffective handling of that problem. The author wishes to acknowledge the support provided by the Upper Canada Brewing Company, and particularly by Frank Heaps, President.

process; all products must be naturally aged to enhance the beer flavour. The products are also unpasteurized since this process adversely affects the taste of beer and may interfere with the natural carbonation process. The result is that beer brewed under these guidelines produces dual benefits for the consumer—true beer taste and no headaches or hangovers.

To determine what product lines of beer to produce, Mr. Heaps did his homework to find out the facts about beer. Research showed that two brewing styles dominated the world production of beer. Almost all beer made was either an ale product or a lager beer product. Indeed, all North American ''light'' beer products were lager beers. Ale was a generic term for English-style top-fermented beers, while lager was a generic term for all bottom-fermented beers. One advantage of brewing ale products as opposed to lager products was that an ale took only half the time to mature — three weeks as opposed to five. Mr. Heaps wondered what product lines he should brew—an ale, or a lager, or both? In addition, he had to decide whether to include a line of light beer. The company was new and therefore had limited resources. But he also wanted to offer a variety of products that would meet the needs of his target market.

An equally important decision concerned the depth of the product lines. Most beer products were available in kegs for the licensee trade and 6-, 12-, and 24-packs for the ultimate consumer. One higher-priced domestic premium beer was also available in a 20-pack to compensate for the higher price. He wondered which of these alternatives would be most advantageous for his company.

Packaging There were a number of packaging decisions facing Mr. Heaps. First he had to decide what bottle size would be most appropriate for his new brew. The traditional bottle size used by the major breweries was 341 mL. The Granville Island Brewery also used this bottle size and the mould was available to Mr. Heaps for use at Upper Canada; one advantage of this alternative was that it avoided the up-front $16,000 expense of a custom-made mould. The other common bottle sizes included the litre-sized bottles used for a number of European beers that were sold in Ontario and the half-litre

size (500 mL) used in Germany. The advantage of these other sizes was the import image that they projected. Other bottle decisions facing Mr. Heaps concerned the shape and colour. Granville Island Brewery used a tall, traditional bottle, a replica of a 30-year-old British Columbia beer bottle design, in amber glass. The bottles of the other breweries were undergoing change, with many of the mass breweries moving to the non-stubby bottles desired by the consumer. The colour of most North American beer bottles was amber. Import bottles varied in shape and colour; most were tall, traditional-styled in either amber or green. The amber glass was preferred by many because it was the best for screening natural or artificial light and thus offered the beer the best protection when it was out of its case.

Mr. Heaps also had to decide on the type of cap to be used on the bottle. There were basically three alternatives: (i) the new twist-off caps being adopted by the mass brewers; (ii) the standard compression caps; and (iii) the corks with wire holders, available on some European beers. The major advantage of the twist-off cap was customer convenience. The problem, however, was that to be tamper-evident a twist-off cap should have a protective foil or paper label around it. This would mean that the company would need a new labeller or foiler — an additional expense. The compression style cap did not have this disadvantage but was considered old-fashioned and inconvenient by some consumers. The cork with the wire holder had the advantage of a European image and convenience but was more expensive.

The final packaging decision concerned the cartons in which the beer would be packed. Mr. Heaps had two objectives which he felt the package must achieve: it had to ''say something,'' and be bright and interesting to attract attention. He proposed including a brief description about the specifications of the product, including a mention of the Bavarian Purity Act of 1516, as well as the company logo — a beaver building a dam with pine forests in the background (see Exhibit 1). The major breweries followed a completely different strategy — their cases featured a brand name and little else.

Positioning Positioning the product(s) correctly in the marketplace was of critical importance if

EXHIBIT 1

THE UPPER CANADA BREWING COMPANY

the Upper Canada Brewing Company was to achieve a competitive advantage. Mr. Heaps felt that the target market wanted a high-quality product with taste. This market segment was not being satisfied by existing mass-produced alternatives, thus the products of the Upper Canada Brewing Company would be positioned to reach and satisfy this market niche. The positioning would be done by product attribute, emphasizing the all-natural, high quality, traditional "beer" taste and price/quality — value for money.

The target date to get the products on the market was only six months away. The product mix decisions, the related packaging decisions, and positioning strategy needed to be finalized soon if Mr. Heaps was to meet this deadline.

QUESTIONS

1. Does the target market identified by Mr. Heaps represent the best market opportunity for this new venture? Why or why not?

2. What would you recommend to Mr. Heaps in each of the following product strategy areas? Substantiate your recommendations.
   a. Breadth of the product mix (number of lines to brew).
   b. Number of package sizes (depth).
   c. Bottle size, shape, and colour.
   d. Type of cap.
   e. Product positioning.

3. Are there any other decisions that Mr. Heaps should make in the product strategy area? What are they?

4. Evaluate the packaging approach Mr. Heaps has proposed for the Upper Canada Brewery. Will the "informative" approach and proposed logo design appeal to the target market?

5. How important is the Bavarian Purity Act of 1516 to the competitive position of the Upper Canada Brewery's product(s)? What advantage will this offer the company in the short and long term?

CASE 3.2   **National Sea Products (A)**

It was late 1989 and National Sea Products was coping with one of the most serious situations ever to face the Canadian fishing industry. The company would lose $32 million during the year, compared with a $5.8 million loss in 1988. Other companies in the industry were facing the same bleak financial picture, brought about largely by an unavailability of raw material. Because of cuts in quotas imposed by the federal government, designed to conserve fish stocks off Canada's coasts, companies such as National Sea Products had much less fish available to them. The situation was causing a number of companies in the industry to look for alternative means of generating sales and profits. Jim Jaques, marketing manager with National Sea, was researching a number of opportunities to take the company into new fields.

THE COMPANY AND THE INDUSTRY

National Sea Products is one of North America's largest seafood companies. It had enjoyed a long history as Canada's best-known processor of fish and other seafood products. The company's Highliner brand was one of the best-known and

Copyright 1991. This case was written by Leanne O'Leary and James G. Barnes of Memorial University of Newfoundland. The case was prepared with the co-operation of National Sea Products Limited to illustrate the marketing activities of that company in launching a new product to the Canadian market and not to indicate a correct or incorrect approach to such marketing initiatives. The authors acknowledge the co-operation and support of Jim Jaques, Director of Marketing, National Sea Products Limited, in the preparation of this case.

most successful brands of frozen food products available in Canadian supermarkets. The advertising character, Captain Highliner, was among the most recognizable advertising symbols in the country. National Sea had also carved out a major position in the food-service industry in North America. Over the past few years, however, the company's total production of groundfish had dropped from 179,000 tonnes in 1986 to approximately 141,000 tonnes in 1989. At the same time, production of shrimp had increased from 5,800 to 7,300 tonnes. Total number of employees had dropped from 8,000 to 6,500 over the same period.

The latter half of the 1980s had presented the Halifax-based corporation with some of the worst times the industry had ever experienced. In addition to quota cuts, National Sea was afflicted by a series of plant closures, protests by union and community leaders, and uncertain markets resulting from the relatively high price of the raw material. The company, with four seafood processing plants in Newfoundland, four in Nova Scotia, and two in the United States, has made aggressive progress in developing a strategy to move from a strictly fish-based enterprise to an international food-processing company.

While National Sea was best known as a major producer and marketer of seafood products, the company had moved into poultry production in 1985 with the launch of Captain's Chicken, which was now the leading brand of frozen processed chicken in Canada. Such efforts on the part of National Sea in recent years to diversify its operations were consistent with the company's mission statement and its corporate commitment to reduce reliance on the troubled Atlantic fish stocks. Most of these actions taken by National Sea have been influenced by the fluctuating supply of fish since 1983.

Until 1986, demand for fish grew significantly because of availability and affordability. Trends towards healthier eating, nutrition consciousness, and "good for you" messages in the media contributed to this rise. Since this time, however, the retail price of fish has increased faster than that of other high-protein foods. Therefore, retail packaged seafood products experienced a dramatic increase in price relative to beef, pork, and poultry, leading to an ongoing decline in the retail sales volume of fish fillets, seafood in batter, and similar products.

The per capita consumption of seafood had, however, been increasing on an annual basis throughout the 1980s, when all forms of seafood are taken into consideration, including seafood consumed outside the home and in the food-service industry. The availability of farmed salmon and other species has contributed to a situation where seafood can be economically prepared and served in restaurants. Although many consumers are unlikely to serve seafood as a main meal for all members of the household, they are much more likely to order seafood when they are out for a meal. As a result, the reduced availability of raw material has become an even more serious problem for National Sea and other companies in the industry, because they have not been able to supply the increased consumer demand.

THE MICROWAVEABLE SEGMENT

One area of the food-preparation market that was gaining much attention from National Sea's competitors was microwaveable food products. Even by 1983, many food companies had entered the frozen entrée market, which included such products as scallops and shrimp in complete meals with rice, pasta, or vegetables. The Stouffer's division of Nestlé had just launched their Lean Cuisine line, including several new seafood entrées, and Campbell's had also announced plans for their frozen, microwaveable entrée meal, Le Menu. National Sea's activity in the microwaveable market was minimal, as was their concentration on new product development.

National Sea had been producing a line of frozen seafood entrées since 1979. For the microwaveable segment, the company had introduced shrimp entrées in 1985. Fish sticks had been National Sea's most successful packaged frozen seafood product since the early 1950s, and a decision was made to relaunch this product in a microwaveable format in 1987. The company did not experience the success that had been expected in its attempt to reposition fish sticks as a microwaveable product, a move that was intended to extend the occasions on which the product might be served. There was no clear product or convenience advantage offered by the microwaveable product since fish sticks require only 15 minutes' preparation time in a conventional oven. In addition, the preparation of the product in a microwave oven negatively affected the taste and texture, so that the product was not a crisp as when it is prepared in a conventional oven.

This lack of success with microwaveable fish sticks led the marketing department at National Sea to begin a search for a new product line that would be developed uniquely for the microwaveable market. Jim Jaques and his marketing colleagues were convinced that the development of microwaveable products was essential for National Sea, in part because close to 70 percent of Canadian homes now had microwave ovens, but also because of a general slowdown in the retail food business brought about by increasing consumer demands for convenience. With more food being consumed outside the home and in time-constrained situations, the microwave oven was widely regarded as offering food manufacturers and supermarkets an opportunity to compete with the fast-food restaurants.

The microwaveable market had witnessed an influx of companies attempting to gain a share of frozen entrée sales, including Stouffer's, Campbell's, Weight Watchers, McCain's, Heinz, and Schneider's. These firms were all working on perfecting a microwaveable product in the entrée segment. A review of the National Sea product line and their history with microwaveable products suggested that the company's participation in this market would require a "perfect" product targeted at a specific market segment. Unlike the fish sticks, the next product offered to this market must have a clear, product advantage and be "truly" microwaveable.

During preparation for their expansion into the microwaveable food market, the National Sea marketing team identified a market gap, a segment that was not currently targeted by any of their current competitors. In late 1988, in part because of their general lack of success in repositioning fish sticks as a microwaveable product, the marketing group had conducted a series of four focus group interviews (two each in Montreal and Toronto) with women who serve fish sticks to their families.

This research produced two clear results relating to fish sticks. First, the consumer already perceived fish sticks to be a convenient product and the use of the microwave oven did little to add to the perceived convenience of preparing them. Second, the preparation of fish sticks in a

microwave oven produced negative effects, in that it failed to crisp the fish sticks, leaving them soggy. As part of the focus group process, however, Jim Jaques and his marketing colleagues also learned that many parents allowed their children to use the microwave oven unsupervised, whereas they would not allow them to turn on the kitchen stove.

A second piece of evidence pointing towards the existence of a market gap came from research conducted in the United States, which showed that a number of large manufacturers of food products were in the process of launching new microwaveable snack items. While a number of companies were producing microwaveable entrées for the Canadian market, none had yet introduced snack items to their lines.

A number of brainstorming sessions conducted within the marketing group determined that no microwaveable product was currently targeted to children. The segment identified as being of particular interest to National Sea was children aged 6 to 11, constituting the "unsupervised after-school snack" segment. Microwaveable entrées currently available were priced in the range of $3.50 or more and were marketed only in packages that were clearly too large for snacks. These products were considered unsuitable for the after-school snack segment.

Targeting children with a new product offered National Sea a new segment opportunity, a basis for product differentiation, and the chance to establish the brand position with a segment that could potentially stay with the company's products over the long term. This was consistent with the concept of life-cycle marketing and the view that, if children could be exposed to fish products and to the Highliner brand at an early age, they would continue to buy the company's products as adults. Without conducting market research to quantify the direction obtained from the focus groups and the internal brainstorming sessions, National Sea decided to develop a range of microwaveable products to be targeted particularly at children.

PRODUCT DEVELOPMENT

Jim Jaques realized that because of the lack of success National Sea had experienced in repositioning its fish-stick product in 1987, there was a need for research and development in designing the next microwaveable product brought to the market. Areas of particular interest to the company's product development staff included the ability to brown the bread crumbs often used in microwaveable food products and the development of a truly microwaveable bun.

In December 1988, National Sea identified a unique microwaveable bun that could be used in the production of burgers and other snack items. The major problem with using regular buns in a microwave oven was the evaporation of moisture during the warming process. Ben's Bakery of Saint John, New Brunswick, had developed a bun with increased emulsifiers; it produced a higher moisture content but did not harden shortly after being removed from the microwave oven. A contract was signed with the bakery to supply these new buns to National Sea on an exclusive basis.

With the signing of the contract with Ben's Bakery in December 1988, National Sea's marketing and product development departments realized they had a relatively short time in which to develop the product concept. The company felt that the market segment was potentially a very large one, but that competing food companies in Canada were probably already working on similar products and would be in the market with their own versions within six months.

What was National Sea going to put into the new, microwaveable bun that had been developed? At the end of 1988, the decision was made to launch a fish filet product, with the objective of being the fastest microwaveable product on the market. The unique bun and the speed of preparation promised to be major differentiating points.

Jim Jaques realized, however, that a single microwaveable snack product was not going to be sufficient to gain a large share of the market in the face of the anticipated competition. He also knew that at least a second variety of the product would be necessary to give the consumer a choice and to provide a minimal level of exposure on retail shelves. As a result, the marketing group decided to introduce a chicken burger, in part because National Sea had gained valuable experience in the chicken business and knew the market and the product. They also had a ready internal source of supply. A conscious

decision was made to stay away from beef, as National Sea had no experience in this market and the product was considered too far removed from fish. Also, the beef market was well developed and very competitive.

In establishing the pricing objective for this product line, National Sea considered the after-school snack market and the amount children or parents would allocate to this expenditure. The objective was to enter the market at less than $2, which was about the price consumers would expect to pay for a snack meal at a fast-food restaurant. In planning for the distribution of the product, National Sea believed that the chain food stores would like the new product and would be eager to carry more microwaveable products as they were losing an increasing percentage of total food sales because of out-of-home eating.

THE LAUNCH DECISION

As the time for the planned launch on May 1, 1989, approached, a major concern for Jim Jaques and the marketing staff at National Sea was the completeness of the product line they were offering to the market. The decision that faced the National Sea marketing team was whether to launch the new line with only two stock-keeping units (SKUs) or delay the launch until other fillings could be developed for the line. As competitors launched lines containing four products (six was the usual number in the United States), it was apparent that the two-SKU line would appear to offer very limited variety to the consumer. Such a limited line presented the potential danger of creating consumer and trade boredom with the new line.

The possibility was considerable that consumers would get bored with the lack of selection in the National Sea line and discontinue purchases of this brand, moving to another brand that offered greater variety. Jim Jaques knew that consumers become bored when product lines lack variety, thereby decreasing the attention retailers are prepared to pay to a particular line. He also realized that the new line would have difficulty surviving in the extremely competitive retail-food business if National Sea was not able to offer the level of product presence that retailers demand.

Name selection for the product line was conducted with limited consumer input. Once again, internal brainstorming resulted in the selection of the name, Fastbreak. National Sea had allocated $300,000 for the May 1989 launch of the product line. This budget was mainly for retail listing fees to support the effort of getting the products into retail stores.

There was a limited budget available for consumer launch support, devoted almost entirely to a coupon campaign in the fall of 1989. Using the Catalina system of producing point-of-sale coupons for retail shoppers, National Sea offered coupons to purchasers of microwaveable products at 500 scanner-equipped food stores, primarily in Ontario and Quebec. The promotion offered $1 coupons for Fastbreak products to purchasers of directly competing products, 50¢ coupons to buyers of other microwaveable food products, and 25¢ coupons to purchasers of Fastbreak products. It planned to offer 40¢ coupons through a coupon drop in home-delivered newspapers outside Ontario and Quebec in January 1990.

THE MICROWAVEABLE SNACK SEGMENT

The spring of 1989 had been a very active time in the microwaveable food market overall. Nestlé's Handwich was announced in Canada, and in the United States there were an increasing number of microwaveable snack items being introduced. Sales in this category were strong despite what many in the industry felt were low-quality products. McCain's introduced their Burgers 'n' Fries with heavy consumer advertising. The period immediately following the launch of the National Sea Fastbreak line was very successful. Measured in sales per SKU, the Fastbreak products were outselling McCain's (which had four SKUs) and were second only to Nestlé/Stouffer's (with six SKUs). Schneider's had also launched a similar line with six SKUs.

By October 1989, share of market in the "portable meal category," as reported by A. C. Nielsen, was:

National Sea Fastbreak (2 SKU)	5.1%
McCain (4 SKU)	6.9
Schneider's (6 SKU)	15.1
Nestlé/Stouffer's (6 SKU)	18.0

Within the Fastbreak line, the chicken burger, with 3 percent of the market, was outselling the fish filet, with 2.1 percent.

Six months after the launch of the Fastbreak line, concerns were raised within National Sea concerning the performance of the new products. The line was considered a fairly low priority by some people within the company because of the limited potential percentage of total sales that it represented. The target market, although representing a market gap, was still a very small category. Approximately 70 percent of households had microwave ovens, but the number of households that might be considered potential purchasers for this product line was limited when the requirement for school-age children to be present was added.

Although there was a commitment for the company to diversify its operations beyond seafood, there was a real question about the extent to which this particular venture should be supported.

The Fastbreak line simply did not warrant the expenditure of large amounts of management and sales time on the line. The sales forecast for the new product showed that it would contribute sales of approximately $700,000 in the eight months of 1989 that it would be in the market, out of total corporate sales of more than $600 million.

The new product line was also experiencing stockouts at the retail level. The support the Fastbreak line was receiving from the trade was not great, as retailers appeared unwilling to invest in a line with only two shelf facings. The two-SKU line could not prevent the predicted consumer boredom from setting in.

The decision facing Jim Jaques and the National Sea marketing group in the late fall of 1989 concerned the future of the Fastbreak line. Should the line be discontinued and a new concept be developed for the microwaveable market? Should the current Fastbreak line be extended? Ideas that were generated internally concerning the future of the line included its extension to include more SKUs, requiring more exposure in the store, side-by-side distribution on retail shelves, and better package design.

CASE 3.3   **The Gillette Sensor Razor: Positioning a New Product***

When you hear "Gillette," one thing comes to mind — *razors*. That's to be expected since the safety razor was invented by King C. Gillette in 1903, and the company that bears his name is one of the foremost manufacturers of razors around the world.

The Gillette Co. had more than a 60 percent share of the Canadian and U.S. markets for razors in the late 1980s and intends to maintain its position of dominance in the 1990s. As a first step towards achieving that objective, Gillette introduced the new Sensor razor in both Canada and the United States in 1990. Its primary goal: Win back men who now use disposable razors (made by Bic, Schick, Wilkinson, and Gillette itself). A second goal: Attract current users of top-of-the-line razors, especially those made by Gillette's competitors.

A major challenge Gillette faced in introducing Sensor was how to position the product in relation to key factors such as its target market, main competitors, other razors, and price and quality. These positioning decisions are likely to determine the success or failure of the new product, which in turn will have a significant impact on the entire company. In terms of product development and positioning, Gillette tries to maintain a single global strategy and this sometimes complicates its positioning decisions.

In a way, Gillette created its own problem. In the mid-1970s Gillette introduced Good News, the first disposable razor. Rather than serving only a small segment of the market, Good News and its imitators have attracted large numbers of customers. What Gillette didn't count on was that the disposable's customers included many people who previously used Gillette's more profitable Atra and Trac II razors.

Disposables currently account for 40 to 50 percent of razor blade sales in Canada and the United States. Shavers who use disposable razors are not seeking the best shave; rather,

they want value and convenience. Value may be a particularly important factor because men think they spend more money on shaving than they actually do. According to Gillette research, men estimate they spend about $50 annually on razors and blades, but the actual figure is less than $20.

Along with the popularity of disposables, Gillette faces two other problems: (1) competitors such as Bic, Wilkinson, and Schick are strong and aggressive; (2) the number of young adults (new shavers) in North America is declining. Gillette's response to these challenges is the new

*Adapted from Dan Koeppel, "Gillette's Rivals Predict a Razor War," *Adweek's Marketing Week*, Oct. 16, 1989, p. 3; Martha T. Moore, "Gillette Arms Itself with Sensor Razor," *USA Today*, Oct. 4, 1989, p. B6; Lawrence Ingrassia, "A Recovering Gillette Hopes for Vindication in a High-tech Razor," *The Wall Street Journal*, Sept. 29, 1989, pp. A1, A6; *Canadian Direct Marketing News*, March 1991, p. 6.

Sensor razor. According to Peter Hoffman, Gillette's marketing VP, "We've found that the three most important attributes of a razor are closeness, comfort, and safety." Hoffman believes the Sensor combines all three features and, as a result, its introduction "will lead to a decline in sales of disposables."

What's new about Sensor? The biggest differences between Sensor and other cartridge razors are: Sensor's twin blades are mounted on tiny springs that allow each blade to move separately; it pivots in a concave (rather than convex) arc in order to remain in close contact with the face; and its skin guard is also spring-mounted to keep the blades on the face. The critical question is whether shavers will perceive these differences as important benefits.

Besides being an innovative product, Sensor differs from other Gillette cartridge razors in price. The razor and three cartridges initially carried a suggested U.S. retail price of $3.75; a pack of five replacement cartridges cost about the same amount. At these prices the Sensor was about 25 percent more expensive than Gillette's Atra Plus razor and cartridges and about twice as costly as a package of disposables. The same price differentials were to be maintained for Canada.

QUESTIONS

1. a. How new a product is Sensor? Is it truly innovative — a significantly different replacement — or simply imitative?

   b. Given your answer to (a), what special marketing challenges does Gillette face?

2. Do you think consumers will view Sensor's new product features as beneficial enough to abandon their present razor? Why or why not?

3. Gillette's executives intend that the primary buyers of the Sensor razor will be people who presently use either the top-of-the-line razors of competitors (Schick, Wilkinson) or disposable razors, rather than other Gillette products. With this goal in mind, how should Gillette position Sensor with respect to (a) competitors, (b) target market, (c) product class, and (d) price and quality?

CASE 3.4 **Segmenting Service Markets: Trading Up and Down American Express Canada Inc.**

In preparation for the 1990s, American Express (AMEX) wanted to broaden the base of its credit-card user market as well as its credit-card accepting market. AMEX is a large, global, financial services organization. American Express Canada Inc. is the U.S. parent's largest and most profitable foreign subsidiary. In Canada, the credit-card business is dominated by VISA (an estimated 13.4 million cardholders charging $20.9 million annually averaging $1,500 per card); followed by MasterCard (estimated 6 million

Case prepared by Montrose S. Sommers, University of Guelph, and adapted, in part, from Daniel Stoffman, "Class for the Mass," *Report on Business Magazine*, February 1990, pp. 42-48.

cardholders charging $9.4 billion with the same average annual charge as VISA); and AMEX (estimated 1.4 million cardholders with an annual average charge of $3,000).

Both VISA and MasterCard are affiliated with chartered banks and trust companies while AMEX has only recently (1988) received a banking charter from the federal government. Credit-card issuers make their money in three ways: annual fees; interest of balances (includes traveller's cheques that people hang onto); and the discount collected from merchants on each transaction. AMEX, unlike banks, does an interesting amount of non-financial product retailing (travel and exclusive products) itself.

With the charter, AMEX can now compete with the banking business as never before. Prior to receiving banking powers, AMEX offered a charge-card service that did not offer credit. You spent, you were billed, and you paid — all in short order. Now if you have the right card, you don't have to pay — all at once, that is. You can take your time and pay your interest. That's the AMEX banking part of the business. While the banks are relatively new at real marketing, AMEX is an old pro. For years, it has been telling its cardholders that they are "members" of an international club of successful people. And it has been doing this even though it really has been offering three different cards to three different sets of people.

The AMEX green, gold, and platinum cards are differentiated by the services package offered to cardholders. Green cardholders are most numerous; the Green is now offered to anyone who graduates from a Canadian university. Greens are said to be more upscale in income, creditworthiness, and expenditures than either VISA or MasterCard holders. Gold is upscale from Green and, of course, Platinum is everybody's favourite customer. It is estimated that there are only 8,000 Platinums in Canada; they are issued to those who charge a minimum of $10,000 a year. The typical Platinum holder is a male university graduate who is a president, CEO, or highly paid professional between the ages of 35 and 55 with an income of more than $150,000 and taking 22 business trips a year as well as nine personal flights. As a result of now being a bank, AMEX has been able to launch its Optima credit card so that it competes directly with the banks on credit terms and associated services. Thus, its ability to earn profits as a result of carrying balances and charging interest becomes greatly enhanced.

During the 1980s, AMEX expanded both its services and its reach on a global basis and most particularly in Canada. Morris Perlis, the president of AMEX Canada, saw his organization sign up more Canadians in 1989-90 than ever before. Canadians are seen as ideal prospects: AMEX sells security and we are security conscious, buying more traveller's cheques per capita than anyone else. Because of our origins, weather, and trade patterns, we are three times as likely to travel abroad as are Americans. While AMEX thinks globally, it acts locally and each country's operation deals with local market conditions in developing new services. Canadian Green cardholders of long standing can now buy, for $600, lifetime memberships. This is part of getting members to feel special — the right to be recognized. Lifetime members will have a separate service unit catering to them, sending them an exclusive newsletter, and designing travel and other products for their interest. What AMEX is promoting to these and all other cardholders is a sense of exclusivity, self-worth, privilege, status, and distinctiveness. With the company's skill at market segmentation and promotion, the approach has worked well.

While it was expanding its services to cardholders and segmenting the card market more finely by offering insurance, magazines, and specialty products, it was also adding retailers to the service firms that would accept the card. The AMEX cards can now be used extensively for purchasing products as well as services. In the past ten years, the number of Canadian retailers who display the blue and white logo has increased from 10,000 to over 70,000. The various cards can now be seen in pizza parlours and other fast-food outlets, service stations, and drug stores. In other words, the cards can be seen in all kinds of places where ordinary as opposed to special goods and services are available — and in competition with VISA and MasterCard.

Some cardholders have been heard to ask, "What's special about standing in line at a fast-food restaurant with a lot of . . . other . . . people who also use your card?" Perlis believes that providing the services that each group is interested in takes care of things, that you really can be special to a lot of different people. It's a matter of how you do it. Others believe AMEX has come to the end of the line in being special to everyone — the claim can no longer be credible and new positioning is in order.

QUESTION

Is the AMEX cardholder expansion program and its positioning inconsistent with the expansion of its service and retailer card accepting base?

P A R T

4

THE
PRICE

The development and use of a pricing structure

as part of the firm's marketing mix

We are in the process of developing a strategic marketing mix to reach our target markets and achieve our marketing goals. With our product planning completed, we now turn our attention to the pricing ingredient in the marketing mix. In the strategic planning for — and development of — the pricing structure, we face two broad tasks. First, we must determine the base price for a product, including a decision on our pricing objectives. These topics are covered in Chapter 12. Second, we must decide on the strategies (such as discounts) to employ in modifying and applying the base price. These strategies are discussed in Chapter 13.

CHAPTER 12 GOALS

In this chapter we discuss the role of price in the marketing mix—what price is, how it can be used, and how it is set relative to product costs, market demand, and competitive prices. This chapter is somewhat more difficult and quantitative than previous ones. After studying this chapter, you should be able to explain:

- The meaning of price.
- The importance of price in our economy and in an individual firm.
- The major pricing goals.
- The idea of an "expected" price.
- The several types of costs that are incurred in producing and marketing a product.
- The cost-plus method of setting a base price.
- The use of break-even analysis in setting a price.
- Prices established by marginal analysis.
- Prices established in relation only to the competitive market price.

C H A P T E R 12

Price Determination

I n 1988 a French company, Société Bic, introduced a line of perfumes in France, Italy, and Belgium. The company then planned to expand its distribution system by exporting to the United States and Canada. This is the same company that produces and markets Bic disposable cigarette lighters, Bic disposable razors, and Bic ballpoint pens, all at very low prices.

Even though Bic enjoyed huge market shares in most of its products—65 percent in lighters and 50 percent in pens—management realized that the company faced some major environmental threats. With cigarette lighters, Bic faced an inevitable long-run decline as people quit smoking. Bic lost the market share in disposable razors after Gillette introduced its MicroTrac razor as a low-priced alternative to Bic. In pens, Japanese imports and Gillette (Paper Mate, Flair, Write Brothers) were growing competitive threats.

Consequently Bic's search for hot, new growth products led the company to French perfumes. Bic estimated that retail sales of perfume in the North American market were about $3 billion a year, and growth prospects were favourable. Perfume is considered a high-priced luxury good. Prices at the time for ¼-ounce bottles of some competitive brands were:

Obsession: $60	Opium: $67.50
Chanel No. 5: $60	Giorgio: $55
Joy: $90	

Bic, however, initially priced its imported French perfume at $5 for a ¼-ounce spray bottle. The perfume was sold through Bic's traditional distribution channels, which included drugstores and supermarkets.

Do you think this product was properly priced at $5? Or will people reject Bic perfume because its price is too low? "It can't be real perfume at only $5." "I'd be embarrassed if my friends knew I was wearing $5 perfume." Such reactions can result in what economists call an inverse demand curve (a concept discussed later in this chapter), which means the lower your price is, the less you sell.

What would be a good brand name for this perfume? How about Eau de Bic? Actually the company exported four scents—two for women and two for men—and named them Nuit, Jour, Bic for Men, and Bic Sport for Men.[1]

"How much will people pay for our perfume?" Société Bic had to answer that question in the course of planning to introduce its perfumes to the North American market. In effect, this question is asked any time an organization introduces a new product or considers changing the price on an existing one. This question also reminds us that *prices are always on trial*. A price is simply an offer or an experiment to test the pulse of the market. If customers accept the offer, then the price is fine. If they reject it, the price usually will be changed quickly, or the product may even be withdrawn from the market. In this chapter we shall discuss some major methods used to determine a price. Before being concerned with actual price determination, however, executives should understand the meaning and importance of price. They must also decide on their pricing objectives.

MEANING OF PRICE

Undoubtedly, many of the difficulties associated with pricing start with the rather simple fact that often we really do not know what we are talking about. That is, we do not know the meaning of the word *price*, even though it is true that the concept is quite easy to define in familiar terms.

In economic theory, we learn that price, value, and utility are related concepts. **Utility** is the attribute of an item that makes it capable of satisfying human wants. **Value** is the quantitative measure of the worth of a product to attract other products in exchange. We may say the value of a certain hat is three baseball bats or 25 litres of gasoline. Because our economy is not geared to a slow, ponderous barter system, we use money as a common denominator of value. And we use the term *price* to describe the money value of an item. **Price** is value expressed in terms of dollars and cents, or any other monetary medium of exchange.

Practical problems arise in connection with a definition of price, however, when we try to state simply the price of a product — say, an office desk. Suppose the price quoted to Helen for an office desk was $625, while Bill paid only $375. At first glance it looks as if Bill got a better deal. Yet, when we get all the facts, we may change our opinion. Helen's desk was delivered to her office, she had a year to pay for it, and it was beautifully finished. Bill bought a partially assembled desk with no finish on it. (He was a do-it-yourself fan.) He had to assemble the drawers and legs and then painstakingly stain, varnish, and hand-rub the entire desk. He arranged for the delivery himself, and he paid cash in full at the time of purchase. Now let us ask who paid the higher price in each case. The answer is not as easy as it seemed at first glance.

This example illustrates how difficult it is to define price in an everyday business situation. Many variables are involved. The definition hinges on the problem of determining exactly what is being sold. This relates to a problem posed in Chapter 8, that of trying to define a product. In pricing, we must consider more than the physical product alone. A seller usually is pricing a combination of the physical product and several services and want-satisfying

---

[1]Adapted from "Will $4 Perfume Do the Trick for Bic?" *Business Week*, June 20, 1988, p. 89; and Andrea Rothman, "France's Bic Bets U.S. Consumers Will Go for Perfume on the Cheap," *The Wall Street Journal*, January 12, 1989, p. B6.

Defining the price of a product can be tricky because of the difficulty of determining exactly what the sale price will buy.

Mercedes-Benz

Mercedes-Benz Canada Inc.

Model 600SEL

V-type, 12 cylinder multivalve
6.0 litre
LH electronic fuel injection
Dual overhead camshafts
4-speed automatic transmission
Independent suspension
4-wheel power disc brakes

$ 169,500.00

Standard equipment:

Adaptive damping system (ADS)	Leather-covered steering wheel
Adjustable steering column	and shift knob
Alloy wheels, 8 hole design	Outside mirrors - electrically
Anti-lock braking system (ABS)	operated
Automatic slip control (ASR)	Power assisted trunk/door closers
Burled walnut trim	Power steering
Central locking system	Radio - Bose Beta sound system
Climate control, automatic	w/11 speakers
Compact disc changer	Rear headrests
Cruise control	Rear window sunshade
Electric seat adjustment - front	Supplemental restraint system (SRS)
and rear seats	including passenger side airbag
Electric sliding roof w/rear lift	Telephone
feature	Theft alarm system
Electric windows	Tinted glass - all around
Headlight wash and wiper system	Visor vanity mirrors - illuminated
Heated front and rear seats	front and rear
Leather upholstery	

Optional equipment:

Metallic paint	No charge

Total suggested retail price of show car FOB Montreal/Toronto $169,500.00
Suggested retail price only - dealer may sell for less.

benefits. Sometimes it is difficult even to define the price of the physical product or service alone. On one model of automobile, a stated price may include radio, power steering, and power brakes. For another model of the same make of car, these three items may be priced separately.

In summary, price is the value placed on goods and services. **Price** is the amount of money and/or products that are needed to acquire some combination of another product and its accompanying services.

IMPORTANCE OF PRICE

In the Economy

Pricing is considered by many to be the key activity within a free enterprise system. The product's price influences wages, rent, interest, and profits. That is, the price of a product influences the price paid for the factors of production —labour, land, capital, and entrepreneurship. Price thus is a basic regulator of the economic system because it influences the allocation of these factors of production. High wages attract labour, high interest rates attract capital, and so on. As an allocator of scarce resources, price determines what will be produced (supply) and who will get the goods and services that are produced (demand).

Criticism of the free enterprise system, and the public's demand for further restraints on the system, are often triggered by a reaction to price or to pricing policies.

M A R K E T I N G   A T   W O R K

FILE 12-1   **PRICE MEANS COST AND VALUE**

There is no question that the pricing decision is a very important one for the company trying to decide what to charge for its product or service. But how important is it to the consumer who is expected to buy that product or service? Marketers occasionally fall into the trap of believing that price is all-important in influencing the consumer's decision of whether or not to buy. Such is not always the case. Just a few years ago, a study was conducted of the retail price of food products in 50 cities and towns in Newfoundland to determine what factors contributed to differences in the prices paid by consumers in different towns. The main conclusion of the study was that the level of food prices is attributable mainly to factors such as the presence of large chain stores, the amount of competition, and the distance from main wholesale distribution centres. What was more surprising was that consumers in small, more isolated towns did not express as much concern about the level of food prices as had been expected. Consumers were more concerned about the variety of food products available and the quality of fresh fruit and vegetables. Many said that they would be prepared to pay even more for better quality and greater variety. Although consumers may complain about *price*, what they really want is better *value*.

THE PRICE IS WHAT YOU PAY FOR WHAT YOU GET

"That which we call a rose by any other name would smell as sweet."
　　　　　　　　　　　　　　　　　　　　—Romeo and Juliet, Act II, Scene 2

Tuition ....Education	Contribution ..Appreciation from your alumni fund
Interest ....Use of money	
Rent ....Use of living quarters or a piece of equipment for a period of time	Toll ....Long-distance phone call or travel on some highways or bridges
	Salary ....Services of an executive or other white-collar worker
Fare ....Taxi or bus ride	
Fee ....Services of a lawyer	Wage ....Services of a blue-collar worker
Retainer ......Accountant's services over a period of time	Commission ..Salesperson's services
Donation .....Thanks from a charity	
Subscription ..Magazines or a concert series	Honorarium ..Guest speaker
	Dues ....Membership in a union or a club
Fine ....Parking on an expired parking meter	

—then in socially undesirable situations, some people pay a price called blackmail, ransom, or bribery.

SOURCE: Suggested, in part, by John T. Mentzer and David J. Schwartz, *Marketing Today*, 4th ed., Harcourt Brace Jovanovich, San Diego, 1985, p. 599.

In the Individual Firm

The price of a product or service is a major determinant of the market demand for the item. Price affects the firm's competitive position and its market share. As a result, price has a considerable bearing on the company's revenue and net profit. It is only through price that money comes into a firm.

At the same time, there usually are forces that limit the importance of pricing in a company's marketing program. Differentiated product features or a favourite brand may be more important to consumers than price. In fact, as noted in Chapter 10, one object of branding is to decrease the effect of price on the demand for a product. To put the role of pricing in a company's marketing program in its proper perspective, then, let us say that price is important, but not all-important, in explaining marketing success.

Price — Toronto Transit calls it 1990 fares, doctors call it a fee, and universities and colleges call it tuition.

TTC Fares

ADULT

CASH FARE	$1.30
TWO-FARE TICKET	$2.50
TOKENS	7 FOR $7.50
TICKETS OR TOKENS (PACKAGED)	28 FOR $30.00
METROPASS (MONTHLY)	$56.50

MUST BE PRESENTED WITH TTC METROPASS PHOTO I.D. WHEN USED.

STUDENT

TTC STUDENT I.D. CARD MUST BE SHOWN WHEN FARE DEPOSITED OR ADULT FARE REQUIRED.

CASH FARE	80¢
TICKETS	7 FOR $3.75

CHILD

12 YEARS OF AGE OR UNDER. CHILDREN UNDER AGE OF 2 — FREE.

CASH FARE	55¢
TICKETS	8 FOR $2.50

SENIOR CITIZEN

MUST SHOW ONTARIO SENIOR CITIZEN PRIVILEGE CARD, ONTARIO HEALTH CARD WITH "65" IN THE TOP RIGHT CORNER, ELIGIBLE WAR VETERAN'S CARD OR TTC SENIORS METROPASS PHOTO I.D. CARD.

TICKETS	7 FOR $3.75
SENIORS METROPASS (MONTHLY)	$36.75

MUST BE PRESENTED WITH TTC SENIORS METROPASS PHOTO I.D. CARD WHEN USED.

DAY PASS $5.00

MONDAY-SATURDAY - GOOD FOR ONE PERSON, UNLIMITED ONE DAY TRAVEL ON ALL REGULAR TTC ROUTES AFTER 9.30 A.M. WEEKDAYS OR ALL DAY SATURDAYS.
SUNDAY & HOLIDAY - GOOD FOR UP TO 6 PERSONS, MAXIMUM 2 ADULTS. UNLIMITED ONE DAY TRAVEL ON ALL REGULAR TTC ROUTES SUNDAYS AND HOLIDAYS.

TRANSFERS ARE FREE AND MUST BE OBTAINED WHERE FARE IS PAID.

EFFECTIVE DECEMBER 31, 1990

MARKETING AT WORK

FILE 12-2   **A NEW ROLE FOR TAXES IN PRICING**

With the advent of the GST (Goods and Services Tax) and the shifting of provincial taxes to either blend with (as in Saskatchewan and Quebec) or hinder the tax, the nature of the tax regime in place, its evolution, and how it affects demand and total costs now play a much more important role in pricing than in the past. The discussion of how the GST raises, lowers, or has no effect on prices has been long and loud. In general, the provinces have avoided any consumer hostility in this discussion even though they deserve it. But what is clear is that these days, the federal and provincial tax effects on consumer perceptions of value for money must be researched and calculated into new approaches to developing pricing strategies. The nature of the cross-border shopping phenomenon underscores at least one vital aspect of this issue.

A second phenomenon associated with new taxes and their effects on prices and consumer response has to do with the "antisocial" products—cigarettes, tobacco, and alcoholic beverages being prime examples. Here again the federal government is seen by some consumers (by 6 million smokers, to be precise) as the villain while provincial governments escape attention. So-called "sin" products have always been heavily taxed simply because increased consumer cost did not affect demand proportionately. But now governments are increasing taxes in an attempt to reduce demand for these products which will reduce the social costs their consumption creates. It is estimated that 35,000 deaths per year are caused by the use of tobacco products; that $2.5 billion is added to health-care costs; and that productivity loss per smoking employee is over $2400 annually. The fact that buying cigarettes in the United States allows consumers to save $3 per pack clearly complicates the matter.

So, the new role of taxes has greater commercial, moral, and ethical implications than ever before—and price and price response is one place where you start to look at these matters.

SOURCE: Adapted, in part, from an editorial in *The Financial Post*, June 21, 1991, p. 8.

Relationship to Product Quality

Consumers rely heavily on price as an indicator of a product's quality, especially when they must make purchase decisions with incomplete information. Some consumers' perceptions of product quality vary directly with price. Thus, the higher the price, the better the quality is perceived to be. Consumers make this judgement, particularly when no other clues as to product quality are available. Consumers' quality perceptions can, of course, also be influenced by such things as store reputation and advertising.[2]

PRICING OBJECTIVES

Every marketing task — including pricing — should be directed towards the achievement of a goal. In other words, management should decide on its

---

[2]For an in-depth discussion of this topic, along with excellent bibliographies, see David J. Curry and Peter C. Riesz, ''Prices and Price/Quality Relationships: A Longitudinal Analysis,'' *Journal of Marketing*, January 1988, pp. 36–51; and Valarie A. Zeithaml, ''Consumer Perceptions of Price, Quality, and Value: A Means-End Model and Synthesis of Evidence,'' *Journal of Marketing*, July 1988, pp. 2–22.

pricing *objective* before determining the price itself. Yet, as logical as this may be, very few firms consciously establish, or explicitly state, their pricing objective. We shall discuss the following pricing objectives:

Profit-oriented:	*Sales-oriented:*	*Status quo-oriented:*
To achieve target return on investment or net sales.	To increase sales.	To stabilize prices.
	To maintain or increase market share.	To meet competition.
To maximize profit.		

The pricing goal that management selects should be entirely compatible with the goals set for the company and its marketing program. To illustrate, let's assume that the company's goal is to increase its target return on investment from the present level of 15 percent to a level of 20 percent at the end of a three-year period. Then it follows that the pricing goal during this period must be to achieve some stated percentage return on investment. It would not be logical, in this case, to adopt the pricing goal of maintaining the company's market share or of stabilizing prices.

Profit-Oriented Goals By selecting profit maximization or a target return, management focuses its attention on profit generation. Profit goals may be set either for the short run or for longer periods of time.

ACHIEVE A TARGET RETURN

A firm may price its products or services to achieve a certain percentage return on its *investment* or on its *sales*. Such goals are used by both middlemen and producers.

Many retailers and wholesalers use target return on *net sales* as a pricing objective for short-run periods. They set a percentage markup on sales that is large enough to cover anticipated operating costs plus a desired profit for the year. Loblaws or Safeway, for example may price to earn a net profit of 1.5 percent of net sales. In such cases, the *percentage* of profit may remain constant, but the *dollar* profit will vary according to the number of units sold.

Achieving a target return on *investment* is typically selected as a goal by manufacturers that are leaders in their industry. Companies such as General Motors and Union Carbide (Prestone antifreeze, Eveready batteries) may price so that they earn a net profit that is 15 or 20 percent of the firm's investment.) Target-return pricing is used frequently by industry leaders because they can set their pricing goals more independently of competition than can the smaller firms in the industry.

MAXIMIZE PROFITS

The pricing objective of making as much money as possible is probably followed by a larger number of companies than any other goal. The trouble with this goal is that the term *profit maximization* may have an ugly connotation. It is sometimes connected in the public mind with profiteering, high prices, and monopoly. Extra billing doctors as well as auto insurers in some provinces are accused of greedy maximizing. In economic theory or business practice, however, there is nothing wrong with profit maximization. Theoretically, if profits become unduly high because supply is short in relation to demand, new competitors will be attracted to the field. This will increase supply and eventually reduce profits to normal levels. Or it can lead to provincial government fee and rate setting. In the marketplace, it is difficult to find many situations

MARKETING AT WORK

FILE 12-3 **PRICE BY ANY OTHER NAME IS STILL PRICE**

In many organizations, particularly in the not-for-profit sector, the objective of pricing decisions may not be the maximization of profits. A public art gallery sets a token admission charge to help it defray some of its expenses, relying on grants from government and public donations for the bulk of its revenues. A public library certainly does not consider the maximization of revenues when it decides what fines to levy on patrons who return books late. The fine is a deterent to encourage the tardy borrower to return books on time. The local amateur theatre group sets its ticket prices so as to generate revenues, while at the same time trying not to discourage any interested member of the public from attending its performances. Universities and colleges set their tuition fees in much the same way — setting them high enough to recoup a reasonable portion of the operating costs, while at the same time wishing to ensure that no student finds it impossible to attend because of the cost. Pricing really is an art, and often not at all scientific.

---

where profiteering has existed over an extended period of time. Substitute products are available, purchases are postponable, and competition can increase to keep prices at a reasonable level. Where prices may be unduly high and entry into the field is severely limited, public outrage soon balances the scales. If market conditions and public opinion do not do the job directly, government restraints will soon bring about moderation.

A profit maximization goal is likely to be far more beneficial to a company and to the public if practised over the *long run*. To do this, however, firms sometimes have to accept short-run losses. A company entering a new geographic market or introducing a new product frequently does best by initially setting low prices to build a large clientele.

The goal should be to maximize profits on *total output* rather than on each single item marketed. A manufacturer may maximize total profits by practically giving away some articles in order to stimulate sales of other goods. Through its sponsored broadcasts and telecasts of athletic events, the Gillette Company frequently promotes razors at very low, profitless prices. Management hopes that once customers acquire Gillette razors, they will become long-term profitable customers for Gillette blades.

Sales-Oriented Goals

In some companies, management's pricing attention is focused on sales volume. In these situations, the pricing goal may be to increase sales volume or to maintain or increase the firm's market share.

INCREASE SALES VOLUME

This pricing goal is usually stated as a percentage increase in sales volume over some period of time, say, one year or three years. Management may decide to increase sales volume by discounting or by some other aggressive pricing strategy, perhaps even incurring a loss in the short run. Thus, clothing stores run end-of-season sales, and auto dealers offer rebates and below-market financing rates on new cars to stimulate sales. Many vacation resorts reduce their prices during off-seasons to increase sales volume.

MAINTAIN OR INCREASE MARKET SHARE

In some companies, both large ones and small ones, the major pricing objective is to maintain or increase the firm's market share. In the late 1980s, for instance, the Japanese yen rose considerably in relation to the Canadian and U.S. dollars. Consequently, Japanese products — autos, for example — became more expensive in dollars and Japanese companies faced the prospect of losing market share. To maintain their market shares, Toyota, Nissan, and Honda accepted smaller profit margins and reduced their costs so that they could lower their selling prices.

Occasionally a price war is started when one firm cuts its price in an effort to increase its market share. A gas station may lower the price of its gasoline below market level, or an airline may cut fares on certain routes. Other gas stations and airlines in those markets usually are forced to cut their prices just to maintain their market shares.

Status Quo Goals

Two closely related goals — **stabilizing prices** and **meeting competition** — are the least aggressive of all pricing goals, because they are designed to maintain the pricing status quo. The primary intention of a firm that adopts these goals is to avoid any form of price competition — to "live and let live."

Price stabilization often is the goal in industries where the product is highly standardized (steel, gasoline, copper, bulk chemicals) and one large firm historically has acted as a leader in setting prices. Smaller firms in these industries simply adopt a follow-the-leader policy (meeting competition) when setting their own prices. A major reason for seeking price stability is to avoid price wars.

Gas stations' pricing goal usually is to meet competition.

Even in industries where there are no price leaders, countless firms consciously price their products to meet the competitive market price. This pricing policy gives management an easy means of avoiding difficult pricing decisions.

Just because firms adopt status quo pricing goals that circumvent price competition does not mean that they are unaggressive in marketing. Quite the contrary! Typically these companies compete aggressively using the other major elements in the marketing mix—product, distribution, and especially promotion. This approach is called nonprice competition.

FACTORS INFLUENCING PRICE DETERMINATION

Knowing its objective, a company then can move to the heart of price management—the actual determination of the base price of a product or service. By **base price** (or list price) we mean the price of one unit of the product at its point of production or resale. This is the price before allowance is made for discounts, freight charges, or any other modification such as those discussed in the next chapter.

The same general procedure is followed in pricing both new and established products. However, the pricing of an established product usually involves little difficulty, because the exact price or a narrow range of prices are usually dictated by consumer and competitive behaviour in the market. In the pricing of new products, though, the decisions called for in the pricing process typically are important and difficult.

In the price-determination process, several factors usually influence the final decision. The key factors, however, are as follows:

- Demand for the product.
- Target share of the market.
- Competitive reactions.
- Other parts of the marketing mix—the product, distribution channels, and promotion.

Estimated Demand for the Product

An important step in pricing a product is to estimate the total demand for it. This is easier to do for an established product than for a new one. Two steps in demand estimation are, first, to determine whether there is a price that the market expects and, second, to estimate the sales volume at different prices.

THE "EXPECTED" PRICE

The "expected" price for a product is the price at which customers consciously or unconsciously value it—what they think the product is worth. The expected price usually is expressed as a *range* of prices, rather than as specific amount. Thus, the expected price might be "between $250 and $300" or "not over $20." Consumers sometimes can be surprisingly shrewd in evaluating a product and its expected price. After all, they "price" across a wide range of products.

A producer must also consider the trade reaction to the price. Middlemen are more likely to give an article favourable treatment in their stores if they approve of its price. Retail or wholesale buyers can frequently examine an item and make an accurate estimate of the selling price that the market will accept.

It is possible to set a price too low. If the price is much lower than that which the market expects, sales may be lost. For example, it would probably be a mistake for a well-known cosmetics manufacturer to put a 99-cent price tag on its lipstick or to price its imported perfume at $2.99 a millilitre. Either

ELASTICITY OF DEMAND
A REVIEW OF A BASIC ECONOMIC CONCEPT

Elasticity of demand refers to the effect that unit-price changes have on the number of units sold and the total revenue. (The total revenue — that is, the total dollar sales volume — equals the unit price times the number of units sold.) We say that the demand is **elastic** when (1) reducing the unit price causes an increase in total revenue or (2) raising the unit price causes a decrease in total revenue. In the first case, the cut in unit price results in a boost in quantity sold and more than offsets the price cut — hence the increase in total revenue.

These situations are illustrated in Fig. 12-A. We start with a situation wherein, at $5 a unit, we sell 100 units and the total revenue equals $500. When we lower the price to $4 a unit, the quantity sold increases to 150 and the resultant total revenue also goes up — to $600. When the unit price is boosted to $6, however, the quantity sold drops off so much (to 70 units) that the total revenue also declines (to $420).

Demand is **inelastic** when (1) a price cut causes total dollar sales volume to decline or (2) a price rise results in an increase in total revenue. In each of these two situations the changes in unit price more than offset the relatively small changes in quantities sold. That is, when the price is cut, the increase in quantity sold is not enough. When the unit price

is raised, it more than offsets the decline in quantity sold, so total revenue goes up.

In Fig. 12-B, again we start with a unit price of $5, we sell 100 units, and our total revenue is $500. When we lower the unit price to $4, our quantity sold increases to 115. But this is not enough to offset the price cut, so our total revenue declines to $460. When we raise our unit price to $6, our quantity sold falls off 90. But the price increase more than offsets the drop in quantity sold, so our total revenue goes up to $540.

As a generalization, the industry demand for necessities (salt, sugar, gasoline, telephone service, gas and electric service) tends to be inelastic. If the price of gasoline, for example, goes up or down say, 4 or 8 cents a litre, the total number of litres sold does not change very much. On the other hand, the demand for products purchased with our discretionary income (luxury items, large appliances, furniture, autos) typically is much more elastic. Moreover, the demand for individual *brands* is much more elastic than is the demand for the broader *product* category. Thus, the demand for Air Canada seats or Hertz rental cars is far more elastic (price-sensitive) than is the demand for air travel or rented cars in general.

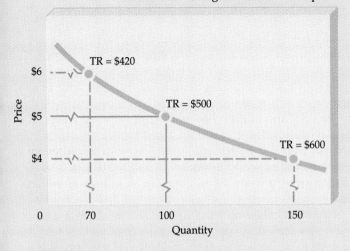

FIGURE 12-A
Elastic demand.

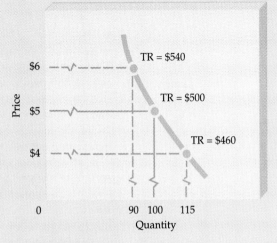

FIGURE 12-B
Inelastic demand.

MARKETING AT WORK

FILE 12-4 EXPECTING THE ALL-YEAR BOXING DAY SALE

It used to be that widespread price slashing during the holiday season came *after* Christmas. It used to be. Not any more. Increasingly, over the last decade, retailers' Christmas sales have been held *before* Christmas. This pre-Christmas price slashing has become such a trend that consumers now wait until the last possible moment in order to get the best bargains on their Christmas gifts as well as nonholiday items. Now that consumer expectations have been re-established, retailers are at a loss as to what to do next.

Source: Adapted from Marina Strauss, ''Price-Slashing a Short Term Solution,'' *Globe and Mail*, November 14, 1990, p. B4.

---

customers will be suspicious of the quality of the product or their self-concepts will not let them buy such low-priced merchandise. More than one seller has raised the price of a product and experienced a considerable increase in sales. this situation is called **inverse demand**—the higher the price, the greater the unit sales. This inverse demand situation usually exists only within a given price range and only at the lower price levels. Once a price rises to some particular point, inverse demand ends and the usual-shaped demand curve takes over. That is, demand then declines as prices rise.

How do sellers determine expected prices? They may submit articles to experienced retailers or wholesalers for appraisal. A manufacturer of business products might get price estimates by showing product models or blueprints to engineers working for prospective customers. A third alternative is to survey potential consumers. They may be shown an article and asked what they would pay for it. Often, however, there is a considerable difference between what people say a product is worth and what they will actually pay for it. A more effective approach is to market the product in a few limited test areas. By trying different prices under controlled test-market conditions, the seller can determine at least a reasonable range of prices.

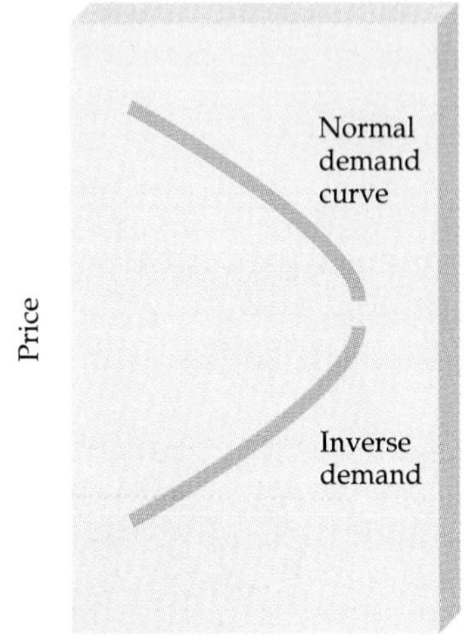

ESTIMATES OF SALES AT VARIOUS PRICES

It is extremely helpful to estimate what the sales volume will be at several different prices. By doing this, the seller is, in effect, determining the demand curve for the product and thus determining its demand elasticity. These estimates of sales at different prices also are useful in determining break-even points—a topic that we discuss later in this chapter.

There are several methods that sellers can use to estimate potential sales at various prices. Some of these methods were suggested in the preceding section on expected prices. Other methods were discussed in the sales forecasting section of Chapter 7. To illustrate, a company can conduct a survey of buyer intentions to determine consumer buying interest at different prices. Or management can conduct test-market experiments, offering the product at a different price in each market and measuring consumer purchases at these different prices. For an established product, management can measure sales of competitors' products, especially when reasonably similar models are offered at different prices.

FIGURE 12-1 Quantity sold
Inverse demand.

A seller may be able to design a computerized model that would simulate field selling conditions and sales responses at various prices. Some firms can get these estimates by surveying their wholesalers and retailers. For some business products, the sales estimates can be generated by using the sales-force composite method of forecasting.

Target Share of Market

The market share targeted by a company is a major factor to consider in determining the price of a product or service. A company striving to increase its market share may price more aggressively (lower base price, larger discounts) than a firm that wants to maintain its present market share.

The expected share of the market is influenced by present production capacity and ease of competitive entry. It would be a mistake for a firm to aim for a larger share of the market than its plant capacity can sustain. So, if management will not expand its plant (because ease of competitive entry will drive down future profits), then the initial price should be set relatively high.

Competitive Reactions

Present and potential competition is an important influence in determining a base price. Even a new product is distinctive for only a limited time, until the inevitable competition arrives. The threat of *potential* competition is greatest when the field is easy to enter and the profit prospects are encouraging. Competition can also come from three other sources:

- *Directly similar products:* Nike running shoes versus Adidas or Reebok shoes.
- *Available substitutes:* Air freight versus truck or rail freight.
- *Unrelated products seeking the same consumer dollar:* Videocassette recorder (VCR) versus a bicycle or a weekend excursion.

Other Parts of the Marketing Mix

The base price of a product normally is influenced considerably by the other major ingredients in the marketing mix.

THE PRODUCT

We have already observed that the price of a product is influenced substantially by whether it is a new item or an older, established one. The importance of the product in its end use must also be considered. To illustrate, there is little price competition among manufacturers of packaging materials or producers of industrial gases, and a stable price structure exists. These industrial products are only an incidental part of the final article, so customers will buy the least expensive product consistent with the required quality. The price of a product is influenced also (1) by whether the product may be leased as well as purchased outright, (2) by whether the product may be returned to the seller, and (3) by whether a trade-in is involved.

CHANNELS OF DISTRIBUTION

The channels selected and the types of middlemen used will influence a manufacturer's pricing. A firm selling both through wholesalers and directly to retailers often sets a different factory price for each of these two classes of customers. The price to wholesalers is lower because they perform activities (services) that the manufacturer otherwise would have to perform itself — activities such as providing storage, granting credit to retailers, and selling to small retailers.

PROMOTIONAL METHODS

The promotional methods used, and the extent to which the product is promoted by the manufacturer or middlemen, are still other factors to consider in pricing. If major promotional responsibility is placed upon retailers, they ordinarily will be charged a lower price for a product than if the manufacturer advertises it heavily. Even when a manufacturer promotes heavily, it may want its retailers to use local advertising to tie in with national advertising. Such a decision must be reflected in the manufacturer's price to these retailers.

COST-PLUS PRICING

We now are at the point in our price determination discussion where we can talk about setting a *specific* selling price. Most approaches used by companies to establish base prices are variations of one of the following methods:

- Prices are based on total cost plus a desired profit. (Break-even analysis is a variation of this method.)
- Prices are based on marginal analysis — a consideration of both market demand and supply.
- Prices are based only on competitive market conditions.

Cost-plus pricing means setting the price of one unit of a product equal to the unit's total cost plus the desired profit on the unit. Suppose a contractor figures that the labour and materials required to build and sell 10 houses will cost $750,000, and that other expenses (office rent, depreciation on equipment, wages of management, and so on) will equal $150,000. On this total cost of $900,000, the contractor desires a profit of 10 percent of cost. The cost plus the profit amount is $990,000, so each of the 10 houses is priced at $99,000.

TABLE 12-1 **Example of cost-plus pricing**
Actual results often differ from the original plans because various types of costs react differently to changes in output.

Costs, selling prices, profit	Number of houses built and sold	
	Planned = 10	Actual = 8
Labour and materials costs ($75,000 per house)	$750,000	$600,000
Overhead (fixed) costs	150,000	150,000
Total costs	$900,000	$750,000
Total sales at $99,000 per house	990,000	792,000
Profit: Total	$90,000	$42,000
Per house	$9,000	$5,250
As % of cost	10%	5.6%

While this is an easily applied pricing method, it has one serious limitation. It does not account for the fact that there are different types of costs, and that these costs are affected differently by changes in level of output. In our housing example, suppose the contractor built and sold only eight houses at the cost-plus price of $99,000 each. As shown in Table 12-1, total sales would then be $792,000. Labour and materials chargeable to the eight houses would total $600,000 ($75,000 per house). Since the contractor would still incur the full $150,000 in overhead expenses, however, the total cost would be $750,000. This would leave a profit of only $42,000, or $5,250 per house instead of the

Should the builder use the cost-plus method when pricing these condominium units?

anticipated $9,000. On a percentage basis, the profit would be only 5.6 percent of total cost rather than the desired 10 percent.

Cost Concepts   The total unit costs of a product is made up of several types of costs that react differently to changes in the quantity produced. Thus the total unit cost of a product changes as output expands or contracts. A more sophisticated approach to cost-plus pricing takes such changes into consideration.

The cost concepts in the nearby box entitled "Different Kinds of Costs" are fundamental to our discussion. These nine cost concepts and their interrelationships may be studied in Table 12-2 and Fig. 12-2, which is based on the table. The interrelationship among the various *average unit* costs is displayed graphically in the figure and may be explained briefly as follows:

- The **average fixed cost curve** declines as output increases because the total of the fixed costs is spread over an increasing number of units.
- The **average variable cost curve** usually is U-shaped. It starts high because average variable costs for the first few units of output are high. Variable costs per unit then decline as the company realizes efficiencies in production. Eventually the average variable cost curve reaches its lowest point, reflecting optimum output as far as variable costs (not total costs) are concerned. In Fig. 12-2 this point is at three units of output. Beyond that point the average variable cost rises, reflecting the increase in unit variable costs caused by overcrowded facilities and other inefficiencies. If the variable costs per unit were constant, then the average variable cost curve would be a horizontal line at the level of the constant unit variable cost.
- The **average total cost curve** is the sum of the first two curves — average fixed cost and average variable cost. It starts high, reflecting the fact that total *fixed* costs are spread over so few units of output. As output increases, the average total cost curve declines, because the unit fixed cost and unit variable cost are decreasing. Eventually the point of lowest total cost per unit is reached (four units of output in the figure). Beyond that optimum point, diminishing returns set in and the average total cost curve rises.
- The **marginal cost curve** has a more pronounced U-shape than the other curves in Fig. 12-2. The marginal cost curve slopes downward until the second unit of output, at which point the marginal costs start to increase.

Now note the relationship between the marginal cost curve and the average

TABLE 12-2 **Costs for an individual firm**

Total fixed costs do not change in the short run, despite increases in quantity produced. Variable costs are the costs of inputs—materials, labour, power. Total variable costs increase as production quantity rises. Total cost is the sum of all fixed and variable costs. The other measures in the table are simply methods of looking at costs per unit; they always involve dividing a cost by the number of units produced.

(1)	(2)	(3)	(4)	(5)	(6)	(7)	(8)
					Average	Average	Average
	Total	Total	Total	Marginal	fixed	variable	Total cost
Quantity	fixed	variable	costs	cost	cost	cost	per unit
produced	costs	costs	(2) + (3)	per unit	(2) ÷ (1)	(3) ÷ (1)	(4) ÷ (1)
0	$256	$ 0	$256		Infinity	$ 0	Infinity
1	256	84	340	$ 84	$256.00	84	$340.00
2	256	112	368	28	128.00	56	184.00
3	256	144	400	32	85.33	48	133.33
4	256	224	480	80	64.00	56	120.00
5	256	400	656	176	51.20	80	131.20

FIGURE 12-2
Unit cost curves for an individual firm.
This figure is based on data in Table 12-2. Here we see how *unit* costs change as quantity increases. Using cost-plus pricing, two units of output would be priced at $184 each, whereas four units would sell for $120 each.

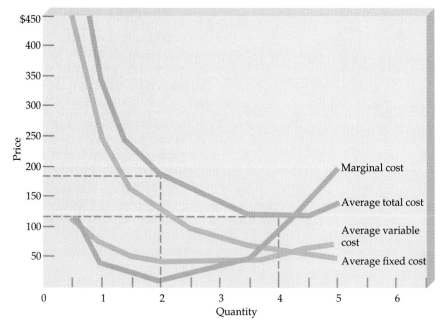

total cost curve. The average total cost curve slopes downward *as long as the marginal cost is less than the average total cost*. Even though the marginal cost increases after the second unit, the average total cost curve continues to slope downward until the fourth unit. This is so because marginal cost—even when it is going up—is still less than average total cost.

The marginal cost and average total cost curves intersect at the lowest point of the average total cost curve. Beyond that point (the fourth unit in the example), the cost of producing and selling the next unit is higher than the average cost of all units. Therefore, from then on the average total cost rises. This occurs because the average variable cost is increasing faster than the average fixed cost is decreasing. Table 12-2 shows that producing the fifth unit reduces the average fixed cost by $12.80 (from $64 to $51.20), but causes the average variable cost to increase by $24.

Different kinds of costs

- A **fixed cost** is an element, such as rent, executive salaries, or property tax, that remains constant regardless of how many items are produced. Such a cost continues even if production stops completely. It is called a fixed cost because it is difficult to change in the short run (but not in the long run).
- **Total fixed cost** is the sum of all fixed costs.
- **Average fixed cost** is the total fixed cost divided by the number of units produced.
- A **variable cost** is an element, such as labour or material cost, that is directly related to production. Variable costs can be controlled in the short run simply by changing the level of production. When production stops, for example, all variable production costs become zero.
- **Total variable cost** is the sum of all variable costs. The more units produced, the higher this cost is.
- **Average variable cost** is the total variable cost divided by the number of units produced. Average variable cost is usually high for the first few units produced. It decreases as production increases due to such things as quantity discounts on materials and more efficient use of labour. Beyond some optimum output, it increases, because of such factors as crowding of production facilities and overtime pay.
- **Total cost** is the sum of total fixed cost and total variable cost for a specific quantity produced.
- **Average total cost** is the total cost divided by the number of units produced.
- **Marginal cost** is the cost of producing and selling one more unit. Usually the marginal cost of the last unit is the same as the variable cost of that unit.

Refinements in Cost-Plus Pricing

Once a company understands that not all costs react in the same way to changes in output, refinements in cost-plus pricing are possible. Let's assume that the desired profit is included either in the fixed cost or the variable cost schedule. That is, profit is included as a cost in Table 12-2 and Fig. 12-2. Then once the quantity to be produced has been determined, management can refer to the table or graph to find the appropriate price. If a firm decides to produce three units in our example, the selling price will be $133.33 per unit. A production run of four units would be priced at $120 per unit.

This pricing method assumes that all the intended output will be produced and sold. If fewer units are produced, each would have to sell for a higher price in order to cover all costs and show a profit. But, obviously, if business is slack and output must be cut, it is not wise to raise the unit price. Thus the difficulty in this pricing approach is that market demand is ignored.

Prices Based on Marginal Costs Only

Another approach to cost-plus pricing is to set a price that will cover only marginal costs, not total costs. Refer again to the cost schedules shown in Table 12-2 and Fig. 12-1, and assume that a firm is operating at an output level of three units. Under marginal cost pricing, this firm can accept an order for one more unit at $80, instead of the total unit cost of $120. The company is then trying to cover only its variable costs. If the firm can sell for any price over $80 — say, $85 or $90 — the excess contributes to the payment of fixed costs.

Not all orders can be priced to cover only variable costs. Marginal cost pricing may be feasible, however, if management wants to keep its labour force employed during a slack season. Marginal cost pricing may also be used when one product is expected to attract business for another. A department store may price meals in its café at a level that covers only the marginal costs. The reasoning is that this café will bring shoppers to the store, where they will buy other, more profitable products.

Cost-Plus Pricing by Middlemen

Cost-plus pricing is widely used by retailing and wholesaling middlemen. At least it seems this way at first glance. A retailer, for example, pays a given amount to buy products and have them delivered to the store. Then the retailer adds an amount (a markup) to the acquisition cost. This markup is estimated to be sufficient to cover the store's expenses and still provide a reasonable profit. Thus a clothing store may buy a garment for $30 including freight, and price the item at $50. The price of $50 reflects a markup of 40 percent based on the selling price, or $66^2/_3$ percent based on the merchandise cost.

Different types of retailers will require different percentage markups because of the nature of the products handled and the services offered. A self-service supermarket has lower costs and thus a lower average markup than a full-service delicatessen. Figure 12-3 shows an example of markup pricing by middlemen. The topic of markups is discussed in more detail in Appendix B.

To what extent is cost-plus pricing truly used by middlemen? At least three significant indications suggest that what seems to be cost-plus pricing is really market-influenced pricing:

1. Most retail prices set by applying average percentage markups are really only price offers. If the merchandise does not sell at the original price, that price will be lowered until it reaches a level at which the merchandise will sell.
2. Many retailers do not use the same markup on all the products they carry. A supermarket will have a markup of 6 to 8 percent on sugar and soap products, 15 to 18 percent on canned fruit and vegetables, and 25 to 30 percent on fresh meats and produce. These different markups for different products definitely reflect competitive considerations and other aspects of market demand.
3. The middleman usually does not actually set a base price but only adds a percentage to the price that has already been set by the producer. The producer's price is set to allow each middleman to add the customary

FIGURE 12-3
Examples of markup pricing by retailers and wholesalers.

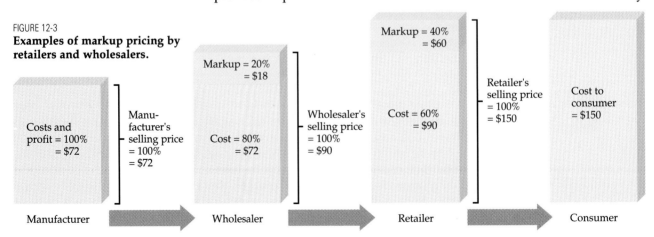

Manufacturer		Wholesaler		Retailer		Consumer
Costs and profit = 100% = $72	Manufacturer's selling price = 100% = $72	Markup = 20% = $18 / Cost = 80% = $72	Wholesaler's selling price = 100% = $90	Markup = 40% = $60 / Cost = 60% = $90	Retailer's selling price = 100% = $150	Cost to consumer = $150

markup and still sell at a competitive retail price. The key price is set by the producer, with an eye on the market.

Evaluation of Cost-Plus Pricing

We have emphasized that a firm must be market-oriented and must cater to consumers' wants. Why, then, are we now considering cost-plus pricing? Cost-plus pricing is mentioned so widely in business that it must be understood. Adherents of cost-plus pricing point to its simplicity and its ease of determination. They say that costs are a known quantity, whereas attempts to estimate demand for pricing purposes are mainly guesswork.

This opinion is questionable on two counts. First, it is doubtful that accurate cost data are available. We know a fair amount about cost-volume relationships in production costs, but what we know is still insufficient. Furthermore, information regarding marketing costs is woefully inadequate. Second, it is indeed difficult to estimate demand — that is, to construct a demand schedule that shows sales volume at various prices. Nevertheless, sales forecasting and other research tools can do a surprisingly good job in this area.

Critics of cost-plus pricing do not say that costs should be disregarded in pricing. Costs should be a determinant, they maintain, but not the only one. Costs are a floor under a firm's prices. If goods are priced under this floor for a long time, the firm will be forced out of business. But when used by itself, cost-plus pricing is a weak and unrealistic method, because it ignores competition and market demand.

BREAK-EVEN ANALYSIS

One way to use market demand in price determination, and still consider costs, is to conduct a break-even analysis and determine break-even points. A **break-even point** is that quantity of output at which total revenue equals total costs, *assuming a certain selling price*. There is a different break-even point for each different selling price. Sales of quantities above the break-even output result in a profit on each additional unit. The further the sales are above the break-even point, the higher the total and unit profits. Sales below the break-even point result in a loss to the seller.

Determining the Break-Even Point

The method of determining a break-even point is illustrated in Table 12-3 and Fig. 12-4. In our hypothetical situation, the company's fixed costs are $250 and its variable costs are constant at $30 a unit. Recall that in our earlier example (Table 12-2 and Fig. 12-2) we assumed that unit variable costs were *not* constant; they fluctuated. Now to simplify our break-even analysis, we are assuming that unit variable costs *are* constant.

Therefore, the total cost of producing one unit is $280. For five units the total cost is $400 ($30 multiplied by 5, plus $250). In Fig. 12-4 the selling price is $80 a unit. Consequently, every time a unit is sold, $50 is contributed to overhead (fixed costs). The variable costs are $30 per unit, and these costs are incurred in producing each unit. But any revenue over $30 can be used to help cover fixed costs. At a selling price of $80, the company will break even if five units are sold because a $50 contribution from each of five units will just cover the total fixed costs of $250.

Stated another way, variable costs for five units are $150 and fixed costs are $250, for a total cost of $400. This is equal to the revenue from five units sold at $80 each. So, for an $80 selling price, the break-even volume is five units.

The break-even point may be found with this formula:

TABLE 12-3 **Computation of break-even point**

At each of several prices we wish to find out how many units must be sold to cover all costs. At a unit price of $100, the sale of each unit contributes $70 to cover overhead expenses. We must sell about 3.6 units to cover the $250 fixed cost. See Figures 12-4 and 12-5 for a visual portrayal of the data in this table.

(1) Unit price	(2) Unit variable costs	(3) Contribution to overhead (1) − (2)	(4) Overhead (total fixed costs)	(5) Break-even point (4) ÷ (3)
$ 60	$30	$ 30	$250	8.3 units
80	30	50	250	5.0 units
100	30	70	250	3.6 units
150	30	120	250	2.1 units

FIGURE 12-4
Break-even chart with selling price of $80 per unit.
Here the break-even point is reached when the company sells five units. Fixed costs, regardless of quantity produced and sold, are $250. The variable cost per unit is $30. If this company sells five units, total cost is $400 (variable cost of 5 × $30, or $150, plus fixed cost of $250). At a selling price of $80, the sale of five units will yield $400 revenue, and costs and revenue will equal each other. At the same price, the sale of each unit above five yields a profit.

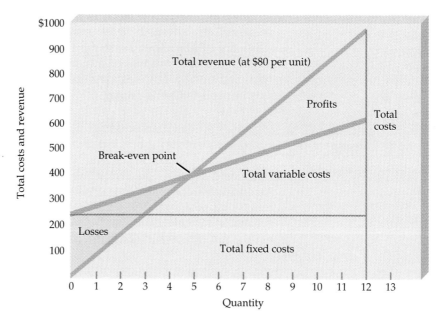

$$\text{Break-even point in units} = \frac{\text{Total fixed costs}}{\text{Unit contribution to overhead}}$$

$$= \frac{\text{Total fixed costs}}{\text{Selling price} - \text{Average variable cost}}$$

The basic assumptions underlying these calculations are as follows:

- Total fixed costs are constant. In reality they may change, although they usually don't in the short run. It is reasonably easy, however, to develop a break-even chart in which fixed costs, and consequently total costs, are stepped up at several intervals.
- Variable costs remain constant per unit of output. In the earlier discussion of cost structure, however, we noted that average variable costs usually fluctuate.
- Figure 12-4 shows a break-even point only where the unit price is $80. It is highly desirable to calculate break-even points for several different selling prices.

MARKETING AT WORK

FILE 12-5   **PRICING FOR EXPORT MARKETING**

How should a company price a product for export? This question cannot be answered easily because it is difficult to generalize about export pricing. Not only are there significant differences among companies' philosophies, cultures, and products, but also pricing is affected by different constraints in the various foreign markets.

For example, intensive negotiations normally occur when selling in the Middle East. When Regal Ware, a producer of kitchen cookware, sells in these markets, the company sets a higher list price to allow room for bargaining. On the other hand, a manufacturer of grain storage and handling equipment refuses to engage in price bargaining in the Middle East. This company is convinced that once you make price concessions, the bargaining process will continue indefinitely through future transactions.

The three major methods of export price determination are rigid cost-plus pricing, flexible cost-plus pricing, and marginal cost pricing. Seventy percent of the firms in one survey used some form of cost-plus pricing when engaging in export marketing. For these firms, pricing was a static, rather than dynamic, element in their marketing mix. In fact, over half the firms practising cost-plus pricing reported that they adhered *rigidly* to this method of price determination. Autotrol, a manufacturer of water treatment and control equipment, has used rigid cost-plus pricing successfully for the past 15 years. This company's major markets include Western Europe, Japan, Australia, and New Zealand.

In recent years, competitive pressures have induced many firms to employ a more flexible cost-plus pricing method. Typically these firms offer some form of discounts or other price concessions to ensure making a sale. The Baughman Company, a producer of grain storage silos, has identical export and domestic prices, before exporting costs are added. However, the company will make price concessions when an important export sale is at stake.

The third export pricing method — marginal costs — was used by about 30 percent of the firms covered in the survey. The price is set at a level that covers only variable production costs plus exporting expenses. This price does not cover fixed costs for manufacturing and research and development, nor does it cover domestic marketing expenses. Firms using this pricing method have unused production capacity and assume that the exported products could not be sold at full cost.

Perhaps the bottom-line answer to our original question is "It all depends." Export price setting is complex, and no single method suits a company at all times.

Adapted from: Tamer Cavusgil, "Unraveling the Mystique of Export Pricing," *Business Horizons*, May/June 1988, pp. 54–63.

Evaluation of Break-Even Analysis

Many of the underlying assumptions in break-even analysis — such as that costs are nonfluctuating — are unrealistic in real-world business operations. Consequently, break-even analysis has limited value in companies where demand and/or average unit costs fluctuate frequently.

Another major drawback of break-even analysis is that it ignores market demand at the various prices. Table 12-3, for example, shows what revenue will be at the different prices *if* (and it is a big if) the given number of units can be sold at these prices. The completed break-even charts show only the amount that must be sold at the stated price to break even. The charts do not tell us whether we *can* actually sell this amount. The amount the market will buy at a given price could well be below the break-even point. For instance, at a selling price of $80 per unit, the break-even point is five units. But competition and/or a volatile market may prevent the company from selling those five units. If the company can sell only three or four units, the firm will not break even. It will show a loss.

These limitations, however, should not lead management to dismiss break-even analysis as a pricing tool. Even in its simplest form, break-even analysis is very helpful because in the short run many firms experience reasonably stable cost and demand structures.[3]

PRICES BASED ON MARGINAL ANALYSIS

Another method of price setting is based on marginal analysis—a consideration of both demand and costs to determine the best price for profit maximization. This policy of price determination is thus best suited for companies whose pricing goal is to maximize profit. However, firms with other pricing goals might use this method in special situations or perhaps to compare prices determined by different means.

Determining the Price

To use marginal analysis, the price setter must understand the concepts of average and marginal revenue, in addition to average and marginal cost. **Marginal revenue** is the income derived from the sale of the last unit. **Average revenue** is the unit price at a given level of unit sales. It is calculated by dividing total revenue by the number of units sold. Referring to the hypothetical demand schedule in Table 12-4, we see that the company can sell one unit at $80. To sell two units, it must reduce its price to $75 for each unit. Thus the company receives an additional $70 (marginal revenue) by selling two units instead of one. The fifth unit brings a marginal revenue of $53. After the sixth unit, however, total revenue declines each time the unit price is lowered to sell an additional unit. Hence there is a negative marginal revenue.

The price-setting process that considers both supply and demand is illustrated in Fig. 12-5. We assume that a firm will continue to produce units as long as revenue from the last unit sold exceeds the cost of producing this last unit. That is, output continues to increase as long as marginal revenue exceeds marginal cost. At the point where they meet (quantity Q in Fig. 12-5*a*), production theoretically should cease. Ordinarily a company will not want to sell a unit at a price less than its out-of-pocket (variable) costs of production. The optimum volume of output is the quantity level at which *marginal cost equals marginal revenue*, or quantity Q.

The unit price is determined by locating the point on the average revenue curve that represents an output of Q units. Remember that average revenue represents the unit price. The average revenue curve has been added in Fig. 12-5*b*. The unit price at which to sell quantity Q is represented by point C. It is price B in Fig. 12-5*b*.

---

[3]For a more sophisticated approach to break-even analysis—one that includes semifixed costs—and is of more practical value in situations typically faced by marketing executives, see Thomas L. Powers, ''Breakeven Analysis with Semifixed Costs,'' *Industrial Marketing Management*, February 1987, pp. 35–41.

TABLE 12-4 **Demand schedule for an individual firm**

At each market price, a certain quantity of the product will be demanded. Marginal revenue is simply the amount of additional money gained by selling one more unit. In this example, the company no longer gains marginal revenue after it has sold the sixth unit at a price of $60.

Units sold	Unit price (average revenue)	Total revenue	Marginal revenue
1	$80	$ 80	
2	75	150	$ 70
3	72	216	66
4	68	272	56
5	65	325	53
6	60	360	35
7	50	350	− 10
8	40	320	− 30

FIGURE 12-5
Price setting and profit maximization through marginal analysis.

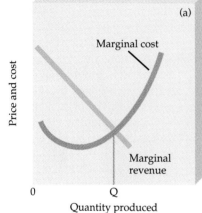 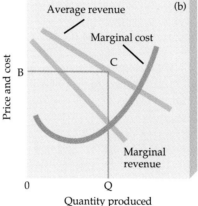 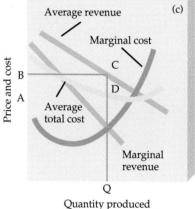

The average unit total cost curve has been added in Fig. 12-5c. It shows that, for output quantity Q, the average unit cost is represented by point D. This average unit cost is A. Thus, with a price of B and an average unit cost of A, the company enjoys a unit profit given by AB in the future. Total profit is represented by area ABCD (quantity Q times unit profit AB).

Evaluation of Marginal Analysis Pricing

Marginal analysis as a basis for price setting has enjoyed only limited use. Business people claim that better data are needed for plotting the curves exactly. Marginal analysis can be used, they feel, to study past price movements, but it cannot serve as a practical basis for setting prices.

On the brighter side, management's knowledge of costs and demand is improving. Computerized data bases are bringing more complete and detailed information to management's attention all the time. Earlier we pointed out that management usually can estimate demand within broad limits, and this is helpful. And experienced management in many firms can do a surprisingly accurate job of estimating marginal and average costs and revenues.

Marginal analysis can also have practical value if management will adjust the price in light of some conditions discussed earlier in this chapter. In Fig. 12-5, the price was set at point B. But, in the short run, management may price below B, or even below A, adopting an aggressive pricing strategy to increase market share or to discourage competition.

PRICES SET IN RELATION TO MARKET ALONE

Cost-plus pricing is one extreme among pricing methods. At the other end of the scale is a method whereby a firm's prices are set in relation *only* to the market price. The seller's price may be set right at the market price to meet the competition, or it may be set either above or below the market price.

Pricing to Meet Competition

Management may decide to price a product right at the competitive level in several situations. One such situation occurs when the market is highly competitive and the firm's product is not differentiated significantly from competing products. To some extent, this method of pricing reflects market conditions that parallel those found under perfect competition. That is, product differentiation is absent, buyers and sellers are well informed, and the seller has no discernible control over the selling price. Most producers of agricultural products and small firms marketing well-known, standardized products ordinarily use this pricing method.

The sharp drop in revenue that occurs when the price is raised above the prevailing level indicates that the individual seller faces a *kinked demand* (see Fig. 12-6). The prevailing price is at A. If the seller tries to go above that price, the demand for the product drops sharply, as indicated by the flat average revenue curve above point P. At any price above A, then, demand is highly elastic—total revenue declines. Below price A, demand is highly inelastic, as represented by the steeply sloping average revenue curve and the negative marginal revenue curve. Total revenue decreases each time the price is reduced to a level below A. The prevailing price is strong. Consequently, a reduction in price by one firm will not increase the firm's unit sales very much—certainly not enough to offset the loss in average revenue.

Up to this point in our discussion of pricing to meet competition, we have observed market situations that involve many sellers. Oddly enough, the same pricing method is often used when the market is dominated by a few firms, each marketing similar products. This type of market structure, called an **oligopoly**, exists in such industries as copper, aluminum, soft drinks, breakfast cereals, auto tires, and even among barber shops and grocery stores within a smaller community.

The demand curve facing an individual seller in an oligopoly is a kinked one, as in Fig. 12-6. An oligopolist must price at market level to maximize profit. Selling *above* market price will result in a drastic reduction in total revenue, because the average revenue curve is so elastic above point P. If an oligopolist cuts its price *below* the market price, all other members of the oligopoly must respond immediately. Otherwise the price cutter will enjoy a substantial increase in business. Therefore, competitors do retaliate with comparable price cuts, and the net result is that a new market price is established at a lower level. All members of the oligopoly end up with about the same share of the market that they had before. However, unit revenue is reduced by the amount of the price cut.

Theoretically, oligopolists gain no advantage by cutting prices. For their own good they should simply set prices at a competitive level and leave them there. In reality, however, price wars are common in an oligopoly because it is not possible to control all sellers of the product. In the absence of collusion, every so often some firm will cut its price. Then all others usually cut prices to maintain their respective market shares.

FIGURE 12-6
Kinked demand curve facing producer of product sold at prevailing price (the same type of curve faces individual oligopolist).
The kink occurs at the point representing the prevailing price A. Above A, demand declines rapidly as price is increased. A price set below A results in very little increase in volume, so revenue is lost. Marginal revenue is negative.

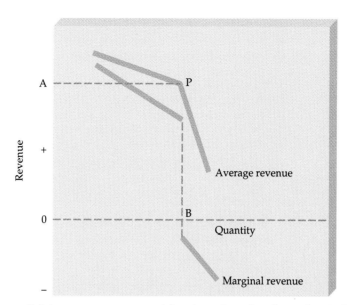

Pricing to meet competition is rather simple to do. A firm ascertains what the market price is, and after allowing for customary markups for middlemen, it arrives at its own selling price. To illustrate, a manufacturer of men's dress shoes knows that retailers want to sell the shoes for $70 ($69.95) a pair. The firm sells directly to retailers, who want an average markup of 40 percent of their selling price. Consequently, after allowing $28 for the retailer's markup, the producer's top price is about $42. This manufacturer then has to decide whether $42 is enough to cover costs and still provide a reasonable profit. Sometimes a producer faces a real squeeze, particularly when its costs are rising but the market price is holding firm.

Pricing below Competitive Level

A variation of market-based pricing is to set a price at some point *below* the competitive level. This is typically done by discount retailers. These stores offer fewer services and operate on the principle of low markup and high volume. They price nationally advertised brands 10 to 30 percent below the suggested retail list price, or the price being charged by full-service retailers. Even full-service retailers may price below the competitive level by eliminating specific services. For example, some gas stations offer a discount to customers who use the self-service pumps or who pay with cash instead of a credit card.

Pricing above Competitive Level

Producers or retailers sometimes set their prices *above* the market level. Usually above-market pricing works only when the product is distinctive or when the seller has acquired prestige in its field. Most cities have an elite clothing or jewellery store where price tags are noticeably above the competitive level set by other stores that handle similar products. Above-market pricing often is practised by manufacturers of prestige brands of expensive products such as autos (Ferrari, Mercedes), watches (Rolex), crystal (Waterford), and leather products (Gucci, Fendi). Above-market pricing is sometimes found even among relatively low-cost products — candies, for example, as in the case of Godiva and other brands of imported Belgian chocolates. A product with a celebrity tie-in may command an above-market price. In perfumes, Elizabeth Taylor's "Passion" was priced above market, yet it was one of the top 10 selling scents in 1989.

Most of the examples in this chapter illustrate the pricing of tangible goods.

> ### Flying from Vancouver to Toronto — the kinked demand curve in the real world
>
> The type of pricing situation discussed in this section is exactly what has occurred throughout the airline industry since deregulation. In an attempt to increase the number of passengers, Canadian Airlines International would cut its price on a heavily travelled route. However, Air Canada usually would match that lower fare immediately. As a result, there was no significant shift in the market share held by each airline on that route. But another result was that the market price settled at the lower level, and the profits of both airlines involved generally suffered. They then both increased their fares.

The basic pricing methods (cost-plus and marginal analysis, for instance) are equally applicable in the marketing of intangible services — a topic that was covered in more detail in Chapter 11.

SUMMARY In our economy, price is a major regulator because it influences the allocation of scarce resources. In individual companies, price is one important factor in determining marketing success. However, it is difficult to define price. A rather general definition is: Price is the amount of money (plus possibly some goods or services) needed to acquire another product.

Before setting the base price on a product, management should identify its pricing goal. Major pricing objectives are to (1) earn a target return on investment or on net sales, (2) maximize profits, (3) increase sales, (4) gain or hold a target share of the market, (5) stabilize prices, and (6) meet competition's prices.

Key factors (besides the firm's pricing objective) that should influence management's decision when setting the base price are: (1) demand for the product, (2) competitive reactions, (3) other major elements in the marketing mix, (4) desired market share, and (5) the product's cost.

Three major methods used to determine the base price are cost-plus pricing, marginal analysis, and setting the price in relation only to the market.

For cost-plus pricing to be at all effective, a seller must consider several types of costs and their reactions to changes in the quantity produced. A producer usually sets a price to cover total cost. In some cases, however, the best policy may be to set a price that covers marginal cost only. The main weakness in cost-plus pricing is that it completely ignores market demand. To partially offset this weakness, a company may use break-even analysis as a tool in price setting.

In real-life situations virtually all price setting is market-inspired to some extent. Consequently, marginal analysis is a useful method for setting price. Prices are set and output level is determined at the point where marginal cost equals marginal revenue.

For many products, price setting is a relatively easy job because management simply sets the price at the market level established by the competition. Two variations of market-level pricing are to price below or above the competitive level.

KEY TERMS AND CONCEPTS

QUESTIONS AND PROBLEMS

1. Two students paid $2.49 for identical tubes of toothpaste at a leading store. Yet one student complained about paying a much higher price than the other. What might be the basis for this complaint?

2. Explain how a firm's pricing objective may influence the promotional program for a product. Which of the six pricing goals involves the largest, most aggressive promotional campaign?

3. What marketing conditions might logically lead a company to set "meeting competition" as a pricing objective?

4. What is the expected price for each of the following articles? How did you arrive at your estimate in each instance?
   a. A new type of cola beverage that holds its carbonation long after it has been opened; packaged in 355-mL and 2-L bottles.
   b. A nuclear-powered 23-inch table-model television set, guaranteed to run for years without replacement of the original power-generating component; requires no battery or electric wires.
   c. An automatic garage-door opener for residential housing.

5. Name at least three products for which you think an inverse demand exists. For each product, within which price range does this inverse demand exist?

6. In Fig. 12-2, what is the significance of the point where the marginal cost curve intersects the average total cost curve? Explain why the average total cost curve is declining to the left of the intersection point and rising beyond it. Explain how the marginal cost curve can be rising, while the average total cost curve is still declining.

7. In Table 12-2, what is the marginal cost of the fifth unit produced?

8. What are the merits and limitations of the cost-plus method of setting a base price?

9. In a break-even chart, is the total *fixed* cost line always horizontal? Is the total *variable* cost line always straight? Explain.

10. In Table 12-3 and Fig. 12-4, what would be the break-even points at prices of $50 and $90, if variable costs are $40 per unit and fixed costs remain at $250?

11. A small manufacturer sold ballpoint pens to retailers at $8.40 per dozen. The manufacturing cost was 50 cents for each pen. The expenses, including all selling and administrative costs except advertising, were $19,200. How many dozen must the manufacturer sell to cover these expenses and pay for an advertising campaign costing $6,000?

12. In Fig. 12-6, why would the firm normally stop producing at Quantity Q? Why is the price set at B and not at D or A?

13. Are there any stores in your community that generally price above the competitive level? How are they able to do this?

14. Evaluate the three methods of export pricing identified in Marketing at Work File 12-5. Under what conditions do you recommend that each be used?

Financial Accounting in Marketing

Marketing involves people—customers, middlemen, and producers. Much of the business activity of these people, however, is quantified in some manner. Consequently, some knowledge of the rudiments of financial accounting is essential for decision making in many areas of marketing. This appendix is intended as a basic review. It contains discussions of three accounting concepts that are useful in marketing: (1) the operating statement, (2) markups, and (3) analytical ratios. Another useful concept—discounts and terms of sale—was reviewed in Chapter 13 in connection with pricing policies.

THE OPERATING STATEMENT

An operating statement—often called a *profit and loss statement* or an *income and expense statement*—is one of the two main financial statements prepared by a company. The other is the balance sheet. An **operating statement** is a summary picture of the firm's income and expenses—its operations—over a period of time. In contrast, a **balance sheet** shows the assets, liabilities, and net worth of a company at a given time, for example, at the close of business on December 31, 1992.

The operating statement shows whether the business earned a net profit or suffered a net loss during the period covered. It is an orderly summary of the income and expense items that resulted in this net profit or loss.

An operating statement can cover any selected period of time. To fulfil income tax requirements, virtually all firms prepare a statement covering operations during the calendar or fiscal year. In addition, it is common for business to prepare monthly, quarterly, or semiannual operating statements.

Table B-1 is an example of an operating statement for a wholesaler or retailer. The main difference between the operating statement of a middleman and that of a manufacturer is in the cost-of-goods sold section. A manufacturer shows the cost of goods *manufactured*, whereas the middleman's statement shows net *purchases*.

Major Sections

From one point of view, the essence of business is very simple. A company buys or makes a product and then sells it for a higher price. Out of the sales revenue, the seller hopes to cover the cost of the merchandise and the seller's own expenses and have something left over, which is called *net profit*. These relationships form the skeleton of an operating statement. That is, *sales minus cost of goods sold equals gross margin*; then *gross margin minus expenses equals net profit*. An example based on Table B-1 is as follows:

	Sales	$80,000
less	Cost of goods sold	− 48,000
equals	Gross margin	32,000
less	Expenses	− 27,200
equals	Net profit	$ 4,800

TABLE B-1 **Alpha-Beta Company Ltd., Operating Statement, for Year Ending December 31, 1992**

Gross sales		$87,000	
Less: Sales returns and allowances	$ 5,500		
Cash discounts allowed	1,500	7,000	
Net sales			$80,000
Cost of goods sold:			
Beginning inventory, January 1 (at cost)		18,000	
Gross purchases	49,300		
Less: Cash discounts taken on purchases	900		
Net purchases	48,400		
Plus: Freight in	1,600		
Net purchases (at delivered cost)		50,000	
Cost of goods available for sale		68,000	
Less: Ending inventory, December 31 (at cost)		20,000	
Cost of goods sold			48,000
Gross margin			32,000
Expenses:			
Sales-force salaries and commissions		$11,000	
Advertising		2,400	
Office supplies		250	
Taxes (except income tax)		125	
Telephone and telegraph		250	
Delivery expenses		175	
Rent		800	
Heat, light, and power		300	
Depreciation		100	
Insurance		150	
Interest		150	
Bad debts		300	
Administrative salaries		7,500	
Office salaries		3,500	
Miscellaneous expenses		200	
Total expenses			27,200
Net profit			$ 4,800

SALES

The first line in an operating statement records the gross sales — the total amount sold by the company. From this figure, the company deducts its sales returns and sales allowances. From gross sales, the company also deducts the discounts that are granted to company employees when they purchase merchandise or services.

In virtually every firm at some time during an operating period, customers will want to return or exchange merchandise. In a *sales return*, the customer is refunded the full purchase price in cash or credit. In a *sales allowance*, the customer keeps the merchandise, but is given a reduction from the selling price because of some dissatisfaction. The income from the sale of returned merchandise is included in a company's gross sales, so returns and allowances must be deducted to get net sales.

NET SALES

This is the most important figure in the sales section of the statement. It represents the net amount of sales revenue, out of which the company will pay for the products and all its expenses. The net sales figure is also the one upon which many operating ratios are based. It is called 100 percent (of itself), and the other items are then expressed as a percentage of net sales.

COST OF GOODS SOLD

From net sales, we must deduct the cost of the merchandise that was sold, as we work towards discovering the firm's net profit. In determining the cost of goods sold in a retail or wholesale operation, we start with the value of any merchandise on hand at the beginning of the period. To this we add the net cost of what was purchased during the period. From this total we deduct the value of whatever remains unsold at the end of the period. In Table B-1 the firm started with an inventory worth $18,000, and it purchased goods that cost $50,000. Thus the firm had a total of $68,000 worth of goods available for sale. If all were sold, the cost of goods sold would have been $68,000. At the end of the year, however, there was still $20,000 worth of merchandise on hand. Thus, during the year, the company sold goods that cost $48,000.

In the preceding paragraph, we spoke of merchandise "valued at" a certain figure or "worth" a stated amount. Actually, the problem of inventory valuation is complicated and sometimes controversial. The usual rule of thumb is to value inventories at cost or market, whichever is lower. The actual application of this rule may be difficult. Assume that a store buys six footballs at $2 each and the next week buys six more at $2.50 each. The company places all 12, jumbled, in a basketball display for sale. Then one is sold, but there is no marking to indicate whether its cost was $2 or $2.50. Thus the inventory value of the remaining 11 balls may be $25 or $24.50. If we multiply this situation by thousands of purchases and sales, we may begin to see the depth of the problem.

A figure that deserves some comment is the *net cost of delivered purchases*. A company starts with its gross purchases at billed cost. Then it must deduct any purchases that were returned or any purchase allowances received. The company should also deduct any discounts taken for payment of the bill within a specified period of time. Deducting purchase returns and allowances and purchase discounts gives the net cost of the purchases. Then freight charges paid by the buyer (called "freight in") are added to net purchases to determine the net cost of *delivered* purchases.

In a manufacturing concern, the cost-of-goods-sold section has a slightly different form. Instead of determining the cost of goods *purchased*, the company determines the cost of goods *manufactured*. (See Table B-2.) Cost of goods manufactured ($50,000) is added to the beginning inventory ($18,000) to ascertain the total goods available for sale ($68,000). Then, after the ending inventory of finished goods has been deducted ($20,000), the result is the cost of goods sold ($48,000).

To find the cost of goods *manufactured*, a company starts with the value of goods partially completed (beginning inventory of goods in process—$24,000). To this beginning inventory figure is added the cost of raw materials, direct labour, and factory overhead expenses incurred during the period ($48,000). The resulting figure is the total goods in process during the period ($72,000).

By deducting the value of goods still in process at the end of the period ($22,000), management finds the cost of goods manufactured during that span of time ($50,000).

TABLE B-2 **Cost-of-Goods-Sold Section of an Operating Statement for A Manufacturer**

Beginning inventory of finished goods (at cost)		$18,000
Cost of goods manufactured:		
Beginning inventory, goods in process	$24,000	
Plus: Raw materials $20,000		
Direct labour 15,000		
Overhead 13,000	48,000	
Total goods in process	72,000	
Less: Ending inventory, goods in process	22,000	
Cost of goods manufactured		50,000
Cost of goods available for sale		68,000
Less: Ending inventory, finished goods (at cost)		20,000
Cost of goods sold		$48,000

GROSS MARGIN

Gross margin is determined simply by subtracting cost of goods sold from net sale. Gross margin, sometimes called *gross profit*, is one of the key figures in the entire marketing program. When we say that a certain store has a "margin" of 30 percent, we are referring to the gross margin.

EXPENSES

Operating expenses are deducted from gross margin to determine the net profit. The operating expense section includes marketing, administrative, and possibly some miscellaneous expense items. It does not, of course, include the cost of goods purchased or manufactured, since these costs have already been deducted.

NET PROFIT

Net profit is the difference between gross margin and total expenses. A negative net profit is, of course, a loss.

MARKUPS Many retailers and wholesalers use markup percentages to determine the selling price of an article. Normally the selling price must exceed the cost of the merchandise by an amount sufficient to cover the operating expenses and still leave the desired profit. The difference between the selling price of an item and its cost is the **markup**, sometimes referred to as the "mark-on."

Typically, markups are expressed in percentages rather than dollars. A markup may be expressed as a percentage of either the cost or the selling price. Therefore, we must first determine which will be the *base* for the markup. That is, when we speak of a 40 percent markup, do we mean 40 percent of the *cost* or of the *selling price?*

To determine the markup percentage when it is based on *cost*, we use the following formula:

$$\text{Markup \%} = \frac{\text{dollar markup}}{\text{cost}}$$

When the markup is based on *selling price*, the formula to use is:

$$\text{Markup \%} = \frac{\text{dollar markup}}{\text{selling price}}$$

It is important that all interested parties understand which base is being used in a given situation. Otherwise, there can be a considerable misunderstanding. To illustrate, suppose Mr. A runs a clothing store and claims he needs a 66⅔ percent markup to make a small net profit. Ms. B, who runs a competitive store, says she needs only a 40 percent markup and that A must be inefficient or a big profiteer. Actually, both merchants are using identical markups, but they are using different bases. Each seller buys hats at $6 apiece and sets the selling price at $10. This is a markup of $4 per hat. Mr. A is expressing his markup as a percentage of cost—hence, the 66⅔ percent figure ($4 ÷ $6 = .67, or 66⅔ percent). Ms. B is basing her markup on the selling price ($4 ÷ $10 = .4, or 40 percent). It would be a mistake for Mr. A to try to get on B's 40 percent markup, as long as A uses cost as his base. To illustrate, if Mr. A used the 40 percent markup, *but based it on cost*, the markup would be only $2.40. And the selling price would be only $8.40. This $2.40 markup, averaged over the entire hat department, would not enable A to cover his usual expenses and make a profit.

Unless otherwise indicated, markup percentages are always stated as percentage of selling price.

Markup Based on Selling Price

The following diagram should help you understand the various relationships between selling price, cost, and markup. It can be used to compute these figures regardless of whether the markup is stated in percentages or dollars, and whether the percentages are based on selling price or cost:

	Dollars	Percentage
Selling price		
less Cost	_____	_____
equals Markup		

As an example, suppose a merchant buys an article for $90 and knows the markup based on selling price must be 40 percent. What is the selling price? By filling in the known information in the diagram, we obtain:

	Dollars	Percentage
Selling price		100
less Cost	90	_____
equals Markup		40

The percentage representing cost must then be 60 percent. Thus the $90 cost is 60 percent of the selling price. The selling price is then $150. [That is, $90 equals 60 percent of the selling price. Then $90 is divided by .6 (or 60 percent) to get the selling price of $150.]

A common situation facing merchants is to have competition set a ceiling on selling prices. Or possibly the sellers must buy an item to fit into one of their price lines. Then they want to know the maximum amount they can pay for an item and still get their normal markup. For instance, assume that the selling price of an article is set at $60 (by competition or by the $59.95 price line). The retailer's normal markup is 35 percent. What is the most that the retailer should pay for this article? Again, let's fill in what we know in the diagram:

		Dollars	Percentage
	Selling price	60	100
less	Cost	_____	_____
equals	Markup		35

The dollar markup is $21 (35 percent of $60). So, by a simple subtraction we find that the maximum cost the merchant will want to pay is $39.

Series of Markups

It should be clearly understood that markups are figured on the selling price at *each level of business* in a channel of distribution. A manufacturer applies a markup to determine its selling price. The manufacturer's selling price then becomes the wholesaler's cost. Then the wholesaler must determine its own selling price by applying its usual markup percentage based on its—the wholesaler's—selling price. The same procedure is carried on by the retailer, whose cost is the wholesaler's selling price. The following computations should illustrate this point:

Producer's cost $ 7 } **Producer's markup = $4, or 30%**
Producer's selling price $10 }

Wholesaler's cost $10 } **Wholesaler's markup = $2, or $16²⁄₃%**
Wholesaler's selling price $12 }

Retailer's cost $12 } **Retailer's markup = $8, or 40%**
Retailer's selling price $20 }

Markup Based on Cost

If a firm is used to dealing in markups based on cost—and sometimes this is done among wholesalers — the same diagrammatic approach may be employed that was used above. The only change is that cost will equal 100 percent. Then the selling price will be 100 percent plus the markup based on cost. As an example, assume that a firm bought an article for $70 and wants a 20 percent markup based on cost. The markup in dollars is $14 (20 percent of $70). The selling price is $84 ($70 plus $14):

		Dollars	Percentage
	Selling price	84	120
less	Cost	70	100
equals	Markup	14	20

A marketing executive should understand the relationship between markups on cost and markups on selling price. For instance, if a product costs $6 and sells for $10, there is a $4 markup. This is a 40 percent markup based on selling price, but a 66²⁄₃ percent markup based on cost. The following diagram may be helpful in understanding these relationships and in converting from one base to another.

If selling price = 100%   *If cost = 100%*

$10 = 100% { 60% →   **Cost = $6.00**   ←100% } $10 = 166²⁄₃%
           { 40% →   **Markup = $4.00**   ←66²⁄₃% }

The relationships between the two bases are expressed in the following formulas:

(1) % markup on selling price $= \dfrac{\% \text{ markup on cost}}{100\% + \% \text{ markup on cost}}$

(2) % markup on cost $= \dfrac{\% \text{ markup on selling price}}{100\% - \% \text{ markup on selling price}}$

To illustrate the use of these formulas, let us assume that a retailer has a markup of 25 percent on *cost*. This retailer then wants to know what the corresponding figure is, based on selling price. In formula 1 we get:

$$\frac{25\%}{100\% + 25\%} = \frac{25\%}{125\%} = .2, \text{ or } 20\%$$

A markup of 33⅓ percent based on *selling price* converts to 50 percent based on cost, according to formula 2:

$$\frac{33⅓\%}{100\% - 33⅓\%} = \frac{33⅓\%}{66⅔\%} = .5, \text{ or } 50\%$$

The markup is closely related to the gross margin. Recall that gross margin is equal to net sales minus cost of goods sold. Looking below the gross margin on an operating statement, we find that gross margin equals operating expenses plus net profit. Normally, the initial markup in a company, department, or product line must be set a little higher than the overall gross margin desired for the selling unit. The reason for this is that, ordinarily, some reductions will be incurred before all the articles are sold. For one reason or another, some items will not sell at the original price. They will have to be marked down, that is, reduced in price from the original level. Some pilferage and other shortages also may occur.

ANALYTICAL RATIOS

From a study of the operating statement, management can develop several ratios that are useful in evaluating the results of its marketing program. In most cases, net sales is used as the base (100 percent). In fact, unless it is specifically mentioned to the contrary, all ratios reflecting gross margin, net profit, or any operating expense are stated as a percentage of net sales.

Gross Margin Percentage

This is the ratio of gross margin to net sales. In Table B-1, the gross margin percentage is $32,000 ÷ $80,000, or 40 percent.

Net Profit Percentage

This ratio is computed by dividing net profit by net sales. In Table B-1, the ratio is $4,800 ÷ $80,000, or 6 percent. This percentage may be computed either before or after federal income taxes are deducted, but the result should be labelled to show which it is.

Operating Expense Percentage

When total operating expenses are divided by net sales, the result is the operating expense ratio. In Table B-1, the ratio is $27,200 ÷ $80,000, or 34 percent. In similar fashion, we may determine the expense ratio for any given cost. Thus we note in Table B-1 that the rent expense was 1 percent, advertising was 3 percent, and salesforce salaries and commissions were 13.75 percent.

Rate of Stockturn

Management often measures the efficiency of its marketing operations by means of the **stockturn rate**. This figure represents the number of times the average inventory is "turned over," or sold, during the period under study. The rate is computed on either a cost or a selling-price basis. That is, both the numerator and the denominator of the ratio fraction must be expressed in the same terms, either cost or selling price.

On a *cost* basis, the formula for stockturn rate is as follows:

$$\text{Rate of stockturn} = \frac{\text{cost of goods sold}}{\text{average inventory at cost}}$$

The average inventory is determined by adding the beginning and ending inventories and dividing the result by 2. In Table B-1, the average inventory is ($18,000 + $20,000) ÷ 2 = $19,000. The stockturn rate then is $48,000 ÷ $19,000, or 2.5. Because inventories usually are abnormally low at the first of the year in anticipation of taking physical inventory, this average may not be representative. Consequently, some companies find their average inventory by adding the book inventories at the beginning of each month, and then dividing this sum by 12.

Now let's assume the inventory is recorded on a *selling-price* basis, as is done in most large retail organizations. Then the stockturn rate equals net sales divided by average inventory at selling price. Sometimes the stockturn rate is computed by dividing the number of *units* sold by the average inventory expressed in *units*.

Wholesale and retail trade associations in many types of businesses publish figures showing the average rate of stockturn for their members. A firm with a low rate of stockturn is likely to be spending too much on storage and inventory. Also, the company runs a higher risk of obsolescence or spoilage. If the stockturn rate gets too high, this may indicate that the company maintains too low an average inventory. Often, a firm in this situation is operating on a hand-to-mouth buying system. In addition to incurring high handling and billing costs, the company is liable to be out of stock on some items.

Markdown Percentage

Sometimes retailers are unable to sell articles at the originally stated prices, and they reduce these prices to move the goods. A **markdown** is a reduction from the original selling price. Management frequently finds it very helpful to determine the markdown percentage. Then management analyzes the size and number of markdowns and the reasons for them. Retailers, particularly, make extensive use of markdown analysis.

Markdowns are expressed as a percentage of net sales and *not* as a percentage of the original selling price. To illustrate, assume that a retailer purchased a hat for $6 and marked it up 40 percent to sell for $10. The hat did not sell at that price, so it was marked down to $8. Now the seller may advertise a price cut of 20 percent. Yet, according to our rule, this $2 markdown is 25 percent *of the $8 selling price.*

Markdown percentage is computed by dividing total dollar markdowns by total net sales during a given period of time. Two important points should be noted here. First, the markdown percentage is computed in this fashion, whether the markdown items were sold or are still in the store. Second, the percentage is computed with respect to total net sales, and not only in connection with sales of marked-down articles. As an example, assume that a retailer buys 10 hats at $6 each and prices them to sell at $10. Five hats are sold at $10. The other five are marked down to $8, and three are sold at the lower price. Total sales are $74, and the total markdowns are $10. The retailer has a markdown ratio of $10 ÷ $74, or 13.5 percent.

Markdowns do not appear on the profit and loss statement because they occur *before* an article is sold. The first item on an operating statement is gross sales. That figure reflects the actual selling price, which may be the selling price after a markdown has been taken.

Return on Investment

A commonly used measure of managerial performance and the operating success of a company is its rate of return on investment. We use both the balance sheet and the operating statement as sources of information. The formula for calculating return on investment (ROI) is as follows:

$$\text{ROI} = \frac{\text{net profit}}{\text{sales}} \times \frac{\text{sales}}{\text{investment}}$$

Two questions may quickly come to mind. First, what do we mean by "investment"? Second, why do we need two fractions? It would seem that the "sales" component in each fraction would cancel out, leaving net profit divided by investment as the meaningful ratio.

To answer the first query, consider a firm whose operating statement shows annual sales of $1,000,000 and a net profit of $50,000. At the end of the year, the balance sheet reports:

Assets	$600,000	Liabilities		$200,000
		Capital stock	$300,000	
		Retained earnings	100,000	400,000
	$600,000			$600,000

Now, is the investment $400,000 or $600,000? Certainly the ROI will depend upon which figure we use. The answer depends upon whether we are talking to the stockholders or to the company executives. The stockholders are more interested in the return on what they have invested—in this case, $400,000. The ROI calculation then is:

$$\text{ROI} = \frac{\text{net profit } \$50,000}{\text{sales } \$1,000,000} \times \frac{\text{sales } \$1,000,000}{\text{investment } \$400,000} = 12\tfrac{1}{2}\%$$

Management, on the other hand, is more concerned with the total investment, as represented by the total assets ($600,000). This is the amount that the executives must manage, regardless of whether the assets were acquired by the stockholders' investment, retained earnings, or loans from outside sources. Within this context the ROI computation becomes:

$$\text{ROI} = \frac{\text{net profit } \$50,000}{\text{sales } \$1,000,000} \times \frac{\text{sales } \$1,000,000}{\text{investment } \$600,000} = 8\tfrac{1}{3}\%$$

Regarding the second question, we use two fractions because we are dealing with two separate elements—the rate of profit on sales and the rate of capital turnover. Management really should determine each rate separately and then multiply the two. The rate of profit on sales is influenced by marketing considerations—sales volume, price, product mix, advertising effort. The capital turnover is a financial consideration not directly involved with costs or profits—only sales volume and assets managed.

To illustrate, assume that our company's profits doubled with the same sales volume and investment because management operated an excellent marketing program this year. In effect, we doubled our profit rate with the same capital turnover:

$$\text{ROI} = \underbrace{\frac{\text{net profit } \$100,000}{\text{sales } \$1,000,000}}_{10\%} \times \underbrace{\frac{\text{sales } \$1,000,000}{\text{investment } \$600,000}}_{1.67} = 16\tfrac{2}{3}\%$$

$$10\% \quad \times \quad 1.67 \quad = 16\tfrac{2}{3}\%$$

As expected this 16⅔ percent is twice the ROI calculated above.

Now assume that we earned our original profit of $50,000 but that we did it with an investment reduced to $500,000. We cut the size of our average inventory, and we closed some branch offices. By increasing our capital turnover from 1.67 to 2, we raised the ROI from 8⅓ percent to 10 percent, even though sales volumes and profits remain unchanged:

$$\text{ROI} = \underbrace{\frac{\$50,000}{\$1,000,000}}_{5\%} \times \underbrace{\frac{\$1,000,000}{\$500,000}}_{2} = 10\%$$

$$5\% \quad \times \quad 2 \quad = 10\%$$

Assume now that we increase our sales volume—let us say we double it—but do not increase our profit or investment. That is, the cost-profit squeeze is bringing us "profitless prosperity." The following interesting results occur:

$$\text{ROI} = \underbrace{\frac{\$50,000}{\$2,000,000}}_{2\tfrac{1}{2}\%} \times \underbrace{\frac{\$2,000,000}{\$600,000}}_{3.33} = 8\tfrac{1}{3}\%$$

$$2\tfrac{1}{2}\% \quad \times \quad 3.33 \quad = 8\tfrac{1}{3}\%$$

The profit rate was cut in half, but this was offset by a doubling of the capital turnover rate, leaving the ROI unchanged.

QUESTIONS AND PROBLEMS

1. Construct an operating statement from the following data, and compute the gross-margin percentage:

Purchases at billed cost	$15,000
Net sales	30,000
Sales returns and allowances	200
Cash discounts given	300
Cash discounts earned	100
Rent	1,500
Salaries	6,000
Opening inventory at cost	10,000
Advertising	600
Other expenses	2,000
Closing inventory at cost	7,500

2. Prepare a retail operating statement from the following data and compute the markdown percentage:

Rent	$ 9,000
Closing inventory at cost	28,000
Sales returns	6,500
Gross margin as percentage of sales	35
Cash discounts allowed	2,000
Salaries	34,000
Markdowns	4,000
Other operating expenses	15,000
Opening inventory at cost	35,000
Gross sales	232,500
Advertising	5,500
Freight in	3,500

3. What percentage markups on cost correspond to the following percentages of markup on selling price?
  a. 20 percent.   c. 50 percent.
  b. 37½ percent.   d. 66⅔ percent.

4. What percentage markups on selling price correspond to the following percentages of markup on cost?
  a. 20 percent.   c. 50 percent.
  b. 33⅓ percent.   d. 300 percent.

5. A hardware store bought a gross (12 dozen) of hammers, paying $302.40 for the lot. The retailer estimated operating expenses for this product to be 35 percent of sales, and wanted a net profit of 5 percent of sales. The retailer expected no markdowns. What retail selling price should be set for each hammer?

6. Competition in a certain line of sporting goods pretty well limits the selling price on a certain item to $25. If the store owner feels a markup of 35 percent is needed to cover expenses and return a reasonable profit, what is the most the owner can pay for this item?

7. A retailer with annual net sales of $2 million maintains a markup of 66⅔ percent based on cost. Expenses average 35 percent. What are the retailer's gross margin and net profit in dollars?

8. A company has a stockturn rate of five times a year, a sales volume of $600,000, and a gross margin of 25 percent. What is the average inventory at cost?

9. A store has an average inventory of $30,000 at retail and a stockturn rate of five times a year. If the company maintains a markup of 50 percent based on cost, what are the annual sales volume and the cost of goods sold?

10. From the following data, compute the gross margin percentage and the operating expense ratio:
  Stockturn rate = 9
  Average inventory at selling price = $45,000
  Net profit = $20,000
  Cost of goods sold = $350,000

11. A ski shop sold 50 pairs of skis at $90 a pair, after taking a 10 percent markdown. All the skis were originally purchased at the same price and had been marked up 60 percent on cost. What was the gross margin on the 50 pairs of skis?

12. A men's clothing store bought 200 suits at $90 each. The suits were marked up 40 percent. Eighty were sold at that price. The remaining suits were each marked down 20 percent from the original selling price, and then they were sold. Compute the sales volume and the markdown percentage.

13. An appliance retailer sold 60 radios at $30 each after taking markdowns equal to 20 percent of the actual selling price. Originally all the radios had been purchased at the same price and were marked up 50 percent on cost. What was the gross margin percentage earned in this situation?

14. An appliance manufacturer produced a line of small appliances advertised to sell at $30. The manufacturer planned for wholesalers to receive a 20 percent markup, and retailers a 33⅓ percent markup. Total manufacturing costs were $12 per unit. What did retailers pay for the product? What were the manufacturer's selling price and percentage markup?

15. A housewares manufacturer produces an article at a full cost of $1.80. It is sold through a manufacturers' agent directly to large retailers. The agent receives a 20 percent commission on sales, the retailers earn a margin of 30 percent, and the manufacturer plans a net profit of 10 percent on the selling price. What is the retail price of this article?

16. A building materials manufacturer sold a quantity of a product to a wholesaler for $350, and the wholesaler in turn sold to a lumberyard. The wholesaler's normal markup was 15 percent, and the retailer usually priced the item to include a 30 percent markup. What is the selling price to consumers?

17. From the following data, calculate the return on investment, based on a definition of *investment* that is useful for evaluating managerial performance:

Net sales	$800,000	Markup	35%
Gross margin	$280,000	Average inventory	$ 75,000
Total assets	$200,000	Retained earnings	$ 60,000
Cost of goods sold	$520,000	Operating expenses	$240,000
Liabilities	$ 40,000		

CHAPTER 13 GOALS

This chapter is concerned with the ways in which a base price can (and sometimes must) be modified. After studying this chapter, you should be able to explain:

- Price discounts and allowances.
- Geographic pricing strategies.
- Skimming and penetration pricing strategies.
- One-price and flexible-price strategies.
- Unit pricing.
- Price lining.
- Resale price maintenance.
- "Leader" pricing.
- Psychological pricing.
- Price competition versus nonprice competition.

Pricing Strategies and Policies

Since airline deregulation in the United States in the 1980s and international airfare discounting as a result of the Gulf War in 1991, Canadian travellers have been awaiting the arrival of deep-cut air fares in Canada. Both Air Canada and Canadian Airlines International offered periodic deep discounts and have also been following the approach of getting more revenue out of existing passengers.

Industry analysts and spokespeople feel that starting fare wars is a risky strategy since, once started, it's difficult to determine when they will stop. Some recall what happened to Wardair in 1987 when it decided to increase its market share of scheduled airline business by starting fare wars across Canada. Air Canada and Canadian Pacific followed suit to protect their positions and by 1989, Wardair was acquired by Canadian Pacific and the new Canadian Airlines International was born.

Now both these Canadian competitors are being very careful with each other. Whereas there are about ten major airlines in the United States and thus a greater incentive to launch fare wars, the two major competitors here—both being under revenue pressures—have chosen to compete on a different basis. Canadian Airlines International, while initiating major seat sales in 1991—which were immediately followed by Air Canada—has also worked to increase customer service and value added. At the same time, both Canadian airlines are following a strategy of cost cutting to increase revenue yields per passenger.

In contrast, many if not all of the major U.S. airlines are involved in consistent deep-discounting to increase both market share and total demand. Many of them believe that increasing revenue through demand expansion will produce a better long-run result. But while all ten major U.S. airlines are discounting, only three of them have increased their traffic. And for some of them, the increase has resulted in revenue losses rather than gains as the yield per passenger dropped drastically.

Some observers maintain that the only way to assure the profitability of Canada's airlines is to market more value added and thus expensive rather than less expensive tickets. The most effective pricing strategy is still a matter of contention.[1]

The strategy of engaging in price competition — as the airlines have been doing—is just one of the pricing strategies that we will discuss in this chapter. In managing the price portion of a company's marketing mix, management first decides on its pricing goal and then sets the base price for a product or service. The next task is to design the appropriate strategies and policies concerning several aspects of the price structure. What kind of discount schedule should be adopted? Will the company occasionally absorb freight costs? In this chapter we shall discuss several pricing topics that require strategy decisions and policy making. We also shall consider some legal aspects of these activities. A company's success in pricing may depend upon management's ability to design creative pricing stategies that reflect a customer orientation, rather than the traditional cost-oriented pricing methodology.

We shall be using the terms *policy* and *strategy* frequently in this chapter. So let's review the meaning of these terms as they were defined in Chapter 3. A **strategy** is a broad plan of action by which an organization intends to reach its goal. A **policy** is a managerial guide to future decision making when a given situation arises. Thus a policy becomes the course of action followed routinely any time a given strategic or tactical situation arises. To illustrate, suppose management adopts the *strategy* of offering certain quantity discounts in order to achieve the goal of a 10 percent increase in sales next year. Then, routinely,

FIGURE 13-1
The price-determination process.

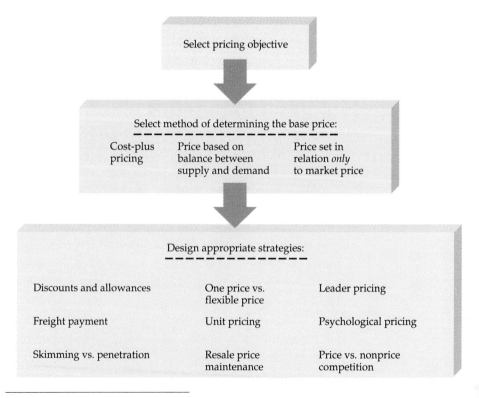

---

[1]Adapted from Geoffrey Rowan, ''Canadian Airlines Avoid Fare Wars,'' *Globe and Mail*, June 3, 1991, pp. B1-2.

every time the company receives an order of a given size, it is company *policy* to grant the customer the prescribed quantity discount.[2]

DISCOUNTS AND ALLOWANCES

Discounts and allowances result in a deduction from the base (or list) price. The deduction may be in the form of a reduced price or some other concession, such as free merchandise or advertising allowances.

Quantity Discounts

Quantity discounts are deductions from the price offered by a seller to encourage resellers to buy in larger amounts or to make most of their purchases from that seller. The discounts are based on the size of the purchase, either in dollars or in units.

A **noncumulative** discount is based upon the size of an *individual order* of one or more products. Thus a retailer may sell golf balls at $1 each or at three for $2.50. A manufacturer or wholesaler may set up a quantity discount schedule such as the following, which was used by a manufacturer of industrial adhesives.

Retailers, too, offer quantity discounts.

Boxes purchased on single order	% discount from list price
1–5	0.0
6–12	2.0
13–25	3.5
Over 25	5.0

Noncumulative quantity discounts are expected to encourage large orders. Many expenses, such as billing, order filling, and the salaries of sales people, are about the same whether the seller receives an order totalling $10 or $500. Consequently, selling expense as a percentage of sales decreases as orders become larger. The seller shares such savings with the purchaser of large quantities.

Cumulative discounts are based on the total volume purchased *over a period of time*. These discounts are advantageous to a seller because they tie customers more closely to that seller. They really are patronage discounts, because the more total business a buyer gives a seller, the greater is the discount. Cumulative discounts are especially useful in the sale of perishable products. These discounts encourage customers to buy fresh supplies frequently so that the merchandise will not grow stale.

Quantity discounts can help a manufacturer effect real economies in production as well as in selling. Large orders can result in lower-cost production runs and lower transportation costs. A producer's cumulative discount based on total orders from all the stores in a retail chain may increase orders from that chain substantially. This enables the producer to make much more effective use of production capacity, even though the individual orders are small and do not generate savings in marketing costs.

TRADE DISCOUNTS

Trade discounts, sometimes called **functional** discounts, are reductions from the list price offered to buyers in payment for marketing functions that they will perform. A manufacturer may quote a retail price of $400 with trade discounts of 40 percent and 10 percent. This means that the retailer pays the

[2]For further discussion of pricing strategies and policies, see Gerard J. Tellis, ''Beyond the Many Faces of Price: An Integration of Pricing Strategies,'' *Journal of Marketing*, October 1986, pp. 146–160.

wholesaler $240 ($400 less 40 percent), and the wholesaler pays the manufacturer $216 ($240 less 10 percent). The wholesaler is given the 40 and 10 percent discounts. The wholesaler keeps the 10 percent to cover the costs of the wholesaling functions and passes on the 40 percent discount to the retailers. Note that the 40 and 10 percent discounts do not constitute a total discount of 50 percent off the list price. Each discount percentage in the "chain" is computed on the amount remaining after the preceding percentage has been deducted.

Cash Discounts

A **cash** discount is a deduction granted to buyers for paying their bills within a specified period of time. The discount is computed on the net amount due after first deducting trade and quantity discounts from the base price. Let's say a buyer owes $360 after the other discounts have been granted and is offered terms of 2/10, n/30 on an invoice dated November 8. This buyer may deduct a discount of 2 percent ($7.20) if the bill is paid within 10 days after the date of the invoice (by November 18). Otherwise the entire bill of $360 must be paid in 30 days (by December 8).

Every cash discount includes three elements: (1) the percentage discount itself, (2) the time period during which the discount may be taken, and (3) the time when the bill becomes overdue. (See Fig. 13-2 below.) There are many different terms of sale because practically every industry has its own traditional combination of elements.

Normally, most buyers are extremely eager to pay bills in time to earn cash discounts. The discount in a 2/10, n/30 situation may not seem like very much. But management must realize that this 2 percent is earned just for paying 20 days in advance of the date the entire bill is due. If buyers fail to take the cash discount in a 2/10, n/30 situation, they are, in effect, borrowing money at a 36 percent annual rate of interest. (In a 360-day year, there are 18 periods of 20 days. Paying 2 percent for one of these 20-day periods is equivalent to paying 36 percent for an entire year.)

FIGURE 13-2
The parts of a cash discount.
SOURCE: Don L. James, Bruce J. Walker, and Michael J. Etzel, *Retailing Today*, 2d ed., Harcourt Brace Jovanovich, Inc., New York, 1981, p. 199)

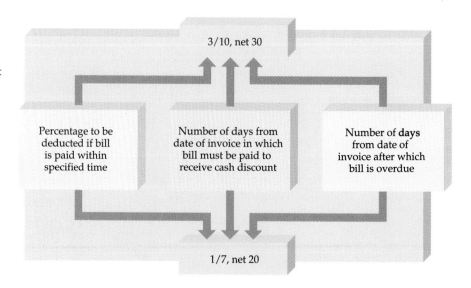

3/10, net 30

| Percentage to be deducted if bill is paid within specified time | Number of days from date of invoice in which bill must be paid to receive cash discount | Number of **days** from date of invoice after which bill is overdue |

1/7, net 20

Other Discounts and Allowances

A firm that produces articles, such as furnaces or air conditioners, that are purchased on a seasonal basis may consider the policy of granting a **seasonal discount**. This is a discount of, say, 5, 10, or 20 percent given to a customer who places an order during the slack season. Off-season orders enable manufacturers to make better use of their production facilities and/or avoid inventory carrying costs.

Forward dating is a variation of both seasonal and cash discounts. A manufacturer of fishing tackle, for example, might seek and fill orders from wholesalers and retailers during the winter months. But the bill would be dated, say, April 1, with terms of 2/10, n/30 offered as of that date. Orders that the seller fills in December and January help to maintain production during the slack season for more efficient operation. The forward-dated bills allow the wholesale or retail buyers to pay their bills after the season has started and some sales revenue has been generated.

Promotional allowances are price reductions granted by a seller in payment for promotional services performed by buyers. To illustrate, a manufacturer of builders' hardware gives a certain quantity of ''free goods'' to dealers who prominently display its line. Or a clothing manufacturer pays one-half the space charge of a retailer's advertisement that features the manufacturer's product.

The Competition Act and Price Discrimination

The discounts and allowances discussed in this section may result in different prices for different customers. Whenever price differentials exist, there is price discrimination. The terms are synonymous. In certain situations, price discrimination is prohibited by the Competition Act. This is one of the most important federal laws affecting a company's marketing program.

BACKGROUND OF THE ACT

Competition legislation in Canada was first introduced in 1888. Small businesses who suffered from the monopolistic and collusive practices in restraint of trade by large manufacturers pressured Parliament into setting up a Combines Investigation Commission. Investigators attempting to verify the allegations of the small businesses unearthed a widespread range of restrictive practices and measures.

The results of the investigation led Parliament in 1889 to pass an Act for the Prevention and Suppression of Combinations Formed in Restraint of Trade. The intent of the Act was to declare illegal monopolies and combinations in restraint of trade. Although the Act was incorporated into the Criminal Code as section 520 in 1892, it proved ineffectual, because to break the law an individual would have to commit an illegal act within the meaning of the ''common law.'' In 1900 the Act was amended to remove this loophole and undue restriction of competition became, in itself, a criminal offence.

Additional legislation was passed in 1910 after a rash of mergers involving 58 business firms, to complement the Criminal Code and assist in the application of the Act. In 1919 the Combines and Fair Prices Act was passed, which prohibited undue stockpiling of the ''necessities of life'' and also prohibited the realization of exaggerated profits through ''unreasonable'' prices.

In 1923, Canadian combines legislation was finally consolidated and important sections remain in force to this day. Following the presentation of a report by the Economic Council of Canada in 1969,[3] the Government of Canada introduced into Parliament, in 1971 and 1975, a number of important amendments to the Combines Investigation Act to form the basis for a new competition policy for Canada. However, it was not until 1986, when the new Competition Act (the successor to the Combines Investigation Act) became law, that major Economic Council recommendations were implemented.

Below are some of the Competition Act implications for common pricing strategies and policies.[4]

FIGURE 13-3

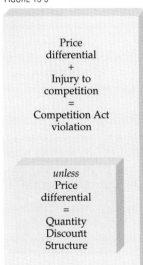

Price differential
+
Injury to competition
=
Competition Act violation

unless
Price differential
=
Quantity Discount Structure

PREDATORY PRICING AS AN OFFENCE

The provisions respecting predatory pricing are contained in paragraph 34(1)(*c*) of the Competition Act, which states:

> 34.(1) Every one engaged in a business who (*c*)
> engages in a policy of selling products at prices unreasonably low, having the effect or tendency of substantially lessening competition or eliminating a competitor, or designed to have such effect; is guilty of an indictable offence and is liable to imprisonment for two years.

In order for a conviction to result under paragraph 34(1)(*c*), it must be shown that prices are unreasonably low and that such prices have the effect of reducing competition. The amendments to the Combines Investigation Act that were passed in 1975 extended the predatory pricing provisions to the sale of both articles and services. The word "products" is now defined in the Competition Act to include articles *and* services.

PRICE DISCRIMINATION AS AN OFFENCE

At present, price discrimination is regulated under paragraph 34(1)(*a*) of the Competition Act, which states:

> 34.(1) Every one engaged in a business who
> (a) is a party or privy to, or assists in, any sale that discriminates to his knowledge, directly or indirectly, against competitors of a purchaser of articles from him in that any discount, rebate, allowance, price concession or other advantage is granted to the purchaser over and above any discount, rebate, allowance, price concession or other advantage that, at the time the articles are sold to such purchaser, is available to such competitors in respect of a sale of articles of like quality and quantity;
> is guilty of an indictable offence and is liable to imprisonment for two years.

This section goes on to state in paragraph 34(2):

> (2) It is not an offence under paragraph (1)(a) to be a party or privy to, or assist in any sale mentioned therein unless the discount, rebate, allowance, price concession or other advantage was granted as part of a practice of discriminating as described in that paragraph.

The following conditions must, therefore, be met in order for a conviction to be registered for price discrimination: (1) a discount, rebate, allowance, price concession, or other advantage must be granted to one customer and not to another; (2) the two customers concerned must be *competitors*; (3) the price discrimination must occur in respect of *articles* of similar quality and

---

[3]Economic Council of Canada, *Interim Report on Competition Policy*, Queen's Printer, Ottawa, July 1969.

[4]The materials presented in this section are based on *Competition Law Amendments*, Ministry of Supply and Services 1986; and *A Guide to Competition Law Amendments*, Ministry of Supply and Services 1985. Both are sponsored by the Department of Consumer and Corporate Affairs.

quantity; (4) the act of discrimination must be part of a *practice* of discrimination.

Not all price discrimination is, *per se*, an offence. It is lawful to discriminate in price on the basis of quantities of goods purchased. The cost justification defence which is used in the United States—that of a seller differentiating the price to a favoured competitor because of a difference in the costs of supplying that customer — is not viewed as an acceptable basis for discrimination in Canada. On the other hand, a seller does not have to demonstrate a cost difference in order to support a quantity discount structure. Rather, the basis for such price discrimination is accepted only on a quantity of goods-purchased basis. Establishing volume discount pricing structures that are available to competing buyers who purchase in comparable quantities is a major basis for discriminating under the provision.

It is also of note that the buyer is seen as being as liable as the seller in cases of discrimination. The legislation applies to those who are party to a sale and this includes both buyer and seller. This wording was intended to restrain large-scale buyers from demanding discriminatory prices. In addition, the buyer (as well as the seller) must know that the price involved is discriminatory.

GRANTING PROMOTIONAL ALLOWANCES AS AN OFFENCE

The Competition Act in section 35 requires that promotional allowances be granted proportionately to all competing customers. This section states:

> 35.(1) In this section "allowance" means any discount, rebate, price concession or other advantage that is or purports to be offered or granted for advertising or display purposes and is collateral to a sale or sales of products but is not applied directly to the selling price.
>
> (2) Every one engaged in a business who is a party or privy to the granting of an allowance to any purchaser that is not offered on proportionate terms to other purchasers in competition with the first-mentioned purchaser, (which other purchasers are in this section called "competing purchasers"), is guilty of an indictable offence and is liable to imprisonment for two years.
>
> (3) For the purposes of this section, an allowance is offered on proportionate terms only if
> (a) the allowance offered to a purchaser is in approximately the same proportion to the value of sales to him as the allowance offered to each competing purchaser is to the total value of sales to such competing purchaser.
> (b) in any case where advertising or other expenditures or services are exacted in return therefor, the cost thereof required to be incurred by a purchaser is in approximately the same proportion to the value of sales to him as the cost of such advertising or other expenditures or services required to be incurred by each competing purchaser is the total value of sales to such competing purchaser, and
> (c) in any case where services are exacted in return therefor, the requirements thereof have regard to the kinds of services that competing purchasers at the same time or different levels of distribution are ordinarily able to perform or cause to be performed.

The provisions of section 35 apply to the sale of both articles and services. Discrimination in the granting of promotional allowances is a *per se* offence, not requiring proof of the existence of either a practice of discrimination or a lessening of competition. A company that wishes to discriminate among its customers may do so through the legal practice of granting quantity discounts.

GEOGRAPHIC PRICING STRATEGIES

In its pricing, a seller must consider the freight costs involved in shipping the product to the buyer. This consideration grows in importance as freight becomes a larger part of total variable costs. Pricing policies may be established whereby the buyer pays all the freight, the seller bears the entire costs, or the two parties share the expense. The chosen strategy can have an important bearing on (1) the geographic limits of a firm's market, (2) the location of its production facilities, (3) the source of its raw materials, and (4) its competitive strength in various market areas.

F.O.B. Point-of-Production Pricing

In one widely used geographic pricing strategy, the seller quotes the selling price at the factory or at some other point of production or origin. In this situation the buyer pays the entire cost of transportation. This is usually referred to as **f.o.b. mill** or **f.o.b. factory** pricing. Of the four strategies discussed in this section, this is the only one in which the seller does not pay *any* of the freight costs. The seller pays only the cost of loading the shipment aboard the carrier—hence the term **f.o.b.**, or **free on board**.

Under the f.o.b. factory pricing strategy, the seller nets the same amount on each sale of similar quantities. The delivered price to the buyer varies according to the freight charge. However, this pricing strategy has serious economic and marketing implications. In effect, f.o.b. mill pricing tends to establish a geographic monopoly for a given seller, because freight rates prevent distant competitors from entering the market. The seller, in turn, is increasingly priced out of more distant markets.

Uniform Delivered Pricing

Under the **uniform delivered pricing** strategy, the same delivered price is quoted to all buyers regardless of their locations. This strategy is sometimes referred to as "postage stamp pricing" because of its similarity to the pricing of first-class mail service. The net revenue to the seller varies, depending upon the shipping cost involved in each sale.

A uniform delivered price is typically used where transportation costs are a small part of the seller's total costs. This strategy is also used by many retailers who feel that "free" delivery is an additional service that strengthens their market position.

Under a uniform delivered price system, buyers located near the seller's factory pay for some of the costs of shipping to more distant locations. Critics of f.o.b. factory pricing are usually in favour of a uniform delivered price. They feel that the freight expense should not be charged to individual customers any more than any other single marketing or production expense.

Zone Delivered Pricing

Under a **zone delivered pricing** strategy, a seller would divide the Canadian market into a limited number of broad geographic zones. Then a uniform delivered price is set within each zone. Zone delivered pricing is similar to the system used in pricing parcel post services and long-distance telephone service. A firm that quotes a price and then says "Slightly higher west of the Lakehead" is using a two-zone pricing system. The freight charge built into the delivered price is an average of the charges at all points within a zone area.

When adopting this pricing strategy, the seller must walk a neat tightrope to avoid charges of illegal price discrimination. This means that the zone lines must be drawn so that all buyers who compete for a particular market are in the same zone. Such a condition is most easily met where markets are widely distributed.

Freight Absorption Pricing

A **freight absorption pricing** strategy may be adopted to offset some of the competitive disadvantages of f.o.b. factory pricing. With an f.o.b. factory price, a firm is at a price disadvantage when it tries to sell to buyers located in markets

M A R K E T I N G   A T   W O R K

FILE 13-1   **THE MODULAR APPROACH TO PRICING**

Interleaf is a producer of high-end publishing software and is a company that uses price bundling as an important part of its marketing strategy. Interleaf sells its core Technical Publishing Software for $2,500. Then there are options that can be added, such as the Advanced Graphics module ($4,500) and the Book Catalogue module ($2,500). The full version of Technical Publishing Software, including other modules, sells for $15,000. Because its product is sold in optional parts, Interleaf is able to adopt a high-price strategy in its less price-sensitive markets (where they have few rivals), while remaining competitive in lower-end markets, where competition is fierce and consumers are more price sensitive. With this strategy, Interleaf is able to standardize on one basic system while catering to the individual needs of specific customers — already they have designed add-on modules that appeal to the graphic arts, technical document, and newspaper market segments. Because potential and future modules can all be added to the core product, Interleaf is constantly able to vertically expand its markets.

Source: Adapted from Denes Bartakovich, "Building Competitive Advantage Through Creative Pricing Strategies," *Business Quarterly*, Summer 1990, pp. 47–48.

nearer to competitors' plants. To penetrate more deeply into such markets, a seller may be willing to absorb some of the freight costs. Thus, seller A will quote to the customer a delivered price equal to (1) A's factory price plus (2) the freight costs that would be charged by the competitive seller located nearest to that customer.

A seller can continue to expand the geographic limits of its market as long as its net revenue after freight absorption is larger than its marginal cost for the units sold. Freight absorption is particularly useful to a firm with excess capacity whose fixed costs per unit of product are high and whose variable costs are low. In these cases, management must constantly seek ways to cover fixed costs, and freight absorption is one answer.

The legality of freight absorption is reasonably clear. The strategy is legal if it is used independently and not in collusion with other firms. Also, it must be used only to meet competition. In fact, if practised properly, freight absorption can have the effect of strengthening competition because it can break down geographic monopolies.

SKIMMING AND PENETRATION PRICING

When pricing a product or service, especially a new market entry, management should consider whether to adopt a market-skimming pricing strategy or a penetration pricing strategy.

Market-Skimming Pricing

The market-skimming strategy involves setting a price that is high in the range of expected prices. This strategy is particularly suitable for new products because:

- In the early stages of a product's life cycle, price is less important, competition is minimal, and the product's distinctiveness lends itself to effective marketing.

MARKETING AT WORK

FILE 13-2   **WHEN PRICE SKIMMING HITS ETHICS**

Price skimming strategies are often used by drug companies. Not only do they cover the high costs of research, development, and production of a drug, but they support R&D work for future drugs while compensating for R&D costs from past products that failed in the laboratory or in the marketplace. It was in keeping with these strategies that in 1989 the Burroughs Wellcome Company (BW) — a British-based pharmaceutical manufacturer — introduced azidothymidine (AZT), a drug that controls advances of the AIDS virus in humans and adopted a price-skimming strategy. BW priced AZT at $8,000 (U.S.) for a year's supply per patient, making it one of the most expensive drugs ever sold. The gross margin on AZT was 70 to 80 percent — high, but equal to what other firms make on major new drugs. Later in 1989 however, the price was reduced to $6,400 for two reasons: the strong protests from AIDS activists and the anticipated market growth provoked by increasing acceptance of AZT as an AIDS treatment. The conclusion reached was that skimming strategies must be shaped to an extent by external environmental factors.

Source: Adapted from Marilyn Chase, ''Burroughs Wellcome Reaps Profits, Outrage from Its AIDS Drug,'' *The Wall Street Journal*, September 15, 1989. p. 1; ''Burroughs Wellcome Cuts Price of AZT under Pressure from AIDS Activists,'' *The Wall Street Journal*, September 19, 1989. p. 3.

- This strategy can effectively segment the market on an income basis. At first, the product is marketed to that segment that responds to distinctiveness in a product and is relatively insensitive to price. Later, the seller can lower the price and appeal to market segments that are more sensitive to price.
- The strategy acts as a strong hedge against a possible mistake in setting the price. If the original price is too high and the market does not respond, management can easily lower it. But it is very difficult to raise a price that has proven to be too low to cover costs.
- High initial prices can keep demand within the limits of a company's productive capacity.

Penetration Pricing   In penetration pricing, a low initial price is set to reach the mass market immediately. This strategy can also be employed at a later stage in the product's life cycle. Penetration pricing is likely to be more satisfactory than market skimming pricing when the following conditions exist:

- The product has a highly elastic demand.
- Substantial reductions in unit costs can be achieved through large-scale operations.
- The product is expected to face very strong competition soon after it is introduced to the market.

The nature of the potential competition will critically influence management's choice between the two pricing strategies. If competitors can enter a market quickly, and if the market potential for the product is very promising, management probably should adopt a policy of penetration pricing. Low initial pricing may do two things. First, it may discourage other firms from entering the field, because of the anticipated low profit margin. Second, low initial pricing may give the innovator such a strong hold on its share of the market that future competitors cannot cut into it. On the other hand, cream skimming may be more feasible when the market is not large enough to attract big competitors.

ONE-PRICE AND FLEXIBLE-PRICE STRATEGIES

Rather early in its pricing deliberations, management should decide whether to adopt a one-price strategy or a flexible-price strategy. Under a **one-price strategy**, a seller charges the *same* price to all similar customers who buy similar quantities of a product. Under a **flexible-price** (also called a **variable-price**) strategy, similar customers may each pay a *different* price when buying similar quantities of a product.

In Canada and the United States, a one-price strategy has been adopted more than variable pricing. Most retailers, for example, typically follow a one-price policy — except in cases where trade-ins are involved, and then flexible pricing abounds. A one-price policy builds customer confidence in a seller, whether at the manufacturing, wholesaling, or retailing level. Weak bargainers need not feel that they are at a competitive disadvantage.

When a flexible pricing policy is followed, often the price is set as a result of buyer-seller bargaining. In automobile retailing — with or without a trade-in — price negotiating (bargaining) is quite common, even though window-sticker prices may suggest a one-price policy. Variable pricing may be used to meet a competitor's price. Airlines have used an aggressive flexible pricing strategy to enter new markets and to increase their market share on existing routes. Their new business comes from two sources — passengers now flying on other airlines and passengers who would not fly at higher prices. In the second group, especially, the demand for air travel is highly elastic. The trick is to keep the market segment of price-sensitive passengers separate from the business-traveller segment, whose demand is inelastic. Airlines keep these segments apart by placing restrictions on the lower-priced tickets — requiring advance purchases, over-the-weekend stays in destination cities, etc.

This seller seems to have a one-price strategy. But at the end of the day, flexible pricing might be used to sell this produce before it spoils.

A considerable amount of flexible pricing does exist in Canada. On balance, however, a flexible-price strategy is generally less desirable than a one-price strategy. In sales, to business firms, but not to consumers, flexible pricing may be in violation of the Competition Act. Flexible pricing also may generate considerable ill will when the word gets around that some buyers acquired the product at lower prices.

UNIT PRICING

Unit pricing is a retail price-information-reporting strategy that, to date, has been employed by most supermarket chains. The method is, however, adaptable to other types of stores and products. The strategy is a business response to consumer protests concerning the proliferation of package sizes (especially in grocery stores). The practice has made it virtually impossible to compare prices of similar products. Regarding canned beans, for example: Is a can labelled "15½ avoirdupois ounces" for 39 cents a better deal than two "1-pound 1-ounce (482 grams)" cans for 89 cents?

In unit pricing, for each separate product and package size there is a shelf label that states (1) the price of the package and (2) this price expressed in dollars and cents per millilitre, litre, kilogram or some other standard measure.

Studies covering the early years of unit pricing showed that consumers — especially low-income consumers — were not using unit-pricing data. More recent studies show an increase in the awareness and usage of unit-pricing information. Unfortunately, however, city residents (typically lower-income markets) still use this information significantly less than do suburban residents (typically higher-income consumers).[5]

Increasingly, supermarkets and other retail stores are using electronic scanners at the checkout stands to read the Universal Product Code on products. Many of these retailers are no longer price-marking each individual item in a store. In such situations, unit-pricing shelf signs clearly are important, if not absolutely essential, to provide consumers with price information.

PRICE LINING

Price lining is used extensively by retailers. It consists of selecting a limited number of prices at which a store will sell its merchandise. A shoe store, for example, sells several styles of shoes at $69.88 a pair, another group at $79.88, and a third assortment at $89.88.

For the consumer, the main benefit of price lining is that it simplifies buying decisions. From the retailer's point of view, the strategy is advantageous because it helps store owners plan their purchases. A dress buyer, for example, can go into a market looking for dresses that can be retailed for $89.95 or $119.95.

Rising costs can put a real squeeze on price lines, because a company hesitates to change its price line every time costs go up. But if costs increase and prices remain stationary, then profit margins are compressed and the retailer may be forced to seek products with lower costs.

---

[5]See David A. Aaker and Gary T. Ford, "Unit Pricing Ten Years Later: A Replication," *Journal of Marketing*, Winter 1983, pp. 118–122.

This store followed a price-lining strategy.

RESALE PRICE MAINTENANCE

Some manufacturers want control over the prices at which retailers resell the manufacturers' products. This is most often done in Canada by following a policy of providing manufacturers' suggested list prices, where the price is just a guide for retailers. It is a list price on which discounts may be computed. For others, the suggested price is "informally" enforced. Normally enforcement of a suggested price, termed resale price maintenance, has been illegal in Canada since 1951. In this country, attempts on the part of the manufacturers to control or to influence upward the prices at which their products are sold by retailers have been considered akin to price fixing.

Section 38 of the Competition Act prohibits a manufacturer or supplier from requiring or inducing a retailer to sell a product at a particular price or not below a particular price. On occasion, a supplier may attempt to control retail prices through the use of a "suggested retail price." Under section 38, the use of "suggested retail prices" is permitted *only* if the supplier makes it clear to the retailer that the product *may* be sold at a price below the suggested price and that the retailer will not in any way be discriminated against if the product is sold at a lower price. Also, where a manufacturer advertises a product, and in the advertisement mentions a certain price, the manufacturer must make it clear in the advertisement that the product *may* be sold at a lower price.

Prior to 1975 it was legal in Canada for a manufacturer to refuse to supply a product to a retailer if that retailer was selling that product as a loss leader or was using the product in "bait advertising" to attract people to his or her store. The 1975 amendments to the Combines Investigation Act eliminated this provision, and it is now illegal for a manufacturer to refuse to supply a product to a retailer because of the pricing policies of the retailer. In other

A manufacturer's suggested price may be a starting point for a reseller's attractive discounts.

words, a retailer is free to sell a product at whatever price he or she deems appropriate, and the manufacturer of that product is not permitted to exert any pressure on the retailer to sell at a particular price.

LEADER PRICING AND UNFAIR-PRACTICES ACTS

Many firms, primarily retailers, temporarily cut prices on a few items to attract customers. This price and promotional strategy is called **leader pricing**, and the items whose prices may be reduced below the retailer's cost are called **loss leaders**. These leader items should be well-known heavily advertised articles that are purchased frequently. The idea is that customers will come to the store to buy the advertised leader items and then stay to buy other regularly priced merchandise. The net result, the firm hopes, will be increased total sales volume and net profit.

Three provinces, British Columbia, Alberta, and Manitoba, have had legislation dealing with loss leader selling. The approach has been to prohibit a reseller from selling an item below invoice cost, including freight, plus a stated markup, which is usually 5 percent at retail.

The general intent of these laws is commendable. They eliminate much of the predatory type of price-cutting; however, they permit firms to use loss leaders as a price and promotional strategy. That is, a retailer can offer an article below full cost but still sell above cost plus 5 percent markup. Under such acts, low-cost, efficient businesses are not penalized, nor are high-cost operators protected. Differentials in retailers' purchase prices can be reflected in their selling prices, and savings resulting from the absence of services can be passed on to the customers.

On the other hand, the laws have some glaring weaknesses. In the first place, the provinces do not establish provisions or agencies for enforcement. It is the responsibility and burden of the injured party to seek satisfaction from the offender in a civil suit. Another limitation is that it is difficult or even impossible to determine the cost of doing business for each individual product. The third weakness is that the laws seem to disregard the fundamental idea

MARKETING AT WORK

FILE 13-3   **VALUE PRICING VERSUS LEADER PRICING**

A common practice among retailers is buying products specifically to put them on sale. Increasingly, however, retailers are finding that such price strategies can backfire. Eaton's department store used to constantly mark down merchandise hoping to increase sales, but then they discovered that their tactics were only creating a credibility gap — customers never knew whether they were buying an item at the right price or if they had paid too much. Hoping to remedy their situation, Eaton's has now adopted a marketing plan of everyday "value pricing," inspired by the success of companies such as Toys 'Я' Us and IKEA, whose fair and stable prices, along with specialized services and a distinct and attractive image, have remained consistently stable and profitable.

Source: Adapted from Marina Strauss, "Price-Slashing a Short-Term Solution," The Globe and Mail. April 24, 1990, pp. 3, 4.

---

that the purpose of a business is to make a profit on the total operation, and not necessarily on each sale of each product.

PSYCHOLOGICAL PRICING — ODD PRICING

We have already briefly discussed some pricing strategies that might be called **psychological pricing**. For example, there is price lining, prestige pricing above competitive levels, and *raising* a too-low price in order to *increase* sales. At the retail level, another psychological pricing strategy is commonly used. Prices are set at odd amounts, such as 19 cents, 49 cents, and $19.95. Automobiles are priced at $14,995 rather than $15,000, and houses are listed at $179,950 instead of $180,000.

In general, retailers believe that pricing items at odd amounts will result in larger sales. Thus, a price of 49 cents or 98 cents will bring greater revenue than a price of 50 cents or $1. There is little concrete evidence to support retailers' belief in the value of odd prices. Various studies have reported inconclusive results. Odd pricing is often avoided in prestige stores or on higher-priced items. Thus more expensive men's suits are priced at $650, not $649.95.

PRICE VERSUS NON-PRICE COMPETITION

In the course of developing its marketing program, management has a choice of emphasizing price competition or nonprice competition. This choice can affect various other parts of the firm's marketing system.

Price Competition

In our economy today, there still is a considerable amount of price competition. A firm can effectively engage in price competition by regularly offering prices that are as low as possible. Along with this, the seller usually offers a minimum of services. In their early years, discount houses and chain stores competed in this way. A firm can also use price to compete by (1) changing its prices and (2) reacting to price changes made by a competitor.

PRICE CHANGES BY THE FIRM

Any one of several situations may prompt a firm to change its price. As costs

MARKETING AT WORK

FILE 13-4 **INSTANT CHANGE PRICING**

Fiercely competing supermarkets in North America and Europe have been engaged in price wars for years. There appears to be a new phase in the battle, however, as fighters lash out at each other armed with the latest weapon in pricing technology—electronic shelf pricing. This pricing system uses radio-frequency waves to transmit price data from an in-store data base to shelf-mounted panels with liquid crystal displays. At the touch of a button, cost per unit by weight or volume can be shown, while at the same time, bar-coding machines linked to the store's data base ensure prices at the cash registers match those on the shelves. The result is a store that can change hundreds of digital price displays instantly—a process that before took three days to carry out. Also eliminated are the labour and printing costs for the thousands of paper labels a typical store has to change every week. With about 30,000 supermarkets capable of benefiting from the system, suppliers are getting ready for their own battle—the one for the biggest possible piece of the estimated $2 billion to $3 billion market.

Source: Adapted from Beppi Crosariol, ''Arming for Grocery Price Wars,'' *Financial Times of Canada*, October 8, 1990, p. 7.

---

increase, for instance, management may decide to raise the price, rather than to cut quality or aggressively promote the product and still maintain the price. If a company's share of the market is declining because of strong competition, its executives may react initially by *reducing* their price. In the long run, however, their best alternative may be to improve their own marketing program, rather than to rely on the price cut. *Temporary* price cuts may be used to correct an imbalance in inventory or to introduce a new product.

From the seller's standpoint, the big disadvantage in price cutting is that competitors will retaliate. This is especially true in oligopolistic market situations. The net result can be a price war, and the price may even settle permanently at a lower level. Note that ''oligopoly'' does not necessarily imply *large* firms. *Oligopoly* means ''a few sellers.'' Thus a neighbourhood group of small merchants—dry cleaners or hair-styling services, for instance—can constitute an oligopoly. These service retailers will try to avoid price competition, because if one reduces prices, all must follow.

REACTION TO COMPETITOR'S PRICE CHANGES

Any firm can assume that its competitors will change prices. Consequently, every firm should be ready with some policy guidelines on how it will react. If a competitor *boosts* prices, a reasonable delay in reacting probably will not be perilous. Advance planning is particularly necessary in case of a competitive price *reduction*, since time is then of the essence.

Only a few years ago, Air Canada, Wardair, and Canadian Pacific faced new pricing strategy challenges under deregulation in Canada. In spite of having the example of what happened during the somewhat earlier U.S. airline price wars—ruinous price cutting resulting in heavy financial losses—these three engaged in similar price wars. Each airline cut its fares on lines competing with the others and while consumers benefited enormously, the result was to financially weaken Wardair to the point that it had to sell out to Canadian Airlines International. As soon as Wardair was acquired, cut-rate fares disappeared and more selective route competition was engaged.

Nonprice Competition

In nonprice competition, sellers maintain stable prices. They attempt to improve their market position by emphasizing other aspects of their marketing programs. Of course, competitive prices still must be taken into consideration, and price changes will occur over time. Nevertheless, in a nonprice competitive situation the emphasis is on something *other than* price.

By using terms familiar in economic theory, we can differentiate nonprice competition from price competition. In price competition, sellers attempt to move up or down their individual demand curves by changing prices. In nonprice competition, sellers attempt to *shift* their demand curves to the right by means of product differentiation, promotional activities, or some other device. This point is illustrated in Fig. 13-4. The demand curve faced by the producer of a given model of skis is DD. At a price of $250, the producer can sell 35,000 pairs a year in a ski market. On the basis of price competition alone, sales can be increased to 55,000 if the producer is willing to reduce the price to $230. The demand curve is still DD.

However, the producer is interested in boosting sales without any decrease in selling price. Consequently, the firm embarks upon a promotional program — a form of nonprice competition. Suppose enough new customers are persuaded to buy at the original $250 price so that unit sales increase to 55,000 pairs a year. In effect, the firm's entire demand curve has been shifted to position D'D'.

Two of the major methods of nonprice competition are **promotion** and **product differentiation**. In addition, some firms emphasize the **variety** and **quality** of their services.

FIGURE 13-4
Shift in demand curve for skis in a market.
The use of nonprice competition can shift the demand curve for a product. A company selling skis used a promotional program to sell more skis at the same price, thus shifting DD to D'D'. Volume increased from 35,000 to 55,000 units at $250 (point X to point Y). Besides advertising, what other devices might this firm use to shift its demand curve?

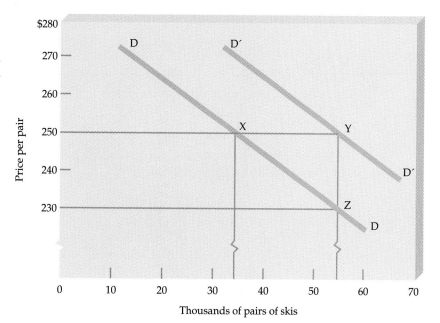

MARKETING AT WORK

FILE 13-5   **PAYING A PRICE TO SEND A MESSAGE**

There is a very important relationship between price and brand name. This is especially obvious in the case of fashion merchandising and personal care items. In some cases, consumers are prepared to pay quite high prices for certain clothing items and then *advertise* the manufacturer's brand name free. The phenomenon of visible brands is an important one in fashion merchandising in recent years and points to the fact that consumers are not particularly interested in the product's functional attributes when they buy some items of clothing. Whereas a student could buy a sweatshirt with a relatively obscure brand name at a local discount clothing store, he or she may be willing to pay two or three times as much for a sweatshirt that has the brand name of Roots, Benetton, or Cotton Ginny. In this case, price seems less important than other motivating factors in influencing the purchase decision. This is a situation where nonprice competition is at work to differentiate one brand from another.

Combining price and nonprice appeals: a suite for the price of a room.

Nonprice competition is being used increasingly in marketing. Companies want, at least to some extent, to be the masters of their own destiny. In nonprice competition, a seller's entire advantage is not removed when a competitor decides to undersell. Furthermore, there is little customer loyalty when price is the only feature that distinguishes the seller. Buyers will stick only as long as that seller offers the lowest price.

PRICING IN NONBUSINESS AND NONPROFIT SETTINGS

Pricing in many nonbusiness organizations is quite different from pricing in a business firm. First, pricing becomes less important when profit making is not an organizational goal. Also, many nonbusiness groups believe there are *no* client-market pricing considerations in their marketing because there is no charge to the client. The organization's basic function is to help those who cannot afford to pay.

Actually, the products or services received by the clients rarely are free — that is, without a price of some kind. True, the price may not be a monetary charge. Often, however, the client pays a charge — in the form of travel and waiting time, and perhaps degrading treatment — that a money-paying client-customer would not incur for the same service. Poor children who have to wear donated, second-hand clothes certainly are paying a price if their classmates ridicule these clothes. Alcoholics Anonymous and some drug rehabilitation organizations that provide "free" services do exact a price. They require active participation by their clients and often a very strongly expressed resolve by clients to help themselves.

Some nonbusiness groups *do* face the same general pricing problems we discussed in Chapter 12. Museums and opera companies must decide on admission prices; fraternal organizations must set a schedule for dues; and colleges must determine how much to charge for tuition. These and other not-for-profit organizations typically face a cash-management problem, the same as in profit-seeking firms. Not-for-profit firms still must generate enough revenue from some source to cover all their costs. For example, an organization may budget a preplanned loss from its own operating revenues. This organization still must price its offerings in such a way that the operating revenues come in at the targeted loss figure. Let's take the case of a private school as an illustration. This school's total operating costs are budgeted at $10 million for next year. The school is expecting to generate $7 million in tuition revenue, leaving a loss of $3 million to be covered by gifts and other grants. Now the school must set its price (tuition) in such a way as to generate enough revenue to meet its $7 million target. Basically this is the same situation that a profit-seeking firm faces when pricing to meet a predetermined profit target. Essentially, not-for-profit organizations must (1) determine the base price for their product offering and (2) establish pricing strategies in several areas of their pricing structure.

SETTING THE BASE PRICE

Here again we are faced with two market situations—pricing in the contributor market and pricing in the client market.

When dealing with the contributor market, nonbusiness organizations really do not set the price of the donation. That price is set by contributors when they decide how much they are willing to pay for the benefits they expect to receive in return for their gifts. However, the organization may suggest a price.

MARKETING AT WORK

FILE 13-6 ALL BENEFITS HAVE COSTS

The concept of price is one that many not-for-profit and nonbusiness organizations often have difficulty using in their marketing programs. Many tend to think of price only in *monetary* terms and conclude that they do not set prices. The Salvation Army does not set a price on a donation. The Boy Scouts do not tell you how much to pay for an apple (although they may suggest a minimum price). Most churches do not exact a set weekly contribution from their parishioners. Some charitable organizations may not deal in very much money at all. Others do have to make more traditional pricing decisions when they set ticket prices, membership dues, and similar charges.

It may be more useful for a not-for-profit organization to think in terms of *costs* rather than prices. Since much of the activity of such organizations involves attracting volunteers, convincing people to support a particular cause, or to donate their time and interest, it is often appropriate to ask, ''What are we costing people to deal with us?'' How much are we asking them to commit, not in monetary terms, but in terms of time, effort, and psychic commitment?

Being a Big Brother or Big Sister or a Red Cross blood donor may not cost us anything in dollar terms, but it certainly takes time and a major psychological commitment. Think about how such organizations can use this definition of price in their marketing programs.

For nonbusiness organizations, price is often left to the consumer.

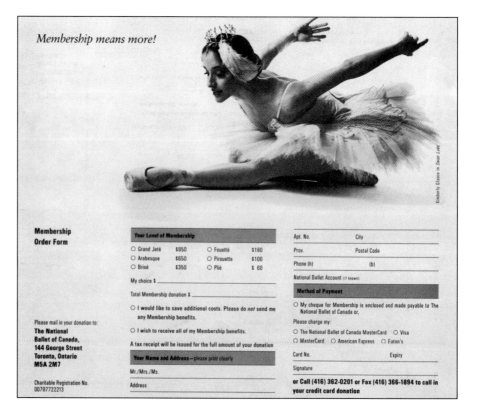

A charitable organization, for example, may suggest that you donate one day's pay or that you donate your time for one day a month.

For the most nonbusiness organizations, the basic pricing methods used by business firms — cost-plus, balance of supply and demand, market alone — simply are not appropriate. Many organizations know they cannot cover their costs with prices charged to client markets. The difference between anticipated revenues and costs must be made up by contributions.

As yet, we simply have not developed any real guidelines — any methodology — for much of our nonbusiness pricing. A major problem here is that most nonbusiness organizations simply do not know the cost of the products and services they offer in their client markets.

PRICING STRATEGIES

Some of the pricing strategies discussed earlier are also applicable in nonbusiness marketing. Discount strategies have widespread use, for example. Some museums offer discount prices to students and to senior citizens. A season ticket for some opera companies or symphony orchestras costs less per performance than tickets purchased on an individual-performance basis. This is a form of quantity discount.

Considerations regarding one price versus variable price also are strategies applicable in nonbusiness marketing. Many nursing homes charge according to the resident's ability to pay—a variable-price strategy. A one-price strategy typically is followed by most universities. That is, all students pay the same tuition for a full load of coursework.

SUMMARY After deciding on pricing goals and then setting the base (list) price, the next task in pricing is to establish specific strategies in several areas of the pricing structure. One of these areas relates to discounts and allowances—deductions from the list price. Management has the option of offering quantity discounts, trade discounts, cash discounts, and other types of deductions. The factor of freight costs must also be considered in pricing strategy. A producer can pay all the freight (uniform delivered price) or let the buyer pay the freight bill (f.o.b. factory price). Or the two parties can share the cost in some proportion (freight absorption). Any decisions involving discounts or freight allowances must be made in conformity with the Competition Act. This is a major law relating to price discrimination and other aspects of a company's marketing program.

When pricing a product, especially a new product, a company should consider whether to use a market-skimming or a penetration pricing strategy. Management also should decide whether to charge the same price to all similar buyers (one-price strategy) or to adopt a flexible (variable) pricing strategy. Unit pricing—a relatively new development—can affect a company's marketing program. Some firms, especially retailers, have adopted price lining as a marketing strategy. Many retailers use leader pricing to stimulate sales. Odd pricing is a psychological pricing strategy commonly used by retailers.

Another basic decision facing management is whether to engage primarily in price competition or in nonprice competition. Most firms prefer to use promotion, product differentiation, and other nonprice marketing activities, rather than to rely only on price as a sales stimulant.

KEY TERMS AND CONCEPTS

Quantity discount: 411
Noncumulative discount 411
Cumulative discount 411
Trade (functional) discount 411
Cash discount 412
Competition Act 413
F.o.b. factory price 416
Uniform delivered price 416
Zone delivered price 416
Freight absorption 416
Market skimming pricing 417

Penetration pricing 418
One-price strategy 419
Flexible-price strategy 419
Unit pricing 420
Price lining 420
Resale price maintenance 421
Leader pricing 422
Odd pricing 423
Price competition 423
Nonprice competition 425

QUESTIONS AND PROBLEMS

1. Carefully distinguish between cumulative and noncumulative quantity discounts. Which of these two types of quantity discounts has the greater economic and social justification? Why?

2. A manufacturer of appliances quotes a list price of $800 per unit for a certain model of refrigerator and grants trade discounts of 35, 20, and 5 percent. What is the manufacturer's selling price? Who might get these various discounts?

3. Company A sells to all its customers at the same published price. A sales executive finds that company B is offering to sell to one of A's customers at a lower price. Company A then cuts its price to this customer but maintains the original price for all other customers. Is this a violation of the Competition Act?

4. Name some products that might logically be sold under a uniform delivered price system.

5. "An f.o.b. point-of-purchase system is the only geographic price system that is fair to buyers." Discuss.

6. An Ontario firm wants to compete in Western Canada, where it is at a significant disadvantage with respect to freight costs. What pricing alternatives can it adopt to overcome the freight differential?

7. For each of the following products, do you recommend that the seller adopt a market-skimming or a penetration pricing strategy? Support your decision in each instance.
   a. Original models of women's dresses styled and manufactured by Alfred Sung.
   b. A new wonder drug.
   c. An exterior house paint that wears twice as long as any competitive brand.
   d. A cigarette *totally* free of tar and nicotine.
   e. A tablet that converts a litre of water into a litre of automotive fuel.

8. Under what marketing conditions is a company likely to use a variable-price strategy? Can you name some firms that employ this strategy, other than when a trade-in is involved?

9. Distinguish between leader pricing and predatory price cutting.

10. How should a manufacturer of prefinished plywood interior wall panelling react if a competitor cuts prices?

11. What factors account for the increased use of nonprice competition?

12. On the basis of the topics covered in this chapter, establish a set of price strategies for the manufacturer of a new glass cleaner that is sold through a broker to supermarkets. The manufacturer sells the product at $10 for a case of a dozen 459 mL bottles.

13. Suppose you are president of a company that has just developed a camera and film process somewhat comparable to Polaroid's. The camera is designed to be used only with film produced by your firm. The chief marketing executive recommended that the camera be priced relatively low and the film relatively high. The idea was to make it easy to buy the camera, because from then on the customer would have to buy the company's film. The company's chief accountant said "no" to that idea. He wanted to price both camera and film in relation to their full cost plus a reasonable profit. You are mulling over these alternative strategies and also wondering whether there is not a third alternative, better than either of those two. Which pricing strategy would you adopt for the new camera and film?

14. Identify the various prices and costs that a neighbourhood child-care clinic should consider in developing its marketing program.

C A S E S   F O R   P A R T   4

CASE 4.1 ## Upper Canada Brewing Company (C): Developing a Pricing Strategy

Frank Heaps, president of the Upper Canada Brewing Company, was preparing the pricing section of his marketing plan for the products of his brewery. He realized that the pricing decisions were especially important because they affected both the level of sales the brewery would achieve and how much profit would be earned. He also realized that price often had a psychological impact on consumers and thus could be used symbolically as an indicator of quality to position the products in the consumer's mind. The decision on price was further complicated by its strong interrelationship with the three other elements of the marketing mix: product and packaging, advertising and promotion, and distribution channels. With these important considerations in mind, Mr. Heaps faced the task of setting the retail selling price for his product(s).

THE PRICING OBJECTIVE

Although the Upper Canada Brewing Company was a relatively small and new organization, Mr. Heaps had taken time to carefully prepare a pricing objective. To ensure that the pricing objectives flowed from — and fit in with — the corporate and marketing objectives, Mr. Heaps chose a sales-oriented pricing goal. The specific objective was to capture a 0.1 percent share of the Ontario beer market, growing to 0.3 percent within five years. To achieve this objective, he anticipated that the company would generate a loss for the first one or two years but would

obtain an adequate profit and return on investment in the long run.

THE RETAIL SELLING PRICE

Given the unique characteristics of the beer market, Mr. Heaps realized that he did not have complete freedom to set the selling price for his products at any level he desired. This "floor" price was used to establish the retail selling price for Ontario domestic brands (see Exhibit C-1). Mr. Heaps also realized that in the beer industry most buyers and sellers were very familiar with beer prices. Thus, consumers had a good idea of the price that they expected to pay for European-style, top-quality beer products. It was his perception that the target market chosen by the Upper Canada Brewing Company was not price sensitive, but he wondered if buyers would be willing to pay a price higher than that established for quality imports. The prices for import beers sold in Ontario in 1983 and 1984 are given in Exhibit C-2.

To set the retail selling price for his products, key information on the costs, both fixed and variable, were needed. Heaps has a clear idea of the cost of the project to date. The total budget for the acquisition and installation of the brewery equipment was $1.1 million, and the building acquisition cost was roughly another $1 million.

To forecast an operating statement for the first two years of operation, Mr. Heaps assumed that he could sell the 175,000 gallons of beer needed to achieve his 0.1 percent market share. He also

EXHIBIT C-1 **ONTARIO DOMESTIC BEER PRICES**

	Keg	24-Pack	12-Pack	6-Pack
1983	$82.00	$15.55	$8.40	$4.50
1984	—	16.50	8.95	4.75

SOURCE: Liquor Control Board of Ontario (L.C.B.O.)

This case was prepared by Donna M. Stapleton and is intended to stimulate discussion of an actual management problem and not to illustrate either effective or ineffective handling of that problem. The author wishes to acknowledge the support provided by the Upper Canada Brewing Company, and particularly by Frank Heaps, President.

EXHIBIT C-2 **ONTARIO IMPORT BEER PRICES**

			1983	1984
Bass Pale Ale	(British)	6-pack	$7.15	$7.25
Beck's	(German)	6-pack	5.45	5.90
Carta Blanca	(Mexican)	6-pack	6.15	6.40
Dortmunder Union	(German)	3-pack	3.20	3.20
Genesee Lager	(American)	6-pack	4.55	4.85
Goesser Export	(Austrian)	6-pack	5.55	5.60
Harp Lager	(Irish)	4-pack*	3.95	—
Heineken Lager	(Dutch)	6-pack*	6.20	6.50
Heineken Lager	(Dutch)	6-pack	6.25	6.50
Holston DiaMalt	(German)	6-pack	5.85	—
Kirin	(Japanese)	6-pack	5.65	6.10
Krakaus	(Polish)	6-pack	4.85	5.45
Kronenbourg	(French)	6-pack	6.60	6.65
Lowenbrau Dark Special	(German)	6-pack	6.25	6.30
Lowenbrau Light Special	(German)	6-pack	6.25	6.30
MacEwan's Export Scotch Ale	(British)	6-pack	7.75	—
Michelob	(American)	6-pack	5.75	5.95
Newcastle Brown Ale	(British)	4-pack*	5.75	5.85
Pilsner Urquell	(Czechoslovakian)	4-pack	4.35	4.35
Schlitz	(American)	6-pack	5.45	5.45
Swan Lager	(Australian)	4-pack*	5.40	5.80
Tsing Tao	(Chinese)	6-pack	—	7.25
Tennant's Lager	(British)	4-pack*	4.75	—
Tuborg	(Danish)	6-pack	5.95	6.40
Whitbread Pale Ale	(British)	6-pack	7.00	—

SOURCE: Liquor Control Board of Ontario (L.C.B.O.)
*cans

projected that the sales would be 23.6 percent of annual production in kegs and 76.4 percent in bottles. This mix will change to 18.0 percent and 82.0 percent in 1986. To complete the forecast, he chose a selling price of his product in kegs to be $95 per keg based on a premium above the 1983 domestic premium brand price of $82 per keg. The selling price for a case of 12 341 mL bottles for the year 1985 was projected to be $13. This was based on the average price of 1983 imported brands. The forecasted operating statement is given in Exhibit C-3 with the notes and assumptions to support the financial projections.

THE DECISION

Selecting the final retail selling price was simplified by the fact that Mr. Heaps did not have to consider what type of discount schedule or geographic pricing policy to use. Price deals to middlemen were prohibited in the Ontario beer market, and all products were distributed with a uniform delivered price to all buyers regardless of their location. Even with this added simplification, establishing the retail selling price was not an easy decision. Mr. Heaps debated whether he should set his price equal to the forecasted selling price of $95 per keg and $13 per 12-pack. He realized that if he set a higher price it would mean larger margins and fewer sales required to break even, but it could prevent him from achieving his pricing goal of 0.1 percent market share. If he set a lower price, it would increase his chances of achieving the desired market share but could lead to profitless success. The dilemma he faced was to determine the price that would optimize his profit (minimize his projected loss), yet ensure that the company market share objective was achieved.

EXHIBIT C-3 **Forecast Operating Statement**

Gallons Sold	175,000	250,000
Gross Sales	$2,348,111	$3,522,167
Less: retail sales tax	(251,583)	(377,375)
Net sales	2,096,528	3,144,792
Cost of sales:		
Opening inventory	$ 0	$ 70,000
Materials and manufacturing	630,000	858,000
Less: closing inventory	(70,000)	(91,500)
	560,000	836,500
Federal excise tax	138,801	198,288
Federal sales tax	183,153	274,729
Provincial ad valorem tax	366,719	550,079
Cost of sales	1,248,673	1,859,596
Gross margin	847,855	1,285,196
Operating costs:		
Distribution	176,199	264,298
Marketing and promotion	175,000	175,000
Management and administration	200,000	225,000
Bank interest	198,333	171,394
Maintenance	5,000	10,000
Depreciation	145,000	130,000
Total operating costs	899,532	975,692
Operating income (loss)	($ 51,677)	$ 309,504

Notes to Support Financial Projections

1. Provincial retail sales tax is 12 percent of net sales.
2. Cost of sales for material and manufacturing was estimated at about $3.20 per gallon (which included materials, supplies, labour, utilities, realty and business taxes, and insurance). A 5 percent per annum increase is projected.
3. Federal excise tax was $0.793152 per gallon sold.
4. Federal sales tax was 12 percent of the gross sales price.
5. Provincial Ad valorem tax was 17.4917 percent of the net sales price.
6. Brewers' warehousing distribution costs were based on an average service charge of $1.00685 per gallon with a 5 percent increase per year.
7. Marketing and promotion costs had been estimated at roughly 7.5 percent of gross sales for the first year and 5 percent in the second year.
8. Management and administration costs included projected salaries for the general manager, office manager, brewmaster and office staff, management fees, professional services, overhead, and sundry office expenses.
9. Interest was a rough estimate based at 14 percent on the total of the net long-term loan and the revolving line of credit.
10. Maintenance cost estimates were in addition to plant maintenance personnel wages, which were included in material and manufacturing costs.

11. Depreciation was estimated at 10 percent on a declining balance basis for equipment and 5 percent for building and improvements.

12. 1 hectolitre = 21.9 gallons
    1 hectolitre = 100 litres
    1 litre = 1,000 millilitres
    1 keg = 25 gallons
    12 – 341 mL bottles = .896 148 gallons

QUESTIONS

1. Evaluate the pricing objective set by Mr. Heaps.

2. What retail selling price would you recommend? What impact will increasing or decreasing the retail selling price have on the company's bottom line and pricing objective?

CASE 4.2   **Hillcrest Products**

The executives of Hillcrest Products were trying to decide what pricing strategy and what retail price they should set for their new product. The new product, a liquid glass cleaner called Shine-Thru, was ready for marketing on a full-scale basis. The product was in liquid form and golden in colour. It was competitive with such brands as Windex, Bon-Ami, and Easy-Off. Market research indicated that Windex held about 70 percent of the market with no other brand reaching over 10 percent of the market.

Management in the Hillcrest company felt that its product was superior to anything else on the market. Market tests had shown that once consumers tried this product, they strongly favoured it over anything they had used previously. The product's main advantage was that it did not leave a film. Also, the Hillcrest product was nontoxic, a distinct advantage in households where there were small children.

The product came in a 500 mL clear plastic bottle with a plunger-type spray dispenser top. The fact that the plastic was unbreakable was another favourable differentiating product feature. The product was packed 12 to a case. Hillcrest marketed through supermarket chains in the Atlantic provinces. The company used a separate food broker to reach the chains in each brokerage area.

In setting its own selling price, the company had to have some intended retail price in mind in order to allow for the necessary broker's fee and retailer's margin. The company planned to allow retailers a margin of 25 percent of their selling price and the brokers a fee of 10 percent of Hillcrest's selling price.

The unit variable cost for Shine-Thru packed in case losts was 93 cents. This included the plastic package, the liquid cleaner itself, the shipping carton, freight, and direct labour for filling the packages and preparing the cartons for shipment. It was difficult to estimate overhead very accurately at this stage. Administrative and office salaries would be about $25,000. Other overhead costs, including travel expense but excluding advertising, were figured at $15,000. Of course, the largest single indirect expense was advertising. The company expected to plough all available funds into advertising and display. If necessary, the company would operate at a loss for a few years rather than skimp on advertising. The advertising budget for the first year was set at $30,000.

The usual retail selling prices of competitive products in supermarkets were as follows:

Windex	600 mL bottle	$1.99
Windex	425 g aerosol can	$1.69
Windex	225 mL bottle	$ .99
Easy-Off	425 g aerosol can	$1.59
Bon-Ami	425 g aerosol can	$1.79

This case was adapted by Lanita Carter. Used with permission.

QUESTIONS

1. What pricing strategy would you recommend for Shine-Thru? Why?
2. What retail price do you recommend for Shine-Thru? Why?
3. What should Hillcrest's selling price for Shine-Thru be?
4. What is the break-even point in units and in revenue given the selling price you recommended?

CASE 4.3 **Horizon Video Company: Pricing a Rental Service**

Henry and Frances Seybold were discussing how they might increase the weekday customer traffic in their store—Horizon Video Company. They had done a limited amount of advertising during the past year and concluded that the slight improvement in store traffic did not justify the advertising costs. Now they were devoting their attention to the current pricing schedule for their products.

Horizon Video was a retail store that rented movies and videocassette recorders (VCRs). The store also sold a line of VCR-related products. It was located in a small shopping centre in a Western college town with a population of about 80,000. Henry's and Frances Seybold had purchased the store from its original owners a little over a year ago.

Horizon carried a rental stock of 1,350 movies and 10 VCRs. Products for sale included used movies, blank videocassette tapes, videocassette holders, VCR connectors, and VCR head cleaners. The inventory of rental films included various categories, such as romance, horror, science fiction, war, comedy, classics, and even some "adult" movies. Horizon purchased two to six new films each month, some in multiple copies, depending on what was available and the store's financial condition. The cost of a new film ranged from $50 to $70.

Horizon's owners identified their market broadly as any person or family that owned a TV set. One segment of this market included people who owned a VCR and rented movies; another segment rented both the VCR and the movies. Henry noted that over half of Horizon's customers were between the ages of 23 and 50, about

equally divided between men and women. The majority seemed to be middle-income adults or lower-income college students. The students were more price-conscious and less store-loyal than the older customers.

Frances said that Horizon faced considerable competition in the city. The Yellow Pages telephone directory listed 21 retail stores under the heading of "videotapes and discs—renting and leasing." Frances also noted that their main competition came from four nearby stores, including a supermarket in the same shopping centre as Horizon. Each of the three video-store competitors had about two and a half times as much store space as Horizon and all were more attractively furnished. However, Frances felt that their store was "a nice clean place with a pleasant, friendly atmosphere." Two of the four competitors offered an annual membership deal that included lower rental charges to members. The pricing schedule in the four competing stores is shown in Exhibit 1.

Adapted from a case prepared by Scott Hansen, under supervision of Professor William J. Stanton.

EXHIBIT 1   **Pricing schedules of Horizon's main competitors**

Store	Annual membership Charge	Movie rental per day, any day			VCR rental per day	
			Member	Nonmember	Member	Nonmember
Sunset Video	$10	One move Additional movies	$3 $2	$5 $4	$6.95 (Mon.–Fri.) $9.95 (Sat.–Sun.)	Same
Laser Sound Video	$40	One movie Additional movies	$3 $2	$5 $4	$7.98 (Mon.–Fri.) $9.98 (Sat.–Sun.)	$9.98 per day
Hollywood-at-Home	None	One movie Additional movies	$2.99 $1.99	— —	$9.95 (Sun.–Thurs.) $12.95 (Fri.–Sat.)	— —
Supermarket	None	One movie Additional movies	$1.99 $ .99	— —	$4.99 any day	—

In Henry's opinion, the most serious difficulty facing Horizon was the lack of store traffic during the week. Many days were extremely slow, and the problem seemed to be getting worse. Weekends, especially Friday nights, were better, but still not what they had hoped for.

The Seybolds had done a limited amount of advertising in the classified section of student newspapers on the college campus in the city. However, the slight improvement in customer traffic was not enough to justify the advertising costs.

As Henry and Frances continued the discussion of the customer-traffic situation, their attention shifted to their pricing structure for rental video movies and VCRs. At the time, their rental schedule was as follows:

For movies:
Monday, Tuesday, Thursday: 2 for $5 or $3 each.
Wednesday: 2 for $3; additional movies $3 each.
Friday, Saturday, Sunday: $3 each with no quantity discount.

For VCRs:
$10.95 per day, any day, including 2 "free" movies.

Horizon did not charge a membership fee, but did use a "punch-card" system. By purchasing a punch card, a customer, in effect, paid for movie rentals in advance and in so doing, received a substantial discount. Punch-card prices were as follows:

7-movie punch card: $15.

12-movie punch card: $25.

17-movie punch card: $30.

The cards had no expiration date and could be used by anyone whose name was listed on the back of the card. The Seybolds believed that the punch cards had helped to increase store loyalty and repeat business. About 150 punch cards had been sold.

The Seybolds also distributed "2 for 1" cards to local appliance stores that sold VCRs. These cards were given to customers who bought a new VCR, and entitled them to 20 "2 for 1" movie rentals. With a "2 for 1" card, the rental price was $3 for two movies any day of the week. Currently about 100 customers were using these cards.

As they reviewed their own pricing structure and compared it with competitors' prices, Henry raised the question of whether their pricing structure was too complicated and thus confusing to customers. He noted that some other video stores in town charged the same rental price every day of the week. He also considered cutting Horizon's price to $2 per movie every day of the week. But Frances said this might upset the punch-card holders.

QUESTION

What changes, if any, should Horizon make in its pricing schedule?

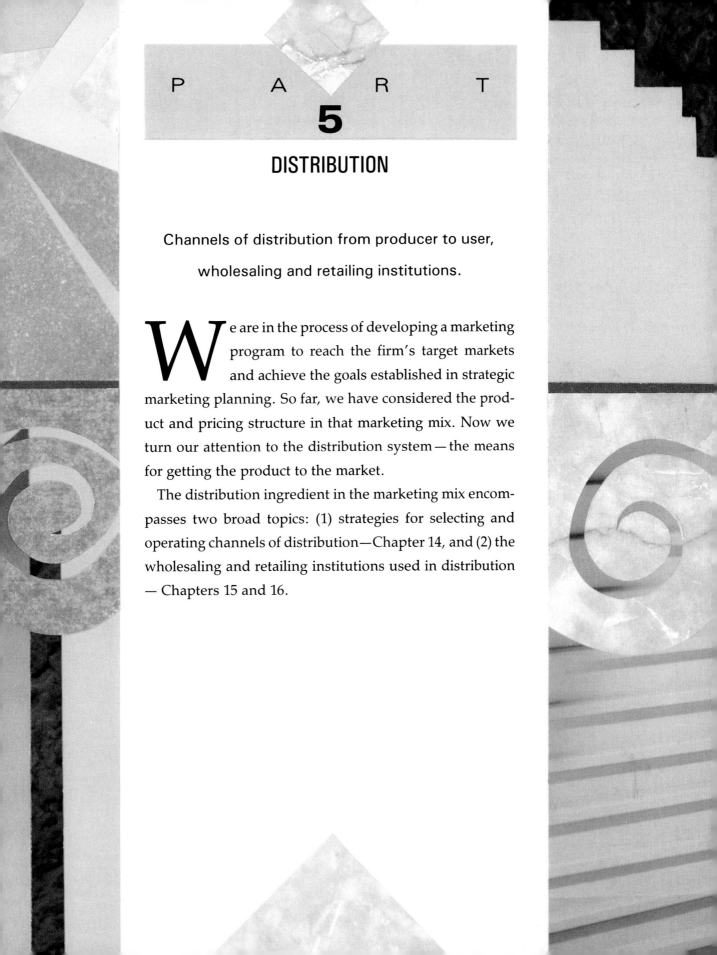

PART

5

DISTRIBUTION

Channels of distribution from producer to user,
wholesaling and retailing institutions.

We are in the process of developing a marketing program to reach the firm's target markets and achieve the goals established in strategic marketing planning. So far, we have considered the product and pricing structure in that marketing mix. Now we turn our attention to the distribution system — the means for getting the product to the market.

The distribution ingredient in the marketing mix encompasses two broad topics: (1) strategies for selecting and operating channels of distribution—Chapter 14, and (2) the wholesaling and retailing institutions used in distribution — Chapters 15 and 16.

CHAPTER 14 GOALS

A distribution channel sometimes is a tightly coordinated system. Other times it consists of independent and competing firms. Whatever the circumstances, for a product to reach its intended market, a channel of distribution must be well managed. After studying this chapter, you should be able to explain:

- The nature and importance of middlemen.
- What a distribution channel is.
- The sequence of decisions involved in designing a channel.
- The major channels of distribution for consumer goods, business goods, and services.
- Multiple channels of distribution.
- Vertical marketing systems.
- Factors affecting the selection of a channel.
- The concept of intensity of distribution.
- The choice of individual middlemen.
- The nature of horizontal and vertical conflicts in distribution channels.
- The concept of channel control.
- Legal considerations in channels management.

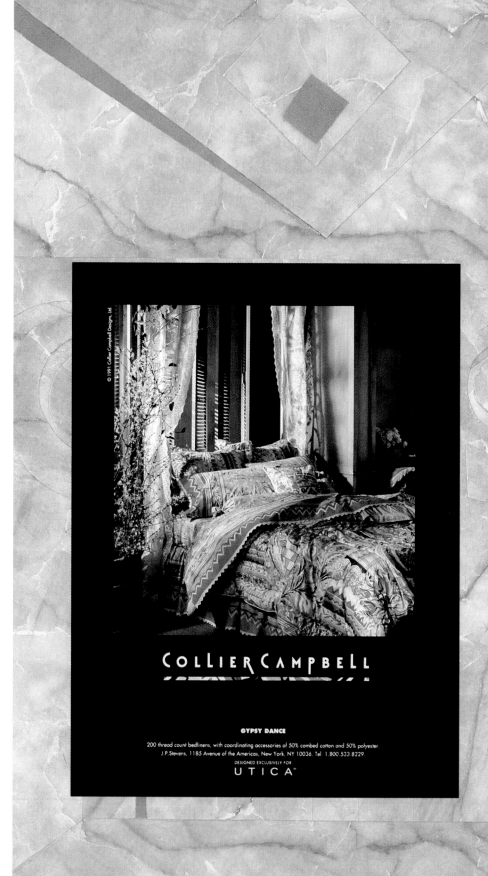

COLLIER CAMPBELL

GYPSY DANCE

200 thread count bedlinens, with coordinating accessories of 50% combed cotton and 50% polyester.
J.P. Stevens, 1185 Avenue of the Americas, New York, NY 10036. Tel. 1.800.533.8229.

DESIGNED EXCLUSIVELY FOR
UTICA

Channels of Distribution: Conflicts, Cooperation, and Management

W hat do channels of distribution have to do with cross-border shopping? More than just the obvious effects of exchange rates, tariffs and taxes (the GST and various PST's — provincial sales taxes). The research into Canadian consumers' cross-border hopping and shopping tells us more than we ever knew about Canada's channels of distribution and the web of operating policies and strategies that hold them together. An Ernst & Young study, prepared for the federal Ministry of Industry, Science and Technology, shows that origin of product, strategy of manufacturer, type of distribution channels, and degree of competition at different channel levels all contribute to Canadian–U.S. price and product assortment differences. And these differences, in addition to exchange rates, tariffs, and taxes, contribute to the cost and price differences.

As an illustration, take the distribution of bedding and linen. Bed sheets and pillowcases have been high on the cross-border shopper's list for a long time, not just recently. Canadian manufacturers supply the low end of the market (about 20 to 30 percent of bedding and linen sales). Mid-priced goods, the major share of the market, are generally imported from the United States. High-priced goods — which are a small share of the market — come primarily from Europe.

The Canadian and U.S. channels are similar for the low-end market: the dominant retailers (department stores and other mass merchandisers) buy mainly from domestic manufacturers and apply a 40 to 60 percent markup. Independents and smaller retailers buy from distibutors who have applied a 30 to 40 percent markup to the manufacturers' price and the retailers, in turn, apply a 30 to 50 percent markup.

But for the huge mid-priced market, while the channels remain the same in the United States, they change in Canada simply because imports supply the bulk of the needs. The imported bedding items move from the U.S. manufacturer to its Canadian subsidiary, which ads a 100 percent markup. This markup covers the manufacturer's price, exchange, tariffs, transportation, subsidiary operating cost, and profit. The subsidiary then sells to Canadian department stores and mass merchandisers, who add a 100 percent markup to their cost. It also sells to Canadian distributors, who add a 30 to 40 percent markup, and they, in turn, sell to independent retailers, who add markups ranging from 50 to 150 percent on their cost. The story is the same for many imported goods, not just bedding and linens.

The Ernst & Young study points to a number of channel-of-distribution differences and practices that distinguish the Canadian and U.S. situations:

- The differences in market size mean that economies of scale are less available in the Canadian distribution system, resulting in higher costs.
- Competition between the manufacturer, distributor, and retailer levels in channels is more intense in the United States because of its larger scale of market, resulting in lower margins and prices.
- Gross margins are higher in Canada partly because of higher product, operating, wage, and tax costs.
- For products imported into Canada and not purchased directly from a foreign manufacturer, an extra level in the distribution system increases costs all through the channel.[1]

Even before a product is ready for market, management should determine what methods and routes will be used to get it there. This task involves establishing a strategy covering distribution channels and physical distribution of the product.

Managing a distribution channel often begins with a producer. Therefore, we will discuss channels largely from the vantage point of the producer. As you will see, however, the channel problems and opportunities of middlemen are similar to those faced by producers. Furthermore, the control of channels used by producers may actually rest with middlemen.

MIDDLEMEN AND DISTRIBUTION CHANNELS

Product ownership has to be transferred somehow from the individual or organization making it to the consumer needing it. Goods also must be transported from the production site to the location where they are needed. (As was discussed in Chapter 11, services ordinarily cannot be shipped but rather are produced and consumed in the same place.)

Distribution's role within a marketing mix is getting the product to its target market. Overall responsibility rests with the distribution channel, with some tasks assumed by middlemen in this channel. Thus we begin by discussing the activities and roles of middlemen and a distribution channel.

Getting a product to market entails a number of activities, most importantly arranging for its sale (and the transfer of title) from producer to final customer. Other common functions are promoting the product, storing it, and assuming some of the risk during the distribution process.

A producer can carry out these functions in exchange for an order (and, ultimately, payment) from a consumer. Or producer and consumer can divide up the activities. Typically firms called middlemen perform these activities on behalf of the producer or consumer.

A **middleman** is a business firm that renders services directly related to the purchase and/or sale of a product as it flows from producer to consumer. A middleman either owns the product or actively aids in the transfer of ownership. Often, but not always, a middleman takes physical possession of the product, whereas others do not physically handle it.

Middlemen are commonly classified on the basis of whether or not they take

[1]Adapted from Kenneth Kidd, "Price Gaps That Drive Canadians to U.S. Shops," p. 1, and "The Costly Steps to Canada's Cash Registers," p. B1-2, *Globe and Mail*, April 23, 1991.

title to the products involved. **Merchant middlemen** actually take title to the goods they are helping to market. **Agent middlemen** never actually own the goods, but they do actively assist in the transfer of title. Real estate brokers, manufacturers' agents, and travel agents are examples of agent middlemen. The two major groups of merchant middlemen are wholesalers and retailers. Middlemen operate as vital links between producers and ultimate consumers or business users.

How Important Are Middlemen?

Marketing's critics sometimes say that prices of products are high because there are too many middlemen who perform unnecessary, duplicate functions. While middlemen can be eliminated in attempting to reduce distribution costs, lower costs may not always be achieved. The reason for this uncertainty lies in a basic axiom of marketing: *You can eliminate middlemen, but you cannot eliminate their functions.* These functions can be shifted from one party to another in an effort to improve efficiency. However, someone has to perform the various activities—if not a middleman, then the producer or final customer.

In certain situations middlemen may be able to carry out distribution activities better or more cheaply than either producers or consumers. In fact, middlemen can be downright indispensable in many situations. It is usually not practical for a producer to deal directly with ultimate consumers. Think for a moment how inconvenient life would be if there were no retail middlemen—no supermarkets, gas stations, or ticket sales outlets, for instance.

As illustrated in Fig. 14-1, middlemen serve as purchasing agents for their customers and as sales specialists for their suppliers. They provide financial services for both suppliers and customers. Middlemen's storage services, abil-

FIGURE 14-1
Typical activities of a middleman.

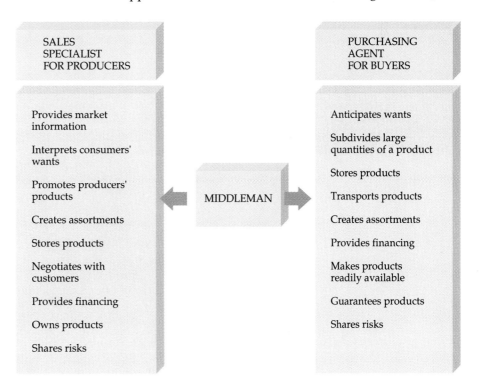

SALES SPECIALIST FOR PRODUCERS	MIDDLEMAN	PURCHASING AGENT FOR BUYERS
Provides market information		Anticipates wants
Interprets consumers' wants		Subdivides large quantities of a product
Promotes producers' products		Stores products
Creates assortments		Transports products
Stores products		Creates assortments
Negotiates with customers		Provides financing
Provides financing		Makes products readily available
Owns products		Guarantees products
Shares risks		Shares risks

ity to divide large shipments into smaller ones for resale, and market knowledge benefit suppliers and customers alike.

What Is a Distribution Channel?

A **distribution channel** consists of the set of people and firms involved in the flow of title to a product as it moves from producer to ultimate consumer or business user. A channel of distribution always includes both the producer and the final customer for the product in its present form as well as any middlemen (such as retailers and wholesalers).

The channel for a product extends only to the last person or organization

Sofas, like many goods, are distributed through a channel consisting of the manufacturer, retailer, and final consumer.

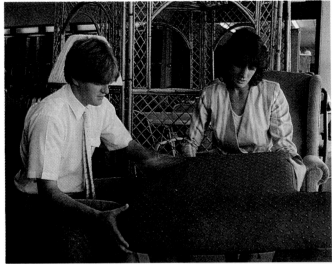

buying it without any significant change in its form. When its form is altered and another product emerges, a new channel is started. When lumber is milled and then made into furniture, two separate channels are involved. The channel for the *lumber* might be lumber mill → broker → furniture manufacturer. The channel for the *finished furniture* might be furniture manufacturer → retail furniture store → consumer.

Besides producer, middlemen, and final customer, other institutions aid the distribution process. Among these intermediaries are banks, insurance companies, storage firms, and transportation companies. However, because they do not take title to the products and are not actively involved in purchase or sales activities, these intermediaries are not formally included in the distribution channel.

This chapter focuses on the flow of ownership of title for a product. These flows are distinct; consequently, different institutions may carry them out. For example, a contractor might order a load of roofing shingles from a local building-materials distributor. The product might be shipped directly from the shingles manufacturer to the contractor to minimize freight and handling costs. But the channel for title (and ownership) would be manufacturer → distributor → contractor.

DESIGNING DISTRIBUTION CHANNELS

Firms that appear to be similar often have dissimilar channels of distribution. For instance, two sellers of auto insurance in Canada and the United States use different channels. State Farm sells through its own sales force working out of branch offices in local communities or through brokers. Allstate sales people typically sell from offices located in Sears stores.

Why do seemingly similar firms wind up with such different channels? One reason is that there are numerous types of channels and middlemen from which to choose. Also a variety of factors related to the market, product, middlemen, and company itself influence which channel is actually used by a firm.

Essentially a company wants a distribution channel that not only meets customers' needs but also provides an edge on competition. This requires an organized approach to designing a channel. As shown in Fig. 14-2, we suggest a sequence of four decisions:

1. *Delineating the role of distribution.* A channel strategy should be designed within the context of an entire marketing mix. First the firm's marketing objectives are reviewed. Next the roles assigned to product, price, and promotion are delineated. Each element may have a distinct role, or two elements may share an assignment. For example, a manufacturer of pressure gauges may use both distribution and promotion to convince prospective customers that it is committed to servicing the product following the sale.

FIGURE 14-2
Sequence of decisions to design a distribution channel.

| Delineate the role of distribution within the marketing mix | → | Select type of distribution channel | → | Determine appropriate intensity of distribution | → | Choose specific channel members | → | WELL-DESIGNED DISTRIBUTION CHANNEL |

A company must decide whether distribution will be used defensively or offensively. If defensive, a firm will strive for distribution that is as good as, but not necessarily better than, other firms' distribution. With an offensive strategy, a firm uses distribution to gain an advantage over competitors. Recently Honda decided to seek an advantage for its Acura line of luxury cars by establishing separate Acura dealerships rather than relying on existing Honda dealerships.

2. *Selecting the type of channel.* Once distribution's role in the overall marketing program has been agreed on, the most suitable type of channel for the company's product must be determined. At this point in the sequence, a firm needs to decide whether middlemen will be used in its channel and, if so, which types of middlemen.

    To illustrate the wide array of institutions available as well as the difficulty of channel selection, consider a manufacturer of compact disc players. If the use of middlemen is deemed appropriate, the company must choose among many different types of middlemen. At the retail level the range of institutions includes specialty audio-video outlets, department stores, discount houses, and mail-order firms. Which single type or combination of types would permit the manufacturer to achieve its distribution objectives? Another choice must be made if the firm has decided to also use wholesaling middlemen. In a subsequent section this decision as well as the major types of channels for goods and services will be discussed in detail.

3. *Determining intensity of distribution.* The next decision relates to **intensity of distribution**, or the number of middlemen used at the wholesale and retail levels in a particular territory. The target market's buying behaviour and the product's nature have a direct bearing on this decision, as we will see later.

4. *Choosing specific channel members.* The last decision is the selection of specific firms, or ''brands'' of middlemen, to distribute the product. For each type of institution, there are usually numerous specific companies from which to choose.

    Recalling our compact disc player example, assume that the manufacturer prefers two types of middlemen: department stores and specialty outlets. If the CD players will be sold in Toronto, the producer must decide which department stores — Eaton's or the Bay — will be asked to distribute its product line. Also one or more audio-video chains — from a group including Multitech, Stereo Express, and Electronic Station — must be selected. Similar decisions must be made for each territory in the firm's market.

    When selecting specific firms to be part of a channel, a producer should assess factors related to the market, product, and company as well as middlemen. Another key factor is the degree of intensity necessary to serve its target market well. Two addition factors are whether the middleman sells to the market that the manufacturer wants to reach and whether its product mix, pricing structure, promotion, and customer service are all compatible with the producer's needs.[2]

---

[2]For further ideas on how to build a good producer-middleman relationship, see James A. Narus and James C. Anderson, ''Distributor Contributions to Partnership with Manufacturers,'' *Business Horizons*, September-October 1987, pp. 34–42.

SELECTING THE TYPE OF CHANNEL

Firms may rely on existing channels or they may use new channels to better serve existing customers, reach new customers, and/or gain an edge on competitors. For instance, to attract new customers, Xerox now distributes some of its products through Sears stores. A small company named New Pig decided not to use conventional middlemen such as supermarkets and hardware stores to sell a new dust cloth that has special dirt-attracting properties. Instead, to reach a primarily female target market, it is distributing its product through beauty salons![3]

Most distribution channels include middlemen, but some do not. A channel consisting only of producer and final customer, with no middlemen providing assistance, is called **direct distribution**. In contrast, a channel of producer, final customer, and at least one level of middleman represents **indirect distribution**. One level of middleman — retailers but no wholesaling middlemen, for example—or multiple levels may participate in an indirect channel. (Sometimes a channel for consumer goods in which wholesalers are bypassed but retailers are used is termed *direct*, rather than indirect, distribution.) With indirect distribution a producer must determine the type(s) of middlemen that will best serve its needs. A wide range of options exists at both the wholesale and retail levels, and these will be described in the next two chapters.

Selection of one type of middleman, such as a discount house, may affect whether another type, such as a specialty retailer, will participate in the channel. Or including one type may influence how much support another type will put behind the manufacturer's product. Their decisions are based on various factors that will soon be discussed.

At this point in the decision sequence, we should look at the major channels traditionally used by producers and at two special channels. Then we can consider the factors that most influence a company's choice of channels.

Major Channels of Distribution

Diverse distribution channels exist today. However, only a handful of channels are used most often. Common channels for consumer goods, business goods, and services are described next and summarized in Fig. 14-3.

DISTRIBUTION OF CONSUMER GOODS

Five channels are widely used in marketing tangible products intended for ultimate consumers:

- *Producer → consumer*. The shortest, simplest distribution channel for consumer goods involves no middlemen. The producer may sell from door to door or by mail.
- *Producer → retailer → consumer*. Many large retailers buy directly from manufacturers and agricultural producers.
- *Producer → wholesaler → retailer → consumer*. If there is a "traditional" channel for consumer goods, this is it. Small retailers and manufacturers by the thousands find this channel the only economically feasible choice.
- *Producer → agent → retailer → consumer*. Instead of using wholesalers, many producers prefer to use agent middlemen to reach the retail market, especially *large-scale* retailers. For example, a manufacturer of a glass cleaner selected a food broker to reach the grocery store market, including large chains.

---

[3]These examples are taken from "Unconventional Channels," *Sales & Marketing Management,* October 1988, p. 38.

FIGURE 14-3
Major marketing channels available to producers.

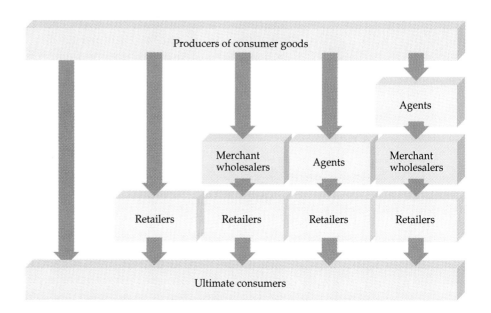

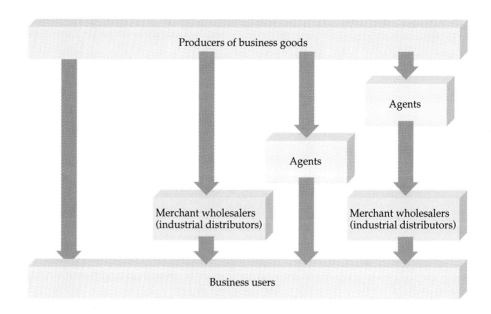

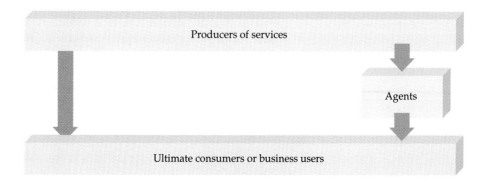

MARKETING AT WORK

FILE 14-1   **AVON IS STILL VERY DIRECT**

Direct marketing has become one of the most effective ways for many companies to attract new customers. This is the case for one of the best known direct selling companies — Avon. Because of sagging sales, Avon decided to conduct a market study. It determined that the increasing number of women entering the work force has diminished the pool of people available to work as Avon sales reps and the number of women at home to receive calls. To combat the problem of reaching working women, Avon has directed its sales force to sell at the workplace during coffee breaks or lunch hours. Avon also has plans to reach customers still isolated from sales representatives by direct mailing. A department has been set up to oversee the implementation of a direct marketing program. However, Avon does not plan on becoming a mail-order company, and the direct marketing will be used to complement the direct-selling system. Their major objective at present is to start a data base of all their customers. From this, Avon can initiate consumer motivation programs such as sweepstakes or enlist the help of representatives in signing people up to mailing lists.

Source: Cheryl Sandys, ''Avon Ladies Building Customer Database,'' *Canadian Direct Marketing News*, Vol. 2, No. 12, September 1990, p. 1.

- *Producer → agent → wholesaler → retailer → consumer*. To reach *small* retailers, producers often use agent middlemen, who in turn call on wholesalers that sell to small stores.

DISTRIBUTION OF BUSINESS GOODS

Once again, a variety of channels are available to reach organizations that will incorporate the products into their manufacturing process or use them in their operations.[4] In the following discussion, the term *industrial distributor* is synonymous with merchant wholesaler. The four most common channels for business goods are:

- *Producer → user*. This direct channel accounts for a greater *dollar* volume of business products than any other distribution structure. Manufacturers of large installations, such as airplanes, generators, and heating plants, usually sell directly to users.
- *Producer → industrial distributor → user*. Producers of operating supplies and small accessory equipment frequently use industrial distributors to reach their markets. Manufacturers of building materials and air-conditioning equipment are two examples of firms that make heavy use of the industrial distributor.
- *Producer → agent → user*. Firms without their own sales departments find this a desirable channel. Also a company that wants to introduce a new

---

[4]An excellent discussion of distribution channels for business goods and services is found in Michael D. Hutt and Thomas W. Speh, *Business Marketing Management*, 3rd ed., The Dryden Press, Chicago, 1989, pp. 379–411.

M A R K E T I N G   A T   W O R K

FILE 14-2   **YOU SELL IT, I'LL SERVICE IT!**

As competition heats up, more computer companies are adding to or bypassing their own high-priced sales staff and relying on cut-rate distribution channels to market their wares. The problem is that for every layer a computer company adds to its distribution system, it adds up to 1.5 percent to the product's cost (overall distribution could constitute 5 percent of the product's cost). And in a market where high-margin, big-ticket hardware aimed at office use has been eroded by the popularity of lower-cost, lower-margin personal computers, concentrating all of a company's energy on the product no longer makes sense. What does make sense is computer services. Which is why Data General Inc. of Mississauga announced that EMJ Data Systems of Guelph, Ontario, would distribute its products—so that Data General itself could focus on service. "Selling the boxes just gives a computer company a foot in the door. . . . The real money is in services. . . in the tying together of disparate pieces of hardware."

Source: Adapted from Geoffrey Rowan, "Feeling the Byte," *Globe and Mail*, August 29, 1990, p. 3.

product or enter a new market may prefer to use agents rather than its own sales force.

- *Producer → agent → industrial distributor → user.* This channel is similar to the preceding one. It is used when, for some reason, it is not feasible to sell through agents directly to the business user. The unit sale may be too small for direct selling. Or decentralized inventory may be needed to supply users rapidly, in which case the storage services of an industrial distributor are required.

DISTRIBUTION OF SERVICES

The intangible nature of services creates special distribution requirements. There are only two common channels for services:[5]

- *Producer → consumer.* Because a service is intangible, the production process and/or sales activity often requires personal contact between producer and consumer. Thus a direct channel is used. Direct distribution is typical for many professional services, such as health care and legal advice, and personal services, such as haircutting and weight-loss counselling. However, other services, including travel, insurance, and entertainment, may also rely on direct distribution.
- *Producer → agent → consumer.* While direct distribution often is necessary for a service to be performed, producer-consumer contact may not be required for key distribution activities. Agents frequently assist a services producer with transfer of ownership (the sales task) or related tasks. Many services, notably travel, lodging, advertising media, entertainment, and insurance, use agents.

---

[5]For an excellent discussion of this topic, see Donald H. Light, "A Guide for New Distribution Channel Strategies for Service Firms," *The Journal of Business Strategy*, Summer 1986, pp. 56–64.

M A R K E T I N G   A T   W O R K

FILE 14-3   **MORE SERVICE WITH FRANCHISES**

In Canada today, franchises account for more than $1 out of every $4 spent on retail goods and services. This phenomenon is a result of several factors: a weakening demand for consumer tangibles, the higher startup costs of inventory, and Canadians' increasing dissatisfaction with the range of available services. In such a market, there is great potential for service franchises and many Canadians are taking advantage of this situation; more than 45,000 people in 1989 (25 percent more than in 1987) are now operating franchises. A successful example is Bob Soulis, an accountant who launched Accounting on Wheels, an office on wheels designed to provide a full range of office services to entrepreneurs working out of their homes. Aside from providing on-the-spot financial statements, payrolls, and tax services, Accounting on Wheels offers mobile computers, printers, phones, and fax machines to clients (most of them in the construction industry) who have no interest or talent in doing their own accounting.

Source: Adapted from Clayton Sinclair, ''Franchise Finds for a Falling Economy,'' *Financial Times of Canada*, August 13, 1990, p. 7.

Multiple Channels of Distribution

Many, perhaps most, producers are not content to use only a single distribution channel. Instead, for reasons such as achieving broad market coverage or avoiding total dependence on a single arrangement, they employ multiple channels. (Similarly, to ensure they have products when needed, many companies establish multiple *supply* channels.)

Use of multiple channels, sometimes called **dual distribution**, occurs in several distinct situations. A manufacturer is likely to use multiple channels to reach *different types of markets* when selling:

- The same product (for example, sporting goods or typewriters) to both consumer and business markets.[6]
- Unrelated products (margarine and paint; rubber products and plastics).

Multiple channels are also used to reach *different segments within a single market* when:

- Size of the buyers varies greatly. To illustrate, a regional airline may sell directly to travel departments in local corporations but use travel agents to reach small businesses and ultimate consumers locally and large firms elsewhere.
- Density differs across parts of the market. For example, a manufacturer of industrial machinery may use its own sales force to sell directly to users in concentrated markets, but may employ agents in sparsely populated markets.

A significant trend is the use of competing channel systems to sell the *same brand to a single market*. Dack's shoes, Sherwin-Williams paints, and Goodyear tires are distributed through the manufacturers' own retail stores as well as

---

[6]For extensive discussion of this strategy, see John A. Quelch, ''Why Not Exploit Dual Marketing?'' *Business Horizons*, January-February 1987, pp. 52–60.

Whom does a travel agent primarily serve — airlines, lodging chains, and cruise lines, *or* final consumers?

through conventional channels of independent retailers and possibly whole-salers. Producers may open their own stores, thereby creating dual distribu-tion, when they are not satisfied with the market coverage provided by existing retail outlets. Or they may establish their own stores primarily as testing grounds for new products and marketing techniques.

Although multiple distribution channels provide various benefits to the pro-ducer, they can aggravate middlemen. Disputes between producers and mid-dlemen may occur. To mention an example, owners of franchised Häagen-Dazs stores rebelled when faced with multiple channels. They claimed their marketing efforts were undermined (and sales and profits reduced) when the producer decided to sell this premium ice cream in supermarkets as well as franchised stores.

Vertical Marketing Systems

Historically, distribution channels stressed the independence of individual channel members. That is, various middlemen were employed to achieve a producer's distribution objectives; however, the producer typically was not concerned with middlemen's needs. In turn, wholesalers and retailers were more interested in maintaining their freedom than in coordinating their activ-ities with a producer. These shortcomings of conventional distribution chan-nels provided an opportunity for a new type of channel.

During the past three decades, the vertical marketing system has become a major force — perhaps *the* dominant force — in distribution. A **vertical mar-keting system** (VMS) is a tightly coordinated distribution channel designed to achieve operating efficiencies and marketing effectiveness.

Vertical marketing systems exemplify the concept of function shifting dis-cussed earlier. No marketing function is sacred to a particular level or firm in the channel. Instead, each function is performed at the most advantageous position in the channel.

The high degree of coordination or control that characterizes a VMS is achieved through one of three means: ownership of successive levels of a channel, contracts between channel members, or the market power of one or more members. As shown in Table 14-1, there are three distinct forms of vertical marketing systems.

In a **corporate VMS**, a firm at one level of a channel owns the firms at the next level or owns the entire channel. Remember that Sherwin-Williams and

TABLE 14-1 **TYPES OF VERTICAL MARKETING SYSTEMS**

Type of system	Control maintained by	Examples
Corporate	Ownership	Singer (sewing machines), Goodyear (tires), Radio Shack (electronics), Bata (shoes)
Contractual:		
Wholesaler-sponsored voluntary chain	Contract	IDA and Guardian drugs, IGA stores
Retailer-owned cooperative	Stock ownership by retailers	Canadian Tire
Franchise systems	Contract:	
	Manufacturer-sponsored retailers	Ford, Chrysler, and other auto dealers
	Manufacturer-sponsored wholesalers	Coca-Cola and other soft-drink bottlers
	Marketers of services	Harvey's Hamburgers, Speedy Muffler, Holiday Inn
Consumer-owned cooperative	Owned by consumers	Calgary Co-op
Administered	Economic power	Samsonite luggage, General Electric, Labatt

Goodyear own retail outlets. Also, a growing number of clothing and sportswear makers such as Benetton and Club Monaco are opening their own retail stores to feature their own brands.

Middlemen may also engage in this type of vertical integration. For example, many grocery chains own food-processing facilities, such as dairies, which supply their stores. And Eaton's, the Bay, and Sears have ownership interests in manufacturing facilities that supply its stores with many goods, including tools and clothing.

In a **contractual VMS**, independent firms — producers, wholesalers, and retailers — operate under contracts specifying how they will try to improve distribution efficiency and effectiveness. Three contractual systems have developed: wholesaler-sponsored voluntary chains, retailer-owned cooperatives, and franchise systems. All three will be discussed in Chapter 16.

An **administered VMS** coordinates distribution activities through the market and/or economic power of one channel member or the shared power of two channel members. This is illustrated by Corning in ovenware, Campbell's in canned soup, and Kraft in food products. Typically a producer's brand and market position are strong enough to gain the voluntary cooperation of retailers in matters such as inventory levels, advertising, and store display.

In the distant past, competition in distribution usually involved two different conventional channels. More recently, competition pitted a conventional channel against some form of VMS. Presently and in the future, the most common competitive battles will be between different forms of vertical marketing systems. For example, a corporate system (such as the stores owned by Goodyear)

In this administered VMS, Ports International and Ogilvy's in Montreal work towards shared goals.

competes with a contractual system (such as Firestone's franchised dealers). Considering the potential benefits of vertical marketing systems with respect to both operating efficiencies and marketing effectiveness, they should continue to grow in number and importance.

Factors Affecting Choice of Channels

If a firm is customer-oriented, its channels should be determined by consumer buying patterns. Thus the nature of the market should be the key influence in management's choice of channels. Other major considerations are the product, the middlemen, and the company itself.

MARKET CONSIDERATIONS

A logical starting point is to consider the needs, structure, and buying behaviour of target markets:

- *Type of market*. Because the buying behaviour of ultimate consumers ordinarily is different than that of business users, separate distribution arrangements normally must be made to reach the different markets. Retailers, by definition, serve ultimate consumers so they are not in channels for business goods.
- *Number of potential customers*. A manufacturer with relatively few potential customers (firms or industries) may use its own sales force to sell directly to consumers or business users. For a large number of customers, the manufacturer would likely use middlemen.

- *Geographic concentration of the market.* Direct sale to the textile or the garment manufacturing industry is feasible because most of the buyers are concentrated in a few geographic areas. Even in the case of a national market, some segments have a higher density rate than others. Sellers may establish sales branches in densely populated markets and use middlemen in less concentrated markets.
- *Order size.* A food products manufacturer would sell directly to large grocery chains because the large order size and total volume of business make this channel economically desirable. The same manufacturer, however, would use wholesalers to reach small grocery stores whose orders are usually too small to justify direct sale.[7]

PRODUCT CONSIDERATIONS

While there are numerous product-related factors to consider, we will highlight three:

- *Unit value.* The price attached to each unit of a product affects the amount of funds available for distribution. For example, a company can afford to use its own employee to sell a nuclear-reactor part that costs, say, more than $10,000, but it would not make sense for a company sales person to call on a household or a business firm to sell a $2 ballpoint pen. Consequently, products with low unit values usually are distributed through long channels (that is, through one or more levels of middlemen). There are exceptions, however. For instance, if order size is large because the customer buys many products at the same time from the company, then a direct (or short) channel may be economically feasible.
- *Perishability.* Some goods, including many agricultural products, physically deteriorate fairly quickly. Other goods, such as clothing, perish in a fashion sense. As was discussed in Chapter 11, services are perishable owing to their intangible nature. Perishable products require direct or very short channels.
- *Technical nature of a product.* A business product that is highly technical is often distributed directly to business users. The producer's sales force must provide considerable presale and postsale service; wholesalers normally cannot do this. *Consumer* products of a technical nature provide a real distribution challenge for manufacturers. Ordinarily, manufacturers cannot sell the goods directly to the consumer. As much as possible producers try to sell directly to retailers, but even then product servicing often poses problems.

MIDDLEMEN CONSIDERATIONS

Here we begin to see that a company may not be able to arrange exactly the channels it desires:

- *Services provided by middlemen.* Each producer should select middlemen that will provide those marketing services that the producer either is unable to provide or cannot economically perform.
- *Availability of desired middlemen.* The middlemen preferred by a producer

---

[7]For more on the idea that market considerations should determine a producer's channel structure, see Louis W. Stern and Frederick D. Sturdivant, "Customer-Driven Distribution Systems," *Harvard Business Review*, July-August 1987, pp. 34–41.

may not be available. They may be carrying competitive products and may not want to add another line.

- *Attitude of middlemen towards producers' policies.* Sometimes manufacturers' choices of channels are limited because their marketing policies are not acceptable to certain types of middlemen. Some retailers or wholesalers, for example, are interested in carrying a line only if they receive assurance that no competing firms will carry the line in the same territory.

COMPANY CONSIDERATIONS

Before choosing a distribution channel for a product, a company should consider relevant factors in its own situation:

- *Desire for channel control.* Some producers establish short channels simply because they want to control the distribution of their products, even though the cost of the more direct channel may be higher than that of an indirect channel. By controlling the channel, producers can achieve more aggressive promotion and can better control both the freshness of merchandise stocks and the retail prices of their products.
- *Services provided by seller.* Some producers base channel decisions in part on their ability to carry out the distribution functions demanded by middlemen. For instance, often a retail chain will not stock a given product unless it is presold through heavy producer advertising.
- *Ability of management.* Channel decisions are affected by the marketing experience and ability of the firm's management. Many companies lacking marketing know-how prefer to turn the distribution job over to middlemen.
- *Financial resources.* A business with adequate finances can establish its own sales force, grant credit, or warehouse its own products. A financially weak firm would have to use middlemen who could provide these services.

In some cases virtually all factors point to a particular length and/or type of channel. In most situations, however, careful assessment results in mixed signals. Several factors may point to the desirability of direct channels, but others to the use of wholesalers and/or retailers. Or the company may find a desired length or type of channel is unavailable. If a company with an unproven product having low profit potential cannot place its product with middlemen, it may have no other option but to try to distribute the product directly to its target market.

DETERMINING INTENSITY OF DISTRIBUTION

At this stage in the design sequence, a firm knows what role within the marketing mix has been assigned to distribution, whether direct or indirect distribution is the better choice, and which types of middlemen will be used (assuming indirect distribution is appropriate). Next the company must decide on the intensity of distribution, that is, how many middlemen will be used at the wholesale and retail levels in a particular territory.

The degrees of intensity span an entire continuum. For ease of discussion and decision making, the continuum typically is broken into three categories, ranging from *intensive* to *selective* to *exclusive*. This continuum is presented in Fig. 14-4.

Distribution intensity ordinarily is thought to be a single decision. For instance, after considering all factors, a firm may opt for intensive distribution. However, if the desired channel has more than one level of middlemen (whole-

FIGURE 14-4
The intensity-of-distribution continuum.

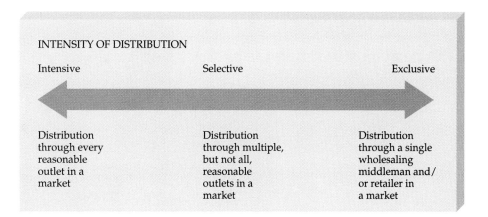

INTENSITY OF DISTRIBUTION

Intensive   Selective   Exclusive

Distribution   Distribution   Distribution
through every   through multiple,   through a single
reasonable   but not all,   wholesaling
outlet in a   reasonable   middleman and/
market   outlets in a   or retailer in
                        market   a market

saler and retailer, for example), then the appropriate intensity must be selected for each level.

Different degrees of intensity may be appropriate at successive levels of distribution. A manufacturer can often achieve intensive retail coverage with selective, rather than intensive, wholesale distribution. Or selective intensity at the retail level may be gained through one wholesaler — that is, exclusive intensity at the wholesale level. Of course, the wholesaling firm(s) will determine which retail outlets actually receive the product. Despite this lack of control, a producer should plan the levels of intensity needed at both the wholesale and retail levels. Making only one decision is simplistic and can create serious problems.

Intensive Distribution

Under a strategy of **intensive distribution**, a producer sells its product through every available outlet in a market where a consumer might reasonably look for it. High intensity is often used by manufacturers of convenience goods. Ultimate consumers demand immediate satisfaction with this class of product and will not defer purchases to find a particular brand. Retailers often control whether this strategy can be implemented. For example, a new manufacturer of toothpaste or a small producer of potato chips may want distribution in all supermarkets, but these retailers may limit their assortments to four fast-selling brands.

Retailers typically will not pay to advertise a product that is sold by competitors. Therefore, intensive distribution places most of the advertising and promotion burden on the producer.

Selective Distribution

In **selective distribution**, a producer sells its product through multiple, but not all possible, wholesalers and/or retailers in a market where a consumer might reasonably look for it. Selective distribution is appropriate for consumer shopping goods, such as various types of clothing and appliances, and for business accessory equipment, such as office equipment and hand-held tools.

A company may decide to adopt a selective distribution strategy after some experience with intensive distribution. The decision to change usually hinges on the high cost of intensive distribution or the unsatisfactory performance of middlemen. Certain customers perennially order in small, unprofitable amounts. Others may be poor credit risks. Eliminating such marginal middlemen may reduce the number of outlets, but it can actually increase a company's

Benetton achieves selective distribution through Eaton's.

sales volume. Many companies have found this to be the case simply because they were able to do a more thorough selling job with a smaller number of accounts.

Exclusive Distribution

Under an **exclusive distribution** strategy, the supplier agrees to sell its product only to a single wholesaling middleman and/or retailer in a given market. An exclusive distributorship with a wholesaler or an exclusive dealership with a retailer sometimes prohibits the middleman from handling a directly competing product line.

Exclusive dealerships are frequently used in the marketing of consumer specialty products such as expensive suits. Producers also often adopt an exclusive distribution strategy when it is essential that the retailer carry a large inventory. This form of distribution is also desirable when the dealer or distributor must furnish installation and repair service. Manufacturers of farm machinery and large construction equipment use exclusive distributorships for this reason.

MARKETING AT WORK

FILE 14-4   DEALING WITH THE JAPANESE DISTRIBUTION SYSTEM

With so many possible combinations of types of institutions, distribution intensity, and specific firms, Canadian producers face serious challenges in arranging effective distribution channels in their own country. But the challenge is much greater, sometimes insurmountable, in Japan!

Distribution in Japan has been characterized by numerous small, family-operated retail stores, an even larger number of wholesalers, and many government regulations protecting traditional distribution channels. Ownership of goods may pass through several wholesalers before reaching retailers.

The 1.6 million "papa-mama" stores, as the Japanese call them, account for 56 percent of retail sales (compared to only 35 percent in North America). And government regulations deter change. One law, for example, stipulates that a chain desiring to open a new store must gain the approval of *all* papa-mama stores within half a kilometre of the proposed store site. If approval is obtained, another law limits the size of the new store.

Changing consumer needs and government attitudes are beginning to modify the complex and, according to many observers, inefficient Japanese distribution system. More Japanese women are employed, and they desire the convenience of one-stop shopping provided by large stores and shopping centres. Also the government considers big stores good for economic growth, so some restrictions are being eased.

Sensing an opportunity, some North Americans are trying to distribute their products in Japan. More success is being achieved by going around — rather than through — traditional channels. For example, importers avoid wholesalers, if possible, and deal directly with retailers. American-style convenience stores (led by 7-Eleven) now compete with the traditional papa-mama stores.

What's on the horizon for Japanese distribution? Apparently, traditional wholesalers and retailers will lose ground to new distribution approaches. Discount houses, large shopping centres, home-shopping channels on TV, and catalogue retailing are finding favour with Japanese consumers who want to save money and/or time. New NIE (*newly industrialized economy*) stores are selling products from South Korea, Hong Kong, and elsewhere at lower prices than comparable Japanese goods sell for. Change is in the air!

Source: Adapted from Carla Rapoport, "Ready, Set, Sell—Japan Is Buying," *Fortune*, Sept. 11, 1989, pp. 159–60ff; C. William Verity, "Piercing the Ultimate Trade Barrier," *Fortune*, Dec. 19, 1988, p. 183; and Damon Darlin, " 'Papa-Mama' Stores in Japan Wield Power to Hold Back Imports," *The Wall Street Journal*, Nov. 14, 1988, pp. A1, A7.

Exclusive distribution helps a manufacturer control the last level of middlemen before the final customer. A middleman with exclusive rights is usually willing to promote the product aggressively. This is because interested customers will have to purchase the product at its outlet since no other outlets in the area carry the same brand. However, a producer suffers if its exclusive middlemen in various markets do not serve customers well. Essentially a manufacturer has "all its eggs in one basket."

A significant advantage of being an exclusive dealer or distributor is the opportunity to reap all the benefits of the producer's marketing activities in a

Plastic wrap plus children's toys equals scrambled merchandising.

particular area. However, an exclusive middleman may become too dependent on the manufacturer. If the manufacturer fails, the middleman also fails (for that product). Another risk is that once sales volume has been built up in a market, the producer may add other dealers.

CONFLICT AND CONTROL IN CHANNELS

Distribution occasionally is characterized by shared goals and cooperative actions. But conflict and struggles for control are more typical. Firms in one channel often compete vigorously with firms in other channels. Even within the same channel, firms argue about operating practices and try to gain control over actions of other members.

Effective management of distribution channels requires an understanding of both conflict and control, including techniques to (1) decrease conflict, or at least its negative effects, and (2) increase a firm's control within a channel. **Channel conflict** exists when one channel member perceives another channel member to be acting in a way that prevents the first member from achieving its distribution objectives. There are two types of conflict — horizontal and vertical.

Horizontal Conflicts

Horizontal conflict occurs among firms on the same level of distribution. Such conflict may occur between:

- *Middlemen of the same type:* Maryvale Home Hardware versus Fred's Friendly Hardware, for example.
- *Different types of middlemen on the same level:* Maryvale Home Hardware versus St. Clair Paint and Wallpaper versus K mart.

The main source of horizontal conflict is **scrambled merchandising**, where middlemen diversify by adding product lines not traditionally carried by their type of business. Supermarkets, for instance, expanded beyond groceries by adding health and beauty aids, small appliances, snack bars, and various services. Retailers that sold these product lines first have become irritated both at supermarkets for diversifying and at producers for using multiple distribution channels.

Scrambled merchandising and the resulting horizontal competition may stem from the market, middleman, or producer. Many consumers (the *market*) prefer convenient, one-stop shopping, so stores broaden their assortments to satisfy this desire. *Middlemen* constantly strive for higher gross margins and more customer traffic by adding new lines. *Producers* seek to expand market coverage and reduce unit production costs by adding new types of outlets. These diversification efforts intensify the degree of horizontal conflict.

Vertical Conflicts

Perhaps the most severe conflicts in distribution involve firms at different levels of the same channel. These **vertical conflicts** typically occur between producer and wholesaler or producer and retailer.

PRODUCER VERSUS WHOLESALER

Tensions occasionally arise between producers and wholesalers. A producer and wholesaler may disagree about aspects of their business relationship. For instance, John Deere has argued with distributors about whether they should sell farm equipment made by other companies or should restrict their efforts to the Deere brand.

Why do conflicts arise? Basically manufacturers and wholesalers have differing points of view. On the one hand, manufacturers think that wholesalers neither promote products aggressively nor provide sufficient storage services. And wholesalers' services cost too much. On the other hand, wholesalers believe producers either expect too much or do not understand the wholesaler's primary obligation to customers.

Channel conflict typically stems from a manufacturer's attempts to bypass wholesalers and deal directly with retailers or consumers. Direct sale occurs because (1) producers are dissatisfied with wholesalers' services or (2) market conditions call for direct sale. Ordinarily battles about direct sale are fought in *consumer* goods channels. Such conflicts rarely arise in channels for business goods because there is a tradition of direct sale to ultimate customers in business markets.

To bypass wholesalers, a producer has two alternatives:

- *Sell directly to consumers.* Producers may employ house-to-house or mail-order selling. They also may establish their own distribution centres in different areas or even their own retail stores in major markets.
- *Sell directly to retailers.* Under certain market and product conditions, selling directly to retailers is feasible and advisable. An ideal retail market for this option consists of retailers that buy large quantities of a limited line of products.

Direct distribution — a short channel — is advantageous when the product (1) is subject to physical or fashion perishability, (2) carries a high unit price, (3) is custom-made, or (4) requires installation and technical service. Direct distribution, however, places a financial and managerial burden on the producer. Not only must the manufacturer operate its own sales force and handle physical distribution of its products, but a direct-selling manufacturer also faces competition from its former wholesalers, which no doubt now sell competitive products.

Some manufacturers, such as Ralph Lauren, risk conflict by distributing their products through their own outlets as well as other retail chains.

Wholesalers too can improve their competitive position and thereby reduce channel conflict. Their options include:

- *Improve internal management.* Many wholesalers have modernized their operations and upgraded the calibre of their management. Functional, single-store warehouses have been built outside congested downtown areas, and mechanized materials-handling equipment has been installed. Computers have improved order processing, inventory control, and billing.
- *Provide management assistance to retailers.* Wholesalers have realized that improving retailers' operations benefits all parties. Wholesalers help meet certain retailers' needs, such as store layout, merchandise selection, promotion, and inventory control.
- *Form voluntary chains.* In a voluntary chain (discussed in Chapter 15), a wholesaler enters into a contract with a group of retailers, agreeing to furnish them with management services and volume buying power. In turn, retailers promise to buy all, or almost all, of their merchandise from the wholesaler.
- *Develop private brands.* Some large wholesalers have successfully established their own brands. A voluntary chain of retailers provides a built-in market for the wholesaler's brand.

PRODUCER VERSUS RETAILER

Another struggle for channel control takes place between manufacturers and retailers. Conflict can arise over terms or conditions of the relationship between the two parties. Or producers may compete with retailers by selling from house to house or through producer-owned stores. A number of apparel makers — including Ralph Lauren, Club Monaco, and Liz Claiborne—have opened retail outlets. In doing so, they have aggravated department stores and specialty retailers that also carry their brands.[8]

---

[8]For details about this trend and the resulting conflicts, see Teri Agins, "Clothing Makers Don Retailers' Garb," *The Wall Street Journal*, July 13, 1989, p. B1.

M A R K E T I N G   A T   W O R K

FILE 14-5   **GETTING ON THE SHELF**

In exchange for shelf space in their stores, some supermarket chains require manufacturers to pay slotting allowances. Part or all of the revenues a chain receives from slotting allowances might be passed on to consumers in the form of lower prices. Or the chain could retain these revenues to cover added labour costs associated with shelving new products and/or to boost profits. Assume you are a supermarket-chain vice-president responsible for establishing policies regarding relationships with suppliers. Do you consider it ethical for your chain to demand slotting allowances from manufacturers? Would your view depend on whether the revenues were passed on to consumers via lower prices?

As discussed throughout this chapter, producers and retailers both have methods to gain more control. Manufacturers can:

- *Build strong consumer brand loyalty.* To accomplish this, creative and aggressive promotion is needed.
- *Establish one or more forms of vertical marketing system.*
- *Refuse to sell to uncooperative retailers.* However, this tactic has to be defensible from a legal standpoint.

Effective marketing weapons are also available to retailers. They can:

- *Develop store loyalty among consumers.* This is done by advertising effectively and/or establishing a store's own brands.
- *Improve computerized information systems.*
- *Plan more sophisticated marketing programs.*[9]

Who Controls Channels?

Every firm would like to determine the behaviour of other companies in the same distribution channel. The ability to influence the behaviour of other channel members is termed **channel control**. Traditionally, manufacturers have been viewed as controlling channels — that is, making the decisions regarding types and number of outlets, participation of individual middlemen, and business practices to be followed by a channel. But this is a one-sided, outdated point of view.

Middlemen often have considerable freedom to establish their own channels. Certainly the names Safeway and Sears mean more to consumers than the names of many brands sold in these stores. Large retailers are challenging producers for channel control, just as many manufacturers seized control from wholesalers years ago. Even small retailers may be quite influential in local markets because their prestige may be greater than that of their suppliers.

The position supporting channel leadership by manufacturers is that they create the new products and need greater sales volume to benefit from economies of scale. The argument favouring leadership by retailers is that they are

---

[9]For further discussion of strategies that either create or offset conflict between manufacturers and retailers, see Allan J. Magrath and Kenneth G. Hardy, ''Avoiding the Pitfalls in Managing Distribution Channels,'' *Business Horizons*, September-October 1987, pp. 29–33.

closest to final customers and, as a result, are best able to know consumer's wants and to design and oversee channels to satisfy them. Various factors have contributed to retailers' growing ability to control channels. To mention one, widespread introduction by retailers of electronic scanning devices has given them access to more accurate information about sales trends of individual products than producers have.[10]

A Channel Viewed as a System

Many producers and middlemen understand that each channel member is part of a *system* designed to provide want-satisfaction to the ultimate consumer. Consequently, coordination is needed throughout a distribution channel.

Sometimes, however, members see a channel as a fragmented collection of independent, competing firms. One possible reason for channel problems is that most producers do not have a person in the organization who is formally in charge of channels. While most firms have an *advertising* manager and a *sales* manager, few have a *channels* manager. Perhaps it is time for manufacturers to create this position. The channels manager would be directly responsible for planning, coordinating, and evaluating the firm's distribution channels.[11]

Channel members frequently do realize that benefits of cooperation and voluntary control often outweigh any reasons for conflict. Producers and middlemen alike must consider the channel as an extension of their own internal organizations.

LEGAL CONSIDERATIONS IN CHANNEL MANAGEMENT

In various ways, organizations may try to exercise control over the distribution of their product as it moves through the channel. Generally speaking, any attempts to control distribution may be subject to legal constraints. In this section, we shall discuss briefly four control methods that are frequently considered by suppliers (usually manufacturers):

- *Dealer selection.* The manufacturer wants to select its customers and refuses to sell to some middlemen.
- *Exclusive dealing.* The manufacturer prohibits its dealers from carrying products of the manufacturer's competitors.
- *Tying contracts.* The manufacturer sells a product to a middleman only under the condition that this middleman also buys another (possibly unwanted) product from the manufacturer. Or, at least, the middleman agrees not to buy the other product from any other supplier.
- *Exclusive (closed) territories.* The manufacturer requires each middleman to sell *only* to customers who are located within the middleman's assigned territory.

None of these arrangements is automatically illegal. The Competition Act deals with such practices under Part VII in which certain dealings between manufacturers and middlemen are deemed illegal if they restrict competition.

---

[10]Customer market power in relation to channel control is covered in Gul Butaney and Lawrence H. Wortzel, ''Distributor Power Versus Manufacturer Power: The Customer Role,'' *Journal of Marketing,* January 1988, pp. 52–63. For more on the struggle for channel control, see Brent H. Felgner, ''Retailers Grab Power, Control Marketplace,'' *Marketing News,* Jan. 16, 1989, pp. 1-2.

[11]Donald W. Jackson, Jr., and Bruce J. Walker, ''The Channels Manager: Marketing's Newest Aide?'' *California Management Review,* Winter 1980, pp. 52–58.

M A R K E T I N G   A T   W O R K

FILE 14-6   SUCCESSFULLY TYING-BACK WITH FRANCHISING

One example of a tying contract takes place when a franchising company requires that a franchisee buy from the franchiser some or all of the raw materials needed for the operation of the franchise. For example, Tim Horton's Donuts franchisees must buy all ''non-fresh'' ingredients from the franchise company; Pizza Delight franchisees buy all ''dry'' ingredients and meats from a food supply company that is owned by the franchiser.

Such arrangements are not in violation of the exclusive dealing or tied selling provisions in Section 49 of the Competition Act because they do not substantially lessen competition. In addition, the Act specifically exempts from these provisions situations in which the companies involved are affiliated, which they clearly are under a franchise agreement.

Dealer Selection

Under Section 47 of the Competition Act, it is illegal for a manufacturer or supplier to refuse to supply a middleman with the supplier's products. Under certain circumstances, however, a supplier may refuse to deal with retailers or other middlemen if they are unwilling or unable to meet the usual trade terms of the supplier. In other words, for example, if the middleman engaged in a practice of selling the supplier's product as a loss leader, or failed to provide adequate postpurchase service, or in some other way failed to support the product, the supplier could refuse to deal with that company. Generally, it would be illegal to refuse to supply a middleman if the company carried a competitor's product or for resisting a tying contract.

Exclusive Dealing

Exclusive dealing contracts have been declared unlawful if the manufacturer's sales volume is a substantial part of the total volume in a market or if the volume done by the exclusive dealers is a significant percentage of the total business in an area. That is, the law is violated when the competitors of a manufacturer are essentially shut out from a substantial part of the market because of this manufacturer's exclusive dealing contract.

By inference, it is clear that exclusive dealing is not illegal in all situations. In fact, where the seller is just getting started in a market or where its share of the total market is so small as to be negligible, its negotiation of exclusive dealing agreements may not only improve its competitive position but also strengthen competition in general.

Ordinarily there is no question of legality when a manufacturer agrees to sell to only one retailer or wholesaler in a given territory, provided there are no limitations on competitive products. Also, a manufacturer can sell to dealers who do not carry competitor's products, as long as this is a voluntary decision on the part of the franchise holder.

Tying Contracts

A supplier is likely to push for a tying agreement when:

• There are shortages of a desired product, and the supplier also wants to push products that are less in demand.

- The supplier grants a franchise (as in fast-food services) and wants the franchisee to purchase all necessary supplies and equipment from this supplier.
- The supplier has exclusive dealers or distributors (in appliances, for example) and wants them to carry a full line of the supplier's products.

With regard to tying contracts, apparently a dealer can be required to carry a manufacturer's full line as long as this does not impede competition in the market. The arrangement may be questionable, however, if a supplier forces a dealer or a distributor to take slow-moving, less attractive items in order to acquire the really desirable products.

Exclusive Territories

Traditionally, the strategy of exclusive (or closed) sales territories has been used by manufacturers in assigning market areas to retailing or wholesaling middlemen. However, closed sales territories can create area monopolies, lessen competition, and restrict trade among middlemen who carry the same brand. Exceptions are generally provided when a company is small or is a new entrant to the market, in order to facilitate market entry.

These limitations on closed sales territories are likely to foster vertical marketing systems, where the manufacturer retains ownership of the product until it reaches the final buyer. That is, the manufacturer could either (1) own the retail or wholesale outlet or (2) consign products on an agency basis to the middlemen but retain ownership. In either of these situations, exclusive territories are quite legal.

SUMMARY

The role of distribution is getting a product to its target market. A distribution channel carries out this assignment with middlemen performing some tasks. A middleman is a business firm that renders services directly related to the purchase and/or sale of a product as it flows from producer to consumer. Middlemen can be eliminated from a channel, but someone still has to carry out their essential functions.

A distribution channel is the set of people and firms involved in the flow of title to a product as it moves from producer to ultimate consumer or business user. A channel includes producer, final customer, and any middlemen that participate in the process.

Designing a channel of distribution for a product occurs through a sequence of four decisions: (1) delineating the role of distribution within the marketing mix; (2) selecting the proper type of distribution channel; (3) determining the appropriate intensity of distribution; and (4) choosing specific channel members. A variety of channels are used to distribute consumer goods, business goods, and services. Firms often employ multiple channels to achieve broad market coverage, although this strategy can alienate some middlemen. Because of deficiencies in conventional channels, vertical marketing systems have become a major force in distribution. There are three forms of vertical marketing systems: corporate, contractual, and administered.

Numerous factors need to be considered prior to selecting a distribution channel for a product. The primary consideration is the nature of the target market; other considerations relate to the product, the middlemen, and the company itself.

Distribution intensity refers to the number of middlemen used at the wholesale and retail levels in a particular territory. It ranges from intensive to selective to exclusive.

Firms distributing goods and services sometimes clash. There are two types of conflict: horizontal (between firms at the same level of distribution) and vertical (between firms at different levels of the same channel). Scrambled merchandising is a prime cause of horizontal conflict. Vertical conflict typically pits producer against wholesaler or retailer. Manufacturers' attempts to bypass middlemen are a prime cause of vertical conflict.

Channel members frequently strive for some control over one another. Depending on the circumstances, either producers or middlemen can achieve the dominant position in a channel. All parties may be served best by viewing channels as a system requiring coordination or distribution activities. Moreover, attempts to control distribution may be subject to legal constraints.

KEY TERMS AND CONCEPTS

Middleman 442
Merchant middleman 443
Agent middleman 443
Shifting of functions 443
Distribution channel 444
Intensity of distribution 446
Direct distribution 447
Indirect distribution 447
Multiple-channel distribution 451
Dual distribution 451
Vertical marketing system 452
Corporate vertical marketing system 452
Contractual vertical marketing system 453

Administered vertical marketing system 453
Intensive distribution 457
Selective distribution 457
Exclusive distribution 458
Channel conflict 460
Horizontal conflict 460
Scrambled merchandising 460
Vertical conflict 461
Channel control 463
Channels manager 464
Dealer selection 465
Exclusive dealing 465
Tying contracts 465
Exclusive territory 466

QUESTIONS AND PROBLEMS

1. ''You can eliminate middlemen, but you cannot eliminate their functions.'' Discuss this statement.
2. Which of the following institutions are middlemen? Explain.
   a. Avon sales person.
   b. Electrical wholesaler.
   c. Real estate broker.
   d. Railroad.
   e. Auctioneer.
   f. Advertising agency.
   g. Grocery store.
   h. Stockbroker.
   i. Bank.
   j. Radio station.

3. Which of the channels illustrated in Fig. 14-3 is most apt to be used for each of the following products? Defend your choice in each case.
   a. Fire insurance.
   b. Single-family residences.
   c. Farm hay balers.
   d. Washing machines.
   e. Hair spray.
   f. An ocean cruise.

4. "The great majority of business sales are made directly from producer to business user." Explain the reason for this first in terms of the nature of the market, and then in terms of the product.

5. Explain, using examples, the differences among the three major types of vertical systems—corporate, administered, contractual. Which is the best kind?

6. A small manufacturer of fishing lures is faced with the problem of selecting its channel of distribution. What reasonable alternatives does it have? Consider particularly the nature of its product and the nature of its market.

7. Is a policy of intensive distribution consistent with consumer buying habits for convenience goods? For shopping goods? Is intensive distribution normally used in the marketing of any type of business goods?

8. From a producer's viewpoint, what are the competitive advantages of exclusive distribution?

9. What are the drawbacks to exclusive distribution from a retailer's point of view? To what extent are these alleviated if the retailer controls the channel for the particular brand?

10. A manufacturer of a well-known brand of men's clothing has been selling directly to one dealer in a small Canadian city for many years. For some time the market has been large enough to support two retailers very profitably. Yet the present dealer objects strongly when the manufacturer suggests adding another outlet. What alternatives does the manufacturer have in this situation? What course of action would you recommend?

11. "Manufacturers should always strive to select the lowest-cost channel of distribution." Do you agree? Should they always try to use the middlemen with the lowest operating costs? Why or why not?

12. What are reasons for producers' dissatisfaction with the wholesalers' performance? Do you agree with the producers' complaints?

13. Why are full-service wholesalers relatively unimportant in the marketing of women's high-fashion wearing apparel, furniture, and large electrical equipment?

CHAPTER 15 GOALS

Although consumers shop regularly at the stores of retailing middlemen, they rarely see the establishments of wholesaling middlemen. As a result, wholesaling and wholesaling middlemen are often misunderstood. Wholesaling middlemen may not always be necessary, but they can be essential members of a distribution channel. After studying this chapter, you should be able to explain:

- The nature of wholesaling and the role of wholesaling middlemen.
- The economic justification of wholesaling.
- Three broad categories of wholesaling middlemen.
- The ranges of expenses and profits in wholesaling.
- Major types of merchant wholesaling middlemen, particularly full-service wholesalers, and the services they render.
- Major types of agent wholesaling middlemen, especially manufacturers' agents, and the services they render.
- Key trends in wholesaling.
- The primary areas in which wholesaling middlemen have to develop marketing strategies.

Wholesaling: Markets and Institutions

Have you ever wondered how all the merchandise that you see in retail stores actually gets there? In the case of the more than 1,000 Home Hardware stores throughout Canada, thousands of products flow through a modern high-tech warehouse and distribution system.

Home Hardware is owned by its retailers and all of the purchasing for the chain is done through head office in St. Jacob's, Ontario. Almost 400 Home Hardware retailers in western Canada are served by a 450,000-square-foot distribution facility in Wetaskiwin, Alberta, with a computerized purchasing, ordering, and shipping system.

A store owner uses an electronic order entry system to identify the items to be ordered each week from the store's inventory system. The order is sent electronically over telephone lines to the central warehouse and computer in St. Jacob's at any time of the day or night. If the order is from a store in the western region, it is transferred to the computer at the regional warehouse in Wetaskiwin. That computer generates a hard copy of the order, which is used by warehouse employees to put the order together.

Each store is served weekly and the shipping department uses colour-coded labels to identify individual orders. More than 300,000 pounds of merchandise a day are shipped from the Wetaskiwin facility. The company uses 25 trucks to make deliveries throughout western Canada.[1]

At various times, consumers, business people, and government officials have proclaimed, ''The middleman makes all the profit in distribution.'' Critics have even suggested a solution: ''Let's eliminate the middleman.'' Such comments are most often focused on the wholesaling part of the distribution process.

As we shall see, most middlemen (especially wholesaling middlemen) typically earn a small profit. Indeed, many are fighting for survival against modified distribution patterns resulting from changing consumer needs and desires. Also, as discussed in the preceding chapter, eliminating middlemen from a distribution channel does not guarantee lower prices or better service.

---

[1]Adapted from Andy Zielinski, ''Hardware Distribution Centre Runs Smoothly,'' *Materials Management and Distribution*, March 1986, pp. 20–23.

In fact, just the opposite may occur. Furthermore, some wholesaling middlemen perform vital services for producers and consumers in a highly efficient manner. This chapter will provide you with greater insight into both wholesale markets and wholesaling institutions as they relate to the broader marketing system.

NATURE AND IMPORTANCE OF WHOLESALING

Wholesaling and retailing stand between production and purchases for consumption. Whereas retailing involves sales to ultimate consumers for their personal use, wholesaling has a different role in the marketing system.

What Are Wholesaling and Wholesaling Middlemen?

Wholesaling, or wholesale trade, consists of the sale, and all activities directly related to the sale, of goods and services to parties for resale, use in producing other goods or services, or operating an organization. Broadly viewed, sales made by one producer to another are wholesale transactions, and the selling producer is engaged in wholesaling. Likewise, a retail variety store is carrying out wholesaling when it sells calculators and office supplies to a business firm.

Thus wholesaling includes sales by any firm to any customer except an ultimate consumer who is buying for personal, nonbusiness use. From this perspective, all sales are either wholesale or retail sales, distinguished only by the purchaser's intended use of the product or service that is bought.

In this chapter, we will concentrate on firms engaged *primarily* in wholesaling. This type of company is called a **wholesaling middleman**. We will not be concerned with retailers that make only occasional wholesale sales. And we will not focus on the sales of manufacturers and farmers because they are primarily engaged in production rather than wholesaling.

Economic Justification for Wholesaling

Many manufacturing companies in Canada are small and specialized. They don't have the capital needed to maintain a sales force large enough to contact the many small retailers that are their customers. Even for producers with sufficient capital, output frequently is too small to justify the necessary sales force. On the other hand, many retailers buy in small quantities and have only a limited knowledge of the market and sources of supply. Thus there is often a gap between the retailer (buyer) and the producer (seller). A wholesaling middleman can fill this gap by pooling the orders of many retailers and so furnish a market for the small producer. At the same time, the wholesaling middleman is performing a buying service for small retailers.

From a broad point of view, wholesaling brings to the total distribution system the economies of skill, scale, and transactions. Wholesaling *skills* are efficiently concentrated in a relatively few hands. This saves the duplication of effort that would occur if many producers had to perform wholesaling functions themselves. Economies of *scale* result from the specialization of wholesaling middlemen performing functions that might otherwise require several small departments run by producing firms. Wholesalers typically can perform wholesaling functions at a lower operating-expense percentage than can most manufacturers. *Transaction* economies come into play when wholesaling or retailing middlemen are introduced between producers and their customers. To illustrate: four manufacturers want to sell to six retailers. As shown in Fig. 15-1, *without* a middleman, there are 24 transactions; *with* one wholesaling middleman, the number is cut to 10. Four transactions occur when all the producers sell to the middleman, and another six occur when the middleman sells to all the retailers.

FIGURE 15-1
The economy of transactions in wholesaling

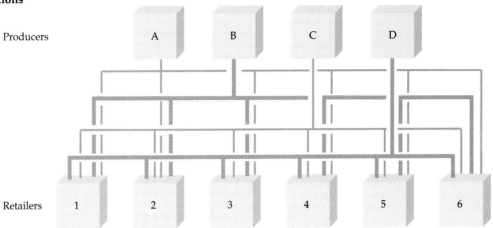

Four producers each sell directly to six retailers, resulting in 24 transactions.

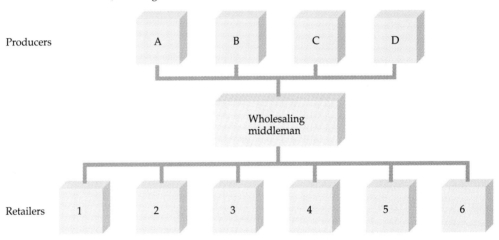

Four producers use the same wholesaling middleman, reducing the number of transactions to 10:

Size of the Wholesale Market

In 1987, there were more than 64,000 wholesaling establishments in Canada, with a total annual sales volume of about $257 billion. As is the case in retailing, the sales generated by wholesaling establishments have increased dramatically in recent years. Part of this increase is accounted for by increases in prices that have occurred during the past ten years or so, but even if sales were expressed in constant dollars, we would still see a substantial increase.

PROFILE OF WHOLESALING MIDDLEMEN

A producer or retailer considering indirect distribution and the use of wholesaling middlemen must know what alternatives are available, whom these middlemen serve, and how they operate. Having this information increases the likelihood of establishing effective distribution arrangements.

Four Major Categories

Classifying wholesaling middlemen is difficult because they vary greatly in (1) products they carry, (2) markets to which they sell, and (3) methods of operation. To minimize the confusion, we will use the classification scheme shown in Fig. 15-2. There, all wholesaling middlemen are grouped into only four broad categories — wholesale merchants, manufacturers' sales branches

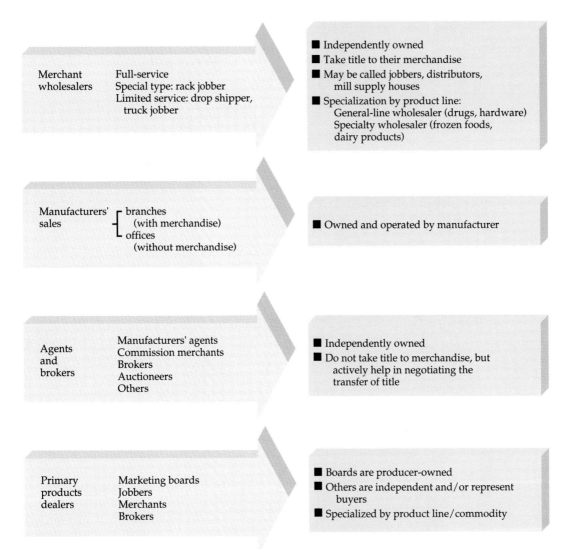

FIGURE 15-2
Types of wholesaling institutions.

and offices, agents and brokers, and primary product dealers. These four groups are the classifications used by Statistics Canada, which is the major source of quantitative data covering wholesaling institutions and markets. Later in this chapter we shall discuss merchant wholesalers, agents and brokers, and primary products dealers in more detail.

MERCHANT WHOLESALERS

These are firms we usually refer to as wholesalers, jobbers, or industrial distributors. They typically are independently owned, and they take title to the merchandise they handle. They form the largest single segment of wholesaling firms when measured either by sales or by number of establishments. Statistics Canada reports that wholesale merchants, along with manufacturers' sales branches and primary-product dealers discussed below, account for almost 85 percent of total wholesale trade.

MANUFACTURERS' SALES BRANCHES AND OFFICES

These establishments are owned and operated by manufacturers, but they are physically separated from the manufacturing plants. The distinction between

MARKETING AT WORK

FILE 15-1 **WHOLESALING GOES RETAILING**

A recent development in Canadian distribution is the wholesale or warehouse club. These large bulk merchandisers are located in large urban areas such as Vancouver, Toronto, Edmonton, and Montreal and sell in volume to retail customers and to small independent businesses, many of whom buy at attractive discounts to resell in their own stores. Costco Wholesale opened the first warehouse club in Burnaby, B.C., in 1985. It now has stores in Edmonton and Calgary. Steinberg opened its first Price wholesale club in Montreal and Titan Warehouse Club is based in Toronto.

The wholesale club stocks food and other merchandise and operates on thin margins and no-frills service. Consumers must be members and they buy in bulk at attractive discounts. About 25 percent of warehouse club sales are from food, 20 percent from appliances, and the rest from a wide range of products including sporting goods, automotive products, and toys. The clubs attract small convenience store operators, professionals, restaurant operators, and other small businesses who have no efficient route to buy supplies wholesale. Provided they can show a commercial licence, they buy at special wholesale prices and pay no sales tax. These business customers typically account for between 50 percent and 70 percent of sales. Warehouse clubs also appeal to consumer groups, such as credit unions and government employees.

TABLE 15-1 **Wholesale Trade in Canada, 1987**

	Number of Establishments	Number of Locations	Sales Volume ($ millions)
Wholesaler merchants	60,537	72,707	220,007.8
Agents and brokers	4,005	4,265	37,727.3
TOTAL	64,542	76,972	257,735.1

SOURCE: *Wholesale Trade Statistics*, cat. no. 63-226, 1987. Reproduced with permission of the Minister of Supply and Services Canada.

a sales branch and a sales office is that a branch carries merchandise stock and an office does not.

AGENTS AND BROKERS

Agents and brokers do *not* take title to the merchandise they handle, but they do actively negotiate the purchase or sale of products for their principals. The main types of agent middlemen are manufacturers' agents, commission merchants (in the marketing of agricultural products), and brokers. As a group, agents and brokers represent less than 20 percent of total wholesale trade.

PRIMARY-PRODUCT DEALERS

These firms are principally engaged in buying for resale primary products such as grain, livestock, furs, fish, tobacco, fruit, and vegetables from the primary producers of these products. On occasion, they will act as agents of the producer. Cooperatives that market the primary products of their members are also included in this category.

Some other subcategories used in classifying the wholesaling business are reflected in Fig. 15-2. For example, wholesaling middlemen may be grouped by:

- *Ownership of products*—wholesale merchants versus agent middlemen.
- *Ownership of establishment* — manufacturers' sales branches versus independent merchants and agents.
- *Range of services offered* — full-service wholesalers versus limited-service firms.
- *Depth and breadth of the line carried*—general-line wholesalers (drugs, hardware) versus specialty firms (frozen foods, dairy products).

Customers of Wholesaling Middlemen

One might expect that total retail sales would be considerably higher than total wholesale trade, because the retail price of a given product is higher than the wholesale price. Also, many products sold at retail never pass through a wholesaler's establishment and so are excluded from total wholesale sales.

Total sales figures belie this particular line of reasoning (see Table 15-2). In each year, the volume of wholesale trade is considerably higher than total retail sales.

The explanation for this situation may be found in an analysis of the customers of wholesaling middlemen (see Fig. 15-3).

Most wholesale merchants' sales are made to customers other than retailers. That is, large quantities of business and industrial products are now sold through wholesale merchants. Moreover, sales by the other types of wholesaling middlemen show this same pattern. Thus, overall, sales to retailers account for much less than total sales by wholesale merchants.

Another trend that has become obvious in recent years is the increase in the percentage of consumer goods sold directly to retailers by manufacturers. Yet, in spite of this increased bypassing of the wholesaler, wholesaling is on the increase, an indication of the usefulness of wholesaling to the business world.

Operating Expenses and Profits of Wholesaling Middlemen

The average total operating expenses for all wholesaling middlemen combined has been estimated at about 17 percent of *wholesale* sales. It has also been estimated that operating expenses of retailers average about 25 percent of *retail* sales (omitting bars and restaurants, which do some processing of products).

TABLE 15-2   **Total Wholesale and Retail Trade, Selected Years**

Year	Wholesale Trade	Retail Trade
1980	128,932.6	84,026.6
1982	170,061.0	97,638.5
1984	213,747.5	116,079.9
1986	171,848.5	146,734.7
1987	191,637.1	156,713.9

SOURCE: Statistics Canada, *Market Research Handbook*, cat. no. 63-224; *Canadian Statistical Review*, cat. no. 11-003E; *Corporate Financial Statistics*, cat. no. 61-207; and *Wholesale Trade Statistics*, cat. no. 63-226 (various years). Reproduced with permission of Supply and Services Canada.

FIGURE 15-3
Wholesale trade customers

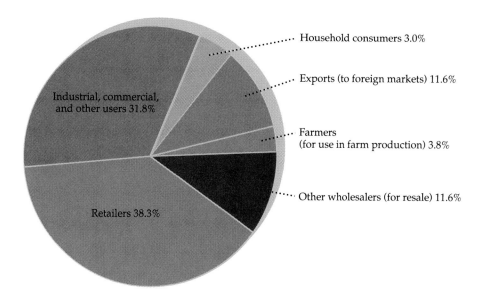

Household consumers 3.0%

Exports (to foreign markets) 11.6%

Farmers
(for use in farm production) 3.8%

Other wholesalers (for resale) 11.6%

Industrial, commercial,
and other users 31.8%

Retailers 38.3%

Therefore, on a broad average, the expenses of wholesaling middlemen take less than 8 percent of the consumer's dollar.

Net operating profit after taxes, expressed as a percentage of total income, is extremely modest for wholesaling middlemen and is considerably lower than that for retailing middlemen. Data collected by Statistics Canada from wholesalers in 1984 showed an average after-tax profit of only 1.7 percent. This compares with an average of 3.3 percent profit after taxes among retailers. The highest after-tax profits were reported by wholesalers of motor vehicles and parts. Several categories of wholesalers reported after-tax profits of less than 1.5 percent of total income. These included petroleum wholesalers and those engaged in the wholesaling of paper, food, and livestock products.

MERCHANT WHOLESALERS

Wholesale merchants are the wholesaling middlemen that take title to the products they handle, and they account for the largest segment of wholesale trade.

Full-Service Wholesalers

Full-service (also called full-function) wholesalers are independent merchant middlemen who generally perform a full range of wholesaling functions. These are the firms that fit the layman's image or stereotype of wholesalers. They may be called simply "wholesalers," or they may be listed as "distributors," "mill supply houses," "industrial distributors," or "jobbers," depending upon the usage in their line of business. They may handle consumer and/or industrial products, and these goods may be manufactured or nonmanufactured, and imported or exported.

Wholesale merchants have accounted for well over one-half of total wholesale trade in Canada for many years. Thus, the full-service wholesalers have held their own in the competitive struggles within the distribution system. In fact, their market share has been relatively constant in the recent past, despite increasing competition from agents and brokers and from direct-selling manufacturers and their sales offices and branches. A presumption is that the wholesalers' existence is maintained by the services they provide both to their customers and to their suppliers.

Full-service wholesalers consider modern, efficient warehouses vital to their success.

This picture of stability in the full-service wholesaler's share of the market may be a bit misleading. It hides the volatility and shifting competitive positions within various industries. Wholesalers have increased their market share in some industries but have lost ground in other markets where they once dominated. Certainly the aggregate market-share figures are misleading in industries where wholesalers are, and always have been, used very little.

Special Types of Merchant Wholesalers

Within the broad category of wholesale merchants, there are a few subclassifications worth observing because of the special nature of their operations. Their titles reflect either the specialized nature of their work or the limited range of wholesaling services that they offer. (Recall Fig. 15-2.)

RACK JOBBERS

These firms are wholesale merchants that began to appear about 40 years ago, primarily to supply grocery supermarkets with nonfood items. Since then, rack jobbers have expanded to serve drugstores, hardware stores, and other stores that have instituted the self-service method of retailing. The many general-line wholesalers carrying these nonfood lines could not easily sell to supermarkets for at least three reasons. First, the wholesalers' regular customers, such as drugstore or hardware stores, would complain loudly and probably withdraw their business. Second, too many different wholesalers would have to call on the supermarket to fill all the nonfood lines, and the retailer would object to seeing so many wholesalers. Third, a single supermarket ordinarily orders too small a quantity in any one nonfood line to make it profitable for a wholesaler to service that line.

TABLE 15-3 **Full-service Wholesalers' Services to Customers and to Producer-suppliers**

Service	Description
Buying	Act as purchasing agent for customers. Anticipate needs and have good knowledge of sources of supply.
Creating assortments	Buy from many suppliers to develop an inventory matching needs of customers. Enable customers to deal with only one wholesaler rather than many producers.
Subdividing	Buy in large quantities (such as a truckload) and then resell in smaller quantities (such as a dozen).
Selling	Provide a sales force for producers to reach small retailers and other businesses, at a lower cost than producers would incur by having their own sales forces.
Transportation	Make quick, frequent deliveries to customers, thereby reducing their risks and investment in inventory. Reduce producers' and customers' freight costs by buying in large quantities.
Warehousing	Store products in facilities that are nearer customers' locations than are manufacturing plants.
Financing	Grant credit to customers, thereby reducing their capital requirements. Aid producers by ordering and paying for products before purchase by customers.
Risk taking	Reduce a producer's risk by taking title to products. Bear the risk of losses due to perishability.
Market information	Supply information to customers on new products and special offers by producers. Provide information to producer-suppliers in many areas, including customers' needs and competitors' activities.
Management assistance	Assist customers, especially small retailers, in areas such as inventory control, allocation of shelf space, and financial management.

Truck jobbers frequently are used in the distribution channels for perishables.

One rack jobber (or a very few) can furnish all the nonfood items in a supermarket. Rack jobbers furnish the racks or shelves upon which to display the merchandise, and they stock only the fastest-moving brands on these racks. They are responsible for maintaining full stocked racks, building attractive displays, and price-marking the merchandise. In essence, the retailers merely furnish floor or shelf space and then collect the money as the customers go through the checkout stands.

LIMITED-FUNCTION WHOLESALERS

A small group of wholesale merchants that have received attention in marketing literature through the years — possibly more attention than their numerical importance merits — are the limited-function wholesalers. These are merchant middlemen who do not perform all the usual wholesaling functions. The activities of most of these wholesalers are concentrated in a few product lines. The major types of limited-function wholesalers are truck jobbers, drop shippers, and retailer cooperative warehouses. The retailer cooperative warehouse was discussed in the preceding chapter.

Truck distributors or jobbers (sometimes still called "wagon jobbers," recalling the days when they used a horse and wagon) are specialty wholesalers, chiefly in the food field. Each jobber carries a nationally advertised brand of fast-moving and perishable or semiperishable goods, such as candies, dairy products, potato chips, and tobacco products. The unique feature of their method of operation is that they sell and deliver merchandising during their calls. Their competitive advantage lies in their ability to furnish fresh products so frequently that retailers can buy perishable goods in small amounts to minimize the risk of loss. The major limitation of truck jobbers is their high operating cost ratio. This is caused primarily by the small order size and the inefficient use of delivery equipment. A truck is an expensive warehouse.

Drop shippers, sometimes called "desk jobbers," get their name from the fact that the merchandise they sell is delivered from the manufacturer to the customer and is called a "drop shipment." Drop shippers take title to the products but do not physically handle them. They operate almost entirely in coal and coke, lumber, and building materials. These products are typically sold in carload quantities, and freight is high in comparison with their unit value. Thus, it is desirable to minimize the physical handling of the product.

AGENT WHOLESALING MIDDLEMEN

Agents and brokers (agent middlemen) are distinguished from wholesale merchants in two important respects: Agent middlemen do *not* take title to the merchandise, and they typically perform fewer services for their clients and principals. (See Table 15-4.) For these reasons, the operating expenses for agents and brokers average only 3 to 4 percent of net sales, compared with 17 percent for wholesale merchants. On the basis of sales volume, the major types of agent middlemen are manufacturers' agents, brokers, and commission merchants. Other types include auction companies, selling agents, import agents, and export agents.

The relative importance of agents and brokers in wholesale trade has declined over the past 40 years. Although the total number of agents and brokers has not changed appreciably, their market share has dropped to approximately 15 percent. In the wholesaling of agricultural products, agent middlemen are being replaced by wholesale merchants, or by direct sales to retailers and food processors. In the marketing of manufactured goods, agent middlemen are being supplanted by manufacturers' sales branches and offices. As manufacturers' markets grow in sales potential, it becomes more effective for them to establish their own outlets and sales force in these markets.

Manufacturers' Agents

Manufacturers' agents (frequently called *manufacturers' representatives*) are agents commissioned to sell part or all of a producer's products in particular territories. The agents are independent and are in no way employees of the manufacturers. They have little or no control over the prices and terms of sale; these are established by the manufacturer. Because a manufacturers' agent sells in a limited territory, say a province or group of provinces, each producer typically uses several agents. Unlike brokers, manufacturers' agents have continuing, year-round relationships with their principals. Each agent usually represents several noncompeting manufacturers of related products. The agent can pool into one profitable sale the small orders that otherwise would go to several individual manufacturers.

TABLE 15-4 **Services Provided by Agent Wholesaling Middlemen**

Services	Manufacturers' agents	Selling agents	Brokers	Commission merchants
Provides buying services	Yes	Yes	Some	Yes
Provides selling services	Yes	Yes	Yes	Yes
Carries inventory stocks	Sometimes	No	No	Yes
Delivers the products	Sometimes	No	No	Yes
Provides market information	Yes	Yes	Yes	Yes
Sets prices and terms of sale	No	Yes	No	No
Grants credit to customers	No	Sometimes	No	Sometimes
Reduces producers' credit risks	No	Yes	No	No
Sells producers' full line	Sometimes	Yes	Sometimes	No
Has continuing relationship with producer throughout year	Yes	Yes	No	No
Manufacturer uses own sales force along with agents'	Sometimes	No	No	No
Manufacturer uses same agent for entire market	No	Yes	No	No

Manufacturers' agents are used extensively in the distribution of many types of consumer and business products. The main service offered to manufacturers by these agent middlemen is selling. They seek out and serve markets that manufacturers cannot profitably reach. Furthermore, a manufacturers' agent does not carry nearly so many lines as a full-service wholesaler. Consequently, the agent can offer a high-calibre, more aggressive selling service. Operating expenses depend upon the product sold and whether the merchandise is stocked. Some representatives operate on a commission as low as 2 percent, while others charge as much as 20 percent. These commissions cover operating expenses and net profit. On an overall basis, the operating expense ratio is about 8 percent for these agents.

There are some limitations to the use of manufacturers' agents. Most agents do not carry merchandise stocks. Also, many agents cannot furnish customers with adequate technical advice or repair service; nor are they equipped to install major products.

Manufacturers' agents are most helpful in three characteristic situations:

- A small firm has a limited number of products and no sales force. Then manufacturers' agents may do all the selling.
- A firm wants to add a new and possibly unrelated line to its existing product mix. But the present sales force either is not experienced in the new line or cannot reach the new market. Then the new line may be given to manufacturers' agents. Thus, a company's own sales force and its agents may cover the same geographical market.
- A firm wishes to enter a new market that is not yet sufficiently developed to warrant the use of its own sales force. Then manufacturers' agents familiar with that market may be used.

Brokers

Brokers are agent middlemen whose prime responsibility is to bring buyers and sellers together. They furnish considerable market information regarding prices, products, and general market conditions. Brokers do not physically handle the goods. Nor do they work on a continuing basis with their principals. Most brokers work for sellers although about 10 percent represent buyers.

Brokers have no authority to set prices. A broker simply negotiates a sale and leaves it up to the seller to accept or reject the buyer's offer. Because of the limited services provided, brokers operate on a very low cost ratio—about 3 percent of net sales.

Brokers are most prevalent in the food field. Their operation is typified by a seafood broker handling the pack from a salmon cannery. The cannery is in operation for possibly three months of the year. The canner employs a broker each year (the same one if relationships are mutually satisfactory) to find buyers for the salmon pack. The broker provides information regarding market prices and conditions, and the canner then informs the broker of the desired price. The broker seeks potential buyers among chain stores, wholesalers, and others. When the entire pack has been sold, the agent-principal relationship is discontinued until possibly the following year.

An evolutionary development in the food brokerage field should be noted. Through the years, many brokers have established permanent relationships with some principals. These brokers are now performing activities that would more accurately classify them as manufacturers' agents. They still call themselves ''food brokers,'' however, and they are classed as brokers by Statistics Canada.

Commission Merchants

In the marketing of many agricultural products, a widely used middleman is the commission merchant, also called a *commission house*. (The term *commission*

Brokers are used in selling not only real estate and securities but sometimes even perishable goods.

merchant is actually a misnomer. This handler is really an agent middleman who, in many transactions, does not take title to the commodities which are handled.)

The commission method of operation, found mainly in large central markets, may be described briefly as follows: Assemblers in local markets (possibly local produce buyers or grain elevators) consign shipments to commission merchants in central markets. (These firms usually have established working relationships over a period of years.) The commission merchants meet trains or trucks and take charge of the shipments. It is their responsibility to handle and sell the goods. They arrange for any necessary storage, grading, and other services prior to the sale. They find buyers at the best possible prices, make the sales, and arrange for the transfer of shipments. They deduct their commissions, freight charges, and other marketing expenses and then remit the balance as soon as possible to the local shippers.

Other Types of Agent Wholesaling Middlemen

Three additional types of agent wholesaling middlemen account for smaller shares of wholesale trade than do manufacturers' reps, brokers, and commission merchants. Nevertheless, for certain products and in specific markets, the services they provide are invaluable. These middlemen are:

- *Auction companies.* Some firms simply help assembled buyers and sellers complete their transactions. Firms that provide (1) auctioneers who do the selling and (2) physical facilities for displaying the sellers' products are called **auction companies**. Although they make up a very small percentage of total wholesale trade, auction companies are extremely important in some markets in the wholesaling of used cars and certain agricultural products (such as tobacco and livestock).
- *Selling agents.* One type of independent middleman, a **selling agent**, essentially takes the place of a manufacturers' marketing department by marketing the producer's entire output. Often a selling agent influences product design and pricing. Although selling agents transact a very small percentage of total wholesale trade, they play a key role in the distribution of textile products and coal and, to a lesser extent, apparel, food, lumber, and metal products.
- *Import-export agents.* Some agents specialize in international marketing by arranging for distribution of goods in a foreign country. Export agents work in the country in which the product is made, whereas import agents are based in the foreign country where the product will be sold. There are many different forms of import and export agents, including export management companies, factors, and managing agents. Each, however, brings together sellers and buyers from different countries.

WHOLESALING CHALLENGES AND OPPORTUNITIES

To survive and prosper in the future, wholesaling middlemen will have to identify and respond to certain trends in their operating environment. They will also need marketing strategies that serve their customers well.

Trends in Wholesaling

Wholesaling middlemen can expect serious challenges to their role in the distribution process, including:

- Direct distribution whereby suppliers and customers bypass wholesaling middlemen and deal directly with each other.
- Continuing growth of vertical marketing systems. Merchant wholesalers,

M A R K E T I N G   A T   W O R K

FILE 15-2   **GREY MARKETS GIVE SOME PRODUCERS AND MIDDLEMEN GREY HAIR**

Products distributed by wholesaling middlemen do not always wind up where producer-suppliers intend. Occasionally products are sold through distribution channels that are not authorized by the manufacturer. This practice, called *grey marketing*, accounts for substantial sales annually around the world.

Diverse products are sold through grey markets: cameras, computer disc drives, perfumes, cars, and personal computers, among others. Ordinarily grey marketing arises when a product with a well-known brand name carries different prices under different circumstances. For example, a product's wholesale price may vary depending on the country to which it is sold or the quantity purchased.

Grey marketing takes many forms and typically has international dimensions. Most commonly a wholesaling middleman, such as an import or export agent, purchases a product made in one country and agrees to distribute it in a second country, but instead diverts the product to a third country, where it is then sold at a discount.

So what's wrong with grey marketing? After spending time and money to promote the product, authorized distributors lose sales to outlets selling grey-market goods. Manufacturers then have to placate these distributors. Grey marketing disrupts a producer's distribution and pricing strategies. And consumers may buy products without warranties or service contracts.

Still, some parties (except authorized distributors) see benefits in grey marketing. Unauthorized distributors are able to sell products they normally cannot acquire. Some manufacturers quietly participate in, or at least do not discourage, grey marketing to sell excess output. Consumers pay lower prices for popular products and may also find the products at more outlets.

Most manufacturers would like to eliminate unauthorized channels. However, some have accepted grey marketing as inevitable because it is too difficult and costly to fight. Other producer-suppliers try very hard to minimize grey marketing. Their tactics include revising pricing schedules and distribution policies and taking unauthorized distributors to court. Grey marketing represents one more complication in channels management for both producers and wholesaling middlemen.

Source: Peter Engardi et al., ''There's Nothing Black-and-White about the Gray Market,'' *Business Week*, Nov. 7, 1988, pp. 172–73ff; and Larry S. Lowe and Kevin McCrohan, ''Gray Markets in the United States,'' *Journal of Consumer Marketing*, Winter 1988, pp. 45–51.

---

in particular, will need to determine how they can become part of such coordinated approaches to distribution.
- Development of new wholesaling institutions that serve suppliers and customers in new and more satisfying ways.

Merchant wholesalers are likely to gain at the expense of agent wholesaling middlemen and manufacturers' sales facilities. This trend would continue the pattern reflected in Statistics Canada data.

Several examples show how dynamic the wholesaling field will be as the

To remain competitive and profitable, many wholesalers use networked computer systems to control inventories.

twenty-first century approaches. The total number of merchant wholesalers is expected to decline due to increasing mergers and acquisitions. The consolidation of merchant wholesalers stems from the belief of some wholesaling firms that they need to be larger in order to maintain their competitive edge. Mergers also add resources that permit wholesalers to invest in the latest technology.[2] Smaller wholesalers will have to decide whether they intend to acquire, be acquired, or somehow isolate themselves from this trend—perhaps by serving small market niches.

To illustrate the impact of a new institution, consider service merchandisers, which supply retail stores (particularly grocery stores) with nonfood items ranging from health and beauty aids to automotive supplies. To develop a strong seller-buyer relationship, service merchandisers ordinarily provide retail outlets with computerized order-entry systems to assist the stores in placing orders with their firms. This new type of company threatens the viability of traditional rack jobbers.

Marketing Strategies

Like all other business firms, wholesaling middlemen must develop effective marketing strategies in the following related areas:

- *Target markets.* Wholesaling firms must decide whether to pursue diversified or niche markets. To make this decision, middlemen should classify markets by size, types of customers, and services needed by customers.
- *Product.* Several strategic decisions relate to this element of the marketing mix. A wholesaling middleman must determine the breadth and depth of assortment of the firm's product mix. A middleman then has to decide whether it will actually carry stocks. A wholesaling firm may want a broad assortment and extensive inventories to satisfy customers' desires to deal with few suppliers and receive goods soon after an order is placed. However, a middleman may want to control its investment in inventory. Another key decision is what services will be performed for suppliers and customers.

---

[2]This trend is reported in Joseph Weber, ''Mom and Pop Move Out of Wholesaling,'' *Business Week*, Jan. 9, 1989, p. 91.

M A R K E T I N G   A T   W O R K

FILE 15-3   **USING GREY SUPPLIERS**

Under grey marketing, products wind up being distributed outside a manufacturer's authorized distribution channels. For example, an exporter may establish a relationship with a European manufacturer to distribute its line of stereo equipment in the United States. However, without the manufacturer's knowledge, the exporter diverts a large order of equipment for sale in Canada. Assume you are the stereo-equipment buyer for a chain of discount houses. The exporter contacts you about purchasing some stereos at prices that are substantially below the normal wholesale price. Would it be ethical for you to buy these stereos for resale in your stores? Would your view depend on whether you knew for sure that the stereos were indeed ''grey market'' goods?

- *Price.* Middlemen's prices should take into account many factors, most notably services performed. Prices are reflected in the size of markups and commissions.
- *Distribution.* The first distribution decision pertains to where the specific wholesaling middleman fits into various distribution channels. In turn, specific suppliers must be chosen. Many wholesaling middlemen face strategic decisions regarding the extent to which the firm will be involved in physical distribution of the product and where they will locate, considering such factors as access to markets, transportation requirements, and costs.
- *Promotion.* This element of the marketing mix concerns the best means of communicating with target markets. Wholesaling middlemen, like other firms, need to create an effective blend of advertising, personal selling, sales promotion, and publicity. For most middlemen, personal-selling activities are of paramount importance.

Successful wholesaling middlemen have a true customer orientation. They identify and then satisfy the needs of their retail customers. Furthermore, they consider their suppliers as customers in that producers must perform or delegate various distribution functions, and wholesaling middlemen have to determine how they can satisfy these needs.

SUMMARY   Wholesaling is the sale, and all activities directly related to the sale, of goods and services to parties for resale, use in producing other goods or services, or operating an organization. In contrast, retailing involves sales to ultimate consumers. Thus all transactions are either wholesale or retail sales, depending on the purchaser's purpose in buying.

Firms primarily engaged in wholesaling are called wholesaling middlemen. Such firms provide participants in the distribution process with economies of skill, scale, and transactions.

The institutional structure of wholesaling middlemen (the all-inclusive term) may be divided into four groups: (1) wholesale merchants, (2) manufacturers' sales offices and branches, (3) agents and brokers, and (4) primary products dealers. Total operating expenses of all wholesaling middlemen average about 17 percent of *wholesale* sales and less than 10 percent of *retail* sales (the consumer's dollar). Net profits in wholesaling average only about 2 percent of sales.

Less than 40 percent of wholesale sales are made to retailers, and approximately the same percentage go to industrial users and other wholesalers.

Wholesale merchants (also called jobbers or distributors) generally fit the layman's stereotype of a wholesaler. They constitute the largest category of wholesaling middlemen, in both sales volume and number of companies. These middlemen offer the widest range of wholesaling services, and consequently incur the highest operating expenses, of the four major groups of wholesaling middlemen. Wholesale merchants have consistently accounted for more than 50 percent of all wholesale sales over the past 40 years. In spite of persistent attempts to "eliminate the middleman" (namely, the wholesale merchant), these middlemen continue to grow and thrive, thus attesting to their real economic value in our economy.

The use of agents and brokers has decreased over the years. These middlemen have been replaced in distribution channels by wholesale merchants and by manufacturers' sales offices and branches. Agent wholesaling middlemen (manufacturers' agents, brokers, and others) remain strong in certain industries, and in geographic areas where the market potential is still too small for a producer's sales force.

In the future, wholesaling middlemen will face challenges to their roles in distribution. To succeed, wholesaling middlemen will have to address significant trends in distribution and develop effective marketing strategies.

KEY TERMS AND CONCEPTS

Wholesaling 472
Wholesaling middlemen 472
Wholesaler 472
Manufacturer's sales office 474
Manufacturer's sales branch 474
Rack jobber 478
Limited-function wholesale 479
Agent wholesaling middleman 480

Manufacturers' agent 480
Broker 482
Commission merchant 482
Auction company 483
Selling agent 483
Import-export agent 483

QUESTIONS AND PROBLEMS

1. A large furniture warehouse is located in a Saskatchewan city. The following conditions exist with respect to this firm:
   a. All merchandise is purchased directly from manufacturers.
   b. The warehouse is located in the low-rent wholesaling district.
   c. Merchandise remains in original crates; customers use catalogues and swatch books to see what the articles look like and what fabrics are used.
   d. About 90 percent of the customers are ultimate consumers, and they account for 85 percent of the sales volume.
   e. The firm does quite a bit of advertising, pointing out that consumers are buying at wholesale prices.
   f. Crates are not price-marketed. Sales people bargain with customers.
   g. Some 10 percent of sales volume comes from sales to furniture stores.
   Is the furniture warehouse a wholesaler? Explain.
2. Which of the following are wholesaling transactions?
   a. St. Clair Paint and Paper sells wallpaper to an apartment building contractor and also to the contractor's family for their home.

b. Canadian General Electric sells small motors to Inglis for its washing machines.

c. A shrimp fisherman sells shrimp to a local restaurant.

d. A family has a friend who is a home decorating consultant. The family orders carpet through the consultant at 50 percent off retail. The carpet is delivered directly to the house.

3. Manufacturers' sales offices and branches have maintained a steadily increasing share of total wholesale trade, while the agents' and brokers' share has declined. What conditions account for this fact?

4. What activities could full-service wholesalers discontinue in an effort to reduce operating costs?

5. What service does a full-service wholesaler provide for a manufacturer?

6. What types of retailers, other than supermarkets, offer reasonable fields for entry by rack jobbers? Explain.

7. Why would a manufacturing firm prefer to use manufacturers' agents instead of its own company sales force?

8. Why is it that manufacturers' agents often can penetrate a market faster and at a lower cost than a manufacturer's sales force?

9. What is the economic justification for the existence of brokers, especially in light of the few functions they perform?

10. Which type of wholesaling middleman, if any, is most likely to be used by each of the following? Explain your choice in each instance.

a. A small manufacturer of a liquid glass cleaner to be sold through supermarkets.

b. A small manufacturer of knives used for hunting, fishing, and camping.

c. A salmon canner in British Columbia packing a high-quality, unbranded product.

d. A small-tools manufacturing firm that has its own sales force selling to the industrial market and that wishes to add backyard barbecue equipment to its line.

e. A Quebec textile mill producing unbranded towels, sheets, pillowcases, and blankets.

11. Looking into the future, which types of wholesaling middlemen do you think will increase in importance, and which ones will decline? Explain.

CHAPTER 16 GOALS

Distribution of consumer products begins with the producer and ends with the ultimate consumer. Between the two there is usually at least one middleman—a retailer. The various markets served by retailers and the many types of retailing institutions are the primary subjects of this chapter. After studying this chapter, you should be able to explain:

- The nature of retailing.
- What a retailer is.
- Different types of retailers classified by form of ownership.
- Different types of retailers classified by marketing strategies.
- Various forms of nonstore retailing.
- Major strategy areas for retailers.
- Key trends in retailing.

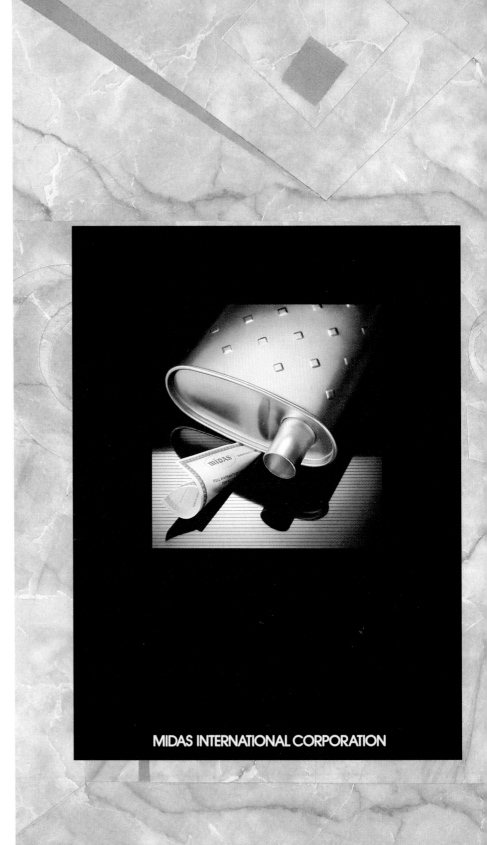

MIDAS INTERNATIONAL CORPORATION

Retailing: Markets and Institutions

I s there a Midas outlet in your town or neighbourhood? Have you or your family ever taken your car to Midas to have a muffler, brakes, or shock absorbers replaced?

With more than 200 Midas outlets across Canada, chances are that most of us are familiar with Midas and its products, even if we haven't brought our cars there for repair. We see the stores as we drive by and we are exposed to national radio and television advertising for Midas and its ''top guns.''

Midas Canada is part of the worldwide chain of Midas International, which now operates more than 2,000 units in many countries, including western Europe, Great Britain, Australia, Mexico, and Panama. Starting from a single store in Georgia in 1955, Midas has grown in many ways, not just in the number of outlets. In addition to being an international operation, it has expanded its business from the time when it was known as ''Midas Muffler'' to include a complete range of automotive service and parts for brakes, suspension, exhaust systems, and front-end repair.

Midas is a good example of franchising in action. Franchising as a form of retailing has blossomed over the past 40 years and franchised operations now dominate many sectors of retailing, including most fast food, automotive repair, car rentals, service stations, and convenience stores. Franchising offers a small business person the opportunity to run his or her own business, while also taking advantage of the expertise and support available from the franchising company.

For example, in return for a franchise fee of $25,000 and initial investment for equipment and inventory in the range of $150,000 to $200,000, a Midas franchisee immediately becomes a member of the Midas International network of stores. The new franchisee can trade on the international recognition and reputation of the Midas name, the extensive advertising and public-relations support offered by the parent company to all franchisers, assistance in site location and financing of facilities, and training at the Midas training centre, MIT (Midas Institute of Technology), in the United States. In return for these services and support, the franchisee pays Midas Canada 5 percent of gross sales as a royalty and an additional 5 percent to cover his or her share of national advertising.

A great deal of the success enjoyed by Midas is attributable to the company's emphasis on quality and excellent customer service. Each franchiser in the Midas organization is expected to live up to the Midas reputation for service and quality. As Midas advertising indicates, the emphasis of the company is not only based on speed of service, but on doing the job properly—"first you get good, then you get fast." This corporate commitment is reinforced by a guarantee on Midas work "for as long as you own your car," by stringent quality control on the 5,900 parts manufactured by Midas, and by a computerized distribution system which ensures that franchisors have parts in stock when they need them.

Midas Canada is but one example of a franchising operation. We will discuss others later in this chapter. Midas serves not only as an excellent example of how franchising operates, but also of how important this form of retailing has become in many retail sectors with which we deal regularly.

There are many examples of the fact that the entrepreneurial spirit still prevails in Canadian retailing. This is a fast-moving field, characterized by innovations and new entrants. The exciting world of retailing provides many entrepreneurial opportunities and career openings for university and college graduates.

We all have a great deal of experience with retailing — as consumers. And many students acquire work experience in retailing. This chapter builds on that experience and provides insights about retail markets, different types of retailers, and key strategies and trends in retailing.

NATURE AND IMPORTANCE OF RETAILING

For every retail superstar like Eaton's, Midas, or Loblaws, thousands of tiny retailers serve consumers only in very limited areas. Despite their differences, all of these firms do have two common features: They link producers and ultimate consumers, and they perform valuable services for both parties. In all likelihood these firms are retailers, but all of their activities may not qualify as retailing. How can that be? Explanations follow.

What Are Retailing and Retailers?

If Safeway or Sobeys sells some floor wax to a gift-shop operator to polish the shop floor, is this a retail sale? When a Shell or Petro-Canada service station advertises that tires are being sold at the wholesale price, is this retailing? Can a wholesaler or manufacturer engage in retailing? When a service such as hair styling or auto repair is sold to an ultimate consumer, is this retailing? Obviously we need to define some terms, particularly *retailing* and *retailer*, to avoid misunderstandings later.

Retailing (or **retail trade**) consists of the sale, and all activities directly related to the sale, of goods and services to ultimate consumers for personal, non-business use. While most retailing occurs through retail stores, it may be done by any institution. A manufacturer selling brushes or cosmetics door to door is engaged in retailing, as is a farmer selling vegetables at a roadside stand.

Any firm — manufacturer, wholesaler, or retailer — that sells something to ultimate consumers for their own nonbusiness use is making a retail sale. This is true regardless of *how* the product is sold (in person or by telephone, mail, or vending machine) or *where* it is sold (in a store or at the consumer's home). However, a firm engaged *primarily* in retailing is called a **retailer**. In this chapter, we will concentrate on retailers rather than on other types of businesses that make only occasional retail sales.

While this chapter focuses primarily on retailers of *goods*, much of what is said — particularly regarding marketing strategies — applies equally well to retailers of *services*. As we discussed in Chapter 11, one of the characteristics of services relates to the inseparability of the service from the individual or company which provides it. Although this is certainly the case, the marketing of services is often delegated to retailers. For example, travel agents are really retailers who sell to end consumers the services offered by airlines, hotels, railways, and car rental companies. Banks and other financial services companies retail Canada Savings Bonds on behalf of the Government of Canada.

Economic Justification for Retailing

All middlemen basically serve as purchasing agents for their customers and as sales specialists for their suppliers. To carry out these roles, retailers perform many activities, including anticipating customers' wants, developing assortments of products, acquiring market information, and financing.

It is relatively easy to become a retailer. No large investment in production equipment is required, merchandise can often be purchased on credit, and store space can be leased with no ''down payment.'' This ease of entry results in fierce competition and better value for consumers.

To get into retailing is easy but to be forced out is just as easy. To survive in retailing, a company must do a satisfactory job in its primary role — catering to consumers — as well as in its secondary role — serving producers and wholesalers. This dual responsibility is both the justification for retailing and the key to success in retailing.

There are about 230,000 retail stores in Canada, and their total sales volume in 1988 was about $182 *billion* (see Fig. 16-1). In spite of growth in population and rising consumer incomes over the past 25 years, the total number of retail outlets has not increased dramatically. The increase in total sales volume, however, has been tremendous — a twelve-fold increase in the 30 years from 1961 to 1990, by which time total retail sales in Canada had reached $195 billion. Even if we adjust for the rate of inflation, we find that total retail sales, and per capita retail sales, have gone up considerably. That is, there has been a huge increase in the volume and value of goods and services sold at the retail level.

FIGURE 16-1
Total retail trade in Canada, selected years.
Sales volume has increased tremendously. In constrast, note the remarkable stability in the number of retail stores. (*Source: Statistics Canada*)

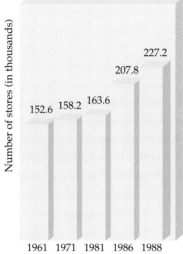

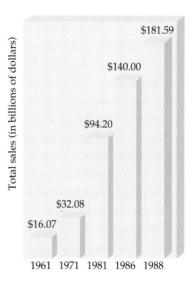

TABLE 16-1   **Total Retail Trade in Canada, 1961–1988**

	1961	1971	1981	1986	1988
Number of stores (thousands)	152.6	158.2	163.6	207.8	227.2
Total sales ($ billions)	$16.07	$32.08	$94.20	$140.00	$181.59
Average sales per store	$105,504	$202,781	$576,363	$673,706	$799,252

SOURCE: Statistics Canada. *Annual Retail Trade*, Catalogue Number 63-223, Annual. Reproduced with permission of Supply and Services Canada.

Costs and Profits of Retailers

Information regarding the costs of retailing is very meagre. By gleaning data from several sources, however, we can make some rough generalizations.

TOTAL COSTS AND PROFITS

As nearly as can be estimated, the total average operating expense for all retailers combined is about 25 to 27 percent of retail sales. Wholesaling expenses are estimated at about 8 percent of the *retail* dollar or about 10 to 11 percent of *wholesaling* sales. Thus, retailing costs are about $2\frac{1}{2}$ times the costs of wholesaling, when both are stated as a percentage of sales of the middlemen in question. (See Fig. 16-2).

FIGURE 16-2
Average costs of retailing and wholesaling.

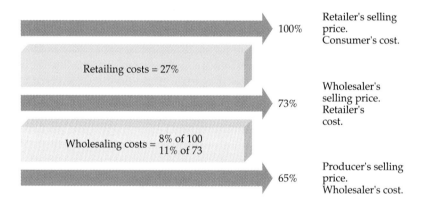

The proportionately higher retailing costs are generally related to the expense of dealing directly with the consumer. In comparison with wholesalers' customers, consumers demand more services. The average retail sale is smaller, the rate of merchandise turnover is lower, merchandise is bought in smaller lots, rent is higher, and expenses for furniture and fixtures are greater. And retail sales people cannot be used efficiently because customers do not come into retail stores at a steady rate.

COSTS AND PROFITS BY KIND OF BUSINESS

The expense ratios of retailers vary from one type of store to another. Table 16-2 shows average gross margins as a percentage of sales for different kinds of stores. These margins range from 15.4 percent for motor vehicle dealers to 51 percent for motor vehicle repair shops. Table 16-2 also shows average net profit (after income taxes) for each type of store.

TABLE 16-2 **Gross Margin and Net Profit as Percentage of Net Sales of Selected Types of Retailers**

Gross margin (net sales minus cost of goods sold) is the amount needed to cover a company's operating expenses and still leave a profit. How do you account for the differences in operating expenses among the various types of retailers?

Line of business	Gross margin %	Net Profit % after income taxes
Food stores	22.3	1.0
Department stores	31.0	1.4
Variety stores	27.4	1.7
General merchandise	20.7	1.7
Automobile accessories and parts	27.0	2.2
Gasoline service stations	14.8	1.4
Motor vehicle dealers	9.1	−0.7
Motor vehicle repair shops	32.5	2.9
Shoe stores	42.7	1.8
Men's clothing stores	40.8	3.5
Women's clothing stores	42.7	1.9
Dry goods stores	39.4	1.3
Hardware stores	31.3	2.5
Book and stationery stores	35.6	2.2
Florist shops	49.1	2.3
Fuel dealers	17.9	3.0
Furniture and appliance stores	29.9	1.9
Jewellery stores	41.3	3.2
Tobacconists	40.0	4.3
Drugstores	27.2	2.2
TOTAL RETAIL TRADE	24.8	3.6

SOURCE: Statistics Canada, *Corporation Financial Statistics*, 1987, cat. no. 61-207. Reproduced with permission of Supply and Services Canada.

Store Size Most retail establishments are very small. In fact, as many as 20 percent of all retailers have annual sales of $100,000 or less. However, despite their numbers, such stores account for a very small percentage of total retail sales.

At the same time, there is a high degree of concentration in retailing. A small number of companies account for a substantial share of total retail trade. These companies, such as Loblaws (part of the George Weston group of companies) and the Hudson's Bay Company (The Bay and Zellers), own many individual stores and account for the considerable degree of concentration in the industry. For example, the ten largest retailers in Canada, as shown in Table 16-3, in 1990 accounted for more than $45 billion in sales, approximately 24 percent of all retail sales in Canada.

Stores of different sizes present different management challenges and opportunities. Buying, promotion, personnel relations, and expense control are influenced significantly by whether a store's sales volume is large or small.

Size, or the lack thereof, brings with it certain advantages, several of which are evaluated in Table 16-4. This assessment suggests that relatively large stores have a competitive advantage over small stores. Small retailers do face

TABLE 16-3 **1990 Sales and Profits of Ten Largest Canadian Retailers**

Rank	Company	1990 revenue $'000	1990 assets $'000	1990 net income $'000
1	George Weston	10,856,000	3,707,000	125,000
2	Provigo	6,525,700	1,347,800	60,700
3	Hudson's Bay	5,041,733	3,100,289	163,282
4	Oshawa Group	4,598,798	994,015	70,301
5	Sears Canada	4,571,100	3,193,700	21,300
6	Canada Safeway	4,317,951	972,492	73,918
7	Canadian Tire	3,060,125	1,984,918	144,366
8	F.W. Woolworth	2,321,791	874,423	55,578
9	Great Atlantic & Pacific	2,299,881	492,584	35,973
10	Métro-Richelieu	2,189,404	503,711	(4,540)

SOURCE: *The Financial Post 500: Canada's Largest Corporations,* Summer 1991, p. 132.

TABLE 16-4 **Competitive Positions of Large and Small Retail Stores**

Selected bases for evalution	Who has the advantage?
Division of labour and specialization of management	Large-scale retailers — their biggest advantage
Flexibility of operations — merchandise selection, services offered, store design, reflection of owner's personality	Small retailers — their biggest advantage
Buying power	Large retailers buy in bigger quantities and thus get lower costs
Access to desirable merchandise	Large retailers promise suppliers access to large numbers of customers whereas a single small retailer may be viewed as insignificant
Development and promotion of retailer's own brand	Large retailers
Efficient use of advertising, especially in citywide media	Large retailers' markets match better with media circulation
Ability to provide top-quality personal service	Small retailers if owners pay personal attention to customers and also to selecting and supervising sales staff
Opportunity to experiment with new products and selling methods	Large retailers can better afford the risks
Financial strength	Large retailers have resources to gain some of the advantages noted above (such as private brands and experimentation)
Public image	Small retailers enjoy public support and sympathy. However, this same public often votes with its wallet by shopping at big stores.

many difficulties. The ones that cannot meet the challenges fail. If that's the case, how do so many small retailers succeed? The answer is twofold:

- Some small retailers have formed or joined contractual vertical marketing systems. These entities—called retailer cooperatives, voluntary chains, or franchise systems — give individual members certain advantages of large stores, such as specialized management, buying power, and a well-known store name.
- Many consumers seek benefits that small stores can often provide better than large stores can. For instance, some people seek high levels of shopping convenience. Small outlets located near residential areas offer such convenience. Other consumers desire high levels of personal service. A small store's highly motivated owner-manager and well-supervised sales staff may surpass a large store on this important shopping dimension.

Many small stores take advantage of their comparative strengths and compete successfully against other retailers of varying sizes and types.

Retailing Structure in Metropolitan Areas

As we might expect, retail sales and retailer location tend to follow the population. The bulk of retail sales is concentrated in very small land masses — the Census Metropolitan Areas. These CMA markets account for more than 60 percent of Canada's population and approximately 65 percent of our retail trade.

Within the central city and its adjacent suburbs in a metropolitan area, there are several discernible types of shopping districts. Together, these constitute a retailing structure that should be recognized by marketers. The hub of retailing activity has traditionally been the central downtown shopping district. This is the location of the main units of department stores, major apparel specialty stores, jewellery stores, and other shopping-goods stores.

Hazelton Lanes in Toronto designs to attract.

In the older, larger cities we often find a secondary shopping district with branches of downtown stores. A third type of shopping district is a "string-street" development, or a cluster of small, neighbourhood stores. None of these three types of shopping districts is planned or controlled for marketing purposes. Thus they are different from planned suburban shopping centres.

During the past 25 years or so, many cities have made a concerted effort to revitalize their downtown shopping districts. An especially successful venture in this respect has been the development of planned, controlled downtown shopping centres—the urban shopping mall. Many cities now have such malls —the Rideau Centre in Ottawa, Scotia Square in Halifax, the Pacific Centre in Vancouver, London Square in London, and Eaton Centres in Toronto, Calgary, and Edmonton, to name just a few. These malls have brought retail customers back to the downtown areas, provided excellent shopping for the many people who work downtown, and rebuilt an urban tax base.

SUBURBAN SHOPPING CENTRES

Another significant type of shopping district in metropolitan areas is the suburban shopping centre—a unit that is planned, developed, and controlled by one organization. These planned centres range from (1) a *neighbourhood* centre built around a supermarket, through (2) a *community* centre featuring a discount store or junior department store, to (3) a *regional* centre anchored by a branch of one or more downtown department stores. In the regional centre, ideally there is at least one limited-line store to compete with each department in the department stores.

Many of the regional centres are giant-sized; in effect, they are miniature downtowns. These supercentres may have as many as three department stores, plus many small stores and service operations. They also include hotels, banks, office buildings, churches, and theatres. These centres integrate retail, cultural, and commercial activities, all enclosed under one roof.

In the late 1970s, the building of giant regional centres slowed considerably as the market for shopping centres became saturated in many parts of the country. In the 1980s, energy shortages and concern for more efficient land uses further discouraged the development of outlying shopping centres. At the same time, increased attention is being devoted to in-city shopping facilities. Many cities from Victoria to St. John's already have built traffic-limited downtown shopping malls or promenades as part of their urban redevelopment programs.

The success of suburban shopping centres lies essentially in their conformity with consumer buying patterns. A wide selection of merchandise is available; stores are open evenings; an informal atmosphere encourages shoppers to dress informally and to bring the children; plenty of free parking space is available. By coordinating their promotional efforts, all stores benefit; one builds traffic for another. Many stores in these centres are too small to do effective, economical advertising on their own. But they can make good use of major advertising media by tying in with the overall shopping-centre advertising.

Classification of Retailers

To understand how retailers serve both suppliers and customers, we will classify retailers on two bases:

1. Form of ownership.
2. Marketing strategies.

Although both are retailers, Eaton's and North's differ in important ways.

Each of these categories will be discussed in turn. Any retail store can be classified according to both bases, as illustrated by the following comparison of Eaton's and a neighbourhood paint store.

	Classification bases	
Sample stores	**1. Form of ownership**	**2. Marketing strategies**
Eaton's	Corporate chain	Department store with broad, relatively deep assortments, affordable prices, and levels of personal service that vary across departments
Neighbourhood paint store	Independent	Limited-line store that has narrow, relatively deep assortments, avoids price competition, and provides extensive personal service

RETAILERS CLASSIFIED BY FORM OF OWNERSHIP

The major forms of ownership in retailing are corporate chain, independent, and vertical marketing system (VMS). Within the VMS category are several types of organizations: wholesaler-sponsored voluntary chains, retailer-owned cooperatives, and franchise systems.

Corporate Chains

A **corporate chain**, sometimes called a *chain-store system*, is an organization of two or more centrally owned and managed stores that generally handle the same lines of products. Three factors differentiate a chain from an independent store and contractual vertical marketing system:

- Technically, two or more units constitute a chain. Today, however, many small-scale merchants have opened two or three units in shopping centres and in newly populated areas. These retailers ordinarily do not think of themselves as chains. Having four or more units is a good definitional basis for discussing chain stores.

- Central ownership distinguishes corporate chains from contractual vertical marketing systems.
- Due to centralized management, individual units in a chain typically have little autonomy. Stategic decisions are made at headquarters, and there is considerable standardization of operating policies for all the units in a chain.

Corporate chains continue to increase their share of total retail trade, as shown in Table 16-5. The predominance of chains varies considerably, however, depending on the kind of business. Organizations with four or more stores did almost 40 percent of all retail business in Canada in 1989. The importance of chains varies considerably from one type of business to another. Chains account for 70 percent or more of total sales in the general merchandise and variety stores categories and in family clothing and shoes. Among grocery stores, hardware stores, and pharmacies, however, chains account for 30 percent of sales or less. In the retail food business, there are several giant food chains (Loblaws, Steinberg, A&P, Provigo, Sobeys, Safeway, etc.), yet chains still account for only about 63 percent of all food sales. This is explained in part by the large number of independent food retailers in small towns and neighbourhoods throughout Canada.

TABLE 16-5 **Chains' Share of Total Retail Sales Volume by Kind of Business, 1966 to 1989**

	Percent of Sales				
Kind of Business	**1966**	**1974**	**1979**	**1986**	**1989**
Total retail sales	33.4	41.1	41.5	41.5	39.3
Grocery and combination stores	44.9	57.5	60.4		
Combination stores (groceries and meat)				64.8	63.5
Grocery, confectionery and sundries				29.8	25.5
Other food stores	8.7	8.1	8.5	9.4	11.2
Department stores*	100.00	100.00	100.00	100.00	100.00
General merchandise	74.7	80.4	79.8	75.6	73.3
Variety stores	86.7	83.2	76.3	87.2	85.4
Men's clothing	13.2	18.6	34.3	54.9	58.8
Women's clothing	26.5	40.9	53.3	65.6	67.4
Family clothing	21.9	28.5	49.9	68.3	70.3
Shoe stores	45.0	51.8	66.0	71.7	73.5
Hardware stores	15.5	19.0	n/a	21.2	14.8
Furniture stores	19.2	19.2	19.5	50.9	58.3
Pharmacy stores	13.4	18.5	22.4	29.6	31.0
Jewellery stores	33.7	39.4	45.4	49.3	48.0

*All department stores are considered chains by Statistics Canada.

SOURCE: Statistics Canada, *Market Research Handbook*, cat. no. 63-224, various years. Reproduced with permission of Supply and Services Canada.

COMPETITIVE STRENGTHS AND WEAKNESSES

Chain-store organizations are large-scale retailing institutions. As such, they are subject to the general advantages and limitations of all large retailers that we discussed earlier in this chapter. Let's look at a few of these points, especially as they relate to chain stores.

Lower selling prices   Chain stores have traditionally been credited with selling at lower prices than independents. But the claim of lower prices needs careful scrutiny because it can be misleading. It was probably more justified in the past than it is today. Many independents have pooled their buying power so that, in many instances, they can buy products at the same price as the chains.

It is very difficult to compare the prices of chains with those of independents. The merchandise is often not exactly comparable, because many chains sell items under their own brands. It is difficult to compare the prices of Del Monte peaches with Loblaws', Steinberg's, or Safeway's brand of peaches. Also, it is not accurate to compare the price of the product sold in a cash-and-carry, no-customer-service store with the price of an identically branded product in a full-service store. The value of services should be included in the comparison.

Multistore feature of chains   Chain stores do not have all their eggs in one basket (or in one store). Even large-scale independent department stores or supermarkets cannot match this advantage of the chains. A multiunit operation has automatically *spread its risks* among many units. Losses in one store can be offset by profits in other units. Multistore organizations can *experiment* quite easily. They can try a new store layout or a new type of merchandise in one store without committing the entire firm.

A chain can make more *effective use of advertising* than even a giant single-unit independent store. To illustrate, a grocery chain may have 15 medium-sized stores blanketing a city. An independent competitor may have one huge supermarket doing three to four times the business of any single unit of the chain. Yet the chain can use the metropolitan daily newspaper as an advertising medium with much less waste in circulation than the independent can. Many chains can also make effective use of national advertising media.

On the negative side   Standardization, the hallmark of a chain-store system and a major factor in its success, is a mixed blessing. *Standardization also means inflexibility.* Often a chain cannot adjust rapidly to a local market situation. Chains are well aware of this weakness, however, and have consequently given local store managers somewhat greater freedom to act in various situations.

Independent Stores

An **independent retailer** is a company with a single retail store that is not affiliated with any type of contractual vertical marketing system. Most retailers are independents, and most independents are quite small. Of course, an independent department store or supermarket can have $10 million or more in annual sales, so it may have more economic power than small chains consisting of only a few stores. Still, independents usually have the characteristics of small retailers that were presented in Table 16-4.

Independents typically are viewed as having higher prices than chain stores. However, due to differences in merchandise and services, it is difficult to directly compare the prices of chains and independents. For instance, chains often have their own private brands that are not sold by independents. Also the two types of retailers frequently provide customers with different levels— and perhaps quality—of services. Many customers are willing to pay extra for services that are valuable to them, such as credit, delivery, alterations, installation, a liberal return policy, and friendly, knowledgeable personal service.

Contractual Vertical Marketing Systems

In a contractual vertical marketing system, independently owned firms join together under a contract specifying how they will operate. The three types of contractual VMS are briefly described next.

RETAILER COOPERATIVES AND VOLUNTARY CHAINS

Cooperatives and voluntary chains have the same basic purposes:

- To enable independent retailers to compete effectively with corporate chains.
- To provide members with management assistance in store layout, employee and management training programs, promotion, accounting, and inventory control systems.

The main difference between these two types of systems is who organizes them. A voluntary chain is sponsored by a wholesaler that enters into a contract with interested retailers. In contrast, a retailer cooperative is formed by a group of small retailers that agree to establish and operate a wholesale warehouse.

Historically these two forms of contractual VMS have been organized for defensive reasons — to maintain a competitive position against large, strong chains. Some differences between the two groups are as follows:

Voluntary chain	Retailer cooperative chain
1. Sponsored by wholesalers, with a contract between wholesalers and independent retailer members.	1. Sponsored by retailers. They combine to form and operate a wholesale warehouse corporation.
2. Wholesaler provides a wide variety of management services — buying, advertising, store layout, accounting, and inventory control. Retailers agree to buy all (or almost all) their merchandise from wholesaler. Members agree to use common store name and design and to follow common managerial procedures.	2. Services to retailer members are primarily large-scale buying and warehousing operations. Members maintain their separate identities.
3. Most prevalent in grocery field (IGA). These chains also exist in hardware and building supplies (Castle), auto supplies (Western Auto), and variety stores.	3. Quite significant in grocery field in local areas, but not in other lines.

FRANCHISE SYSTEMS

Franchising involves a continuing relationship in which a franchiser (the parent company) provides the right to use a trademark and management assistance in return for financial considerations from a franchisee (the owner of the individual business unit). The combination of franchiser and franchisees is called a **franchise system**. This type of contractual VMS is growing rapidly.

There are two kinds of franchising:

- *Product and trade name.* Historically the dominant kind, product and trade name franchising is most prevalent in the automobile (Ford, Honda) and petroleum (Esso, Ultramar, Petro-Canada) industries. It is a distribution agreement wherein a franchiser authorizes a franchisee-dealer to sell a

product line, using the parent company's trade name for promotional purposes. The franchisee agrees to buy from the franchiser-supplier and also to abide by specified policies. The focus in product and trade name franchising is on *what is sold*.

- *Business format*. Much of franchising's growth and publicity over the past two decades has been associated with business-format franchising (including names such as Kentucky Fried Chicken, Harvey's, Midas, and H & R Block). This kind of franchising covers an entire format for operating a business. A firm with a successful retail business sells the right to operate the same business in different geographic areas. Quite simply, the franchisee expects to receive from the parent company a proven business format; in return, the franchiser receives from the individual business owner payments and also conformance to policies and standards. The focus here is on *how the business is run*.

  In business-format franchising, the franchiser may be a manufacturer that provides franchisees with merchandise. More often, though, this is not the case. For example, some such franchisers do not sell products to their franchised stores; rather the stores buy their inventory from wholesalers. What the franchiser provides to franchisees in this case is management assistance, especially marketing expertise.

For a successful retail business that wants to expand, franchising provides critical advantages:

- Rapid expansion is facilitated because franchisees provide capital when they purchase franchises.
- Because they have an investment at risk, franchisees typically are highly motivated to work hard and adhere to the parent company's proven format.

For an independent store facing stiff competition from chains and for a prospective new retail store, franchising offers advantages:

- Franchisees can use the parent company's well-known name, which should help attract customers.

**Numerous products reach consumer markets through
business-format franchises**

Product/Service Category	Sample franchises
Fast Food	McDonald's, Tim Horton's, A. L. Van Houtte, Harvey's, Druxy's, Pizza Hut, Second Cup, Grandma Lee's, Pizza Pizza, Treats
Auto Rental	Avis, Hertz, Tilden, Thrifty, Budget
Auto Repair	Midas, Speedy, Apple Auto Glass, Jiffy Lube, Thruway Muffler, Mister Transmission, Ziebart
Personal Care/Services	Magicuts, Body Shop, H & R Block, Faces, Money Concepts, Uniglobe Travel, Nautilus Fitness
Home Decor/Services	Color Your World, St. Clair, The Bathtub Doctor, College Pro Painters, Molly Maid, Weed Man, The Lawn Rangers
Printing/Photography	Kwik-Kopy Printing, Japan Camera, U Frame It, The Frame UP, Direct Film
Clothing	Athlete's Foot, Benetton, Cotton Ginny, Kettle Creek Canvas, Mark's Work Wearhouse, Tabi, Rodier
Computers and Video	Compucentres, Computerland, Jumbo Video, Captain Video, Radio Shack
Health and Personal Care	Nutri/system, Shoppers Drug Mart, Optical Factory, Tridont Health Care, People's Drug Mart
Convenience Stores	7-Eleven, Mac's, Beckers, Red & White

- Various forms of management assistance are provided to franchisees prior to, as well as after, opening the store, including site selection and store-layout guidance, technical and management training, promotional programs, and inventory control systems.

Continued growth in franchising is expected. Entrepreneurs will use it as an offensive tool — for rapid expansion — and many small retailers will use it defensively — to achieve a viable competitive position in battles against corporate chains.

RETAILERS CLASSIFIED BY MARKETING STRATEGIES

Whatever its form of ownership, a retailer must develop target-market and marketing-mix strategies. In retailing, the marketing mix typically emphasizes product assortment, price, location, promotion, and customer services. This last element consists of services designed to aid in the sale of a product. They include credit, delivery, gift wrapping, product installation, merchandise returns, store hours, parking, and — very importantly — personal service. (When this last form of customer service is aimed *directly* at creating a sale, then it is personal selling — a type of promotion.)

In this section we will describe the major types of retail stores, paying particular attention to three elements of their marketing mixes:

- Breadth and depth of product assortment.
- Price level.
- Number and level of customer services.

MARKETING AT WORK

FILE 16-1   **SECOND TO NONE IN NORTH AMERICA**

From zero to 160 outlets in 15 years — that's Second Cup, the largest coffee retail franchise in Canada (originating in Etobicoke, Ontario) and the United States. The secret of success is said to be simple — concentrate on one area, be the best at it, maintain very high standards. This means that instead of diversifying into agricultural products or other noncoffee-related ventures, Second Cup deals only with 55 types, flavours, and blends of fresh brewed coffee, coffee beans, brewed and packaged teas, as well as filters, mugs, coffee makers, and a limited number of specialty items that complement coffee and teas (muffins, danishes, hot chocolate).

Being good and maintaining standards means that Second Cup franchisees are trained, trained, and trained so that they appreciate what good value and customer service is all about. All attend Coffee College, a five-day intensive training program in retailing and coffee know-how, which ensures that they understand how quality, consistency, and service operate to bring people back to the franchise the next day.

Source: Adapted from Michael Rozek, "Second to None," *Canadian*, vol. 6, no. 4, October, 1990.

Table 16-6 classifies retail stores on the basis of these three elements.

Some types of retail stores, such as off-price retailers, are new and growing rapidly. Others, notably variety stores, are diminishing in importance. And still others, particularly department stores, are under competitive pressure to modify some strategies. We will see that certain retailers are similar to others because new or modified institutions have filled the "strategic gaps" that once separated different types of retail institutions.

Department Stores

A mainstay of retailing in Canada is the **department store**, a large-scale retailing institution that has a very broad and deep product assortment, tries not to compete on the basis of price and provides a wide array of customer services. Familiar department store names include Eaton's, Woodward's, Sears, and The Bay.

Traditional department stores offer a greater variety of merchandise and services than any other type of retail stores. They feature both "soft goods" — such as apparel, sheets, towels, and bedding — and "hard goods" — including furniture, appliances, and consumer electronics. Department stores also attract — and satisfy — consumers by offering many customer services. The combination of distinctive, appealing merchandise and numerous customer services is designed to allow the stores to maintain the manufacturers' suggested retail prices. That is, department stores strive to charge "full" or "nondiscounted" prices.

Department stores face mounting problems, however. Largely due to their prime locations and customer services, their operating expenses are considerably higher than those of most other kinds of retail business. Many manufacturers' brands that used to be available exclusively through department stores are now widely distributed and often carry discounted prices in other

TABLE 16-6 **Retail Stores Classified by Key Marketing Strategies**

Type of store	Breadth and depth of assortment	Price level	Amount of customer services
Department store	Very broad, deep	Avoids price competition	Wide array
Discount house	Broad, shallow	Emphasizes low prices	Relatively few
Catalogue showroom	Broad, shallow	Emphasizes low prices	Few
Limited-line store	Narrow, deep	Traditional types avoid price competition; newer kinds emphasize low prices	Vary by type
Specialty store	Very narrow, deep	Avoids price competition	At least standard and extensive in some
Off-price retailer	Narrow, deep	Emphasizes low prices	Few
Category killer store	Narrow, very deep	Emphasizes low prices	Few to moderate
Supermarket	Broad, deep	Some emphasize low prices; others avoid price disadvantages	Few
Convenience store	Narrow, shallow	High prices	Few
Warehouse club	Very broad, very shallow	Emphasizes very low prices	Few (open only to members)
Hypermarket	Very broad, deep	Emphasizes low prices	Some

outlets. And the quality of personal service, especially knowledgeable sales help, has deteriorated in some department stores.

Intense horizontal competition is also hurting department stores. Other types of retailers are aiming at consumers who have long supported department stores. Specialty stores, off-price retailers, and even some discount houses have been particularly aggressive in trying to lure shoppers away from department stores. To varying degrees, retail chains such as K mart, Woolco, and Zellers compete directly against the department stores.

Consequently, many department stores have modified their target markets or elements of their marketing mixes. In 1991, the Hudson's Bay Company, which owned Simpson's and The Bay department stores, as well as the Zellers discount chain, announced that it was closing all Simpson's stores and converting approximately half of them to Bay outlets. The remaining stores would be sold to Sears. The rationale was that the stores that would become Sears outlets were in locations where a directly competing Bay outlet was in operation, and that Sears and The Bay compete in different segments of the market. The Bay would be positioned to compete directly with Eaton's.

Other participants in the department store market have taken positioning decisions so that they occupy a well-defined place in the market. Bretton's, an Ontario-based chain, is more of a "junior department store" operation, with stores that cater to fashions and avoid "hard goods" such as furniture and appliances. Efforts to return the Vancouver-based Woodward's chain to profitability in 1990 included moving the chain slightly away from the upscale image it had acquired in the 1980s and reducing the variety available in departments such as toys and sporting goods.[1]

Discount Houses

Discount retailing uses price as a major selling point by combining comparatively low prices and reduced costs of doing business. Several institutions, including off-price retailers and warehouse clubs, rely on discount retailing as their main marketing strategy.

Not surprisingly, the prime example of discount retailing is the **discount house**, a large-scale retailing institution that has a broad, shallow product assortment, emphasizes low prices, and offers relatively few customer services. A discount house normally carries a broad assortment of soft goods (particularly apparel) and well-known brands of hard goods (including appliances and home furnishings). It also advertises extensively. K mart, Zellers, and Woolco are leading discount-house chains.

The success of discount houses can be attributed to two factors: First, other types of retailers normally had large markups on appliances and other merchandise, thereby providing discount houses with the opportunity to set smaller margins and charge lower prices. Second, consumers were receptive to a low-price, limited-service format. Discount houses have had a major impact on retailing, prompting many retailers to lower their prices.

Some discount chains have, in recent years, been trading up their operations to the point where they are virtually indistinguishable from some department stores. For example, Woolco, which started life as the discount arm of the variety chain F. W. Woolworth, has gradually moved closer to becoming a mainstream department store by offering value-priced, high-quality merchandise, much of which carries well-known brand names. Such upgrading or trading up brings discount houses into direct competition with certain department stores. Such a strategy moves the traditional discount store into a situation where it may enjoy higher profit margins, but it also involves higher expenses as higher-quality facilities and certain customer services are added.

Catalogue Showrooms

By placing a complete catalogue and a number of sample items in a showroom and the remaining inventory in an attached warehouse, a **catalogue showroom** sets itself apart from other types of stores. If offers a broad but shallow assortment of merchandise, low prices, and few customer services. Catalogue showrooms stress selected product lines, such as photographic equipment, consumer electronics, jewellery, small appliances, luggage, and gift items.

Shoppers examine the samples and catalogue available in the showroom. Or they may have already received an abridged catalogue in the mail or

---

[1]Kenneth Kidd, "Woodward's Getting a New 'Culture'," *Globe and Mail Report on Business*, June 24, 1991, p. B3.

inserted in their newspapers. To purchase an item, the consumer fills out an order form and gives it to a clerk at the central counter. An employee takes the form and goes to the warehouse to obtain the desired merchandise.

The unopposed leader in the Canadian catalogue showroom business is Consumers Distributing Limited, which operates outlets across the country. Although Consumers pioneered the market in this country and successfully defended itself against a number of competitors in its early days, in the 1980s the company faced tough competition. Their price advantage disappeared as large discounters and new "category killer" stores (discussed shortly) also stressed low prices. Consequently, as the 1990s began, catalogue showrooms were trying to figure out whether to seek a price advantage or to trade up and encourage shoppers to spend more time in their stores.

Limited-Line Stores

Much of the "action" in retailing in recent years has been in **limited-line stores**. This type of institution has a narrow but deep product assortment and customer services that vary from store to store. Traditionally, limited-line stores strived for full or nondiscounted prices. Currently, however, new types of limited-line retailers have gained a foothold by emphasizing low prices.

Breadth of assortment varies somewhat across limited-line stores. A store may choose to concentrate on:

- Several related product lines (shoes, sportswear, and accessories),
- A single product line (shoes), or
- Part of one product line (athletic footwear).

We identify limited-line stores by the name of the primary product line — furniture store, hardware store, clothing store, for example. Some retailers such as grocery stores and drugstores that used to be limited-line stores now carry much broader assortments because of scrambled merchandising.

SPECIALTY STORES

A very narrow and deep product assortment, often concentrating on a specialized product line (baked goods) or even part of a specialized product line (cinnamon rolls), is offered to consumers by a **specialty store**. Examples of specialty stores are bake shops, furriers, athletic footwear stores, meat markets, and dress shops. (Specialty *stores* should not be confused with specialty *goods*. In a sense, specialty stores are misnamed because they may carry any category of consumer goods, not just specialty goods.)

Most specialty stores strive to maintain manufacturers' suggested prices and provide at least standard customer services. Some specialty stores, however, emphasize extensive customer services, particularly knowledgeable and friendly sales help. The success of specialty stores depends on their ability to attract and then serve well customers whose two primary concerns are deep assortments and extensive, top-quality services.

OFF-PRICE RETAILERS

While many discount houses attempted to trade up during the 1980s, **off-price retailers** positioned themselves below discount houses with lower prices on selected product lines. These new discount retailers are most in evidence in the areas of clothing and consumer electronics; they offer a narrow, deep product assortment, emphasize low prices, and offer few customer services. Store names such as BiWay, Future Shop, and Majestic Electronic Superstore are now well known to consumers in many cities in Canada. A number of chains of off-price retailers now operate in various regions of the country.

Off-price retailers often buy manufacturers' excess output, inventory remaining at the end of a fashion season, or irregular merchandise at lower-than-normal wholesale costs. In turn, their retail prices are much lower than those for regular, in-season merchandise sold in other stores. Customers are attracted by the low prices and fairly current fashions.

Factory outlets are a special type of off-price retailer. They are owned by manufacturers and usually sell a single manufacturer's clearance items, regular merchandise, and perhaps even otherwise unavailable items. Many well-known and popular brands such as L. L. Bean, Esprit, Calvin Klein, Royal Doulton, and Wabasso can be found in factory outlets in the United States, and occasionally in Canada. This is a retailing form that is well established south of the border, but that has not yet made its presence felt in this country. As Canadian consumers become more familiar with shopping at factory outlets in the United States and as cross-border shopping continues to be part of the retailing scene in this country, we can expect the factory outlet to emerge here as well.

CATEGORY KILLER STORES

Another phenomenon of the 1980s, a **category killer store** has a narrow but very deep assortment, emphasizes low prices, and has few to moderate customer services. It is so named because it is designed to destroy all competition in a specific product category. Highly successful category killers include Ikea in assemble-it-yourself furniture, Majestic, and Future Shop in consumer electronics, and Toys "Я" Us. Other product areas where category killers tend to operate include office supplies, sporting goods, housewares, and records, tapes and discs.[2]

---

[2]Kenneth Kidd, "Future Shop Wins at Pricing Game," *Globe and Mail Report on Business*, June 24, 1991, p. B3.

MARKETING AT WORK

FILE 16-2 **ANOTHER CATEGORY KILLER CONCEPT: FOR THE OFFICE**

As is frequently the case, the U.S. market, because of its size and degree of competition, spins off a succession of new retailing concepts—some of which work in Canada, some of which don't. The boom in office equipment super-stores in the United States has now come to Canada. The concept began in the United States in the mid-1980s, and national companies as well as regional ones grew rapidly as the concept took hold in the marketplace. Office Depot out of Florida grew to over 100 stores in a matter of three years. The first entry into Canada came in British Columbia in 1990—Great Canadian Office Supplies Warehouse of Richmond, B.C. H Q Office Supplies now has stores in Edmonton, Victoria, and Calgary. New stores are planned for Winnipeg and Burnaby with a Toronto store planned for 1992. The stores range in size from 20,000 to 25,000 square feet with inventory of over $1 million—they occupy former supermarkets. H Q Office is owned by a California organization that retained Canadian consultants to domesticate the concept, since our geography and business climate are quite different from that of California.

Meanwhile, in Eastern Canada, both Canadian and American firms from the Eastern United States are also moving quickly with the concept. Canadian office equipment chains already offer volume discounts to corporate buyers, and they have opened some warehouse stores of their own. Staples, from United States, is backing a Canadian group with plans to open warehouse stores shortly.

Will the concept translate?

Source: Adapted from John Schreiner, "Office Superstores Try Luck in Canada," *The Financial Post*, July 8, 1991, p. 18.

This relatively new form of retail institution concentrates on a single product line or several closely related lines. The distinguishing feature of a category killer is a combination of many different sizes, models, styles, and colours of the product, *coupled with* low prices. For example, Ikea stocks literally thousands of furniture and home furnishing items. Record retailers such as the major stores of Sam's, A&A, and HMV carry such an assortment that the consumer needs to make only one stop to ensure that he or she can find a particular tape or compact disc.

That is the objective of the category killer in retailing, to dominate a category in such a way that the consumer believes that this is the first store to visit and that the value will be better there. Although the major category killers tend to be found in large metropolitan markets such as Toronto, Montreal, and Vancouver, it is in fact easier for a major retailer to dominate a category in a smaller market, where the competition is not likely to be as fierce and where competitors tend to be smaller, local independents.

Sustained growth is forecast for category killers. However, most kinds of merchandise as well as many geographic areas will not generate the large sales levels that permit low prices through high-volume buying power. Furthermore, existing category killers are not without problems. In particular, they face a major challenge in maintaining inventories that are large enough to satisfy customer demand but not so large as to result in excess inventories requiring significant markdowns.

Supermarkets

As was the case with *discount*, the word *supermarket* can be used to describe a method of retailing *and* a type of institution. As a method, **supermarket retailing** features several related product lines, a high degree of self-service, largely centralized checkouts, and competitive prices. The supermarket approach to retailing is used to sell various kinds of merchandise, including building materials, office products, and—of course—groceries.

The term *supermarket* usually refers to an institution in the grocery retailing field. In this context a **supermarket** is a retailing institution that has a moderately broad, moderately deep product assortment spanning groceries and some nonfood lines and offers relatively few customer services. Most supermarkets emphasize price. Some use price *offensively* by featuring low prices in order to attract customers. Other supermarkets use price more *defensively* by relying on leader pricing to avoid a price disadvantage. Since supermarkets typically have very thin gross margins, they need high levels of inventory turnover to achieve satisfactory returns on invested capital.

Supermarkets originated in the early 1930s. They were established by *independents* to compete with grocery chains. Supermarkets were an immediate success, and the innovation was soon adopted by chain stores. In recent decades supermarkets have added various nonfood lines to provide customers with one-stop shopping convenience and to improve overall gross margins.

Today stores using the supermarket *method* of retailing are dominant in grocery retailing. However, different names are used to distinguish these institutions by size and assortment:

- A *superstore* is a larger version of the supermarket. It offers more grocery and nonfood items than a conventional supermarket does. Many supermarket chains are emphasizing superstores in their new construction.
- *Combination stores* are usually even larger than superstores. They, too, offer more groceries and nonfoods than a supermarket but also most product lines found in a large drugstore.

For many years the supermarket has been under attack from numerous competitors. For example, a grocery shopper can choose among not only many brands of supermarkets (Loblaws, Safeway, A&P, Sobey's and Steinbergs) but also various types of institutions (warehouse stores, gourmet shops, meat and fish markets, and convenience stores). Supermarkets have reacted to competitive pressures primarily in either of two ways: Some cut costs and stressed low prices by offering more private brands and generic products and few customer services. Others expanded their store size and assortments by adding more nonfood lines (especially products found in drugstores), groceries attuned to a particular market area (foods that appeal to a specific ethnic group, for example), and various service departments (including video rentals, restaurants, delicatessens, financial institutions, and pharmacies).

Convenience Stores

To satisfy increasing consumer demand for convenience, particularly in suburban areas, the **convenience store** emerged several decades ago. This retailing institution concentrates on convenience groceries and nonfoods, has higher prices than most other grocery stores, and offers few customer services. Gasoline, fast foods, and selected services (such as car washes and automated teller machines) can also be found in many convenience stores.

The name *convenience store* reflects its main appeal and explains how the somewhat higher prices are justified. Convenience stores are typically located near residential areas and are open extended hours; in fact, some never close. Examples of convenience-store chains are 7-Eleven (originally open from 7 A.M. to 11 P.M. but now open 24 hours in most locations), Mac's, and Beckers.

Convenience stores compete to some extent with both supermarkets and fast-food restaurants. Furthermore, in the 1980s, petroleum companies modified many service stations by phasing out auto repairs and adding a convenience groceries section.

Warehouse Clubs

Another institution that mushroomed during the 1980s is the **warehouse club**, sometimes called a **wholesale club**. A combined retailing and wholesaling institution, it has very broad but very shallow product assortments, extremely low prices, and few customer services, and is open only to members. This format originated in Europe many years ago and was first applied successfully in the United States in the mid-1970s by the Price Club. In this country, Price Club Canada operates stores primarily in eastern Canada, while Costco Wholesale Corp, a Washington-based company, operates in the Western provinces.[3]

Warehouse clubs' target markets are small businesses (some purchasing merchandise for resale) and select groups of employees (government workers and school personnel, for example) as well as members of credit unions. Prices paid by ultimate consumers are usually about 5 percent higher than those paid by business members.

A warehouse club carries about the same breadth of assortment as a large discount house but in much less depth. For each item, the club stocks only one or two brands and a limited number of sizes and models. It is housed in a warehouse-type building with tall metal racks that display merchandise at ground level and store it at higher levels. Customers pay cash (credit cards are not accepted) and handle their own merchandise — even bulky, heavy items.

Further growth of warehouse clubs is expected during the 1990s. As with other retailing institutions, modifications and refinements can be anticipated as competition intensifies. Some warehouse clubs, for instance, are already experimenting with more service departments.

NONSTORE RETAILING

A large majority — perhaps 85 percent — of retail transactions are made in stores. However, a growing volume of sales is taking place away from stores. Retailing activities resulting in transactions that occur away from a retail store are termed **nonstore retailing**.

We will consider four types of nonstore retailing: direct selling, telemarketing, automatic vending, and direct marketing. (These names may be confusing so don't worry about the names. Focus instead on the distinctive features and competitive standings of the four types.) Each type may be used by producers and/or retailers.

Direct Selling

Statistics Canada defines direct selling as the retail marketing of consumer goods to household consumers by other than the regular retail store outlet. This represents a major growth area in Canadian retailing, as consumers increasingly turn to nonstore retailers for the purchase of many products. In

---

[3]Mark Evans, "Warehouse 'Clubs' Revolutionizing Retail," *The Financial Post*, June 3, 1991, p. 3.

Canada, sales by direct selling exceeded almost $3 billion in 1989, a figure that does not include sales by foreign mail-order retailers, direct sales made to Canadians by the mail-order divisions of department stores (such as the Sears catalogue), or direct sales through vending machines or by wholesalers. We can expect the impact of nonstore retailers to increase through the 1990s as consumers demand the convenience of shopping from locations that are convenient *to them* and at times at which *they* are available.

The annual volume of direct selling in Canada has increased from approximately $772 million in 1969 to more than $3 billion in 1989.[4] An increasing number of companies are turning to the direct-selling route to reach consumers in their own homes. There are many well-known direct-selling companies, including Avon, Tupperware, Mary Kay, Amway, Electrolux, and Encyclopedia Britannica. Many diverse products are sold through the direct-selling route, most of which require some form of testing or demonstration (cosmetics, water purifiers, vacuum cleaners). Essentially, the direct-selling approach involves a sales person contacting potential customers outside of a conventional retail store environment. Direct selling—as well as other forms of nonstore retailing—is also used in other countries. In Japan, for example, Nissan used 2,500 white-collar employees to sell cars door to door. With the unification of the European market in 1992, direct selling is expected to become a major channel for satisfying the needs of various market segments across national boundaries.[5]

The two major kinds of direct selling are door to door and party plan. Sometimes door-to-door selling simply involves ''cold canvassing'' without any advance selection of prospects. More often there is an initial contact in a store, by telephone, or by a mailed-in coupon. A relatively new form of direct selling has emerged in recent years, known as network marketing.[6] This approach to non-store retailing involves a series of levels of sales personnel, each of whom reports to an area or territory manager or captain. Sales are generated by sales people contacting prospects directly, usually in their homes. Commissions on sales are paid to each level in the sales hierarchy. Products currently sold by this method include cosmetics (Nu-Skin) and water purification systems (NSA).

With the party-plan approach, a host or hostess invites some friends to a party. These guests understand that a sales person—say, for a cosmetics or a housewares company—will make a sales presentation. The sales rep has a larger prospective market and more favourable selling conditions than if these people were approached individually door to door. And the guests get to shop in a friendly, social atmosphere.

With so many women now working outside the home, direct-selling firms have had to find new ways of making contact with prospective customers. For instance, Avon has moved in recent years to reach their target customers at their place of work by distributing catalogues at offices. Tupperware, possibly the best known of the party-plan retailers, continues to market its extensive range of plastic houseware products primarily through in-home parties,

---

[4]Statistics Canada, *Direct Selling in Canada*, cat. no. 63-218, annual.

[5]Derek Suchard, ''Direct to Play Vital Role in 1992: Study,'' *Playback Strategy*, March 12, 1990, p. 27.

[6]Jamie Hubbard, ''Low-risk chance to score big fast,'' *The Financial Post*, Sept. 2, 1991, p. 6.

involving its 374,000 dealers in more than 40 countries. However, because of the changing nature of the North American market, Tupperware is now also marketed through catalogues and Tupperware parties held at the office.[7]

There are other drawbacks to direct selling. It is the most expensive form of retailing, with sales commissions as high as 40 to 50 percent of the retail price. Also, good sales people are extremely hard to recruit and retain. Some sales people have been too persistent or even fraudulent. As a result, a number of provinces have ''cooling off'' laws that permit consumers to nullify a door-to-door or party-plan sale during a period up to several days after the transaction.

Direct selling does give consumers the opportunity to buy at home or another convenient nonstore location. For the seller, direct selling provides the most aggressive form of retail promotion as well as the chance to demonstrate a product in the shopper's (rather than the seller's) environment.

Telemarketing

Sometimes called *telephone selling*, **telemarketing** refers to a sales person initiating contact with a shopper and also closing a sale over the telephone. As with door-to-door selling, telemarketing may mean cold canvassing from the phone directory. Or it may rely on prospects who have requested information from the company or whose demographics match those of the firm's target market.

The telemarketing business has really developed only within the past ten years, as marketers found it increasingly difficult to reach consumers through conventional means. Also, the development of computerized mailing or calling lists and auto-dialling technology have meant that literally hundreds of calls can be made during a day by a single telemarketer. Many products that can be bought without being seen are sold over the telephone. Examples include home cleaning and pest-control services, magazine subscriptions, credit-card and other financial services, and athletic club memberships.

Telemarketing's reputation has been damaged by the unethical sales practices of some firms. These firms tell consumers that they are conducting marketing research and ''are not selling anything.'' Such unethical procedures hurt other telemarketing companies as well as legitimate research firms that conduct telephone surveys. Such practices are known as ''sugging''—selling under the guise of research. The approaches used by some telemarketing companies, coupled with a desire on the part of many consumers not to be bothered at home, has led to a consumer backlash against telemarketing in some areas.[8]

Despite this problem, telemarketing sales have been increasing for several reasons. Certain consumers appreciate the convenience of making a purchase by phone. Also, the introduction of outgoing WATS lines about 20 years ago made telemarketing to consumers in distant locations more cost effective. Finally, computer systems today can automatically dial a telephone number or, going a step further, play a taped message and then record information that the consumer gives to complete the sale. Such systems reduce the normally high labour costs associated with telemarketing. These advances in

[7]Kathy Hogan Trocheck, ''The Party's Not Over,'' *Globe and Mail Report on Business*, March 21, 1991, p. B8.

[8]Michael W. Miller, ''You're Selling What? Hold on, I'll Let You Speak to My Dog,'' *Globe and Mail Report on Business*, June 29, 1991, p. B18.

technology, despite their obvious contribution to the efficiency of the process, contribute further to the negative feeling that many consumers have towards being sold products and services in such an intrusive manner. The truly effective telemarketing programs are being run by companies that have adopted an approach to telemarketing that involves doing a better job of targeting those customers who are likely to be interested in the products or service being offered (rather than the blanket calling of all households in a region) and conveying the message to the consumer in a polite and caring manner.

Automatic Vending

The sale of products through a machine with no personal contact between buyer and seller is called **automatic vending** (or *automated merchandising*). Most products sold by automatic vending are convenience-oriented or are purchased on impulse. They are usually well-known, presold brands with a high rate of turnover. For many years, the bulk of automatic vending sales has come from four main product categories: coffee, soft drinks, confectionery items, and cigarettes. In Canada, sales made through more than 200,000 vending machines now total approximately $450 million annually and come increasingly from hot and cold drinks and confectionery. Sales of cigarettes through vending machines have followed the same downward trend as is evident in the sales of tobacco products generally.[9]

Vending machines can expand a firm's market by reaching customers where and when it is not feasible for stores to do so. Thus they are found virtually everywhere, particularly in schools, workplaces, and public facilities. Automatic vending has to overcome major challenges, however. Operating costs are high because of the need to continually replenish inventories. The machines also require occasional maintenance and repairs.

The outlook for automatic vending is uncertain. Some observers predict the difficulties just cited will deter further growth. Others are more optimistic owing to vending innovations. Some machines are now equipped to sell "vending debit cards" that can be used to make vending purchases. When one of these cards is inserted into a vending machine, the amount of the

The product selection available keeps expanding.

---

[9]Statistics Canada, *Vending Machine Operators*, Catalogue Number 63-213, Annual.

purchase is deducted from the card's credit balance. Also there is a continuing flow of new products for vending machines, including pizza and other micro-waveable meals, gourmet coffee, and video movies.

Direct Marketing

There is no consensus on the exact nature of direct marketing; in a sense, it comprises all types of nonstore retailing other than the three already discussed. We define **direct marketing** as the use of nonpersonal media to contact consumers who, in turn, purchase products without visiting a retail store. (Be sure to distinguish among the terms direct *marketing*, direct *selling*, and direct *distribution*.)

To contact consumers, direct marketers use one or more of the following media: radio, TV, newspapers, magazines, catalogues, and mailings (direct mail). Consumers typically place orders by telephone or mail. Direct marketing is big business. Everywhere we go today, we are exposed to direct-marketing efforts. We see advertisements on television from direct-marketing retailers of records and exercise aids, and we are encouraged to telephone a 1-800 number with our VISA or MasterCard number. We receive ''bill stuffers'' with our monthly gasoline bills, retail store, and credit-card statements. We order clothing and other items from mail-order catalogues, by either mailing back an order form, or more likely calling a toll-free long-distance telephone number. A large volume of direct-marketing effort is rarely seen by end consumers as it is directed as the business-to-business market, where direct marketers have relied on catalogues and mailing pieces for many years.

Given its broad definition, there are many forms of direct marketing. The major types are as follows:

- *Direct mail.* Companies mail consumers letters, brochures, and even product samples, and ask that orders be placed by mail or telephone.
- *Catalogue retailing.* Companies mail catalogues to consumers and to businesses or make them available at retail stores. Examples of the latter include Tilley Endurables, Canadian Tire, and Consumers Distributing.
- *Television shopping.* There are basically two approaches to retailing through television. One we have mentioned above, in which individual products are advertised and the consumer places an order by telephoning a toll-free number and giving his or her credit card number. The second involves the use of a dedicated television channel such as the Canadian Home Shopping Network, which represents a continuous advertisement for a variety of products such as housewares, jewellery, and other items that can be sold without the need for demonstration or trial.

Some companies operate mail-order divisions as components of their department store operations—Sears being the best example. Others have launched catalogues as an additional vehicle for the distribution of their products. Others, such as The Added Touch, distribute only through their catalogues. Direct marketers can be classified as either general-merchandise firms, which offer a wide variety of product lines, or specialty firms, which carry merchandise in only one or two product categories.

Direct marketing represents a major growth area in retailing. Its advantages relate particularly to its ability to direct the marketing effort to those consumers who are most likely to respond positively. Also, it offers products and services in a way that is most convenient for the consumer. Companies that are using catalogues and direct mail to reach their target customers maximize the effectiveness of their marketing programs by having the most accurate and complete mailing list possible. In fact, the success of most direct-marketing programs lies to a very great extent in the preparation and maintenance of an accurate mailing list.[10]

Technology has kept pace with (or even led) developments in the direct-marketing field as companies are now developing sophisticated computer data bases of customers and prospective customers. These data bases contain not only mailing addresses, but other data on the characteristics of the consumer and his or her household, and a history of purchases that the consumer has made. Companies such as American Express make very effective use of such data bases to direct mailings to cardholders in their monthly statements. The types of advertisements that are sent to certain customers are determined to an extent by an analysis of their purchasing history using the American Express card.[11]

Like other types of nonstore retailing, direct marketing provides consumers with shopping convenience. Direct marketers often benefit from relatively low operating expenses because they do not have the overhead of retail stores. There are drawbacks to direct marketing, however. Consumers must place orders without seeing or trying on the actual merchandise (although they may see a picture of it). To offset this limitation, direct marketers must offer liberal return policies. Furthermore, catalogues and, to some extent, direct-mail pieces are costly and must be prepared long before they are issued. Price changes and new products can be announced only through supplementary catalogues or brochures.

In addition, some consumers have reacted negatively to receiving unsolicited mailing pieces at their homes, in much the same way that they are not exactly delighted to receive telemarketing solicitations. This negative reaction to direct-mail advertising in particular is exacerbated by the opinion shared by many that direct mail is ''junk mail'' in that much of it is wasted and represents a waste of paper at a time when more and more people are interested in conserving forest products. Some equate the receiving of ''junk mail'' to killing a tree and request that their names are taken off mailing lists to reduce the amount of unsolicited printed materials sent through the mail. The Canadian Direct Marketing Association has encouraged its 450 members to comply with these requests.[12]

RETAILING MANAGEMENT

Fundamental to managing a retailing firm is the planning of sound strategies. Central to strategic planning are the selection of target markets and development of a marketing mix. Also, during the turbulent 1990s, a factor called retail positioning will probably be critical. Let's briefly discuss these topics.

Target Markets and Marketing Mix

As department stores are now discovering, retailers can no longer be ''all things to all people.'' Therefore, many retail firms of various sizes are looking for unsatisfied niches that can be served profitably. However, some types of

[10]George Whitbread, ''The Promise of Direct Marketing . . . Has Its Time Finally Come?'' *Canadian Direct Marketing News*, a series of three articles: January 1990 (p. 10), February 1990 (p. 11), and April 1990 (p. 16).

[11]Daniel Stoffman, ''Class for the Mass,'' *Report on Business Magazine*, February 1990, pp. 42–48.

[12]Marina Strauss, ''Marketers Battling Junk Mail,'' *Globe and Mail Report on Business*, February 14, 1991, p. B1.

retailers — notably department stores and hypermarkets — still have fairly broad, rather than highly focused, target markets.

We have paid much attention to product assortments, price strategies, and promotional methods in preceding sections. Physical facilities, the fourth element of a retailer's marketing mix, also deserve some mention.

PHYSICAL FACILITIES

Firms that operate retail stores, rather than relying solely on nonstore retailing, must consider three aspects of physical facilities:

- *Location*. It is frequently stated that there are three keys to success in retailing: location, location, and location! Although overstated, this axiom does suggest the importance that retailers attach to location. Thus the store's physical site should be the first decision made about facilities. Considerations such as surrounding population, traffic, and cost determine where a store should be located.
- *Design*. This factor refers to exterior and interior appearance.
- *Layout*. The amount of space allocated to various product lines, specific locations of products, and a floor plan of display tables and racks comprise the store's layout.

As might be expected, retail locations tend to follow the population. Consequently, the bulk of retail sales occur in urban areas. And suburban shopping areas have become more and more popular while many downtown areas have declined.

Planned shopping centres have become the predominant type of retail location in many suburban areas. A **shopping centre** consists of a planned grouping of retail stores that lease space in a multiunit structure typically owned by a single organization. Shopping centres can be classified by size and market served:

- *Convenience centre*. Usually consists of 5 to 10 outlets such as a dry cleaner, branch bank, convenience grocery store, and video rental store.

Vancouver's Granville Island offers both unique assortments and sights.

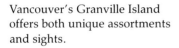

MARKETING AT WORK

FILE 16-3   **CANADIAN TIRE TESTS WAREHOUSE AUSTERITY DESIGN AND AMBIENCE**

Canadian Tire believes that price competition will continue to grow and it wants to both cut costs to be more competitive and be seen and felt to be more competitive. This is where a new store design called All Out Retail comes into the picture. Management believes that its current stores, all 422 of them, are too finished, too polished as hardware stores, too much like traditional retailers who have higher margins and prices. It wants to know if the stores give the wrong impression—and if looking more like a U.S.-style warehouse club store would be good for sales.

The first test store is in St. Hubert, Quebec; it has 38,000 square feet (most Canadian Tire stores are 21,000) and will feature concrete floors rather than tile. Traditional shelving with storage shelving on top to reduce stocking costs give warehouse appearance. Store selling space will be expanded to 70 percent of space compared with the previous store arrangement, which provided only 40 percent (the remainder being used for storage of stock).

After extensive consumer testing of the store concept, as well as testing of an expanded home-decorating department called The Works, Canadian Tire is prepared to have 200 stores using the warehouse format and The Works concept within five years.

Source: Adapted from Kenneth Kidd, "Canadian Tire Opts for Austerity," *Globe and Mail*, July 17, 1991, p. B1-2.

- *Neighbourhood centre*. Has 10 to 25 tenants including a large supermarket and perhaps a drugstore.
- *Community centre*. Includes 25 to 50 stores and features a discount house or junior department store. It may also include a supermarket. Given its composition of stores, a community centre draws shoppers from a larger area than does a neighbourhood centre.
- *Regional centre*. Anchored by one or more department stores and supermarkets and complemented by as many as 200 smaller retail outlets; typically an enclosed climate-controlled mall.

Many regional shopping centres are very large. They have become the hub of shopping and social activities in many communities; in fact they are "the meeting place" for many seniors and high school students. During the 1980s, construction of new regional centres slowed considerably as the market became saturated. It is expected that relatively few shopping malls will be built in the 1990s, but many existing ones will be renovated and modernized.

The growth of suburban shopping, especially in regional malls, led to decreased retail sales in many urban downtown areas. In recent years, therefore, some cities have worked to revitalize their downtown shopping districts. Often historical buildings or neighbourhoods are converted to shopping areas (for example, St. Lawrence Market in Toronto and the Cours de Mont Royal in Montreal). Enclosed shopping malls featuring distinctive designs have also been build in a number of cities. Possibly the best known of these shopping centres is the West Edmonton Mall, which has become something of a tourist attraction in Western Canada.

Positioning

Retailers are increasingly thinking about positioning as they develop marketing plans. **Positioning** is a retailer's strategies and actions designed to favourably distinguish itself from competitors in the minds (and hearts) of targeted groups of consumers. Positioning centres on the three variables we have stressed in this chapter: product assortment, price, and customer services.

Let's briefly examine several positioning strategies.[13] When only price and service levels are considered, two strategies that have potential value are *high price–high service* and *low price–low service*. The former is difficult to implement because it requires skilled, motivated employees (especially sales people); the latter necessitates careful management of operating expenses because gross margins are small.

When all three variables—product assortment, price, and customer services —are considered, two new options emerge. One is *product differentiation*, in which a retailer offers different brands or styles than those sold in competing stores. A second is *service and personality augmentation*, where a retailer offers similar products but sets itself apart by providing special services and also creating a distinctive personality or atmosphere for its stores.

A retailer's positioning strategy may include one or a combination of these options. Retail executives need to exhibit creativity and skill in selecting positioning strategies and then in implementing them.

Customer Retention

In recent years, marketers in many businesses, and especially in retailing, have begun to subscribe in increasing numbers to the philosophy that it makes considerably greater sense to retain the customers we have rather than having to compete vigorously to attract new ones. This viewpoint acknowledges what should have been obvious to all marketers, namely that a company's most valuable assets are loyal customers. While not denying the importance of going out to attract new customers, this approach to doing business places at least equal emphasis on keeping existing customers happy.

Two elements of a customer-retention strategy involve getting to know customers in as much detail as possible and rewarding those who are loyal and continue to give us their business. The former implies that development and maintenance of a customer data base and the latter often involves the establishment of a bonus program for frequent shoppers. Some of the most effective customer-retention programs combine these elements.

The best example of a customer-retention program in Canadian retailing is Club Z, operated by Zellers, the successful discount arm of the Hudson's Bay Company. Established in 1986 as a frequent-buyer program, modelled along the lines of the airlines' frequent-flyer programs, Club Z awards ''points'' to Zellers' shoppers based upon the amount of their purchases. These points may be redeemed for premiums from a Club Z gift catalogue. The program has been wildly successful in differentiating Zellers from the competition and

---

[13]Positioning based on price and service is discussed in George H. Lucas, Jr., and Larry G. Gresham, ''How to Position for Retail Success,'' *Business*, April-June 1988, pp. 3–13. Positioning that combines all three variables is presented in Lawrence H. Wortzel, ''Retailing Strategies for Today's Mature Marketplace,'' *The Journal of Business Strategy*, Spring 1987, pp. 45–56.

in creating a very loyal customer base, as now close to half of all Canadian households are Club Z members.[14]

Other retailers have had or have recently established similar programs to encourage shopper loyalty. Canadian Tire has issued its well-known "Canadian Tire money" for many years, essentially giving customers discounts of up to 5 percent on purchases made in the store. Sears Canada relaunched its Sears Club, a frequent-shopper program that rewards users of the Sears credit card with savings of up to 4 percent on purchases. These reward programs are really modern-day, electronic versions of trading stamps, which were distributed by many retailers primarily in the 1940s and 1950s.

TRENDS IN RETAILING

In the 1990s, retailers face challenges perhaps unequalled since the Depression of the 1930s. Dozens of noteworthy trends present threats or, alternatively, provide opportunities for retailers. We will illustrate how dynamic retailing is by focusing on eight diverse, but highly significant trends.[15]

- *Changing demographics and industry structure.* The Canadian population is growing older, with proportional decreases in the 16-to-34 age group and increases in the 45-and-over age group. Real growth in retail sales is expected to be substantially less than in the 1970s and 1980s. Thus there may be too many shopping centres and retail stores in the 1990s.
- *Expanding computer technology.* Advancing technology dramatically affects both consumer behaviour and retail management. In particular, sophisticated computer systems that capture sales and inventory data influence the items retailers stock as well as what and when they reorder. Newer systems permit retailers to automatically place orders and reorders with suppliers that are linked to them via computer.
- *Emphasis on convenience and service.* Consumers are increasingly busy, generally older, and have more money to spend. Such consumers desire products and methods of purchase that provide maximum convenience and service. Convenience is exemplified by nearby locations, extended hours, short waiting times, and other factors that make shopping easier. Service includes some convenience factors and also friendly, knowledgeable sales help, easy credit, liberal return policies, and postsale service.
- *Scrambled merchandising.* Although not new, scrambled merchandising remains a major trend. In the constant search for higher-margin items, one type of store adds products that traditionally were handled by other retail stores. This move intensifies retail competition and forces adjustments in distribution channels.
- *Increasing polarity in retail trade.* At one end are large stores with a tremendously wide variety of products; at the other extreme are small limited-line stores. As retailers carefully identify and segment their markets, specialized stores are increasing in importance.

---

[14]For more on the use of frequent-shopper programs and other techniques designed to encourage customer retention, see: Kenneth R. Wightman, "The Marriage of Retail Marketing and Information Systems Technology: The Zellers Club Z Experience," *MIS Quarterly*, December 1990, pp. 359–366; and Mark Evans, "Retailers in Battle for Frequent Buyer," *The Financial Post*, May 13, 1991, p. 8.

[15]Some of these trends as well as others are described in Richard V. Sarkissian, "Retail Trends in the 1990s," *Journal of Accounting*, December 1989, pp. 44–46ff.

M A R K E T I N G   A T   W O R K

FILE 16-4   **CANADIAN RETAILERS RESPOND TO THE CROSS-BORDER SHOPPING TREND**

It is just not possible that there is anyone left in the country who does not know more than they want to about cross-border shopping. It has always been a fact of life, but these days seems to have moved from a trickle to a torrent.

At first, taxes and exchange rates were the culprits that caused Canadian prices to be comparatively high and thus the federal government was to blame. Then the lack of Sunday shopping was seen as a contributor and this caused provincial governments to be blamed. But some research has shown that retail strategies on loss-leader selling and positioning, limited assortments, and abysmal service can also take some of the blame. And this means retailers must respond. Some argue that had they responded a long time ago instead of waiting for the government rescue brigades, the torrent would be much less.

Now, Bata Shoes proclaims in its advertising that a war is underway and the battleground is price. It will match any U.S. or Canadian price on comparable goods. And Bay Bloor Radio, a Toronto-based company, says in a full-page ad: "Celestian British speakers for less than American prices." Ramsay Bike, a family-owned business in Ontario, is promoting the fact that its prices have been lower all along by advertising "Cross the Border into Canada." The Montreal clothing chain, Cohoes, advertises that its prices have been lower than those in adjoining U.S. cities. Both companies will advertise direct price comparisons as well. Some retailers point out to consumers that shopping in the United States means waiting in line for three hours, others point to patriotism — "Dollars that leave home are gone forever."

It would seem that more marketing, more positioning, more good promotion, more sensible assortment management, and more service will result in a greater degree of incomparable Canadian value, eh? And then there's the government . . .

Source: Abstracted, in part, from Ann Gibbon, "Retailers Trumpet Low Canadian Prices," *Globe and Mail*, June 25, 1991, p. B4.

- *Experimentation.* Largely because of competitive pressures, many retailers are experimenting with new or modified formats and also with nontraditional locations. For example, department stores are scaling back product assortments by eliminating "commodity" lines (such as fabrics and matresses) and stressing fashion and quality. Discount houses are either trading up to become so-called promotional department stores or are digging in for price battles. Some retailers are expanding their markets through new types of locations, or by moving towards more nonstore retailing.
- *Emphasis on productivity.* Extremely small profits are forcing retailers to squeeze more revenues out of their resources (floor space, people, and inventories). Hence, virtually all products are being sold, at least to some extent, on a self-service basis. To boost motivation, some retailers have put sales people completely on commissions rather than salaries plus commissions. Computer systems, as discussed above, can also help achieve greater productivity.

- *Continuing growth of nonstore retailing.* Retail stores will continue to be dominant. But more and more retailers are complementing their stores with one or more types of nonstore retailing. Many consumers prefer the novelty or convenience of nonstore retailing.

As consumers change, so do forms of retailing. Retail executives would like to anticipate changes in retailing before they occur. To some extent this is possible, as many of the evolutionary changes in retailing have followed a cyclical pattern called the **wheel of retailing**.[16] This theory states that a new type of retailer often enters the market as a low-cost, low-price store. Other retailers as well as financial firms do not take the new type seriously. However, consumers respond favourably to the low prices and shop at the new institution. Over time this store takes business away from other retailers that initially ignored it and retained their old strategies.

Eventually, according to the wheel of retailing, the successful new institution trades up in order to attract a broader market, achieve higher margins, and/ or gain more status. Trading up entails improving the quality of products sold and adding customer services. Sooner or later, high costs and, ultimately, high prices (at least as perceived by its target markets) make the institution vulnerable to new retail types as the wheel revolves. The next innovator enters as a low-cost, low-price form of retailing, and the evolutionary process continues.

There are many examples of the wheel of retailing. To mention a few, chain stores grew at the expense of independents during the 1920s, particularly in the grocery field. In the 1950s, discount houses placed tremendous pressure on department stores, which had become staid, stagnant institutions. The 1980s saw the expansion of warehouse clubs and off-price retailers, which have forced many institutions — supermarkets, specialty stores, and department stores — to modify their marketing strategies.

What will be the retailing innovations of the 1990s? Perhaps electronic retailing, some other form of nonstore retailing, or a new type of low-cost, low-price store. The wheel of retailing can help retailers identify changes in retail institutions. Retail firms must identify and respond to significant trends that affect retailing, including institutional changes, by developing customer want-satisfying marketing strategies.

SUMMARY   Retailing is the sale of goods and services to ultimate consumers for personal, nonbusiness use. Any institution (such as a manufacturer) may engage in retailing, but a firm engaged primarily in retailing is called a retailer.

Retailers serve as purchasing agents for consumers and as sales specialists for wholesaling middlemen and producers. They perform many specific activities such as anticipating customers' wants, developing product assortments, and financing.

Almost 250,000 retail stores in Canada collectively generate almost $200 billion in annual sales. Retailers' operating expenses run about 27 percent of the retail selling price; profits are usually a very small percentage of sales.

Most retail firms are very small. However, small retailers can survive — and

---

[16]The wheel of retailing was first described in M. P. McNair, ''Significant Trends and Developments in the Postwar Period,'' in A. B. Smith (ed.), *Competitive Distribution in a Free, High-Level Economy and Its Implications for the University*, Pittsburgh: The University of Pittsburgh Press, 1958, pp. 17–18.

even prosper—if they remain flexible and pay careful attention to personally serving customers' needs.

Retailers can be classified in two ways: (1) by form of ownership, including corporate chain, independent store, and various kinds of contractual vertical marketing systems such as franchising; and (2) by key marketing strategies. Retailer types are distinguished according to product assortment, price levels, and customer service levels: department store, discount house, catalogue showroom, limited-line store (including specialty store, off-price retailer, and category killer store), supermarket, convenience store, warehouse club, and hypermarket. Mature institutions such as department stores, discount houses, and supermarkets face strong challenges from new competitors, particularly different kinds of limited-line stores.

Although the large majority of retail sales are made in stores, an increasing percentage now occur away from stores. And this proportion is growing steadily. Four major forms of nonstore retailing are direct selling, telemarketing, automatic vending, and direct marketing. Each type has advantages as well as drawbacks.

Retailers need to carefully select markets and plan marketing mixes. Besides product, price, promotion, and customer services, executives also must make strategic decisions regarding physical facilities. Specific decisions concern location, design, and layout of the store. Downtown shopping areas have suffered while suburban shopping centres have grown in number and importance. Retailers also should consider positioning — how to favourably distinguish their stores from competitors' stores in the minds of consumers.

Various trends present opportunities or pose threats for retailers. Institutional changes in retailing can frequently be explained by a theory called the wheel of retailing. To succeed, retailers need to identify significant trends and ensure that they develop marketing strategies to satisfy consumers.

KEY TERMS AND CONCEPTS

QUESTIONS AND PROBLEMS

1. Explain the terms *retailing, retail sale,* and *retailer* in light of the following situations:
   a. Avon cosmetics sales person selling door to door.
   b. Farmer selling produce door to door.
   c. Farmer selling produce at a roadside stand.
   d. Sporting goods store selling uniforms to a semiprofessional baseball team.

2. How do you explain the wide differences in operating expenses among the various types of retailers shown in Table 16-2?

3. What recommendations do you have for reducing retailing costs?

4. Reconcile the following statements, using facts and statistics where appropriate:
   a. ''Retailing is typically small-scale business.''
   b. ''There is a high degree of concentration in retailing today; the giants control the field.''

5. Of the criteria given in this chapter for evaluating the competitive positions of large-scale and small-scale retailers, which ones show small stores to be in a stronger position than large-scale retailers? Do your findings conflict with the fact that most retail firms are quite small?

6. The ease of entry into retailing undoubtedly contributes to the high failure rate among retailers, which — in the view of some — creates economic waste. Should entry into retailing be restricted? If so, how could this be done?

7. What course of action might small retailers take to improve their competitive position?

8. In what ways does a corporate chain (Loblaws, Zellers, or Sears) differ from a voluntary chain such as IGA?

9. What can department stores do to strengthen their competitive positions?

10. ''The supermarket, with its operating expense ratio of 20 percent, is the most efficient institution in retailing today.'' Do you agree with this statement? In what ways might supermarkets futher reduce their expenses?

11. ''Door-to-door selling is the most efficient form of retailing because it eliminates wholesalers and retail stores.'' Discuss.

12. What is the relationship between the growth and successful development of regional shopping centres in suburban areas and the material you studied in Chapters 4 and 5 regarding consumers?

13. Which of the retailing trends discussed in the last section of the chapter do you think represents the greatest opportunity for retailers? The greatest threat?

14. Do you agree with the axiom that there are three keys to success in retailing — location, location, and location? How do you reconcile this axiom with the fact that there is so much price competition in retailing at the present time?

15. Of the types of retail stores discussed in the chapter, which one(s) do you think have been or would be most successful in foreign countries? Which one(s) have been or would be unsuccessful in other countries? Explain your answers.

C A S E S   F O R   P A R T   5

CASE 5.1   ## The Upper Canada Brewing Company (D): Developing a Distribution Strategy

Frank Heaps, president of the Upper Canada Brewing Company, carefully reviewed the decisions for the distribution element of the marketing plan. He sensed that these decisions were of vital importance to the success of the new brewery; if the products were not available where the customers wished to purchase them, it was likely that the sale would be lost. As well, he realized the importance of coordinating the distribution strategies with the other three elements of the marketing mix. The decisions he faced concerned the intensity of distribution, the geographic scope of the initial as well as future distribution, and the type of licensee establishments to serve. The critical decision on the channel structure was solved; in Ontario there existed a very efficient distribution network exclusively for brewery products called Brewers' Warehousing Company Limited ("Brewers' Warehousing").

BREWERS' WAREHOUSING

The sale of beer in Ontario is conducted in almost all cases by Brewers' Warehousing. This company, which is owned by five brewing companies (Labatts, Molson, Carling O'Keefe, Heineken, and Northern Breweries), has the exclusive franchise to distribute domestically produced beer in Ontario. The producers bring their products to the Brewers' Warehousing depot, from there the products are distributed to the Brewers' Retail outlets, the Liquor Control Board of Ontario (L.C.B.O.) stores, and licensee establishments. The empty bottles and kegs are also returned to the Brewers' Warehousing depot where they are sorted and picked up by the appropriate owner. The charge for this service varied with the distribution agreement. The type of agreement negotiated by the Upper Canada Brewing Company involved the payment of a service charge of $21 per hectolitre (75 percent Brewers' Retail and 25 percent licensee) with a 5 percent increase per year.

THE DECISIONS

The first major distribution decision facing Mr. Heaps was to determine the geographic scope of the market he wished to serve at present and in the future. The alternatives he considered were: (i) Toronto; (ii) Toronto Census Metropolitan Area; and (iii) Southern Ontario. He wondered which of these alternatives was most realistic to help him reach his market share objective of 0.1 percent of the Ontario market (see Exhibit A-2, page 73, for details on the Toronto and Toronto CMA marketplace). He also considered exporting to the United States and Germany as soon as he achieved viability in the Ontario marketplace. Given the fact that there were no taxes on beer in the U.S., the beer could sell at approximately half the domestic selling price, despite the small duty imposed on Canadian beer. He felt that this price differential would help launch the beer on the U.S. market. He also wanted to export the beer to Germany with the hope of being the first Canadian beer to meet the rigid German standards. This achievement would further enhance the quality image of the brewery's product(s).

A related decision concerned the intensity of distribution. Should he have the products available in all locations where beer products were sold or should he use more selective distribution? The obvious advantage of using a more selective approach would be to provide a more exclusive image for the product(s) and to concentrate on areas where he felt the target market was located, in areas with the highest socioeconomic profiles, and neighbourhoods with significant ethnic components.

This case was prepared by Donna M. Stapleton and is intended to stimulate discussion of an actual management problem and not to illustrate either effective or ineffective handling of that problem. The author wishes to acknowledge the support provided by the Upper Canada Brewing Company, and particularly by Frank Heaps, President.

As well, he wondered if he should distribute to all Brewers' Retail outlets. Given the fact that Brewers' Retail stores did not stock imported beer, buyers of imported brands had to go to L.C.B.O. outlets. He wondered if he should concentrate on the Brewers' Retail outlets located adjacent or very close to L.C.B.O. stores. The rationale to support this move was that patrons of Brewers' Retail would be able to buy a quality premium beer (already chilled) in the ''Beer Store'' without having to make a special trip to the L.C.B.O.; conversely, those who were in the habit of going to an L.C.B.O. store for imported products would be able to buy the import-quality Upper Canada Brewery product(s) at the adjacent store. As well, he wondered if he should distribute to the L.C.B.O. stores themselves, given that the Brewers' Retail stores were nearby. If he did decide to distribute at these

L.C.B.O. outlets, only one product line from each brewing company could be carried on their shelves.

A final distribution decision centred on the licensee trade — restaurants and taverns. Mr. Heaps projected that the licensee trade would contribute at least 15 percent of gross sales. He wondered which type of establishment he should serve and indeed what intensity of distribution would be ideal for these outlets.

QUESTIONS

1. What geographic market should Mr. Heaps serve initially and in the future? Why?

2. What intensity of distribution would you recommend?

3. What types of licensee establishments should Mr. Heaps use? Why?

CASE 5.2   **Charlie's Laundry Factory**

Charlie Thorne is the owner/manager of Charlie's Laundry Factory, a laundromat located on the corner of Pleasantville Avenue and Boundary Road, approximately four kilometres west of the campus of the University of the Atlantic. Charlie had been in business for more than three years and had established a regular clientele among residents of the immediate residential area, which was generally a middle- to lower-income neighbourhood. There was very little competition in the immediate area and none of the laundromats in the city did any advertising. It appeared that most seemed content to draw their business from their immediate areas. It was July and business was a little slow. Charlie was considering the introduction of a laundry pick-up and delivery service aimed directly at the student market.

Charlie's Laundry Factory operated with 10 automatic heavy-duty washers and 12 dryers. All were coin-operated. Charlie kept the business open seven days a week, opening from 9:00 A.M. to 11:00 P.M. on weekdays and from 10:00 A.M. to 6:00 P.M. on Saturdays and Sun-

days. The laundromat was located in the west-central area of the city in a primarily residential area. The location was not near the central business district of the city of 150,000, although two strip shopping centres, each containing a large supermarket, were located nearby.

Charlie Thorne had recently experienced an increase in his operating costs, as the owner of the converted house in which the Laundry Factory was located had just increased his rent. This, coupled with the need to replace two of his washing machines, led Charlie to consider how he might increase his business. He observed that there were certain times each day when several of the washers and dryers were not in use. It was clear that the volume of business picked up in the evenings when people were home from work.

The University of the Atlantic is one of Eastern Canada's largest universities, with approximately 15,000 students, half of whom are from outside the immediate area. Of those students, only 2,000 or so live on campus. The city also contains McCaskill Community College, with

3,000 students, located approximately two kilometres east of the university campus. McCaskill provides no residences on its campus for those of its students who come to the college from other parts of the province.

Charlie has always been aware of the potential of the student business in the city. He realized that students generally worked long hours and didn't always have access to laundry facilities where they lived. He currently offered a service to students whereby they could drop off their laundry and pick it up later; it would be washed, dried, folded and sorted, with no extra charges for the additional services of folding and sorting. This program had been quite successful in drawing more students to the Laundry Factory, although Charlie was of the opinion that he was still attracting only students who lived in the area.

In order to continue to increase his business and to establish his laundromat more firmly in the student market, Charlie had recently developed an idea for a laundry pick-up and delivery service. He felt this was a logical extension of his business, to reach students who didn't currently have easy access to his laundromat. He also felt that such a service would firmly establish Charlie's Laundry Factory as the most ''student-friendly'' laundry service in the city.

Charlie was at the stage where he felt the concept was a good one and that there was a ready market in the city. He had discussed the idea with several university students who were regular customers of his laundromat, and they seemed to feel that the concept would be well received. He had decided that he could implement the service with very little additional expense. He already had his panel van, which could be used for pick-up and delivery, and he planned to hire one full-time employee who could handle pick-ups and deliveries and the washing, drying, and sorting of student laundry.

Despite his optimism that his idea was sound, Charlie did not want to rush into the establishment of the service without making sure that he was doing things right. Consequently, he felt that he needed to have a better feel for the size of the potential market for this service, what students would be willing to pay for such a service, and how exactly the service should be offered and promoted.

QUESTIONS

1. What information do you feel Charlie Thorne needs to make a decision on whether to establish his new pick-up and delivery laundry service for students? How should he obtain this information (keeping in mind that he probably doesn't have a lot of money to spend)?

2. Develop a profile of the student market for such a service. What student groups should Charlie consider his principal target segments for this service? How should he design and promote the service so as to have maximum appeal?

CASE 5.3 **Toronto Dominion Bank**

It was 7:30 on a very warm morning in early July 1991. Although the thermometer on the clock at the service station across the street read 26 degrees, Marilyn Krauss had not minded walking the three blocks from the hotel to the branch. There were already a number of people on the streets of Melfort. She couldn't help thinking how much earlier people started the day here, as compared with Saskatoon. She was eager to get to the branch as she had scheduled a meeting at 8 o'clock with her senior staff to learn more about the Melfort area and to begin the process

Copyright 1991. This case has been prepared by James G. Barnes of Memorial University of Newfoundland. It has been written to illustrate and stimulate discussion of a hypothetical marketing situation, and not to indicate either effective or ineffective handling of that situation. The author wishes to thank Al Cotton, David Thomson, and David Ross of the Toronto Dominion Bank for providing advice and data on the rural market for financial services; Gérard Cussom of Statistics Canada in Ottawa, and Dr. John Leyes, Director of the Small Area and Administrative Data Division of Statistics Canada. The preparation of this case was made possible through a grant from Statistics Canada.

of preparing a marketing plan for the branch. It was her third week in her new job, and she had not had an opportunity to meet with her staff as she had spent the first two weeks familiarizing herself with the town and the branch.

Marilyn had been transferred from main office in Saskatoon to the position of manager of the Toronto Dominion Bank's branch in Melfort. She was looking forward to the new assignment, as she was happy to be in rural Saskatchewan. Marilyn had grown up near Regina, but moved to Saskatoon to attend the University of Saskatchewan. After graduation, she had joined the TD Bank as a management trainee. That was nine years ago, and she had moved steadily up the management ladder in two branches in Saskatoon, serving first as a loans officer and later as an account manager. Two years ago, she had moved to main office as a senior account manager. She expected the Melfort assignment to be a challenging one, as she knew that rural bank customers were likely to be different in many ways from those with whom she had been dealing in Saskatoon for the past nine years.

Marilyn was taking over the manager's job in Melfort from Fred Simpson, who had retired at the end of June. Fred had worked for the TD for more than 40 years, the last 15 as manager in Melfort. Marilyn wished that she had been able to spend more time with Fred before he and his wife had left for Regina, but the Simpsons had wanted to move as soon as possible after Fred retired, to be closer to their children and grandchildren, all of whom lived in Regina. In May, when Marilyn had visited Melfort to meet the staff of the branch, she and Fred had spent one afternoon meeting in Fred's office. Marilyn remembered that at the time she wondered whether she would ever be able to know the community as well as Fred did.

MELFORT, SASKATCHEWAN

Melfort is a small Saskatchewan city located in the northeast part of the province, in the heart of the Carrot River Valley. Although there has not been much population growth in the city itself in the past ten years, Melfort is an economically stable community, located as it is in one of the richest and most productive farming areas of Canada. The city is an agriculture service centre, and most of the businesses in Melfort are related to the agriculture industry. The farmers in the area grow primarily grains, including wheat, oats, barley, rye, flax, and rapeseed. There are four grain elevators in Melfort.

The Melfort Union Hospital was replaced with a completely new facility in 1985–86 at a cost of $8 million. The 85-bed hospital is staffed by 14 physicians. In addition, three long-stay nursing homes accommodate 226 residents. Although only 38 permits for residential construction were issued in Melfort in 1990, construction in the city was booming as more than $8 million had been spent on the first phase of the new North East Leisure Centre, including a gymnasium, meeting rooms, crafts areas, exercise rooms, and catering facilities. The second phase, containing a 25-metre swimming pool, whirlpool, saunas, waterslide, snack bar, and spectator area, was scheduled for completion in late 1991.

Although she had not yet found a place to live, Marilyn had noted in the *Melfort Journal* that there were a small number of homes available for sale. As she had driven around the town over the Canada Day weekend, she had made a number of enquiries. At the local Realty World real estate office, she had been advised that homes in Melfort generally sold in the range of $50,000 to $75,000 and that there was a small number currently on the market. Alternatively, she could rent a two-bedroom home quite near the business district for $400 per month. She had to make a decision on housing soon as she did not want to stay at the hotel more than another few days.

Marilyn was already aware that the TD Bank's competition in Melfort came from branches of the Bank of Nova Scotia and Royal Bank of Canada, and from the Melfort Credit Union. There were four small investment company offices in town, including The Co-operators, and four real estate companies. In addition to the downtown business and retail district, there were three small shopping plazas in Melfort and a 30-store enclosed shopping mall.

Several weeks ago, when she had been informed that the manager's position in Melfort was to be offered to her, she had asked the bank's regional office to send her information about the city. Data on Melfort's population (Exhibit 1) and the mix of businesses in the city (Exhibit 2) were of particular interest to her. She had also called the office of Statistics Canada in Regina to send her information about the population of the Melfort area.

EXHIBIT 1 **Population, City of Melfort, 1980–1990**

Population				Age Groups			
	Total	Male	Female	0–19	20–44	45–64	65 and over
1980	6136	2960	3176	2006	1977	1146	1007
1985	6542	3154	3388	1922	2361	1108	1151
1988	6296	3022	3274	1812	2175	1084	1225
1990	6211	2954	3257	1785	2079	1095	1252

SOURCE: Saskatchewan Department of Rural Development, *Community Profile, Melfort*, 1990

EXHIBIT 2 **Profile of Businesses, City of Melfort 1990**

Type of Business	No. of Firms	Employment	Employment of Largest
Agriculture			
Nurseries	1	3	3
Feedlots	1	4	4
Dairy Farms	3	7	3
Hatcheries	1	6	6
Others	13	67	20
Construction			
General Building Contractors	3	20	6
Plumbing and Heating	5	20	6
Painting and Decorating	5	15	—
Electrical	3	15	5
Masonry	1	2	2
Plastering and Drywall	2	5	3
Carpenters	1	2	2
Others	9	46	15
Manufacturing			
Food Products	5	61	21
Printing, Publishing	1	27	27
Chemical Products	4	5	5
Metal Products	2	3	3
Others	2	17	12
Retail Trade			
Bulk Oil	3	12	4
Lumber Yards	2	18	8
Hardware Stores	2	11	7
Farm Equipment	7	84	25
General Merchandise	6	56	26
Grocery Stores	9	40	—
Meat and Fish Markets	2	18	14
Confectioneries	4	15	3
Bakeries	3	11	6
Motor Vehicle Dealers	5	70	26
Auto Supply Stores	4	20	7
Service Stations	5	30	15

Type of Business	No. of Firms	Employment	Employment of Largest
Men's and Boys' Clothing	4	6	3
Women's Clothing	4	10	3
Children's Clothing	1	2	—
Family Clothing	3	20	6
Furniture Stores	1	8	—
Eating Places	23	168	50
Drug Stores	3	25	7
Sporting Goods	1	4	4
Jewellery Stores	2	5	—
Gift Shops	1	4	4
Book and Stationery	4	12	3
Others	8	17	4
Transportation			
Local and Suburban Transit	1	6	6
Taxicabs	1	3	3
Motor Freight Transport			
Local Trucking Firms	7	12	5
Non Local Trucking	2	13	7
Aircraft Servicing	1	1	1
Personal Services			
Coin Laundries	1	3	3
Dry Cleaners	2	8	4
Photo Studios	3	6	3
Beauty Shops	6	16	5
Barber Shops	3	4	2
Funeral Parlours	1	6	6
Other Personal Services	1	4	4
Business Services			
Cleaning and Maintenance	3	7	4
Real Estate	3	27	8
Insurance Agencies	5	27	8
Accounting Firms	6	17	8
Other Business Services	4	20	10
Auto Services			
Auto Body Repair Shops	3	18	6
Auto Repair	8	25	6
Car Washes	2	4	4
Other Auto Services	5	16	4
Repair Shops			
Radio and Television	3	3	2
Furniture and Repair	2	1	1
Other Repair Shops	1	1	1
Entertainment and Recreation			
Movie Theatres	1	6	6
Pool Halls	2	2	1
Bowling Alleys	1	3	3
Public Golf Courses	2	25	25
Others	10	130	45

SOURCE: Saskatchewan Department of Rural Development, *Community Profile, Melfort*, 1990

THE STAFF MEETING

Precisely at 8 o'clock, Marilyn was joined in her office by Wendy Parmiter and Tony Wroblewski, the most senior members of the staff of 12. Wendy is the assistant manager of the Melfort branch and Tony had come to the branch as accountant just six months ago. Marilyn explained that she would like to spend the next two hours or so discussing the Melfort area and reviewing some of the data she had been able to compile on the area. She knew that they would soon have to begin preparing plans for 1992 and she wanted to make sure that they were ready and as well informed as possible.

Since Wendy had worked in the branch for more than ten years, Marilyn asked her to begin the discussion by providing an overview of the bank's customers and the way business is done in the area. Wendy explained that Melfort, with a population within the city itself of only approximately 6,000, was really quite a small market where business often was done on a more informal basis than would be the case in a larger city. As Wendy explained, "Everyone here knows each other, and it's hard to keep a secret in this town." As a result, she explained, many people are quite concerned about the confidentiality of their banking arrangements. They want to make sure that they can trust their banker to keep their financial affairs totally confidential.

Tony added that most of the TD customers are in the branch at least once a week, generally combining a visit to the bank with a shopping trip. Marilyn observed that this was quite different from her experience in Saskatoon, where the increased use of automated banking machines has meant that many customers rarely come into the branch. Tony also added that many of the customers also want to see the manager when they visit, even for relatively minor matters. He suggested that Marilyn should expect to be quite busy meeting customers, as maintaining the relationship with customers is an important element in keeping their business.

Marilyn asked Wendy and Tony to give her an overview of the competition in Melfort and the position that the TD is perceived to occupy. They explained that the three banks in town were quite competitive, each with its own solid core of loyal customers. Wendy observed that there

had been some indication in recent years that some of the small investment companies in Melfort had been building business in the financial planning area, in some cases taking away business by providing services that she felt could have been provided by the banks. Tony felt that this may reflect something that he had noted since coming to Melfort, namely that some of the business customers in the city seemed to want to keep their business and personal banking separate.

Marilyn wanted to know whether Wendy and Tony felt that there were any particular opportunities she could address in the short term that might bring additional business to the branch. Both felt that the market for financial services in the area was quite stable and slow to change, although there had been a rumour recently that one of the other banks was planning to move its commercial lending department out of its Melfort branch to centralize it in a regional office in Prince Albert, 97 km away. Tony felt that this might open up some commercial credit business.

THE PLANNING PROCESS

As 10 o'clock approached, Wendy could not help feeling that she had a challenge ahead of her. She was new to Melfort and the first woman to be manager of a bank in the city. In addition to wondering whether she would be accepted in her new role, she was concerned about how she would be able to build business for the bank in a market that seemed to be quite stable.

To demonstrate her commitment to planning and to the development of the Melfort branch, she had decided to send a report by the end of August to the TD Bank's divisional marketing manager in Regina, outlining her views on the prospects and opportunities facing the Melfort branch. To begin the process of preparing this report, she took out of her briefcase the information she had obtained from the office of Statistics Canada in Regina.

The data presented in Tables 3 to 10 represent information obtained from Statistics Canada's FSA and Postal Code Data Bank System on the Forward Sortation Area (FSA) around Melfort, the province of Saskatchewan, and all of Canada. Marilyn had asked for these data so that she could compare the postal area around Melfort (the S0E 1A0 postal area) with the province and the rest of the country. She was particularly interested in being able to identify any obvious areas where the Melfort area was different from Saskatchewan as a whole on various data obtained from tax returns.

The data from Statistics Canada were for the 1989 taxation year; that is, tax returns filed before April 30, 1990. The information indicated that there were 5,600 people who had filed tax returns from the Melfort area (Exhibit 3), and that the median income for all Melfort tax filers was $14,500, compared with $15,600 for Saskatchewan and $18,100 for all of Canada (Exhibit 4). She also noted that only 4 percent of Melfort taxfilers reported income of more than $50,000 in 1989, compared with 5 percent in Saskatchewan and 8 percent in the country as a whole (Exhibit 10a). She was also interested in the fact that, of the 5,600 taxfilers in Melfort, 2,950 had declared income from interest on investments (Exhibit 10b), 475 had declared income from dividends (Exhibit 10c), and 1,200 had made a contribution to a Registered Retirement Savings Plan (Exhibit 10d).

Marilyn concluded that there was a great deal of information contained in the data that she had obtained from Statistics Canada. She was looking forward to having an opportunity to interpret the tables in greater detail and to incorporate the results of her analysis into her report to the divisional marketing manager.

QUESTIONS

1. Identify as many factors as you can that would contribute to Marilyn Krauss's analysis of the differences between the marketing of financial services in rural as compared with urban markets.

2. Prepare a detailed analysis of the characteristics of the Melfort area as compared with the rest of Saskatchewan and Canada as a whole that would assist Marilyn Krauss in developing a profile of her market area.

3. Suggest a number of marketing strategies she should employ in developing business for the Toronto Dominion Bank in the Melfort area.

EXHIBIT 3   **Number of Taxfilers by Total Income by Sex, 1989**

(Thousands of Dollars)	Melfort Males	Melfort Females	Melfort Total	Saskatchewan Males	Saskatchewan Females	Saskatchewan Total	Canada Males	Canada Females	Canada Total
$ Under 5.0	275	625	900	32,775	72,800	105,575	841,250	1,947,025	2,788,275
5.0 – 9.9	475	625	1,100	43,675	62,075	105,750	979,250	1,610,325	2,589,575
10.0 – 14.9	450	450	900	41,500	49,650	91,150	955,850	1,323,175	2,279,025
15.0 – 19.9	350	325	700	35,150	36,625	71,775	931,625	1,083,800	2,015,400
20.0 – 24.9	325	300	625	31,925	29,950	61,900	889,575	900,750	1,790,325
25.0 – 34.9	450	250	700	55,725	31,900	87,600	1,638,125	1,082,150	2,720,275
35.0 – 49.9	375	125	500	48,975	16,400	65,375	1,658,000	582,675	2,240,675
50.0 – 74.9	125	—	150	21,700	3,450	25,150	857,050	181,825	1,038,875
75.0 – 99.9	25	—	25	4,150	525	4,675	167,800	31,000	198,800
100.0 +	—	—	—	3,075	350	3,425	161,325	25,950	187,275
Total	2,875	2,725	5,600	318,650	303,725	622,375	9,079,850	8,768,650	17,848,500
Median, 1984	16,700	10,000	13,100	18,800	9,200	13,600	20,400	9,800	14,500
Median, 1989	18,500	11,400	14,500	21,000	11,600	15,600	24,700	13,000	18,100
% Change, 1984–89	11	14	11	12	26	15	21	33	25

Table includes only the taxfilers who reported some income.

SOURCE: Statistics Canada

EXHIBIT 4 **Number of Taxfilers in the Labour Force, 1984 and 1989**

	Melfort			Saskatchewan			Canada		
	1984	1989	% Change 1984–89	1984	1989	% Change 1984–89	1984	1989	% Change 1984–89
MALES									
With Employment Income	2,375	2,425	2	279,225	270,650	−3	7,027,800	7,650,425	9
With Unemployment Insurance Income	425	425	0	48,675	46,800	−4	1,699,225	1,451,025	−15
Total	2,375	2,450	3	282,025	273,425	−3	7,144,825	7,731,500	8
Median Employment Income	14,000	15,300	9	16,300	18,100	11	19,500	24,600	26
FEMALES									
With Employment Income	1,675	1,875	12	195,625	211,125	8	5,216,025	6,255,450	20
With Unemployment Insurance Income	250	300	20	33,550	36,175	8	1,298,900	1,365,175	5
Total	1,675	1,925	15	199,250	214,900	8	5,352,075	6,375,600	19
Median Employment Income	9,800	11,300	15	9,500	11,400	20	10,500	13,700	30
BOTH									
With Employment Income	4,025	4,300	7	474,875	481,775	1	12,243,825	13,905,875	14
With Unemployment Insurance Income	675	725	7	82,200	83,000	1	2,998,125	2,816,225	−6
Total	4,075	4,350	7	481,250	488,300	1	12,496,900	14,107,100	13
Median Employment Income	12,000	12,800	7	12,700	14,400	13	14,700	18,700	27

''Total'' includes those with employment income and/or U.I. income. Because a number of taxfilers report both sources of income, the ''Total'' may be less than the sum of the counts for the two sources.

All counts are rounded to the nearest multiple of 25.

SOURCE: Statistics Canada

EXHIBIT 5 **Number of Taxfilers Reporting Each Source of Income, 1989**

Source of Income	Melfort			Saskatchewan			Canada		
	Males	Females	Total	Males	Females	Total	Males	Females	Total
Wages/Salaries/Commissions	1,750	1,700	3,450	210,575	193,425	404,000	6,990,350	5,969,400	12,959,750
Self-Employment	1,200	375	1,575	103,250	33,575	136,825	1,264,325	559,000	1,823,325
Dividends	325	125	475	27,200	16,575	43,750	867,975	633,325	1,501,300
Interest	1,775	1,575	3,350	179,450	162,450	341,925	4,473,100	4,326,325	8,799,425
Family Allowances	800	400	1,225	91,375	51,200	142,575	2,440,775	1,291,075	3,731,850
Unemployment Insurance	425	300	725	46,800	36,175	83,000	1,451,025	1,365,175	2,816,225
Pensions	750	725	1,475	70,475	68,100	138,575	1,670,650	1,751,700	3,422,375
Other Income	600	450	1,050	70,925	53,875	124,825	1,980,575	1,601,775	3,582,350
Child Tax Credit	25	925	975	2,975	101,625	104,600	69,250	2,193,800	2,263,025
Federal Sales Tax Credit	800	900	1,725	89,200	97,775	186,950	2,170,425	2,662,500	4,832,950

All counts are rounded to the nearest multiple of 25.
Taxfilers can report more than one source of income.

EXHIBIT 6   **Income Reported by Source of Income, 1989**

(Millions of Dollars)	Melfort			Saskatchewan			Canada		
	Males	Females	Total	Males	Females	Total	Males	Females	Total
Wages/Salaries/Commissions	35.7	23.4	59.1	5,046.1	2,821.5	7,867.6	203,002.8	99,590.2	302,592.7
Self-Employment	10.6	1.5	12.0	997.6	162.3	1,159.9	17,086.1	3,726.3	20,812.4
Dividends	1.1	0.2	1.3	89.0	44.1	133.1	4,403.8	2,287.8	6,691.6
Interest	6.2	4.8	11.0	647.7	526.4	1,174.1	13,328.4	14,373.5	27,701.9
Family Allowances	0.6	0.3	0.9	70.9	36.7	107.6	1,725.0	795.9	2,520.9
Unemployment Insurance	1.7	0.8	2.5	192.4	102.5	295.0	6,293.1	4,359.3	10,652.4
Pensions	7.0	4.5	11.5	784.1	482.4	1,266.5	20,893.4	12,751.2	33,644.5
Other Income	1.7	1.0	2.8	210.6	152.7	363.3	5,655.2	4,845.1	10,500.2
Child Tax Credit	0.0	1.0	1.0	2.7	113.2	115.8	52.1	2,041.3	2,093.4
Federal Sales Tax Credit	0.1	0.1	0.2	11.2	13.9	25.1	250.5	329.3	579.8

Totals are independently rounded and do not necessarily equal the sum of individual rounded figures in the distribution.

SOURCE: Statistics Canada

EXHIBIT 7 **Number of Taxfilers by Marital Status, 1989**

Marital Status	Melfort			Saskatchewan			Canada		
	Males	Females	Total	Males	Females	Total	Males	Females	Total
Single	700	450	1,150	91,600	67,350	158,950	2,899,275	2,405,650	5,304,950
Married	1,950	1,675	3,625	202,100	177,025	379,125	5,315,275	4,545,475	9,860,750
Separated/Divorced	150	175	325	17,950	23,825	41,775	680,100	919,875	1,599,975
Widow/Widower	75	425	500	7,525	36,200	43,750	206,875	929,325	1,136,200
Total Taxfilers, 1989	2,875	2,725	5,600	319,200	304,400	623,600	9,101,525	8,800,325	17,901,850
% Change 1984–89	7	21	14	3	11	7	14	19	16

All counts are rounded to the nearest multiple of 25.
Marital status is reported as of December 31, 1989.

SOURCE: Statistics Canada

EXHIBIT 8 **Demographic and Income Data for Postal Code Areas, 1989**

	Melfort	Saskatchewan	Canada
All taxfilers			
Number	5,600	623,600	17,901,850
% Change, 1984–89	14	7	16
% Female	49	49	49
% Married	65	61	55
% By age			
< 25	13	15	15
25–44	40	45	47
45–64	26	24	25
> 64	20	16	13
% Apartment	—	—	—
Taxfilers reporting income			
Number	5,600	622,375	17,848,500
% With income			
> $ 15,000	48	51	57
> $ 25,000	25	30	36
> $ 35,000	13	16	20
> $ 50,000	4	5	8
> $ 75,000	1	1	2
> $100,000	—	1	1

	Melfort	Saskatchewan	Canada
Median total income			
Male	18,500	21,000	24,700
Female	11,400	11,600	13,000
Both Sexes	14,500	15,600	18,100
Canadian Index	80	86	100
Provincial Index	93	100	—
% Change, 1984–89	11	15	25
Taxfilers reporting employment income and/or U.I.			
Number	4,350	488,300	14,107,100
% Female	44	44	45
% U.I.	17	17	20
Median employment income			
Male	15,300	18,100	24,600
Female	11,300	11,400	13,700
Both Sexes	12,800	14,400	18,700
Taxfilers reporting Family Allowance income			
Number	1,225	142,575	3,731,850
Dollars ($'000)	922	107,575	2,520,860

SOURCE: Statistics Canada

EXHIBIT 9 **Age Distribution of Taxfilers, 1989**

Age group	Melfort Males	%	Females	%	Total	%	Saskatchewan Males	%	Females	%	Total	%	Canada Males	%	Females	%	Total	%
Under 20	125	4	125	5	225	4	14,450	5	13,150	4	27,600	4	479,375	5	417,875	5	897,225	5
20–24	250	9	225	8	475	8	31,825	10	32,350	11	64,175	10	931,375	10	936,800	11	1,868,175	10
25–29	275	9	300	11	550	10	38,075	12	39,800	13	77,875	12	1,137,125	12	1,157,000	13	2,294,125	13
30–34	300	10	300	11	600	11	38,950	12	39,250	13	78,225	13	1,122,250	12	1,136,000	13	2,258,250	13
35–39	300	10	325	12	625	11	34,225	11	33,750	11	67,975	11	1,010,975	11	1,015,325	12	2,026,300	11
40–44	275	9	225	8	500	9	28,325	9	27,450	9	55,775	9	914,100	10	888,425	10	1,802,525	10
45–49	250	9	225	8	475	8	21,875	7	20,525	7	42,400	7	714,550	8	655,725	7	1,370,275	8
50–54	150	5	150	5	325	6	19,575	6	17,450	6	37,025	6	591,875	7	509,000	6	1,100,875	6
55–59	175	6	175	6	350	6	19,875	6	16,250	5	36,125	6	566,550	6	450,450	5	1,017,025	6
60–64	200	7	150	5	350	6	19,450	6	14,950	5	34,375	6	516,025	6	407,525	5	923,575	5
65+	600	21	550	20	1,150	20	52,525	16	49,525	16	102,050	16	1,117,300	12	1,226,225	14	2,343,525	13
Total	2,875	100	2,725	100	5,600	100	319,200	100	304,400	100	623,600	100	9,101,525	100	8,800,325	100	17,901,850	100

All counts are rounded to the nearest multiple of 25.
Age is calculated as of December 31, 1989.

SOURCE: Statistics Canada

EXHIBIT 10 **Interest and Investment Income**

(a) Demographic and Income Report

Postal Areas	Number Taxfilers	% Age <25	% 25–44	% 45–59	% >60	Median Tot Inc	% >35K	% >50K
Melfort	5600	13	41	20	26	14,600	13	4
Saskatchewan	619,125	15	45	19	21	15,700	16	5
Canada	17,716,325	15	47	20	18	18,200	21	8

(b) Report on Savers

Postal Areas	Number Taxfilers	Number of Interest Filers	Amount Interest (000$)	Median Interest ($)	Median Age of Interest Filers
Melfort	5600	2950	8667	900	50
Saskatchewan	619,125	301,025	906,280	800	48
Canada	17,716,325	7,436,500	18,448,377	700	45

(c) Report on Investors

Postal Areas	Number Taxfilers	Number of Dividend Filers	Amount Invested (000$)	Median Invested ($)	Median Age of Dividend Filers
Melfort	5600	475	3478	3300	50
Saskatchewan	619,125	43,700	396,280	3500	51
Canada	17,716,325	1,490,000	15,587,673	3000	49

(d) RRSP Report

Postal Areas	Number Taxfilers	Number RRSP Filers	Amount RRSP (000$)	Median Age RRSP Filers
Melfort	5600	1200	3415	42
Saskatchewan	619,125	145,050	435,405	42
Canada	17,716,325	4,136,650	13,337,526	42

SOURCE: Statistics Canada

CASE 5.4   **Tapis Royale: Setting a Brand Apart Through Retail Merchandising**

Mr. Phillipe Gagnon is president of Tapis Royale Inc., a Canadian manufacturer of carpeting with head offices in a city in eastern Quebec. Mr. Gagnon was giving serious thought to a retail merchandising support program that members of his senior management group had developed. He was not sure how retailers would react to the proposed program; nor was he sure what competing retailers and manufacturers would do if Tapis Royale retailers made effective use of it. He was also giving considerable thought to whether the proposed program would give his firm an edge in the highly competitive retail carpet market.

Tapis Royale is one of the largest manufacturers of carpeting in Quebec and would be considered mid-sized among Canadian-owned manufacturers. The company produces a complete line of household and commercial carpeting, in a range of fabrics and colours. It also manufactures carpet tiles, primarily for the commercial and industrial markets. The company operates four mills in Quebec, one in Ontario and one in rural New Hampshire, from which carpeting is distributed to retailers in the eastern United States. The Tapis Royale product line is manufactured from a variety of fabrics, including wool and various synthetics such as nylon and Antron and is available at independent carpet retailers and department stores throughout Canada.

The Canadian carpeting industry is characterized by considerable fragmentation, with a large number of companies operating, ranging in size from large multinational companies to somewhat smaller regional firms such as Tapis Royale. Mr. Gagnon was concerned that most consumers who wanted to purchase carpeting for their homes were generally unaware of the brand names available in carpeting stores and department stores. He felt that the lack of awareness might even be greater in the case of Tapis Royale, which would probably not be as well known as some of the large carpet manufacturers, including Burlington, Kraus, and Coronet. He was sure that there was little if any brand loyalty and that consumers generally sought out the retailer first and then decided on the carpet.

Phillipe Gagnon and his management team were concerned that too much reliance in the marketing of carpet was left to the retailer. He knew how important the retailer is in attracting the customer and in directing him or her towards (or away from) a particular fabric or type of carpet. He was also very concerned about the high variability across the country in the manner in which carpet retailers displayed, promoted, and merchandised the carpet that they carried in their stores.

Most carpet retailers point to the high cost of producing effective merchandising programs for particular brands of carpet that they carry in their stores. Other reasons for a less than satisfactory level of support at the retail level included a lack of merchandising expertise on the part of some retailers and time constraints in what is undoubtedly a very competitive business at the retail level. But Mr. Gagnon was confident that the relatively poor quality of promotional activity on the part of independent retailers was hurting the sales of his company. In late 1987, he decided to do something about it. He wanted to bring more customers into Canadian carpet retail stores and he wanted to make sure that they bought Tapis Royale carpeting.

Working with the Tapis Royale management group, Mr. Gagnon wanted to develop a new concept in carpet retail merchandising, one that would allow Tapis Royale carpet to stand out in the confusion that exists in most carpet outlets and carpet departments of department stores. Tapis Royale would create a new retail environment that would be much more conducive to the creation of a somewhat unique image for the Tapis Royale brand. It was obvious that the retailers were going to have to be compensated if they were to cooperate in an improved merchandising program for the Tapis Royale line.

This case was prepared by James G. Barnes and is intended to present a marketing problem, rather than to illustrate either effective or ineffective handling of that problem.

The concept developed by Phillipe Gagon and his team was named the "Tapis Royale Suite." The objective of the program was to set up a display environment in larger carpet stores across Canada in which only Tapis Royale carpet was to be displayed. In the vast array of carpet that now is featured in most retail carpet stores, with racks and displays of carpet samples, Tapis Royale wanted to create an island devoted exclusively to the Tapis Royale line.

It was decided that the first phase of the "Tapis Royale Suite" program would be the establishment of "suites" in more than 100 retail stores across Canada, working first with stores in major markets in Quebec and Ontario where Tapis Royale sales were better developed, and which were within easy contact by the company's sales staff. The program would then be moved east and west as market acceptance was established over a three-year period. Each "Tapis Royale Suite" was to feature only Tapis Royale carpet and was to look like a small room, with a variety of types of carpeting on floors, stairs, and walls. Each "suite" would be approximately three metres square. The finished look of the room would be enhanced with the use of appropriate furniture, lighting, and pictures on walls. The result would be an "oasis" effect, where Mr. Gagnon was confident Tapis Royale carpet would be more attractively displayed.

The second phase of the retailer merchandising program for Tapis Royale carpet was to involve the distribution of printed flyers that would be made available to retailers by Tapis Royale and that would feature only Tapis Royale carpet, attractively presented and priced. Tapis Royale would prepare four-page, four-colour flyers that qualifying retailers could purchase for $75 per 1,000 flyers. These flyers could be used by the retailers to distribute in their stores or to mail to prospective customers to promote special Tapis Royale sales events. This stage of the merchandising program was to be introduced only after 50 "Tapis Royale Suites" had been established. Mr. Gagnon was convinced that this promotional program, coupled with the "suites," would attract customers to the retail outlets and to the Tapis Royale brand.

The Tapis Royale management group felt it would be a distinct advantage for their company if they could convince Canadian carpet retailers to display and promote their carpet. In order to encourage retailers to participate in the program, Tapis Royale would assume the entire cost of the "Tapis Royale Suite" program — each "suite" was to cost an estimated $1,000. Each retailer who agreed to install a suite would sign an agreement that the store would display only Tapis Royale carpet within the suite and that the area would be properly decorated in a manner consistent with the image of the store and the Tapis Royale line.

Phillipe Gagnon was confident that Tapis Royale was about to make a major breakthrough in the retail merchandising of carpet in Canada. As preparations were being made to install the first Tapis Royale Suites in Montreal and Quebec City, he was looking forward to expanded sales over the next three years.

QUESTIONS

1. Do you agree with Mr. Gagnon's assessment of the process that consumers follow in the purchase of carpet for their homes? How does the proposed Tapis Royale program address the problems inherent in Mr. Gagnon's overview of how consumers buy carpet?

2. Evaluate the "Tapis Royale Suite" concept. How willing would you expect retailers to be to participate in the program? How would you expect consumers to react?

3. To what extent can Tapis Royale exercise control over the "Suite" program once the suites are installed in stores across the country?

4. Can Tapis Royale extend the suite concept into other lines that the company manufacturers? Will it or some variation work for industrial and commercial carpeting? Can other manufacturers of carpet do the same thing? Would you now expect manufacturers of furniture, appliances, and other major items for the home to implement similar programs?

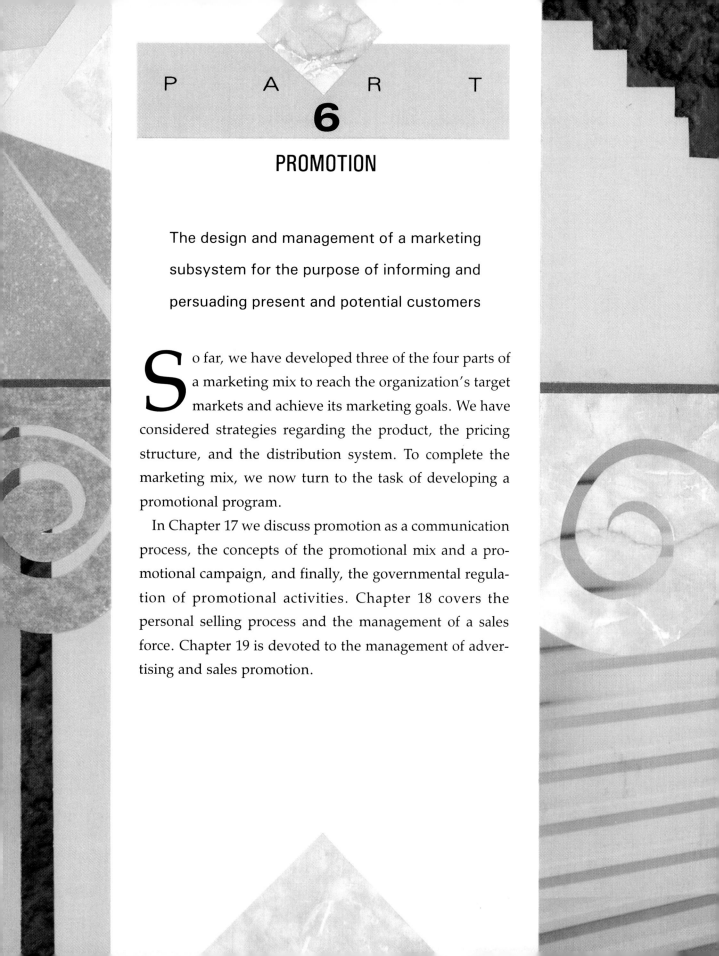

P A R T

6

PROMOTION

The design and management of a marketing subsystem for the purpose of informing and persuading present and potential customers

So far, we have developed three of the four parts of a marketing mix to reach the organization's target markets and achieve its marketing goals. We have considered strategies regarding the product, the pricing structure, and the distribution system. To complete the marketing mix, we now turn to the task of developing a promotional program.

In Chapter 17 we discuss promotion as a communication process, the concepts of the promotional mix and a promotional campaign, and finally, the governmental regulation of promotional activities. Chapter 18 covers the personal selling process and the management of a sales force. Chapter 19 is devoted to the management of advertising and sales promotion.

CHAPTER 17 GOALS

This chapter discusses what promotion is and how it fits into a firm's total marketing program. After studying this chapter, you should be able to explain:

- The components of promotion and how they differ.
- The importance of promotion to an organization and to the economy.
- What makes promotion a special case of communications.
- The concept of the promotional mix.
- Factors that shape a company's promotional mix.
- Methods and problems in determining the promotional budget.
- The concept of the promotional campaign.
- Governmental regulation of promotion.

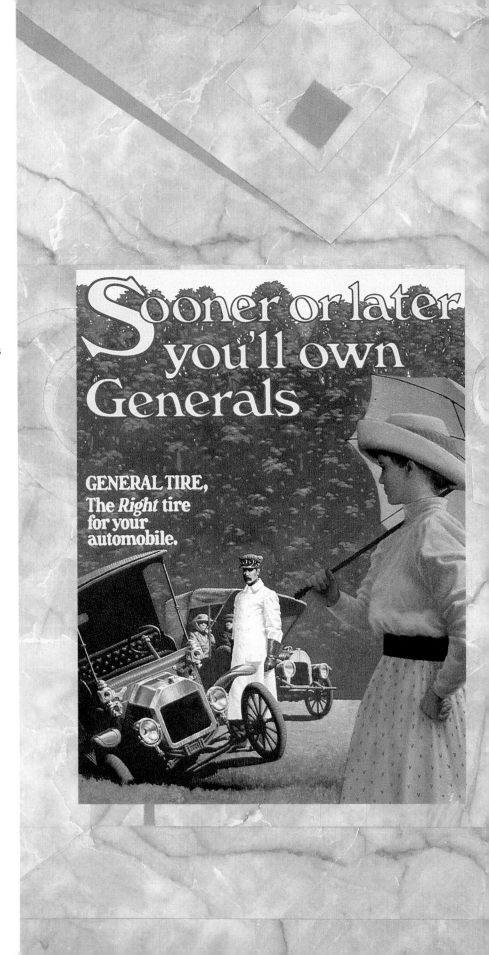

The Promotional Program

There is more to promotion than advertising. When most of us think of the promotional side of a marketing program, we are likely to think of advertising in the mass media — radio and television commercials, print advertising in magazines and newspapers, outdoor billboards — but these represent the side of promotion that is most visible to the end consumer. There is a great deal of promotional activity involved in marketing that many of us never see.

One example of such a promotional activity is a campaign directed to its dealers by General Tire Canada to celebrate the company's seventy-fifth anniversary. Founded in 1915, General Tire has enjoyed a reputation for quality and dependability with North American motorists, supported by its widely recognized advertising slogan, ''Sooner or later, you'll own Generals.''

In 1990, to commemorate the seventy-fifth anniversary, General Tire launched a dealer promotion that involved spring and fall components. In both cases, the principal target market for the campaign were General Tire dealers, with consumers representing a secondary target. The main objective of the promotional program was to motivate dealers to sell more General tires. Research that General had carried out showed that consumers perceive tire dealers to be the ultimate authority on tires and the main source of recommendations on which tire to buy. General was also aware that tire dealers regularly add and drop brands of tires from the range they carry and that they tend to be quite responsive to dealer promotions.

The promotional program developed by General Tire gave both dealers and consumers an incentive to buy General tires and gave the General brand greater visibility at dealerships. The spring campaign ran from March 15 to June 30 and reflected a nostalgic theme. Consumers who purchased General tires during that period were presented with a card in the shape of a 1915 General Tire store. Opening the perforated ''door'' of the store revealed which prize the customer had won. The list of prizes included brass money clips, poster reproductions, yo-yos, antique radios, and children's ''car fun books.'' The dealer was provided with point-of-sale materials to support the campaign, including window banners, posters, counter cards, and buttons.

The fall component of the dealer campaign ran from August 1 to November

30 and gave customers at General Tire dealerships a chance to win an antique-style, gold-plated pocket watch. Each dealer also received a pocket watch. Customers who purchased tires were given a ballot to complete, giving them a chance to win a watch. Dealers were again provided with point-of-sale materials and various customer give-aways, including "fun books" and wind-shield sun screens.

The 1990 General Tire dealer promotion achieved the company's objectives. Top-of-mind awareness of General Tire increased from 5 percent in March to 11 percent in May, and from 10 percent in September to 20 percent in November. Total awareness of the brand rose from 16 percent to 52 percent over the course of the entire campaign. In addition, a major increase was noted in the percentage of consumers who perceived General Tire as having "the most trusted name" in tires.

MEANING AND IMPORTANCE OF PROMOTION

The marketing-mix activities of product planning, pricing, and distribution are performed mainly within the organization or between the organization and its marketing "partners." However, with promotional activities, the firm communicates directly with potential customers. And as the chapter-opening example illustrates, marketers may in certain circumstances wish to communicate not only with end consumers, but with other parties as well, including the members of the distribution channel.

Promotion is the element in an organization's marketing mix that serves to inform, persuade, and remind the market of the organization and/or its products. Basically, promotion is an attempt to influence. Whether a particular promotional activity is designed to inform, persuade, or remind, the ultimate objective is to influence the recipient's feelings, beliefs, or behaviour. In our socioeconomic system, this is not only acceptable, it is essential. One of the attributes of a free society is the right to use communication as a tool of influence. The only constraint is that it be done in a nondeceptive fashion.

Promotion Methods

The **promotional mix** is the combination of personal selling, advertising, sales promotion, publicity, and public relations that helps an organization achieve its marketing objectives. These five methods of promotion and the manner in which they are integrated into the marketing mix are shown in Fig. 17-1. The five methods are defined as follows:

- **Personal selling** is the presentation of a product to a prospective customer by a representative of the selling organization. Across all businesses, more money is spent on personal selling than on any other form of promotion.

FIGURE 17-1

Role of promotion in the marketing mix.
To reach the target market, coordinate the elements in the promotional mix, and coordinate promotion with the other components in the marketing mix.

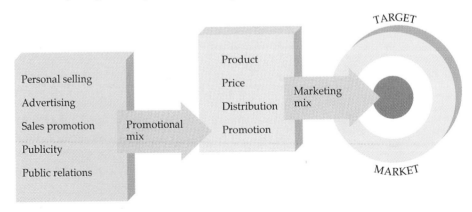

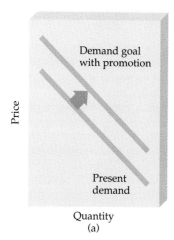

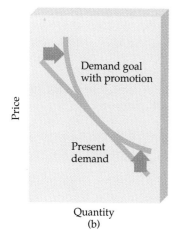

FIGURE 17-2
The goal of promotion: to change the pattern of demand for a product.
Through promotion a company attempts to (a) shift a product's demand curve to the right and (b) change the shape of the curve.

- **Advertising** is a paid-for type of impersonal mass communication in which the sponsor is clearly identified. The most common forms are broadcast (TV and radio) and print (newspapers and magazines).
- **Sales promotion** is designed to supplement advertising and coordinate personal selling. Included in sales promotion are such activities as contests for sales people and consumers, trade shows, in-store displays, samples, premiums, and coupons.
- **Publicity** is similar to advertising in that it is a mass communication type of demand stimulation. Publicity usually consists of a favourable news presentation—a ''plug''—for a product or organization presented in any medium. The unique features of publicity are that it is *not* paid for and it has the credibility of editorial material. Organizations frequently provide the material for publicity in the form of news releases, press conferences, and photographs.
- **Public relations** is more targeted than publicity. It is a planned effort by an organization to influence the attitudes and opinions of a specific group. The target may be customers, shareholders, a government agency, or a special interest group. Public relations efforts are seen in newsletters, annual reports, lobbying, and sponsorship of charity events.

Promotion is a critical ingredient of many marketing strategies. Product differentiation, market segmentation, positioning, trading up and trading down, and branding all require promotion.

Promotion and Imperfect Competition

The North American marketplace operates under conditions of imperfect competition, characterized by product differentiation, emotional buying behaviour, and less-than-complete market information. Under these conditions, promotional activities are essential. A company uses promotion to assist in differentiating its product, to persuade potential buyers, and to bring more information into the buying-decision process.

In economic terms, the basic purpose of promotion is to change the location and shape of the demand (revenue) curve for a company's product. (See Fig. 17-2 and recall the discussion of nonprice competition in Chapter 7.) Through promotion, a company strives to increase a product's sales volume at any given price (17-2a). It also hopes that promotion will affect the demand elasticity for the product (17-2b). The intent is to make the demand *inelastic* when price increases, and *elastic* when price decreases. In other words, management wants the quantity demanded to decline very little when prices go up (inelastic demand). However, when the price goes down, management would like sales to increase considerably (elastic demand).

Purposes of Promotion   Promotion—informing, persuading, and reminding—is essential for several reasons. Distribution channels are often long, and so a product may pass through many hands between a producer and consumers. Therefore, a producer must *inform* middlemen as well as the ultimate consumer or business users about the product. Wholesalers, in turn, must promote the product to retailers, and retailers must communicate with consumers. As the number of potential customers grows and the geographic dimensions of a market expand, the problems of market communication increase. The most useful product will be a failure if no one knows it is available! Thus, a major purpose of promotion

GOOD PROMOTION TAKES MORE THAN HORSE SENSE

Some people fail to recognize that promotion is more than just advertising, thus overlooking the important role the other four methods can play in strategy. The following illustrates a promotional program with almost no advertising.

Horse meat, which is low in cost and high in nutritional value, has long been eaten by Europeans. A decade ago, Europeans consumed about half a kilogram per capita annually. However, rising prices and pressure from animal protection groups have cut sales in half in Belgium, France, Spain, and Italy. Most industries faced with a sales slump of this magnitude would undertake an aggressive ad campaign to stimulate demand. But the horse meat industry was afraid that such a strategy would be too blunt, alienating more consumers than it would win. Therefore, a broad but subtle promotional program was launched using several components of the promotional mix, including:

- A cookbook with recipes using horse meat (sales promotion).
- Demonstrations on TV cooking shows of horse meat dishes, including horse tartare, horse spaghetti, and horse pizza (publicity).
- Mailings to physicians detailing the low-fat, high-protein nutritional benefits of horse meat (public relations).
- Posters featuring healthy middle-aged people and the slogan ''Horse Meat: For Energy'' (advertising).

The campaign is relatively inexpensive, highly targeted to reach the potential market, and discreet enough to avoid the ire of animal rights groups.

SOURCE: Mark M. Nelson, ''A Horse Is a Horse, Of Course, Of Course, Unless It's a Dinner,'' *The Wall Street Journal*, Sept. 26, 1989, pp. A1, A17.

is to disseminate information — to let potential customers know.

Another function of promotion is *persuasion*. The intense competition among different industries, as well as among different firms in the same industry, puts tremendous pressure on the promotional programs of sellers. In our economy of abundance, even a product designed to satisfy a basic physiological need requires strong persuasive promotion since consumers have many brands to choose from. For a want-satisfying or luxury product, for which demand depends on a seller's ability to convince consumers that the product's benefits exceed those of other luxuries, persuasion is even more important.

Consumers also must be *reminded* about a product's availability and satisfaction potential. Sellers bombard the marketplace with thousands of messages every day in the hope of attracting new consumers and establishing markets for new products. Given the intense competition for consumers' attention, even an established firm must constantly remind people about its products in order to retain a place in their minds. Much promotion, therefore, is intended simply to offset competitors' marketing activity by keeping the firm's products in front of the market.

Promotion and Strategic Marketing Planning

In line with the strategic approach to marketing planning, a company should treat personal selling, advertising, and other promotional activities as a coordinated effort within the total marketing program. These activities are fragmented in many firms, with potentially damaging consequences. For example, advertising managers and sales force managers may come into conflict over resources.

To be effective, promotional activities also must be coordinated with product

Red Rose responded to the Tetley round tea bag with indirect comparative advertising.

planning, pricing, and distribution. Promotion is influenced, for instance, by the uniqueness of a product and whether a price is above or below the competition. A manufacturer or middleman must also consider its promotional interdependency with other firms in the distribution channel. For example, when developing a retail store display, a manufacturer must take into account the space constraints of the store, the availability of store personnel to assemble the display, and the presence of adequate inventory at the retail level.

Promotion should also strongly reflect a firm's strategic marketing plan.

An ad that grabs your attention and then informs you.

GREAT WESTERN GARMENT COMPANY
RILEY PANTS

The way we were and can be again.

Suppose a company faces production limitations imposed by material shortages. This firm's marketing goal is simply to hold on to its present customers and market share. Its strategic marketing planning and promotional program will be geared toward attaining that objective. The promotional activities will be quite different from those of a company with bright prospects for market expansion brought about by new technology.

Retail displays must get consumers' attention without disrupting the store's operation.

THE COMMUNICATION PROCESS

As noted earlier, promotion is an exercise in communication. **Communication** is the verbal and/or nonverbal transmission of information between a sender and a receiver. A conversation, an ad, and even a shrug are examples of communication.

Fundamentally, the communication process requires only four elements—a *message*, a *source* of the message, a *communication channel*, and a *receiver*. In practice, however, important additional components come into play. The information that the sending source wants to share must first be *encoded* into a transmittable form. In marketing this means changing an idea into words, pictures, or both. Once the message has been transmitted through some communication channel, the symbols must be given meaning, or *decoded*, by the receiver. If the message has been transmitted successfully, there is some change in the receiver's knowledge, beliefs, or feelings. As a result of this change the receiver *responds* in some way. The final element in the process, *feedback*, tells the sender whether the message was received and how it was perceived by the recipient. Through feedback, the sender learns how to improve communication. All stages of the process can be affected by *noise*—that is, any external factor that interferes with successful communication.

Figure 17-3 illustrates these elements of a general communication process, using as examples typical promotion activities. The information source may be a marketing executive with a sales idea or proposition to communicate. After being encoded into a transmittable message, such as an ad, a display, or a sales presentation, the idea is carried by a sales force or by advertising media (the communication channel) to the receivers—perhaps different target markets. These receivers decode the message in light of their frames of reference, experiences, and memories of similar messages. The message changes the recipients' knowledge, beliefs, or feelings in some way and the recipients respond. In a successful marketing communication, the response might be interest in the product, a desire for it, or possibly the purchase of it. By evaluating the receivers' words or actions, often through marketing research, the sender gets feedback on the effectiveness of the communication. At various stages in the process, the message is subject to interference or noise from competitors' messages, errors in transmission, or other distractions.

MARKETING AT WORK

FILE 17-1   **DO OENOLOGISTS KNOW HOW TO COMMUNICATE?**

An *oenologist* (also spelled *enologist*) is a specialist in the science and study of wines. Perhaps two oenologists can understand each other. But to the uninitiated outsider, the oenologist's language often seems to be a snobbish jargon that tries to impress us, but really tells us nothing. Consider, for example, the following descriptions of seven French wines displayed at an exhibition:

1. A sturdy, well-balanced white wine.
2. Fresher and with more grace than wine #1. An underlying soundness and sturdiness. Not fresh but more serious in tone.
3. A lively rosé.
4. (Same wine as #3, but a vintage from two years earlier.) This wine has more colour and a more serious rosé (than #3). Exquisite balance and finish, with a nice complexity.
5. A quiet, subdued, elegant wine. But not for greatness.
6. More forward in bouquet. A big wine. A lasting finish.
7. A wine with an earthly quality. A light vintage with deep tones.

Now you tell us what they—the experts—are talking about. The name of the game in promotion is to communicate. If you cannot inform and persuade us, then you can't sell to us. And with wines, we wonder if the oenologists' message is really coming through.

FIGURE 17-3

The communication process in promotional programs.

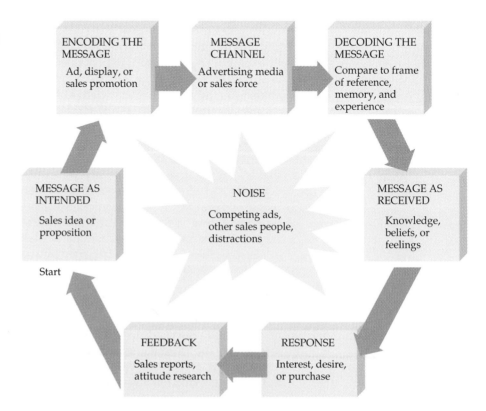

DETERMINING THE PROMOTIONAL MIX

Management has to design the **promotional mix**—the combination of personal selling, advertising, sales promotion, publicity, and public relations that will make the most effective promotional program for a firm. This is a difficult task requiring a number of strategic decisions.

Factors Influencing the Promotional Mix

Four factors should be taken into account when determining the promotional mix. They are (1) the nature of the market, (2) the nature of the product or service, (3) the stage of the product's life cycle, and (4) the amount of money available for promotion.

NATURE OF THE MARKET

As is true in most areas of marketing, decisions on the promotional mix will be greatly influenced by the nature of the market. As least three variables affect the choice of a promotional method for a particular market:

- *Geographic scope of the market.* Personal selling may be adequate in a small local market, but as the market broadens geographically, greater emphasis must be placed on advertising. The exception would be a firm that sells nationally, but finds its customers concentrated in relatively few areas. For example, the market for certain plastics is heavily concentrated in Southern Ontario because these plastics are used by component suppliers to the auto industry. In this case, emphasis on personal selling may be feasible.
- *Type of customer.* Promotional strategy depends in part on what level of the distribution channel the organization hopes to influence. Final consumers and middlemen alike may buy a product, but they require different promotion. To illustrate, a promotional program aimed at retailers will probably include more personal selling than a program designed to attract final consumers. In many situations, middlemen may strongly affect a manufacturer's promotional strategy. Large retail chains may refuse to stock a product unless the manufacturer agrees to do a certain amount of advertising.

  Another consideration is the variety of final customers for a product. A market with only one type of customer will call for a different promotional mix than a market with many customer groups. A firm selling large power saws used exclusively by lumber manufacturers may have to rely only on personal selling. In contrast, a company selling portable hand saws to consumers and to construction firms will probably include a liberal portion of advertising in its mix. Personal selling would be prohibitively expensive in reaching the firm's many customers.
- *Concentration of the market.* The total number of prospective buyers is another consideration. The fewer potential buyers there are, the more effective personal selling is, compared with advertising.

NATURE OF THE PRODUCT

Several product attributes influence promotional strategy. The most important are:

- *Unit value.* A product with low unit value is usually relatively uncomplicated, involves little risks for the buyer, and must appeal to a mass market to survive. Advertising would be the appropriate promotional tool. In contrast, high-unit-value products often are complex and expensive. These features suggest the need for personal selling.

FILE 17-2   **IF YOU KNOW HOW THEY WALK AND TALK, YOU CAN PROMOTE TO THEM**

A lot of companies such as Frito-Lay, Nike, Benetton, Levi Strauss, and Pepsi-Cola are trying to work out promotional programs that get the attention of and say the right things to Canada's 2.5 million teenagers who appear to be spending an estimated $6 billion. Not only do today's teens have money to spend, but they influence their parents' spending on food, cars, home electronics, and computer equipment, according to the president of Echo Advertising and Marketing of Toronto.

It is said that today's teens are different from those of the sixties; they're more realistic, tolerant of others, and although rebellious, they want to conform. They also get bored easily and like change and having fun. In a commercial for Pepsi-Cola Canada Ltd., a principal scolds a pupil for drinking Coke in class. Then the taste-test patrol arrives and the principal chooses Pepsi over Coke in a blind test. In the final scene, the principal and the boy are sitting together, drinking their Pepsis. Pepsi Canada's director of marketing feels that if this commercial had been shot in the sixties, the teenager would have rejected the principal for not knowing that Pepsi was cool.

The makers of Doritos spent a year studying the way teenagers dress, talk, and think. The result was the Bob commercial with 18 fast-paced spots built around a cool mystery man named Bob who never appears. Each spot attracts teen attention, speaks in teen language, and represents teen fun and irreverence. For example, a girl in a bathing suit chants, ''He's hot. He's hot,'' — followed by the on-screen words ''Bob's Favorite Snacks'' and a crumpled Doritos bag; a boy lies on the floor of a bowling alley kicking his legs in excitement with the same on-screen ending. Hostess Canada's vice-president of marketing believes that Bob and Doritos are now part of teen culture. Of course, the ads have to be coordinated with other elements of the promotional program to make sure the message gets through.

Source: Adapted, in part, from Marina Strauss, ''First, You Have to Get the Attention of Teens,'' *Globe and Mail*, July 12, 1991, pp. B1, B2.

- *Degree of customization*. If a product must be fitted to the individual customer's needs, personal selling is necessary. However, the benefits of standardized products can be effectively communicated in advertising.
- *Presale and postsale service*. Products that must be demonstrated, for which there are trade-ins, or that require frequent servicing to keep them in good working order lend themselves to personal selling.

Beyond these conditions, certain products are simply more ''advertisable'' than others. Many years ago, advertising authority Neil Borden identified five product criteria that suggest when advertising might be most effective. If all these criteria are met, there is an excellent opportunity to advertise. When a product meets some, but not all, of these conditions, advertising may be less effective. The five criteria are as follows:

- The primary demand trend for the product should be favourable. In spite of public opinion to the contrary, advertising cannot successfully sell a product that people do not want. Nor can advertising reverse declining primary demand.

- There should be considerable opportunity to differentiate the product. Then it is easier to advertise because the company has something to say. For this reason, automobiles or cosmetics are easier to advertise than salt or sugar. Products that are not easy to differentiate by *brand* may still be advertised by a trade association, such as the Dairy Bureau of Canada or the Canadian Cattlemen's Association.
- The product should have hidden qualities. This condition affords the seller grounds for educating the market through advertising. For instance, a reclining chair or a television set is simpler to advertise than greeting cards.
- Powerful emotional buying motives should exist for the product. Buying action can be stimulated by appeal to these motives. It is easier to build an effective advertising campaign for Weight Loss Centres than for clotheslines or hammers.
- The company must have sufficient funds to support an advertising program adequately.

A summary of how the major financial, market, and product factors affect the decision to emphasize advertising or personal selling is shown in Fig. 17-4.

FIGURE 17-4

Financial, market, and product factors that affect the promotional mix.

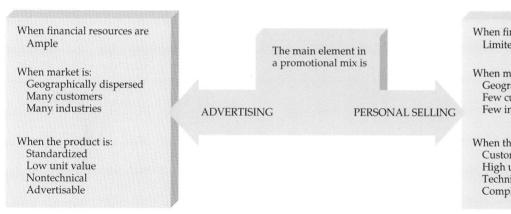

STAGE OF THE PRODUCT LIFE CYCLE

Promotion strategies are influenced by the life-cycle stage a product is in at a given time. When a new product is introduced, prospects must be informed about its existence and its benefits. Also, middlemen must be convinced to carry it. Thus both advertising (to consumers) and personal selling (to middlemen) are critical in a product's introductory stage. At this time, a product also may be something of a novelty, and excellent opportunities exist for publicity. Later in a successful product's life, as competition intensifies, more emphasis is placed on persuasive advertising. Table 17-1 shows how promotional strategies change as a product moves through its life cycle.

FUNDS AVAILABLE

Regardless of what may be the most desirable promotional mix, the amount of money available for promotion is the ultimate determinant of the mix. A business with ample funds can make more effective use of advertising than

TABLE 17-1 **Promotional Strategies for Different Product Life-Cycle Stages**

Market situation	Promotional strategy
Introductory stage	
Customers do not realize that they want the product, nor do they understand how it will benefit them.	Inform and educate potential customers. Tell them that the product exists, how it might be used, and what want-satisfying benefits it provides.
	In this stage, a seller must stimulate *primary demand* — the demand for a type of product — as contrasted with *selective demand* — the demand for a particular brand. For example, producers had to sell consumers on the value of compact discs in general before it was feasible to promote a particular brand.
	Normally, heavy emphasis must be placed on personal selling. Trade shows are also used extensively in the promotional mix. Rather than calling on customers individually, the company can promote its new product at a trade show where prospective customers come to the seller's exhibit. Manufacturers also rely heavily on personal selling to attract middlemen to handle a new product.
Growth stage	
Customers are aware of product benefits. The product is selling well and middlemen want to handle it.	Stimulate selective (brand) demand. Increase emphasis on advertising. Middlemen share more of the total promotional burden.
Maturity stage	
Competition intensifies and sales level off.	Advertising is used as a tool to persuade rather than only to provide information. Intense competition forces sellers to devote larger sums to advertising and thus contributes to the declining profits experienced in this stage.
Sales-decline stage	
Sales and profits are declining. New and better products are coming into the market.	All promotional efforts should be cut back substantially, except when attempting to revitalize the product.

an enterprise with limited financial resources. Small or financially weak companies are likely to rely on personal selling, dealer displays, or joint manufacturer-retailer advertising. Lack of money may even force a company to use a less efficient promotional method. For example, advertising can carry a promotional message to far more people and at a lower cost *per person* than can a sales force. Yet the firm may have to rely on personal selling because it lacks the funds to take advantage of advertising's efficiency.

M A R K E T I N G   A T   W O R K

FILE 17-3   **THE COOKIE WARS: BREATHING NEW LIFE INTO AN OLD CATEGORY**

Cookie consumption in Canada has been stagnant for a few years, but then again, cookies have been around for a long time. But when Loblaws entered the market with its President's Choice brands and varieties—Decadent Chocolate Chip, Peanut Butter First, and Butter First Oatmeal—the market was invigorated by the superior products as well as the new competition.

Now, Keebler, the second largest U.S. cookie maker, plans to enter Canada's $650-million cookie market with 11 top-selling cookie and cracker brands. Keebler has acquired a Canadian distributor and has developed an aggressive pricing program as well as a coordinated promotional program comprising ads, coupons, and point-of-purchase materials. Keebler intends to promote low introductory prices to help secure retail shelf space.

Competitors in the Canadian market—Nabisco with 50 percent share, Culinar with 21 percent, Dare 11 percent, Beatrice Foods at 7 percent—have already been shaken up by the President's Choice brands and are preparing promotional programs to protect themselves in this mature market. The Loblaws product and promotion is so effective that it now sells $150 million in Canada and exports $20 million worth of cookies to American retailers.

Nabisco has already reacted by lowering prices on some of its best-selling brands—it produces nine of the top ten national brands, including Oreo and Chips Ahoy. Look for more aggressive distributor-retailer promotion, more advertising, more couponing, more retailer case deals and price specials, and more creative point-of-purchase material. Maybe lots more sampling. Perhaps growth can return to the cookie market.

Source: Adapted, in part, from Mark Evans, "How Cookie Market Crumbles," *The Financial Post*, July 1, 1991, p. 4.

The Choice of a Push or Pull Strategy

As we have seen, in designing the promotional mix, producers aim their efforts at both middlemen and end users. Promotion aimed at middlemen is called a **push strategy** and promotion directed at end users is called a **pull strategy**. Figure 17-5 contrasts these two strategies.

Using a push strategy means a producer directs promotion primarily at the middlemen that are the next link forward in the producer's distribution channel. The product is "pushed" through the channel. Take the case of a lawn fertilizer producer that sells some of its products in bags through wholesalers and retailers to household consumers. This producer will promote heavily to wholesalers, which then also use a push strategy to retailers. In turn, the retailers promote to consumers. A push strategy usually involves a lot of personal selling and sales promotion, including contests for sales people and displays at trade shows. This promotional strategy is appropriate for many manufacturers of business products, as well as for various consumer goods.

With a pull strategy, a producer aims promotion at end users — usually ultimate consumers. The intention is to motivate people to ask retailers for the product. The retailers, in turn, will request the product from wholesalers, and wholesalers will order it from the producer. In effect, promotion to consumers

FIGURE 17-5
Push and pull promotional strategies.

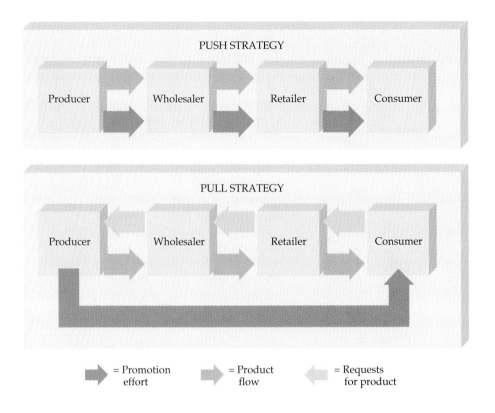

PUSH STRATEGY

Producer · Wholesaler · Retailer · Consumer

PULL STRATEGY

Producer · Wholesaler · Retailer · Consumer

= Promotion effort   = Product flow   = Requests for product

is designed to ''pull'' the product through the channel. This strategy typically calls for heavy use of advertising and possibly various forms of sales promotion such as premiums, samples, or in-store demonstrations. Manufacturers of consumer packaged goods often use a pull strategy to get products stocked on supermarket shelves.[1]

DETERMINING THE PROMOTIONAL BUDGET

It is extremely challenging to establish promotional budgets. Management lacks reliable standards for determining (1) how much to spend altogether on advertising or personal selling and (2) how much to spend on specific activities within each area. A serious problem is that management normally cannot assess the results of promotional expenditures. A firm may decide to add ten sales people or increase its trade show budget by $200,000 a year, but it cannot determine precisely what increase in sales or profits to expect from these moves. Nor can anyone measure with a high degree of certainty the relative values of the two expenditures.

Promotional activities generally are budgeted as current operating expenses, implying that their benefits are used up immediately. Through the years, however, several economists and executives have proposed treating advertising (and presumably other promotional efforts) as a capital investment. Their reasoning is that the benefits and returns on these investments often are not immediately evident and are spread over several years.

There are four methods of determining the budget for promotion. These are

---

[1]The move from pull to push strategies is discussed in Alvin A. Achenbaum and F. Kent Mitchel, ''Pulling Away from Push Marketing,'' *Harvard Business Review*, May–June 1987, pp. 38–40.

frequently discussed in connection with the advertising budget alone, but they may also be applied to the total promotional budget.

Percentage of Sales

The promotional budget may be related in some way to company income. The expenditures may be set as a percentage of past or anticipated sales. However, some businesses prefer to budget a fixed amount of money per *unit* of past or expected future sales. Manufacturers of products with a high unit value and a low rate of turnover (automobiles or appliances, for example) frequently use the unit method.

This *percentage-of-sales method* is probably the most widely used of all those discussed here. It has achieved broad acceptance because it is simple to calculate. Moreover, it sets the cost in relation to sales income and thus has the effect of being a variable rather than a fixed expense.

Actually, this method is unsound and illogical if promotional expenditures are based on past sales. Management is saying that promotion is a *result* of sales when, in fact, it is a *cause* of sales. Another undesirable result of using a percentage of past sales method is that it reduces promotional expenditures when sales are declining. And this is just when promotion usually is most needed.

Use of All Available Funds

A new company frequently ploughs all available funds into its promotional program. The objective here is to build sales for the first few years. After that period, management expects to earn a profit and will budget for promotion in a different manner.

Follow Competition

A weak method of determining the promotional budget, but one that is used occasionally, is to match the promotional expenditures of competitors. Sometimes only one competitor is followed. In other cases, if management has access to industry averages through a trade association, these become company benchmarks. There are at least two problems with this approach. First, a firm's competitors may be just as much in the dark regarding how to set a promotional budget. Second, one company's promotional goals and strategies may be quite different from those of its competitors because of differences in strategic marketing planning.

Task or Objective

The soundest basis for establishing the promotional budget is to decide what tasks or objectives the promotional program must accomplish and then determine what they will cost. Various forms of this method are widely used today. The *task method* forces management to realistically define the goals of its promotional program.

Sometimes this approach is called the *buildup method* because of the way it operates. For example, a company may elect to enter a new geographic market. Management decides that this venture will require ten additional sales people. Compensation and expenses of these people will cost a total of $520,000 per year. Salary for an additional sales supervisor and expenses for an extra office and administrative needs will cost $70,000. Thus in the personal selling part of the promotional mix, an extra $590,000 must be budgeted. Similar estimates can be made for the anticipated cost of advertising, sales promotion, and other promotional tools. The promotional budget is *built up* by adding up the costs of the individual promotional tasks needed to reach the goal of entering a new territory.

THE CAMPAIGN CONCEPT

In planning the total promotional program for an organization, management should think in terms of the campaign concept. A **campaign** is a coordinated series of promotional efforts built around a single theme and designed to reach a predetermined goal. In effect a campaign is an exercise in strategic planning.

Although the term *campaign* is probably thought of most often in connection with advertising, we should apply the campaign concept first to the entire promotional program. Then the total promotional campaign can be subdivided into its advertising, personal selling, and sales promotion components. These subcampaigns can be planned in more detail, to work towards the program goal.

Many types of promotional campaigns may be conducted by a company, and some may run concurrently. Depending on available funds and objectives, a firm may have a local, regional, national, or international campaign. One campaign may be aimed at consumers, another at wholesalers and retailers. The stage of a product's life cycle may determine whether a primary or a selective demand campaign will be conducted.

The user's comfort is the central theme.

A firm should first establish the goal(s) of the promotional campaign. This goal, and the buying motives of customers, will determine the selling appeals to be stressed. Assume that the goal of an airline's promotional campaign is to introduce its new Toronto to Paris service. The appeals might be to the customers' desire for speed, a quiet and restful trip, or fine food and courteous service. If the same airline wanted to increase its plane loadings of air freight, then the ads and personal selling might emphasize speed of delivery, reduction in losses due to spoilage and handling, or convenient schedules.

A campaign revolves around a central idea or focal point. This "theme" permeates all promotional efforts and helps to unify the campaign. A **theme** is simply the promotional appeals dressed up in a distinctive, attention-getting form. It expresses the product's benefits. Frequently the theme takes the form of a slogan. Some companies use the same theme for several campaigns; others develop a different theme for each new campaign.

For a promotional campaign to be successful, the efforts of participating groups must be carefully coordinated. This means that:

- The *advertising program* will consist of a series of related, well-timed, carefully placed ads that reinforce personal selling and sales promotional efforts.
- The *personal selling effort* will be coordinated with the advertising program. The sales force will explain and demonstrate the product benefits stressed in the ads. The sales people will also be fully informed about the advertising part of the campaign—the theme, media used, and schedule for the appearance of ads. The sales people, in turn, should carry this information to middlemen so that they take part in the campaign.
- The *sales promotional devices*, such as point-of-purchase display materials, will be coordinated with other aspects of the campaign. For each campaign, new display materials must be prepared. They should reflect the ads and appeals used in the current campaign to maximize the campaign's impact at the point of sale.
- *Physical distribution management* will ensure that adequate stocks of the product are available in all outlets prior to the start of the campaign.

REGULATION OF PROMOTIONAL ACTIVITIES

Because the primary objective of promotion is to sell something by communicating with a market, promotional activities attract attention. Consequently, abuses by individual firms are easily and quickly noted by the public. This situation in turn soon leads to (1) public demand for correction of the abuses, (2) assurances that they will not be repeated, and (3) general restraints on promotional activities. To answer public demand, laws and regulations have been enacted by the federal government and by most provincial governments. In addition, many private business organizations have established voluntary codes of advertising and promotional standards to guide their own promotional activities. In addition, the advertising industry itself, through the Advertising Advisory Board and its Advertising Standards Councils, does a considerable amount of self-regulation.

The Federal Role

A number of departments of the federal government administer Acts aimed at controlling various aspects of promotion, particularly advertising. The Broadcasting Act established the Canadian Radio-television and Telecommunications Commission (CRTC) in 1968 and provided for sweeping powers of advertising regulation. Under section 16 of the Act, the Commission may make regulations concerning the character of broadcast advertising and the amount of time that may be devoted to it. While the potential for substantial control exists, the Commission does not in reality pass on each commercial message. What it has done is to delegate authority in certain fields to other agencies such as the Health Protection Branch of the Department of Health and Welfare and the Combines Investigation Branch of the Department of Consumer and Corporate Affairs.

The Health Protection Branch deals with advertising in the fields of drugs, cosmetics, and devices (officialese for birth-control products), and it has sweeping powers to limit, control, rewrite, or ban promotion for the products under its authority. The authority itself is embodied in such Acts, and regulations associated with them, as the Health and Welfare Department Act, the Proprietary or Patent Medicine Act, the Food and Drug Act, the Criminal Code of Canada, and the Broadcasting Act. The various Acts and regulations result in general types of prohibition aimed at preventing the treatment, processing, packaging, labelling, advertising, and selling of foods, drugs, and devices in such a manner as to mislead or deceive, or even to be likely to create an erroneous impression concerning the nature of the products.

The Branch also prohibits the advertising of whole classes of drugs. It has developed a list of diseases or conditions for which a cure may not be advertised under any circumstances. This prohibition stands even if a professionally accepted cure exists. The logic for the prohibition of advertising, in spite of the existence of a cure, is that the Branch does not wish members of the general public to engage in self-diagnosis of the condition that can be treated.

By virtue of the powers delegated to it by the Commission, the Branch has absolute control over radio and television advertisements for the products under its jurisdiction. All such advertisements must be submitted to it at least 15 days prior to airing, and no radio or television station can air an ad without its having been approved by the Branch and, thereby, the Commission. In practical terms, the Health Protection Branch, even though an appeal route to the CRTC is available, has complete authority and advertisers have no resource of any consequence.

In contrast to the delegated review powers the Health Protection Branch has over advertisements using the broadcast media, its position with reference to the print media is weak. Its formal control is in terms of alleged Food and Drug violations, which must be prosecuted in court. Given the lack of jurisprudence in this area, the Branch is loath to go to court in case it loses and thus sets a precedent or in case its regulations (many of which have not been tested in court) are found to be illegal. What the Branch does is advise advertisers of its opinion of advertisements that are prepared for the print media. This opinion is not a ruling, and ads submitted, as well as those that are not, are still subject to the regulations for which the Branch has responsibility. This does not mean that the Branch does not monitor the print media. Newspapers and magazines are sampled and advertisements examined.

The Department of Consumer and Corporate Affairs has substantial and major responsibility in the area of regulating promotion. The Bureau of Competition Policy of the Department carries the major burden of promotional regulation. The Acts administered include: (1) the Hazardous Products Act (concerning poisonous compounds for household use), (2) the Precious Metals Marketing Act (i.e., definitions of sterling and carat weight), (3) the Trade Marks Act, (4) the Consumer Packaging and Labelling Act, and of greatest significance, (5) the Competition Act. Within the Competition Act, a number of sections pertain directly to the regulation of advertising and promotional activities. Section 35, for example, requires that manufacturers or wholesalers who offer promotional allowances to retailers must offer such allowances on proportionate terms to all competing purchasers. Section 36 of the Act regulates misleading advertising in general, while section 37 pertains specifically to "bait and switch" advertising.[2]

Section 36 of the Competition Act makes it illegal for an advertiser to make any false or misleading statement to the public in advertising or promotional materials or with respect to warranties. This section also regulates the use of false statements regarding the expected performance or length of life of a product and the use of testimonials in advertising. Section 36.2 of the Act regulates the use of "double ticketing" in retail selling and requires that, where a retailer promotes a product at two different prices or where two prices appear on a product or at the point of sale, the retailer must sell the product at the lower of the prices. Businesses or individuals who are convicted of violating section 36 are subject to fines as large as $25,000 or to imprisonment for up to one year.

Paragraph 36(1)(*d*) of the Competition Act regulates "sale" advertising and would apply particularly to retail advertisers. Section 37 requires that an advertiser who promotes a product at a "sale" price have sufficient quantities of the product on hand to satisfy reasonable market demand. Section 37.1 prohibits an advertiser from selling a "sale" item at a price higher than the advertised "sale" price. Finally, section 37.2 regulates the conduct of contests, lotteries, and games of chance. This section requires that advertisers who promote such contests disclose the number and value of prizes and the areas in which prizes are to be distributed, and further requires that prizes be distributed on a basis of skill or on a basis of random selection.

The provisions of the Competition Act relating to misleading advertising do not apply to publishers and broadcasters who actually distribute the advertising in question to the general public, provided that these publishers have accepted the contents of the advertising in good faith. In essence, this means that a newspaper cannot be prosecuted for misleading advertising if it accepted the advertising on the assumption that its contents were not misleading. Although no newspaper can be prosecuted for misleading advertising if it accepted the advertising in good faith, there is still some question concerning whether media production departments and advertising agencies, which actually participate with the advertiser in the production of misleading advertising, might not in the future be considered jointly responsible with the advertiser for the contents of the offending advertisement. This is a question with which the Canadian courts may deal in the future.

The Provincial Role

In each of the provinces, a considerable variety of legislation exists that is aimed at controlling various promotional practices. For instance, in Ontario, various degrees of control are exercised by the Liquor Control Board of Ontario, the Ontario Board of Film Censors, the Ontario Superintendent of Insurance, the Ontario Human Rights Commission, the Ontario Securities

---

[2]For a review of court decisions in misleading advertising cases in Canada, refer to James G. Barnes, "Advertising and the Courts," *The Canadian Business Review*, Autumn 1975, pp. 51–54. The Misleading Advertising Division of the Department of Consumer and Corporate Affairs also publishes a quarterly review of misleading advertising cases entitled the *Misleading Advertising Bulletin*. Individuals interested in receiving this bulletin can have their names placed on the mailing list simply by writing to the Department of Consumer and Corporate Affairs.

M A R K E T I N G   A T   W O R K

FILE 17-4   **RUNNING AFOUL THE MISLEADING ADVERTISING PROVISIONS OF THE COMPETITION ACT: A WORD FROM THE DIRECTOR**

SECTION 52(1)(a): all representations, in any form whatever, that are false or misleading in a material respect are prohibited.

In promoting the sale of radios, K mart Canada Ltd. represented on in-store signs:

"OUR PRICE 19.99 SALE PRICE 9.99"

Investigation revealed that "19.99" represented neither the regular selling price in the relevant market nor K mart's regular selling price. The accused pleaded guilty and was fined $10,000.

SECTION 52(1)(b): Any representation in the form of statement, warranty or guarantee of the performance, efficacy or length of life of a product, not based on an adequate or proper test, is prohibited. The onus is on the one making the claim to prove that it is so based.

Remington Products (Canada) Inc., in promoting the sale of electric shavers, represented in television commercials:

"Shaves as close as a blade and closer than any other electric shaver . . . Gets whiskers other shavers leave behind . . . Remington Ultimate *tests prove it*. In independent tests approximately 70 percent said it shaves closer than any other electric shaver."

Investigation revealed that these claims were not based on adequate and proper tests. The accused pleaded guilty and was fined $75,000.

SECTION 59: Any contest that does not disclose the number and approximate value of prizes or important information relating to the chances of winning in the contest, that does not select participants or distribute prizes on the basis of skill or on a random basis, or in which the distribution of prizes is unduly delayed, is prohibited.

In promoting the sale of health club memberships, Hatcher and Jay represented on a ballot:

"SUNSHINE SWEEPSTAKES — No Purchase Necessary.
Limit One per person. . ."

Investigation revealed that the accused unduly delayed the distribution of prizes. Hatcher and Day pleaded guilty and were each fined $2,500 for a total of $5,000.

SOURCE: Adapted from Director of Investigation and Research, *Misleading Advertising Bulletin*, Consumer and Corporate Affairs Canada, January, 1991, pp. 11, 16, 18, 19.

Commission, the Ontario Police Commission, the Ontario Racing Commission, various ministries of the Ontario government responsible for financial, commercial, consumer, and transportation functions and services, and yet more. Most of the provinces have similar sets of legislation, regulatory bodies, and provincial departments. While much of the federal regulation must in the end result in argument and prosecution in a courtroom, the provincial machinery would appear to be much more flexible and potentially regulatory in nature, and if pursued, may have a more substantial effect on undesirable practices.

The powers of provincial governments in relation to the regulation of misleading advertising have been increased considerably in recent years. Since the mid-1970s, a number of provinces have passed legislation dealing with unfair and unconscionable trade practices. The ''trade practices'' Acts passed by British Columbia, Alberta, and Ontario contain ''shopping lists'' of practices that are made illegal by these Acts. In reality, these pieces of legislation write into law practices that have been considered illegal by federal prosecutors for a number of years. Relating to advertising, these Acts prohibit such practices as advertising a product as new when it is in fact used; advertising that fails to state a material fact, thereby deceiving the consumer; and advertising that gives greater prominence to low down payments or monthly payments rather than to the actual price of the product. The Alberta Unfair Trade Practices Act also contains a provision for corrective advertising. This provision means that a court, upon convicting an advertiser for misleading advertising, can order that advertiser to devote some or all of its advertising for a certain period to informing customers that the advertiser had been advertising falsely in the past and to correcting the misleading information that had been communicated in the offending advertisements.

The Province of Quebec has within its Consumer Protection Act a section that regulates advertising directed at children. This section forbids the use of exaggeration, endorsements, cartoon characters, and statements that urge children to buy. Quebec's Official Language Act also contains a number of sections that govern the use of French and English in advertising in that province.

Regulation by Private Organizations

Several kinds of private organizations also exert considerable control over promotional practices of businesses. Magazines, newspapers, and radio and television stations regularly refuse to accept advertisements that they feel are false, misleading, or generally in bad taste, and in so doing they are being ''reasonable'' in the ordinary course of doing business. Some trade associations have established a ''code of ethics'' that includes points pertaining to sales-force and advertising activities. Some trade associations regularly censor advertising appearing in their trade or professional journals. Better Business Bureaus located in major cities all over the country are working to control some very difficult situations. The Advertising Advisory Board administers the Canadian Code of Advertising Standards, a number of other advertising codes, including the Broadcast Code for Advertising to Children (on behalf of the Canadian Association of Broadcasters), and a code regulating the advertising of over-the-counter drugs, which was developed in cooperation with the Proprietary Association and Health and Welfare Canada.

SUMMARY

Promotion is the fourth component of a company's total marketing mix. Its purpose is to inform, persuade, and remind. It is a basic ingredient of nonprice competition and an essential element of modern marketing. The three primary methods of promotion are personal selling, advertising, and sales promotion. Other forms include publicity and public relations.

Promotional activity is essentially an exercise in communication. Fundamentally the communication process consists of a source sending a message through a channel to a receiver. The success of communication depends on the encoding and decoding of the message and the noise that may interfere with transmission. Feedback is a measure of how effective a communication has been.

Promotion must be integrated into a firm's strategic planning because all elements of the marketing mix—product, price, distribution, and promotion —must be coordinated in order to be effective. When deciding on the appropriate promotional mix (the combination of advertising, personal selling, and other promotional tools), management should consider four factors: (1) nature of the market, (2) nature of the product, (3) stage of the product's life cycle, and (4) money available. A push strategy involves concentrating promotional effort on the next link forward in the distribution channel. The alternative is a pull strategy, in which promotion is focused on the final buyer.

It is difficult to set a dollar figure for the total promotional budget. The most commonly used method is to set the budget as a percentage of sales, but a better approach is to establish the promotional goals and then figure out how much it will cost to achieve them. The promotional efforts of the firm should be coordinated in a campaign built around a single theme and designed to reach a predetermined goal.

As a result of criticism and concern regarding the use of advertising and promotional techniques, the federal government has enacted legislation that regulates promotion. The main federal laws are the Competition Act and the Broadcasting Act. The Department of Consumer and Corporate Affairs and the Canadian Radio-Television and Telecommunications Commission are charged with administering the legislation in this area. Promotional practices are also regulated at the provincial level through trade practices legislation, through voluntary codes of businesses and trade associations, and by the advertising industry itself.

KEY TERMS AND CONCEPTS

Promotion 550
Promotional mix 550
Personal selling 550
Advertising 551
Sales promotion 551
Publicity 551
Public relations 551
Promotion and demand
  elasticity 551
Communication process 555
Encoding 555
Decoding 555
Feedback 555

Noise 555
Primary demand 558
Push strategy 561
Pull strategy 561
Promotional budgeting
  methods 562
Campaign 564
Campaign theme 565
Broadcasting Act 565
Competition Act 567
Provincial role in regulating
  promotion 567
Regulation by industry itself 569

QUESTIONS AND PROBLEMS

1. For each of the following promotional objectives, find one example of a print ad:
   a. Primarily designed to inform.
   b. Primarily designed to persuade.
   c. Primarily designed to remind.

2. Describe and explain a communication process in the following situations:
   a. A college student trying to convince her father to buy her a used car.
   b. A sales person trying to sell a car to a college student.

3. Explain how the nature of the market affects the promotional mix for the following products:

    a. Contact lenses.
    b. Golf balls.
    c. Plywood.
    d. Take-out fried chicken.
    e. Compact discs.
    f. Mainframe computers.

4. Describe how classifying consumer goods as convenience, shopping, or specialty goods helps determine the best promotional mix.

5. Using the criteria for advertisability, evaluate each of the following products. Assume sufficient funds are available.
    a. Automobile tires.
    b. Revlon cosmetics.
    c. Light bulbs.
    d. Ten-minute automobile oil changes.
    e. College education.
    f. Luggage.

6. Explain why personal selling is or is not likely to be the main ingredient in the promotional mix for each of the following products:
    a. Chequing accounts.
    b. Home swimming pools.
    c. Liquid laundry detergent.
    d. Large order of McDonald's french fries.

7. Explain why retailer promotional efforts should or should not be stressed in the promotional mix for the following:
    a. Levi's 501 jeans.
    b. Sunkist oranges.
    c. Women's cosmetics.
    d. Bank credit card.

8. Why is the percentage-of-sales method so widely used to determine promotional budgets when, in fact, most authorities recognize the task or objective method as more desirable?

9. Identify the central idea — the theme — in three current promotional campaigns.

10. Assume you are marketing a liquid that removes creosote (and the danger of fire) from chimneys used for wood-burning stoves. Briefly describe the roles you would assign to advertising, personal selling, sales promotion, and publicity in your promotional campaign.

11. Explain the term *proportionally equal basis* in connection with manufacturers' granting promotional allowances. Consider especially the situations where retailers vary in size.

12. Do you think we need additional legislation to regulate advertising? To regulate personal selling? If so, explain what you would recommend.

13. Sports are increasingly being seen as a vehicle for international promotion by multinational corporations. What issues related to the *other* marketing mix elements must be resolved before the full potential of this opportunity can be realized?

CHAPTER 18 GOALS

In this chapter we look at personal selling from the viewpoints of both the sales person and the sales manager. After studying this chapter, you should be able to explain:

- The importance of personal selling in our economy and in a company's marketing program.
- How sales jobs differ from other jobs.
- The wide variety of sales jobs.
- The steps involved in the selling process.
- The sales management activities of staffing, training, evaluating, and compensating a sales force.

C H A P T E R 18

Management of Personal Selling

Today's top young sales people are a diverse group, but they do have some things in common. They are trained professionals who see sales experience as an important part of a total business career. Let's meet some sales people, aged 25 to 30, and find out what else they think about selling:

- Catherine Hogan is an account manager for Bell Canada. When she graduated from college, technical sales was not in her career plans. Now she is involved in cooperative selling, teaming up with Bell account executives to bring long disance voice or data services to customers. Hogan, a black woman, has succeeded in an environment dominated by white, middle-aged males. She says, ''Minorities shouldn't overlook sales. You can adapt to your environment and make decisions that let you comfortably maintain your sense of self.''

- Mark DeAngelis, an industrial distribution graduate, is a sales engineer with Canadian General Electric. He feels that the way to learn a business is to be in front of the customer. ''He'll [the customer] tell you exactly what he likes or doesn't like about your product.'' He also finds sales a good way to learn about his own company. In the course of a sales project, DeAngelis talks to marketing, manufacturing, and engineering personnel at GE plants in Canada and the United States. Viewing selling in a professional manner, he says, ''This is not a back-slapping sort of business. Actually, selling is more of a service than it is 'selling.' ''

- Kathy Serfilippi is a college graduate and sales representative for corporate sales at Air Canada. It is her job to build relationships with travel agents and corporate travel managers. She says, ''When you come down to it, I guess I'm a people person.'' But liking people isn't enough. Persistence is the name of the game in her business. Serfilippi says you have to ask for the business and not be afraid to go back and ask again if you're turned down. To keep up her selling skills, she attends at least ten training seminars a year.

- Jacques Murphy majored in marketing and is now a group vice-president responsible for five divisions at The Gallup Organization, Inc. In addition to being a manager, Murphy sells marketing research services to banks, trust companies, and credit unions. He recognizes that selling is more than just making a transaction. "When we win a contract at Gallup, that's when the selling really starts. We're constantly reinforcing the buying decision by keeping ahead on deadlines and showing how the research is useful to the buyer."[1]

Selling is essential to the well-being of our economic system, and it probably offers more job opportunities than any other single vocation. Personal selling is not easy, nor is it something everyone is capable of doing. Yet, as the comments above indicate, it can be an exciting and challenging occupation.

THE NATURE OF PERSONAL SELLING

The goal of all marketing efforts is to achieve the organization's performance objectives by offering want-satisfaction to the market over the long run. **Personal selling**, the personal communication of information to persuade a prospective customer to buy a good, service, or idea, is the major promotional tool used to reach this goal. How well an organization manages its sales force often has a direct bearing on the success of its entire marketing program.

The efforts of sales people go far beyond simply making transactions. They concern making and retaining customer relationships and include:

- Explaining product benefits.
- Demonstrating the proper operation of products.
- Answering questions and responding to objections.
- Organizing and implementing point-of-purchase promotions.
- Arranging the terms of a sale.
- Following up the sale to ensure that the buyer is satisfied and remains a buyer.
- Collecting market and competitive information to improve marketing strategy.

Advantages and Disadvantages of Personal Selling

Compared to the impersonal promotional tools — advertising, sales promotion, publicity, and public relations — personal selling has the advantage of greater *flexibility*. Sales people can tailor sales presentations to fit the needs and behaviours of individual customers. Also, sales people can see the prospect's immediate reaction to a sales approach and make adjustments on the spot. For example, if a prospective customer appears skeptical about a particular point or shows a special interest in one product feature, the sales person can alter the presentation accordingly.

A second merit of personal selling is that it usually can be *focused* on prospective customers, thus minimizing wasted effort. By contrast, in most forms of advertising, much of the cost is devoted to sending the message to people who are not real prospects.

In most instances, a third benefit of personal selling is that it *results in the actual sale*. Other forms of promotion have as their objective moving the prospect closer to the sale. Advertisements, for example, can attract attention, provide information, and even stimulate desire, but seldom do they actually cause the prospective customer to complete the transaction.

---

[1]Adapted, in part, from Martin Everett, "Selling's New Breed: Smart and Feisty," *Sales & Marketing Management*, October 1989, pp. 52–64.

Telemarketing provides inexpensive access to customers, but its success depends on the skill, training, and supervision of the callers.

A fourth benefit, and a major challenge for personal selling, is the development and maintenance of the sales representative–customer relationship. It is the nature and quality of this relationship that has a great impact on the perception of quality and evaluation of service that a customer makes. This applies equally in consumer and business-to-business marketing.

The major limitation of personal selling is its *high cost*. Using a sales force does minimize wasted effort because sales people can concentrate on legitimate prospects. However, the costs of operating a sales force are high. The average cost of a sales call in business-to-business selling, including salary, benefits, commissions, travel expenses, and sales promotion materials, ranges from $180 to $200.[2] Excluded from this calculation are costs such as training, support staff, and supervision.

One alternative to the high cost of face-to-face personal selling is **telemarketing**. Instead of the traditional sales call, a growing number of firms are using telephones or computers to talk with customers. Particularly appropriate for straight rebuy situations as well as accounts for which orders are too small to justify a personal visit, telemarketing has expanded to include providing product operating instructions and technical advice. Major auto manufacturers have progressed to the point where their computers order directly from the computers of suppliers without human intervention.

Another disadvantage of personal selling is that companies often are unable to *attract the calibre of people needed* to do the job well. At the retail level, in particular, many firms have eliminated sales forces and shifted to self-service for this reason.

Nature of the Sales Job

It is difficult to generalize about sales jobs because there are so many varieties. However, one trend is the broadening of the sales person's responsibilities. With greater acceptance of the marketing concept by manufacturing firms, for instance, a new type of sales position—the **territory manager**—has been cre-

---

[2]"What Is the Average Cost of a Personal Sales Call?" Carr Report No. 541.1F, Cahners Publishing Co., July 1989.

ated. A territory is treated as an individual profit centre with the territory manager in charge. Rather than just pushing what the factory produces, this new breed of sales person works closely with customers to understand and interpret their wants. The territory manager then either fills these wants with existing products or communicates them to the producer so that adjustments can be made or new products developed. Today's territory manager engages in a total selling job — identifying customer needs, qualifying prospects, developing sales promotions, servicing customers, managing expenses, and collecting market intelligence. The job includes selling to new customers, obtaining reorders from repeat customers, selling new products, helping customers find new uses for existing products, and teaching customers to use products properly.

Due to increased responsibility, the territory manager experiences problems of **role ambiguity** and **role conflict**. Ambiguity is caused by the many different tasks modern sales people are called on to perform. Among other things they persuade prospective customers, negotiate with manufacturing, service accounts, set up displays, expedite orders, coordinate deliveries, gather information, collect past-due accounts, and help solve customers' problems. Frequently sales people must make quick decisions in the field, without all pertinent information and far removed from the advice of superiors at headquarters. The result is ambiguity about how much responsibility to assume and uncertainty about the risks of undesirable outcomes.

Role conflict occurs because several groups often place conflicting demands on the sales person. The marketing concept emphasizes satisfying the customer. But, on occasion, the best interests of the customer are inconsistent with the short-term interests of the sales person's company. As a result, sales people experience conflicts regarding whose position—the firm's or the customer's — they should support. Also, within the company, different departments (credit and production, for example) may view customers' requests from a very different perspective than does the sales person. Another potential source of conflict involves the sales person's family. The demands of sales jobs often include overnight travel, entertaining customers, and doing paperwork at home or in the evening. If the sales person feels that family obligations are at odds with the expectations of the firm, role conflict ensues. Given the nature of the sales job, it is unlikely that such conflicts can ever be completely eliminated. However, many organizations are becoming aware of the emotional stress stemming from these conflicts and try to prepare sales people for them. Some companies even conduct training for spouses or partners so they will better understand the demands of the sales job.

Distinctive Features of Sales Jobs

Sales jobs have a number of features that distinguish them from most other business positions:

- Sales people represent their organizations to the outside world. Consequently, attitudes about a company and its products often are based on the impressions left by sales people. The public seldom judges a firm by the appearance of its office or the behaviour of its production employees.
- Sales people typically operate with little or no direct supervision. Therefore, to be successful, sales people must be creative and persistent, and show great initiative—all of which requires a high degree of motivation.
- Sales people are authorized to spend company funds. To do their jobs, sales people spend money for transportation, food, housing, entertain-

ment, and other expenses. Spending too little can be as counterproductive as spending too much. The secret is to spend profitably.

- Sales people frequently must travel a considerable amount. Many companies have successfully reduced the number of nights sales people must be away from home by redesigning sales territories, better routing their trips, and relying more on telemarketing. However, the fact remains that most sales jobs do require travel.
- Sales people often have profit responsibility. Today's sales people may do much of the strategic planning for their individual territories. In cooperation with sales managers, they decide what target markets they will pursue, how they will deal with each market segment as well as with each individual customer, and which products they will emphasize.

Wide Variety of Sales Jobs

No two selling jobs are alike. Even when grouped on some basis, the types of jobs and the skills needed to fill them cover a wide spectrum. Consider, for example, the job of a sales person for a Pepsi-Cola bottler who calls routinely on a group of retail stores. That job is totally different from the role of an IBM computer sales person, an Avon representative selling cosmetics door to door, or a London Life agent selling health and disability insurance to business firms.

A way to understand the broad array of sales jobs is to think of selling as ranging from *order filling* to *order getting* positions. The following are examples of positions along such a continuum:

- Positions in which the job is primarily to deliver a product—for example, a **driver–sales person** for soft drinks, dairy products, bakery items, or fuel oil. Many of these jobs involve merchandising tasks such as arranging displays and setting up point-of-purchase material. Selling responsibilities are secondary to seeing that orders are filled correctly and on time.
- Positions in which the sales person is primarily an **inside order taker**—for example, a retail clerk behind a counter at Sears or a telephone representative at a catalogue retailer such as a Mark's Work Wearhouse special unit or Consumers Distributing. Most customers have already decided to buy and the sales person's job is to serve them efficiently. Some selling may be done through suggestions, but ordinarily the sales person cannot do much more.
- Positions in which sales people are mainly **outside order takers**, going to customers in the field—for example, Procter & Gamble sales reps who call on retail stores or radio advertising sales people who sell time on their stations to local businesses. The majority of sales are of established products to repeat customers, though these sales people do introduce new products to customers and make presentations to prospects.
- Positions in which the sales people are not expected to solicit orders. Rather, their job is to influence decision makers by building goodwill, performing promotional activities, and providing service to customers. These are called **missionary sales people** in food products companies and **detail sales people** in pharmaceutical firms.
- Positions in which the major emphasis is on the sales person's ability to explain the product to a prospect as well as possibly adapt it to the customer's particular needs. A **sales engineer** is an example of this type of technically trained individual who usually sells some kind of sophisticated equipment.

MARKETING AT WORK

FILE 18-1   **THE TELEMARKETING CUSTOMER CONTACT**

The job of outside selling — the kind where the sales person goes to the customer, in contrast to inside (or across-the-counter) selling — is changing dramatically these days. Instead of the traditional in-person sales call, a growing number of sales reps are using the telephone and/or the computer to talk with customers. In effect, outside selling—especially outside *industrial* selling—is going electronic.

The prime factor accounting for this change is the dramatic increase in the cost of keeping sales people on the road. Some companies estimate that their travel expenses—transportation, hotel, and meals—are higher than their sales reps' compensation (salary, commission, and bonus).

Telephone selling, of course, has been used by many companies for decades. What is new today, however, is the innovative use of communications systems involving the telephone, television, and sometimes the computer to aid a company's selling effort and other marketing activities. The term **telemarketing** has been coined to describe these marketing communication systems.

Some companies have increased sales and reduced costs by taking their field sales people away from their travelling jobs and bringing them into the office. There these reps have been trained to sell by telephone. In effect, personal selling and order taking are being moved from the field to a well-trained inside sales force. The field selling in these firms is shifting to sales promotion work such as instructing customers or providing technical advice and service.

Some companies have turned the telemarketing function around and initiate the customer contact through television or other forms of advertising, relying on the telephone to receive orders. Many direct marketing companies now sell through advertising, rather than through sales people, promoting everything from records to exercise equipment to self-sharpening knives. Interested customers telephone a toll-free 1-800 number, where "operators are standing by" to accept VISA and MasterCard numbers. The purchase price (plus cost of shipping) is charged to the customer's account and the merchandise is mailed.

In some cases, the telemarketing system is tied in to a sophisticated computer system that is able to determine inventory status and shipping dates. All of these examples will save millions of dollars in personal selling and other communications expenses.

- Positions that require **creative selling** of either goods or services. Often customers are not aware of their need for the product, or they may not realize how the product can satisfy their wants better than the product they are using. Creative selling often means designing a system to fit the needs of the particular customer and may require the expertise of several people who make up a sales team. Examples are construction by Alberta Government Telephone of a communications system for a hospital and development of a vertical lift system by Otis Elevator for a new office complex.

An organization may employ several different types of sales people. For instance, IBM has sales people who fit into all categories except driver–sales person.

THE PERSONAL SELLING PROCESS

The personal selling process is a logical sequence of four steps that a sales person takes in dealing with a prospective customer. The process applies equally well to any face-to-face attempt at persuasion. So whether the objective is to sell a product to a consumer, gain a retailer's participation in a sales promotion program, or convince someone of the correctness of a cause, these four steps, diagrammed in Fig. 18-1, should be followed.

FIGURE 18-1
The personal selling process.

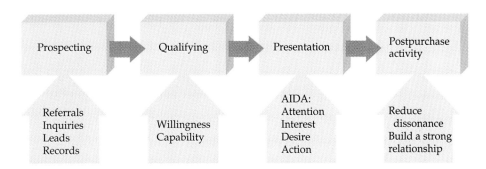

Prospecting → Qualifying → Presentation → Postpurchase activity

Referrals
Inquiries
Leads
Records

Willingness
Capability

AIDA:
Attention
Interest
Desire
Action

Reduce dissonance
Build a strong relationship

Prospecting for Potential Buyers

The first task of the seller is to identify prospects. If the organization has a well-designed marketing strategy, the segment(s) with the greatest potential have been identified. The sales person must take this general description (based on such descriptors as demographics, attitudes, and past purchasing behaviour) and then identify specific individuals or firms that may be prospects. For example, prospects may be found in trade-association and industry directories; among people who have mailed in inquiry cards or called a 1-800 number featured in an advertisement; and among existing customers, suppliers, and social or professional contacts. Frequently, a little thought will suggest logical prospects. For instance, sellers of home or office furnishings and telephone equipment find prospects in regularly published lists of building permits issued. Insurance, real estate, and diaper service sellers find leads in engagement, marriage, and birth announcements in newspapers.

Qualifying the Prospect

A sales person must determine whether the prospect is qualified to buy. Qualifications include both a reasonable *willingness* to buy and the *capability* to buy. To qualify the prospect, the sales person must gather information from a wide variety of sources. To detemine willingness to buy, information about a business prospect's customers, competitors, and suppliers is important. If the prospect has a special relationship with an existing supplier, for instance, there may be little possibility of getting the business, so the sales person's time would be better spent elsewhere. Also, the sales person must objectively compare the prospect's needs with the product's features. Sometimes, in their enthusiasm, sales people are unrealistic about how well a product fits a customer's situation.

The capability of a prospect to buy includes an evaluation of both short-term and long-term profit potential. The sales person, often with the aid of others in the organization, must determine whether the prospect has sufficient immediate demand for the offering to justify the selling and order-processing costs and is a reasonable credit risk. An assessment also must be made of long-term potential in deciding how much time and effort to devote to cultivating the prospect. Is the prospect's business likely to grow? Is the prospect a candidate for other products in the line?

Presenting the Sales Message

Before preparing a presentation, sales people need to learn all they can about the individual or company to which they hope to sell. Past purchasing behaviour, product preferences, and special needs are all very pertinent details. If the prospect is an organization, the sales person should discover how purchase decisions are made and who in the organization makes them. (Recall the discussion in Chapter 6 on purchase decision roles.) Knowing who is the information gatekeeper, who is likely to influence the choice of suppliers, and who ultimately will make the purchase decision allows the sales person to target the right people.

With this background information a sales person can design a presentation that will attract the prospect's *attention*. The sales person will then try to hold the prospect's *interest* while building a *desire* for the product. When the time is right, the sales person will attempt to stimulate *action* by closing the sale. This approach, called **AIDA** (an acronym formed by the first letters of *attention, interest, desire,* and *action*), is commonly used by many organizations. Each step is described next.

ATTRACT ATTENTION

The initial objective is to generate curiosity. In some cases, for example when the prospect is already aware of the need and is seeking a solution, simply mentioning the sales person's company or product will be enough. However, more creativity is often required. If the sales person was referred to the prospect by a third party, the best approach might be to begin by mentioning this common acquaintance. An alternative is to begin with a startling statement that emphasizes the product's benefits. For instance, it would be difficult to ignore the question, "Would you give me five minutes to explain how I can cut your selling costs in half while doubling your sales volume?" Another method of gaining attention, particularly when the product has an unusual or novel aspect, is simply to place it in the prospect's hand. Obviously there is no limit to the variety of presentation openers. The key is remembering that attention is very valuable and can be granted only by the prospect. Therefore, the sales person must be sensitive to both the prospect's personality and circumstances in opening a presentation.

HOLD INTEREST AND AROUSE DESIRE

After attracting the prospect's attention, the sales person can hold this interest and stimulate a desire for the product by means of the presentation itself. There is no standard pattern to follow. A number of presentation methods, each suitable for particular situations, are described in texts on selling.

Many companies insist that their sales people memorize the presentation to ensure that all key points are covered in a particular order. The problem with these "canned" presentations is that they do not permit the sales person to adapt to the customer's needs or desires. Whatever sales presentation approach is followed, the sales person must always concentrate on showing how the product will benefit the prospect.

MEET OBJECTIONS AND CLOSE THE SALE

Closing means obtaining agreement to buy. It is the action step. Clearly this is the objective of the personal selling effort. On the average, it takes four personal sales calls to close a business-to-business sale. At a cost of, say, $240 per call, the average cost of a sale is $960.[3] Thus, sellers are interested in closing sales as quickly as possible.

As part of the presentation, the sales person may periodically venture a **trial close** to measure the prospect's willingness to commit. By posing some ''either-or'' questions, to which both answers will result in a sale, the sales person can move the presentation towards closure. That is, the sales person might ask, ''Would you prefer the red or the blue model?'' or ''Would you like to charge this or pay cash?''

The sales person must uncover and resolve any objections before a sale is possible. Of course, the toughest objections to answer are those that are unspoken. The trial close is useful because it frequently brings out such objections. Then the sales person has the opportunity to point out additional product features and reemphasize previously stated benefits.

As the prospect gets closer to a decision, the sales person can often finalize the sale with the **assumptive close**. In this technique the sales person assumes the prospect is going to buy and begins asking questions that will settle the details of the purchase. For example, questions like ''When would you want this delivered?'' and ''Would one truckload be enough to get started?'' indicate that the process has progressed beyond the decision to buy.

Servicing Customers after the Sale

An effective selling job does not end when the order is written up. The final stage of the selling process is a series of postpurchase services that can build customer goodwill and lay the groundwork for future business. The alert sales person will follow up sales to ensure that no problems occur in delivery, financing, installation, routine maintenance, employee training, billing, and other areas important to customer satisfaction. Note this is not obtaining a sale, it is ensuring that a strong valuable relationship exists so that future sales ''come naturally.''

STRATEGIC SALES-FORCE MANAGEMENT

The management tasks of planning, implementing, and evaluating must be applied to the sales force. Sales executives begin by setting sales goals and planning sales-force activities. This involves forecasting sales, preparing sales budgets, establishing sales territories, and setting sales quotas.

When a plan is established, a sales force must be organized to carry it out. This means selecting, training, and supervising the people who will do the actual selling. The final element—performance evaluation—includes assessing the performance of individual sales people and providing compensation.

Effective sales-force management starts with a qualified sales manager. Finding the right person for this job is not easy. In many organizations, the common practice when a sales management position becomes available is to reward the most productive sales person with a promotion. The assumption is that as a manager, an effective sales person will be able to impart the necessary wisdom to make others equally successful. However, as the following statements suggest, the qualities that lead to effective sales management are often diametrically opposed to the attributes of a successful person.[4]

---

[3]''How Many Personal Sales Calls Does It Take to Close a Sale?'' Carr Report No. 542.5A, Cahners Publishing Co., July 1989.

[4]Adapted from Jack Falvey, ''The Making of a Manager,'' *Sales & Marketing Management*, March 1989, pp. 42–47, 83.

MARKETING AT WORK

FILE 18-2   **THE BIG GAINS ARE IN FOLLOWING UP**

Some companies fall down on the job of closing sales by not following up on sales leads. They may spend thousands of dollars generating enquiries from coupons in advertisements, from trade shows, sales calls, telephone calls, direct mail or other sources. In these days when a sales call may cost $240, it is reasonable to expect a company to put a system in place to ensure that sales leads are followed up quickly and efficiently.

A study completed for the Center for Marketing Communications revealed the following startling statistics:

- of all requests for information, 18 percent of those inquiring received no material at all;
- in the case of 43 percent of inquiries, the material was received too late to be of any use;
- a total of 59 percent of those who had received material said they considered some of the material useless and threw it away;
- only 28 percent were ever contacted by a sales person;
- of those who specifically requested a sales person to call, only 25 percent were contacted.

The people who respond to advertising by sending in coupons or calling to request information are interested in buying. In fact, the study showed that 40 percent of those leads resulted in the sale of a product—either the company's or a competitor's. To not respond is to ignore an excellent opportunity to close a sale—often to a customer who is already pre-sold.

Source: Adapted from Michael E. Liepner, ''Turning Lead into Gold,'' *Business to Business Marketing*, September 22, 1986, p. B 22.

- A sales person must be self-driven in order to achieve results. A sales manager must be careful not to drive people to achieve results.
- A sales person must be impatient. A sales manager must let situations develop and ripen.
- A sales person requires constant recognition for results. A sales manager must learn to give recognition and accept a secondary role.
- A sales person must ''make the numbers'' in the short run. A sales manager must take a longer-term view of business growth and personnel development.
- A sales person must be self-reliant. A sales manager must rely almost completely on others.
- A sales person is a doer. A sales manager is an organizer.
- A sales person builds account loyalty. A sales manager builds company loyalty.
- A sales person must be tenacious, confident that with enough time and effort any prospect can be sold. A sales manager must learn to cut losses quickly and move resources to more productive opportunities.
- A sales person has considerable freedom as long as results are forthcoming.

What similarities and differences between the jobs of sales people and sales managers does this sales meeting suggest?

A sales manager must conform to policies and procedures and play by the rules.

Success in sales management typically requires a blend of sales experience, knowledge of the selling process, and management skill. It might be wise to identify individuals with management potential and groom them with sales training rather than selecting sales people for management positions in the hope they will develop the necessary management ability.

OPERATING A SALES FORCE

We will focus here on the areas of sales-force operation that take up the bulk of sales executives' time. These tasks, outlined in Fig. 18-2, are recruitment and selection, training, supervision, performance evaluation, and compensation. Sales forecasting is discussed in Chapter 5. The topics of sales budgeting, territory design, and quotas are too specialized for treatment in this text.

Recruiting and Selecting the Sales Force

Staffing is the most important activity in the management process in any organization. This is true whether the organization is a business, an athletic team, or a college faculty. Consequently, the key to success in managing a sales force is selecting the right people. No matter what the calibre of sales management, if a sales force is distinctly inferior to that of a competitor, the competitor will win.

The three steps in sales force recruitment and selection are:

1. Determine the number and type of people wanted by preparing a written job description.
2. Recruit an adequate number of applicants.
3. Select the most qualified persons from among the applicants.

The turnover rate in sales personnel averages about 20 percent across all industries, with a high in auto and truck sales of 87 percent and a low in paper

FIGURE 18-2
Operating a sales force.

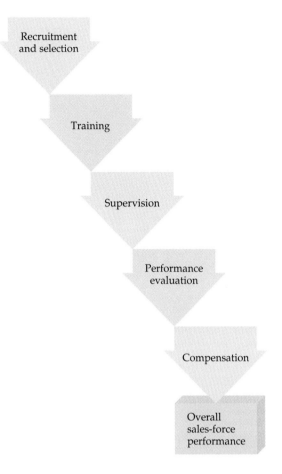

and allied products of 5.6 percent.[5] That means that on the average, one in five sales people leave their jobs every year. Weaknesses in recruitment and selection are major contributors to this high rate.

WHAT MAKES A GOOD SALES PERSON?

An organization must begin the recruitment process by determining what qualifications are needed to fill the job. Many sales managers have developed general guidelines through experience for identifying potentially successful sales people. Among the common attributes sought in prospects are a high energy level, self-confidence, competitiveness, and personal sensitivity.

Researchers have also attempted to identify generalizable traits of successful sales people. However, their efforts have not met with much success. In a review of 400 studies of relationships between personal characteristics and sales performance, six sets of variables were investigated:

- Demographic and physical attributes.
- Background and experience.
- Current marital and financial status and life-style.
- Intellectual aptitude and cognitive ability.

[5]"1989 Survey of Selling Costs," *Sales & Marketing Management*, Feb. 20, 1989, p. 22.

MARKETING AT WORK

FILE 18-3   AUTOMATING THE SALES FORCE FOR THE NINETIES

Sales executives today are faced with a decision that has the potential of changing how the sales job is performed—whether to automate sales forces. With automation, sales people are provided with desktop or laptop computers. Firms that have automated their sales forces report the following benefits:

- *Increased information accessibility.* Some insurance agents can directly access the company's mainframe computer to compare coverage options or get immediate answers about the effect of changing a customer's policy.
- *Customized customer information.* With personal computers many reps track customer buying habits, sales performance, and inventories more efficiently.
- *Reduced paperwork.* Sales people at Owens-Corning Fiberglas are able to electronically input and access data. Before automation, each sales person received 20 pounds of reports a month.
- *Improved internal communications.* Details of new sales promotions at Black & Decker are put on the computer and are available to sales people as soon as they log on to their portable machines.
- *Strengthened sales presentations.* A Du Pont sales person, challenged by a new competitive product, can tap into a data base to see how fellow sales people in other territories have countered it.
- *Increased selling time.* IBM has found that laptops save sales people 4.4 hours per week by allowing them to avoid such tasks as travelling to a branch office to get answers to customers' questions.

What are the drawbacks of automation? Among those noted are:

- *Cost.* The necessary hardware, software, training, and support cost about $7,500 per sales person. Then there are additional costs for upgrading each year.
- *Difficulty in measuring contribution.* Though costs can be measured in dollars and cents, benefits such as time saved and improvements in information quantity and quality are harder to translate to the bottom line.
- *Sales-force resistance.* Some sale people don't want to change their behavior.

Source: Adapted, in part, from Thayer C. Taylor, "How the Best Sales Forces Use PCs and Laptops," *Sales & Marketing Management*, April 1988, pp. 64–74; Joe Ferreira and Michael E. Treacy, "How to Justify Computers for Your Sales Force," *Sales & Marketing Management*, December 1988, pp. 46–48. The growing popularity of sales-force automation is reflected in the December issues of *Sales & Marketing Management*, which include an annual directory of PC software.

- Personality traits.
- Interpersonal, presentation, and management skills.[6]

Though intuitively it would seem that these factors are related to sales performance, none proved to be consistently related across industries and sales

---

[6]Neil M. Ford, Orville C. Walker, Jr., Gilbert A. Churchill, Jr., and Steven W. Hartley, "Selecting Successful Salespeople: A Meta-Analysis of Biographical and Psychological Selection Criteria," in Michael J. Houston, *Review of Marketing*, American Marketing Association, Chicago, 1987, pp. 90–131.

M A R K E T I N G   A T   W O R K

FILE 18-4   **SOME SALES INCENTIVES ARE A PROBLEM**

Sales contests require that sales people produce a certain volume of sales during a specified period. In order to win contests and qualify for the incentives, some sales people will build up customers' inventories beyond what is necessary. The result is that sales are shifted from a future period into the contest period and the customers have higher inventory costs than are necessary (though they will use the products eventually). Assume you are a sales manager and you suspect one of your sales people is shifting sales to earn incentives. What would you do about it?

---

jobs. The apparent explanation is found in the wide variety that exists among sales jobs. The positions simply differ so much that the factors leading to success in one may be much less important in another.

The conclusion that can be drawn regarding sales person selection is that each organization must examine its own situation and determine what the particular sales job entails. This calls for a detailed job analysis and a written job description that includes specific job duties and appropriate qualifications.

RECRUITING APPLICANTS

A planned system for recruiting a sufficient number of applicants is the next step in selection. A good recruiting system:

- Operates continuously, not only when there are vacancies on the sales force.
- Is systematic in reaching and exploiting all appropriate sources of applicants.
- Provides a flow of qualified applicants in numbers greater than the company's needs.

To identify recruits, large organizations often use placement services on college campuses or professional employment agencies. Smaller firms needing fewer new sales people may place classified advertisements in trade publications and daily newspapers and solicit recommendations of existing employees as well as referrals from customers, suppliers, or other business contacts.

MATCHING APPLICANTS WITH HIRING SPECIFICATIONS

Sales managers use a variety of techniques to determine which applicants possess the desired qualifications, including application forms, interviews, references, credit reports, psychological tests, aptitude tests, and physical examinations. Virtually all companies ask candidates to fill out application forms. In addition to providing basic screening information, the application indicates areas that should be explored in an interview.

No sales person should be hired without at least one personal interview. And it is usually desirable to have several interviews conducted by different people in different physical settings. Pooling the opinions of a number of people increases the likelihood of discovering any undesirable characteristics

M A R K E T I N G   A T   W O R K

FILE 18-5   RECRUITING SALES PEOPLE OVERSEAS—THE CHALLENGE

Corporations engaged in global marketing often encounter shortages of qualified sales personnel abroad. To complicate matters, cultural, educational, ethnic, and religious differences make the use of standardized hiring criteria risky. As the following cross-national comparisons suggest, multinational companies need to be sensitive to these differences when selecting sales people for foreign markets:

- In Canada, 25 percent of 18- to 21-year-olds go to college, and many study career-oriented professional subjects. In Europe there is a greater emphasis on the liberal arts and sciences, and higher education is restricted to a smaller percentage of the population. The number of educated people in developing countries is still quite small.
- Even with its various ethnic subcultures, the United States is relatively homogeneous compared to Canada, which is 25 percent French-speaking. Other countries—such as Zaire with 250 dialects and India with over 300 dialects—seem to have more ethnic differences than similarities.
- Religious friction in Canada is mild compared to other countries. Protestantism, the dominant religion, exerts little daily influence on the lives of its followers. Religions such as Hinduism, Buddhism, and Islam have a much greater influence on their adherents' behaviour. Conflicts between Sunni and Shiite groups in the Middle East, Muslims and Hindus in India, and Muslims and Buddhists in Malaysia testify to the strong role that religion plays in many people's lives.
- Social class, which for the most part is based on economic considerations in North America, has very different bases in other countries. Heredity, ethnic background, and age help determine social class in various cultures.

An examination of how these differences affect selection of sales personnel by multinationals in overseas locations showed that:

- Selection criteria, though generally the same as those used at home, are weighted differently overseas.
- Social class, religion, and ethnic background influence as many as a quarter of the selection decisions sales departments make abroad.
- Social class, religious, and ethnic criteria are applied in both developed and developing countries.

Source: Adapted, in part, from John S. Hill and Meg Birdseye, ''Salesperson Selection in Multinational Corporations: An Empirical Study,'' *Journal of Personal Selling & Sales Management*, Summer 1989, pp. 39–47.

and reduces the effects of one interviewer's possible bias. An interview helps an employer to determine (1) the applicant's degree of interest in the job, (2) the match between the requirements of the job and the applicant's skills, and (3) the applicant's motivation to work hard. Interviews can be **unstructured** or **patterned**. For relatively inexperienced interviewers, the patterned interview is usually preferable because the questions are planned in advance to make sure that all important issues are covered.

To recruit applicants, Century 21 uses a coordinated program of mass media advertising and personal presentations.

Testing for intelligence, attributes, or personality is somewhat controversial. Some companies avoid testing for fear that they will be accused of discrimination. However, employment tests are legitimate selection tools as long as they can be validated. A **valid test** is one that accurately predicts job performance.

Sales Force Training

Sales training is a major expense for many organizations. According to figures developed by Dartnell Corporation, initial training costs range from $11,600 per sales person at consumer products firms to $22,200 for an industrial-products sales person, and the training period lasts from five to eight months.[7] These figures may seem high, but keep in mind that, in addition to the direct costs of training (training personnel, supplies, facilities), a firm pays the trainee a salary during this period.

Newly hired sales people know very little about the details of the job, their fellow workers, and their status in the firm. Thus the first training task is indoctrination and guidance to assimilate the person into the organization.

Designing a training program involves answering the following questions:

- What are the goals of the program? In very general terms, the aim of the program is to increase productivity and stimulate the sales force. In addition, executives must determine what specific ends they want to reach. For instance, the goal may be to increase sales of high-profit items or to improve prospecting methods for generating new accounts.

---

[7]"1989 Survey of Selling Costs," *Sales & Marketing Management*, Feb. 20, 1989, p. 23.

- Who should do the training? The training program may be conducted by line sales executives, by a company training department, by outside training specialists, or by some combination of the three.
- What should be the content of the program? A well-rounded sales training program should cover three general topics: product knowledge, company policies, and selling techniques.
- When and where should training be done? Some companies believe in training new people before they go into the field. Others let new people prove that they have the desire and ability to sell first and then bring them back into the office for intensive training. Firms may employ either centralized or decentralized training programs. A centralized program, usually at the home office, may take the form of a periodic meeting attended by all sales people. A decentralized program may be held in branch offices or during on-the-job training. Decentralized programs typically cost less than centralized programs; however, the quality of instruction is often inferior.
- What instructional methods should be used? The lecture method may be employed to inform trainees about company history and practices. Demonstrations may be used to impart product knowledge or selling techniques. Role playing is an excellent device for training a person in proper selling techniques. On-the-job training may be used in almost any phase of the program.

After becoming familiar with the new work environment, sales people — both new and experienced — need regular training to enhance and refine their selling skills, to learn about new products, and to improve their time and territory management practices. The frequency and duration of refresher training depends on the company and the situation. However, most organizations recognize that learning and improving are a continuous, career-long process.

Supervising the Sales Force

Supervision of a sales force is difficult but essential. It is difficult because sales people often work independently where they cannot be continually observed.

Training is often a combination of motivation and instruction.

And yet supervision serves both as a means of continuing training and as a device to ensure that company policies are being carried out. Another value of supervision is that it creates a two-way communications channel between management and the sales force.

An issue that management must resolve is how close supervision should be. If it is too close, it will create role conflict for the sales person. One of the attractions of selling is the freedom it affords sales people to develop creative solutions to customers' problems. However, close supervision will stifle that sense of independence. Sales people will have difficulty seeing themselves as problem solvers if supervisors are constantly checking up on them. Conversely, too little supervision will contribute to role ambiguity. Sales people who are not closely supervised lack an understanding of the expectations of their supervisors and companies. They may not know, for example, how much time should be spent servicing existing accounts and how much developing new business. If they do something wrong, it may not be brought to their attention until after it has become a serious problem. As a result, they may become tentative and avoid risks.

The most effective supervisory method is personal observation in the field. Typically, at least half of a sales manager's time is spent travelling with sales people. Other supervisory tools are reports, correspondence, and sales meetings.

Evaluating Performance

Managing a sales force includes evaluating the efforts of the sales people. Sales executives must know what the sales force is doing to be in a position to reward them or to make constructive proposals for improvement. By establishing performance standards and studying sales people's activities, management can develop new training programs for upgrading the sales force's efforts. And, of course, performance evaluation should be the basis for salary decisions and other rewards.

Performance evaluation can also help sales people identify opportunities for improving their efforts. Employees with poor sales records know they are doing something wrong. However, they may not know what the problem is if they lack objective standards by which to measure their performance.

Both quantitative and qualitative factors should serve as bases for performance evaluation. **Quantitative bases** generally have the advantage of being specific and objective. **Qualitative factors**, although often reflecting broader dimensions of behaviour, are limited by the subjective judgement of the evaluators. For management, the challenges are selecting measures and setting standards against which the performance measures can be compared.

Sales performance should be evaluated in terms of both **inputs** (or effort) and **outputs** (or results). Together, inputs such as call rate and customer service activity and outputs such as sales volume and gross margin provide a measure of a person's selling effectiveness.

Some *output* measures that are also *quantitative* evaluation criteria are:

- Sales volume by product, customer group, and territory.
- Sales volume as a percentage of quota or territory potential.
- Gross margin by product line, customer group, and territory.
- Orders — number and average dollar amount.
- Closing date — number of orders divided by number of calls.
- Accounts — percentage of existing accounts sold and number of new accounts opened.

Useful *quantitative input* measures include:

- Call rate—number of calls per day or week.
- Direct selling expenses—total dollars or as a percentage of sales.
- Nonselling activities — promotion displays set up, training sessions held with distributors or dealers.

The importance of output factors in a performance evaluation is readily recognized. Sometimes, however, the value of input factors is underestimated. Actually an analysis of input measures helps to pinpoint trouble spots. If a person's output performance is unsatisfactory, very often the cause lies in the handling of the various input factors over which the sales person has control.

One key to a successful evaluation program is appraisal of the sales person's performance on as many different bases as possible. Otherwise management may be misled. A high daily call rate may look good, but it tells us nothing about how many orders per call are being written up. A high closing rate (orders divided by calls) may be camouflaging a low average order size or a high sales volume on low-profit items.

Performance evaluation would be much easier if it could be based only on quantitative criteria. It would minimize the subjectivity and personal bias of the evaluators. However, many *qualitative* factors must be considered because they influence a sales person's performance and help in the interpretation of quantitative data. Some of these factors are:

- Knowledge of products, company policies, and competitors.
- Time management and preparation for sales calls.
- Strength and quality of customer relationships.
- Personal appearance.
- Personality and attitude—cooperation, creativity, resourcefulness.

Compensating Sales People

To compensate their sales forces, companies offer both financial and nonfinancial rewards. *Nonfinancial rewards* include opportunities for advancement, recognition of efforts, and a feeling of belonging. *Financial rewards* may take the form of *direct* monetary payment or *indirect* monetary payment (paid vacations, pensions, and insurance plans).

Establishing a compensation system entails decisions concerning the *level* of compensation as well as the *method* of compensation. The level refers to the total dollar income that a sales person earns over a period of time. Level is influenced by the type of person required and the competitive rate of pay for similar positions. The method is the system or plan by which the sales person will reach the intended level.

There are three widely used methods of compensating a sales force: straight salary, straight commission, and a combination plan. Today well over half the firms in the country use some kind of combination plan.

The **straight-salary plan** offers maximum security and stability of earnings for a sales person. Management can expect sales people to perform any reasonable work assignment because they receive the same pay regardless of the task performed. Under a straight salary, sales reps can consider the customers' best interests and are less likely to use high-pressure selling tactics.

A drawback of straight-salary compensation is that it does not offer adequate incentive. Thus management has the added burden of motivating and directing sales people. The pay plan itself does not provide any appreciable direction or control. Also, under this plan compensation is a fixed cost unrelated to sales revenue. Straight-salary plans typically are used:

- For new sales people or missionary sales people.
- When opening new territories.
- When sales involve a technical product and a lengthy period of negotiation.

A **straight commission** has just the opposite merits and limitations. It provides tremendous incentive for sales people, and commission costs can be related directly to sales or gross margin. Sales representatives have more freedom in their work, and their level of income is determined largely by their own efforts. On the other hand, it is difficult to control sales people and get them to perform tasks for which no commission is paid. There is always the danger that they will oversell customers or otherwise incur customer ill will. Straight-commission plans may work well if:

- Great incentive is needed to get the sales.
- Very little nonselling missionary work is required.
- The company is financially weak and must relate its compensation expenses directly to sales or gross margin.
- The company is unable to supervise its sales force.

The ideal **combination salary plan** has the best features of both the straight-salary and straight-commission plans, with as few of their drawbacks as possible. To come close to this ideal, the combination plan must be tailored to the particular firm, product, market, and type of selling.

Which organizations are the best at performing all of these sales management tasks? That is a difficult question. However, the results of a survey of sales managers suggest that some companies have particularly noteworthy sales forces.

SUMMARY   Personal selling is the main promotional method used in Canadian business — whether measured by number of people employed, by total expenditures, or by expenses as a percentage of sales. Sales differs from other jobs because sales people represent the organization to the outside world, operate without close supervision, are authorized to spend company funds, and frequently travel. The great variety of sales jobs can be viewed as a continuum from order filling to order getting. Examples along the continuum range from driver–sales person through jobs like inside order taker, outside order taker, missionary seller, sales engineer, and creative seller.

There are four steps in the sale of a product. The first is prospecting, or identifying potential customers. In the second step, prospects are qualified to determine their willingness and capability to buy. Next the qualified prospects are presented with the sales message. Messages are often designed using a framework called AIDA, which stands for creating Attention, generating Interest, stimulating Desire, and requesting Action. The final step consists of post-purchase activities intended to reduce anxieties and increase the likelihood of repeat purchases.

Sales force management involves planning, supervising, and evaluating a sales force within guidelines set by strategic marketing planning. Major sales force operations include recruitment and selection, training, supervision, performance evaluation, and compensation. Recruiting begins with a written job description to identify necessary qualifications. In the selection process, the most common tools are the job application and the interview. Sales training is an ongoing process that should conform to guidelines delineating goals, methods, content, instructors, and timing. Performance evaluation requires quantitative and qualitative measures of both inputs (effort) and outputs (results). Compensation consists of financial and nonfinancial rewards. The most common forms of financial rewards are straight salary, straight commission, and a combination of the two.

KEY TERMS AND CONCEPTS

Personal selling 574
Advantages of personal selling 574
Disadvantages of personal selling 574
Telemarketing 575
Territory manager 575
Role ambiguity 576
Role conflict 576
Driver–sales person 577
Inside order taker 577
Outside order taker 577
Missionary sales person 577
Detail sales person 577
Sales engineer 577
Creative selling 578
Prospecting 579
Qualifying 579
AIDA 580
Meeting objections 580

Closing a sale 580
Trial close 581
Assumptive close 581
Postpurchase service 581
Patterned interview 581
Unstructured interview 587
Valid test 588
Quantitative performance bases 590
Qualitative performance bases 590
Input performance measures 590
Output performance measures 590
Nonfinancial rewards 591
Financial rewards 591
Straight-salary compensation 591
Straight-commission compensation 592
Combination salary plan 592

QUESTIONS AND PROBLEMS

1. The cost of a full-page, four-colour advertisement in one issue of a national magazine may be more than the cost of employing a sales person for a full year. A sales-force executive is urging her company to eliminate a few of these ads and, instead, to hire a few more sales people. This executive believes that one good sales person working for an entire year can sell more than one ad can. How would you respond?

2. "The often conflicting demands of a sales manager, an employer, customers, and family can create heavy emotional stress for a sales person." Explain.

3. Refer to the classification of sales jobs from driver–sales person to creative seller and answer the following questions:
   a. In which types of jobs are sales people most likely to be free from close supervision?
   b. Which types are likely to be the highest paid?
   c. Which are likely to involve the most overnight travelling?
   d. For which types of jobs is the highest degree of motivation necessary?

4. What are some sources you might use to acquire a list of prospects for the following products?
   a. Bank accounts for new area residents.
   b. Dental X-ray equipment.
   c. Laptop computers.
   d. Contributors to the United Way.
   e. Baby furniture and clothes.

5. If you were preparing a sales presentation for the following products, what information about a prospect would you seek as part of your preparation?
   a. Two-bedroom condominium.
   b. New automobile.
   c. Carpeting for a home redecorating project.

6. How should a sales person respond when a prospect says the price of a product is too high?

7. ''A good selection program is desirable, but not essential. Improper selection of sales people can be offset by a good training program, by good compensation, and by proper supervision.'' Discuss this statement.

8. What source should be used for recruiting sales applicants in each of the following firms? Explain your choice in each case.
   a. A Marriott hotel that wants companies to use the hotel for conventions.
   b. Avon or Mary Kay Cosmetics for sales directly to consumers.
   c. IBM, for sales of mainframe (large) computers.

9. ''It is best to hire experienced sales people because they don't require training.'' Discuss this statement.

10. How can a sales manager evaluate the performance of sales people in getting new business?

11. What factors should be considered in determining the level of sales-force compensation?

12. Compare the merits of straight-salary and straight-commission plans of sales compensation. What are two types of sales jobs in which each plan might be desirable?

13. How might a firm determine whether a sales person is using high-pressure selling tactics that might injure customer relations?

14. For a multinational corporation hiring a sales force in a developing country, what applicant characteristics should be added to its selection criteria?

This chapter examines nonpersonal promotional tools—advertising, sales promotion, public relations, and publicity. After studying this chapter, you should be able to explain:

- The nature of advertising and its importance in our economy and in individual firms.
- Characteristics of the major types of advertising.
- How to develop advertising campaigns and select advertising media.
- The nature and role of sales promotion.
- How to evaluate the effectiveness of advertising and sales promotion.
- The roles of public relations and publicity in the promotional mix.

Management of Advertising, Sales Promotion, Public Relations, and Publicity

The value of advertising is widely acknowledged and is reflected in its use in creating positive and distinctive images for brands and companies. One of the most important roles of advertising is to differentiate the company's products and brands from those of the competition, to position them in the minds of potential customers. To accomplish this goal, marketers make use of a number of advertising techniques and tools.

When the Everfresh Juice Company was launching its new line of sparkling mineral water with pure fruit juice, their objectives were to create a distinctive image for the new product and to position it as an alternative beverage for certain segments of the market. The company used three phases of qualitative research to work its way to a positioning strategy.

All three stages of the research involved one-on-one depth interviews, lasting one hour, with respondents who had been screened on the basis of their attitude towards health and life-style. All had made some recent minor change in their behaviour, such as switching from regular to decaffeinated coffee. The objectives of the research were: (1) to review attitudes towards and usage of all beverages; (2) to focus on juice and what it would take to make juice an alternative to soft drinks; and (3) to review various creative advertising concepts.

Everfresh used the results of these three research projects to build the concept of the new product from the ground up. They found that consumers really like juice, provided that it is pure, but that they tend to take juice for granted. To make it really distinctive and competitive as a "mainstream" beverage, juice would have to be carbonated. Consumers who were interviewed also reacted very positively to the straightforward description "pure fruit juice with sparkling mineral water."

With regard to positioning and creative concepts, the research indicated that traditional "healthy life-style" images had been used over such a wide range of product categories that they would not contribute to distinctive communication for Everfresh. The concept of a "sparkling juice" product tended to be associated by consumers with a more tranquil, passive life-style, as compared with the high-energy and sociability themes more relevant for soft drinks such as Coke and Pepsi. Many consumers viewed the idea of a healthy life-style in a broader context, which included getting control of their lives; many spoke of leading a more balanced life.

These research results led Everfresh to the conclusion that advertising for its sparkling juice product should build upon the company's image as a producer of pure, fresh juices and create a strong emotional link with contemporary attitudes to healthy, balanced life-styles. The benefits of the concept were considered self-evident. What was needed was a new kind of advertising that would depict Everfresh as a New Age beverage company with a very special emotional link with its target consumers, who are real people (not "health nuts") who enjoy real things and who are looking for substitutes for their regular beverages, from soft drinks to alcohol.

Mass communication is needed to reach mass markets at reasonable costs. Advertising, sales promotion, public relations, and publicity are the tools for this job. It is too costly and time-consuming to use only sales people in large, geographically diverse markets. However, whereas personal selling can be tailored to the individual prospect, mass communicators try to reach many people with a common message. And as the chapter-opening example illustrates, finding images that consumers can relate to is very valuable.

NATURE OF ADVERTISING

Advertising consists of all activities involved in presenting to a target audience a non-personal, sponsor-identified message about a product or organization. This message, called an **advertisement**, can be verbal and/or visual, and is disseminated through one or more media. Two factors differentiate advertising from publicity. The public knows who is doing the advertising because the sponsor is openly identified. And payment is made by the sponsor to the medium that carries the message.

Types of Advertising

An organization's advertising objectives determine, to a great extent, what type of advertising should be used. Consequently, it is essential to understand the different classifications of advertising.

PRODUCT AND INSTITUTIONAL ADVERTISING

All advertising may be classified as product or institutional. In **product advertising**, advertisers inform or stimulate the market about their products. Product advertising is subdivided into direct-action and indirect-action advertising:

- **Direct-action advertising** seeks a quick response. For instance, a print ad with a coupon or a 1-800 telephone number may urge the reader to send or call immediately for a free sample or to place an order.
- **Indirect-action advertising** is designed to stimulate demand over a longer period of time. It is intended to inform or remind consumers that the product exists and to point out its benefits. Most television advertising is of this type.

Institutional advertising presents information about the advertiser's business or tries to create a good attitude—build goodwill—towards the organization. This type of advertising is not intended to sell a specific product. Two forms of institutional advertising are:

- **Customer service advertising**, which presents information about the advertiser's operations. Advertisements describing the variety of automobile repairs and services available at Petro-Canada stations are an example.
- **Public service advertising**, which is designed to improve the quality of life

Many manufacturers of alcoholic beverages are promoting responsible use of their products.

and show that the advertiser is a responsible member of the community. Such ads may urge the public to avoid drugs or to support a local antipollution campaign.

PRIMARY AND SELECTIVE DEMAND ADVERTISING

Primary demand advertising is designed to stimulate demand for a generic category of a product such as Colombian coffee, B.C. apples, or garments made from cotton. This is in contrast to **selective demand advertising**, intended to stimulate demand for individual brands such as Nabob Coffee, Sunkist oranges, and Club Monaco sportswear.

Primary demand advertising is used in either of two situations. The first is when the product is in the introductory stage of its life cycle. This is called **pioneering advertising**. A firm may run an ad about its new product, explaining the product's benefits, but not emphasizing the brand name. The objective of pioneering primary demand advertising is to inform, not to persuade, the target market. The buying decision process model explains why such ads are limited to information. Recall from our discussion in Chapter 6 that a consumer must first be made *aware* of a product before becoming *interested* in or *desiring* it. Combine this with the fact that only so much information can be communicated in a single ad, and it becomes clear that only one objective can be accomplished at a time. In recent years, pioneering demand ads have been run for cellular telephones and video camcorders.

The second use of primary demand advertising occurs throughout the product life cycle. It is usually done by trade associations trying to stimulate demand for their industry's product. Thus the Dairy Bureau of Canada's ads urge us

Canada Pork changes the image of pork to increase primary demand.

If you still think pork's too fat, you're living in the past.

Today's pork is 23% leaner. This delightful Pork and Apple Stir Fry has only 300 calories per serving.

PORK

Lighten your fork with pork.

to drink more milk. The bureau doesn't care what brand of milk and dairy products we buy, just that we use more of them. Similarly, the Pork Council encourages us to eat more pork.

Selective demand advertising essentially is competitive advertising—it pits one brand against another. This type of advertising typically is employed when a product has gone beyond the introductory life-cycle stage. The product is reasonably well known and in competition for market share with several brands. The objective of selective demand advertising is to increase the demand for a brand. To accomplish this goal, it emphasizes the particular benefits—the **differential advantages**—of the brand being advertised.

Comparative advertising is an important kind of selective demand advertising that is used for a wide variety of products. In comparative advertising, the advertiser either directly—by naming a rival brand—or indirectly—through inference—points out differences between the brands. We have all seen the comparative advertising for Coke and Pepsi, both of which show the competitor's brand. Red Rose tea responded to the introduction of Tetley's round teabag with advertisements featuring the Red Rose ''diamond'' teabag—comparing its product to Tetley by implication only. Sometimes comparative advertising becomes fairly nasty. In response to the launch of Procter & Gamble's Ultra Tide, Lever Brothers, maker of rival Sunlight detergent, advertised that P&G's new product, while meant to be more effective, had actually become more expensive. The president of Lever Brothers said that P&G had started the comparative advertising battle, by issuing their own advertising for Ultra Tide, comparing it to "the Number 2 brand" (Sunlight).[1]

The Bureau of Competition Policy of the federal Department of Consumer and Corporate Affairs has taken the position that truthful comparative advertising can be a pro-competitive force in the marketplace. In fact, the Bureau has periodically published guidelines for the consideration of advertisers.[2] The main point to be learned from the discussion of comparative advertising and its regulation is that a company planning to use the technique had better be very sure that what is being said in its advertising about the competition is completely accurate.

COOPERATIVE ADVERTISING

Cooperative advertising promotes products of two or more firms that share the cost of the advertising. There are two types — vertical and horizontal. **Vertical cooperative advertising** involves firms on different levels of distribution. For example, a manufacturer and a retailer share the cost of the retailer's advertising of that manufacturer's product. Frequently the manufacturer prepares the actual ad, leaving space for the retailer's name and location. Then the manufacturer and retailer share the media cost of placing the ad. Many retail ads in newspapers are cooperative ads. Cooperative ads are also common on radio but appear less frequently on TV.

Another type of vertical cooperative advertising uses an **advertising allowance**, or cash discount offered by a manufacturer to a retailer, to encourage the retailer to advertise or prominently display a product. The difference between cooperative advertising and allowances is the amount of control exerted by the manufacturer over how the money is actually spent.

These arrangements benefit retailers by providing them with extra funds for promotion. Manufacturers benefit from advertising at the local level. In addition, ad dollars go farther because rates for local media are typically lower for ads placed by local firms than for ads placed by national advertisers.

Horizontal cooperative advertising is undertaken by firms on the same level of distribution — such as a group of retailers — that share the costs of advertising. For example, all stores in a suburban shopping centre may run a joint newspaper ad. The principal benefit is that by pooling their funds, the firms can achieve much greater exposure than if they advertised individually.

Companies that normally would not have a close association often cooperate in joint promotions. More and more companies are realizing that they can stretch their promotion dollars, benefit from the reputation of noncompeting successful brands, and open new markets with joint promotional programs. Evian, the French spring water company, recently launched a special promotion with Kellogg's Special K breakfast cereal, the main focus of which was a sweepstakes with trips to the French Alps as grand prizes. By entering into the joint arrangement, Evian had two objectives in mind. The company wanted to increase sales in the short term but, more importantly, was interested in

---

[1] Bob Papoe, "Laundry Detergent Firms in Dustup Over Ad Claims," *The Toronto Star*, May 22, 1991, pp. F1, F4.

[2] See for example "Comparative Price Advertising," in *Misleading Advertising Bulletin*, Ottawa: Consumer and Corporate Affairs Canada, no. 3, 1987, April/June 1987, pp. 1–5.

Marlin Travel promotes itself and its preferred suppliers in this cooperative ad.

increasing brand awareness and spreading the message of proper hydration. By associating with Kellogg, Evian moved from being a ''niche'' brand to a major player in the competitive bottled water market.[3] In another joint promotion, Campbell's Soup and Shell gasoline collaborated on a self-liquidating cross-promotion which offered consumers free Campbell's soups mugs when they visited Shell stations in Ontario.[4]

Cost of Advertising

Advertising in one form or another is used by most marketers. The significance of advertising is indicated by the amount of money spent on it. In 1990, the gross expenditures on advertising in Canada totalled $10.86 billion, up from $7.3 billion just three years earlier. Table 19-1 shows the total expenditure by medium and the percentage of the total accounted for by each of the major advertising media. For many years, daily newspapers have been the most widely used medium, but the percentage of total expenditures accounted for by newspapers has been declining steadily from approximately 30 percent in the mid-1970s to 22.9 percent in 1990. In fact, the percentage of total advertising expenditures going to the traditional mass media — radio, television, newspapers, and magazines—has been declining steadily, as many advertisers have

---

[3]David Chilton, ''Evian, Kellogg's a Healthy Union,'' *Strategy*, July 29, 1991, p. 18.

[4]Ken Riddell, ''Campbell Sends Kids to Shell,'' *Marketing*, February 11, 1991, p. 2.

TABLE 19-1 **Advertising Expenditures in Canada, by medium**

	Dollars spent, 1990 in millions	1990* %	1985* %	1980 %
Radio	751	8.0	9.0	10.4
Television	1,456	15.6	16.6	16.2
Daily newspapers	2,233	22.9	23.9	27.2
Weekly newspapers	690	7.0	6.3	5.5
General magazines	252	2.6	3.4	4.4
Business/Farm press	176	1.8	2.5	3.8
Directories	1,109	11.3	7.8	5.9
Religious/School media	54	0.5	0.4	0.5
Catalogues/Direct mail	2,204	22.4	22.4	19.7
Outdoor	764	7.8	7.5	6.4

* Tables do not add to 100% because of rounding.

SOURCE: Stan Sutter, "Advertising Revenues Continue to Climb, MH Research Finds," *Marketing*, May 20, 1991, p. 1. (data provided by the Maclean Hunter Research Bureau)

been switching at least part of their advertising budgets to media such as direct mail, directories, and weekly papers, which can often do a better job of reaching targeted segments.[5]

ADVERTISING AS A PERCENTAGE OF SALES

When gauging the importance of advertising, we should measure expenditures against a benchmark rather than simply look at the total. Frequently, advertising expenses are expressed as a percentage of a company's sales. Table 19-2 shows the ten largest advertisers in Canada for 1990. Note how these large advertisers differ in the way they allocate their advertising expenditures across the major advertising media. It is important also to note that some of

TABLE 19-2 **Top 10 National Advertisers in Canada, with expenditures by medium, 1990**

	Total* (in $000s)	Television	Daily Newspapers	Magazines	Out-of-Home	Radio
1. The Thomson Group	75,777.2	15,906.8	54,521.1	2577.0	685.1	2087.3
2. General Motors of Canada	68,332.9	40,612.0	17,540.7	7392.7	2339.8	447.7
3. Government of Canada	67,313.8	27,552.1	19,292.0	5637.7	4589.2	10,242.8
4. Procter & Gamble	67,224.1	55,220.9	171.9	9044.1	454.4	2332.8
5. Sears Canada	63,937.6	17,154.8	39,084.1	2711.3	7.4	4979.9
6. Molson Breweries of Canada	52,664.5	37,584.9	3454.9	633.2	1984.0	9077.6
7. Paramount Communications	44,705.2	3630.3	39,157.9	419.7	702.2	795.2
8. Unilever	43,799.9	33,154.0	494.4	6007.1	1845.7	2298.7
9. Cineplex Odeon	42,865.2	1184.3	41,328.5	119.3	—	233.0
10. John Labatt Limited	40,849.5	24,550.1	2,549.5	1,318.1	2,477.0	9,954.7

*Figures have been rounded off.

SOURCE: Martin Mehr, "Thomson Overtakes Government as Top Advertiser," *Marketing*, April 8, 1991, pp. 1, 47.

[5]Marina Strauss, "Marketers Shift to Coupons, Contests," *Globe and Mail*, November 3, 1990, p. B3; and John Partridge, "Magazines Starved for Ads," *Globe and Mail*, May 18, 1991, p. B1.

the advertisers who spend a large amount of money on advertising each year actually devote a very small percentage of their total sales to advertising. Data collected by Statistics Canada indicate that the largest percentage of sales spent on advertising is by companies that manufacture health and beauty aids and soaps and cleaning products. In general, companies in the consumer products field spend a higher percentage of sales on advertising than do manufacturers of industrial products. In general, major companies spend an average of about 2 percent of total sales on advertising, with companies that manufacture consumer products spending approximately 3 percent on average.

ADVERTISING COST VERSUS PERSONAL SELLING COST

While we do not have accurate totals for the costs of personal selling, we do know they far surpass advertising expenditures. In manufacturing, only a few industries, such as drugs, toiletries, cleaning products, tobacco, and beverages, spend more on advertising than on personal selling. Advertising runs 1 to 3 percent of net sales in many firms, whereas the expenses of recruiting and operating a sales force are typically 8 to 15 percent of sales.

At the wholesale level, advertising costs are very low. Personal selling expenses, however, may run 10 to 15 times as high. Even among retailers in total — and this includes those with self-service operations — the cost of personal selling is substantially higher than that of advertising.

OBJECTIVES OF ADVERTISING

The fundamental purpose of advertising is to sell something—a good, service, idea, person, or place. This broad goal is reached by setting specific objectives that can be incorporated into individual advertising campaigns. Recall again our discussion of the buying decision process. Buyers go through a series of stages from unawareness to purchase in the process of making a decision. Thus the immediate objective of an ad may be to move target customers to the next stage in the hierarchy, say from awareness to interest. Note also that advertising seldom is the only promotional tool used by a firm. Rather, it is typically one part of a strategy that may also include personal selling, sales promotion, and other tools. Therefore, the objective of advertising may be to ''open doors'' for the sales force.

Specific advertising objectives will be determined by the firm's overall marketing strategy. Typical objectives are:

- *Support personal selling*. Advertising may be used to acquaint prospects with the seller's company and products, easing the way for the sales force.
- *Reach people inaccessible to the sales force*. Sales people may be unable to reach top executives or may be uncertain who in the company makes the buying decisions. A well-placed ad may attract the attention of these executives.
- *Improve dealer relations*. Wholesalers and retailers like to see a manufacturer support its products.
- *Enter a new geographic market or attract a new market segment*.
- *Introduce a new product*.
- *Expand the use of a product*. Advertising may be used to lengthen the season for a product (as has been done by Lipton for iced tea); increase the frequency of replacement (as was done for oil filters); or increase the variety of product uses (as was done for baking soda by Cow Brand).
- *Expand industry sales*.
- *Counteract substitution*.
- *Build goodwill for the company*.

M A R K E T I N G   A T   W O R K

FILE 19-1   **THE VIDEO INSTRUCTION BOOKLET**

The Braun Company, well-known multinational appliance manufacturer and marketer, often uses Canada as its test market—rather than the United States, as do many other firms — before moving product and advertising programs into its markets in 16 other countries. This makes Braun Canada Ltd. extremely active in high-priced, high-quality new product development (19 new products in 1991), launch, advertising program development, and spending.

Braun has developed an expresso coffee maker—the Expresso master—that produces cappuccino the way the French do. Its market research found that people who had expresso machines didn't use them because the written instructions were not useful or were unclear. The solution, provided by Braun's ad agency, Backer Spilvogel Bates Canada Ltd., is a 15-minute video that shows consumers how to make good expresso and cappuccino. Not only does the video help consumers make better use of the product and thus increase user satisfaction, but it also supports dealers and sales people to be effective with new products and new markets. Video instructions thus become an important part of the total advertising campaign and, in this instance, the Canadian video will be appearing in a number of Braun's international markets.

Source: Adapted from Marina Strauss, ''Braun Likes Smell of Expresso How-To Video,'' *Globe and Mail*, April 23, 1991, p. B4.

Johnson attempts to expand the use of its baby products by targeting other age categories.

HOW THOSE WHO'VE GOT IT
GET IT

Some girls overdo it. Others keep it natural with JOHNSON'S Baby Powder, Lotion and Moisturizing Body Mousse. They feel pure and soft on your skin, so you always smell fresh and look good.

The only ones, from day one.

DEVELOPING AN ADVERTISING CAMPAIGN

Once a company decides to advertise (based on the factors discussed in Chapter 17), management develops an advertising campaign. An **advertising campaign** has the same characteristics as a total promotional campaign — that is, coordination, a central theme, and a specific goal.

Initial Planning

An advertising campaign must be planned within the framework of the overall strategic marketing program and promotional campaign. When the advertising campaign is designed, presumably management has already made decisions in several areas. Promotional goals have been established and the role of advertising in the promotional campaign has been determined. Also, the central campaign theme that will stress the product's benefits in light of the market's buying motives and habits has been chosen. The total promotion budget has been set and allocated among specific promotional methods. With these tasks completed, management can move on to the selection of advertising media and the creation and production of individual ads.

Media Selection

Three levels of decision making enter into advertising media selection. First, the type of medium must be selected. Of the major media, will newspaper, television, radio, or magazines be used? What about the less prominent media of direct mail, billboards, specialty items, and yellow pages? Second, a particular category of the desired medium must be chosen. Television offers network and local; magazines include general-interest (*Maclean's, Time*) and special-interest categories (*Chatelaine, Canadian Business*); and there are national and local newspapers available. Finally, a specific vehicle must be chosen. An advertiser who decides first on radio and then on local stations must determine which stations to use in each city.

Factors to consider in making media decisions are:

OBJECTIVES OF THE AD

Media choice is influenced by the purpose of a particular ad and by the goals of an entire campaign. For example, if the campaign goal is to generate appointments for sales people, the company may rely on direct mail. If an advertiser wants to induce quick action, newspaper or radio may be the way to go.

AUDIENCE COVERAGE

The audience reached by the medium should fit the *geographic* distribution patterns of the product. Furthermore, the selected media should reach the desired *types of prospects* with a minimum of wasted coverage. Many media — even national and other large-market media — can be targeted at small, specialized market segments. For example, *Maclean's* magazine publishes regional editions with different ads in the Atlantic, Ontario, and the West.

REQUIREMENTS OF THE MESSAGE

The medium should fit the message. For example, food products, floor coverings, and apparel are best presented visually. If the advertiser can use a very brief message (the rule of thumb is six words or less), as is possible with reminder advertising, billboards may be a good choice.

TIME AND LOCATION OF THE BUYING DECISION

The medium should reach prospective customers near the time they make the buying decisions and the places where they make them. For this reason, outdoor advertising often does well for gasoline products. Many grocery store ads are placed in newspapers on Wednesdays or Thursdays in anticipation of heavy weekend buying.

MEDIA COST

The cost of advertising media should be considered in relation to the amount of money available and the reach or circulation of the media. For example, the expense of network television exceeds the available funds of many advertisers. To determine the relationship between the cost of the medium and the size of the audience, there is a standard measure provided to prospective advertisers by all media—*cost per thousand (CPM)* persons reached. Of course, it is essential to estimate what proportion of all persons reached are truly prospects for the advertiser's product.

Media Characteristics   When selecting media, management must consider their advertising characteristics. We have carefully chosen the term *characteristics* instead of advantages and disadvantages because a medium that works well for one product is not necessarily the best choice for another product. To illustrate, a characteristic of radio is that it makes its impressions through sound. For many products, this feature is an advantage. For products that benefit from colour photography, however, this characteristic of radio is a drawback.

NEWSPAPERS

As an advertising medium, newspapers are flexible and timely. They account for the largest portion of total advertising dollars spent in Canada. They can be used to cover a single city or a number of urban centres. With the development of computer technology and regional printing in the publishing industry, once-local newspapers may now be printed in regional centres for distribution across the country. The daily *Financial Post* and the *Globe and Mail*, for example, are headquartered in Toronto, but are printed regionally and are now true national daily papers.

While newspapers are becoming more attractive to the national advertiser, they remain the principal advertising vehicle for the local advertiser. Ads can be cancelled on a few days' notice or inserted on one day's notice. Newspapers can give an advertiser an intense coverage of a local market because almost everybody reads newspapers. The local feature also helps in that the ads can be adapted to local social and economic conditions. Circulation costs per prospect are low. On the other hand, the life of a newspaper advertisement is very short.

TELEVISION

Television is probably the most versatile of all media. It makes its appeal through both the eye and the ear; products can be demonstrated as well as explained. It offers considerable flexibility in the geographic market covered and the time of message presentation. By making part of its impression through the ear, television can take advantage of the personal, dramatic impact of the spoken word.

On the other hand, television is an extremely expensive medium. The message is not permanently recorded for the message receiver. Thus the prospect who is not reached the first time is lost forever, as far as a particular message is concerned. Television does not lend itself to long advertising copy, nor does it present pictures as clearly as magazines do. As with direct mail and radio, television advertisers must create their own audiences.

Cable is also changing television as an advertising medium. Canada is among the most heavily ''cabled'' nations in the world, with well over 80 percent of homes in many urban areas wired for cable. In this country, having cable television has given Canadians access to as many as 30 channels, many of which originate in the United States or carry specialized programming, including sports, movies, youth programs, arts and entertainment, and popular music videos. This increased access to television channels has resulted in a dramatic change in the nature and effect of television as an advertising medium.

In households with cable, television is now a much more focused medium, offering specialized television channels to people with particular interests. The sheer variety of channels has led to a situation described as fragmentation, where viewers regularly ''zap'' their way through the range of channels available, often when a commercial appears. This proliferation of channels through cable, coupled with the use of VCRs, remote control devices, and video games, has meant that the audience likely to be exposed to a television commercial is reduced, thereby limiting the effectiveness of television in reaching a mass market. As a result, some advertisers have begun to use shorter, more attention-getting commercials, or have moved some of their advertising budgets away from television to other media.

DIRECT MAIL

Direct mail is probably the most personal and selective of all the media. Because it reaches only the market that the advertiser wishes to contact, there is a minimum of waste circulation. Direct mail is not accompanied by articles or other editorial matter, however, unless the advertiser provides it. That is, most direct mail is pure advertising. As a result, a direct-mail ad creates its own circulation and attracts its own readers. The cost of direct mail per prospect reached is quite high compared with other media. But other media reach many people who are not real prospects and thus have higher waste-circulation costs. A severe limitation of direct mail is the difficulty of getting and maintaining good mailing lists. Direct-mail advertising also suffers from the stigma of being classed as ''junk mail.''

The effectiveness of direct mail has been increased in recent years through the application of technology to the process of identifying prospects to whom advertising materials are to be mailed. Highly specialized mailing lists can be purchased from mailing-list brokers. These lists can be expensive, but do offer the advertisers the ability to target precisely the group in which they are interested. Many companies have developed their own mailing lists through effective design of their internal information systems. By capturing sales data in an appropriate way, for example, a travel agency can produce a list of all the clients who made a business trip to Europe in the past year, or took a vacation in the southern United States, or made more than 15 business trips. These individuals then represent target segments for special-interest mailings. Wastage is dramatically reduced because the advertising reaches precisely those people who are most likely interested.

RADIO

Radio is enjoying a renaissance as an advertising and cultural medium and as a financial investment. When interest in television soared after World War II, radio audiences (especially for national network radio), declined so much that people were predicting radio's demise. But for the past ten years or so, this medium has been making a real comeback. Local radio (as contrasted with national networks) is especially strong. Radio accounts for almost 10 percent of all advertising revenues in Canada, attracting more than $600 million in sales annually.

As an advertising medium, radio's big advantage is its relatively low cost. You can reach almost everybody with radio. At the same time, with special-interest, targeted programming, certain radio stations can do a very effective job of reaching specific target market segments. In recent years, for example, a number of Canadian radio stations began to pay more attention to the growing segment of the population in the 30-to-50 age segment. By 1990, teens accounted for less than 10 percent of the Canadian population, down from 15 percent in 1970. On the other hand, the big bulge of aging baby boomers represented an increasingly lucrative target market, leading many stations to change from their teen-oriented top-20 hits format, which had been successful through the 1970s and early 1980s, to adopt a much mellower, "oldies" music format, featuring hits of the 1960s and early 1970s.

Although radio is one of the more targeted of the mass media and can deliver an audience at a fairly low CPM (cost per thousand), it does have its limitations. Firstly, it makes only an audio impression, so it is of limited value where a visual impact is needed. On the other hand, some advertisers who believe in the value of radio consider this to be one of radio's strong points, that it is able to stimulate the imagination of the listener. Radio also does not have a captive audience, in that many people listen to the radio for "background" entertainment while they are working around the house, driving in their cars, or doing homework! The exposure life of a radio commercial is quite short, resulting in a need to deliver multiple exposures to gain impact.[6]

MAGAZINES

Magazines are an excellent medium when high-quality printing and colour are desired in an ad. Magazines can reach a national market at a relatively low cost per reader. Through special-interest or regional editions of general-interest magazines, an advertiser can reach a selected audience with a minimum of waste circulation. Magazines are usually read in a leisurely fashion, in contrast to the haste in which other print media are read. This feature is especially valuable to the advertiser with a lengthy or complicated message. Magazines have a relatively long life, anywhere from a week to a month, and a high pass-along readership.

With less flexible production schedules than newspapers, magazines require ads to be submitted several weeks before publication. In addition, because they are published weekly or monthly, it is more difficult to use topical messages. Magazines are often read at times or in places—on planes or in doctors'

---

[6]For an interesting overview of the value of radio advertising, see: Marina Strauss, "Advertisers Neglect Potential of Radio," *Globe and Mail*, March 29, 1990, p. B8.

M A R K E T I N G   A T   W O R K

FILE 19-2   **THE MAYTAG MAN: BORN ON CANADIAN RADIO!**

In Canada, Maytag is the most popular brand of washer, dryer, and dishwasher. In the United States, the washer and dryer are number 1 and the dishwasher is number 2. Maytag management attributes the relative success of the dishwasher here to heavier advertising in the Canadian market. The Maytag marketing strategy has been to promote superior quality right from the beginning—almost 100 years ago. While quality is very "in" in marketing circles these days, it has been in place at Maytag for so long that it is recognized as part of normal business culture.

In order to market its quality culture, Maytag ads use the bored repairman, dressed in a uniform and cap, ready for service calls but never receiving any since Maytag appliances "are built to last longer and need fewer repairs." Presenting a superior quality claim in a credible fashion is important since Maytag products sell for 15 to 20 percent more than other brands. And Maytag has the independent surveys to substantiate the claim.

The Maytag man was created as a result of a company-sponsored Canadian radio program in the mid-sixties. An appliance repairman who offered advice was the program theme. Maytag's Chicago ad agency picked up the theme, added loneliness, and the result is an effective and award-winning campaign that has been running for more than 20 years—and in both French and English in Canada.

Source: Adapted from Marina Strauss, "Maytag Makes No. 1 Out of Loneliness," *Globe and Mail*, June 18, 1990, p. B4.

---

offices, for instance—far removed from where a buying impulse can be acted on.

OUTDOOR ADVERTISING

Outdoor advertising has a low cost per exposure. Because of the mobile nature of our society, outdoor ads reach a large percentage of the population. But because it is typically seen by people "on the go," billboard advertising is appropriate only for brief messages. It is excellent for reminder advertising, and it carries the impact of large size and colour. Motion and three-dimensional figures can be incorporated in a billboard's design for increased attention-getting ability. Billboards provide flexibility in geographic coverage and intensity of market coverage within an area. However, unless the advertised product is a widely used good or service, considerable waste circulation will occur. Although the cost of reaching an individual person is low, the total cost of a national billboard campaign can be quite high. Finally, the landscape-defacing aspect of outdoor advertising has aroused considerable public criticism.

ALTERNATIVE MEDIA

Don't be misled into thinking that there are only a few mass media used to reach consumers with advertising messages. While there is still a strong reliance on the traditional print and broadcast media, advertisers in Canada have recently been faced with a dazzling array of new media. There are now more

Balancing getting attention with reducing distraction.

alternatives than ever for getting your message in front of the customer. Many of these media have developed in response to a fragmentation of the mass media. With the proliferation of alternatives competing for the attention of the customer, advertisers have had to look for new ways of getting the message to the target market and getting it there closer to the point of sale. Some of the innovations represent modifications of the existing mass media, others ''piggyback'' on new technologies, while still others are part of the burgeoning out-of-home advertising business.

- Many advertisers are turning to 15-second television commercials, priced at 60 percent to 70 percent of the cost of a 30-second commercial.
- Bothered by the erosion of their network television audience by videos, some national advertisers have moved their advertising to reach the video watchers by placing ads on rental video movies or by co-sponsoring or co-producing them.
- Transit ads now appear on the exterior as well as the interior of buses and subway cars, both on the rear and the front of the bus; in fact, one of the newest forms of transit advertising is to paint the entire bus as a mobile billboard.
- The out-of-home advertising media are the fastest growing. These encompass outdoor billboards, posters in airports, malls, and railway stations, ads on shopping carts, on golf courses, ski lifts, washroom walls, and garbage cans.
- Pixsell is an in-store interactive computer that allows customers to call up recipes or discount coupons, which are then printed right in the store. This system has been tested in supermarkets with considerable success, again reaching the customer at the point of sale.
- Coupons and advertising materials are included in egg cartons; home computer owners can access an on-line database called ''Free Access Network,'' complete with news, sports, weather, and classified and display advertising. Tele-Direct, the publication arm of Bell Canada which publishes the

MARKETING AT WORK

FILE 19-3 **ACCOUNTANTS PROMOTE SMALL, BUT WITH PIZZAZ**

The Canadian accounting profession, until lately, has not been much involved in the kinds of marketing and promotion efforts that are commonly used by other service providers or product marketing organizations. But now, many accounting firms are learning their markets and developing well-focused marketing strategies and very effective promotional materials. The profession now has an annual competition — the Bottom Line Awards for Marketing Excellence. The awards are organized into four categories, three of which are for brochures (specialty services, corporate image, recruitment) with the fourth being for print advertising in the business press. Brochures are clearly an important vehicle for the advertising and promotion of professional services. They are not necessarily expensive to develop and thus are ideal for small service organizations. New desktop publishing technology allows anyone to do a very good job — creativity and clarity are more important than size of firm.

The Corporate Image Brochure category was won by an eight-partner chartered accounting firm that produced a small humorous brochure shaped like a pin-striped jacket adorned with a yellow daisy and colourful tie. The purpose of the brochure was to creatively communicate ''self-expression, responsible participation, pride, respect, creativity and humour, coupled with a strong collective commitment to excellence and service. . . .'' The judges found that the firm effectively ''communicated itself as an approachable, fresh, innovative, accounting firm of real people. . . .'' Brochures are small items when it comes to budgets, but they can mean everything when it comes to making sense to new clients.

Source: Adapted from Gundi Jeffrey, ''Pinstripes Get Pizzaz,'' *The Financial Post*, August 1, 1991, p. 14.

Yellow Pages, has introduced its Talking Yellow Pages service. Users dial a phone number and punch in a four-digit code that is included in a Yellow Pages ad to hear recorded messages that provide more details on the advertiser's products and services.

These represent a small sample of the ''new media'' being developed for Canadian advertisers. The choice of where to place one's advertising dollars becomes more difficult all the time.

Creating Advertisements

Remember that the ultimate purpose of advertising is to sell something and that the ad itself is a sales message. The ad may be a fast-paced sales talk, as in a direct-action TV ad by a car dealership. Or it may be a very long-range, low-key message, as are many institutional ads. Whatever the method, the goal is to sell something sooner or later. Consequently advertising involves the same *AIDA* steps used in personal selling (as discussed in Chapter 18). The ad must first attract *attention* and then hold *interest* long enough to stimulate a *desire* for the product. Finally, the ad must move the prospect to some kind of *action*.

Attention can be achieved in many ways. (Recall our discussion of perception in Chapter 6). The most common approach is to present the material in an unexpected manner or using an unconventional technique to capture the attention of the audience. Thus a print ad may be mostly white space or a television commercial might show the product in an unusual setting or address a topic from a new perspective. Thus, William Neilson Limited gained attention when they raised the question of how they were able to get the filling inside the Caramilk bar. Some beer commercials have departed from the rock music and party scene and Molson has advertised Canadian Light in commercials showing a young couple leaving their family with a babysitter to go out for the evening.[7] Catelli has even showed a single mother serving her children pasta.[8]

Maintaining interest once the audience recognizes that the communication is an ad is a challenge for advertisers. Except for people very involved with the product, most of us will quickly transfer our attention elsewhere. Therefore, advertisers must make the ad interesting through the use of humour, an attractive spokesperson, or some other device to hold the audience.

Desire for a product is stimulated by effectively presenting the product's benefits. This is the heart of the ad. Through words, pictures, and/or sounds, the advertiser must make the consumer imagine experiencing the product's benefits. The desired consumer action may be retention of new knowledge about the product or company, a change in attitude, a request for additional information, or the actual purchase of the product.

Creating an advertisement involves writing the copy, selecting the illustration (for visual media), preparing the visual or verbal layout, and reproducing the ad for the selected media. The **copy** in an ad is all the written or spoken material in it. Copy in a print ad includes the headline, coupons, advertiser's identification, and the main body of the message. In a broadcast ad the copy is the script.

For visual ads, the **illustration** is a powerful feature. The main points to consider about illustrations are (1) whether they are totally appropriate to the product advertised and (2) despite the adage ''a picture is worth a thousand words,'' whether they are the best use of the space. The **layout** is the physical arrangement of all the elements in an advertisement. In print ads, it is the appearance of the page. For television, layout is the set as well as the positioning of actors and props. The layout of a radio ad is the sequence in which information is presented. A good layout can hold interest as well as attract attention. It should lead the audience through the entire ad in an orderly fashion.

The cost of creating an ad can vary from almost nothing for a local radio spot written by the staff at a radio station to as much as $400,000 for a television commercial. In recent years, production costs for network TV ads have escalated dramatically. As a result, fewer ads are being made and they are kept on the air longer.

EVALUATING THE ADVERTISING EFFORT

In managing its advertising program, a company should carefully evaluate the effectiveness of previous and future ads. Shrinking profit margins and increasing competition—both foreign and domestic—force management to appraise

---

[7]Marina Strauss, ''Brewers Pitching a Responsible Home Run,'' *Globe and Mail*, April 18, 1991, p. B4; and Sandra Porteus, ''Ale Ads Break the Mold,'' *Marketing*, April 1, 1991, p. 11.

[8]Ted Wood, ''Get Rid of Heavy-Handed Niceness,'' *Marketing*, October 29, 1990, p. 44.

all expenditures. Top executives want proof that advertising is justified. They want to know whether dollars spent on advertising are producing as many sales as could be reaped from the same dollars spent on other activities.

Difficulty of Evaluation

It is very hard to measure the sales effectiveness of advertising. By the very nature of the marketing mix, all elements — including advertising — are so intertwined that measurement of any one by itself is nearly impossible. Factors that contribute to the difficulty of measuring the sales impact of advertising are:

- *Ads have different objectives.* Though all advertising is ultimately intended to increase sales, individual ads may not be aimed at producing immediate results. For example, some ads simply announce new store hours or service policies. Other ads build goodwill or contribute to a company's image.
- *Ads can have an effect over time.* Even an ad designed to have an immediate sales impact may product results days, weeks, or months after it appears. A consumer may be influenced by an ad but not be able to act on it immediately. Or an ad may plant in the consumer's mind a seed that doesn't blossom into a sale for several weeks. It is impossible to determine, with the exception of mail-order advertising, when a particular ad or campaign produced results.
- *Measurement problems.* In most instances consumers can't say when or if a specific ad influenced their behaviour, let alone caused them to buy. Human motivation is too complicated to be explained by a single factor.

In spite of these problems, advertisers do attempt to measure advertising effectiveness because they must do so — and some knowledge is better than none at all. Effectiveness may be tested before an ad is presented, while it is being presented, or after it has completed its run.

Methods Used to Measure Effectiveness

Methods of measuring ad effectiveness can be categorized as direct and indirect. **Direct tests** measure or predict the sales volume stemming from the advertisement or campaign being tested. Tabulating the number of redemptions of a reduced-price coupon incorporated in an ad will indicate its effectiveness. Coupons frequently are coded so they can also be traced to the publications from which they came. Another type of direct test measures the number of enquiries that are received from an ad that offers additional information to prospects who call or write in.

Most other types of measures are **indirect tests** of effectiveness, or measures of something other than actual sales. *Recall tests* are based on the premise that an advertisement can have an effect only if it is remembered. Three common recall tests are:

- Recognition—showing people an ad and asking if they have seen it before.
- Aided recall—asking people if they can recall seeing any ads for a particular brand.
- Unaided recall—asking people if they can remember seeing any ads within a product category.

A well-known indirect measure is the Starch Readership Test, which measures exposure to print ads. The Starch researcher pages through magazines with people who have previously read them and notes whether the subjects remember noticing the ads, how much of the copy they read, and whether they associated the ads with the sponsors.

This ad combines sales promotion with advertising. By coding coupons and tabulating the number of coupons redeemed, manufacturers can gauge the effectiveness of a particular campaign.

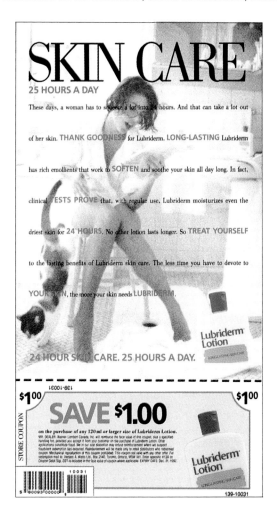

Ads may also be tested before they are presented to the general public. Advertisements in nearly finished form (to save production costs) are presented to panels of consumers for their reactions. This is often done in theatre settings for television ads, with the test ad shown along with other ads, in the context of a regular TV program. After viewing the program and the ads, the consumers are quizzed about the ad being tested.

Refinements are constantly being made in advertising testing. Developments in areas such as laboratory test markets and computer simulations hold promise for the future. However, the complexity of decision making combined with the multitude of influences on the buyer will continue to make measuring the effectiveness of advertising a difficult task.

ORGANIZING FOR ADVERTISING

Now let's consider what kind of organization is needed to perform and manage advertising activities. Management has three alternatives: (1) develop an internal advertising department, (2) use an outside advertising agency, or (3) use both an internal department and an advertising agency. Regardless of which alternative is selected, generally the same specialized skills are necessary to do the advertising job. Creative people are needed to prepare the copy, generate illustrative material, and design the layouts. Media experts are required to select the appropriate media, buy the time or space, and arrange for the scheduled appearance of the ads. And managerial skills are essential to plan and administer the entire advertising program.

Internal Departments

All of these advertising tasks, some of them, or just overall direction can be performed by an internal department. When advertising is a substantial part of the marketing mix, a company usually has its own advertising department. If the company is to implement the marketing concept, the head of this department should report to the head of marketing. Large retailers, for example, have their own advertising departments and may not use advertising agencies at all.

Advertising Agencies

Many companies, especially manufacturers, use advertising agencies to carry out some or all of their advertising activities. An **advertising agency** is an independent company that renders specialized services in advertising in particular and in marketing in general.

Advertising agencies plan and execute entire advertising campaigns. They employ more advertising specialists than their clients do because they spread the cost over many accounts. A company can benefit from an agency's experience with other products and clients. Many advertising agencies offer a wide range of services including research, public relations, and new product development assistance. In fact, many of these firms are becoming *marketing* agencies, offering services heretofore performed by other outside specialists or by the advertisers themselves.[9]

Using Both a Department and an Agency

Many firms have their own advertising department and also use an advertising agency. The internal advertising department acts as a liaison between the agency and the company, giving the company greater control over this major expenditure. It approves the agency's plans and ads, is responsibile for preparing and administering the advertising budget, and coordinates advertising with personal selling. The department may also handle direct mail, dealer displays, and other promotional activities if they are not handled by the agency.

NATURE AND IMPORTANCE OF SALES PROMOTION

Sales promotion is one of the most loosely used terms in the marketing vocabulary. We define **sales promotion** as those promotional activities (other than advertising, personal selling, public relations, and publicity) that are intended to stimulate customer demand and improve the marketing performance of sellers. Sales promotion includes coupons, premiums, in-store displays, trade shows, samples, in-store demonstrations, and contests. Sales promotion activities may be conducted by producers or middlemen. The target for producers' sales promotion may be middlemen or end users—households, business users —or the producer's own sales force. Middlemen direct sales promotion at their sales people or prospects further down the channel of distribution.

Sales promotion is distinct from advertising and personal selling, but all three activities often are interrelated. In fact, a major function of sales promotion is to serve as a bridge between advertising and personal selling — to

---

[9]For an interesting perspective on the competitiveness of the advertising agency business, see: Jan Matthews and Greg Boyd, ''The Hardest Sell,'' *Canadian Business*, April 1991, pp. 60–65.

supplement and coordinate efforts in these two areas. For example, an in-store display (sales promotion) furnished by the manufacturer to stores selling Michelin tires may feature a slogan and illustrations from Michelin's current advertising campaign. This effective display makes retailers more receptive to talking with Michelin sales people. Or prospecting leads may be generated from people who visited the Canon copy-machines exhibit at an office equipment trade show.

Recently sales promotion has been the fastest-growing method of promotion, with dollars being shifted from advertising. Total annual expenditures for sales promotion are estimated to parallel or even exceed those for advertising. Sales promotion is also being integrated into the total marketing strategy in many firms. It is being introduced at the inception of a promotion campaign, not tacked on as an afterthought.

The numbers attached to some sales promotion activities are mind-boggling. More than 23 billion cents-off coupons were distributed in Canada in 1990, of which more than 19 billion were distributed through the weekly newspaper advertising and in-store flyers of retailers. Canadians redeemed a total of 248 million coupons in 1990, with an average face value of 53 cents.[10] Millions of people attend Canadian and international trade shows each year and millions of dollars are spent on point-of-purchase displays in retail stores. The number of contests and the value of their prizes have increased dramatically in recent years.

Several factors in the marketing environment contribute to the surging popularity of sales promotion:

- *Short-run orientation.* Sales promotions such as couponing and trade allowances produce quicker, more measurable sales results. However, critics of this strategy argue that these immediate benefits come at the expense of building a strong brand image in consumers' minds and condition buyers to expect incentives. Thus they feel an overemphasis on sales promotion will undermine a product's future.
- *Competitive pressure.* If competitors are offering buyers price reductions, contests, or other incentives, a firm may feel forced to retaliate with its own sales promotions.
- *State of the economy.* Rising prices have made consumers more price-conscious. Thus, sales promotions become more attractive to them.
- *Low quality of retail selling.* Many retailers have switched to self-service or use sales clerks who are inadequately trained. For these outlets sales promotion devices such as product displays and information booklets often are the only effective promotional tools available at the point of purchase.

STRATEGIC MANAGEMENT OF SALES PROMOTION

Sales promotion should be included in a company's strategic marketing planning, along with advertising and personal selling. This means setting sales promotion goals, selecting appropriate strategies, and establishing a separate sales promotion budget. Management should also eveluate the performance of sales promotion activities.

One problem management faces is that many sales promotion tools are short-run, tactical actions. Coupons, premiums, and contests, for example, are designed to produce immediate (but short-lived) responses. As a result, they

[10]Wayne Mouland, ''Couponing Thrives in Recessionary Market,'' *Marketing*, April 8, 1991, p. 24.

are frequently used as stopgap measures to shore up unexpected sales declines rather than as integrated parts of a marketing program.

Determining Objectives and Strategies

Early in the strategic planning for sales promotion, management should (1) set goals for the current sales promotion program, (2) identify target markets, and (3) select appropriate strategies.

We identified three broad objectives of sales promotion when defining the term:

- Stimulating end-user demand (either business user or household).
- Improving the marketing performance of middlemen and sales people.
- Supplementing and coordinating advertising and personal selling.

More specific objectives of sales promotion are much like those for advertising and personal selling. Examples are:

- *To gain trial for a new or improved product*. Procter & Gamble or Lever Brothers might send a free sample through the mail.
- *To disrupt existing buying habits*. A coupon offering a large discount might cause a consumer to switch brands of a product that is viewed as generic, such as orange juice or motor oil.
- *To attract new customers*. Financial institutions have offered small appliances and other premiums to encourage consumers to open accounts.
- *To encourage greater use by existing customers*. Air Canada and most other airlines have "frequent flyer" programs to encourage travelers to use their airlines more often.
- *To combat a competitor's promotional activity*. One supermarket chain runs a lottery or game to attract shoppers and a competitor retaliates by offering triple-value coupons.
- *To increase impulse buying*. End-of-aisle and island displays in supermarkets can increase sales of a product by as much as 50 percent.
- *To get greater retailer cooperation*. A sporting-goods manufacturer gets additional shelf space by setting up excellent point-of-purchase displays, training retailers' sales people, and providing tote bags to be given away with purchases.

The choice of sales promotion tools derives directly from the objectives of the total marketing program. Consider the following situations and the different strategies available:

- A firm's objective is to increase sales, which calls for entering new geographic markets using a *pull strategy*. To encourage product trial and attract consumers away from familiar brands, possible sales promotion tactics are coupons, cash rebates, free samples, and premiums.
- A firm's objective is to protect market share in the face of intense competition. This goal suggests a *push strategy* to improve retailer performance and goodwill. Training retailers' sales forces, supplying effective point-of-purchase displays, and granting advertising allowances would be appropriate sales promotion options.

Determining Sales Promotion Budgets

The sales promotion budget should be established when the budget for the total promotional mix is determined. Combining sales promotion with advertising or public relations for budgetary purposes or lumping it together with an appropriation labelled "advertising" is likely to prevent the development of a separate sales promotion strategy. Sales promotion may then be overlooked or poorly integrated with the other components of promotion. Setting a separate budget for sales promotion forces a company to recognize and manage this important activity.

Consistent with developing an integrated strategy, the amount budgeted for sales promotion should be determined by the task method. This forces management to consider specific objectives and the sales promotion techniques that will be used to accomplish them.

Selecting the Appropriate Tools

A key step in sales promotion management is deciding which tools will help the organization reach its promotional goals. As shown in Table 19-3, these tools may be divided into three categories, based on the target audience: end users, middlemen, or the producer's own sales force. The same tool may be used to reach more than one audience category. For example, there are automobile shows held in major cities across Canada. The displays of new models, sports cars, racing cars, and custom vehicles attract large audiences—250,000 to the annual shows held at Olympic Stadium in Montreal and the Metro Toronto Convention Centre and SkyDome. Such events have the ability to create high levels of interest for exhibitors.[11]

Factors that influence the choice of promotional tools include:

- *The organization's promotional objectives*. Does it want to use a pull or a push strategy?

TABLE 19-3 **Major sales promotion tools, grouped by target audience**

End users (consumer or business)	Middlemen and their sales forces	Producers' own sales force
Coupons	Trade shows and exhibitions	Sales contests
Cash rebates	Point-of-purchase displays	Sales training manuals
Premiums (gifts)	Free goods	Sales meetings
Free samples	Advertising allowances	Packets with promotional materials
Contests and sweepstakes	Contests for sales people	Demonstration model of product
Point-of-purchase displays	Training middlemen's sales force	
Product demonstrations	Product demonstrations	
Trade shows and exhibitions	Advertising specialties	
Advertising specialties		

- *Target market for the promotion*. Is promotion aimed at ultimate consumers, middlemen, or the firm's own sales force?
- *Nature of the product*. Does it lend itself to sampling or demonstration?
- *Cost of the tool*. Sampling a large market is very expensive.
- *Current economic conditions*. Coupons, premiums, and rebates are good options during periods of recession or inflation.

SALES PROMOTION DIRECTED AT FINAL CONSUMERS

Many of the tools in Table 19-3 probably are quite familiar to you, but a brief discussion of some of them will give you a better sense of their significance.

---

[11]Derek Suchard, ''Trade Shows Under-utilized, Says Expert,'' *Strategy*, August 26, 1991, p. 17.

This trade show is targeted at both consumers and distributors.

In just four years the number of coupons distributed by marketers has increased by over 400 percent (from 6.8 billion in 1986 to 23.4 billion in 1990) with no end in sight.

"Advertising specialties" is a miscellaneous category of small, usually inexpensive items imprinted with a company's name or logo that are given or sold by producers or middlemen to customers and prospects. Examples are pens, calendars, key rings, paperweights, coffee cups, hats, and jackets.

SALES PROMOTION DIRECTED AT MIDDLEMEN

Some of the tools just discussed may also be directed at middlemen and their sales forces. In addition, trade associations in industries as diverse as shoes, travel, and furniture sponsor trade shows that are open only to wholesalers and retailers. Many producers also spend considerable time and money to train the sales forces of their wholesalers and retailers.

SALES PROMOTION DIRECTED AT A PRODUCER'S OWN SALES FORCE

Again, there is overlap between the tools directed at middlemen and those designed for the producer's own sales force. Sales contests are probably the most significant of these tools, with many firms offering one kind or another. The most common incentive is cash, used in over half of all contests. Other incentives include merchandise, plaques, jewellery, and travel. Visual sales aids (flipcharts, slides) are prepared for sales people and brochures are developed to reinforce sales presentations.

EVALUATING SALES PROMOTION

As with other components of the promotional mix, management should try to evaluate the productivity or effectiveness of sales promotion. For many sales promotion tools, this task is much easier and the results more accurate than is the case with advertising. For example, responses to a premium offer or a coupon with a specified closing date can be counted and compared to a similar period when there were no sales promotions underway. Elements that contribute to this ease of measurement are:

- Sales promotions have definite starting and ending points. Coupons must be redeemed by a certain date. Contest entries must be submitted before a particular deadline. Sales contests for the sales force count only the sales made during a specified period. This is quite different from advertising, where there can be significant residual effects and the results of one campaign may overlap another.
- Most sales promotions are designed to affect sales directly. It is more difficult to measure a change in attitude or an increase in information about a product or brand than it is to count sales.

However, there are some pitfalls in measuring sales promotion effects. First, not all sales promotions meet the conditions just mentioned. For instance, training given to a distributor's sales force may be valuable, but may not produce immediate results. Second, sales promotion results may be inflated by sales cannibalized from the future. That is, a sales promotion may get buyers to act now when they would have bought the product in the future anyway. An indication of cannibalization is a lower level of sales *after* the promotion ends compared to *before* the promotion began. Third, any attempt at measurement must take into consideration external conditions such as the behaviour of competitors and the state of the economy. A firm's market share may not increase following an expensive sales promotion, for example, but the promotion may have offset the potentially damaging impact of a competitor's promotional activity.

PUBLIC RELATIONS AND PUBLICITY

Public relations and publicity are the last two methods of promotion that we shall discuss in connection with an organization's total promotional program. In most organizations, these promotional tools typically are relegated to stepchild status behind personal selling, advertising, and sales promotion. There are several reasons for management's lack of attention to these areas:

- *Organizational structure.* In most companies, public relations and publicity are not the responsibility of the marketing department. If there is an organized effort, it is usually handled by a small public relations department that reports directly to top management.
- *Inadequate definitions.* The terms public relations and publicity are loosely used by businesses and the public. There are no generally accepted definitions of the two terms, nor is there a clear-cut distinction between them.
- *Unrecognized benefits.* Only recently have many organizations come to appreciate the tremendous value of good public relations and publicity. As the cost of promotion has gone up, firms are realizing that positive exposure through the media or as a result of community involvement can produce a high return on the investment of time and effort.
- *Adverse publicity.* In a society that is increasingly sensitive about the environment and where news media are quick to report mistakes, organizations tend to focus on the negative dimension of publicity. As a result, managers are so concerned with avoiding bad publicity that they overlook the potential of publicity for improving the firm's image.[12]

---

[12]For an interesting view of how public relations specialists deal with difficult situations, see: Jared Mitchell, ''The Bad News Bearers,'' *Report on Business Magazine*, November 1990, pp. 91-94.

Nature and Scope of Public Relations

Public relations is a broad, overall communications effort to influence various groups' attitudes towards the organization. Public relations activities typically are designed to build or maintain a favourable image for an organization and a favourable relationship with its various publics — customers, prospects, stockholders, employees, labour unions, the local community, and the government. Note that this description is quite similar to our definition of institutional advertising. However, unlike advertising, public relations need not use the media to communicate its message.

Good public relations can be achieved by supporting charitable projects (by supplying volunteer labour or other resources), participating in community service events, sponsoring athletic teams, funding the arts, producing an employee or customer newsletter, and disseminating information through exhibits, displays, and tours. Major companies often sponsor public events or special programs on television as part of their public relations efforts. Cultural organizations such as ballet companies and symphony orchestras would not survive without the support they receive from major corporations. As a result, we see interesting sponsorships such as the support the Hongkong Bank of Canada gave to an exhibition of photographs of children that appeared in art galleries across Canada.

A group of financial services companies sponsors an exhibit of Canadian art.

PUBLICITY AS A FORM OF PUBLIC RELATIONS

Publicity is any promotional communication about an organization or its products that is presented by the media but is *not* paid for by the organization. Publicity usually takes the form of a news story appearing in a mass medium or an endorsement provided by an individual informally or in a speech or interview.

There are three channels for gaining publicity. One is to prepare a story (called a news release) and circulate it to the media. The intention is for the selected newspapers, television stations, or other media to report the information as news. The second channel is personal communication with a group. A press conference will draw media representatives if they feel the subject or speaker has news value. Company tours and speeches to civic or professional groups are other forms of individual-to-group communications. The third channel is one-on-one personal communication, often called lobbying. Companies lobby legislators or other powerful people in an attempt to influence their opinions, and subsequently their decisions. In addition, firms will give products to highly visible people in hopes that the people will be seen using them.

Publicity can help to accomplish any communication objective. It can be used to announce new products, publicize new policies, recognize employees, describe research breakthroughs, or report financial performance—if the message is viewed by the media as newsworthy or by the group or individual recipient as interesting or useful. This is what distinguishes publicity from advertising—publicity cannot be "forced" on the audience. This is also the source of its power. The credibility level of publicity typically is much higher than advertising. If we tell you our product is great, you may well be skeptical. But if an independent, objective third party says our product is great, you are more likely to believe it.

BENEFITS AND LIMITATIONS OF PUBLICITY

Recognizing the value of publicity, some organizations have special units or programs to generate information. For example, Campbell Soup Company sponsors a major national survey of the attitudes of Canadians towards health and nutrition; Christie's, the cookie company, sponsor the Christie Children's Book Awards; and The Body Shop actively supports the World Wildlife Fund and other environmental groups.[13] All of these activities are designed to link the companies involved with causes and activities consumers believe to be important. Through their association, the companies intend to improve their corporate image. To fulfil its potential, however, publicity must be treated as part of the promotional strategy of the firm and be coordinated with the other promotional tools. The benefits of publicity are:

- *Lower cost than advertising or personal selling.* Publicity usually costs much less than advertising and personal selling because there are no media space or time costs for conveying the message.
- *Greater credibility than advertising.* Because the source of the message is an uninvolved third party, the message is more believable than an ad.
- *Increased readership.* Many consumers are conditioned to ignore advertising

---

[13]Pat McNamara, "PR Moves to the Front of Marketing Repertoire," *Marketing*, June 3, 1991, p. 21.

or at least pay it scant attention. Publicity is presented as editorial material or news, so it gets greater readership.

- *More information.* Again, because it is presented as editorial material, publicity can contain much more detail than a standard ad. Thus more information and persuasive content can be included in the message.
- *Timeliness.* A company can put out a news release very quickly when some unexpected event occurs.

Of course, publicity also has some limitations:

- *Loss of control over the message.* An organization has no guarantee that a publicity release will appear in the media. In fact, only a small proportion of all publicity messages prepared are ever used. In addition, there is no way to control how much or what portion of a publicity release the media will print or broadcast.
- *Limited exposure.* The media will typically use publicity material only once. If the target audience misses the message when it is presented, there is no second or third chance. Thus there is no opportunity for repetition as in advertising.
- *Publicity is not free.* Even though there are no media time and space costs, there are expenses in staffing a publicity department and in preparing and disseminating messages.

Evaluating Public Relations and Publicity

Although few executives would argue that having a good image and staying in touch with an organization's publics are unimportant, evaluating public relations and publicity is difficult. In the past, evaluation usually involved a report of inputs or activities rather than outputs or results. Public relations departments maintained ''scrapbooks'' to show management what was being done. These days, to justify expenditures, more organizations are requiring departments to provide specific public relations objectives and show measurable results. Because it is impossible to relate public relations and publicity directly to sales, other measures must be used. One is behavioural research to show, for example, increased awareness of a product or brand name or changes in attitudes and beliefs about a firm.

SUMMARY

Advertising is the nonpersonal, mass-communications component in a company's promotional mix. The firm has the option of running product or institutional types of advertising. Product ads may call for direct or indirect action. Another useful classification of advertising is primary demand and selective demand stimulation, which include pioneering, competitive, and comparative advertising. Manufacturers and their retail dealers often employ vertical cooperative advertising, in which they share the cost of advertising the manufacturer's product at the local level. Horizontal cooperative advertising involves joint sponsorship of ads by firms at the same level of distribution.

Advertising expenditures are large, but the average cost of advertising in a firm is typically 1 to 3 percent of sales. This is considerably less than the average cost of personal selling. Most advertising dollars are spent in newspapers, with television a close second. Other important media are radio, magazines, direct mail, and outdoor displays.

Management should create an advertising campaign as part of the firm's total promotional program. The first step is to set specific goals for the particular campaign. A major task in developing a campaign is to select the advertising media — the general medium type, the particular category, and the specific vehicle. The choice should be based on the characteristics of the media and the way they fit the product and the market. The advertising message — consisting of the copy, illustration, and layout — is an integral part of an advertisement.

An especially important yet difficult task in advertising management is evaluating the effectiveness of the advertising effort — both the entire campaign and individual ads. Except for sales results tests, commonly used techniques measure only the extent to which the ad was read or recalled. To operate an advertising program, a firm may rely on its own advertising department, an advertising agency, or a combination of the two.

Sales promotion is the third major promotional tool. It is used to coordinate and supplement the advertising and personal selling programs. Sales promotion has increased considerably in importance in recent years as management has sought measurable, short-term sales results. Sales promotion should receive the same strategic attention that a company gives to advertising and personal selling. This means establishing objectives and appropriate strategies. A separate budget should be set for sales promotion. Sales promotion can be directed towards final consumers, middlemen, or a company's own employees. To implement its strategic plans, management can choose from a wide variety of sales promotion tools. Sales promotion performance also should be evaluated.

Public relations and publicity were the final promotional methods discussed. Public relations is the broad, overall promotional vehicle for improving or maintaining an organization's image and its favourable relationship with its publics. Publicity, a part of public relations, is any promotional communication regarding an organization and/or its products that is not paid for by the company benefiting from it. Typically these two activities are handled in a department separate from the marketing department in a firm. Nevertheless the management process of planning, implementing, and evaluating should be applied to their performance in the same way it is applied to advertising and personal selling.

KEY TERMS AND CONCEPTS

Advertising 598
Advertisements 598
Product advertising 598
Direct-action advertising 598
Indirect-action advertising 598
Institutional advertising 598
Customer service advertising 598
Public service advertising 598
Primary demand advertising 599
Selective demand advertising 599
Pioneering advertising 599
Differential advantage 600
Comparative advertising 600
Cooperative advertising 601
Vertical cooperative advertising 601
Advertising allowance 601

Horizontal cooperative advertising 601
Advertising campaign 606
Advertising media 606
Cost per thousand (CPM) 607
Copy 613
Illustrations 613
Layout 613
Direct tests 614
Indirect tests 614
Advertising agency 616
Sales promotion 616
Sales promotion tools 619
Public relations 622
Publicity 623

QUESTIONS AND PROBLEMS

1. Businesses in different industries demonstrate quite different patterns in their advertising expenditures. Some are heavy advertisers on television, while others use no television at all. Some advertise heavily in daily newspapers, while others rely on magazines. Some firms, such as those in the consumer products field, spend as much as 15 percent of sales on advertising, while others, including many industrial marketers, spend less than 1 percent. How do you account for such variations in advertising expenditures?

2. Several specific advertising objectives were outlined early in the chapter. Bring to class print ads that illustrate at least four of these goals. As an alternative, be prepared to describe four radio or television ads that attempt to achieve these objectives.

3. Which advertising medium would you recommend as best for each of these products?
   a. Wooden pallets.
   b. Pantyhose.
   c. Tax preparation service.
   d. Funeral services.
   e. Toys for young children.
   f. Plastic clothespins.

4. Many grocery product and candy manufacturers earmark a good portion of their advertising budgets for use in magazines. Is this a wise choice of media for these firms? Explain.

5. Why do department stores use newspapers more than local radio stations as an advertising medium?

6. Why is it worthwhile to pretest advertisements before they appear in the media? How could a test market be used to pretest an ad? (You may want to refresh your memory with a review of test marketing in Chapter 3.)

7. What procedures can a firm use to determine how many sales dollars resulted from a direct-mail ad? How would you determine whether any sales were cannibalized.

8. If a manufacturing firm finds a good ad agency, should it discontinue its own advertising department? Should it consider any changes?

9. Visit a supermarket, a hardware store, or a movie theatre and make a list of all the sales promotion tools that you observe. Which do you feel are particularly effective and why?

10. Is sales promotion effective for selling expensive consumer products such as houses, automobiles, or cruise trips? Is your answer the same for expensive business products?

11. Explain how sales promotion might be used to offset weak personal selling in retail stores.

12. Describe a recent public relations event in your community. How did it benefit the sponsor?

13. How does publicity differ from advertising?

14. Bring to class an article from a daily newspaper that appears to be the result of a firm's publicity efforts. Summarize the points made in the article that may benefit the firm. Could the same benefits be obtained through advertising?

15. Give a recent example of a company or other organization with which you are familiar that encountered unfavourable publicity. How well do you feel the organization handled the situation? What public relations or publicity tools did they use?

C A S E S   F O R   P A R T   6

CASE 6.1   ## The Upper Canada Brewing Company (E): Developing a Promotion Strategy

The final decision confronting Frank Heaps, president of the Upper Canada Brewing Company, involved the promotion element of the marketing plan. He realized that even the most useful and satisfying product would be a dismal failure if no one knew it was available. It was essential to let the target customers know that the product, with the desired benefits, was available at the price they were willing to pay, in the locations where they would wish to purchase it. Indeed, any promotion decision could be effective only if it was coordinated with strategies for the other three elements of the marketing mix: product, pricing, and distribution.

THE PROMOTION BUDGET

The first decision in planning the promotional strategy was to determine the budget. Mr. Heaps proposed that the promotional appropriation would be 7.5 percent of forecasted gross sales in Year One and 5 percent in Year Two. He felt that these expenditures would support the achievement of the company's market share objectives (see Exhibit E-1). He realized, however, that this proposed promotion investment was dwarfed by the marketing outlays of the three major breweries — Molson, Labatts, and Carling O'Keefe. In fact, research showed that their combined 1984 national advertising expenditures was $87.8 million. Given these massive outlays, he pondered the adequacy of his proposed budget. Knowing that his company could not

realistically increase this budget significantly, he knew he had to get real value for each dollar spent. The only problem was, how?

THE PROMOTION STRATEGY

To guide the development of an effective strategy, Mr. Heaps knew that he needed a clear set of objectives. The objectives that he identified were: (i) to inform the target audience about the brewery's product(s) and methods; (ii) to persuade the target customer to try the product(s); and (iii) to position the product(s) in the consumer's mind as truly unique, with significantly different benefits. To achieve these objectives, and to prevent head-to-head competition with the major breweries, Mr. Heaps knew that the promotional approach and appeal had to be significantly different from that used by the giant competitors.

A key decision in being different rested with the blend of the promotional mix chosen by the Upper Canada Brewing Company. To decide on the appropriate blend of activities, Mr. Heaps evaluated the different promotional methods at his disposal: advertising, personal selling, sales promotion, and general publicity and public relations. He realized that, given his limited budget, he would not be able to produce expensive print and broadcast advertisements like those of the competition. He felt, however, that some advertising was necessary for a successful entry into this market. As well, given the importance of the licensee trade to the achievement of

EXHIBIT E-1   **Promotion Budget 1985–86**

	1985	1986
Market Share Objective	0.1%	0.15%
Forecasted Gross Sales	$ 2.M	$ 3.5M
Promotion Budget	$175,000	$175,000

This case was prepared by Donna M. Stapleton and is intended to stimulate discussion of an actual management problem and not to illustrate either effective or ineffective handling of that problem. The author wishes to acknowledge the support provided by the Upper Canada Brewing Company, and particularly by Frank Heaps, President.

company sales (projected licensee trade was 15 percent of gross sales), he concluded that some personal selling was also critical.

The location of the brewery site, adjacent to Toronto's booming downtown with visibility from the Gardiner Expressway, the GO Train system, and the C.N.E./Ontario Place complex provided an excellent vehicle to provoke public interest and awareness. Mr. Heaps wondered if he should use this strategic location as a sales promotion tool and actively encourage public tours and sampling of the plant product(s). He knew that Molson offered tours to the public; however, Carling O'Keefe and Labatts did not.

One final activity that he considered using was company-stimulated media coverage such as news releases and articles on the new brewery; he wondered if these methods would be cost effective ways to influence the target market's opinion of the new company and its product(s). Given the nature of the market, the promotional funds available, and the competitive environment, Mr. Heaps wondered what blend of these promotional methods would provide the optimal mix, and indeed how he should allocate his budget among the different mix items.

A related question, to ensure that the approach used at the Upper Canada Brewing Company was different, centred on the marketing theme or appeal to use. Mr. Heaps decided that the primary marketing emphasis was to be on the Upper Canada brand's freshness, natural quality and unique taste, made in a ''hands-on'' brewery. The slogan he proposed was, ''Our beer is as good as the best in the world!'' To communicate this message, he wanted to advertise informatively rather than with a life-style appeal. General advertising of a life-style nature was to be avoided because of the cost and Mr. Heaps' conviction of its incompatibility with the Upper Canada Brewing Company corporate and product image. To further support this different market appeal, he decided to promote artistic and cultural activities rather than the sports activities supported by the major breweries. Given the characteristics of his target market and the desired position of the brewery product(s) in the marketplace, he analyzed the appropriateness of

this appeal before finalizing decisions on the launch of an advertising campaign.

One final promotion decision to be made concerned media strategy. To ensure that the message reached the target audience, it was necessary to clearly identify the media vehicles to use; the choices available included television, radio, newspaper, magazine, and outdoor. Related to the task of determining media classes and vehicles was the choice of media scheduling and concentration: at what periods throughout the year should the advertising campaign run and should the advertising be concentrated in one medium to gain impact or several media classes to increase reach?

Mr. Heaps realized that any new business must first create awareness and then attract trial if it was to gain customers. The promotional strategy differentiated its products from those of the major competitors, and thus persuaded buyers to give trial support to the products of this new brewery. Ultimately, the success or failure of the venture largely rested with the care taken to devise an appropriate promotion strategy to allow the brewery to obtain 0.1 percent of the market, the estimated market share needed to be viable. Upon gaining initial entry into the market, Mr. Heaps hoped to rely primarily on word-of-mouth advertising for market share development.

QUESTIONS

1. Evaluate the percentage-of-sales method used to establish the promotion budget.

2. Is the promotional budget allocated for the first two years of operation adequate? Why or why not?

3. What blend of promotional methods should Mr. Heaps use? Why?

4. Evaluate the appropriateness of the marketing appeal identified for the product(s) of this new brewery.

5. Which media class(es) should Mr. Heaps choose? Why? What periods of the year should the campaign run? Why?

CASE 6.2 # W. K. Buckley Limited (A)

It was April 1985, and Frank Buckley was faced with an important decision concerning the advertising program for Buckley's Mixture for the 1985-86 advertising season. At the suggestion of his advertising agency, Mr. Buckley had done no advertising during 1984-85 for the principal product in the Buckley product line, using that year to conduct consumer research and to prepare an advertising strategy for the future. The research was now complete and Mr. Buckley had received the recommendations of the agency. The approach they were proposing would involve a major departure from the approach that had been used to advertise Buckley's Mixture in the past.

W. K. BUCKLEY LIMITED

The over-the-counter drug industry is constantly changing. With continuous advances in the treatment of illness, many pharmaceutical products become outdated in a very short time. Continual success of a formula over any extended period in this industry would seem almost impossible. Apparently, W. K. Buckley discovered a product that has maintained its success even after more than 70 years of treating Canadians who suffer from coughs and colds. The product is Buckley's Mixture.

W. K. Buckley Limited is a privately owned, Toronto-based company founded by William K. Buckley in 1920. The founder's son, Frank Buckley, joined the company in 1946 and is the current owner and president. It was 1919 when W.K. Buckley, the owner of a small Toronto drugstore, noticed the increasing popularity of one of his cough remedies. He decided to introduce the product to a wider market as Buckley's Mixture, a sugar-free, expectorant-type, non-prescription product, developed as an effective relief from coughs, colds, and bronchitis. The product was known for its distinctive taste and its effective-

ness in combating coughs and colds. Among the ingredients that Mr. Buckley included and that are still found in Buckley's Mixture are ammonium carbonate, potassium bicarbonate, menthol, camphor, Canada Balsam, and pine needle oil. When other over-the-counter preparations were selling at 25 to 35 cents each, Mr. Buckley introduced Buckley's Mixture to the Toronto market at 75 cents. This higher price allowed him to advertise the product widely and gave him a better financial return. He continued this pricing policy when he expanded distribution to a network of retail drugstores in Toronto. Because it was so successful, he also priced Buckley's higher than competitive products when he began to distribute it throughout Ontario.

Although known primarily as the manufacturer of Buckley's Mixture, now available in 100 mL and 200 mL sizes, W. K. Buckley Limited today also produces and distributes a variety of other cough and cold remedies, as well as a veterinary line. Some of the company's other products include Jack & Jill cough syrup, Lemon Time, and Buckley's White Rub. A 1984 report indicated that 65 to 70 percent of Buckley's volume was sold through non-pharmacy outlets, including supermarkets and convenience stores. This was considerably different from sales patterns of cough medicines generally in Canada, as a recent Gallup study revealed that 84.5 percent of cough and cold remedies are sold through drugstores.

W. K. Buckley Limited distributes its products in Canada, the United States, and the Caribbean, and operates under licensing agreements in Australia, New Zealand, and Holland. The company has remained small, employing only 20 people, all at the company's Toronto plant. Brokers and agents are employed on a regional basis across Canada, eliminating the requirement for the company to employ a sales force.

Numerous changes have taken place in the proprietary medicine industry since the intro-

©1991. This case was written by Leanne O'Leary and James G. Barnes of Memorial University of Newfoundland. The case was prepared with the cooperation and permission of W. K. Buckley Limited to illustrate the marketing initiatives of that company and not to indicate a correct or incorrect approach to the solution of marketing problems. The authors acknowledge the cooperation and support of Frank C. Buckley, President, John J. Meehan, Vice-President, and David Rieger, Manager of Sales and Marketing, of W. K. Buckley Limited, and Jackie Robertson of Ambrose Carr Linton Kelly, Inc., in the preparation of this case.

duction of Buckley's Mixture. As the role of the independent drugstore began to decline in the 1960s, large drug supermarkets emerged as the principal outlet for health and personal care products. Another significant change occurred in the 1970s when national and international pharmaceutical companies began to use some of the marketing and creative advertising strategies that had been employed successfully by W. K. Buckley. Fierce competition from large multinational companies and the introduction of many new products to the Canadian market caused a decline in popularity for Buckley's products during the 1970s and early 1980s.

EARLY MARKETING STRATEGIES

Always one to take advantage of every opportunity, the founder of the company realized the potential that advertising offered for increased sales. During an era when advertising was a relatively new and poorly understood business tool, W. K. Buckley invested in newspaper space and used radio extensively to promote his product. Efficient use of national radio helped establish Buckley's Mixture as a household name in the 1930s and 1940s. Radio spots were purchased adjacent to the news each morning at 8 o'clock, and just before the CBC Noon Farm Broadcast to reach rural areas. Mr. Buckley maintained that this timing and continuity were more economical, equalling more media buys, built market loyalty, and reached his audience. People in rural Canada may be too busy to listen to the radio, but W. K. Buckley knew they stopped everything to listen to the CBC Farm Broadcast. Even today, the sales of Buckley's Mixture in rural Canada reflect the loyalty established over 50 years ago.

The 1920s was a period of rapid growth at W. K. Buckley Limited, with new products introduced and distribution expanded into Quebec, the Maritimes, and the Prairies. With the Depression of the 1930s, the company consolidated its operations in what it did best, the manufacture of cold and cough preparations. By the end of that decade, W. K. Buckley had also recruited commission sales representatives, hand-picked and trained, to establish a sales force for the company's product line. A business graduate from the University of Toronto, Frank Buckley joined the company in 1946, about the

same time his father was expanding its operations into international markets, and the domestic market began to pose increasing challenges. The growth of the non-drugstore market was an early indicator of major changes to come later in the decade. Two major changes swept the industry in the 1960s and 1970s: the transition from the small, independent drugstore to the larger drug supermarket, and the impact of marketing and creative advertising strategies on the promotion of the industry and its products. Frank Buckley believed that the 1980s represented an opportunity for his company to return to a "back to the basics" strategy.

THE MARKET

The Canadian market for cough and cold remedies is highly competitive. In 1984, the industry generated approximately $70 million in sales. Within this total market, the over-the-counter category had remained relatively stable during the preceding ten years. However, this sector of the market was dominated by large multinational pharmaceutical companies who used their size to gain a lead in product development, media spending, and shelf positioning. The key competitive brands in this industry include Benylin (Parke Davis), Novahistine (Dow), Triaminic (Ancalab), Robitussin (A. H. Robins), Vicks (Procter & Gamble), and Buckley's Mixture (W. K. Buckley Ltd.).

Exhibit 1 presents some of the results of a 1984 research study of the liquid cough remedy market, carried out with the objective of defining the national market. The research, conducted by Butler Research Associates, using the data collection services of the Gallup National Omnibus, surveyed 2,100 adults across the country in their own homes. The exhibit presents market share and level of awareness data for the top seven brands in the market. Benylin was the leading brand in all five regions of Canada where data were collected. While Vicks had very high levels of awareness, it had considerably lower incidence of usage. The leading brands of cough and cold remedies listed in this exhibit must also compete with antihistamine and cold products, such as Tylenol, Hismanal, Sudafed and Contac-C, for the same consumer dollar.

Buckley's, with an estimated share of market of 5.2 percent nationally, was strongest on the

EXHIBIT 1 **Research Results**
Canadian Cough Remedy Market, 1984

	Top of Mind	Share of Mind	Total Awareness	Market Share*
Buckley's Mixture	5.4%	12.1%	64.6%	5.2%
Benylin	22.9	33.8	73.0	29.2
Vicks	19.5	36.8	86.8	14.3
Triaminic	6.4	12.9	42.1	13.6
Dimetapp	2.0	4.8	33.3	6.1
Robitussin	4.1	9.1	46.8	5.8
Novahistine	1.2	3.6	45.4	4.0

* brand bought most recently

Prairies and in Ontario. The brand held an 8.6 percent share of market among users aged 60 and older, 5.5 percent with those in the 45-to-59 age bracket, but only 3.6 percent among those aged 18 to 29. When asked what they liked most about the product, users of Buckley's Mixture most often referred to its effectiveness, the fact that it relieves cold symptoms and soothes a cough, that it relieves congestion and is fast-acting. When asked to list what they disliked about the product, users mentioned its taste and its bitter, menthol flavour.

Advertising campaigns in the liquid cough remedy industry are conducted primarily in the winter season, when most colds and coughs are likely to occur. Advertising for Buckley's Mixture in the early 1980s was focused on a "tastes strong" message. To a large extent, the advertising budget consisted of national radio spots aimed at the working person (both male and female) in the 39 and over bracket. The advertising was also directed to rural areas where it was thought that most frequent users of Buckley's Mixture lived. Advertisements were also placed in *Reader's Digest* and *TV Guide*. Exhibit 2 presents radio scripts of three commercials for Buckley's Mixture that were used in the early 1980s.

In April 1984, a new advertising agency was appointed to handle Buckley's advertising, replacing the previous agency, which had closed operations. The new agency, Ambrose, Carr, DeForest, and Linton, Ltd. of Toronto (later to become Ambrose Carr Linton Kelly, Inc.), determined that, although a specific target market had been defined for Buckley's products, there was no market research to confirm the accuracy of that definition. Considering the recent decline in the market share enjoyed by Buckley's Mixture, Ambrose Carr recommended that, before the $250,000 advertising budget was spent on promotion, it should be determined if the budget was being allocated effectively. Following the suggestion of his new advertising agency, Frank Buckley decided to do no advertising during the 1984-85 season; instead the company commissioned marketing research to learn more about its market.

RESEARCH RESULTS

The research project was conducted by Butler Research Associates, a Toronto marketing research company, using the data-collection capabilities of the Gallup National Omnibus service. The data were collected during a two-week period in November 1984. The project was a national survey and involved interviews with 2,100 adults, 18 years of age and over, in their own homes, in population centres of at least 1,000. A random block sampling procedure was used in urban centres, and a quota sample based on sex and age in rural areas. The research objectives established for this project included: (1) determining the level of awareness and share of market of Buckley's Mixture and of competitive brands; (2) determining the strengths and weaknesses of Buckley's Mixture; (3) examining the usage and purchase patterns of the users of liquid cough remedies; and (4) developing a profile of Buckley's users. Some of the significant findings were:

- The liquid-cough-remedy market was strongest in Ontario and Quebec, which together represented 63.1 percent of users.

EXHIBIT 2 **Radio Commercial Scripts —
Buckley's Mixture**

1:

SOUNDS OF TRAFFIC IN BACKGROUND

CAB DRIVER:

"I drive a cab, and when I get a cough from a cold, I don't want to cough all over the customers.

"I take Buckley's Mixture, 'cause it works. It checks my coughing, but it doesn't stop me driving. Buckley's loosens congestion, helps me breathe easy, and clears that stuffy feeling; you know what I mean?

"Personally, I take it straight, but some people mix it with honey. Either way, when you take Buckley's Mixture, you know you've taken cough medicine.

"It tastes strong (HORN BLOWS) but it beats coughing."

2:

SOUND OF VACUUM CLEANER IN BACKGROUND

HOMEMAKER:

"When I get a cough from a cold, I take Buckley's Mixture, because it works and you can't let a cough stop you when there are meals to cook and children to worry about.

"Buckley's Mixture loosens congestion and helps clear that stuffy, chesty feeling. It helps during the day, and it helps at night.

"No point pretending I like the taste; I don't. So, I mix it with honey. Even so, you know you've taken cough medicine when you take Buckley's.

"It tastes strong, but it beats coughing."

3.

SOUNDS OF FACTORY MACHINERY OPERATING IN BACKGROUND

EQUIPMENT OPERATOR:

"When I get a cough from a cold, I take Buckley's Mixture; because it works and because you can't operate machinery if you are coughing all the time.

"Buckley's loosens congestion, helps me breathe without wheezing and spluttering. It checks my coughing, but it doesn't stop me working, and it's sugar-free, which is important to me.

"The thing is that when you've taken Buckley's Mixture, you know you've taken cough medicine.

"It tastes strong (WHISTLE BLOWS) but it sure beats coughing."

- The largest user segments were 18 to 44 years of age (67.2 percent) and families with children (55.4 percent).
- 52 percent of respondents had a cold during the 1983-84 winter.
- 75 percent of cough sufferers decided on and bought their own remedy.
- 66 percent of cough and cold remedies were bought by an individual for his/her own use.
- Almost all purchases were made after a cough and/or cold had started.
- The market was not homogeneous nationally and brand preferences differed across regions.
- Usage of and preference for Vicks was skewed towards the younger age segment (18 to 19).
- Benylin and Triaminic had the highest incidence of usage among families with children.
- Approximately 85 percent of liquid cough remedies are purchased in drugstores, and this statistic is even higher in urban centres.
- The most recent purchase was made by the female head of the household (73 percent).
- Consumers do not generally stock cough syrup, preferring to purchase it as required.

The research revealed some valuable information for the marketing of Buckley's Mixture. From the research, Frank Buckley and the creative staff of Ambrose Carr concluded that Buckley's Mixture was performing best in small communities (population fewer than 30,000), sales were skewed towards the less well educated, were strongest in the Prairies and Ontario, but were extremely weak in Quebec. Preference for Buckley's Mixture tended to be strongest among males and the oldest age segment. The research revealed that the total awareness of Buckley's was 64.6 percent, but the brand's market share was only 5.2 percent nationally. This invited the conclusion that Buckley's Mixture was either failing to elicit trial among consumers or failing to deliver after trial and was not being repurchased. Among current users, the strongest feature of Buckley's Mixture was its effectiveness in relieving coughs and congestion. This attribute was mentioned significantly more often by Buckley's users than by users of other liquid cough remedies. Buckley's sugar-free feature, however, was not particularly important to users in general or to Buckley's users.

In addition to the quantitative Gallup survey, W. K. Buckley Limited also commissioned a qualitative study of the market. A series of focus groups were conducted, two each in Montreal and Toronto. The principal objectives of the focus group discussions were to reveal usage and purchase patterns, identify key variables influencing brand selection, and determine the perceptions of and attitudes towards Buckley's Mixture in relation to competing brands. Consumers appeared to be loyal to a specific brand, with neither the price nor the ingredients of the product being particularly important in the selection of the brand. The discussions revealed that differences in usage patterns appeared not to be related to gender or culture. In most cases, consumers revealed that they used one brand for children and a different brand for adults. Heavy users of cough remedies were more likely than were light users to believe that the products were effective in dealing with a cold or cough. When the preferred brand could not be purchased, a pharmacist was consulted for recommendations. It was also noted that few consumers purchased liquid cough remedies on the basis of packaging.

The qualitative research revealed some key factors about Buckley's Mixture. Most of the participants recognized the brand, though few had tried the product recently. The focus group participants commented that the name had a connotation of old-fashioned reliability, trustworthiness, and security. Its major strengths, as indicated by focus group participants, included effective, old-fashioned strength, based upon its sugar-free, natural ingredients. The participants commented that the product works well as a decongestant, coats the throat, and does not cause drowsiness. They also discussed the brand's weaknesses, which included its aroma, colour, taste, and consistency.

CONCLUSIONS

Once the research had been conducted and results analyzed, a strategy document presented to the Buckley management team by Ambrose Carr in March 1985 identified five key problems with Buckley's Mixture that were apparent from the consumer research:
1. Low top-of-mind awareness,
2. Low rate of trial,
3. Low awareness of its strength and effectiveness,
4. Perception of the product as being old-fashioned,
5. Negative perception of the taste, aroma, and texture.

After a comprehensive review of the results of both the national study and the qualitative focus groups, Peter Byrne, creative director of Ambrose Carr, presented several advertising campaign recommendations to Frank Buckley and his management team. One of the suggested campaigns involved Frank Buckley promoting his own product. This would continue the tradition of a face behind the name of W. K. Buckley Limited, a tradition that had been maintained over seven decades. The agency believed that Frank Buckley would portray the desired image of an honest businessman who believes in the effectiveness of his product and who promotes it on the basis of its true attributes. Another proposal was intended to turn the negative perceptions of the strong taste, aroma, and texture of Buckley's Mixture into positive aspects for the promotion efforts. The proposal from the agency involved the use of humorous phrases to illustrate the ''awful'' taste of Buckley's Mixture, simultaneously establishing it as an effective remedy.

QUESTIONS

1. What objectives should Frank Buckley and his management team have in determining the marketing program to support Buckley's Mixture in 1985-86?

2. As a fairly small company, operating in an industry where the competition consists primarily of large companies with many products in their product lines, what strategy would be most appropriate for Mr. Buckley to adopt for Buckley's Mixture?

3. Considering the recent slippage in the market share of Buckley's Mixture and the limited advertising budget available to W. K. Buckley Limited, would you recommend to Frank Buckley that he accept the recommendations of this advertising agency?

4. What are the implications for Mr. Buckley of appearing in his own advertising and of promoting negative aspects of the product? What consumer or market characteristics or trends would such an approach address?

CASE 6.3   # The Tea Council of Canada (A)

The Tea Council of Canada is a non-profit organization with an international flavour. The concept of a tea council emerged in 1954 when the International Tea Agreement lapsed and was not renewed. Under that agreement, the International Tea Market Extension Board (ITMEB) had promoted tea globally. Major tea producers felt the need to continue the work started by the ITMEB, in cooperation with the tea trade in importing companies.

The Tea Council of Canada was among the first collaborative efforts to be established and, in 1954, it undertook the job of generic tea promotion. The council, funded by Sri Lanka and India as producer members, was chartered and supported by well-known tea importers and processors, including Salada, Brooke Bond, Lipton, and Mother Parker's. The council had since expanded its membership to include Kenya, Nestlé Enterprises, Northern Tea, North American Tea and Coffee, Inc., National Importers Canada Limited, and the Tetley Tea Company. Members of the council serve on its various committees and as financial supporters of its promotional programs.

In 1981, the Tea Council embarked on a planned promotional program with concentrated activities in four key areas: promotion and publicity, school education, special events, and the food services sector. These activities have come to be known as the "core program." Several committees within the council help ensure that the continuity and synergy of message are maintained under this program. These committees are the Marketing Committee, the Food Service Committee, and the Tea Grading Committee.

THE TEA INDUSTRY

Just as the Tea Council has experienced changes over the years, so too has the tea industry as a whole. Although Europe (especially Britain) and tea often seem synonymous, tea originated in China. The first tea pots on record were discovered near Shanghai around 1500 A.D. Tea was then produced by India, Sri Lanka, and Java and these nations soon became major tea producers for the world's consumers. The first tea to arrive in Canada was brought by the Hudson's Bay Company to its trading posts as early as 1716. It soon became one of the company's most important trading commodities.

It was not until the end of the nineteenth century, however, that producers began to package tea in the now familiar tea bag. Today, many types, varieties, and blends of tea in tea bags are enjoyed daily in Canada. The industry has also become highly competitive, with an increased number of companies competing for segments of the market. A number of packaging innovations, including drinking boxes, envelope packs, and round tea bags, have been introduced by companies in an effort to carve out a larger share of the tea market.

TRENDS IN TEA CONSUMPTION

Herbal and specialty teas have been enjoying a growth in popularity in the Canadian market in recent years. A study conducted in 1990 detailed a 5-to-7 percent annual increase in sales in this sector of the market. This positive movement has been a welcome development from the perspective of the tea industry as hot-drink consumption, and more specifically regular black tea consumption, has shown a clear downward trend since 1985. Black tea is also known as Orange Pekoe, and the term is used to describe domestic blends marketed by the various tea packers. Generally, hot beverages are losing sales to cold, light, unsweetened drinks. This is in part a result of dramatically increased promotion and publicity by marketers of certain

©1991. This case was written by Robert Power and Leanne O'Leary of Memorial University of Newfoundland, under the direction of Dr. James G. Barnes. The case was prepared with the cooperation and permission of the Tea Council of Canada to illustrate the marketing initiatives of that organization and not to indicate a correct or incorrect approach to the solution of marketing problems. The authors acknowledge the cooperation and support of Gordon F. Reynolds, Executive Director of the Tea Council of Canada, in the preparation of this case.

drinks within the beverage industry, including milk, soft drinks, fruit juices, and mineral waters.

During the period from 1980 to 1988, tea sales in retail grocery stores declined from 26 percent to 21 percent of the beverage market, while coffee experienced a drop from 36 percent to 31 percent. During this same period, however, soft drink sales jumped from 17 percent to 23 percent, and juice and other non-alcoholic beverages climbed from 20 percent to 24 percent of this market.

In an industry that claims overall world-wide growth in tea volume per year of approximately 3 percent, Canada still manages to remain one of the world's leading tea-consuming nations with a per capita consumption of 1.6 pounds (0.72 kg) annually or the equivalent of one cup per day. In fact, Canada is the foremost tea-drinking country in the western hemisphere. While this may be true, Canadian consumption has seen better days. The mid-1970s saw annual tea consumption in Canada hit an all-time high of 1.3 kg per person. Canadian consumption is well behind that of residents of Qatar, a part of the United Arab Emirates. This nation consumes 12 pounds of tea annually or the equivalent of eight cups per person per day.

THE MARKETING COMMITTEE'S PROPOSAL

In 1981, the Tea Council of Canada embarked upon a planned promotional program with concentrated activities in three key areas. Members agreed that tea was likely to gain in image and consumption from improved awareness, through the provision of information about the social, cultural, geographic, and historic implications of the tea industry. The promotional activities of the council were, therefore, geared to increasing general knowledge and attitudes, as well as improving the quality of tea and service in the out-of-home market.

For some time, however, there had existed a desire among some Tea Council members to test the effectiveness of a carefully planned, strategically defined, generic advertising campaign. In late 1989, the marketing committee of the Tea Council of Canada developed a proposal outlining their goals and methodology to undertake such a campaign. Following some revisions, the proposal was approved by the board of directors and each council member was assessed incremental funding of 0.25 cents per pound, in addition to their regular contribution; this yielded approximately $250,000. While this funding certainly helped defray the costs associated with the project, the campaign would be primarily funded from core program budgets in 1990 and 1991.

Having received the approval of the board, the marketing committee began by undertaking a comprehensive usage and attitude study of the Canadian population. In conducting this research, the objective of the committee was to obtain information that would allow them to develop the marketing and communications strategy for their future promotional campaign. The research was conducted by the Custom Research Division of ISL—International Surveys Limited. The objectives of the research were to:

1. ascertain the prevalent images and attitudes that exist towards tea and tea drinking, and

2. test with consumers several strategic concepts in order to provide direction regarding an advertising and communications approach for tea in the near future.

In order to achieve this, a telephone survey was conducted in which randomly selected individuals were surveyed. The following quotas were followed in selecting the sample for the survey:

1. 60 percent of respondents were to be female and 40 percent male;

2. a total of 600 interviews were to be completed in five regional markets as follows: Halifax, Calgary, and Vancouver, 100 each; Montreal and Toronto, 150 each;

3. 54 percent of respondents were to drink tea daily; 18 percent at least weekly; and 28 percent at least occasionally.

SUMMARY OF FINDINGS

Upon completion of the research, the conclusions presented by ISL reaffirmed some known facts and also provided key directional information for the council's marketing committee. The following conclusions were a result of the ISL research:

1. Hot drink consumption, and more specifi-

cally the consumption of tea, has been in decline since 1985.

2. Water, fruit juice, and milk appear to be the most obvious growth beverages.

3. While tea is not currently viewed as an overly healthy beverage, it clearly carries some health-related connotations.

4. Positioning tea on a health platform would require a considerable effort and a substantial budget since it would necessitate the changing of currently held beliefs, rather than the reinforcement of existing ones.

5. Promoting tea among those aged 60 and over had obvious limitations and promoting it among those aged under 30 means competing in a group of beverages that is already heavily targeted by competing products. The 30-to-49 age segment would therefore appear to be the most appropriate segment on which to concentrate.

6. With limited resources, the most appropriate strategy may be to focus on the soothing, refreshing, and natural taste elements against an executional background of health.

7. Recognizing the move by Canadians towards cold drinks, it may still be best to sell tea on the basis of what it is, a hot drink.

Other life-style research available to the Tea Council provided additional insights and input into the development of the committee's strategies. One survey, for example, found that consumers believe that life is too chaotic and turbulent and that people are looking for anchors and controls of life. Today, consumers want to "relax and take the edge off." People are searching for balance and moderation in their lives.

Another survey found people are working long hours, experiencing high levels of stress, and spending little time with their families. Women, in particular, are juggling the demands of a career and family. Unfortunately, consumers' real and perceived time pressures are likely to get worse during the next decade.

Having reached these conclusions, the council's marketing committee proceeded to prepare their case for approval of a formal promotional campaign for presentation to the board of directors.

QUESTIONS

1. As chairman of the board of directors of the Tea Council of Canada, would you approve the council launching an advertising and promotional campaign designed to increase consumption of tea among Canadians?

2. What do you feel the objectives of such a campaign should be?

3. To whom should such a campaign be directed and what should be its principal messages and components?

CASE 6.4 **Pasquini's Pizzeria: Promotional Program for a Small Business**

About two months ago Tony Pasquini purchased a small pizzeria, which he promptly renamed Pasquini's Pizzeria. The location had housed a pizzeria for about 2½ years with two previous owners. The first owner had operated the pizzeria successfully. Under the most recent owner, however, both in-house sales and home-delivery volume had declined considerably. In effect, Tony Pasquini had acquired an ailing business.

Tony had some experience in the pizza business. As a teenager and college student, he had worked in various capacities in a pizzeria his family owned and operated. In his current situation, Tony faced a problem that commonly confronts young entrepreneurs who have recently acquired a small business. That is, Tony was wondering what would be the most effective way to promote his products.

Pasquini's Pizzeria sold an assortment of freshly made pizzas and other products. The main product was a thick-crusted, New York-style pizza available with a choice of toppings.

Adapted from a case prepared by Anthony Pasquini, under the direction of Professor William J. Stanton.

The restaurant also made and sold calzones (folded pizza dough stuffed with pizza toppings), submarine sandwiches, and salads. No alcoholic beverages were sold by Pasquini's Pizzeria. The restaurant provided a place to eat as well as free home delivery of all menu items within a radius of 20 blocks from the location.

Pasquini's Pizzeria was located in Regina, Saskatchewan, on a major north-south thoroughfare about two miles south of the central downtown business district. The restaurant was about the same distance from the University of Regina with an enrollment of about 7,500.

According to Tony Pasquini, the pizza restaurant business had boomed during the past five years — especially in the area of home delivery. Franchises were proliferating and Regina had followed the national trend with an increase in pizza restaurants. In Pasquini's delivery area alone, there were five pizzerias including Pizza Hut and Little Caesar's. Three of these five competitors featured home delivery. Two of them had the ability to deliver within 30 minutes, in contrast to Pasquini's 45 minutes. However, these two competitors did not deliver all the items listed on their menus. The national chains also had the advantage of large budgets for advertising and other promotion.

During the first two months after Tony acquired the pizzeria, he concentrated on selecting and training a team of dependable employees. Now he was ready to devote his attention to the task of increasing the pizzeria's sales volume. Currently Pasquini's was taking in $3,600 a month at lunchtime and $5,500 during the evenings. "During the next six months," he said, "my goal is to triple our lunch business and quadruple our evening business. That should give us a sales volume of close to $400,000 per year. I realize that the increase in evening business will have to come from home-delivery sales, because at nighttime, this location is dead."

Tony believed that the key to achieving these sales goals was to get people to try Pasquini's pizza. "Our pizzas taste great and their quality is top-notch. We just need to make people aware of Pasquini's Pizzeria and get them to try our pizza. Then I am sure that we will have the repeat business we need to reach our sales goal." However, to generate this customer awareness and product sampling, Tony understood that he needed a good promotional program — yet one that would not cost too much. "We are loaded with dough," he said, "but it's the pizza kind and not the financial kind."

Tony decided that he could spend $2,500 on promotion at this time. When selecting promotional media, Tony knew he should consider the characteristics of each medium as well as the cost of reaching prospective customers (CPM — cost per thousand). Some of the promotional media that he was considering were:

- *Flyers:* Flyers cost $150 per 1,000 (in lots of 10,000) for printing one page on one side, plus $35 per thousand for door-to-door distribution. Pasquini estimated that 2 to 4 percent of the households receiving a flyer would patronize his pizzeria.
- *Direct-mail flyers:* The costs were 9.3 cents per piece for postage, a $240 set-up charge, $100 for a first-time-only postal permit charge, plus the cost of the flyers ($150 per 1,000).
- *Coupon booklets:* A form of co-op advertising that included coupons for other nearby businesses. Booklets cost 30 cents each to print plus 12 cents for postage. Thus the cost per 1,000 was $420. If Tony could get 20 local businesses to pay $210 each to advertise in the booklet, he could include his own coupon and distribute 10,000 booklets at no cost to him.

- *Special business cards:* A variation of the flyer medium, 3-×-5 cards with a special offer on each side, to be personally distributed to businesses in the area. Printing cost was $420 for 5,000 cards. A trial run of these cards led Tony Pasquini to believe that he would get as high as a 50 percent response.
- *Newspaper ads:* A University of Regina student paper with a circulation of 10,000 cost $75 for a quarter-page ad. A neighbourhood paper with a circulation of 3,000 cost $120 for a half page. *Westword*, a paper distributed throughout Regina with heavy circulation (10,000) in Tony's delivery area, cost $180 for a quarter page.
- *Neon signs:* In the front window at a cost of $780. On the side of the building with 3-km clear view at a cost of $1,200.

Tony also wondered whether he should use radio, television, or possibly some other media. He considered personal selling to promote to groups and other customers who bought large quantities of pizza, such as clubs at the university, bars in the area that featured "happy hours," and big companies that ordered food for special events.

Tony was fully aware that his time and financial budget were limited. But he also knew that he had better do an effective promotional job, or all his hard work and investment to date would be wasted.

QUESTION

What promotional program should Tony Pasquini adopt for his pizzeria?

P A R T

7

MANAGING THE MARKETING EFFORT

Planning and implementing a company's
marketing program in its home and global
markets, evaluating the marketing performance
of a company, appraising the role of marketing
in our society, and considering marketing
activities in the future

U p to this point, we have dealt with target market
selection and the development and management of the four elements of the marketing mix
in an individual organization.

Now it is time to take an overview of the firm's marketing
program by examining the implementation and evaluation
aspects of such programs as they are perceived from a
marketing management perspective. Our approach in Part
7 is to introduce the elements of marketing planning and
implementation as they pertain to international marketing
efforts in Chapter 20. In Chapter 21, we take a complete
look at marketing management implementation and evaluation issues regardless of market location. Then in Chapter 22, we conclude by appraising the current position of
marketing in our society and looking to the future.

CHAPTER 20 GOALS

As you will see, international marketing is more than simply marketing in a foreign language. After studying this chapter, you should be able to explain:

- The importance of international marketing to Canadian businesses.
- Major organizational structures for operating in foreign markets.
- The nature and problems of international marketing research.
- The importance of recognizing cultural and environmental differences in various foreign markets.
- International marketing programs—product planning, pricing, distribution, and advertising.
- Government support for international marketing.

C H A P T E R **20**

International Marketing

s trade barriers fall and industries deregulate, powerful trading blocs are forming in Europe, Asia, and North America that will make life more difficult for international marketers. In the 1990s, it is crucial that Canadians build up new markets abroad in order to survive the increasing global competition. Although many companies have a long way to go, there are several big firms who have already succeeded.

Bombardier, the Montreal-based transportation and aerospace firm, now earns 90 percent of its $2.8 billion in net sales internationally. The first key to its success stems from exploiting specialized markets—it provides urban transportation for New York, Boston, and Amtrak and aerospace for the Pentagon and France's Airbus. The second key is to get a foothold in Europe before 1992, through acquisitions or joint ventures; to this end, Bombardier bought the second largest maker of railway equipment in France, while it already owns railway car makers in Belgium and Austria. Also in 1989, Bombardier acquired Short Brothers, a Northern Ireland manufacturer of civil and military aircraft, aero structures and defence systems.

Northern Telecom — the world's fourth-largest telecommunications equipment maker with products sold in 90 countries, a 1990 revenue of $6.8 billion (U.S.), and a 7.5 percent global market share — has concentrated on R & D, investing enormous amounts of money to keep itself on the cutting edge of technology. Northern's marketing teams have also gained success by studying the local political and cultural biases of their clients (with many telephone companies being state-controlled, politics can take precedence over prices and products).

McCain Foods' strategy is probably the most basic: know your customer. Operating out of Florenceville, N.B., the firm has grown into a multinational with 45 plants in eight countries. It has won over half of the french-fry market in France, as well as major market shares in Britain, Holland, Belgium, and Australia by paying attention to what the customer wants — good food that saves time and money.[1]

As we can see from the experience of these three aggressive Canadian companies, business in more involved in international marketing than ever before. And by the same token, Canadian consumers are aware of American, European, Japanese, and other foreign products, brands, and companies as well as their advertising. Canadians have also always been sensitive to exchange rates and the export prices available for our resources. But the rush to globalization of markets and marketing forces us to pay new attention to what we have always known and to look more closely at the international perspective and international marketing.

What do we mean by international marketing? For an organization, marketing is international if its products or services are marketed in two or more countries. We also hear such terms as multinational, transnational (a term used by the United Nations), and globally applied to cross-border marketing. In this book we — along with most business executives — consider the word international in marketing to be synonymous with those other terms.

DOMESTIC MARKETING AND INTERNATIONAL MARKETING

Marketing fundamentals are universally applicable. Every preceding chapter can be applied in an international context. Whether ATCO, an Alberta firm that produces portable and mobile homes and buildings, sells in Toronto, Trois Rivières, Toledo, Taiwan, or Timbuktu, its marketing program should be built around a good product that is properly priced, promoted, and distributed to a market that has been carefully selected. However, strategies used to implement marketing programs in foreign countries often need to be quite different from domestic marketing strategies. And, of course, the international strategies have to be developed in the context of the domestic ones.

Canada's historic major foreign market has been the United States. Because of language, cultural, and social similarities between English-speaking Canadians and Americans, the American market has not been perceived as being very foreign — although it qualifies as such since it is another country. At the same time, the Quebec market — as described in Chapter 6 — is not usually perceived as being foreign. And yet, except for the legal and monetary status of Quebec, the province exhibits for companies outside that province many of the characteristics of a foreign market. As Canadians, we are able to have a unique perspective on international marketing and its opportunities and pitfalls. We engage in "near" international marketing domestically in Quebec with all the problems of translation, different meanings, different values, and different preferences — and we have seen examples of how well or badly we have recognized the differences. On the other hand, we also seem to engage in "near" domestic marketing internationally when dealing with the United States. Here again, we have seen examples of how we have failed to recognize differences.

Our domestic history provides us with a basic message: we have two major language and culture groups and numerous smaller ones; insofar as we recognize our multiculturalism in domestic marketing stategies and tactics, this provides us with the ability to do so in an international marketing context. For

---

[1]Adapted from James Fleming, "Conquering Canadians," *Report on Business Magazine*, January 1990, pp. 30–32.

us, compared with many other countries that are much more homogeneous domestically, there is no reason not to be sensitive to the nuances of international marketing and less reason not to be successful at it. We have the domestic advantages and experience to deal with such issues as understanding foreign markets, determining the strategic question of degree of involvement in them, and being able to organize for operating in each.

Can We Standardize International Marketing?

A continuing controversy in international marketing concerns the extent to which a company can standardize its marketing program in its various foreign markets. Two large multinational firms — Coca-Cola and Nestlé — have been immensely successful, yet they have quite opposite managerial philosophies regarding global standardization. On the one hand, Coca-Cola, following American troops around the world during World War II, established a global marketing program based on one product with one promotional message. This program was tightly managed from the company's world headquarters in Atlanta, Georgia. On the other hand, the Switzerland-based Nestlé Company historically has decentralized much of its management and marketing programs. This was done to avoid wartime disruptions in Europe and also to respond to the wants and preferences of diverse local markets. Nestlé Canada responds quite differently to domestic matters than does Nestlé U.S. Both provide their experiences to the Swiss headquarters for the benefit of other country operations.

We can make a few broad generalizations regarding global standardization in marketing. The best bet for standardization is in the area of durable business goods. In such industries as aircraft, computers, telecommunications, and tractors, the worldwide market (at least among industrialized nations) is quite uniform. This has helped both Northern Telecom and Canadair to be successful in business markets. Somewhere in the middle of our standardization spectrum, we can place consumer durable goods such as cameras, watches, pocket calculators, small appliances, and television sets. The most difficult goods to standardize globally are food and drink products and wearing apparel. (Here Coca-Cola is an exception.) This difficulty can be traced to national tastes and

Benetton's "United Colors of Benetton" ads reach out to young people in many cultures. This campaign is an example of a standardized approach to international marketing.

MARKETING AT WORK

FILE 20-1 **HIGH TECHNOLOGY STANDARDIZATION BREEDS SUCCESS**

In early 1991, the Indonesian government granted permission to Canadair to sell its Challenger business jet in that country. Canadair was pleased as this event places them in a stronger competitive position within the fast-growing Pacific Rim market (already ten jets have been sold to Japanese investors, five to China, five to Australia, and two to Malaysia). The Challenger has now been certified to operate in 14 countries, with military certification in three more. Aside from focusing on the Asian market, Canadair is hoping to win markets in Germany, and especially France — a difficult feat in that France produces the Challenger's main rival, the Dassault Falcon. Canadair has already begun to deliver planes to corporate customers in these two countries. This recent success in global competitiveness means that 22 to 24 Challengers will be sold in 1991, an accomplishment that will allow Canadair to own one-third of the world market.

Adapted from "Challenger Jet Breaks New Ground," *Toronto Star,* Janury 12, 1991, p. 7.

---

habits. Even within national markets such as our own and that of the United States, we often find strong regional differences in food and clothing preferences.

Interestingly enough, the newer a product is, the more likely it will lend itself to standardized marketing across national borders. Traditional apparel such as dress shoes, business suits, and formal wear still are noticeably different from one country to another. But newer items such as T-shirts, blue jeans, athletic shoes, and sweatshirts have readily been accepted across many national borders and cultures.

We support the strategy and philosophy of market segmentation that recognizes cultural differences. It is true that satellite communications, improvements in transportation, and international travel all have contributed to greater familiarity with our neighbours around the world, but strong cultural differences remain.[2]

Different strategies are needed in foreign markets primarily because those markets exist in a different set of environments. Recall that a company operates its marketing program within the economic, political, and cultural environment of each of its markets—foreign or domestic. And none of these environments is controllable by the firm. International marketing is complicated by the fact that these environments — particularly the cultural environment — often consist of elements unfamiliar to Canadian marketing executives. A further complication is the tendency for people to use their own cultural values

---

[2]Part of this section was adapted from J.J. Boddewyn, Robin Soehl, and Jacques Picard, "Standardization in International Marketing: Is Ted Levitt in Fact Right?" *Business Horizons*, November-December 1986, pp. 69–75; John A. Quelch and Edward J. Hoff, "Customizing Global Marketing," *Harvard Business Review*, May–June 1986, pp. 59–68; and Martin van Mesdag, "Winging It in Foreign Markets," *Harvard Business Review*, January–February 1987, pp. 71–74.

as a frame of reference when in a foreign environment. This is particularly the case when Canadians operate in the United States. Throughout this chapter, we shall point out how cultural and other environmental differences among foreign markets strongly affect an organization's international marketing program.[3]

IMPORTANCE OF INTERNATIONAL MARKETING

Canadians have known for a long time that our economic welfare depended, to an important degree, on our success as international traders and marketers. For many years, our exports have ranged from 22 to 25 percent of our gross national product, compared with such current proportions as 6 percent for the United States, 17 percent for France, 26 percent for Germany, 44 percent for the Netherlands, 19 percent for the United Kingdom and 10 percent for Japan. Clearly, how we do abroad is important to our welfare.

Our most important markets continue to be: (1) the United States—accounting for about 75 percent of our international trade; (2) Japan with 7 percent; (3) the European Community (EC) countries with 7 percent and, (4) all other countries of the world with about 11 percent. These proportions have not changed appreciably in the last few years. The overwhelming importance of the American market to each and every one of us is clearly obvious. A very high proportion of the sales made to the United States are of a business marketing nature involving raw materials, components, and parts rather than completely fabricated products. Direct consumer marketing activity plays a minor but growing role. Both forms of international marketing, business and consumer, are increasingly being pursued by more and more Canadian firms as our home market becomes more competitive and as the attractiveness of United States and other opportunities becomes more apparent.

International marketing is a two-way street, however. The same expanding foreign markets that offer growth opportunities for Canadian firms also have their own producers. Foreign firms are providing substantial competition in Canada, the United States, and abroad. Consumers in Canada and around the world have responded favourably, for example, to Japanese radio and TV products (Sony), motorcycles (Yamaha), cameras (Canon, Nikon), and autos (Nissan, Toyota). We continue to buy Italian shoes, German autos, Dutch electric razors, French wines, Austrian skis, Swiss watches, Chinese textiles, and so on.

Especially strong competition is coming from the United States, Japan, and the companies in the European Community, popularly known as the Common Market. The EC is a group of 12 Western European nations that have banded together in a multinational economic union. Competitive challenges are also being encountered from countries in other multinational economic organizations.

The Changing International Scene

Through the 1990s, there will be excellent marketing opportunities abroad for Canadian companies. But the scene has changed. Several factors make international marketing much tougher for our firms than it was from 1945 to 1975. The most significant has been worldwide marketing by foreign companies of

---

[3]For an expansion of this thesis and a more complete treatment of international marketing using the environmental approach, see Philip R. Cateora, *International Marketing*, 7th ed., Richard D. Irwin, Homewood, Ill., 1991.

low cost resources, parts and components, and a wide variety of high-quality, relatively low-priced products. By now we are quite familiar with the flood of products from the United States and Japan. In the late 1980s, however, markets in both Canada and the United States began to swell with imports from four other Asian countries—Korea, Taiwan, Hong Kong, and Singapore—sometimes referred to as Asia's "Four Tigers" or "Four Dragons." And Thailand and China are not far behind as exporters of some products to Canada. In fact, by the year 2000, Asia probably will have replaced Western Europe as the biggest trading partner of both Canada and the United States.[4]

Another major change has been the shift in international investment pat-

Members of the European Common Market.

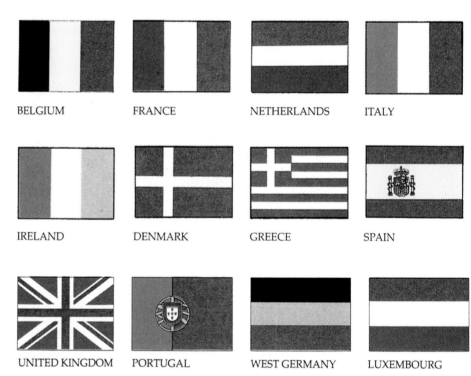

| BELGIUM | FRANCE | NETHERLANDS | ITALY |

| IRELAND | DENMARK | GREECE | SPAIN |

| UNITED KINGDOM | PORTUGAL | WEST GERMANY | LUXEMBOURG |

Multinational economic organizations

EC (European Community, also known as the *Common Market)*: Belgium, France, Germany, Netherlands, Luxembourg, Italy, Ireland, Great Britain, Denmark, Greece, Spain, Portugal.

EFTA (European Free Trade Association): Norway, Sweden, Finland, Iceland, Austria, Switzerland.

OPEC (Organization of Petroleum Exporting Countries): Saudi Arabia, Kuwait, United Arab Emirates, Qatar, Iran, Iraq, Libya, Algeria, Nigeria, Venezuela, Indonesia.

SERA (Latin American Economic System): 25 nations in Central and South America.

---

[4]See Liz Murphy and Richard Kern, "The Pacific Age," *Sales & Marketing Management*, April 1987, p. 64; and "Can Asia's Four Tigers Be Tamed?" *Business Week*, Feb. 15, 1988, p. 46.

A Pepsi-Cola billboard in China.

terns, which assumed significant proportions in the late 1980s. Previously the pattern was for American firms, and some Canadian ones, to invest abroad. At one time it was feared that U.S. firms would eventually own much of Europe's industry. Today it is the other way around. The pattern now is for foreign companies to invest in the United States and Canada. These firms are attracted by political stability, economic growth potential, access to the U.S. market, and limited government regulation compared to Europe. Investment alternatives for foreign companies are either to build new production facilities or to acquire existing firms. Most of our provincial and municipal economic development agencies are busy wooing such investment and providing many incentives—in competition with American agencies—to secure the plants and domestic jobs that will result from the North American market potential.

Of course, the most significant event for Canadians, given the globalization of marketing and the shifts in investment patterns, has been the advent of the Canada-U.S. Free Trade Agreement, a development that was designed to deal with both forms of change and to create an enhanced Canadian advantage in operating in the U.S. market.

THE CANADA-U.S. FREE TRADE AGREEMENT (FTA)

After three failed tries during this century, Canada and the United States negotiated and signed a free trade agreement that went into effect on January 1, 1989. A sectoral free trade arrangement had existed for the automobile industry for the last 24 years and this has proven to be very effective. The new agreement created a single comprehensive market that was 10 percent larger than that of the United States on its own and 15 percent larger than that of the European Community. As a result of the agreement, duties between the two countries are to be eliminated in three stages: (1) immediately, (2) five equal annual cuts of 20 percent beginning January 1, 1989, and (3) ten equal annual cuts of 10 percent beginning January 1, 1989. The first round consisted of such tariff cuts as 4.9 to 22 percent on whiskey, skates, furs, and unprocessed fish. Other sectors, such as textiles, steel, and agricultural products, will not face tariff cuts until late in the ten-year transitional period thereby providing

DEALING WITH FREE TRADE: Adjusting to Reduce Tariffs and New Opportunities
One Answer Is Product Specialization and Market Niching

With clothing tariffs abolished, Peter Nygard of Nygard International Inc., Canada's largest fashion designer, plans to manufacture a new specialized quality line of garments in Canada for sale in both Canadian and American markets. The premium prices and high margins on this line can absorb the high costs of production. At the same time, Nygard plans to produce his medium-priced casual clothes in Los Angeles for sale in both Canada and the United States. Here the more mass-market, medium-price levels and smaller margins dictate a lower-cost larger-scale U.S. production facility. Nygard views his adjustments as a step towards North American specialization to serve medium-priced middle-of-the-road markets as well as higher-priced specialized market niches.

Saskatoon-based Intercontinental Packers, Canada's fourth largest meat processor, uses niche marketing by focusing on sales of gourmet meats (a narrow line of fresh pork, cold ham, roast ham, and bacon) in a single geographic area (Southern California supermarkets).

Another Answer Is Meeting the Competition Head-on

Du Pont Canada Inc. spent $150 million annually for three years to upgrade its Canadian plants in order to take care of an expected double of sales to the United States. The increases are expected as a direct result of tariff reductions allowing lower prices and costs.

Foreign-Owned Subsidiaries Look for North American Product Mandates

Many Canadian subsidiaries of U.S. and other parents are examining how the Canadian facilities and expertise can be used to focus on segments of both the Canadian and U.S. markets. The most common answer seems to be for the Canadian business to serve the large number of specialized markets that exist to the south and leave the mass markets to the large-scale organizations. Procter & Gamble Canada is examining this approach as is Ferro Corp. (producer of industrial coatings) and Camco (Canada's largest appliance manufacturer, owned by Canadian General Electric). American-owned Reynolds and Reynolds, previously focused on a Canadian market with a Toronto plant, will begin serving the New York state and adjacent border states market with its line of computer software and business forms. Robin Hood Multifoods is building a new Canadian bakery to compete across North America with its line of bread, pizza, and muffin mixes.

The Joint Venture—Another Answer

Small and medium-sized Canadian companies can gain access to the U.S. market throughout joint ventures with compatible American firms. Nordco Ltd. of Newfoundland, an innovative producer of underwater sensing equipment and signal processors, formed a joint venture with Ship Analytics, a Connecticut-based producer of ship-bridge simulators. Sales were to be made not only throughout North America but also on a global basis.

Adapted from D'Arcy Jenish, ''Continental Destiny,'' *Maclean's*, July 3, 1989, pp. 68–74.

a long adjustment period in which Canadian and U.S. firms can meet new competition as well as take advantage of new opportunities.[5]

For those Canadian firms that have operated in the United States market without any tariff or non-tariff barriers in the past, nothing has changed as a result of the FTA. For those firms that have successfully hurdled existing barriers and now face a further, phased-in decline in them, they will need to pay more attention to their competitive positioning as well as their market, monitoring of any segment or region of activity. As these firms move to take advantage of gains in gross margin resulting from the elimination of tariffs, they may meet new competition and new competitors. Finally, for those Canadian firms of all sizes who have previously not targeted any segment or region of the U.S. market because they could not deal with the tariff barriers — or simply did not pay attention—new opportunities exist if they can be properly approached. And one of the most important factors to consider is that the American market is actually quite different from the Canadian one in its consumers, competition, and their environment. It is a foreign market regardless of the language spoken.

THE NEW EUROPE

Another significant development that offers new challenges for Canadian firms is the forthcoming economic unification of the 12-nation European Community.

By the end of 1992, the EC will have removed all tariffs along with a maze of nontariff barriers within the 12 participating nations. An economically unified EC with 320 million consumers will present awesome market opportunities and challenges to companies within the EC, as well as to Canadian, American, Japanese, and other foreign firms.

While the EC economic unification will eliminate internal trade barriers, non-European firms fear that external trade barriers may restrict entry of products from outside the EC. These organizations anticipate a "Fortress Europe" that will limit outside competition in EC countries. At the same time, the EC will be a major competitive force as an exporter in world markets. Consequently, Canadian and American firms have moved to establish production facilities, sales branches, and other forms of business presence in the EC prior to 1992.[6]

Looking ahead to the year 2000 and thereafter, perhaps the greatest unknown factor with tremendous international marketing potential is China with its *1 billion* consumers. And, conversely, China has significant potential as an exporter of many low-priced products. Already we have seen glimpses of these possibilities. By 1990, China was a major exporter of clothing. Foreign cosmetic sales in China, unheard of a few years ago, are soaring. Kentucky Fried Chicken opened the largest store in its chain on the square across from Chairman Mao's mausoleum in Beijing. And Coca-Cola and Pepsi-Cola are aggressively competing for larger Chinese market shares.

---

[5]"Summary of the U.S.-Canada Free Trade Agreement," *Export Today*, November-December 1988, pp. 57–61.

[6]See Richard I. Kirkland, Jr., "Outsider's Guide to Europe in 1992," *Fortune*, Oct. 24, 1988, p. 121; and Shawn Tully, "Europe Gets Ready for 1992," *Fortune*, Feb. 1, 1988, p. 81.

STRUCTURES FOR OPERATING IN FOREIGN MARKETS

Once a company has decided to market in foreign countries, management must select an organizational structure for operating in those markets. There are several distinct methods of entering a foreign market. Each represents successively greater international involvement, leading ultimately to a truly global operation. The same firm may use more than one of these operating methods at the same time. To illustrate, it may export products to one country, establish a licensing arrangement in another, and build a manufacturing plant in a third. (See Fig. 20-1.)

The simplest way of operating in foreign markets is by exporting through **import-export agent middlemen**. Very little risk or investment is involved. Also, minimal time and effort are required on the part of the exporting producer. However, the exporter has little or no control over its agent middlemen. Furthermore, these middlemen generally are not aggressive marketers, nor do they generate a large sales volume.

To counteract some of these deficiencies, management can move to the second stage—exporting through **company sales branches** located in foreign markets. Operating a sales branch enables a company to (1) promote its products more aggressively, (2) develop its foreign markets more effectively, and (3) control its sales effort more completely. Of course, management now has the time- and money-consuming task of managing a sales force. The difficulty here is that these sales people are either Canadian sales people unfamiliar with the local market or foreign nationals unfamiliar with the product and the company's marketing practices. New York state has seen a tremendous growth in sales branches that have been established by Quebec- and Ontario-based small and medium-sized firms.

As foreign markets expand, management may enter into licensing arrangements whereby foreign manufacturers produce the goods. **Licensing** means granting to another producer—for a fee or royalty payment—the right to use one's production process, patents, trademarks, or other assets. For example, in Japan, the Suntory brewery is licensed by Anheuser-Busch to produce Budweiser beer, while in England, Budweiser is brewed under licence by the Watney brewery. In Canada, Molson brews both Miller and Lowenbrau under licence from their American and German parent companies.

Contract manufacturing is related to licensing. A Canadian marketer, such as a retail-chain organization, contracts with a foreign producer to supply products that the Canadian firm will market in that producer's country. Shoppers Drug Mart, for instance, contracts with local manufacturers to supply many products for its drugstores in the United States.

Licensing offers companies flexibility with minimal investment. Through licensing or contract manufacturing, producers can enter a market that might otherwise be closed to them because of exchange restrictions, import quotas,

FIGURE 20-1

Structures for operating in a foreign market.

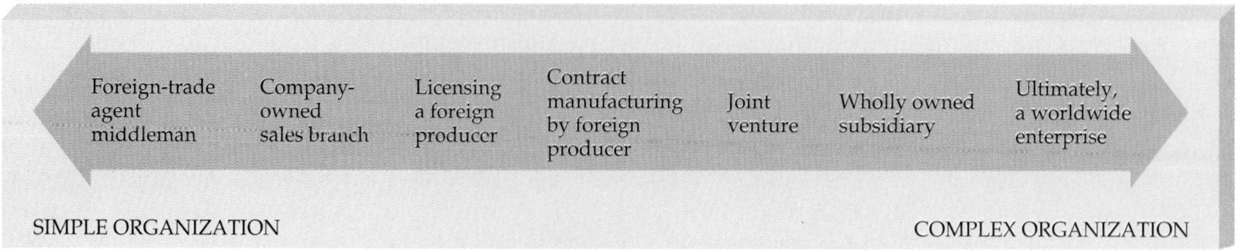

| Foreign-trade agent middleman | Company-owned sales branch | Licensing a foreign producer | Contract manufacturing by foreign producer | Joint venture | Wholly owned subsidiary | Ultimately, a worldwide enterprise |

SIMPLE ORGANIZATION   COMPLEX ORGANIZATION

or prohibitive tariffs. At the same time, by licensing, producers may be building future competitors. A licensee may learn all it can from the producer and then proceed independently when the licensing agreement expires.

In the fourth method, the company builds or otherwise acquires its own production facilities in a foreign country. The structure can be a joint venture or a wholly owned foreign subsidiary. A **joint venture** is a partnership arrangement in which the foreign operation is owned in part by the Canadian company and in part by a foreign company.

When the controlling interest (more than 50 percent) is owned by foreign nationals, the Canadian firm has no real control over any of the marketing or production activities. However, a joint venture may be the only structure (other than licensing) through which a Canadian firm is allowed to enter a given foreign market.

Wholly owned subsidiaries in foreign markets are commonly used by companies that have evolved to an advanced stage of international business. With a wholly owned foreign subsidiary, a company has maximum control over its marketing program and production operations. This type of international structure, however, requires a substantial investment of money, labour, and managerial attention.

This leads us to the final evolutionary stage — one reached by very few companies as yet. It is the stage of the truly multinational corporation — the **worldwide enterprise**. Both the foreign and the domestic operations are integrated and are no longer separately identified. The regional sales office in Montreal is basically the same as the one in Paris. Business opportunities abroad are viewed in the same way as those in Canada. That is, opportunities in Canada are not automatically considered to be better. A true multinational firm does *not* view itself as a Canadian firm (Varity Corp.), or a Swiss firm (Nestlé), or a Dutch firm (Shell Oil) that happens to have plants and markets in a foreign country. In a truly worldwide enterprise, strategic marketing planning is done on a global basis.

A STRATEGIC PROGRAM FOR INTERNATIONAL MARKETING

Firms that have been very successful in marketing in Canada have no assurance whatsoever that their success will be duplicated in foreign markets. A key to satisfactory performance overseas lies in gauging which domestic marketing strategies and tactics should be transferred directly to foreign markets, which ones modified, and which ones not used at all. In other words, foreign markets, too, require strategic marketing planning.

International Marketing Research

Only limited funds are invested in marketing research in foreign countries other than the U.S. and the EC. This is because the costs, relative to the value received, are greater abroad than at home. The reason is that environmental conditions in foreign markets often have a negative influence on some of the basic elements of marketing research.

Fundamental to marketing research is the idea that problems should be solved in a *systematic, analytical manner*. However, an orderly, rational approach runs counter to the business practices found in many locations throughout the world. In some cultures, people are guided by intuition or tradition. And neither of these is particularly conducive to the scientific approach. A second element in marketing research — *customer information* — depends on the willingness of people to respond accurately when researchers pose questions about attitudes or buying habits. In some societies, suspicion of strangers, distrust of government, and an individualism that holds that these things are "none of your business" compound the difficulty of gathering information.

The scarcity of *reliable statistical data* is frequently the single biggest problem in certain foreign markets. Figures on population, personal income, and production may be only crude estimates. Few studies have been made of such things as buying habits or media coverage. In the design of a research project, the lack of reliable data makes it very difficult to select a meaningful sample. Lack of uniformity makes intercountry comparisons very unreliable.[7]

Analysis of Foreign Markets

Nowhere in international marketing is the influence of the cultural and economic environments seen more clearly than in an analysis of market demand. Throughout the world, market demand is determined by population, economic ability to buy, and buying behaviour. Also, human wants and needs have a universal similarity. People need food, clothing, and shelter. They seek a better quality of life — lighter work loads, more leisure time, and social recognition and acceptance. But at about this point, the similarities in foreign and domestic markets end, and the differences in cultural and economic environments must be considered.

When analyzing consumers' *economic ability to buy* in a given foreign market, management may study the (1) distribution of income, (2) rate of growth of buying power, and (3) extent of available consumer financing. In emerging economies, large portions of the population have very low incomes. A much different income-distribution pattern—with resulting differences in marketing programs — is found in industrialized markets of Western Europe. In those countries there are large working-class, middle-income markets. Thus many of the products commonly in demand in Belgium or the Netherlands would find very small markets in many African or Asian countries. In Asia, Japan is an exception, of course. Rising incomes in Japan have generated huge markets for travel, sports, and other leisure-time activities. In response, some shops in London, Paris, and Rome now display window signs saying (in Japanese) "Japanese is spoken here."[8] In western Canada, many resorts such as Banff, Jasper, and Whistler cater to large numbers of Japanese tourists.

Here are some cultural elements that can influence a company's marketing program. The importance of specific elements in marketing varies from country to country.

- *Family.* In some countries the family is an extremely close-knit unit, whereas in others the family members act more independently. Each of these situations requires a different type of promotion, and perhaps even different types of products.
- *Social customs and behaviour.* Some cultural differences are illustrated in the boxed material on page 657.

---

[7]See John Monaco, "Overcoming the Obstacles to International Research," *Marketing News*, Aug. 29, 1988, p. 12; and "Third World Research Is Difficult, but It's Possible," *Marketing News*, Aug. 28, 1987, p. 51. For sources of secondary data on foreign markets, see Cateora, *International Marketing*, Chapter 9.

[8]For some guidelines in determining foreign market opportunities and potential, see S. Tamer Cavusgil, "Guidelines for Export Market Research," *Business Horizons*, November-December 1985, pp. 27–33.

**Northern Telecom helps you fly
to some of the hottest places on earth.**

**And we'll help keep you cool
when you get there.**

It's probable that at any given moment, day or night, there'll be UTA aircraft in the sky ferrying passengers to any of 43 destinations on 5 continents. People on business, others visiting family, but mostly travellers in search of the sun on the beaches of Africa, the Far East and the tropical islands of the Pacific.

Such an operation requires high performance telecommunications. So UTA chose Northern Telecom's Meridian system. A 5000-line network connects several locations to provide a single dialling scheme with Automatic Call Distribution for reservations listings, plus integrated services such as interactive voice messaging.

It's a telecommunications package that easily accommodates the ever changing demands of a modern international airline.

Since 1854, Vittel have been meeting another kind of demand. The demand for natural mineral water. So successful have they been that Vittel has become one of France's top industrial enterprises. And today Vittel water is sold around the globe, including naturally, in places where the sun shines most.

To handle the communications aspects of such a constantly expanding business, Vittel decided to install two of our Meridian systems in their head offices in Vittel itself, to provide integrated telecommunications, interactive voice messaging plus network connectivity for their PC's.

These are just some of the ways that Northern Telecom's advanced telecommunications technology is helping people in more than 100 countries worldwide. Can we help you?

nt northern telecom

TECHNOLOGY THE WORLD CALLS ON.

Quel est le fil conducteur

entre un amateur d'évasion en route pour Tahiti et une eau minérale des Vosges?

Northern Telecom équipe UTA et Vittel.

UTA, compagnie du groupe Air France, dessert 43 destinations sur les 5 continents dont la plupart font rêver car elles se trouvent sous les tropiques. Sur son réseau long courrier, UTA achemine près d'un million de passagers par an et, de jour comme de nuit, elle s'efforce de répondre à leurs nombreuses attentes.

C'est la raison qui a conduit UTA à choisir des systèmes Meridian de Northern Telecom pour son réseau de télécommunications. Ce réseau, d'une capacité de plus de 5 000 lignes comporte, outre un plan de numérotation commun, des listings de réservation des places, un logiciel intégré de distribution automatique des appels et des prestations centralisées

telles qu'une messagerie vocale interactive. Si UTA vous met l'eau à la bouche, Vittel vous désaltérera!

Pour mieux relier ses équipes, Vittel a choisi les systèmes Meridian de Northern Telecom pour son réseau. L'installation "sur mesure" comporte une messagerie vocale interactive, la taxation en réseau et assure la connexion des systèmes informatiques de l'entreprise.

Développer et améliorer le potentiel de communication d'une entreprise, c'est participer à sa réussite. Tel est le but de Northern Telecom, premier fournisseur mondial de systèmes de communation entièrement numériques.

nt northern telecom

LA TECHNOLOGIE QUI FAIT PARLER LE MONDE.

What cultural adjustments do you think Northern Telecom made when entering the market in France? (The French heading translates as: What is the connection between a vacationer on the way to Tahiti and mineral water from the Vosges mountains? Northern Telecom equips both UTA and Vittel.)

- *Educational system.* The educational system affects the literacy rate, which in turn influences advertising, branding, and labelling. The brand may become all-important if potential customers cannot read and must recognize the article by the picture on the label.
- *Language differences.* Language differences also pose problems. Literal translations of English or French advertising copy or brand names may result in ridicule of, or even enmity towards products. Even some English words have different meanings in Canada, Britain, and the United States.
- *Religion.* Religion is a major influence on value systems and behavioural patterns.[9]

A few examples illustrate how buying habits are influenced by cultural elements. One-stop shopping is still unknown in most parts of the world. In many foreign markets, people buy in small units, sometimes literally on a meal-to-meal basis. Also, they buy in small specialty stores. To buy food for a weekend, a *hausfrau* in Germany may visit the chocolate store, the dairy store, the meat market, the fish market, a dry-grocery store, the greengrocer, the bakery, the coffee market, and possibly other specialty food stores. While this may seem to be an inefficient use of her time, we must recognize that a shopping trip is more than just a chore to be done as fast as possible. It is a major part of her social life. She will visit with her friends and neighbours in these shops. Shopping in this fashion is a foreign version of our bridge club or neighbourhood coffee break. In Japan and in Western European countries, some of the traditional shopping patterns are changing, however. Supermarkets now account for a significant and increasing percentage of retail trade in these countries.

So far in this chapter, we have stressed that significant environmental differences do exist between and within foreign countries. Yet we also see movement towards standardization of tastes, wants, and buying habits, especially in Western Europe. In some product lines there are cross-cultural similarities in demand. Pizzerias do business in Germany, lasagna is sold in Stockholm supermarkets, British fish-and-chips are wanted on the Continent, and Scotch whisky sales are large in France. To some extent travel, television, and trade are serving to homogenize European culture. But — and this should be well understood — a German is still a German, and an Italian is still an Italian. The EC may be economically unified after 1992, but a homogeneous Euro-consumer is hardly a reality.[10]

Product Planning for International Markets

Most companies would not think of entering a domestic market without careful, extensive product planning. Yet some Canadian firms typically enter a foreign market with essentially the same product they sell at home. Even when

---

[9]For cultural guidelines on doing business in Asia, see Frederick A. Katayama, ''How to Act Once You Get There,'' *Fortune*, special issue, Fall 1989, p. 87; ''The Delicate Art of Doing Business in Japan,'' *Business Week*, Oct. 2, 1989, p. 120; and John A. Reeder, ''When West Meets East: Cultural Aspects of Doing Business in Asia,'' *Business Horizons*, January-February 1987, pp. 69–74.

[10]For an excellent discussion of this point with many examples, see Barbara Toman, ''Now Comes the Hard Part: Marketing,'' *The Wall Street Journal*, Sept. 22, 1989, p. R10.

Marketing problems may be created by cultural differences

BODY LANGUAGE
- Standing with your hands on your hips is a gesture of defiance in Indonesia.
- Carrying on a conversation with your hands in your pockets makes a poor impression in France, Belgium, Finland, and Sweden.
- When you shake your head from side to side, that means "yes" in Bulgaria and Sri Lanka.
- Crossing your legs to expose the sole of your shoe is really taboo in Muslim countries. In fact, to call a person a "shoe" is a deep insult.

PHYSICAL CONTACT
- Patting a child on the head is a grave offence in Thailand or Singapore, since the head is reversed as the location of the soul.
- In an Oriental culture, touching another person is considered an invasion of privacy, while in Southern European and Arabic countries it is a sign of warmth and friendship.

PROMPTNESS
- Be on time when invited for dinner in Denmark or in China.
- In Latin countries, your host or business associate would be surprised if you arrived at the appointed hour.

EATING AND COOKING
- It is rude to leave anything on your plate when eating in Norway, Malaysia, or Singapore.
- In Egypt, it is rude *not* to leave something.
- In Italy and Spain, cooking is done with oil.
- In Germany and Great Britain, margarine and butter are used.

OTHER SOCIAL CUSTOMS
- In Sweden, nudity and sexual permissiveness are quite all right, but drinking is really frowned on.
- In Spain, there is a very negative attitude towards life insurance. By receiving insurance benefits, a wife feels that she is profiting from her husband's death.
- In Western European countries, many consumers still are reluctant to buy anything (other than a house) on credit. Even for an automobile, they will pay cash after having saved for some time.

a product is changed expressly for an international market, modification is apt to be minor. A producer may convert an appliance for use with 220-volt electrical systems, or paint and package a product to protect it against a destructive tropical climate, for example.

A critical question today in product planning concerns the extent to which a company can market the same product in several different countries. While standardization obviously cannot be applied to all products, or to all international markets, certainly the situation has changed over the past 20 to 30 years. As we indicated, international communication is reducing cultural differences among some markets.

For a number of products in some markets, there is a strong common demand. One survey identified eight product categories that were highly in demand in eight major markets around the world. These products and markets are:[11]

Products	Markets
Personal computers	Australia
Video equipment	Brazil
Healthful food	Britain
Beer and low-alcohol beverages	France
Convenience foods	Germany
Toys	Japan
Financial services	South Africa

These lists still leave a lot of products and markets unaccounted for. Undoubtedly, many products have to be especially adapted for markets in a less-developed country. And by the year 2000, these countries are expected to contain 80 percent of the world's population.

In short, any marketer would be well advised to study carefully the cultural and economic environment of any market—foreign or domestic—before planning products for that particular market. In Europe, for example, a 6-cubic-foot refrigerator is the most popular size, in contrast to the larger units preferred in Canada and the United States. True, the cost difference and the prevalence of smaller kitchens in Europe are decision factors. However, the basic reasons lie in cultural behaviour patterns of the consumers. As noted earlier, many European housewives shop for food daily and thus do not buy large quantities that must be stored for several days in a refrigerator. Many also do not have a car, so they walk to the store and therefore cannot carry large quantities. Frozen foods are not purchased to any great extent, so freezer storage space is not needed.

Branding and labelling are especially important in foreign marketing. As suggested earlier, the brand picture may be the only part of the product that a consumer can recognize. Foreign consumers' preference for well-recognized North American products often overcomes their nationalistic feelings. So in many instances, a company can use the same brand overseas as in the domestic or North American market.[12]

Pricing in International Markets

In earlier chapters, we recognized that determining the base price and formulating pricing strategies are complex tasks, frequently involving trial-and-error decision making. These tasks become even more complex in international marketing. An exporter faces variables such as currency conversion, a variety of bases for price quotations, and often a lack of control over middlemen's pricing.

Cost-plus pricing is probably more common in export marketing than at home. Consequently, foreign prices usually are considerably higher than

---

[11]Carolyn Hulse, ''Popular Categories Cross Cultural Boundaries,'' *Advertising Age*, Dec. 24, 1984, p. 17.

[12]For an excellent discussion of positioning a product in foreign markets through branding and promotion, along with an extensive bibliography, see Teresa Domzal and Lynette Unger, ''Emerging Positioning Strategies in Global Marketing,'' *Journal of Consumer Marketing*, Fall 1987, pp. 23–40.

MARKETING AT WORK

FILE 20-2   **ADAPTING TO THE THIRD WORLD**

To meet the demand in Third World markets, the Gillette Company:

- Packaged its double-edged razor blades so they can be sold one at a time.
- Packaged Silkience shampoo in half-ounce plastic bubbles, instead of the standard 7-ounce bottles.
- Packaged Right Guard deodorant in plastic squeeze bottles, instead of aerosol cans.
- Introduced plastic tubs of shaving cream that sold for half the price of the aerosol-canned cream.

As a result of these and other marketing moves from 1970 to the late 1980s, the proportion of Gillette's sales from Third World countries doubled (to 20 percent) and dollar volume increased sevenfold.

In a quite different vein, researchers at the National Autonomous University in Mexico City developed a miniature cow to help families in Third World markets. This minicow stands about 2 feet tall, and it gives one gallon of milk per day (about two-thirds the amount given by its 6-foot ancestor). Moreover, it needs only one-tenth the amount of grassland required by larger cows.

Sources: David Wessel, ''Gillette Keys Sales to Third World Tastes,'' *The Wall Street Journal*, Jan. 23, 1986, p. 36; and Emily T. Smith, ''A Miniature 'Cow' to Help Third World Families,'' *Business Week*, Dec. 14, 1987, p. 81.

---

domestic prices for the same product. This is because of additional physical distribution expenses, tariffs, and other export costs. At the retail level, price bargaining is quite prevalent in many foreign markets — especially in Asia, Africa, and South America.[13]

Occasionally a firm's foreign price is lower than its domestic price. The price may be lowered to meet foreign competition or to dispose of outmoded products. Sometimes companies engage in **dumping**—that is, selling products in foreign markets at prices below the prices charged for these goods in their home market. Through the years, surplus production of certain raw materials has led to government control of world market prices. For example, individual governments have tried to stabilize the prices of coffee, nitrates, sugar, and rubber. Also, the governments of several countries have established joint agreements covering the prices of such commodities as oil, tin, potash, and cocoa.

Foreign middlemen are sometimes not aggressive in their pricing strategies. They prefer to maintain high unit margins and low sales volume, rather than develop large sales volume by means of lower prices and smaller margins per unit sold. In fact, there is considerable price rigidity in many foreign markets.

---

[13]For a report on price bargaining by consumers in ten developing countries, which concluded that buyer satisfaction was lower with retailers that bargain than with retailers that used a fixed-price policy, see Laurence Jacobs, Reginald Worthley, and Charles Keown, ''Perceived Buyer Satisfaction and Selling Pressure versus Pricing Policy: A Comparative Study of Retailers in Ten Developing Countries,'' *Journal of Business Research*, March 1984, pp. 63–74.

MARKETING AT WORK

FILE 20-3 **ONE BRAND ONE MESSAGE–EIGHT LANGUAGES**

This is the package for Bircher Müsli, a popular cereal in some Western European countries. The flags and respective countries, from top to bottom, are Germany, Great Britain, France, Spain, Italy, Netherlands, Sweden, Norway. In addition, the same package can be read in Ireland, Switzerland, Austria, Belgium, and some say in Canada as well.

The best known of such international marketing combinations is the cartel. A **cartel** is a group of companies that produce similar products and that have combined to restrain competition in manufacturing and marketing. Cartels exist to varying degrees in steel, aluminum, fertilizers, electrical products, petroleum products, rayon, dyes, and sulfur.

Prices may be quoted in Canadian or U.S. dollars or in the currency of the foreign buyer. Here we encounter problems of foreign exchange and conversion of currencies. As a general rule, a firm engaged in foreign trade—whether it is exporting or importing — prefers to have the price quoted in its own national currency. Risks from fluctuations in foreign exchange then are shifted to the other party in the transaction. One way to get around currency problems, especially when dealing with some Eastern European or developing nations, is through a barter agreement in which there is an exchange of goods rather than money.

In some cases the inflexibility stems from agreements among firms that restrain independent pricing. The rigidity also sometimes results from price-control legislation that prevents retailers from cutting prices at their own discretion.

Combinations of manufacturers and middlemen are tolerated to a far greater extent in many foreign countries than in Canada. This occurs even when the avowed purpose of the combinations is to restrain trade and reduce competition.

International Distribution Systems

Understanding the environment in a foreign market helps in understanding the distribution system, because these marketing institutions result from their environment. Perceptive, and thus usually successful, retailers will capitalize on environmental change by introducing innovations that anticipate trends in the environment. Several European retailers have done a good job of innovating. Within a relatively few years, they have moved from the stage of "mom and pop" stores to a variety of retailing concepts as advanced as anything in North America.

These innovative retailers leapfrogged several stages of institutional development. In mass retailing, the *hypermarché* in France and the *verbrauchermarkt* in Germany are huge self-service superstores operating very profitably and at much lower gross margins than similar Canadian stores. Distribution systems in Japan, however, are another story. Producers, both foreign and Japanese, must contend with an antiquated, culture-bound, high-cost channel structure composed of "papa-mama" retail stores and a multilevel wholesaling distribution system.[14]

MIDDLEMEN AND CHANNELS OF DISTRIBUTION

Four groups of middlemen operating in foreign trade are:

- Canadian foreign trade middlemen.

In Japan, foreign as well as large domestic retailers operate in an environment dominated by government-protected "papa-mama" retailers.

---

[14]For a brief but good description of the Japanese retailing system, see "A Land of Papa-Mama Shops," *U.S. News & World Report*, April 24, 1989, p. 47.

M A R K E T I N G   A T   W O R K

FILE 20-4 **CANADIAN RETAILERS ASSUME TOO MUCH**

Canadian retailers often describe the intensity of competition in the United States as warfare. Many of them have problems in the U.S. market by failing to take into account the country's profoundly different cultural and market dynamics (a University of Western Ontario study of 18 Canadian companies operating in the United States revealed that 15 of the firms had retreated from the U.S. market or were undergoing chronic losses). Companies accustomed to the Canadian market have had great difficulty adjusting to the more sophisticated demands of U.S. consumers, who want greater quality, service, convenience, and variety and are prepared to go out of their way to get it at the cheapest possible price. They have also failed to recognize that Americans have different tastes and buying patterns, preferring specialty stores with "deep" product choices to general merchandise outlets, favouring cookies over muffins. Because of these differences, Canadians find competition with American firms intense. U.S. retailers are much more innovative and aware of local tastes. They are also managed more aggressively, with lower prices and margins and greater emphasis on promotional items, hard-sell advertising, and store location. Entering and adapting to the U.S. market is time consuming and expensive, requiring the full commitment and support of the Canadian organization.

Adapted from Beppi Crosariol, "What Makes the U.S. So Tough," *Financial Times of Canada*, October 8, 1990, p. 14.

- Foreign trade middlemen located abroad.
- Wholesalers and retailers operating within foreign markets.
- Manufacturers' sales branches and sales offices located in foreign countries.

These middlemen were introduced briefly earlier in this chapter in connection with organizational structures for international marketing. Middlemen operating *within* foreign countries can be in general, less aggressive and perform fewer marketing services than their Canadian counterparts. The foreign marketing situation, however, usually argues against bypassing these foreign middlemen. Often the demand is too small to warrant the establishment of a sales office or branch. Also, in many foreign countries knowledge of the market may be more important than knowledge of the product, even for high-technology products. And sometimes government controls preclude the use of a sales organization abroad. Thus, middlemen in foreign countries ordinarily are a part of the channel structure.

PHYSICAL DISTRIBUTION

Various aspects of physical distribution in foreign marketing are quite different from anything found on the domestic scene. Generally, physical distribution expenses account for a much larger share of the final selling price in foreign markets than in domestic markets. Packing requirements, for example, are more exacting for foreign shipment. Problems caused by humidity, pilferage, breakage, and inadequate marking of shipments must be considered. Requirements regarding commercial shipping and governmental documents complicate the paperwork in foreign shipping. Marine insurance and the traffic management of international shipments are specialized fields. They involve institutions that are not ordinarily used in domestic marketing.

BRIBERY IN INTERNATIONAL DISTRIBUTION

Bribes, kickbacks, and related payments are facts of life in many international distribution systems. Bribery has existed to varying degrees in buying and selling since time immemorial. It is so rooted in many cultures that special slang words are used to designate it. In Latin America it is called the *mordida* (small bite). It is *dash* in West Africa and *baksheesh* in the Middle East. The French call it *pot de vin* (jug of wine). In Italy there is *la bustarella* (the little envelope) left on a bureaucrat's desk to cut the red tape.

Bribery in marketing became an international scandal in the mid-1970s. Subsequent political sensitivity in various countries resulted in several companies' establishing written ethical guidelines.

What complicates this situation is the fact that bribery is not a sharply defined activity. Sometimes the lines are blurred between a bribe, a gift to show appreciation, a reasonable commission for services rendered, and a "facilitating" payment to grease the distribution channel. Realistically, in some foreign markets a seller must pay a facilitating fee or commission to an agent in order to get in touch with prospective buyers. Without paying such fees, there is simply no effective access to those markets.[15]

Advertising in Foreign Markets

Rather than discuss promotion in its entirety, we limit our discussion to advertising as being illustrative of the strategic problems in international promotion. Advertising is selected because it is probably used by more firms in international marketing than a company sales force or any sales promotion technique.

A controversial issue in international advertising is the extent to which advertising can be standardized in foreign markets. In years gone by, the consensus was that a separate program (copy, appeals, and media) had to be tailored for each country, or even for regions within a country. Today there is much support for the idea of commonality in international ad campaigns. Many companies are using basically the same appeals, theme, copy, and layout in all their international advertising—particularly in Western European countries. Such standardization of advertising is spurred by the increase in international communication. Hordes of Europeans travel from one country to another while on vacation. Many radio and TV broadcasts from one country reach audiences in another country. The circulation of many European magazines and newspapers crosses national borders.

Perhaps the issue comes down to this point: The goal of advertising is essentially the same at home and abroad, namely, to communicate information and persuasive appeals effectively. It is only the media strategy and the specific messages that must be fine-tuned to each country's cultural, economic, and political environment. For some products, the appeals are sufficiently universal and the market is sufficiently homogeneous to permit the use of uniform

---

[15]For more on this subject, see Jeffrey A. Fadiman, "A Traveler's Guide to Gifts and Bribes," *Harvard Business Review*, July–August 1986, pp. 122–26 ff.

MARKETING AT WORK

FILE 20-5 **FIGHT OR JOIN?**

In some countries, it is generally not possible for a foreign marketer to sell directly to a branch of the government or to local private firms. Invariably, sales are made through local agents who have personal contacts (often family members) in the buying organizations. To make sales under these conditions, some foreign firms pay these agents commissions well beyond what is reasonable for the tasks they perform. If your firm wished to expand into international markets, would you consider it ethical to make such payments to agents?

---

advertising in several countries. In general, however, each country has its own national identity and characteristics that must be recognized when advertising in the given country.

ATTITUDE OF FOREIGN MARKETS AND GOVERNMENTS TOWARD ADVERTISING

In other parts of the world, the traditionally negative attitude towards marketing in general and towards advertising in particular is a hardship for foreign firms. Some foreign consumers feel that a product is of dubious value if it has to be advertised. People in many foreign countries object especially to some forms of North American hard-sell advertising.

Many countries have stringent laws regulating advertising. In those countries with government regulation of radio, television, and newspapers, the use of media as advertising vehicles is tightly controlled. For example, on government-controlled TV channels in Europe, commercials are run in 15- or 20-minute blocks of time periodically during the evening. They are not interspersed in 15-, 30-, or 60-second intervals during the programs as in Canada and the United States.

In the late 1980s, however, the winds of change (or at least slight breezes) started blowing through advertising in Western Europe. The growth of private and satellite-beamed cable TV stations is generating pressure to permit commercial advertising on state-owned TV stations. The United Kingdom now allows accountants and lawyers (but still not physicians) to advertise. Carrefour, the largest superstore (*hypermarché*) in France, began to run comparative-price ads, even though French law is unclear on the legality of this strategy.

PREPARATION OF ADVERTISEMENTS

Most of the mistakes in writing copy and preparing individual advertisements can be traced to a lack of knowledge about the foreign market. The wrong colour or a poor choice of words can completely nullify an otherwise good ad. Illustrations are of prime importance in many markets where illiteracy is common. They are, of course, effective in all markets, but they must be accurate, believable, and in accord with local cultures. The translation of advertising copy into the appropriate foreign language — especially for radio — is a major problem. The advertiser must have someone both adept and current in the idioms, dialects, and other nuances of the foreign language.

GOVERNMENT SUPPORT FOR INTERNATIONAL MARKETING

In most of the decision-making areas in international marketing, the federal government, as well as many provincial governments, provide contacts, information, guidance, and even financing for Canadian firms. For example, international marketing efforts are aided by the Department of Industry, Trade and Commerce and the Export Development Corporation. The department attempts to assist firms from the research and development stage through to the international marketing of finished products. The Export Development Corporation provides insurance, guarantees, loans, and other financial facilities to help Canadian exporters.

Within the federal department, a number of units exist that work on specific problems associated with international marketing. The Office of General Relations is responsible for advance planning of Canada's external trade policies and general policy affecting primary and secondary industry. The Office of Area Relations protects and improves the access of Canadian goods to export markets. The Industry, Trade and Traffic Services Branch deals with shipping problems and trade control and provides information on Canadian products and companies. The Fairs and Missions Branch coordinates all departmental activities designed to promote the sale of Canadian products and services abroad. The International Defence Programs Branch promotes defence and export trade. The Trade Commissioners Service, with 76 offices in 55 countries, promotes export trade and protects commercial interests abroad. The Publicity Branch supports foreign trade promotion programs. The operational branches within the department (Aerospace; Marine and Rail; Agriculture; Fisheries and Food Products; Apparel and Textiles; Chemicals; Electrical and Electronics; Machinery; Materials; Mechanical Transport; and Wood Products) work to promote the sales of products and services in international markets.

Lest anyone think that Canadian government support for international trade and marketing is merely verbal, Fig. 20-2 shows quite clearly how we fare in the international context. These data, put together by the U.S. Department of Commerce, indicate quite clearly that our governments are heavy facilitators in encouraging international economic activity with financial expenditures and human resource allocations.

SUMMARY

For countless Canadian companies, the marketing opportunities and challenges of the future lie in international marketing to the United States, Europe, the Far East, and beyond. This conclusion seems inevitable as management views its home markets being saturated, and the intensified competition in Canada coming from both domestic and foreign firms. This broadening of marketing horizons, however, will be a new experience in most cases. Many companies in Canada have never realized that export markets provide them with an opportunity to increase sales volume and profits significantly. Even the increasing competition from foreign imports has usually served only to intensify Canadian sellers' competitive efforts at home, rather than turning their interest to international markets. With the FTA in place and the EC coming together in 1992, it is now that the challenges must be faced.

In terms of organizational structure, the simplest way to operate in a foreign market is by exporting through foreign trade middlemen. Another method is to export through company sales branches located in foreign countries. More sophisticated structures involve licensing a foreign manufacturer, engaging in a joint venture, or forming a wholly owned subsidiary.

To develop an international marketing program, a company follows basically the same procedures it uses for domestic programs. But each step along the

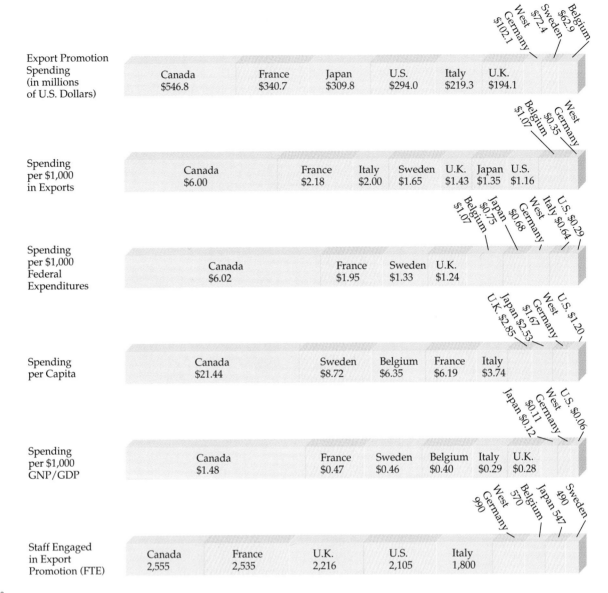

Export Promotion Spending (in millions of U.S. Dollars)

Canada $546.8	France $340.7	Japan $309.8	U.S. $294.0	Italy $219.3	U.K. $194.1	West Germany $102.1	Sweden $72.4	Belgium $62.9

Spending per $1,000 in Exports

Canada $6.00	France $2.18	Italy $2.00	Sweden $1.65	U.K. $1.43	Japan $1.35	U.S. $1.16	West Germany $1.07	Belgium $0.35

Spending per $1,000 Federal Expenditures

Canada $6.02	France $1.95	Sweden $1.33	U.K. $1.24	Japan $1.07	Belgium $0.75	West Germany $0.68	Italy $0.64	U.S. $0.29

Spending per Capita

Canada $21.44	Sweden $8.72	Belgium $6.35	France $6.19	Italy $3.74	U.K. $2.85	Japan $2.53	West Germany $1.67	U.S. $1.20

Spending per $1,000 GNP/GDP

Canada $1.48	France $0.47	Sweden $0.46	Belgium $0.40	Italy $0.29	U.K. $0.28	Japan $0.12	West Germany $0.11	U.S. $0.06

Staff Engaged in Export Promotion (FTE)

Canada 2,555	France 2,535	U.K. 2,216	U.S. 2,105	Italy 1,800	West Germany 990	Belgium 570	Japan 547	Sweden 490

FIGURE 20-2

Canadian rank for selected export promotion indicators.

way involves problems and operating methods that may be different for each country, and that must take into account the foreign market environment. Marketing research is more limited overseas. Product planning, pricing, distribution, and advertising all require modification based on cultures and custom—the marketing environment.

Let us move for a moment from the level of the individual firm to the level of the total economy. It is increasingly apparent that the rate of economic growth in less-developed nations will depend largely upon how effective the marketing systems established in these countries are. Typically in these countries the economic development effort has been concentrated in production. Now governments recognize the role that marketing can play in their national economic growth. This attitude offers countless marketing opportunities (but not without attendant problems) to the internationally oriented business firm.

Particularly, a marketing executive must understand the government's role in business in each country.

Permeating this chapter has been the theme that marketing management in Canadian firms must become more globally minded. We conclude with five reasons why it is mandatory to be successful in international marketing.

1. We cannot adequately expand our economy at home without meeting competition abroad.
2. We cannot eliminate large-scale unemployment in this country unless we do smaller-scale employing in other countries.
3. To achieve a higher tide of prosperity here, we must be willing to develop trade with those whose prosperity is still at a very low ebb.
4. Balancing our international payment books at home requires filling many more order books abroad.
5. If we are to remain dominant and competitive in our home market, we must compete successfully in the world market.

KEY TERMS AND CONCEPTS

QUESTIONS AND PROBLEMS

1. Report on export marketing activities of companies where your school is located. Consider such topics as the following. What products are exported? How many jobs are created by export marketing? What is the dollar value of exports? How does this figure compare with the value of foreign-made goods imported into the province?
2. A luggage-manufacturing company with annual sales over $12 million has decided to market its products in Western Europe. Evaluate the alternative structures this company should consider.
3. Select one product—manufactured or nonmanufactured—for export, and choose the country to which you would like to export it. Then prepare an analysis of the market for this product in the selected country. Be sure to include the sources of information you used.
4. Interview some of the foreign students at your school to determine how their native buying habits differ from yours. Consider such patterns as when, where, and how people in their country buy. Who makes the family buying decisions?

5. Many countries have a low literacy rate. In what ways might a company adjust its marketing program to overcome this problem?

6. Why should special attention be devoted to labelling and branding when products are sold in foreign markets?

7. If a Canadian company uses foreign middlemen, it must usually stand ready to supply them with financial, technical, and promotional help. If this is the case, why is it not customary to bypass these middlemen and deal directly with the ultimate foreign buyers?

8. Why do exporters normally prefer to have prices stated in U.S. dollars? Why should foreign importers prefer that quotations be in the currency of their country?

9. Study the advertisements in foreign newspapers and magazines available in your library. Particularly note the ads for European products, and compare these with the advertisements of the same products in Canadian newspapers and magazines. In what respect do the foreign ads differ from the domestic ads? Are there significant similarities?

10. Are Canadian manufacturers being priced out of world markets because of their high cost structures?

CHAPTER 21 GOALS

This chapter is concerned with two parts of managing a company's total marketing program—implementation and evaluation. After studying this chapter, you should be able to explain:

- The importance of implementation in the management process.
- The relationship among strategic planning, implementation, and performance evaluation.
- Organizational structures used to implement marketing efforts.
- The importance of personnel selection.
- Delegation, coordination, motivation, and communication in the implementation process.
- The concept of a marketing audit as a complete evaluation program.
- The meaning of misdirected marketing effort.
- Sales volume analysis.
- Marketing cost analysis.

Marketing Implementation

M ajor organizational changes are occurring in the packaged consumer goods industries as producers prepare for the future. Procter & Gamble provides a good example of this restructuring.

Sixty years ago P & G instituted the brand-management system. Under this system, each brand had its own manager who served as the brand's advocate within the company. Brands competed against each other as intensely as if they belonged to separate firms. Two problems were inherent in this system. First, there was internal competition for scarce resources. Camay and Ivory, for example, competed for advertising funds. Second, brand managers were responsible for a brand's success, but they were not given corresponding authority in advertising, pricing, and other marketing areas.

Nevertheless, as its markets expanded over the decades, P & G prospered. However, the company also became very bureaucratic and infamous for slow, highly centralized decision making.

Then, in the 1980s, the balance of power in the packaged consumer goods fields shifted from large manufacturers to large retailers such as K mart and Loblaws. These trends adversely affected P & G. The company's gross margins and earnings declined, and flagship brands such as Crest and Pampers lost market share. Retailers became increasingly unhappy with P & G's autocratic, arrogant behaviour.

In the late 1980s, P & G underwent a major organizational restructuring designed to push authority down into middle management levels, speed up decision making, and bring the company closer to its customers. A significant organizational change in marketing was the establishment of a category-management system. P & G's brands were grouped into 39 product categories, among them laundry detergents, bar soaps, deodorants, and diapers. A "category manager" took charge of each category, and all brand managers now report to one of these executives. The intent is to look at a product group as a whole, thus strategically fitting the individual brands together, rather than having them compete against one another.

The category manager acts as the chief executive officer of a small company, with total profit responsibility for the entire category product line and authority to make quick decisions. All areas involved in producing and marketing products within a category—advertising, sales, manufacturing, research, and engineering—report to the category manager.

Procter & Gamble's restructuring is designed to increase the speed and effectiveness of the implementation stage in the company's management process. In Chapter 1 we defined the management process in marketing as planning, implementing, and evaluating the marketing effort in an organization. Most of this book has dealt with *planning* a marketing program. We discussed the selection of target markets and the strategic design of a program to deliver want-satisfaction to those markets. This program was built around the components of a marketing mix—the product, price structure, distribution system, and promotional program.

Now we are ready to devote a chapter to the implementation and evaluation stages of the management process in marketing. Implementation is the operational stage—the stage during which an organization attempts to carry out (that is; implement or execute) its strategic plan.

At the end of an operating period (or even during the period), management needs to evaluate the organization's performance. In this way management can determine how effectively the organization is achieving the goals set in the strategic planning phase of the management process.

IMPLEMENTATION IN MARKETING MANAGEMENT

There should be a close relationship among planning, implementation, and evaluation in the management process. Without planning, a company's operational activities — its implementation — can go off in any direction like an unguided missile. In the 1970s and into the early 1980s, there was tremendous interest in strategic planning, sparked primarily by leading management consulting firms. Then as we progressed through the 1980s, disenchantment with strategic planning set in. This cooling off occurred as many companies came to realize that strategic *planning* alone was not enough to ensure a company's success. These plans had to be *effectively implemented*. Management began to realize that planners were great at telling them *what* to do—that is, designing a strategy. But planners often fell short when it came to telling *how* to do it— that is, how to implement the strategy.[1]

> "Too often those hot-shot planners could not sell a pair of shoes to a guy who is standing barefooted on a very hot sidewalk with a $50 bill in his hand."

No matter how good an organization's strategic planning is, it is virtually useless if those plans do not lead to action—are not implemented or executed. Stated another way, good planning cannot overcome poor implementation, but effective implementation often can overcome poor planning or inappropriate strategies. At this point, therefore, we shall discuss implementation in more detail because, despite its importance, it ordinarily receives so little attention. Much has been written about strategic planning, but very little has been said about *implementing* those strategies.[2]

---

[1]For some guidelines to aid in identifying implementation difficulties and suggestions for remedying them, see Thomas V. Bonoma, "Making Your Marketing Strategy Work," *Harvard Business Review*, March–April 1984, pp. 69–76.

[2]See Thomas V. Bonoma, "Enough about Strategy! Let's See Some Clever Executions," *Marketing News*, Feb. 13, 1989, p. 10.

Often a sales person in the field carries the burden of *implementing* a company's strategic planning.

The implementation stage in the marketing management process includes three broad activities: (1) organizing for the marketing effort; (2) staffing this organization; and (3) directing the operational efforts of these people as they carry out the strategic plans.

Organizing for Implementation Activities

The first major activity in implementing a company's strategic marketing plan is to organize the people who will be doing the actual implementation. We must establish an organizational relationship among marketing and the other major functional areas in a firm. And, within the marketing department, we must decide on the form of organization that will most effectively aid our implementation efforts.

COMPANY-WIDE ORGANIZATION

In Chapter 1 we stated that one of the three foundation stones of the marketing concept is to organizationally coordinate all marketing activities. In firms that are production-oriented or sales-oriented, typically we find that marketing activities are fragmented. A sales force is quite separate from advertising; physical distribution is handled in the production department and not well coordinated with marketing; and sales training may be under the personnel department.

In a marketing-oriented enterprise, all marketing activities are coordinated under one marketing executive, who usually is at the vice presidential level. This executive reports directly to the president and is on an equal organizational footing with top executives in finance, production, and other major functions, as shown in Fig. 21-1. Under the top marketing executive, the marketing activities may be grouped into line activities and staff activities. In most firms the primary line activity is personal selling. Supporting staff activities include advertising, marketing research, sales promotion, sales analysis, and sales training.

MARKETING AT WORK

FILE 21-1 **ORGANIZING TO SOLVE PROBLEMS**

For decades, IBM Canada's employees have been accustomed to predictable growth, predictable work, predictable promotion and compensation. However, in the ever-increasing competitive nature of the technology industry, predictable is no longer good enough.

IBM has traditionally relied on the prestige of its name and has researched, manufactured, and marketed products according to its own technology-driven vision of the computer business, largely ignoring customer services. Ignoring customers, however, has been a mistake in an industry that has moved from large main frames to high-growth, low-end niches such as the laptop market segment. In failing to do so, IBM has been challenged by thousands of small, more flexible competitors.

In fighting back, IBM has revolutionized its inner organization to revolve around the consumer and his or her needs. It has introduced an enormous migration of staff from middle management to customer support functions such as software development and systems customization and has created internal task forces to cut through waste and duplication to improve speed and continuity in customer service. It has also stratified a once hierarchical administration, encouraging all employees to make decisions in order to speed up performance and do away with bureaucratic inefficiency. IBM hopes that if employees feel they can make a difference, they will be more motivated and responsible. Three years after the beginning of this "revolution," the company's revenue was up 13 percent to more than $4 billion and earnings were up 34 percent. Technology comes a distant second in this business. "Customers are no longer buying boxes, but solutions to their problems." IBM management now recognizes this.

Source: Adapted from David Evans, "IBM Canada Rediscovers Its Customers," *Canadian Business*, November 1990, pp. 37–47.

ORGANIZATION WITHIN THE MARKETING DEPARTMENT

Within the marketing department—especially in medium-sized or large firms—the sales force frequently is specialized in some organizational fashion. This is done in order to effectively implement the company's strategic marketing plan. One of three forms of organizational specialization of line authority typically is adopted. The sales force may be organized by (1) geographical territory, (2) product line, or (3) customer type. In very large companies, other marketing activities such as advertising or sales promotion may also be organizationally specialized in one of these three categories.

Geographical specialization.   Probably the most widely used method of specializing selling activities is to organize a sales force on the basis of geographical territories. Under this type of organization, each sales person is assigned a specific geographical area — called a *territory* — in which to sell. Several sales people representing contiguous territories are placed under a territorial sales executive, who reports directly to the general sales manager.

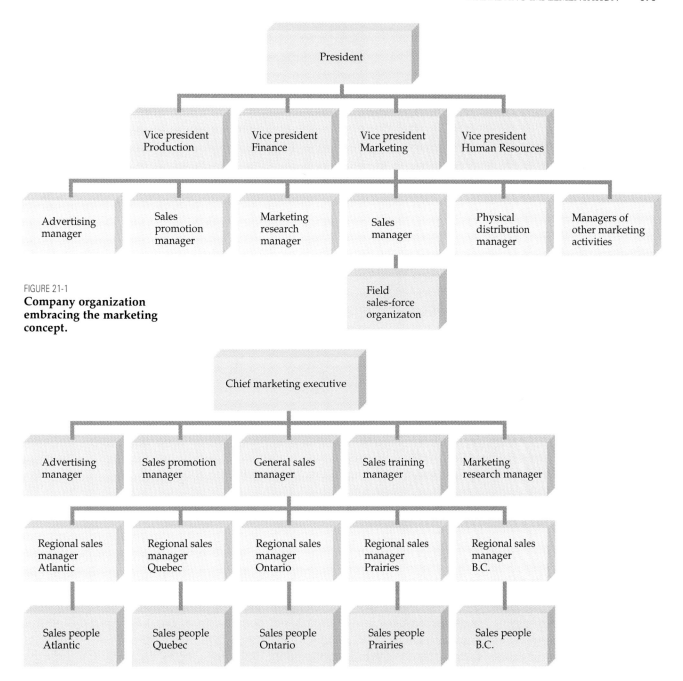

FIGURE 21-1
Company organization embracing the marketing concept.

FIGURE 21-2
Sales organization specialized by geographic territories.

These territorial executives usually are called *district* or *regional* sales managers, as shown in Fig. 21-2.

A territorial organization usually ensures better implementation of sales strategies in each local market and better control over the sales force. Customers can be serviced quickly and effectively, and local sales reps can respond better to competitors' actions in a given territory.

Product specialization.   Another commonly used basis for organizing a sales force is some form of product specialization. As illustrated in Fig. 21-3, a

FIGURE 21-3
**Sales organization specialized
by product.**

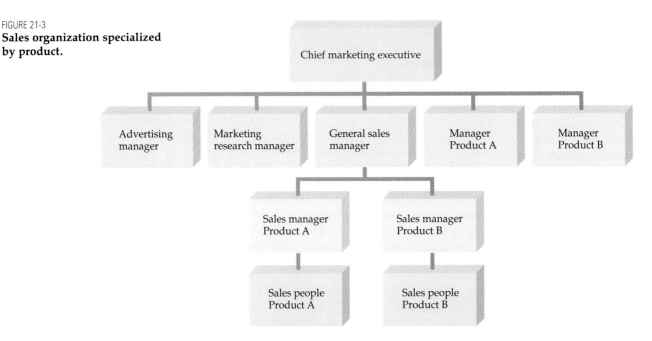

company may divide all of its products into two lines. Then one group of sales reps will sell only the products in line A. All sales people in group A will report to a sales manager for product A, who in turn will report to a general sales manager.

This type of organization is especially well-suited to companies that are marketing:

- A variety of complex technical products—for example, electronics.
- Dissimilar or unrelated products — for example, luggage, folding chairs, and toy building blocks.
- Many thousands of items—for example, hardware.

The main advantage of this form of organization is the specialized attention each product line can get from the sales force. A potential drawback is that more than one sales rep from a company may call on the same customer. This duplication of effort not only is costly but also may irritate the customers.

A variation of product specialization is the product-manager system that we discussed previously. Each product manager is given the responsibility of planning and developing a marketing program for a separate group of products. The product managers report to the chief marketing executive. Typically product managers have no direct authority over a sales force, but act only in an advisory relationship with the sales force and line sales executives.

Customer specialization. Many companies today have divided their sales departments according to type of customer. Customers may be grouped either by type of industry or by channel of distribution. Thus an oil company may divide its markets into such industry customer groups as railroads, auto manufacturers, and farm equipment producers, as shown in Fig. 21-4. A firm that specializes its sales operations by channel of distribution may have one sales force selling to wholesalers and another that deals directly with large retailers.

FIGURE 21-4
**Sales organization specialized
by customer.**

FIGURE 21-4
**Sales organization specialized
by customer.**

As more companies fully implement the marketing concept, the customer-specialization type of organization is likely to increase. Certainly the basis of customer specialization is commensurate with the customer-oriented philosophy that underlies the marketing concept. That is, the organizational emphasis is on customers and markets rather than on products.

Combination of organizational bases. Many medium-sized and large companies typically combine a territorial sales organization with either product or customer specialization. Thus, a hardware wholesaler operating out of a home base in Winnipeg may establish geographical sales districts for its sales reps. This same sales force may be divided on a product basis. Consequently, in the one sales district that covers southern Manitoba and southern Saskatchewan, there may be two or three of this company's sales reps. Each rep sells a different group of the wholesaler's products.

Staffing the Organization

A key step in implementing strategic planning is to staff the organization—to select the people who will be doing the actual implementation work. *Of all the specific stages in the management process, we believe selection of people is the most important.* We strongly feel this is true no matter what organization is being staffed. A college volleyball coach's success depends greatly on her ability to recruit the right players. A political party's success depends on its ability to select the candidate who will attract the most votes. A sales manager's success depends in great measure on the sales people whom the manager selects.

Managing the Marketing Operations

The third activity in the implementation stage of the management process is actually directing and operating a marketing program. This activity is the guts of the entire implementation process—where strategic plans are actually carried out; where the revenue-generating activity occurs in the firm; where

MARKETING AT WORK

FILE 21-2   **EASY MARKET STAFFING?**

Organizations have a hard-time finding qualified sales people. Even more difficult is finding *experienced* sales people who are familiar enough with an industry to begin making a contribution immediately. One way to get such sales people is to aggressively recruit them from competitors. Not only do they know the business, but they might also bring along a few customers. If you were a sales manager, would you adopt this practice?

Yes, selection is critically important in *any* organization. And, tragically, most people do a horrible job of recruiting and selection. Most of us don't know how to pick appropriate people for the position being filled.

In most marketing organizations, the implementation task is done largely by the sales force. So let's identify the reasons why it is important to have a good process for selecting sales people:

- Good sales people are often hard to find. There is a scarcity of prospects who have the necessary skills, experience, and interest in the work.
- Within limits, managers are no better than the people working under them. And managers are judged by the way their subordinates perform.
- A good selection job makes other managerial tasks easier. Well-chosen workers are easier to train, supervise, and motivate.
- Good selection typically reduces the turnover rate with all its attendant costs.

Regardless of the field of endeavor, the selection of people is the most important stage in the management process.

management directs the efforts of the people who have been selected and organized.

The guidelines for operating marketing-mix components (product, price, distribution, promotion) are probably pretty well set by virtue of the strategic marketing plan. It is up to the operating executives in the marketing department to follow these guidelines. The key to success in this stage depends on how well the executives have put into practice four concepts concerning the management of people. These four concepts are delegation, coordination, motivation, and communication.

DELEGATION

Very often an executive's success is measured by the ability to ably delegate authority and responsibility. Executives who try to do everything themselves —who for some reason are reluctant to delegate—invariably fail to maximize the potential of their programs or their subordinates in the company.

COORDINATION

Effective coordination will bring about a synergy in the organization whereby people working together will accomplish more than if they go off on their own in a rudderless fashion. For example, sales peoples' efforts should be coordinated with advertising activities. New-product introduction needs to be coordinated with the physical distribution of the product, and middlemen must be prepared to handle the new product.

MOTIVATION

The success enjoyed by a leader of people in any field—athletics, education, politics, the military, business—is greatly dependent on that leader's ability to motivate people. Here we can consider economic motivation in the form of monetary payments as well as psychological motivation in the form of non-monetary rewards.

COMMUNICATION

Finally, all implementation activities will come together in an effective manner only if the executives involved communicate effectively with their employees. In early chapters we spoke often about effectively communicating with the market. Now we are concerned with doing a good job of internal communication. It is imperative that an organization maintain open communication channels both upward and downward in the company's hierarchy. Management must communicate with sales people, and these reps must have an open channel to communicate upward to management. Often it is easier to say these things than to do them. Companies spend untold sums of money to improve the communication abilities of their executives, but the staff frequently still misunderstands management's messages. Yet this is no reason to stop trying to improve communication.

EVALUATING MARKETING PERFORMANCE

As soon as possible after a firm's plans have been set in operation, the process of evaluation should begin. Without evaluation, management cannot tell whether a plan is working and what factors are contributing to success or failure. Evaluation logically follows planning and implementation. Planning sets forth what *should be* done, and evaluation shows what *really was* done. A circular relationship exists, as illustrated in Fig. 21-5. Plans are made, they are put into action, the operational results are evaluated, and new plans are prepared on the basis of this appraisal.

Previously we discussed evaluation as it relates to individual parts of a marketing program—the product-planning process, the performance of the sales force, and the effectiveness of the advertising program, for instance. At this point let's look at the evaluation of the *total marketing effort*.

MARKETING AT WORK

FILE 21-3   **FINDING PROBLEMS AND TAKING CARE OF THEM**

In 1988, Scarborough Town Centre, a regional mall in a Toronto suburb, was surprised by the results of the research surveys they carried out on their customers. Customers complained about dirty washrooms, lack of information, and an absence of customer services. For a mall with major competitors nearby, the survey's results meant that the mall would have to develop and implement new and improved strategies that would please their dissatisfied clients.

Scarborough Town Centre's new efforts were directed primarily towards the people living within a five-kilometre radius of the mall and who were frequent and stable shoppers; to date the renewed plans have paid off, raising the mall's combined retail sales by 5 percent in the first year, at a time when the sales at most other Ontario mall retailers were decreasing. Baby-sitting was introduced, as was a customer-service kiosk with free coat check, strollers, wheelchairs, gift wrapping, and a community bulletin board featuring local job openings and items for sale. Young people were hired as "runners and greeters," to give customers directions and carry their bags. Finally, the washrooms were renovated and staffed by attendants with vanity trays of free toiletries. The mall's return on its investment is far greater than advertising by flyers or radio. So far the only problem has been the frequent theft of flowers from the washrooms—which men steal to give to women.

Source: Adapted from Kenneth Kidd, "Little Extras a Hit with Shoppers," *Globe and Mail*, November 26, 1990, p. 2.

FIGURE 21-5
The circular relationship among management tasks.

The Marketing Audit: A Total Evaluation Program

A marketing audit is the essential element in a total evaluation program. An audit implies a review and an evaluation of some activity. Thus a **marketing audit** is a comprehensive review and evaluation of the marketing function in an organization — its philosophy, environment, goals, strategies, organizational structure, human and financial resources, and performance. A complete marketing audit is an extensive and difficult project. Therefore, it is conducted infrequently—perhaps every two or three years. However, a company should not delay a marketing audit until a major crisis arises.

The rewards of a marketing audit can be great. Management can identify problem areas in marketing. By reviewing its strategies, the firm is likely to keep abreast of its changing marketing environment. Successes can also be analyzed, so the company can capitalize on its strong points. The audit can spot lack of coordination in the marketing program, outdated strategies, or unrealistic goals. The marketing audit allows management to correctly place responsibility for good or poor performance. Furthermore, an audit should anticipate future situations. It is intended for "prognosis as well as diagnosis. . . . It is the practice of preventive as well as curative marketing medicine."[3]

Misdirected Marketing Effort

One of the primary benefits of evaluation activities is that they can help correct misdirected or misplaced marketing effort.

THE "80-20" PRINCIPLE

In most firms, a large proportion of the orders, customers, territories, or products accounts for only a small share of sales or profit. Conversely, a small proportion produces a large share of sales or profit. This relationship has been characterized as the **80-20 principle**. That is, 80 percent of the orders, customers, territories, or products contribute only 20 percent of sales or profit. On the other hand, 20 percent of these selling units account for 80 percent of the volume or profit. The 80-20 figure is used simply to epitomize the misplacement of marketing efforts. In reality, of course, the percentage split varies from one situation to another.

The basic reason for the 80-20 situation is that almost every marketing program includes some misdirected effort. Marketing efforts and costs are proportional to the *number* of territories, customers, or products, rather than to their actual sales volume or profit. For example, in a department store, approximately the same order-filling, billing, and delivery expenses are involved whether a mink coat or a necktie is sold. Or a manufacturer such as Xerox may assign one sales person to each territory. Yet there may be substantial differences in the potential volume and profit from the various territories. In each case, the marketing effort (cost) is not in line with the potential return.[4]

REASONS FOR MISDIRECTED MARKETING EFFORT

Many executives are unaware of the misdirected marketing effort in their firms. They do not know what percentage of total sales and profit comes from a given product line or customer group. Frequently, executives cannot uncover their misdirection of effort because they lack sufficiently detailed information. The analogy of an iceberg in an open sea has been used to illustrate this situation. Only a small part of an iceberg is visible above the surface of the water, and the submerged 90 percent is the dangerous part. The figures representing total sales or total costs on an operating statement are like the visible part of an iceberg. The detailed figures representing sales, costs, and other performance

[3]Abe Schuchman, "The Marketing Audit: Its Nature, Purpose, and Problems," in *Analyzing and Improving Marketing Performance: "Marketing Audits" in Theory and Practice*, American Management Association, New York, Management Report no. 32, 1959, p. 14. This article is the classic introduction to the marketing audit concept. For a process that proposes different uses of a marketing audit to promote strategic organizational change, see Michael P. Mokwa, "The Strategic Marketing Audit: An Adoption/Utilization Perspective," *Journal of Business Strategy*, Spring 1986, pp. 88–95.

[4]For suggestions on how to develop and manage a program to achieve benefits from the 20 percent of marketing units that generate the 80 percent of sales volume and profit, see Richard T. Hise and Stanley H. Kratchman, "Developing and Managing a 20/80 Program," *Business Horizons*, September–October 1987, pp. 66–73.

measures for each territory or product correspond to the important and dangerous submerged segment.

Total sales or costs as presented on an operating statement are too general to be useful in evaluation. In fact, total figures are often inconclusive and misleading. More than one company has shown satisfactory overall sales and profit figures. But when these totals were subdivided by territory or products, serious weaknesses were discovered. A manufacturer of audio equipment showed an overall annual increase of 12 percent in sales and 9 percent in net profit on one product line one year. But management wasn't satisfied with this "tip of the iceberg." When it analyzed the figures more closely, it found that the sales change within territories ranged from an increase of 19 percent to a decrease of 3 percent. In some territories profits increased as much as 14 percent, and in others they were down 20 percent.

An even more important cause of misplaced marketing effort is the fact that executives must make decisions based on inadequate knowledge of the exact nature of marketing costs. In other words, management often lacks knowledge of: (1) the disproportionate spread of marketing effort; (2) reliable standards for determining what should be spent on marketing; and (3) what results should be expected from these expenditures.

As an illustration, a company may spend $250,000 more on advertising this year than last year. But management ordinarily cannot state what the resultant increase in sales volume or profit should be. Nor do the executives know what would have happened if they had spent the same amount on (1) new-product development, (2) management training seminars for middlemen, or (3) some other aspect of the marketing program.

The Evaluation Process

The evaluation process—whether it is a complete marketing audit or only an appraisal of individual components of the marketing program—is essentially a three-stage task. Management's tasks in this process are as follows:

1. Find out *what* happened. Get the facts and then compare actual results with budgeted goals to determine where they differ.
2. Find out *why* it happened. Determine what specific factors in the marketing program accounted for the results.
3. Decide *what to do* about it. Plan the next period's program so as to improve

Data collection systems from companies such as Panasonic allow retailers to keep track of everything from lettuce to employees.

MARKETING AT WORK

FILE 21-4   **A NEW BIRKS MEANS A NEW REVIEW**

Birks has been manufacturing and selling jewellery in Canada for more than 120 years. As time has passed, the Birks name has become synonymous with the traditional elegance of the old world, as prestigious and Canadian as the CPR. It is an image that Birks has long cultivated, but which has failed it recently. After Jonathan Birks took over the organization, he ordered a review into what, why, and how things went awry. The evaluation of the Birks strategy and implementation showed that it desperately needed to modernize all aspects of its inefficient organization, while reconsolidating its vision. So now Birks is adjusting to the 1990s.

The first priority was to cut costs — reducing staff by 289 employees saved the company $7 million alone — and making changes in management and personnel. The second was to refocus Birks's image as a purveyor of high-end jewellery, a message that had been long lost on customers who saw them selling chintzy giftware such as porcelain blue jays. Hoping to make the company more accessible, Birks held its first-ever press conference; hoping to make it more efficient, it computerized an inventory that had been completely uncontrolled. Last, but not least, Birks has begun emphasizing customer service. It is attempting to woo back its traditional clientele by revamping its distinguished, wholly owned "destination" shopping boutiques and moving away from the suburban mall locations that tarnished its image and lost the company its previous clients by introducing less expensive, middle-of-the-road product lines and discount prices that would attract neighbourhood shoppers.

Source: Adapted from Jennifer Wells, "Jonathan's Mean Season," *Financial Times of Canada*, December 10, 1990, pp. 8–10.

---

on unsatisfactory performance and capitalize on the things that were done well.

An effective way to evaluate a total marketing program is to analyze performance results. To do this, two useful tools are available — sales volume analysis and marketing cost analysis. These tools are examined in the next two sections.

Our discussion of sales volume and marketing cost analyses is built around the Great Western Company Ltd. (GW) — a firm that markets office furniture. This company's market is divided into four sales districts, each with seven or eight sales people and a district sales manager. The company sells to office equipment wholesalers and directly to large business users. Great Western's product mix is divided into four groups — desks, chairs, filing equipment, and office accessories (wastebaskets and desk sets, for example). Some of these products are manufactured by GW and some are purchased from other firms.

SALES VOLUME ANALYSIS

A **sales volume analysis** is a detailed study of the "net sales" section of a company's profit and loss statement (operating statement). Management should analyze its *total* sales volume, and its volume by *product lines* and *market segments* (territories and customer groups). These sales should be compared with company goals and industry sales.

Sales Results versus Sales Goals

We start with an analysis of Great Western's total sales volume, as shown in Table 21-1. The company's annual sales doubled from $18 million to $36 million during the ten-year period ending in 1990. Furthermore, they increased each year over the preceding year, with the exception of 1987. In most of these years, the company met or surpassed its planned sales goals. Thus far the company's situation is very encouraging. When industry sales figures are introduced for comparison, however, the picture changes. But let's hold the industry-comparison analysis until the next section.

A study of total sales volume alone is usually insufficient, and maybe even misleading, because of the iceberg principle. To learn what is going on in the "submerged" parts of the market, we need to analyze sales volume by market segments—sales territories, for example.

Table 21-2 is a summary of the planned sales goals and actual sales results in Great Western's four sales districts. A key measurement figure is the *performance percentage*—actual sales divided by sales goal. A performance percentage of 100 means that the district did exactly what was expected of it. Thus, from the table we see that B and C did just a little better than was expected. District A passed its goal by a wide margin, but D was quite a disappointment.

So far in our evaluation process, we know a little about *what* happened in GW's districts. Now management has to figure out *why* it happened and *what should be done* about it. These are the difficult steps in evaluation. Great Western's executives need to determine why district D did so poorly. The fault may lie in some aspect of the marketing program, or competition may be especially strong there. They also should find out what accounts for district A's success, and whether this information can be used in the other regions.

This brief examination of two aspects of sales volume analysis shows how this evaluation tool may be used. However, for a more useful evaluation GW's executives should go much further. They should analyze their sales volume by individual territories within districts and by product lines. Then they should carry their territorial analysis further by examining volume by product line and customer group *within* each territory. For instance, even though district A did well overall, the iceberg principle may be at work *within* the district.

TABLE 21-1 **Annual sales volume of Great Western Company, industry volume, and company's share of market**

Year	Company volume (in millions of dollars)	Industry volume in company's market (in millions of dollars)	Company's percentage share of market
1990	36.0	300	12.0
1989	34.7	275	12.6
1988	33.1	255	13.0
1987	30.4	220	13.8
1986	31.7	235	13.5
1985	28.0	200	14.0
1984	24.5	170	14.4
1983	22.5	155	14.5
1982	21.8	150	14.8
1981	18.0	120	15.0

TABLE 21-2 **District sales volume in Great Western Company, 1990**

District		Sales goals (in millions of dollars)	Acutal sales (in millions of dollars)	Performance percentage (actual ÷ goal)	Dollar variation (in millions)
A		10.8	12.5	116	+ 1.7
B		9.0	9.6	107	+ .6
C		7.6	7.7	101	+ .1
D		8.6	6.2	72	− 2.4
	Total	$36.0	$36.0		

The fine *total* performance in district A may be covering up weaknesses in an individual product line or territory.

Market-Share Analysis

Comparing a company's sales results with its goal certainly is a useful form of performance evaluation. But it does not tell how the company is doing relative to its competitors. We need a **market-share analysis** to compare the company's sales with the industry's sales. In effect, we should analyze the company's share of the market in total, as well as by product line and market segment.

Probably the major obstacle encountered in market-share analysis is in obtaining industry sales information in total and in the desired detail. Trade associations and government agencies are excellent sources for industry sales volume statistics in many fields.

Great Western Company is a good example of the utility of market-share analysis. Recall from Table 21-1 that GW's total sales doubled over a ten-year period, with annual increases in nine of those years. *But*, during this decade the industry's annual sales increased from $120 million to $300 million (a 150 percent increase). Thus the company's share of this market actually *declined* from 15 to 12 percent. Although GW's annual sales increased 100 percent, its market share declined 20 percent.

The next step is to determine *why* Great Western's market position declined. The number of possible causes is virtually limitless—and this is what makes management's task so difficult. A weakness in almost any aspect of GW's product line, distribution system, pricing structure, or promotional program may have contributed to the loss of market share. Or it may be that the real culprit was competition. There may be new competitors in the market that were attracted by the rapid growth rates. Or competitors' marketing programs may be more effective than Great Western's.

MARKETING COST ANALYSIS

An analysis of sales volume is quite helpful in evaluating and controlling a company's marketing effort. A volume analysis, however, does not tell us anything about the *profitability* of this effort. Management needs to conduct a marketing cost analysis to determine the relative profitability of its territories, product lines, or other marketing units. A **marketing cost analysis** is a detailed study of the operating expense section of a company's profit and loss statement. As part of this analysis, management may establish budgetary goals, and then study the variations between budgeted costs and actual expenses.

Types of Marketing Cost Analyses

A company's marketing costs may be analyzed:

- As they appear in the ledger accounts and on the profit and loss statement.
- After they are grouped into functional (activity) classifications.
- After these activity costs have been allocated to territories, products, or other marketing units.

ANALYSIS OF LEDGER EXPENSES

The simplest and least expensive marketing cost analysis is a study of the "object of expenditure" costs as they appear in the firm's profit and loss statement. These figures, in turn, come from the company's accounting records. The simplified operating statement for the Great Western Company on the left side of Table 21-3 is the model we shall use in this discussion.

The procedure is to analyze each cost item (salaries and media space, for example) in some detail. We can compare this period's total with the totals for similar periods in the past and observe the trends. We can compare actual results with budgeted expense goals. We should also compute each expense as a percentage of net sales. Then, if possible, we should compare these expense ratios with industry figures, which are often available through trade associations.

ANALYSIS OF FUNCTIONAL EXPENSES

Marketing costs should be allocated among the various marketing functions, such as advertising or warehousing, for more effective control. Management can then analyze the cost of each of these activities.

The procedure here is to select the appropriate groups, and then to allocate each ledger expense among those activities. As indicated in the expense distribution sheet on the right-hand side of Table 21-3, we have decided on five activity cost groups in our Great Western example. Some items, such as the cost of media space, can be apportioned directly to one activity (advertising).

TABLE 21-3 **Profit and loss statement and distribution of natural expenses to activity cost groups, Great Western, 1990**

Profit and loss statement ($000)			Expense distribution sheet ($000)				
			Activity (functional) cost groups				
			Personal selling	Advertising	Warehousing and shipping	Order Processing	Marketing administration
Net sales		$36,000					
Cost of goods sold		23,400					
Gross margin		12,600					
Operating expenses:							
Salaries and commissions	$2,710 →		$1,200	$ 240	$ 420	$280	$ 570
Travel and entertainment	1,440 →		1,040				400
Media space	1,480 →			1,480			
Supplies	440 →		60	35	240	70	35
Property taxes	130 →		16	5	60	30	19
Freight out	3,500 →				3,500		
Total expenses		9,700	$2,316	$1,760	$4,220	$380	$1,024
Net profit		$2,900					

For other expenses, the cost can be prorated only after management has established some reasonable basis for allocation. Property taxes, for instance, may be allocated according to the proportion of total floor space occupied by each department. Thus the warehouse accounts for 46 percent of the total area (square feet) of floor space in the firm, so the warehousing and shipping function is charged with $60,000 (46 percent) of the property taxes.

A functional cost analysis gives executives more information than they can get from an analysis of ledger accounts alone. Also, an analysis of activity expenses in total provides an excellent starting point for management to analyze costs by territories, products, or other marketing units.

ANALYSIS OF FUNCTIONAL COSTS BY MARKET SEGMENTS

The third and most beneficial type of marketing cost analysis is a study of the costs and profitability of each segment of the market. This type of analysis divides the market by territories, products, customer groups, or order sizes. Cost analysis by market segment enables management to pinpoint trouble spots much more effectively than does an analysis of either ledger-account expenses or activity costs.

By combining a sales volume analysis with a marketing cost study, a researcher can prepare a complete operating statement for each of the product or market segments. These individual statements can then be analyzed to determine the effectiveness of the marketing program as related to each of those segments.

The procedure for a cost analysis by market segment is similar to that used to analyze activity expenses. The total of each activity cost (the right-hand part of Table 21-3) is prorated on some basis to each product or market segment being studied. Let's walk through an example of a cost analysis, by sales districts, for Great Western, as shown in Tables 21-4 and 21-5.

First, for each of the five GW activities, we select an allocation basis for distributing the cost of that activity among the four districts. These bases are shown in the top part of Table 21-4. Then we determine the number of allocation ''units'' that make up each activity cost, and we find the cost per unit. This completes the allocation scheme, which tells us how to allocate costs to the four districts:

- Personal selling activity expenses pose no problem because they are direct expenses, chargeable to the district in which they are incurred.
- Advertising expenses are allocated on the basis of the number of pages of advertising run in each district. GW purchased the equivalent of 88 pages of advertising during the year, at an average cost of $20,000 per page ($1,760,000 ÷ 88).
- Warehousing and shipping expenses are allocated on the basis of the number of orders shipped. Since 10,550 orders were shipped during the year at a total activity cost of $4,220,000, the cost per order is $400.
- Order-processing expenses are allocated according to the number of invoice lines typed during the year. Since there were 126,667 lines, then the cost per line is $3.
- Marketing administration — a totally indirect expense — is divided equally among the four districts, with each district being allocated $256,000.

The final step is to calculate the amount of each activity cost to be allocated to each district. The results are shown in the bottom part of Table 21-4. We see

TABLE 21-4 **Allocation of activity to sales districts, Great Western, 1990**

Activity		Personal selling	Advertising	Warehousing and shipping	Order processing	Marketing administration
Allocation scheme						
Allocation basis		Direct expense to each district	Number of pages of advertising	Number of orders to be shipped	Number of invoice lines	Equally among districts
Total activity cost		$2,316,000	$1,760,000	$4,220,000	$380,000	$1,024,000
Number of allocation units			88 pages	10,550 orders	126,667 lines	4 districts
Cost per allocation unit			$20,000	$400	$3	$256,000
Allocation of costs						
District A	units	—	27 pages	3,300 orders	46,000 lines	one
	cost	$650,000	$540,000	$1,320,000	$138,000	$256,000
District B	units	—	19 pages	2,850 orders	33,000 lines	one
	cost	$606,000	$380,000	$1,140,000	$99,000	$256,000
District C	units	—	22 pages	2,300 orders	26,667 lines	one
	cost	$540,000	$440,000	$1,920,000	$80,000	$256,000
District D	units	—	20 pages	2,100 orders	21,000 lines	one
	cost	$520,000	$400,000	$840,000	$63,000	$256,000

that $650,000 of personal selling expenses were charged directly to district A and $606,000 to district B, for example. Regarding advertising, the equivalent of 27 pages of advertising was run in district A, so that district is charged with $540,000 (27 pages × $20,000 per page). Similar calculations provide advertising activity cost allocations of $380,000 to district B; $440,000 to district C; and $400,000 to district D.

Regarding warehousing and shipping expenses, 3,300 orders were shipped to customers in district A, at a unit allocation cost of $400 per order, for a total allocated cost of $1,320,000. Warehousing and shipping charges are allocated to the other three districts as indicated in Table 21-4.

To allocate order-processing expenses, management determined that 46,000 invoice lines went to customers in district A. At $3 per line (the cost per allocation unit), district A is charged with $138,000. Each district is charged with $256,000 for marketing administration expenses.

After the activity costs have been allocated among the four districts, we can prepare a profit and loss statement for each district. These statements are shown in Table 21-5. Sales volume for each district is determined from the sales volume analysis (Table 21-2). Cost of goods sold and gross margin for each district is obtained by assuming that the company gross margin of 35 percent (12,600,000 ÷ $36,000,000) was maintained in each district.

Table 21-5 now shows, for each district, what the company profit and loss statement shows for overall company operations. For example, we note that district A's net profit was 11.8 percent of sales ($1,471,000 ÷ $12,500,000 = 11.8 percent). In sharp contrast, district D did rather poorly, earning a net profit of only 1.5 percent of net sales ($91,000 ÷ $6,200,000 = 1.5 percent).

At this point in our performance evaluation, we have completed the "what

TABLE 21-5 **Profit and loss statements for sales districts ($000), Great Western, 1990**

	Total	District A	District B	District C	District D
Net sales	$36,000	$12,500	$9,600	$7,700	$6,200
Cost of goods sold	23,400	8,125	6,240	5,005	4,030
Gross margin	12,600	4,375	3,360	2,695	2,170
Operating expenses:					
Personal selling	2,316	650	606	540	520
Advertising	1,760	540	380	440	400
Warehousing and shipping	4,220	1,320	1,140	920	840
Order processing, billing	380	138	99	80	63
Marketing administration	1,024	256	256	256	256
Total expenses	9,700	2,904	2,481	2,236	2,079
Net profit (in dollars)	$ 2,900	$ 1,471	$ 879	$ 459	$ 91
Net profit (as percentage of sales)	8.1%	11.8%	9.2%	6.0%	1.5%

happened'' stage. The next stage is to determine *why* the results are as depicted in Table 21-5. As mentioned earlier, it is extremely difficult to answer this question. In district D, for example, the sales force obtained only about two-thirds as many orders as in district A (2,100 versus 3,300). Was this because of poor selling ability, poor sales training, more severe competition in district D, or some other reason among a multitude of possibilities?

After a performance evaluation has determined why district results came out as they did, management can move to the third stage in its evaluation process. That final stage is, *what should management do about the situation?* This stage will be discussed briefly after we have reviewed major problem areas in marketing cost analysis.

Problems in Cost Analysis

Marketing cost analysis can be expensive in time, money, and manpower. In particular, the task of allocating costs is often quite difficult.

ALLOCATING COSTS

The problem of allocating costs becomes most evident when activity cost totals must be apportioned among individual territories, products, or other marketing units.

Operating costs can be divided into direct and indirect expenses. Direct, or separable, expenses are those incurred totally in connection with one market segment or one unit of the sales organization. Thus salary and travel expenses of the sales representative in district A are direct expenses for that territory. The cost of newspaper space to advertise product C is a direct cost of marketing that product. Allocating direct expenses is easy. They can be charged in their entirety to the marketing unit that incurred them.

The allocation difficulty arises in connection with indirect, or common, costs. These expenses are incurred jointly for more than one marketing unit. Therefore, they cannot be charged totally to one market unit.

Within the category of indirect expenses, some costs are *partially* indirect and some are *totally* indirect. Order filling and shipping, for example, are partially indirect costs. They would *decrease* if some territories or products were eliminated. They would *increase* if new products or territories were added. On the other hand, marketing administrative expenses are totally indirect. The cost of the chief marketing executive's staff and office would remain about the same, whether or not the number of territories or product lines was changed.

Any method selected for allocating indirect expenses has obvious weaknesses that can distort the results and mislead management. Two commonly used allocation methods are to divide these costs (1) equally among the marketing units being studied (territories, for instance) or (2) in proportion to the sales volume in each marketing unit. But each method gives a different result for the total costs for each marketing unit.

FULL-COST VERSUS CONTRIBUTION-MARGIN APPROACH

In a marketing cost analysis, two means of allocating indirect expenses are the (1) contribution-margin (also called contribution-to-overhead) method and (2) full-cost method. A controversy exists regarding which of these two approaches is better for managerial control purposes.

In the **contribution-margin approach**, only direct expenses are allocated to each marketing unit being analyzed. These costs presumably would be eliminated if that marketing unit were eliminated. When direct expenses are deducted from the gross margin of the marketing unit, the remainder is the amount which that unit is contributing to cover total direct expenses (or overhead).

All expenses—direct and indirect—are allocated among the marketing units under study in the **full-cost approach**. By allocating *all* costs, management can determine the net profit of each territory, product, or other marketing unit.

For any given marketing unit, these two methods can be summarized as follows:

Contribution margin	Full cost
Sales $	Sales $
less	*less*
Cost of goods sold	Cost of goods sold
equals	*equals*
Gross margin	Gross margin
less	*less*
Direct expenses	Direct expenses
equals	*less*
Contribution margin (the amount available to cover overhead expense plus a profit)	Indirect expenses
	equals
	Net profit

Proponents of the *full-cost* approach contend that a marketing cost study is intended to determine the net profitability of the units being studied. They feel that the contribution-margin method does not fulfil this purpose and may be misleading. A given territory or product may be showing a contribution to overhead. Yet, after indirect costs are allocated, this product or territory may actually have a net loss. In effect, say the full-cost proponents, the contribution-margin approach is the iceberg principle in action. That is, the visible tip of the iceberg (the contribution margin) looks good, while the submerged part may be hiding a net loss.

Contribution-margin supporters contend that it is not possible to accurately allocate indirect costs among product or market segments. Furthermore, items such as administrative costs are not all related to any one territory or product. Therefore, the marketing units should not bear any of these costs. Advocates of the contribution-margin approach also point out that a full-cost analysis may show that a product or territory has a net loss, whereas this unit may be contributing something to overhead. Some executives might recommend that the losing product or territory be eliminated. But they are overlooking the fact that the unit's contribution to overhead would then have to be borne by other units. With the contribution-margin approach, there would be no question about keeping this unit as long as no better alternative could be discovered.

USE OF FINDINGS FROM COMBINED VOLUME AND COST ANALYSIS

So far in our discussion of marketing performance evaluation, we have been dealing generally with the first two stages in the process. That is, we have been finding out *what happened* and *why*. To conclude this chapter, let's look at some examples of how management might use the results from a combined sales volume analysis and marketing cost analysis.

Territorial Decisions

Once management knows the net profit (or contribution to overhead) of territories in relation to their potential, there are several possibilities for managerial action. It may decide to adjust (expand or contract) territories to bring them into line with current sales potential. Or territorial problems may stem from weaknesses in the distribution system, and changes in channels of distribution may be needed. Some firms that have been using manufacturers' agents may find it advisable to establish their own sales forces in growing markets. Intense competition may be the cause of unprofitable volume in some districts, and changes in the promotional program may be necessary.

Of course, a losing territory might be abandoned completely. An abandoned region may have been contributing something to overhead, however, even though a net loss was shown. Management must recognize that this contribution must now be carried by the remaining territories.

Product Decisions

When the relative profitability of each product or group of products is known, unprofitable models, sizes, or colours can be eliminated. Sales people's compensation plans may be altered to encourage the sale of high-margin items. Channels of distribution may be changed. Instead of selling all its products directly to business users, for instance, a machine tools manufacturer shifted to industrial distributors for standard products of low unit value. The company thereby improved the profitability of these products.

In the final analysis, management may decide to discontinue a product. Before this is done, however, consideration must be given to the effect this will have on other items in the line. Often a low-volume or unprofitable product must be carried simply to round out the line. Customers may expect a seller to carry the item. If it is not available, the seller may lose sales of other products.

Decisions on Customer Classes and Order Sizes

By combining a volume analysis with a cost study, executives can determine the relative profitability of each group of customers. If one group shows an unsatisfactory net profit, changes in the pricing structure for these accounts may be required. Or perhaps accounts that have been sold directly should be turned over to middlemen.

A common difficulty plaguing many firms today is the **small-order problem**. Many orders are below the break-even point. Revenue from each of these orders is actually less than allocated expenses. This problem occurs because several costs, such as billing or direct selling, are essentially the same whether the order amounts to $10 or $10,000. Management's immediate reaction may be that no order below the break-even point should be accepted. Or small-volume accounts should be dropped from the customer list. Such decisions may be harmful, however. Management should determine first *why* certain accounts are small-order problems and then adopt procedures to correct the situation. Proper handling can often turn a losing account into a satisfactory one. A small-order handling charge, which customers would willingly pay, might change the profit picture entirely.

SUMMARY

The management process in marketing may be defined as the planning, implementation, and evaluation of the marketing effort in an organization. Implementation is the operational stage in which an organization attempts to carry out its strategic planning. Strategic planning is virtually useless if these plans are not implemented effectively.

The implementation stage includes three broad areas of activity—organizing, staffing, and operating. In organizing, the company first should coordinate all marketing activities into one department whose top executive reports directly to the president. Then, within the marketing department, the company may utilize some form of organizational specialization based on geographical territories, products, or customer types. Selecting people is the most important step in the entire management process. To operate an organization effectively, management also needs to do a good job in delegation, coordination, motivation, and communication.

The evaluation stage in the management process involves measuring performance results against predetermined goals. Evaluation enables management to determine the effectiveness of its implementation efforts and to plan future corrective action where necessary.

A marketing audit is extremely important in a total marketing evaluation program. Most companies are victims of at least some misdirected marketing effort. That is, the 80–20 and iceberg principles are at work in most firms because marketing efforts (costs) are expended in relation to the number of marketing units, rather than to their profit potential. Fundamentally, companies do not know how much they should be spending for marketing activities, or what results they should get from these expenditures.

Two useful tools for identifying and correcting misdirected marketing efforts are a sales volume analysis and a marketing cost analysis. Given appropriately detailed analyses, management can study sales volume and marketing costs by product lines and market segments (sales territories, customer groups). One major problem in marketing cost analysis is that of allocating costs—especially indirect costs—to the various marketing units. But the findings from these analyses are extremely helpful in shaping decisions regarding several aspects of a company's marketing program.

KEY TERMS AND CONCEPTS

Brand-management system 671
Category-management system 671
Implementation (in the management process) 672
Organizational structures for implementing strategic planning 673

Importance of good selection 677
Delegating authority and responsibility 679
Coordinating marketing activities 679
Motivating people 679
Communicating inside a company 679

QUESTIONS AND PROBLEMS

1. Explain the relationship among planning, implementation, and evaluation in the management process.

2. "Good implementation in an organization can overcome poor planning, but good planning cannot overcome poor implementation." Explain, using examples.

3. How is the organizational placement of marketing activities likely to be different in a marketing-oriented firm as contrasted with a production-oriented firm?

4. What benefits can a company expect to gain by organizing its sales force by geographical territories?

5. Give some examples of companies that are likely to organize their sales force by product groups.

6. What organizational structures should each of the following companies use when marketing in Western Europe?
   a. Franchised chain of real estate brokerage firms such as Re/Max or Century 21.
   b. Medium-size manufacturer of women's cosmetics.
   c. Manufacturer of outboard motors.

7. What are some reasons why this book's authors believe that selecting people is such a critical aspect of the management process?

8. Why is effective delegation of authority and responsibility so important in operating a marketing program?

9. Give examples of how advertising and personal selling activities might be coordinated in a company's marketing department.

10. A sales volume analysis by territories indicates that the sales of a manufacturer of roofing materials have increased 12 percent a year for the past three years in the territory comprising Alberta and British Columbia. Does this indicate conclusively that the company's sales volume performance is satisfactory in that territory?

11. A manufacturer found that one product accounted for 35 to 45 percent of the company's total sales in all but 2 of the 18 territories. In each of those two territories, this product accounted for only 15 percent of the company's volume. What factors might account for the relatively low sales of this article in the two districts?

12. Explain how the results of a territorial sales volume analysis may influence a firm's promotional program.

13. What effects may a sales volume analysis by product have on training, supervising, and compensating the sales force?

14. "Firms should discontinue selling losing products." Discuss.

15. Should a company stop selling to an unprofitable customer? Why or why not? If not, then what steps might the company take to make the account a profitable one?

CHAPTER 22 GOALS

Throughout the book we have examined marketing within the individual firm. Now, in this final chapter, we will look more closely at marketing within our social system. After studying this chapter, you should be able to explain:

- The ideal basis for evaluating marketing performance.
- Major criticisms of marketing.
- Consumer, government, and business responses to consumer discontent.
- The significance of consumerism.
- The ethical responsibilities of marketers.
- Trends that will likely influence future marketing activity.

A CLEAN WASH IS IMPORTANT. SO IS A CLEAN CONSCIENCE.

Sunlight. Now 100% Phosphate Free.

Marketing: Societal Appraisal and Prospect

Marketers face a dynamic and constantly changing environment. Firms large and small encounter threats from all directions that require constant vigilance and quick responses. Consider these recent challenges:

- Avon Products, a $3-billion-direct marketer of cosmetics, whose success was built on in-home sales, suffered earnings setbacks when women began joining the labour force in large numbers and became less accessible.
- Canada's major national brewers, Molson and Labatt, in response to an increasing concern on the part of Canadians towards the effects of excessive consumption of their products, have been running advertisements encouraging consumers not to drink and drive.
- McDonald's, Burger King, and other fast-food marketers have responded to a public outcry by environmentalists and ordinary consumers about excessive packaging and have abandoned their polystyrene containers in favour or more biodegradable paper and cardboard.
- reacting to the changing food-consumption patterns of Canadians, McCain Foods, the world's leading supplier of french fries, has introduced a new cholesterol-free version of their staple product.
- to encourage efforts towards greater conservation of energy resources, the power utilities of Canada have combined efforts to launch "Power Smart," a program to educate consumers on how they can save on their use of electricity and to subsidize the purchase of energy-saving devices such as shower heads and fluorescent light bulbs.
- manufacturers of disposable diapers have come in for considerable criticism in recent years from environmental groups who are concerned about the fact that the products add to the content of landfill sites. This prompted a battle between manufacturers of the disposable product and companies who supply cloth diapers, and also led Procter & Gamble, makers of Pampers and Luvs, to launch an aggressive advertising campaign arguing that there is environmental damage from both cloth and disposable diapers, but that the disposable variety is more healthy for babies.

As the opening examples indicate, for even the largest firms, change and challenge are probably the only certainties in marketing. Successful responses depend on understanding the proper role of marketing in business and in society.

Recall in Chapters 1 and 2 that our discussion touched on the societal dimensions of marketing as we briefly examined marketing's role in the total economy. For the most part, however, we have approached marketing from the viewpoint of the firm as we addressed the challenges facing an individual producer or middleman in managing its marketing activity. In this final chapter, we will look once again at marketing from a broader, societal perspective. We will appraise our system by identifying the major criticisms of marketing and responses to these criticisms. We conclude our discussion of marketing by looking into the crystal ball and considering some prospects for the future.

EVALUATING THE MARKETING SYSTEM

A major goal of this chapter is to appraise marketing. Before we can do this, however, we have to agree on what the objective of marketing should be. Recall from Chapter 1 our discussion of the marketing concept. We said the objective of an organization is to accomplish its goals through the determination and satisfaction of consumers' wants. Thus, from the point of view of the *individual organization*, if the firm's target market is satisfied and the organization's objectives are being met, then the marketing effort can be judged successful.

However, this standard makes no distinction between organizations whose behaviour is detrimental to society and those whose activities are socially acceptable. Firms that pollute the environment or stimulate unwholesome demand would qualify as good marketers right along with firms that behave responsibly. Therefore, we must take a broader, societal view that incorporates the best interests of others as well as the desires of a particular target market and the objectives of the marketer. In other words, marketing must strike a balance among the wants of consumers, the objectives of the organization, *and* the welfare of society.

There is evidence all around us of the interrelationship of these three criteria. If a product does not *meet consumers' needs* or if a firm is unable to *provide the level of service* that customers want, the consumer will not buy that product or service. The business world is littered with companies that have gone out of business because they were unable to satisfy their customers. Likewise, if a firm behaves in a fashion that is viewed by consumers or the public to be *detrimental to society*, government will likely intervene, as it does in regulating the advertising of tobacco and other products judged to be potentially damaging to the health and safety of consumers. Finally, companies regularly change their advertising and promotional campaigns as their *organizational objectives* change.

CRITICISMS OF MARKETING

Criticisms of marketing centre on actions (or inaction) that relate to the balance between organizational objectives and the wants of customers and/or the well-being of society. These issues can be categorized as follows:

- *Exploitation.* Marketers are sometimes accused of taking unfair advantage of a person or situation. Examples of exploitation are price gouging during a shortage and misleading prospects with false or incomplete information. These behaviours may meet the organization's goal of sales and profits,

Customers can be numbers in a computer or real people. Amex points to the difference.

but they are detrimental to consumers, society, or both, and are clearly in conflict with marketing's goal of long-term customer satisfaction.

- *Inefficiency*. Some critics feel that marketing uses more resources than necessary. Accusations include ineffective promotional activity, unnecessary distribution functions, and excessive numbers of brands in many product categories. Inefficiency results in higher costs to organizations, higher prices to consumers, and a waste of society's resources.

- *Stimulating unwholesome demand*. A number of marketers have been accused of encouraging consumers or businesses to purchase products that are detrimental to the individual or the organization. For example, most people believe that the marketing of pornographic material is socially unacceptable. Though it may meet the needs of some consumers and satisfy the objectives of organizations that produce and sell it, the marketing of pornography is discouraged because society views it as detrimental.

- *Illegal behaviour*. Laws are passed to protect individuals, organizations, and society in general. Marketers are expected to abide by these laws, even when violating a law may benefit consumers or an organization. Price collusion, for instance, is likely to meet the needs of the organizations involved and might even result in lower prices for consumers than price competition. However, it is detrimental to competitors of the colluding firms. Therefore, since the behaviour is unfair to others in society, it is unacceptable.

WHAT BUSINESS PRACTICES MOST ANNOY CONSUMERS?

A survey sponsored by *The Wall Street Journal* indicated that consumers are most annoyed by actions that are designed to benefit the seller at the expense of the consumer. That is, a balance of benefits to both parties in the exchange is absent. The seven things that bother consumers the most, followed by the intended benefit to the seller, are:

1. Waiting in line while other windows or registers are closed.
   (Keeps the seller's costs down.)
2. Solicitation using prerecorded messages.
   (Gives the seller greater control over the message and reduces costs.)
3. Being quoted one price, then finding the real price is higher.
   (Generates interest and store traffic.)
4. Getting a sales call during dinner.
   (Reduces the number of ''not at homes,'' lowering the seller's cost.)
5. Discovering that sale items aren't in stock.
   (Generates store traffic.)
6. Dealing with complicated health insurance forms.
   (Reduces claims and comparisons.)
7. ''Urgent'' mail that is only trying to sell something.
   (Increases the likelihood of the advertisement being read.)

In contrast, marketing-oriented organizations are careful to balance buyer and seller benefits.

Source: David Wessel, ''Sure Ways to Annoy Consumers,'' *The Wall Street Journer*, Nov. 6, 1989, pp. B1, B6.

The major charges against marketing can be grouped according to the components of the marketing mix—product, price, distribution, and promotion. Keep in mind that these are *allegations*. Some are unsubstantiated by facts and others apply only to specific situations.[1]

Product

INGREDIENTS: Wheat Flour, Rye Flour, Coconut Oil, Dehydrated Onions, Salt, Dextrose, Hydrogenated Vegetable Oil (soybean, cottonseed and/or palm), Yeast, Yeast Nutrients (flour, calcium sulfate, salt, ammonium chloride, calcium carbonate, potassium bromate), Sodium Diacetate (to preserve freshness), Dough Conditioner (proteolytic enzymes derived from Aspergillus Oryzae), Ferrous Sulfate (source of iron), Niacin (a B-Vitamin), Thiamine Hydrochloride (Vitamin B₁), Riboflavin (Vitamin B₂).

What do food ingredient lists tell us?

Criticisms of products generally centre on how well they meet buyers' expectations. Critics charge that too many products are of poor quality or are unsafe. Examples cited include products that fail or break under normal use; prepared food that contains chemical preservatives, flavour enhancers, and colouring; airlines and trains that run late; and wash-and-wear clothing that needs ironing. Also, according to some observers, products are often backed by confusing, inadequate warranties and repair service is unsatisfactory.

Other accusations include packages that appear to contain more of a product than they actually do, labels that provide insufficient or misleading information, and products advertised as ''new'' that appear to offer only trivial improvements. Critics also argue that style obsolescence encourages consumers to discard products before they are worn out, and that there is an unnecessary proliferation of brands in many product categories. As a result, buyers are confused and production capacity is wasted.

Price

Everyone would like to pay less for products, but most buyers are satisfied with an equitable exchange. Complaints about prices usually stem from the

---

[1]For an interesting perspective on the criticisms of marketing, see Steven H. Star, ''Marketing and Its Discontents,'' *Harvard Business Review*, November-December 1989, pp. 148–54.

perception that the seller is making an excessive profit, that the buyer has been misled about prices, or that the consumer does not receive good value. We hear that prices are too high because they are controlled by the large firms in an industry. Sellers are sometimes accused of building in hidden charges or advertising false markdowns. Many critics feel that price competition has been largely replaced by nonprice competition in the form of unnecessary frills that add more to the cost than the value of a product.

Distribution
Of the four marketing mix variables, the least understood and appreciated is distribution. This is probably because channels can take so many forms. In addition, a buyer comes in direct contact with only one level of the distribution channel, so it is difficult to appreciate the functions performed at other levels. Criticisms related to channels reflect this complexity. Channel members are accused of performing needless functions or performing them inefficiently.

Promotion
The most common accusations against marketing focus on promotion—especially in personal selling and advertising. Most of the complaints about personal selling are aimed at the retail level and the allegedly poor quality of retail selling and service.

Criticisms of advertising may be divided into two groups—social and economic. From a social point of view, advertising is charged with overemphasizing material standards of living and underemphasizing cultural and moral values. Advertising is also accused of manipulating impressionable people, especially children. Another social criticism is that many advertising statements are false, deceptive, or in bad taste. Specifically, some say that too many of the claims made in ads are exaggerated, and fear and sexual appeals are overused. Critics also argue there is simply too much advertising and that ad placement is often offensive. For example, many people resent promotional messages and advertisements on home videos.

The economic criticism of advertising—that it unnecessarily increases the cost of products—is based on two arguments. One is that advertising, particularly persuasive as opposed to informative ads, simply shifts demand from one brand to another. Thus it only adds to the individual firms' marketing costs without increasing aggregate demand. Since the advertising must be paid for, prices go up. The other argument is that large firms can afford to differentiate their products through advertising. In this way, they create barriers to market entry for new or smaller firms. The result is a high level of market concentration that leads to higher prices and higher profits. This charge was carefully refuted some years ago. A study of the effect of advertising on competition concluded that there is no relationship between advertising intensity and high concentration.[2] Nor does there seem to be any link between advertising intensity and price increases or profitability. Advertising is highly competitive, not anticompetitive. In fact, there is a school of thought that encourages professionals (dentists and lawyers, for example) to advertise in order to *increase* price competition.

---

[2]The topic of the economic effects of advertising in Canada is dealt with in O.J. Firestone, *The Economic Implications of Advertising*, Methuen Publications, Toronto, 1967; and in Jules Backman, *Advertising and Competition*, New York University Press, New York, 1967.

M A R K E T I N G   A T   W O R K

FILE 22-1   **POLICE HUMOUR NOT ALWAYS FUNNY**

Culinar Inc. is a Quebec snack-cake firm. The firm developed a series of advertisements that underscored the fact that Culinar cakes and other products are *not* health foods. One of their slogans was "Grains: they're for the birds." Another was "Doughnuts — they're for the police." The doughnut slogan appeared in an ad for Culinar's Jos. Louis doughnuts and is said to play on the standing joke in Quebec that "if you can't find a cop, check out the local doughnut shop: He's probably there."

The ad is inspired by a Quebec comedy group that created a well-known skit that pokes fun at police eating doughnuts. But the secretary of the provincial association that represents police officers thought the ad was in bad taste and an error in judgement. The police representative thought that although comedians could mock police, a company was not being responsible if it helped "to destroy the image and credibility of a public organization" and the use of stereotypes should no longer be tolerated by society.

Because of the police reaction and other public-relations issues that had cropped up for Culinar, the firm decided to withdraw the doughnut ads from more than 1,500 billboards, subway platforms, and cars and buses.

Source: Adapted from Ann Gibbon, "Doughnut Campaign Proves Sticky for Culinar," *Globe and Mail*, August 28, 1991, p. B3.

Understanding the Criticisms

To evaluate the charges against marketing, we must understand what actually is being criticized. Is the object of the complaint ultimately the economic system, an entire industry, or a particular firm? If the criticism applies to a firm, is the marketing department or some other department the cause? Our free enterprise system encourages competition, and government regulatory bodies for many years have judged competition by the number of competitors in an industry. Thus when we complain about the number of toothpaste or cereal brands on the market, we are really criticizing the system. Within a particular firm, a faulty product may result from production, not marketing problems. Clearly, though this explanation does not make the complaints less valid, it does indicate that marketing is not always to blame.

It is also instructive to consider the sources of criticism. Some critics are well-intentioned, well-informed individuals and groups. They point out legitimate weaknesses or errors that need correction, such as deceptive packaging, misleading advertising, and irresponsible pricing. A second type of detractor is simply ill-informed. For example, these people may not understand the functions associated with distribution or appreciate the costs of producing and selling a product. Although their criticisms may have some popular appeal, they cannot withstand careful scrutiny. A third group is made up of those whose views do not reflect the general sentiments of society. These people vociferously criticize behaviour they find objectionable in the hope of changing public opinion. Protests against the use of persuasive advertising in political campaigns come from such sources. Thus we must examine criticism carefully to separate the legitimate from the erroneous and self-serving.

Operating in a socially undesirable manner, even for a short time, is unacceptable. However, instances of this kind of behaviour, though widely publicized, are few, relative to the totality of marketing effort. More common, and therefore more disturbing, are the situations that are not clear-cut. These are debatable issues such as full disclosure in advertising (What is the meaning of "full"?); planned obsolescence (How long should a product last?); and the subject of our next section, the cost of marketing.

Does Marketing Cost Too Much?

Many of the criticisms of marketing can generally be summarized in the statement that marketing costs too much. If there is too much advertising, not enough competition, too many middlemen, or too many brands, marketing *does* cost too much. But how can we go about making those judgements? Our approach is to address the question from two points of view. The first is within the context of our total socioeconomic system, and the second is within the context of an individual firm.

IN OUR SOCIOECONOMIC SYSTEM

It is estimated that the total cost of producing all products is about 50 percent of the final price paid by consumers. If this is the *average*, then marketing's share of the costs for some products is considerably more than 50 percent. Critics also observe that in many instances the physical product is virtually unchanged from the time it leaves the factory until the consumer buys it. Thus, though marketing costs are a substantial proportion of the final price of most products, it is unclear what value has been added by marketing efforts.

The question of whether marketing costs too much can be asked only in comparative terms. In other words, what would be the effect of spending more or less? There is insufficient accurate information with which to make that comparison. As noted in Chapter 21, we have not yet developed adequate tools to measure the return derived from a given marketing expenditure. However, in qualitative terms, saying marketing costs too much implies that one or more of the following situations must prevail:

- Firms have large amounts of money that they are willing to spend on marketing without concern for the returns produced.
- Firms benefiting from marketing expenditures (the media, advertising agencies, middlemen) are enjoying abnormally high profits.
- More services are being provided than consumers and business people demand.
- Marketing activities are being performed in a grossly inefficient manner.
- Consumption is declining, requiring more marketing effort.

The fact is that none of these situations exists. Competitive pressure ensures that the first four do not occur, and the desire for more and better products has led to continual *increases* in demand (the fifth item). What marketing expenditures produce are time, place, possession, image, and sometimes form utility (as described in Chapter 1). Thus the general criticism that marketing costs too much seems to stem from opinions more than hard evidence.

IN AN INDIVIDUAL ORGANIZATION

Unquestionably, marketing does cost too much in firms that market inefficiently or are production-oriented. Marketing costs are too high and marketing efficiency is too low in firms that:

- Do not offer a product mix desired by customers.
- Have a high rate of new product failures.
- Use improperly designed distribution channels.
- Base prices on cost rather than demand.
- Mismanage the sales force.
- Sponsor ineffective advertising and sales promotions.

In many firms, however, marketing does not cost too much. These firms have strategically planned and implemented customer-oriented marketing programs, as discussed and advocated throughout this book.

It is also important to note that examining marketing costs in isolation is misleading. A total cost approach should be adopted. In many instances, a firm can reduce total costs by increasing marketing costs. To illustrate, an increase in advertising expenditures may sufficiently expand a firm's market so that unit production costs decrease due to economies of scale. If production costs go down more than marketing costs go up, *total* cost is reduced.

There is some justification for most of the criticisms of marketing. Many of these situations do occur, but not with the regularity that many critics charge. Some individuals and organizations do indeed take advantage of an economic system that places a high value on freedom. However, many of the issues are more complicated than they seem. In addition, there is in place a system of checks and balances made up of consumer activists, responsible businesses (the majority of all businesses), and government to ensure that abuses are minimized.

RESPONSES TO MARKETING PROBLEMS

Efforts to address the problems that exist in or result from the exchange process have come from consumers, the government, and business organizations.

Consumer Responses

One response to marketing misdeeds, both actual and alleged, has come from consumer activists. The term *consumerism* was popularized in the 1960s when, in response to increasing consumer protests against a variety of business practices, Canada became the first country in the world to establish a government department at the federal level to be responsible for the rights of consumers. There had been earlier ''consumer movements'' in this country — in the early 1900s and again during the Great Depression of the 1930s. In these, the emphasis had been on protecting consumers from harmful products and from false and misleading advertising.

The movement that began in the 1960s, however, is different in three ways from earlier consumer movements. First, the consumerism of the past 20 years has occurred in a setting of higher incomes and largely fills subsistence needs, in contrast to the harsher economic conditions that surrounded earlier movements. Second, the consumer-movement legislation since the 1960s has been intended first and foremost to protect the consumer's interests. Emphasis in earlier legislation was placed on the protection of competition and competitors.

Third, today's consumerism is much more likely to endure, because it has generated an institutional structure to support it. Government agencies have been established to administer the consumer-oriented laws and to protect consumer interests. The social sensitivity of many businesses has increased, and various consumer- and environment-oriented organizations have developed.

MEANING AND SCOPE OF CONSUMERISM

The consumerism movement protests perceived injustices in exchange relationships and attempts to remedy them. Generally consumers feel that the balance of power in exchange relationships lies with the seller. Consumerism is an expression of this opinion and an effort to obtain a more equal balance of power between buyers and sellers.

Consumerism includes three broad areas of dissatisfaction and remedial effort:

- Discontent with direct buyer-seller exchange relationships between consumers and businesses. This is the original and still main focus of consumerism. Efforts to ban MSG, a flavour enhancer and preservative that can cause a severe allergic reaction in some people, would be an example.
- Discontent with nonbusiness, nonprofit organizations and governmental agencies. Consumerism extends to all exchange relationships. The performance of such diverse organizations as schools (quality of education, performance of students on standardized tests, number of class days per year), hospitals (medical care costs, smoking in rooms, malpractice), and public utilities (rate increases, eliminating service to people unable to pay their bills) has been scrutinized and subjected to organized and spirited consumer protests.
- Discontent of those indirectly affected by the behaviour of others. An exchange between two parties can sometimes have a negative impact on a third party. For example, farmers buy insecticides and pesticides from chemical companies. However, these products may pollute water supplies, rivers, and the air. Thus an exchange has created a problem for a third party or group.

CONSUMER ACTIONS

Consumer reactions to marketing problems have ranged from complaints registered with offending organizations to boycotts (refusing to buy a particular product or shop at a certain store). Consumer groups have recognized their potential power and have become more active politically than ever. They organize mass letter-writing campaigns to editors, legislators, and business executives. They support consumer-oriented political candidates, conduct petition drives, and gain media attention through sit-ins and picketing.

In recent years, many organized groups at both the local and national levels have become involved in a more broadly defined consumer movement. Some of these groups represent a variety of interests, dealing with the direct interaction of consumers with businesses as well as with broader issues such as environmentalism and animal rights. Others represent particular interest groups, including retired and elderly consumers, the urban poor, and victims of crime and fraud by businesses.

CONSUMERISM IN THE FUTURE

Cultural conditions that provided impetus for the heightened level of consumerism in the 1960s are again coming into place. In our advanced stage of economic development, consumers are more sensitive to social and environmental concerns. Along with sources of dissatisfaction already described, the plight of the poor, air and water pollution, waste disposal, treatment of animals, and health and safety are other social and environmental issues that are receiving greater attention.

In addition, more people are willing and able to take active roles in consumer issues. Compared to earlier generations, young people are better educated, more articulate, and more inclined to speak out. People of all ages are generally less intimidated by large organizations and less willing to accept the status quo. Responding to this increased public sensitivity, many politicians are also demonstrating greater concern for societal issues.

Since problems remain, consumerism in the 1990s will focus on some of the same areas as in the past. It is safe to predict, for example, that fair treatment for consumers, personal well-being, and safety will be major concerns. In addition, waste management, utilization of resources, and the preservation of natural beauty and environmental issues will likely draw increased attention.

Government Responses

Consumerism is not likely to fade away. The main reason for this forecast is that today it is politically popular to support consumers. Politicians may generally have been unresponsive to consumer needs in the years prior to the mid-1960s. Since then, however, consumer-oriented activity at both the federal and provincial levels has been carried on at an unprecedented rate. All the provinces and some cities have created some kind of office for consumer affairs.

Since the mid-1960s, federal and provincial legislatures have passed laws whose primary purpose is to aid the consumer. In contrast, very often in the past marketing legislation was generally business-oriented, not consumer-oriented. As we have pointed out earlier, often the intent of such legislation was to protect competition or to benefit some segment of business, and any benefit or protection to the consumer occurred in an indirect manner, if it occurred at all. In contrast, recent years have seen the introduction of a large number of pieces of consumer-oriented legislation at both the federal and provincial levels in Canada.

A significant number of these laws are designed to protect the consumer's "right to safety"—especially in situations where consumers cannot judge for themselves the risk involved in the purchase and use of particular products. In Canada, we have such legislation as the Food and Drugs Act, which regulates and controls the manufacture, distribution, and sale of food, drugs, and cosmetic products. A very important piece of legislation, which also protects the consumer's right to safety, is the Hazardous Products Act. This law establishes standards for the manufacture of consumer products designed for household, garden, personal, recreational, or child use. Regulations under the Hazardous Products Act require that dangerous products be packaged as safely as possible and labelled with clear and adequate warnings. This law also makes provision for the removal of dangerous products from the marketplace.

One controversial area of product safety legislation is the paternalistic type of law that is intended to protect the consumer, whether he or she wants that protection. Thus, it is now mandatory to equip automobiles with seat belts, and in most provinces it is illegal to operate an automobile unless the seat belts are fastened. In effect, somebody else is forcing a consumer to accept what the other person feels is in the consumer's best interests—truly a new and broadening approach to consumer legislation.

Another series of laws and government programs supports the consumer's "right to be informed." These measures help in such areas as reducing confusion and deception in packaging and labelling, identifying the ingredients and nutritional content in food products, advising consumers of the length of life of certain packaged food products, providing instructions and assistance in the care of various textile products, and determining the true rate of interest.

At the federal level, government has passed a number of pieces of legislation designed to provide consumers with more information. Possibly the most important of these is the Consumer Packaging and Labelling Act, which regulates the packaging, labelling, sale, and advertising of prepackaged products. The Textile Labelling Act requires manufacturers of textile products to place labels on most articles made from fabrics. These labels must name the fibres, show the amount of each fibre in the product by percentage, and identify the company for whom or by whom the article was made.

At the provincial level, a number of programs exist that provide information to consumers. For example, all provinces have passed consumer protection legislation, which requires that all consumer lending agencies and retail stores provide consumers with information concerning the true rate of interest that they are paying on borrowed money and on purchases made on credit.

Also at the provincial level, all provinces have passed a general Consumer Protection Act, which deals primarily with the granting of credit. All provinces also have legislation that provides for a "cooling off" period during which the purchaser of goods or services in a door-to-door sale may cancel the contract, return any merchandise, and obtain a full refund. In addition, most provinces have legislation that provides for the disposal of unsolicited goods and credit cards received through the mail. All provinces also administer legislation that regulates particular industries such as collection agencies, automobile dealerships, and insurance agents.

The consumer is also protected at both the federal and provincial levels in Canada in the area of misleading and dishonest advertising. The federal Competition Act contains a number of provisions dealing with misleading advertising; these have been discussed in Chapter 17.

One of the most significant responses to the consumer movement on the part of government has been a strengthened and expanded role of regulatory agencies involved in consumer affairs. At the provincial level, Public Utilities Boards hold public hearings and receive briefs from concerned citizens and consumer groups whenever a telephone or hydro company is seeking a rate increase or a change in its services. It has become quite common for organized consumer associations and ratepayer groups to intervene at such hearings as representatives of consumer interests.

Federally, two major regulatory agencies have emerged as powerful arms of government in recent years. The Canadian Transport Commission (CTC) regulates all aspects of interprovincial travel and companies that operate nationally, such as railways and the major airlines. Applications for route changes and fare increases must be filed with the CTC, and opportunities are presented at public hearings for consumer groups to make representations. Similarly, the Canadian Radio-television and Telecommunications Commission (CRTC) regulates the broadcasting industry in this country. This regulatory body has become very much involved in marketing-related areas in recent years. It is responsible for awarding broadcasting licences to AM and FM radio stations, television stations, and cable television operators. The CRTC also regulates these broadcasters in the content of the programming they use and also administers numerous codes of advertising standards in its role as the agency responsible for regulating broadcast advertising.

Also, at the federal level, many government departments play important regulatory roles that have a major impact on the way in which marketers do business. From the point of view of a marketer of consumer products, the two most important would likely be the Department of Consumer and Corporate Affairs and Health and Welfare Canada. Various branches of these departments administer federal regulations and legislation such as the Competition Act, the Hazardous Products Act, the Consumer Packaging and Labelling Act, and the Food and Drugs Act.

Finally, in all provinces and at the federal level in Canada there exist marketing boards that, to varying degrees, control the production, distribution, and pricing of products. These marketing boards, such as the Ontario Milk Marketing Board, the British Columbia Fruit Board, and the Canadian Egg Marketing Agency, wield considerable power over the marketing of the products that fall under their responsibility. Most of these boards are involved in the distribution of agricultural products and were established to represent the interests of producers. However, through their efforts to promote marketing efficiency, marketing boards generally attempt to represent the best long-term interests of consumers.[3]

It is difficult to judge the effectiveness of government effort since it depends on one's perspective. From the point of view of many consumer advocates, the government is too slow and too many issues ignored or overlooked. Alternatively, some free-market spokespersons would prefer less regulation and view government activity as interference. In evaluating consumer protection, it is important to recognize that there are trade-offs. For example, there are costs involved in providing consumers with more information, designing and manufacturing products to eliminate all hazards, and keeping the environment clean. These must be weighed against the expected benefits. Often these are difficult comparisons; some, for instance, involve costs that will be incurred now for benefits that may not be realized until some time in the future.

Business Responses

An increasing number of businesses are making substantive responses to consumer problems. Here are a few examples:

- *Better communications with consumers.* Many firms have responded positively to the desire of consumers to be heard. Toll-free 1-800 phone numbers have become an integral part of customer service because they are easy to use and allow consumers to speak directly to a representative of the business.
- *More and better information for consumers.* Point-of-sale information is constantly improving. Manufacturers' instruction manuals on the use and care of their products are more detailed and easier to read. In many instances, package labels are more informative than in the past.
- *Product improvements.* More marketers are making a concerted effort to incorporate feedback from consumers in the designs of their products. As a result of consumer input or complaints, many companies have made

---

[3]For an interesting discussion of the pros and cons of marketing boards, see: Mary Janigan, "Why Chickens Don't Come Cheap," *Report on Business Magazine*, October 1990, pp. 87–99.

improvements in their products. For example, detergent manufacturers have produced concentrated products which are more environmentally safe. Soft drink manufacturers have improved the design of the caps on their one- and two-litre bottles so that the product will retain its carbonation after opening.

- *Service quality measurement*. Many companies have realized that it is becoming increasingly difficult to gain a competitive advantage through product design, and that the key to success is to offer the customer the best possible service. Realizing also that they need feedback so that they know how well they are doing, many have developed and introduced programs that allow them to measure consumers' perceptions of the level of service they are receiving.

- *More carefully prepared advertising*. Many advertisers are extremely cautious in approving agency-prepared ads, in sharp contrast to past practices. Advertisers are involving their legal departments in the approval process. They are sensitive to the fact that the CRTC may reject a commercial or the Advertising Standards Council may find that the advertisment violates some particular code of advertising standards. The advertising industry and the media are doing a much more effective self-regulation job than ever before, especially through the Advertising Advisory Board and its Advertising Standards Councils.

- *Customer service departments*. A growing number of companies have separate departments to handle consumer enquiries and complaints. Some even encourage customers to complain, or at least to provide feedback, by distributing short questionnaires in hotel rooms, airline seat pockets, and restaurants. In addition to dealing with complaints, customer service departments also gauge consumer tastes, act as sounding boards for new ideas, and often gain feedback on new products.

Some trade associations see themselves as defenders of their respective industry or profession. In that capacity, they try to moderate government antibusiness legislation through lobbying and head off criticism with arguments to justify almost any behaviour. More enlightened associations have recognized the necessity for responsible corporate behaviour. Though they still engage in lobbying, these groups actively respond to consumer problems by setting industry ethical standards, conducting consumer education, and promoting research among association members.

ETHICS AND MARKETING

Ethics are standards of conduct. To act in an ethical fashion is to conform to an accepted standard of moral behaviour. Undoubtedly, virtually all people prefer to act ethically. It is easy to be ethical when no hardship is involved — when a person is winning and life is going well. The test comes when things are not going so well — when pressures build up. These pressures arise in all walks of life, and marketing is no exception.

Marketing executives face the challenge of balancing the best interests of consumers, the organization, and society into a workable guide for their daily activities. In any situation, they must be able to distinguish what is ethical from what is unethical and act accordingly, regardless of the possible consequences. However, there are many circumstances in which what constitutes ethical behaviour is far from straightforward.

Reasons for Ethical Behaviour

Marketing executives should practice ethical behaviour simply because it is morally correct. While this is simple in concept, it is far more difficult to put into operation. Let's look at four pragmatic reasons for behaving ethically.

TO REVERSE DECLINING PUBLIC CONFIDENCE IN MARKETING

Marketing's image is tarnished in many people's eyes. In addition to negative attention produced by consumer issues, highly questionable practices periodically come to light. For example, we hear about misleading package labels, false claims in ads, phony list prices, and infringements on well-established trademarks. Though such practices are limited to only a small proportion of all marketing, the reputations of marketers in general are damaged.

How can this situation be reversed? Business leaders must demonstrate convincingly that they are aware of their ethical responsibility and will fulfil it. Companies must set high ethical standards and then enforce them. Moreover, it is very much in management's interest to be concerned with the well-being of consumers since they are the lifeblood of business.

TO AVOID INCREASES IN GOVERNMENT REGULATION

Marketing executives must act in an ethical manner to justify the privilege of operating in our relatively free economic system. Nothing worthwhile comes without a price. Our economic freedoms sometimes have a high price, just as our political freedoms do. Business apathy, resistance, or token responses to unethical behaviour simply increase the probability of more government regulation. Indeed, most of the governmental limitations on marketing are the result of management's failure to live up to its ethical responsibilities at one time or other. Moreover, once some form of government control has been introduced, it is rarely removed.

TO RETAIN THE POWER GRANTED BY SOCIETY

The concept that social power begets social responsibility helps explain why marketing executives have a major responsibility to society. Managers wield a great deal of social power as they influence markets and speak out on economic issues. However, there is responsibility tied to that power. Thus it is logical that unethical behaviour will result in an erosion of social power. If marketers do not use their power in a socially acceptable manner, that power will be lost in the long run.

TO PROTECT THE IMAGE OF THE ORGANIZATION

Buyers of goods and services are most likely to come in contact with someone representing the marketing function, and that interaction forms their impression of the entire organization. You may base your opinion of a retail store on the behaviour of a single sales clerk. As Procter & Gamble put it in an annual report: "When a Procter & Gamble sales person walks into a customer's place of business . . . that sales person not only represents Procter & Gamble, but in a very real sense, that person is Procter & Gamble."

Setting Ethical Guidelines

Many organizations have formal codes of ethics for their employees that identify specific acts (bribery, accepting gifts) as unethical. These guidelines lessen the chance that employees will knowingly or unknowingly get into trouble. Ethics codes strengthen a company's hand in dealing with customers or prospects that invite unethical behaviour. For young or inexperienced executives, they can also be valuable guides, helping them to resist pressure to compromise personal ethics in order to move up in the firm.

However, determining what is right and what is wrong can be extremely difficult. It is not realistic for an organization to construct a two-column list of all possible practices, one headed ''ethical'' and the other ''unethical.'' Rather, an executive must personally evaluate the ethical status of many actions. One simple but effective approach is to answer the following questions:

- Would I do this to a friend?
- Would I be willing to have this done to me?
- Would I be embarrassed if this action were publicized nationally?
- Is the action sound from a long-run point of view?

The last question deserves some elaboration. Marketing managers must understand that ethical behaviour is not only morally right but also, over the long run, practically sound. For example, deceiving or pressuring buyers to consummate a sale can alienate customers and eliminate repeat business.

Ethics and the Consumer

Acting ethically is not a one-way street. Consumers also have a responsibility to behave ethically in exchange situations. Business firms are increasingly experiencing unethical behaviour on the part of consumers. Shoplifting, fraudulent coupon redemption, vandalism, fraudulent cheque cashing, and other consumer abuses have become major expense items for organizations. Although determining exactly how much consumer fraud occurs is virtually impossible, reliable estimates place the annual cost to business in the billions of dollars.

Of course, the high incidence of unethical consumer behaviour does not excuse inappropriate business practices. These examples simply illustrate how

A ''fish-eye'' camera may deter shoplifting, but the problem requires a more basic solution.

widespread unethical behaviour has become. What the facts make abundantly clear is the need for a system-wide exploration of ways to reduce this problem in business, among consumers, and within all other social institutions.

The Broadened Marketing Concept

At this point you may wonder about the relationship between the broadened marketing concept and the problems we have been describing. Recall the components of the broadened marketing concept:

- An emphasis on customer orientation.
- Coordination of marketing activities.
- Achieving the organization's performance objectives.
- Satisfying societal wants affected by the organization's activities.

If firms follow this approach, there shouldn't be any criticisms. Yet there are many. How can this be explained?

The major factors affecting the implementation of the broadened marketing concept revolve around the *interpretation of consumer orientation* and the *conflict in goals experienced by consumers*.

Who is the consumer, and what does it mean to be consumer-oriented? Answers to these questions have been too narrow and too short-run. It seems to be human nature to be shortsighted. We often fail to see or choose to ignore the long-run impact of our actions. For example, firms pollute the environment by making nonbiodegradable products, the effects of which won't be felt for two or three generations. However, to fully adopt the marketing concept, it is necessary to look beyond the short-run gratification of consumers or the organization. Adopting the broadened marketing concept requires that one strategic goal be defined as a consumer orientation *in the long run*. That is, we must extend the time dimension used to describe customer orientation.

We also need to expand the *breadth* of the notion of consumers. To view only the direct buyers of a company's product as consumers is too narrow. We must expand our definition of target markets to include other groups affected by the buyer-seller exchange. Someone may buy a car and be satisfied with it. But the negative effects of pollution from the auto endanger others. In the broader context, the automobile maker has not generated customer satisfaction and thus has not successfully implemented the broadened marketing concept. We must define consumers to include not only the purchasers of a product, but also the other parts of society affected by the firm's activities. Until marketing decisions incorporate the long run and an expanded definition of consumers, criticism will continue.

The other problem area is the goal conflict experienced by many consumers. It is difficult to shift from personal to socially oriented goals. As consumers, we have not abandoned our desires for possessions, but we have complicated our wants with social concerns. A simplified example illustrates the difference between our goals of the past and those of today. In the past we wanted big cars that would go fast. We paid little attention to air pollution, traffic congestion, oil reserves depletion, and water pollution. Now we still want the cars, but we also want clean air, an end to traffic jams, clean water, and independence from foreign oil resources. The former goal — a desire for autos only — was much easier to achieve because a conflict in goals was largely absent.

A related problem is the great number of publics a company must deal with and the difficulty of satisfying them all. Often the goals of the different publics are in conflict. One group may want a paper mill closed because it pollutes

MARKETING AT WORK

FILE 22-2   **USING THE MARKETING WAY TO BACK THE UNITED WAY**

There are 122 United Way agencies across Canada, and most of them make an annual appeal for funding. While it is true that the various agencies share advertising and promotional materials, particularly expensive television commercials, much of what is created for campaigns is donated locally.

The Halifax-area Metro United Way had created for it the equivalent of a $500,000 advertising campaign. All the design, materials, air time, and print space were provided by Metro Halifax people and organizations. What is significant in these situations is the commitment that creative people give to the campaign development. Chuck Mora of Corporate Communications, the person who created the campaign, believes that ''creative people will always jump at the chance to do public service work since its a unique chance to talk about something intrinsically emotional. . . . It's hard to get emotional about toilet paper or a bag of potato chips.''

The campaign was significant for it was one of the first to move from the traditional ''soft sell'' advertising approach to what can be called a ''gut-wrenching'' series of stark advertisements for TV, newspapers, and posters. Carol Anne Esnard, vice-president of marketing for United Way Canada in Ottawa, believes that soft sell works well in Western Canada and most small communities but in Toronto and Montreal, and now in Halifax, people need to be jolted from their own preoccupations.

The ads covered four main themes: drug and alcohol addiction, problems of the elderly, family abuse, and housing. They are portraits of despair with those designed for the mass media placement outlining the social problems but not providing the happy endings that donations could provide. Only a poster designed for offices, where research shows that 75 percent of donations are raised through workplace contributions, portrays how money can help. Although the ads are not joyful to see, they reflect reality and have been well received in focus groups.

Source: Adapted from Deborah Jones, ''Halifax United Way Pitch Not Fun to Watch,'' *Globe and Mail*, September 12, 1991, p. B4.

---

the air and the water. But another public wants it kept open because it provides jobs.

PROSPECTS FOR THE FUTURE

Predicting the future is always difficult. Consider, for example, the marketing successes, failures, and fads shown in Table 22-1. The firms that produced these products all had high hopes. But some products succeeded while many products that appeared to have considerable potential in the beginning fizzled in the marketplace.

The challenge of making accurate predictions in marketing is compounded by the fact that change is so rapid. However, none of the prospects described here should surprise you. What we have done is simply evaluate the strength of current trends and extend the strongest into the future. Most marketing successes are accomplished in the same fashion. Managers monitor what is happening in the marketplace, identify opportunities, and respond with want-satisfying products.

Esso demonstrates its environmental awareness by launching a reduced-emission gasoline.

TABLE 22-1 **Market successes, failures, and fads of the 1980s**

Successes	Failures	Fads
VCR's	Videotext	Trivial Pursuit (game)
Minivans	Disposable contact lenses	Cross-training shoes
NutraSweet	New Coke	Oat bran
CD players	Merkur automobile	Mountain bikes
Frozen yogurt	Home banking	Wine coolers
Fax machines	Disk cameras	Granola
Sunscreen lotion	TV home shopping	Bottled water
Light beer		
Laptop computers		
Cellular telephones		
Microwaveable food		
Automated banking machines		

Changes in Consumer Demographics

Changes in demographics — the population's age distribution, income, education, ethnic composition, and household structure — all affect marketers' activities. For example, the population is getting older and senior citizens are the fastest-growing age group.[4] This shift creates expanded marketing opportunities in such areas as travel and tourism and health and medical care. Another demographic change is the greater ethnic diversity resulting primarily from increases in the level of immigration from Asia and other areas. These groups are large enough to attract the attention of marketers, but they present interesting challenges.[5]

Another important development is the decrease in household size. More people than ever live alone. Therefore, marketers of many consumer products must consider the impact of smaller households on meal preparation, the size of appliances, and package sizes, to cite several examples. Small households also mean fewer people to perform normal maintenance functions. Therefore, time has for many become the currency of the 1990s.

What do these demographic changes tell us? They indicate that some markets will disappear and new ones will emerge. Marketers must remain abreast of these developments and adjust strategies accordingly. For example, the aging population has created opportunities for products modified to accommodate the physical limitations of the elderly (labels and instructions in large print, easy-to-open containers), and time pressure has spawned firms that will do routine errands (getting the car serviced, picking up the dry cleaning, grocery shopping).[6]

Changes in Consumer Values

Values change slowly, but when they do, the impact on existing institutions and the opportunities for innovative marketers can be great. A good indicator of value shifts is the amount of coverage given to a particular development by the media. Three examples are discussed below.

ENVIRONMENT

Some forecasters see a shift away from a self-orientation to an "other-orientation." Indicators are that people are disturbed by the excess of the past decade or so, a period when self-gratification governed many choices. For example, volunteerism is on the upswing. What does this mean for marketing? Public opinion surveys have consistently shown an increase in the percentage of Canadians who are concerned about environmental matters. These concerned consumers have been putting pressure on business to act more responsibly; in some cases this pressure has affected business in an indirect way. For example, concern about the amount of paper being wasted has led many consumers to protest the volume of direct mail flyers, coupons, and advertising materials that are distributed through our mailboxes. Some Canadian cities, led by Montreal, have passed local by-laws restricting the amount of such material that can be distributed and allowing homeowners to indicate that they do not wish to receive it.

---

[4]"Those Aging Boomers," *Business Week*, May 20, 1991, pp. 106–112.

[5]Gillian Pritchard, "Polyglot Profits," *Canadian Business*, February 1988, pp. 47–50, 84, 88, 92.

[6]A number of specific implications are described in Anne B. Fisher, "What Consumers Want in the 1990s," *Fortune*, Jan. 29, 1990, pp. 108–12.

There is also evidence of heightened interest in the future quality of life. International concern over the dissipation of the atmosphere's ozone layer, acid rain, and the "greenhouse effect" shows a shift in sentiment. Of more direct interest to marketers are concerns about waste disposal and landfills, air and water pollution, and biodegradability.

Environmentally sensitive product packaging, alternatives to fossil fuel, and energy conservation are excellent marketing opportunities. Other prospects are not so obvious. One industry spawned by environmental interests and a desire to visit unspoiled, exotic locations is leisure travel to unusual destinations. But even this may have its downside. For example, there has been such an increase in the number of whale-watching tours in various parts of the world that some environmentalists are becoming concerned that the number of tourists may represent a threat to the animals they wish to protect.

The issues in the environmental debate are not at all clear. The complexity of the ecosystem means that it is possible for interest groups to argue that recyclable paper and cardboard containers are environmentally safer than polystyrene, while some scientists can make an equally rational case that the total use of energy is greater in the manufacture of the paper products. The net effect is that the consumer is probably confused. Inherently, however, the consumer is more likely to come down on the side of apparently "natural" products; therefore, cloth diapers are perceived to be less harmful to the environment than are disposables; cardboard fast-food containers are perceived to be less harmful than their "plastic" counterparts. Consequently, some companies have been accused of jumping on the bandwagon with respect to the environmental issue by labelling "green" some products that do not really offer an environmental advantage.[7]

Government responds to consumer concerns about environmental matters through the voluntary Environmental Choice program.

[7]For an interesting discussion of the confusion caused by the environmental debate, see Arthur Johnson, "Ecohype—Consumer Beware: 'Green' Products May Not Be What They Seem," *The Financial Post Magazine*, May 1991, pp. 17–23; and Jaclyn Fierman, "The Big Muddle in Green Marketing," *Fortune*, June 3, 1991, pp. 91–101.

MARKETING AT WORK

FILE 22-3   **WHAT LOOKS GREEN AND SMELLS GREEN MAY NOT BE GREEN AT ALL**

Among those products that are labelled "recyclable," "made from re-cycled paper" (or plastic), "ozone friendly," "environment friendly," and "biodegradable," there are some that are and some that are not. While many marketers are sincere in trying to help with the problems, frequently their intentions outrun their performance and it is difficult for many consumers to determine that this is the case.

The manufacturers of disposable diapers are blamed for destroying forests and helping to create Canada's garbage mountains. With the increase in public awareness of the problems, the sales of disposables are slipping and those of cloth re-usables are climbing. Pampers are now made 50 percent thinner than in the past and although this does not eliminate the problem, it does slow it down. P&G tells consumers that demonstration projects have shown that disposable diapers are compostable in closed-vessel composting units. But such units are very scarce in Canada and so a note on the package wrapper that says, "This package is recyclable where plastic bag recycling facilities are available" is accurate but with more of a sales effect than a recycling one.

A similar situation exists for E-Z Foil disposable aluminum roasting trays—used largely at Christmas, Easter, and Thanksgiving. The package states that it is made of recyclable aluminum—and aluminum is eminently recyclable. But most Canadian communities do not have aluminum recycling programs.

There are 900 million Tetra Paks sold annually in Canada. These little airtight boxes, made of layers of plastic, paper, and aluminum, are very popular with retailers and consumers. Tetra Pak advertises that they are 100% recyclable. But again, only a handful of Canadian communities have programs for gathering Tetra Paks through curbside collection programs. Generally, millions of the boxes end up in dumps because they are disposed of in places that aren't part of recycling programs. It becomes a question of what recyclable means.

In each of these cases, and many more, the product is actually recyclable—but it is not recycled to any great extent. Is it recyclable or contingently recyclable?

Source: Adapted from Arthur Johnson, "Eco-Hype," *The Financial Post Magazine*, May, 1991, pp. 17–21.

The federal government has tried to make some sense of the environmental debate by establishing the Environmental Choice program.[8] This is a program that sets certain standards for the testing of products and their impact on the environment. The logo of the program now appears on more than 500 products from 80 companies, including cloth diapers, re-refined motor oil, and environmentally safe paint. Canada's program is an example of similar initiatives that have been launched by many countries around the world. One challenge that comes out of such an initiative, which is all the more important as world trade increases, is the consistency of standards among countries. In other words, will a product that is considered environmentally friendly in Canada

---

[8]John Godfrey, "EcoLogo Program Puts Canada in Lead," *The Financial Post*, August 2, 1991, p. 9.

Eveready features the "ecologo" in the advertising for its low-mercury batteries.

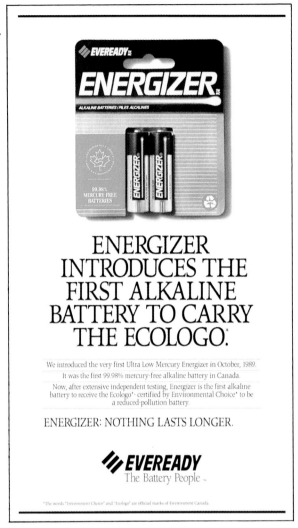

meet the environmental standards of the European Community or Japan? Some business people and economists are concerned that environmental restrictions may become trade barriers of the 1990s.

HOME

There are several indications that consumers will focus more on the home in the years ahead. Stressful jobs and time constraints have led people to seek a place where they can relax in comfort and security.[9] A home fulfils the desire for something stable in a dynamic world. As a result, consumers are spending more on their homes and on products that make their homes enjoyable. For instance, computerized television that will identify and record programs in preselected categories will probably be available in the 1990s. Home remodelling, lower-cost construction methods such as modular homes and prefab

---

[9]Michael Posner, "The Death of Leisure," *Globe and Mail*, May 25, 1991, p. D1.

housing components, and fibre-optic systems to monitor lighting, security, and fire protection are predicted growth markets, as are traditional forms of leisure time activities.[10]

SERVICE

The success of businesses such as Four Seasons Hotels and Bell Canada makes it clear that consumers reward good service. It is also apparent that many firms recognize this opportunity. The effective "lonely Maytag repairman" ad campaign that has run for many years and airline ads emphasizing on-time arrival records are just two examples. Recognizing the need to offer good service is often easier than finding and training employees to provide it. A major challenge for organizations in the 1990s will be to design and implement systems that provide consumers with high-calibre service.[11]

The Development of Fragmented Markets

One outcome of consumer demographic and value changes is fragmented markets. There was a time when a packaged-goods manufacturer could develop a good product, advertise it nationally using the primary media, stock retailers' shelves, and be successful. But the situation has changed. Only 10 percent of women can be considered traditional housewives who stay home and raise children. Highly active consumers are less accessible through the media, and their tastes have gone in many directions. Pressed for time, many consumers are making decisions at the point of purchase. To keep up, marketers are engaging in a variety of tactics from brand extensions to new ways of conveying advertising messages.

Market fragmentation is not something new. Marketers have known about segments within markets for many years. As we discussed in Chapter 4, techniques have been developed using demographic, behavioural, and geographic data to identify market segments to enable marketers to better target their efforts.

What has changed as our society has become more complex and diversified is the number and size of market segments. Marketers can no longer expect large numbers of consumers to compromise their needs and wants and buy standardized products. Rather, they must tailor goods and services to meet the needs of these small segments. **Niche marketing** significantly complicates the marketer's job. One version of a product is replaced by several. Different ads must be produced and new media found to reach different consumers (see box). Retailers must choose among many product variations, not all of which can be stocked. The added variety complicates inventory management, distribution, and personal selling.

Evidence of this fragmentation is everywhere. McDonald's, the king of hamburgers, not only has expanded its variety of burgers, but has also test marketed fish-and-chips, lobster sandwiches, Mexican food, fried chicken, and pizza. From 1947 to 1984 Procter & Gamble had only one Tide. Today there are five versions including Tide Ultra, Phosphate Free Tide, Liquid Tide, and

---

[10]Geoffrey Scotton, "Gardening a Growth Industry," *The Financial Post*, May 20, 1991, p. 16.

[11]For an insight into the efforts of progressive companies to improve the level of service provided to their customers, see: Jim Clemmer, *Firing on All Cylinders: The Service/Quality System for High-Powered Corporate Performance*, Toronto: Macmillan of Canada, 1990; and William A. Band, *Creating Value for Customers: Designing and Implementing a Total Corporate Strategy*, Toronto: John Wiley & Sons, Inc., 1991.

Tide with Bleach. The prices of BMW autmobile models range from $25,000 to $70,000.

There are no indications that the trend to niche marketing will end. In fact, with more sophisticated electronic data collection methods being developed and the diversity of the population increasing, all indications point to even greater fragmentation in the future.

The Expansion of Information and Education

Consumers' choices and marketers' decisions are greatly influenced by the amounts and types of information they have. The quantity of information available to all segments of society continues to grow at what seems to be geometric rates. Consumers have access to dozens of television channels via cable and satellite dishes, news is available 24 hours a day, an unprecedented number of magazines and newspapers are published today, and advertising is presented in forms and places never imagined.

Businesses have amassed more detailed demographic and behavioural data about consumers, competitors, and prospects than previously imaginable (or usable!). Product sales are tracked hourly through electronic scanners. Complex systems have been designed to monitor the competition. The potential of prospects is gauged by their past purchasing tendencies, demographic characteristics, and expressed attitudes.

Of course, technology has made most of these advances possible. For example, using computer files, politicians are better able to match voters with issues on which they are sensitive in order to target more accurately their marketing efforts. Packaged-goods firms can adjust the value of coupons individual consumers receive based on data predicting their likelihood of redeeming them. Regular users receive lower-value coupons; infrequent users and nonusers are sent coupons in larger denominations.

Global Marketing

The cliché that we live in a "small world" is a reality for marketers. Virtually instantaneous communications have greatly increased global awareness. Economic, social, and political developments on one side of the world have an impact everywhere else. On the evening television news we are as likely to hear about developments on the Japanese stock market as we are about activity on Bay Street.

As a result, foreign firms are now major investors in Canada and Canadian firms in search of new mass markets have a renewed interest in opportunities overseas. Growing buying power in Asia, the elimination of trade restrictions in the European Community in 1992, and political changes in Eastern Europe and the Soviet Union have created interest among many Canadian businesses who are establishing their positions or launching initiatives to enter these markets. Canadian companies such as Northern Telecom and Bombardier now manufacture and export telecommunications and transportation equipment to many countries. McDonald's of Canada was responsible for that company's entry into Moscow, and the property company Olympia and York has developed a vast new office complex on the Thames in London. With the enormous potential established by the performance of the pioneering firms, many organizations are eagerly investigating global marketing. However, significant problems exist and the risks may well exceed the benefits in some cases.

Probably the biggest mistake global marketers make is a failure to recognize the diversity that exists in a target area. Some marketers, for example, envision the 320 million consumers in the European Community as a single market.

They ignore the language, cultural, political, and historical differences that transcend any economic agreement. Even in a country as small as Finland, the population is a mixture of natives and immigrants from Russia, Germany, Sweden, and other Western European countries. There are two official languages and many dialects, as well as distinctive regional food preferences. These and other differences, within just one small country, suggest that global marketing faces many of the same challenges as domestic marketing.

A study of global marketing successes and failures identified five key reasons for poor performance.[12]

- Insufficient formal marketing research.
- Failure to adapt marketing to specific market differences.
- Lack of sustained marketing effort.
- Failure to decentralize decision making.
- Lack of local commitment and confidence.

Despite problems, the trend towards global marketing will accelerate. The lure of millions of consumers, combined with improved understanding of the markets and marketing practices necessary to be successful, will increase the attractiveness of such opportunities.

You have now completed your introduction to marketing (with the possible exception of a final exam!). If we have been successful, you will come away from this course with a sense of the excitement and challenges in the field. It would be great if you have been inspired to consider a career in marketing — the field can always use capable, enthusiastic people. However, whether your studies lead you to specialized marketing topics or into other areas, you now know what marketing entails and its importance to every individual and organization involved in exchanges. We hope you put the knowledge to good use!

SUMMARY   A firm's marketing performance should be appraised from a broad, societal perspective. When evaluating the marketing efforts of an organization, we must consider how well the firm satisfies the wants of target customers, meets the needs of the organization, and recognizes the best interests of society.

Marketing has been attacked for being exploitative, inefficient, and illegal and for stimulating unwholesome demand. Several of the criticisms are rooted in the complex question "Does marketing cost too much?" Though truly objective measures are not available, for organizations adopting the marketing concept, costs are not unreasonable. Many of the objections to marketing are valid. However, the offensive behaviour is confined to a small minority of marketers, and some of the issues are more complicated than they appear.

Responses to criticisms have come from consumers, government, and business. Consumerism — protests against institutional injustices and efforts to remedy them — has had a significant impact on business behaviour.

Consumer responses to marketing problems have included protests, political activism, and support of special-interest groups. Conditions providing an impetus for widespread consumerism, sensitivity to social and environmental concerns, and the willingness to become actively involved are present today.

---

[12]These factors are adapted from Kamran Kashani, "Beware the Pitfalls of Global Marketing," *Harvard Business Review*, September-October 1989, pp. 91–98.

Government at all levels passes and enforces consumer protection legislation. Businesses have responded to criticism by improving communications, providing more and better information, upgrading products, producing more sensitive advertising, and enhancing customer service.

Ethical behaviour by business is the best answer to the charges against marketing. Besides being morally correct, ethical behaviour by organizations can restore public confidence, avoid government regulation, retain the power granted by society, and protect the image of the organization. A method of judging the ethics of a particular act is to ask four questions: Would I do this to a friend? Would I be willing to have this done to me? Would I be embarrassed if this action were publicized nationally? Is the action sound from a long-run point of view?

Consumers also have a responsibility to act ethically. The volume of credit-card misuse, cheque fraud, coupon misredemption, and shoplifting suggests that a system-wide exploration of ways to reduce unethical behaviour is needed.

The numerous criticisms directed at marketing suggest the broadened marketing concept has not been widely adopted. If the concept is to be generally implemented, it is essential that marketers change their notion of consumer orientation. The marketing concept has been defined too narrowly and has been too short-run oriented. In addition, consumers must resolve their conflicts between personal and societal goals.

Prospects for marketing are difficult to predict, but the strongest current trends are projected into the future. Developments likely to have major marketing implications are consumer demographic and value changes, fragmentation of markets, information expansion, and global marketing.

KEY TERMS AND CONCEPTS

Basis for evaluating performance 696
Nature of marketing criticisms 696
The cost of marketing 701
Consumerism 702
Scope of consumerism 703
Responses to consumer problems 704

Reasons for ethical behaviour 707
Evaluating ethical merit 708
Consumer ethics 709
Broadened marketing concept 710
Fragmented markets 717
Niche marketing 717

QUESTIONS AND PROBLEMS

1. Can all the criticisms of marketing be dismissed on the basis of critics' being poorly informed or acting in their own interest?

2. What indicates that middlemen make reasonable profits?

3. Some people believe there are too many fast-food outlets in their communities. Suggest a method for reducing the number of these outlets.

4. React to the following criticisms of advertising:
   a. It costs too much.
   b. It is in bad taste.
   c. It is false and deceptive.
   d. It creates monopolies.

5. What proposals do you have for regulating advertising to reduce the occurrence of false or misleading claims?

6. What specific recommendations do you have for reducing the cost of advertising?

7. What information do you think should be included in ads for each of the following goods or services?
   a. Snack foods.
   b. Jogging shoes.
   c. Nursing homes.
   d. Credit cards.

8. What are the social and economic justifications for ''paternalistic'' laws such as seat-belt regulations and warnings on cigarette packages and alcoholic beverage containers?

9. How would you respond to the argument that companies can absorb the cost of coupon misredemption?

10. Describe a firm whose behaviour you feel reflects the adoption of the broadened marketing concept.

11. Within the overall college student segment, describe a smaller or fragmented market that you believe exists.

12. What does global marketing have in common with domestic marketing?

C A S E S   F O R   P A R T   7

CASE 7.1 **W. K. Buckley Limited (B)**

It was the early summer of 1990, and a decision had to be made soon concerning the advertising approach to be used to promote Buckley's Mixture to the Canadian public during the 1990-91 "cough and cold" season. Frank Buckley and John Meehan realized that the advertising strategy adopted in 1985 had been very successful, contributing to dramatic increases in the sales of Buckley's Mixture. But the advertising that featured Frank Buckley and drew attention to the "awful" taste of the product had now been used for five seasons. While sales continued to increase, the management team at W. K. Buckley Limited wondered how much longer this advertising campaign would continue to work. Was 1990 the year when a new approach should be considered?

BUCKLEY'S MIXTURE ADVERTISING

"It tastes awful. And it works." In 1984, Frank Buckley and his management team at W. K. Buckley Limited accepted the recommendation of its advertising agency and decided to use this simple yet honest advertising statement for their most important product, Buckley's Mixture. Since then, it has become a widely recognized and successful marketing slogan and has helped Buckley's Mixture increase its market share in the cough and cold remedy category. In the year ending February 1990, a time when the market for cold remedies had slipped by 2 percent, Buckley's Mixture had enjoyed a 16 percent increase in market share.

W. K. Buckley Limited is a privately owned Canadian company, founded in 1920 by William Buckley. The founder's son, Frank Buckley, joined the company in 1946 and is current owner and president. Primarily known for its flagship product, Buckley's Mixture, W. K. Buckley Limited also manufactures and distributes a variety of other cough and cold products, as well as a veterinary line. The Buckley product line includes Jack & Jill cough syrup, Buckley's White Rub, and Lemon Time. W. K. Buckley Limited operates in Canada, the United States, and the Caribbean and has products marketed under licensing agreements in Holland, Australia, and New Zealand.

First introduced by William Buckley from his Toronto corner drugstore in 1919, Buckley's Mixture became a household name in the 1930s and 1940s, especially in rural areas of western Canada. Its sales were enhanced in the early years by the innovative use of advertising. Extensive promotion in the form of radio advertisements have been key to the success of Buckley's Mixture. Having realized the power of advertising in the consumer marketplace, major international pharmaceutical companies began using aggressive marketing and advertising strategies in the 1970s. This fierce competition contributed to a decline in the market share enjoyed by Buckley's flagship product.

THE 1984-85 ADVERTISING DECISION

The peak season for the liquid cough remedy market is September to April. Before the beginning of the 1984-85 season, W. K. Buckley Limited appointed a new advertising agency, Ambrose, Carr, DeForest & Linton Limited (later to become Ambrose Carr Linton Kelly, Inc.) to coordinate the advertising programs for its products. Following its initial review of the W. K. Buckley account, the agency recommended marketing research to facilitate the definition of target market segments. For the 1984-85 season, on the advice of the new advertising agency, the company did not launch an advertising cam-

© 1991. This case was written by Leanne O'Leary and James G. Barnes of Memorial University of Newfoundland. The case was prepared with the cooperation and permission of W. K. Buckley Limited to illustrate the marketing initiatives of that company and not to indicate a correct or incorrect approach to the solution of marketing problems. The authors acknowledge the cooperation and support of Frank C. Buckley, President, John J. Meehan, Vice-President, and David Rieger, Manager of Sales and Marketing, of W. K. Buckley Limited, and Jackie Robertson of Ambrose Carr Linton Kelly, Inc., in the preparation of this case.

paign, but undertook extensive research into the Canadian cough and cold remedy market.

From this research, five key problems became apparent. For Buckley's Mixture there was:

1. low top-of-mind awareness,
2. low rate of trial,
3. low awareness of its strength and effectiveness,
4. perception of it being old-fashioned,
5. negative perception of its taste, aroma, and texture.

Faced with a decreasing market share for Buckley's Mixture, the advertising agency decided that a different approach was required for the 1985-86 season. On the recommendation of Ambrose Carr, Frank Buckley took an unusual approach in promoting Buckley's Mixture. The agency recommended the use of radio and *Reader's Digest* as the chosen media for the season. The "It tastes awful. And it works" campaign actually drew attention to what some would consider a negative feature of Buckley's Mixture, its taste. The agency described this approach as an attempt to get away from the sameness of many ads that accentuate the positives and praise a product's good points. The objective was to draw attention to the advertisements and create a greater awareness of the product. Frank Buckley, the company's president, was to be featured in the advertisements to develop the concept of established effectiveness and trustworthiness. The agency proposed that Frank Buckley would represent an honest businessman who believed in his product and its attributes and was therefore willing to promote it straight, without gimmicks to hide its awful taste.

Traditionally, the market for Buckley's Mixture was in rural areas and in the lower income segment (less than $30,000 annual household income). While the maintenance and development of this current market segment was important, its definition left a large non-user market that could now be targeted. Based on market research conducted by the agency for W. K. Buckley Limited, the primary target group was redefined to be men aged 18 to 34 and, secondarily, women in the same age category, living in markets of more than 100,000 in Ontario only. The secondary target group remained adults aged 49 and older, living in markets with populations under 30,000. Although W. K. Buckley Limited was operating on a very limited advertising budget, both groups were targeted during the first year of the campaign. (See W. K. Buckley Limited [A] for a review of the 1984-85 marketing research and the recommended advertising strategy.)

ADVERTISING CAMPAIGNS: 1985-86 TO 1989-90

For the 1985-86 advertising season, two radio commercials were produced, featuring lyrics promoting Buckley's Mixture with accompanying music and sung to the tune of a popular song. These were tested with 15 people from the target group (ages 18-34). Most liked the style of music (soft rock), found the lyrics interesting, and felt it was successful in encouraging listeners to try the product. The favourable reaction to these commercials was based on the appeal of using a song for advertising, rather than an announcer's voice. Respondents claimed that the terms "rot your socks," "strong taste," and "make you swoon" were creative in describing the taste of Buckley's Mixture and in catching the listener's attention. These commercials were subsequently launched in the Golden Horseshoe region of Toronto and southern Ontario.

Accompanying the product advertising campaign in the 1985-86 season was promotional support for new packaging for Buckley's Mixture. This represented the first package modification for the product in eight years. The new Buckley's Mixture package, although still available in 100 mL and 200 mL sizes, highlighted its sugar-free attribute. Advertisements ran in both English and French in *Reader's Digest* (see Exhibit 1).

During the 1986-87 season, transit advertisements were used extensively on a national basis. The transit campaign employed the same creative direction as the 1985-86 print campaign, with the reassurance that Buckley's Mixture is the same dependable product that Canadians had known since the 1920s. These advertisements featured Frank Buckley and used quotes such as, "I have recurring nightmares in which someone gives me a taste of my own medicine" and "I'm dedicated to ensuring that every new batch of Buckley's tastes as bad as the last" (see Exhibit 2). The main objectives for that season were to create consumer awareness of the Buckley's Mixture name, to increase awareness of the

EXHIBIT 1 **Buckley's Mixture Print Advertisement 1985-86**

WE'VE HAD A FACELIFT. BUT OUR PERSONALITY IS JUST AS NASTY AS EVER.

Most people who choose Buckley's Mixture will agree on two things. It tastes strong. It works hard. So the Buckley's Mixture you buy today is the same Buckley's Mixture that has been helping relieve coughs due to colds for 65 years.

The only thing we've changed is our package, so it will be easier to spot on the shelf. And that's good. Because the sooner you spot it, the sooner you can start to get rid of that nasty cough that comes with a cold.

W.K. Buckley Limited. A Canadian company.

EXHIBIT 3 **Buckley's Mixture Print Advertisement 1986-87**

"I came by my bad taste honestly. I inherited it from my father."

Fortunately, Buckley's Mixture works on coughs just the way it worked when my dad created it back in 1919.

Unfortunately, it also tastes just the way it tasted back in 1919. But dad always said, "I'll tell you two things about Buckley's. It tastes awful. And it works."

EXHIBIT 2 **Buckley's Mixture Transit Advertisement 1986-87**

"I'm dedicated to ensuring every new batch of Buckley's tastes as bad as the last."

I could add artificial flavouring and sugar to Buckley's Mixture. It might even make it taste better. But like they say, "If it ain't broke, don't fix it." And like dad always said, "I'll tell you two things about Buckley's. It tastes awful. And it works."

new package, and to retain trust in the brand as an effective, reliable product. National magazines *TV Guide* and *TV Hebdo* were used for the print component of the campaign (see Exhibit 3).

A television campaign was also initiated in Atlantic Canada in 1986-87, featuring a single commercial with a sea captain. It was felt that the association between the cold sea and coughs and colds would be appropriate to appeal to consumers in the Atlantic provinces.

This increased awareness also provided a foundation for the introduction of the "Buckley's DM" (Dextromethorphan) product. This addition to the Buckley's line was projected for a 1987-88 launch, but was postponed for a year because of product stability problems.

Transit advertising was continued for the 1987-88 season, as it provided good reach and high frequency with the target group and presented a strong, visual advertising message. Preparing for the upcoming announcement of the DM product, Buckley's redefined the target market to include higher income groups, as they were felt to represent the greatest sales opportunity for DM products. The 1987-88 transit ads were similar to those used during the previous year, with a picture of Frank Buckley and quotes such as "Four of the most dreaded words in the

English language: Get out the Buckley's" and "Since 1919 we've been leaving Canadians with a bad taste in their mouths" (see Exhibit 4). The print advertising was continued in *TV Guide* and *TV Hebdo*, and the television campaign was used again in the Atlantic provinces.

In the 1988-89 season, Buckley's DM was introduced. This product was identical to the original Buckley's Mixture except it had added Dextromethorphan Hydrobromide (DM), an antitussive used for fast-acting suppression of a nonproductive cough. DM products, although new to the Buckley product line, had been on the market for several years and were well known to consumers. Transit ads were used, which now promoted the DM product (see Exhibit 5).

W. K. Buckley's advertising agency, Ambrose Carr Linton Kelly, believed that interior transit was an efficient, strategically correct medium for reaching the target group. During this season, radio was used for the first time in three years and television was introduced as a new medium for Buckley's advertising. Commercials on radio featured Frank Buckley describing the taste of Buckley's Mixture and referring to its effectiveness (see Exhibit 6). These were run in major urban markets across the country. The campaign also involved regional efforts that were custom-

EXHIBIT 4   **Buckley's Mixture Transit Advertisement 1987-88**

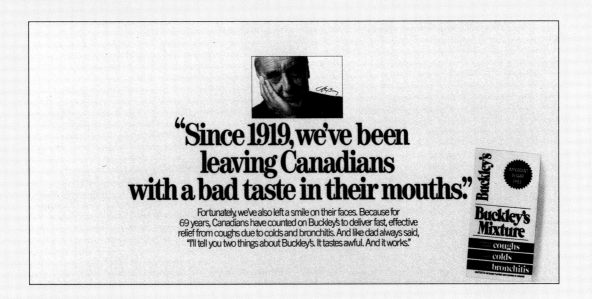

EXHIBIT 5 **Buckley's DM Transit Advertisement**
1988-89

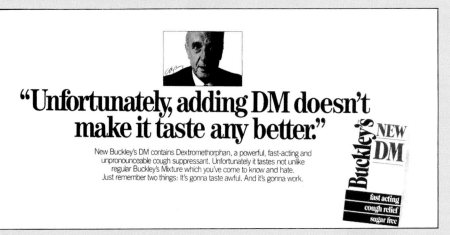

EXHIBIT 6 **Buckley's Mixture Radio Commercial**
Scripts
1988-89 and 1989-90

Dedicated

Hi, I'm Frank Buckley, and I'm dedicated to ensuring that every batch of Buckley's Mixture tastes as bad as the last. You see, back in 1919 when my dad developed Buckley's Mixture, he used only ingredients that would make Buckley's Mixture provide fast, effective relief from coughs due to colds. He didn't particularly care how the stuff tasted. So just remember two things about Buckley's Mixture. It's going to taste awful and it's going to work.

Nightmares

Hi, I'm Frank Buckley, and I have recurring nightmares in which someone gives me a taste of my own medicine. That medicine is Buckley's Mixture. Now, I'd be the first one to admit Buckley's Mixture has a taste that will rot your socks. But when you've got a nasty cough due to a cold, close your eyes, brace yourself, and remember just two things. It's going to taste awful and it's going to work.

Honestly

My name is Frank Buckley and I came by my bad taste honestly. I inherited it from my father. Back in 1919 he developed Buckley's Mixture. Buckley's Mixture became known for two things, how well it worked and how badly it tasted. But 69 years later, when folks have a cough due to a cold or bronchitis, they pucker up and remember what Dad always said about Buckley's Mixture. It's going to taste awful and it's going to work.

1919

Hi, I'm Frank Buckley for Buckley's Mixture. My father came up with Buckley's Mixture back in 1919. About the same time my folks came up with me. Back then, people expected medicine to taste like . . . well, medicine. So, to be real honest, it tastes real bad. But if you do have a nasty hacking cough, but don't have time to pamper it, try Buckley's Mixture. Just remember two things. It tastes awful and it works.

Surprise

Hi, I'm Frank Buckley for Buckley's Mixture. If you've never tried Buckley's Mixture before, you're going to be very surprised, twice. You'll be surprised at how quickly and effectively Buckley's relieves the nastiest coughs due to colds, bronchitis, and even smoker's cough. But, just before you're surprised by how effective Buckley's Mixture is, you'll be very surprised by how it tastes. Buckley's Mixture, it tastes awful and it works.

ized for regional market segments. For example, the television campaign in Atlantic Canada was continued in 1988-89.

For the 1989-90 season, W. K. Buckley Limited expanded the advertising campaign by using television in the Toronto region for the first time. Commercials were aired nine times a week for four weeks on a Buffalo, N.Y., station that beamed its signal into the Toronto area. These commercials featured Frank Buckley, seated in a chair, holding a package of Buckley's Mixture. He explained in a lighthearted way how awful Buckley's tastes but how effectively it works. These TV commercials were also aired in the Atlantic provinces and featured a similar dialogue to the radio commercials, which were run in major markets across the country. The budget allocated to transit advertising was increased and aimed at a better-educated group. ''It contains oil of pine needles. What did you expect it to taste like?'' was one of the advertising slogans created for the campaign that demonstrates the continued focus on the actual attributes of Buckley's Mixture (see Exhibit 7).

Exhibit 8 contains a detailed overview of the advertising budget allocations at W. K. Buckley Limited for the years from 1983 to 1990. The chart details the season, media used, market and target group, and the allocated budget.

MARKETING RESEARCH

Marketing research remained an essential component of the marketing program at W. K. Buckley Limited. In 1988, with the objective of acquiring further information about the consumer of Buckley's Mixture, the company distributed 10,680 survey cards to purchasers in packages of Buckley's Mixture. Although the cards were distributed only in Ontario, among the 357 replies were some cards returned by purchasers from other provinces and two from the United States.

Some of the more significant information from this research came in the form of demographics. Fifty-five percent of purchasers who returned survey cards were aged over 40 and 30 percent were over 60. In addition, 26 percent were retired and 19 percent were homemakers, with only 8 percent at the white-collar or executive level. The most common annual household income mentioned by those who returned cards was $20,000 or less (36 percent), while 53 percent made less than $30,000.

Nearly half the respondents had been using Buckley's Mixture for more than ten years (49 percent) and only 22 percent had used it for two years or less. The ''sugar-free'' factor was important to 69 percent, while 14 percent were not aware of it. In addition, only 7 percent first

EXHIBIT 7 **Buckley's Mixture Transit Advertisement 1989-90**

"It contains oil of pine needles. What did you expect it to taste like?"

When my father came up with the formula for Buckley's Mixture, he didn't particularly care how it tasted. What he did care about was how it worked. Buckley's Mixture works. It's been working for 70 years. And like dad always said, "I'll tell you two things about Buckley's. It tastes awful. And it works."

EXHIBIT 8 **Advertising Overview—Buckley's Mixture**

Year	Media	Market	Target Group	Execution	Budget
1983/84	Radio	National excluding Atlantic	Adult 39 +, Rural	N/A	$228,000
	Television	Atlantic Canada	Adults 18-44	N/A	$22,000
1984/85 1 Year Advertising Hiatus for Market Research					
1985/86	Radio	Southern Ontario	Men 18-34 (Vicks users) (secondary: women 18-34)	All I Want [:60]	$172,000
		Ontario	Urban 100M + population Household income <$30M Education: high school or less	Feelin' Low [:60]	
	Magazine *Reader's Digest*	National Markets	Adults 49 + (Buckley's users) Under 30M population Household income <$30M High school and less	We've Had a Facelift (E&F)	$74,000
	Trade Brochure Developed for sales force and Shelf Talker				
1986/87	Interior Transit	National English only	Adults, 18-44 (Triaminic DM users) Married, no children Urban 100M + population Clerical or labourer	I have recurring nightmares . . . I'm dedicated to ensuring . . . I came by my bad taste . . .	$151,000
	Magazine *TV Guide/ TV Hebdo*	National English/French		We've Had a Facelift I came by my bad taste . . .	$85,000
	Television	Atlantic Canada	Adults, 18-44	Sea Captain	$19,000
1987/88*	Interior Transit	National English/French	Adults, 18-44 Married, with/without children Urban 100M + population Household income $30M +	Since 1919 . . . Four of the Most . . .	$134,000
	Magazine	National		I came by my bad taste . . .	$77,000
	Trade Magazine	National—English	Pharmacists/Drugstore owners	Here's Your Chance . . .	$10,000
	Television	Atlantic Canada		Sea Captain	$24,000

(continued)

1988/89	Transit	National English/French	Adults, 18-49 Household income $25M+ Average education Urban 100M+ population	Sometimes Just the Right . . . Unfortunately, adding DM . . .	$171,000
	Radio	Major Markets		Dedicated [:30] Nightmares [:30] Honesty [:30]	$186,000
	Television	Atlantic Canada		Sea Captain	$30,000
1989/90	Transit	National English/French	Adults, 18+ Household income $25M+ High school education + Professional	It contains oil of pine . . . How bad does it taste . . .	$193,000
	Radio	Major Markets		1919 [:30] Surprise [:30]	$223,000
	Television	Atlantic Canada Toronto spill (WUTV Buffalo)		1919 [:30] Surprise [:30]	$40,000 $5,000

*Buckley's Mint Flavour DM was scheduled for market introduction in 1987, but a decision was made not to launch because of problems with product instability.

became aware of Buckley's Mixture through advertisements (either bus, subway, or radio), while 61 percent learned of the product through friends or family. Ninety percent liked it most because of its effectiveness, 39 percent for its strength, and 7 percent actually liked the taste.

A qualitative study was conducted in 1989 to determine the public's attitudes towards Buckley's Mixture and the advertising approach for the brand. Three focus group interviews were conducted by Ambrose Carr Linton Kelly. Two extended groups were conducted lasting two and one half hours. One of these groups contained current Buckley's users, the other non-triers of the brand. The third focus group consisted of one half triers and one half non-tries. This group discussion lasted three and one half hours.

Each group discussed exposure to other Buckley's products, the DM mixture, and price sensitivity in the market. The research concluded that a strong advertising foundation was being built on the message of honesty and efficacy, which is delivered in a humorous approach by Frank Buckley. In addition, it was found that Mr. Buckley successfully projects the strength of traditional values (honesty and sincerity) and also appears a contemporary businessman who understands today's needs. Participants concluded that, as a brand spokesperson, he is an honest champion of a product he believes in. The discussions concluded that the message was delivered most strongly in the transit medium, as the consumer could visually fit Frank Buckley's style to their expectations. Participants felt that the image tended to lose a little of its impact on radio, as the advertisement moves faster and is filled with more detail than most feel was necessary. However, participants did believe that radio was a "logical" extension to the transit ads and the message was clearly understood by listeners.

Research participants were open to the idea of advertising for Buckley's Mixture on television and radio, expecting the same relaxed but confident presentation. They felt that future advertising, particularly on radio, should portray a softer-spoken, slower-paced, less professional voice. The message communicated should concentrate on heightened efficacy (i.e., bronchitis, serious coughs) and reference to the taste should be softened somewhat. The study revealed that the participants were also receptive to the use of other settings and new generations of the Buckley family.

When questioned about Buckley's DM, few participants in the group interviews were aware of it. Many did not understand the difference between the original Buckley's Mixture and the DM product. Others were concerned that an addition of another ingredient would take away Buckley's "natural" image and would contradict some of the advertising. However, some felt it showed that W. K. Buckley Limited was "keeping up with the times."

The sales of Buckley's Mixture have improved markedly since the launch of the "Tastes Awful" advertising campaign. Some areas of the country are more responsible for the sales increase than are others. Ontario, Alberta, and the Atlantic provinces account for almost 70 percent of the sales of Buckley's Mixture. Alberta and the Atlantic provinces have accounted for the largest sales increases in recent years. Consistent with historic results, Quebec has had very low sales compared to the size of its market.

Percentage of Total Sales of Buckley's Mixture

	Year to date January 1989	Year to date January 1988	Regional Change
Atlantic	14.3%	13.7%	+22.6%
Quebec	8.8	9.3	+13.0
Ontario	36.6	38.4	+13.0
Man./Sask.	11.9	12.5	+13.1
Alberta	17.8	13.9	+52.1
British Columbia	10.5	12.1	+ 2.8
TOTAL	100	100	+18.5

Qualitative research conducted for Ambrose Carr by CRT Information Services involved creative testing of Buckley's Mixture transit advertisements. The research involved personal, indepth inverviews with 13 English-speaking and 13 French-speaking respondents. Among the French-speaking respondents, the "bad taste" emphasis and its communication were not perceived to be particularly humorous and had a negative effect on the desire to purchase. This response interfered with the perception of Buckley's Mixture as an efficient product. Also the word "mixture" in French does not properly communicate the fact that the product is a cough syrup. These factors, as well as difficulty encountered in the consumers' ability to remember the name Buckley's, created very low stimulation to purchase in the Quebec market.

THE 1990-91 CAMPAIGN

The time had come to decide on the advertising campaign for Buckley's Mixture for the 1990-91 season. Frank Buckley and vice-president John Meehan felt the company should give considerable thought to its future advertising efforts. The "Tastes Awful" campaign had been a great success, contributing to increased awareness of Buckley's Mixture and large increases in market share. Both Mr. Buckley and Mr. Meehan agreed that some of the key points that must be conveyed in advertising include:
- Buckley's Mixture is a natural product with no artificial flavours or sugar, and
- the product has enjoyed a good established name since 1919.

In addition to the development of an advertising campaign for the upcoming season, the Buckley's management team had established several business objectives for the coming year. The company is aiming to build awareness and interest in Buckley's Mixture, to increase the trial of their products, while increasing sales by 5 percent real growth during the year and market share by 10 percent by 1991-92. The achievement of these marketing goals would occur while maintaining profitability at current levels.

Since Buckley's Mixture is W. K. Buckley's best-known product, it is expected to lead the way in meeting these objectives. Recognizing that users of Buckley's Mixture are very brand loyal, Frank Buckley and John Meehan agreed that the best way to increase sales would be to attract new users.

QUESTIONS

1. Evaluate the advertising strategy, use of budget, and media allocation used to promote Buckley's Mixture during the period from 1983 to 1990.

2. Recognizing the history of the Buckley's product line and the corporate goals established by W. K. Buckley Limited, what approach should be taken for promoting Buckley's Mixture in 1990-91?

3. Should Mr. Buckley and Mr. Meehan consider making a major change in the advertising strategy? Why?

4. What approach can W. K. Buckley Limited take to gain increased market share in Quebec?

CASE 7.2   **The Tea Council of Canada (B)**

Canada is one of the world's leading tea-consuming countries. However, recent research on consumption habits indicates that, while tea is still a very popular drink in Canada, the historical "hard-core" tea drinkers are moving away from the beverage. Demographic changes in the Canadian market, complemented by trends towards cold, light, unsweetened beverages and drinks, demonstrate that competition in the beverage industry is likely to intensify.

© Copyright 1991. This case was written by Robert Power and Leanne O'Leary of Memorial University of Newfoundland, under the direction of Dr. James G. Barnes. The case was prepared with the cooperation and permission of the Tea Council of Canada to illustrate the marketing initiatives of that organization and not to indicate a correct or incorrect approach to the solution of marketing problems. The authors acknowledge the cooperation and support of Gordon F. Reynolds, Executive Director of the Tea Council of Canada, in the preparation of this case.

In the early 1980s, the Tea Council of Canada, a non-profit generic promotion organization, commenced a promotional program to improve awareness of tea and to facilitate an increase in the consumption of tea, to improve attitudes towards tea and the image of the product, and to contribute to increases in the quality of tea and in how it is served in the out-of-home market. In 1989, the marketing committee of the Tea Council of Canada established their objectives for testing the effectiveness of a strategically defined, generic advertising campaign. The committee proceeded to undertake a detailed usage and attitude study of the Canadian tea market. This research, conducted by ISL—International Surveys Limited, was designed to ascertain the images and attitudes held by the Canadian population towards tea and tea drinking. It was also intended to accumulate information that would provide direction to the advertising and communications approach for promoting regular black tea in the near future. The Tea Council's marketing committee received the results of the ISL usage and attitude study in October 1989. The findings, supplemented with other life-style research, reaffirmed some known facts about the market and provided key directional information for the council's marketing committee.

DEVELOPING THE STRATEGY

After reviewing the conclusions reached through the usage and attitude study, the marketing committee's next step was to identify clearly the marketing and consumer communications strategies for the future campaign. The marketing strategy consisted of a clear definition of tea's current position in the beverage market. Hot tea would be positioned to tea drinkers as the only beverage that offers a calming, soothing respite from the rigours and routines of contemporary daily life. The marketing strategy would also incorporate the focus of the overall campaign to build awareness of hot tea in a contemporary manner. The communications strategy developed by Anderson Advertising of Toronto for the Tea Council of Canada consisted of three key factors: (1) communications focus; (2) target consumers; (3) basic consumer benefit. The council's marketing effort was targeted at adult consumers, aged 25 to 49, primarily female, in middle-income households whose life-styles have become considerably more demanding and compromising. Communication efforts were intended to persuade these consumers to reconsider tea over other beverages. Upon clarification of these points, the committee presented a second proposal to the board of directors of the Tea Council, outlining the potential opportunities for the promotional campaign. This proposal was accepted by the council and the committee was given permission to continue with the implementation process.

To launch the project, the council invited a number of advertising agencies to submit an integrated marketing communications plan with principal emphasis to be centred on an appropriate theme line or slogan to support the advertising position. Five agencies presented their positioning approach to the marketing committee and two were subsequently selected. The Tea Council decided to research these two approaches to determine the level of consumer understanding and acceptability. The two most appropriate theme lines chosen were:

"Tea. It also refreshes the mind."

"Tea. The break you savour."

Elliott Research Corporation was contacted to prepare a research proposal for a survey designed to investigate consumers' interpretations of the theme lines, their reactions towards them, and the images of tea conveyed through these advertising slogans. The results obtained through this consumer study would be used to decide the most effective theme line for promoting the desired black tea image.

METHODOLOGY

The research study was completed by means of personal interviews with 100 adult females, 25 to 49 years of age, who drink tea at least once a month. Individual respondents were recruited among shoppers in the enclosed malls of shopping centres in Toronto and London, Ontario. Qualified respondents were interviewed at Elliott Research Corporation's permanent research facilities in those shopping centres.

Two versions of the questionnaire were prepared so that each of the theme lines to be tested was shown first to one-half of the respondents.

Each of the theme lines was exposed at first with just the line, but later with appropriate additional copy related to the line. As each theme line was exposed, the respondent was asked to express in her own words the messages that she believed the advertiser is attempting to communicate. Additional questions were asked to investigate the suitability of the advertisement's body copy (text) with the theme line and the reasons for the participants' responses.

After each of the theme lines was evaluated, both with and without supporting copy, the respondent was asked to choose the theme line that she believed most effectively described her image of and attitude towards tea. The respondent was then asked to detail, using a list of selected attributes, her impressions of the beverage that would be promoted by that specific theme line.

RESEARCH CONCLUSIONS

The study demonstrated that both of the proposed theme lines successfully conveyed the ideas expressed in the marketing strategy of the Tea Council of Canada: ''Tea is the beverage which offers a calming, soothing respite from the rigours and routine of contemporary daily life.''

Both of the advertising slogans conveyed a variety of relevant sales messages to the tea drinkers as they read them. While either theme line could be used, the research study showed the line, ''Tea. The break you savour'' to be superior in communicating a broader range of product attributes or consumer benefits, without eliciting a significant level of negative thoughts or ideas about the marketing messages. To a majority of respondents, this headline conveyed the desired idea that tea is refreshing. The theme line was also considered to be superior in the degree to which the words used were suited to the remainder of the advertisement, including the body copy. The message conveyed by the slogan and the additional body copy was related mainly to relaxation, enjoying a break, or a pleasurable moment.

As a result, the new theme line for the test advertising campaign and ultimately all other Council promotional activities became:

Tea—The Break You Savour

A break is a brief moment of the day set aside to relax—and that moment can be enhanced by the soothing, natural refreshment of tea.

And, unlike any other break, the time for tea is a simple, yet special, pleasure that is not just enjoyed but savoured.

Anderson Advertising of Toronto was also selected by the Tea Council of Canada to develop the promotional campaign.

TEST ADVERTISING

Based upon the conclusions of the Elliott research, the Anderson team developed an advertising campaign which was scheduled to undergo a market test from September 1990 through May 1991. A test period was required to measure the effectiveness of a carefully planned, strategically defined generic advertising campaign. The results of this test would assist in evaluating the viability of this campaign for use on a national level. Ontario was selected as the most suitable test market because of its importance to total hot tea consumption in Canada and because the region is representative of national tea drinking habits.

Considering the restricted budgets of the Tea Council for this program, television, radio, and newspapers were considered inappropriate and unaffordable vehicles to implement the plan. Other media that took into account vital, creative requirements were selected. Consumer magazines were recommended as the primary medium for the Tea Council's advertising campaign, with transit shelters, mall posters, and direct marketing as the support media. Consumer magazines would provide a cost-efficient means of fulfilling the established media objectives. Transit shelters and mall posters promised broad reach of all segments and another cost-efficient means to establish a high level of frequency. Within Ontario, Toronto offered the means to duplicate most closely the national campaign since it offered both transit shelters and mall poster space and quality market-specific publications, such as *Toronto Magazine*, *Toronto Life*, and the Toronto edition of *Maclean's*. Exhibit 1 shows advertisements developed for the Tea Council's test campaign.

The test, supplemented by a comprehensive public relations campaign, as well as opportunistic marketing activities by the council's corpo-

EXHIBIT 1

rate members, is tremendously important to the future viability of the campaign at a national level. Pre- and post-campaign research will ultimately help determine the extent to which the new campaign affects the opinions and attitudes of target segments, and more importantly, the consumption of "quality" black tea.

QUESTIONS

1. Evaluate the process, as demonstrated in this case, for translating the objective into the advertising materials or campaigns.

2. Recognizing the research results and recommendations presented to the Tea Council of Canada, comment on the appropriateness of the advertising campaign with respect to target segment, slogan, and medium used.

3. What research would you advise the Tea Council of Canada to carry out before and after the test advertising campaign, so that they might be able to evaluate its success?

CASE 7.3   **National Sea Products (B)**

BACKGROUND

National Sea Limited, with headquarters in Halifax, Nova Scotia, is North America's largest seafood company. Aware of the competitive nature of the industry and realizing the declining availability of fish stocks, National Sea has taken aggressive steps towards its goal of developing from a solely fish-based company to an international food-processing enterprise.

The decision at National Sea Products to diversify its activities in the food industry came at a time when the microwaveable market segment was attracting increasing attention from other food companies. The frozen entrée market had attracted many competitors since the early 1980s, including McCain's, Schneider's, the Stouffer's division of Nestlé, and Canada Packers. National Sea's initial offering in this market sector was shrimp entrées in 1985. Fish sticks had been National Sea's most successful packaged frozen seafood product since the early 1950s, and a decision was made to relaunch fish sticks as a microwaveable product in 1987.

Having met with less success with this repo-sitioning of fish sticks than had been expected, Jim Jaques, National Sea's Marketing Manager, turned his attention to the development of other microwaveable products to compete in what was expected to be a rapidly growing sector of the market for food products consumed at home. Internal brainstorming sessions at National Sea Products led Mr. Jacques and his colleagues to the conclusion that no products on the Canadian market were targeted to the "after-school snack segment" for unsupervised school-aged children. The marketing group at National Sea believed that this segment offered a target with great sales potential and a group of customers that could be expected to stay with National Sea products as they grew older.

The product development process for the new products included the search for a truly microwaveable bun that did not harden shortly after removal from the microwave oven. In December 1988, a contract was signed with Ben's Bakery of Saint John, New Brunswick, to supply the buns for the microwaveable snack line. With this contract arranged, and with the competitive advantage represented by the new bun, Jim Jaques felt

---

Copyright 1991. This case was written by Leanne O'Leary and James G. Barnes of Memorial University of Newfoundland. The case was prepared with the cooperation of National Sea Products Limited to illustrate the marketing activities of that company in launching a new product to the Canadian market and not to indicate a correct or incorrect approach to such marketing initiatives. The authors acknowledge the cooperation and support of Jim Jaques, Director of Marketing, National Sea Products Limited, in the preparation of this case.

that National Sea had no more than six months to develop the product concept before competing products would be introduced.

A decision was made to launch the new Fastbreak product line in May 1989 with two stockkeeping units (SKUs) in the line. The product line, including a fish filet and a chicken burger, went to market with relatively little consumer support or input, and with a promotional budget of approximately $300,000 for the 1989 fiscal year. The company planned to spend more than $400,000 for brand support in fiscal 1990.

Initial market reaction to the Fastbreak line was superb. With relatively little promotional support, the product performed very well against the heavy advertised McCain's and Nestlé lines. Six months after the launch of the Fastbreak line, problems began to develop for the line. The limited line did not receive strong support at the retailer level because of the lack of breadth in the line. Anticipated consumer boredom with such a limited line was also a major concern for the company. The targeted segment, although representing a market gap that was expected to grow rapidly, was still a relatively small segment when the age of the after-school consumer and the requirement that the home be equipped with a microwave oven are taken into consideration. (For a comprehensive examination of the activities leading to the launch of the Fastbreak line, see the National Sea Products [A] case on page 355.)

PRODUCT LINE DECISION

Jim Jaques realized that the two stock keeping units in the Fastbreak line would not be enough to guarantee long-term success for the brand. It simply did not allow the brand to have a major presence in retail stores, which would allow it to gain the attention of the customer. Faced with the modest success of the Fastbreak line in the competitive microwaveable snack-food sector, Jim Jaques was forced to make some important decisions regarding the future of the company's participation in that market. Should the Fastbreak line be discontinued, leaving the sector of the market to the competition? Should the line be replaced with a new microwaveable product concept? Or should National Sea extend the current Fastbreak line? Mr. Jaques knew that he

could not expect the brand to be given a very large marketing budget because, even if very successful, it would not account for more than a very small percentage of the company's total sales. Nevertheless, Jim Jaques believed that the Fastbreak line represented a winning concept and prepared to salvage the line.

The National Sea marketing team began the process of modifying the Fastbreak concept with a comprehensive review of the current line and the problems it was facing. The line, limited as it was to two SKUs, received poor support at the retail level, including poor placement in the store. This raised the possibility that the company would encounter difficulties in getting a modified line listed because of the failure of the initial Fastbreak product line to gain the support of the retailer. Jim Jaques knew that the retail trade could not be expected to provide great support for such a limited line. Consumer boredom with the limited variety represented in the line was another reason for considering the extension of the current line.

Jim Jaques and his marketing team wondered if the Fastbreak product was too much a niche item to sell in certain parts of the country, including western Canada, where the penetration of microwave ovens was not as high in the eastern provinces and where households were more rural and traditional in character. He felt that the line did enjoy a good reputation through its association with the Captain Highliner brand and its image of quality and trust. These attributes presented a good basis for positioning a relaunched line. He and his colleagues believed that new life could be brought to the line through the addition of more SKUs and new packaging to catch the attention of consumers and to create the image of an expanded product line. This was thought to be especially important in light of the fact that National Sea was competing in this growing segment with some very large competitors, each of whom offered four to six SKUs in their microwaveable snack line and had the resources to provide merchandising and promotional support.

MARKETING RESEARCH

Considering the limited success of the initial product offering in the microwaveable snack market, management at National Sea recognized the importance of consumer input into the product design process. Although the budget allocated to the Fastbreak line remained limited, a budget was prepared for consumer product research. The market and consumer research for the Fastbreak line was conducted in three stages. The first stage of the research was a test of concepts and involved a series of in-mall interviews with 50 respondents. This project produced a list of the five products that consumers thought to be most appropriate for inclusion in the Fastbreak line. The respondents were asked a series of questions related to their interest in buying a particular product, of which they were provided a brief description. The proposed product line at this stage of research included turkey, tuna, sea pizza, seafood western, and chicken Mexicali burgers. The respondents were asked how interested they would be in buying each product, rating each on a scale from "definitely buy it" to "definitely not buy it." Qualitative responses from the respondents explaining their choice were then recorded. Using this information, National Sea refined the product line to reflect the consumers' responses. The product line was modified to include burgers with turkey, tuna, Bar-B-Que chicken, pizza, and Italian cheese fillings. These additional products were in addition to the current fish and chicken products that had been launched in May 1989.

The modified product line was subsequently tested through the second stage of the consumer research. Following its commitment to consumer input, National Sea interviewed 50 female heads of households in another in-mall survey. The sample for this stage of the research was chosen to reflect the group that National Sea considered to be the decision makers and/or influencers in the purchase of microwaveable snack food products. Again, the respondents were asked to rate descriptions of the individual product concepts within the line, including the two products currently on the market. This wave of consumer research resulted in two products receiving very good reviews or potential purchase ratings. Through the research, pizza burgers, followed by the Bar-B-Que chicken burger, were identified as two possible line extensions of this product. The Bar-B-Que chicken burger actually outscored the chicken burger already on the market.

At this point, Jim Jaques decided to conduct a third wave of research to test consumer reaction to the taste of the pizza and Bar-B-Que chicken burgers. Diversified Research Laboratories Limited of Toronto was commissioned to conduct the consumer taste-testing in April 1990. Two prototype samples of each of the pizza and Bar-B-Que chicken burgers were prepared in small production batches. The two samples of pizza burgers consisted of either 25 percent or 30 percent tomato sauce. The two Bar-B-Que chicken burger samples were prepared with the breading currently being used on the existing chicken burger and with spiced breading. To provide a control for the overall liking of the pizza and Bar-B-Que chicken burger, the current chicken burger was also rated by respondents during the test.

The study was conducted with children between the ages of 8 and 14 who had consumed single-serve microwaveable burgers or snacks currently on the market. Eighty-three children participated and rated the current chicken burger, 42 of the children evaluated the pizza burger, and 41 rated the Bar-B-Que chicken burger. The research was designed to compare the two samples of each product; to determine the overall rating of the current chicken burger; and to identify areas for improvement of the pizza and Bar-B-Que chicken burgers.

Based on the results of the taste test with children who were consumers of microwaveable single-serve burgers and snacks, it was concluded that the pizza and Bar-B-Que chicken burgers were inferior to the current Highliner Fastbreak chicken burger. Exhibit 1 presents the overall liking rating for the various products that were tested. The results showed a tendency on the part of the children who participated to prefer the pizza burger consisting of 30 percent tomato sauce over the 25 percent tomato sauce sample, as shown in Exhibit 2. There was also a tendency for respondents to choose the Bar-B-Que chicken burger made with the current breading over the version with spiced breading. These results are presented in Exhibit 3.

Based on the taste testing results, Diversified Research Laboratories recommended that the perception of a "burger" could be portrayed with both the pizza and Bar-B-Que chicken burgers by making them slightly thicker, with a

EXHIBIT 1 **Overall Liking Rating Comparison**

Sample	Average Rating*
Current Chicken Burger	6.3
Pizza Burgers:	
25% Tomato Sauce	5.2
30% Tomato Sauce	5.3
Bar-B-Que Chicken Burgers:	
Current Breading	5.3
Spiced Breading	5.3

* All samples were rated on a seven-point scale, where 7 = excellent and 1 = terrible.

EXHIBIT 2 **Overall Preference — Pizza Burger**

Total number of children	42
Number preferring 25% Tomato Sauce	15 (36%) +
Number preferring 30% Tomato Sauce	25 (59%)
Number stating no preference	2 (5%)

+ indicates no statistically significant difference in preference.

EXHIBIT 3 **Overall Preference — Bar-B-Que Chicken Burgers**

Total Number of Children	41
Number Preferring Current Breading	23 (56%) +
Number Preferring Spiced Breading	18 (44%)

+ indicates no statistically significant difference in preference.

firmer, drier texture to hold together better. The researchers also suggested that the pizza burger would require more visible pizza-type ingredients such as pepperoni and cheese. The sauce and chicken flavours of the Bar-B-Que chicken product also needed improvement, as a few children commented on the excessive quantity of sauce and the appearance of the patty, which was also thought to lack Bar-B-Que flavour.

Upon completion of the third stage of the new product research in April 1990, Jim Jaques and his marketing team at National Sea Products were faced with a very important decision concerning the future of the Fastbreak product line. The research had provided a great deal of important information about the current product line and possible improvements or extensions. With

the summer season about to begin, Mr. Jaques had to make a series of decisions concerning the future of the Fastbreak line.

QUESTIONS

1. What should Jim Jaques recommend to senior management at National Sea concerning the future of the Fastbreak line?

2. Should he expand the line to include additional SKUs? If so, how many and which ones?

3. Should further steps be considered to reposition the Fastbreak line? If so, what steps and how should the line be positioned in the changing marketplace?

CASE 7.4 # Cooper Supply Company Ltd.: Distribution Channel to Reach a Foreign Market

"You know as well as I do, Ralph, that customers in Saudi Arabia, especially ARAMCO, have been our bread and butter for over 10 years. That's why I'm concerned about this new statement on procurement policy that we just received from ARAMCO. Now the Saudi government may or may not have been behind this new policy. In any case, I think we darned well better come up with the appropriate channel-of-distribution decision that will enable us to comply with this new policy. That is, if we want to continue to compete in the Saudi Arabian market." These words were spoken by Frank Broderick, the senior sales rep in the Cooper Supply Company Ltd. in a conversation with Ralph Karras, the company's vice president of sales.

The Cooper Supply Company was a large independent distributor (wholesaler) of electrical supplies. The company had its main office and warehouse in Hamilton, Ontario, and a smaller office and warehouse in Calgary, Alberta. Since its founding in 1930, the firm had grown slowly but steadily until 1973, when its sales volume reached $12 million. About 25 percent of this volume was in export business, primarily to large oil companies.

Then, in the mid-1970s, the price of oil increased dramatically, thus stimulating the exploration and drilling for oil. This situation sharply increased the demand for products carried by Cooper. Consequently, since 1973, Cooper's sales had increased considerably. By 1990, the company's annual sales volume was $50 million and net profit was $5 million. Almost one-half of this business came from export sales to companies in Saudi Arabia.

Cooper Supply carried a wide variety of electrical supplies and small electrical equipment. "We represent the finest names in the industrial electrical supply and equipment industry," Karras said. "And we got there because of our reputation for honesty and integrity in an industry that often is laced with payoffs, price fixing, and price cutting."

One particular group of products was classified as explosion-proof, hazardous-application products. This group accounted for 50 percent

of Cooper's total sales and about 80 percent of its export sales volume. Intended for use in hazardous environments where toxic or inflammable particles or fumes might be in the atmosphere, these items permitted the safe transfer of electricity without the danger of igniting volatile gases or particles.

These products included switches, circuit breakers, telephones, lighting equipment, receptables, timers, and thermostats. Cooper also carried a complete line of the same goods in the non-explosion-proof category. Other products distributed by Cooper were batteries, flashlights, light bulbs, wire, conduit, transformers, fans, and electric welders.

The large number of competitors, plus the fact that an essentially similar product could be supplied by several manufacturers, made electrical supply wholesaling an intensely competitive industry with low profit margins. However, as Ralph Karras pointed out, "Typically, export customers will pay higher prices, which makes the export business more lucrative and obviously *very* important to us. Of course, the export business is a lot more complicated and risky than is domestic selling."

Many of Cooper's customers preferred to deal with only one electrical goods supplier in order to reduce procurement costs and also to give the buyer some influence with the supplier. Cooper easily adapted to this industrial buying pattern by being able to handle a customer's total electrical supply needs. Cooper sold to firms in a variety of industries including railroads, utilities, manufacturing, engineering, construction, federal and state governments, and petroleum.

Many of Cooper's petroleum accounts were medium and large oil companies that bought electrical merchandise in Canada for use in their foreign operations. In fact, sales to one customer alone — the Arabian-American Oil Company (ARAMCO)—accounted for 30 percent ($15 million) of Cooper's sales in 1990.

Because the ARAMCO account was so important to Cooper Supply, Frank Broderick was greatly concerned about ARAMCO's recently issued statement regarding its procurement policy. In effect, the statement said that, starting the first of the following year, all ARAMCO purchase orders exceeding $50,000 would be placed either through (1) a Saudi Arabian national or (2) agents or companies based in Saudi Arabia. That is, ARAMCO would no longer place orders directly with Cooper or other foreign-based suppliers.

The reason stated for the new policy was ARAMCO's dissatisfaction with the situation in which so much capital was leaving Saudi Arabia without adequately benefiting the country. In view of this line of reasoning Broderick believed that other large Cooper customers in Saudi Arabia would soon adopt a similar purchasing policy.

Despite its rapid growth since the mid-1970s, Cooper Supply still had only 10 outside sales reps and another 10 who comprised the inside sales force. The outside sales people called on customers' offices in Canada, even though many of the orders were shipped to foreign locations. The inside sales force handled all inquiries, mail orders, and telephone orders. Karras preferred to limit the size of his sales force. He wanted Cooper Supply to retain the image of being a medium-sized company that offered personalized service and quick delivery in competition with its large competitors.

Several weeks before receiving ARAMCO's statement, Karras had received a proposal from a Saudi Arabian agent offering to represent Cooper Supply in Saudi Arabia. Karras responded to the agent's letter, saying that Cooper would study the proposal and reply within a reasonable period of time. In fact, Karras had been wondering how to respond to the Saudi's proposal when he (Karras) received the ARAMCO notice.

The proposed agency agreement was to cover a period of three years, and was subject to renewal in three-year time segments. The agent would receive a commission of 2 percent of all orders shipped to Saudi Arabia. This commission was to be paid even if the agent had not been instrumental in soliciting the business or obtaining the order. In return, the agent would (1) supply local sales people in Saudi Arabia, (2) provide contacts with potential customers, and (3) use his good reputation to solicit inquiries and orders for Cooper Supply. The agent also enclosed supporting letters of recommendation from ARAMCO and Saudi government officials.

Ralph Karras was discussing the agent's proposal and the ARAMCO statement with Frank Broderick. Broderick pointed out that Cooper's annual sales to ARAMCO alone amounted to $15 million, and another $8 to $10 million came from sales to other Saudi Arabian construction projects. On the ARAMCO sales alone, the agent's 2 percent commission would amount to $300,000. "And that assumes that the agent can sell at least as much as we've been selling to ARAMCO from our Canadian offices," Broderick stated.

"I don't like this agent's deal at all," he continued. "We tie ourselves up in an exclusive-agency contract for three years. That makes us vulnerable if the guy turns out to be ineffective. Competition could kill us during that period. I think we simply ought to open our own sales office in Saudi—either in Riyadh or in Jiddah. In that way we'd have our own people on the scene. We would avoid paying an agent's commission. We would get better market coverage and still be operating within the terms of the new ARAMCO policy."

"Frank, I'm a little leery of the financial and personnel commitment involved in establishing our own sales office over there," countered Karras. "Salaries and expenses could cost us a bundle, and with no guarantee of success. Maybe we can open an office some time in the future, but for now this agency proposal maybe is our best bet. The guy comes highly recommended, and his 2 percent fee won't put our bids above competitive level. And he will know the territory better than we do. As you well know, the hardest part of obtaining business over there is to make the initial contact — that is, to obtain inquiries from prospective accounts.

"I really don't know which way to go," concluded Karras. "Maybe there is a better alternative that we are overlooking. All I do know is that we have to do something and do it soon."

QUESTION

What channel of distribution should the Cooper Supply Company use to reach the Saudi Arabian market?

GLOSSARY

accessory equipment   In the business market, capital goods used in the operation of an industrial firm.

actual self   The way you really see yourself. To be distinguished from *ideal self*.

ad   See *advertisement*.

administered vertical marketing system   A distribution system in which channel control is maintained through the economic power of one firm in the channel.

administration   See *management*.

adoption process   The stages that an individual goes through in deciding whether or not to accept an innovation.

advertisement   A sponsor-identified message regarding a product or organization that can be verbal and/or visual, and is disseminated through one or more media. Same as *ad*.

advertising   All activities involved in presenting to a group a nonpersonal, sponsor-identified message regarding a product or organization.

advertising agency   An independent company rendering specialized services in advertising in particular and in marketing in general.

advertising allowance   A payment or cash discount offered by a manufacturer to a retailer to encourage the retailer to advertise or prominently display the manufacturer's product.

advertising campaign   The total advertising program for a product or brand that involves coordination, central theme, and specific goals.

advertising media   The communications vehicles (such as newspapers, radio, and television) that carry advertising.

agent middleman   A firm that never actually owns products that are being distributed but does actively assist in the transfer of title.

agent wholesaling middleman   An independent firm that primarily engages in wholesaling and does not take title to the products being distributed but does actively negotiate their sale or purchase on behalf of other firms.

agents and brokers   A broad category of wholesaling middlemen that do not take title to products. The category includes manufacturers' agents, selling agents, commission merchants, auctioneers, brokers, and others.

agribusiness   The business side of farming. Usually involves large, highly mechanized farming operations.

AIDA   A sequence of steps in various forms of promotion, notably personal selling and advertising, consisting of attracting Attention, holding Interest, arousing Desire, and generating buyer Action.

annual marketing plan   A written document that details the planned marketing activities for the given business unit or product for the given year.

assumptive close   In personal selling, the stage in the selling process when the sales person can often finalize the sale by asking questions that will settle the details of the purchase.

attitude   A learned predisposition to respond to an object or class of objects in a consistently favourable or unfavourable way.

auction company   An agent wholesaling middleman that provides (1) auctioneers who do the selling and (2) physical facilities for displaying the sellers' products.

automated merchandising   See *automatic vending*.

automatic vending   A form of nonstore retailing where the products are sold through a machine with no personal contact between the buyer and seller. Same as *automated merchandising*.

average revenue   The unit price at a given level of unit sales. It is calculated by dividing total revenue by the number of units sold.

average total cost   The total cost divided by the number of units produced.

balance of trade   In international business, the difference between the value of a nation's imports and the value of its exports.

base price   The price of one unit of the product at its point of production or resale. Same as *list price*.

battle of the brands   Market competition between producers' brands and middlemen's brands. In recent years, generic products have entered this competitive struggle.

benefit segmentation   A basis for segmenting a market. A total market is divided into segments based on the customers' perceptions of the various benefits provided by a product.

brand   A name, term, symbol, special design, or

some combination of these elements that is intended to identify the products of one seller or a group of sellers.

brand competition Competition among marketers of branded products that are very similar and may be substituted for each other.

brand licensing See *trademark licensing*.

brand manager See *product manager*.

brand mark The part of a brand that appears in the form of a symbol, picture, design, or distinctive colour or type of lettering.

brand name The part of a brand that can be vocalized — words, letters, and/or numbers.

breadth of product mix The number of product lines offered for sale by a firm.

break-even point The level of output at which revenues equal costs, assuming a certain selling price.

broadened marketing concept A marketing philosophy that incorporates consumer orientation, coordination of marketing activities, achieving the organization's objectives, and satisfying societal wants affected by the organization's activities.

broker An independent agent wholesaling middleman that brings buyers and sellers together and provides market information to either party.

build-up method See *task method*.

business marketing The marketing of goods and services to business users.

business product A product that is intended for purchase and use in producing other products or in rendering services in a business.

business user An organization that buys goods or services to resell, use in its own business, or make other products.

buy classes Three typical buying situations in the business market — namely new-task buying, modified rebuy, and straight rebuy.

buyers The people in a buying centre who select the suppliers, arrange the terms of sale, and process the actual purchase orders.

buying centre All of the people in an organization who participate in the buying-decision process.

buying-decision process The series of logical stages a prospective purchaser goes through when faced with a buying problem. The stages differ for consumers and organizations.

buying motive The reason why a person buys a specific product or shops at a specific store.

campaign A coordinated series of promotional efforts built around a single theme and designed to reach a pre-determined goal.

campaign theme In promotion, the central idea or focal point in a promotional campaign.

cartel A group of companies that produce similar products and combine to restrain competition in manufacturing and marketing.

cash discount A deduction from list price for paying a bill within a specified period of time.

catalogue showroom A type of retail institution that offers a complete catalogue and some sample items in the showroom and the remaining inventory in an attached warehouse. It offers a broad but shallow assortment of merchandise, emphasizes low prices, and offers few customer services.

category killer store A type of retail institution that has a narrow but very deep assortment, emphasizes low prices, and few to moderate customer services. It is designed to "destroy" all competition in a specific product category.

category-management system A form of marketing organization in which an executive position called a category manager is established for each product category, and all the competing brand managers in each group report to this executive.

Census Metropolitan Area The major population centres of Canada as defined by Statistics Canada; generally containing population centres of 100,000 or more.

chain store One in a group of retail stores that carry the same type of merchandise. Corporate chain stores are centrally owned and managed. Voluntary chains are an association of independently owned stores.

channel conflict A situation in which one channel member perceives another channel member to be acting in a way that prevents the first member from achieving its distribution objectives.

channel control The ability to influence the behaviour of other channel members.

channels manager A person who is formally in charge of an organization's channels.

client market Individuals and/or organizations that are the recipients of a nonprofit organization's money and/or services. Same as *recipient market*.

closing In personal selling, the stage in the selling process when the sales person gets the buyer to agree to buy.

cognitive dissonance The anxiety created by the fact that in most purchases the alternative selected has some negative features and the alternatives not selected have some positive features.

combination salary plan The method of sales force compensation that combines a base salary with a commission related to some task(s).

commercial environment   All of the marketing organizations and individuals who attempt to communicate with consumers.

commission merchant   An independent agent wholesaling middleman, used primarily in the marketing of agricultural products, that may physically handle the seller's products in central markets and has authority regarding prices and terms of sale.

communication process   A system of verbal and/or nonverbal transmission of information between a sender and a receiver. The four elements are message, source, communication channel, and receiver.

community shopping centre   A shopping *centre* that is larger than a neighbourhood centre but smaller than a regional centre. Usually includes one or two department stores or discount stores, along with a number of shopping-goods stores and specialty stores.

comparative advertising   Selective demand advertising in which the advertiser either directly (by naming a rival brand) or indirectly (through inference) points out how the advertised brand is better.

Competition Act   The major piece of federal legislation in Canada that governs the marketing and advertising activities of companies and organizations operating in Canada.

concept testing   The first three stages in the new-product development process — pretesting of the product idea, in contrast to later pretesting of the product itself and the market.

Consumer Packaging and Labelling Act   Federal legislation that regulates the packaging and labelling of consumer products in Canada.

consumer product   A product that is intended for purchase and use by household consumers for non-business purposes.

consumerism   Protests by consumers against perceived injustices in marketing, and the efforts to remedy these injustices.

contract farming   In advance of growing season, a grower contracts to sell all or part of the crop to a food processor or a middleman.

contract manufacturing   An arrangement in which a firm in one country arranges for a firm in another country to produce, and perhaps distribute, the product in the foreign country.

contractual vertical market system   An arrangement under which independent firms — producers, wholesalers, and retailers — operate under a contract specifying how they will try to improve their distribution efficiency and effectiveness.

contribution-margin allocation   In marketing cost analysis, an accounting approach in which only direct expenses are allocated to the marketing units being studied. A unit's gross margin minus its direct costs equals that unit's contribution to covering the company's indirect expenses (overhead).

contributor market   Individuals and/or organizations that donate money, labour, services, and/or materials to a nonprofit organization. Also called *donor market*.

convenience goods   A class of consumer products that the consumer has prior knowledge of and purchases with minimum time and effort.

convenience store   A type of retailing institution that concentrates on convenience-oriented groceries and nonfoods, has higher prices than found at most other grocery stores, and offers few customer services.

"cooling-off" laws   Provincial or municipal laws that permit a consumer to cancel an order for a product —usually within a period of three days after signing the order.

cooperative advertising   Advertising in which two or more firms share the cost.

copy   The written or spoken material in an ad that makes up the primary message.

corporate chain   An organization of two or more centrally owned and managed stores that generally handle the same lines of products.

corporate vertical marketing system   An arrangement under which a firm at one level of a distribution channel owns the firms at the next level or owns the entire channel.

correlation analysis   A method of sales forecasting that is a statistical refinement of the direct-derivation method.

cost per thousand (CPM)   The media cost of gaining exposure to 1,000 persons with an ad.

cost-plus pricing   A major method of price determination in which the price of a unit of a product is set at a level equal to the unit's total cost plus a desired profit on the unit.

creative selling   A selling job that often requires designing a system to fit the needs of the particular customer and may depend upon the expertise of several people who make up a sales team.

cues   In learning theory, signals from the environment that determine the pattern of response.

culture   A complex of symbols and artifacts created by a given society and handed down from generation to generation as determinants and regulators of human behaviour.

cumulative discount   A quantity discount based on the total volume purchased over a period of time.

custodian warehousing   See *field warehousing*.

customer service advertising   Advertising that presents information about the advertiser's operations.

deciders   The people in a buying centre who make the actual buying decision regarding a product and/or supplier.

decoding   The process of a receiver giving meaning to words, pictures, or both that have been transmitted by a sender.

Delphi method   A forecasting technique, applicable to sales forecasting, in which a group of experts individually and anonymously assesses future sales and after which each member has the chance to offer a revised assessment as the group moves towards a consensus.

demand forecasting   The process of estimating sales of a product during some future time period.

demography   The statistical study of human population and its distribution.

department store   A large-scale retailing institution that has a very broad and deep product assortment, prefers not to compete on the basis of price, and offers a wide array of customer services.

depth of product line   The assortment within a product line.

derived demand   A situation in which the demand for one product is dependent upon the demand for another product.

descriptive label   A label that gives information regarding the use, care, performance, or other features of a product.

differential advantage   Any feature of an organization or brand perceived by customers to be desirable and different from the competition.

diffusion of innovation   A process by which an innovation is spread through a social system over time.

direct-action advertising   Product advertising that seeks a quick response.

direct costs   Separate expenses that are incurred totally in connection with one market segment or one unit of the sales organization.

direct-derivation method   A sales forecasting method used to translate market-factor behaviour into an estimate of future sales.

direct distribution   A channel consisting only of producer and final customer with no middlemen providing assistance.

direct mail   An advertising medium whereby the advertiser contacts prospective customers by sending some form of advertisement through the mail.

direct marketing   A form of nonstore retailing that uses nonpersonal media to contact consumers who, in turn, purchase products without visiting a retail store.

direct purchase   A situation in which a customer makes a purchase directly from a producer.

direct selling   A form of nonstore retailing in which personal contact between a sales person and a consumer occurs away from a retail store.

direct tests (in advertising)   Measures of the sales volume produced by an ad or an entire advertising campaign.

discount house   A large-scale retailing institution that has a broad and shallow product assortment, emphasizes low prices, and offers relatively few customer services.

discount retailing   A retailing approach that uses price as a major selling point by combining comparatively low prices and reduced costs of doing business.

discretionary purchasing power   The amount of disposable income remaining after fixed expenses and essential household needs are paid for.

dispersion   In distribution, the middlemen's activities that distribute the correct amount of a product to its market.

disposable personal income   Personal income remaining after all personal taxes are paid.

distribution centre   A concept in warehousing that develops under one roof an efficient, fully integrated system for the flow of products — taking orders, filling them, and delivering them to customers.

distribution channel   The set of people and firms involved in the flow of the title to a product as it moves from producer to ultimate consumer or business user.

diversification   A product-market growth strategy in which a company develops new products to sell to new markets.

donor market   See *contributor market*.

drive   See *motive*.

driver sales person A selling job in which the job is primarily to deliver the product. Selling responsibilities, if any, are secondary to seeing that orders are filled correctly and on time.

drop shipper A limited-function merchant wholesaler that does not physically handle the product.

dual distribution The use by a producer of multiple and competing channels of distribution.

dumping The process of selling products in foreign markets at prices below the prices charged for these goods in their home market.

early adopters The second group (following the innovators) to adopt something new. This group includes the opinion leaders, is respected, and has much influence on its peers.

early majority A more deliberate group of innovation adopters that adopts just before the ''average'' adopter.

economic order quantity (EOQ) The optimal quantity for reorder when replenishing inventory stocks, as indicated by the volume at which the inventory-carrying cost plus the order-processing cost are at a minimum.

ego In Freudian psychology, the rational control centre in our minds that maintains a balance between (1) the uninhibited instincts of the id and (2) the socially oriented, constraining superego.

80-20 principle A situation in which a large proportion of a company's marketing units (products, territories, customers) accounts for a small share of the company's volume or profit, and vice versa.

elastic demand A price-volume relationship such that a change of one unit on the price scale results in a change of more than one unit on the volume scale.

encoding The process of translating an idea into a message in the form of words, pictures, or both in order that it can be transmitted from a sender to a receiver.

evaluation The process of determining what happened, why it happened, and what to do about it.

exchange The voluntary act of providing a person or organization something of value in order to acquire something else of value in return.

exclusive dealing The practice by which a manufacturer prohibits its dealers from carrying products of competing manufacturers.

exclusive distribution A strategy in which a producer agrees to sell its product to only a single wholesaling middleman and/or retailer in a given market.

exclusive territory The practice by which a manufacturer requires each middleman to sell only to customers located within the middleman's assigned territory.

executive judgement A method of sales forecasting that consists of obtaining opinions regarding future sales volume from one or more executives.

expected price The price at which customers consciously or unconsciously value a product — what they think the product is worth.

experimental method A method of gathering primary data in which the researcher is able to observe the results of changing one variable in a situation while holding all others constant.

express warranty A statement in written or spoken words regarding restitution from seller to customer if the seller's product does not perform up to reasonable expectations.

fabricating materials Business goods that have received some processing and will undergo further processing as they become part of another product.

fabricating parts Business goods that already have been processed to some extent and will be assembled in their present form (with no further change) as part of another product.

factory outlet A special type of off-price retail institution that is owned by a manufacturer and usually sells only that manufacturer's clearance items, regular merchandise, and perhaps even otherwise unavailable items.

fad A short-lived fashion that is usually based on some novelty feature.

family A group of two or more people related by blood, marriage, or adoption living together in a household.

family brands A branding strategy in which a group of products is given a single brand.

family life cycle The series of life stages that a family goes through, starting with young single people and progressing through married stages with young and then older children, and ending with older married and single people.

fashion A style that is popularly accepted by groups of people over a reasonably long period of time.

fashion-adoption process The process by which a style becomes popular in a market; similar to diffusion of an innovation.

fashion cycle Wavelike movements representing the introduction, rise, popular acceptance, and decline in popularity of a given style.

fashion obsolescence See *style obsolescence*.

field experiment An experiment in which the researcher has only limited control of the environment because the experiment is conducted in a real-world setting.

field warehousing A form of public warehousing that provides a financial service for a seller. Same as *custodian warehousing*.

fixed cost A constant cost regardless of how many items are produced or sold.

flexible-price strategy A pricing strategy in which a company sells similar quantities of merchandise to similar buyers at different prices. Same as *variable-price strategy*.

F.O.B. (free on board) factory price A geographic pricing strategy whereby the buyer pays all freight charges from the F.O.B. location to the destination. Same as *F.O.B. mill price*.

F.O.B. mill price See *F.O.B. factory price*.

focus group A preliminary data-gathering method involving an interactive interview of four to ten people.

form utility The utility that is created when a good is produced.

forward dating A combination of a seasonal discount and a cash discount under which a buyer places an order and receives shipment during the off-season but does not have to pay the bill until after the season has started and some sales revenue has been generated.

fragmented markets Small market segments that can be identified and isolated through increasingly sophisticated demographic, behavioural, and geographic data.

franchise system The combination of franchisor, franchisees, and franchisor-owned business units.

franchising A type of contractual vertical marketing system that involves a continuing relationship in which a franchisor (the parent company) provides the right to use a trademark plus various management assistance in opening and operating a business in return for financial considerations from a franchisee (the owner of the individual business unit).

freight absorption A geographic pricing strategy whereby the seller pays for (absorbs) some of the freight charges in order to penetrate more distant markets.

freight forwarder A specialized transportation agency that consolidates less-than-carload or less-than-truckload shipments into carload or truckload quantities and provides door-to-door shipping service.

full-cost allocation In a marketing cost analysis, an accounting approach wherein all expenses — direct and indirect — are allocated to the marketing units being analyzed.

full-service wholesaler An independent merchant middleman that normally performs a full range of wholesaling functions.

functional discount See *trade discount*.

gatekeepers The people in a buying centre who control the flow of purchasing information within the organization and between the buying firm and potential vendors.

generic product A product that is packaged in a plain label and is sold with no advertising and without a brand name. The product goes by its generic name, such as "tomatoes" or "paper towels."

generic use of brand names General reference to a product by its brand name — cellophane, kerosene, zipper, for example — rather than its *generic name*. The owners of these brands no longer have exclusive use of the brand name.

goal See *objective*.

good A set of tangible physical attributes assembled in an identifiable form to provide want-satisfaction to customers.

government market The segment of the business market that includes federal, state, and local units buying for government institutions such as schools, offices, hospitals, and military bases.

grade label Identification of the quality (grade) of a product by means of a letter, number, or word.

heterogeneity of a service A characteristic of a service indicating that each unit is somewhat different from other "units" of the same service.

high involvement A purchase decision that involves all six stages of the buying decision process.

horizontal business market A situation where a given product is usable in a wide variety of industries.

horizontal conflict A form of channel conflict occurring between firms on the same level of distribution — between middlemen of the same type or between different types of middlemen.

horizontal cooperative advertising Advertising that involves firms on the same level of distribution sharing the cost.

household A single person, a family, or any group of unrelated persons who occupy a housing unit.

hypermarket A type of exceedingly large-scale retailing institution that has a very broad and moderately deep product assortment, emphasizes low prices, and offers some customer services.

hypothesis A tentative supposition or a possible solution to a problem.

iceberg principle A concept related to performance evaluation stating that the summary data (tip of the iceberg) regarding an activity may hide significant variations among segments of this activity.

id In Freudian psychology, the part of the mind that houses the basic instinctive drives, many of which are antisocial.

ideal self The way you want to be seen or would like to see yourself. To be distinguished from *actual self*.

illustration The pictorial portion of an ad.

image utility The emotional or psychological value that a person attaches to a product or brand because of the reputation or social standing of that product or brand.

implementation The process of organizing for the marketing effort, staffing this organization, and directing the operational efforts of these people as they carry out the strategic plans.

implied warranty An intended but unstated assurance regarding restitution from seller to customer if the seller's product does not perform up to reasonable expectations.

import-export agent An agent wholesaling middleman that arranges for distribution of goods in a foreign country.

impulse buying Purchases made with little or no advance planning.

independent retailer A company with a single retail store that is not affiliated with any type of contractual vertical marketing system.

indirect-action advertising Product advertising that is intended to inform or remind consumers about a product and its benefits.

indirect costs Expenses that are incurred jointly for more than one marketing unit and therefore cannot be totally charged to one market segment.

indirect distribution A channel consisting of producer, final customer, and at least one level of middleman.

indirect tests (in advertising) Measures of advertising effects that use something other than sales volume.

inelastic demand A price-volume relationship such that a change of one unit on the price scale results in a change of less than one unit on the volume scale.

influencers The people in a buying centre who set the specifications and aspects of buying decisions because of their technical expertise, financial position, or political power in the organization.

informal investigation The stage in a marketing research study at which information is gathered from people outside the company — middlemen, competitors, advertising agencies, and consumers.

in-home retailing Retail selling in the customer's home. A personal sales representative may or may not be involved. In-home retailing includes door-to-door selling, party-plan selling, and selling by television and computer.

innovators The first group—a venturesome group— of people to adopt something new (good, service).

input performance measures In sales force performance, indications of effort expended.

inseparability A characteristic of a service indicating that it cannot be separated from the creator-seller of the service.

inside order taker A selling job in which the primary function of the sales person is to take orders in person or by phone inside a store or other type of business.

installations In the business market, long-lived, expensive, major industrial capital goods that directly affect the scale of operation of an industrial firm.

institutional advertising Advertising designed either to present information about the advertiser's business or to create a good attitude — build goodwill — towards the organization.

intangibility A characteristic of a service indicating that it has no physical attributes and, as a result, is impossible for customers to taste, feel, see, hear, or smell before buying.

intensity of distribution The number of middlemen used by a producer at the retailing and wholesaling levels of distribution.

intensive distribution A strategy in which a producer sells its product in every available outlet where a consumer might reasonably look for it. Same as *mass distribution*.

inverse demand A price-volume relationship such that the higher the price, the greater the unit sales.

involvement level The amount of time and effort the consumer invests in a buying decision.

joint venture A partnership arrangement in which a foreign operation is owned in part by a Canadian company and in part by a foreign company.

"just-in-time" concept An inventory control system that involves buying parts and supplies in small quantities just in time for use in production and then producing in quantities just in time for sale.

label The part of a product that carries verbal information about the product or the seller.

laboratory experiment An experiment in which the researcher has complete control over the environment during the experiment.

laggards Tradition-bound people who are the last to adopt an innovation.

late majority The skeptical group of innovation adopters who adopt a new idea late in the game.

layout The physical arrangement of all of the elements of an ad.

leader pricing Temporary price cuts on well-known items. The price cut is made with the idea that these "specials" (loss leaders) will attract customers to the store.

learning Changes in behaviour resulting from previous experiences.

leasing A situation, found in both business and consumer markets, in which a good is rented rather than purchased outright.

licensing A business arrangement whereby one firm sells to another firm (for a fee or royalty) the right to use the first company's brand, patents, or manufacturing processes.

limited-function wholesaler A merchant wholesaler that performs only selected wholesaling functions.

limited-line store A type of retailing institution that has a narrow but deep product assortment, and its customer services tend to vary from store to store.

list price See *base price*.

logistics See *physical distribution*.

loss leaders Products whose prices are cut with the idea that they will attract customers to the store.

low involvement A purchase decision in which the consumer moves directly from need recognition to purchase, skipping the stages in between.

mail-order selling A type of nonstore, nonpersonal retail or wholesale selling in which the customer mails in an order that is then delivered by mail or other parcel-delivery system.

mall-intercept interview Personal interview conducted in a shopping centre mall.

mail survey The method of gathering data by means of a questionnaire mailed to respondents and, when completed, returned by mail.

management The process of planning, implementing, and evaluating the efforts of a group of people working towards a common goal. Same as *administration*.

manufacturers' agent An independent agent wholesaling middleman that sells part or all of a manufacturer's product mix in an assigned geographic territory.

manufacturer's sales branch A manufacturer's sales facility that carries a stock of the product being sold.

manufacturer's sales facility An establishment that primarily engages in wholesaling and is owned and operated by a manufacturer but is physically separated from manufacturing plants.

manufacturer's sales office A manufacturer's sales facility that does not carry a stock of the product being sold.

marginal analysis A method of price setting that considers both demand and costs to determine the best price for profit maximization.

marginal cost The cost of producing and selling one more unit; that is, the cost of the last unit produced or sold.

marginal revenue The income derived from the sale of the last unit.

markdown A reduction from the original retailing selling price, usually made because the store was unable to sell the product at the original price.

market People or organizations with wants to satisfy, money to spend, and the willingness to spend it.

market aggregation A strategy whereby an organization treats its total market as a unit — that is, as one mass market whose parts are considered to be alike in all major respects.

market development A product-market growth strategy in which a company continues to sell its present products, but to a new market.

market factor An item or element that (1) exists in a market, (2) may be measured quantitatively, and (3) is related to the demand for a good or service.

market-factor analysis A sales forecasting method based on the assumption that future demand for a product is related to the behaviour of certain market factors.

market index A market factor expressed as a percentage, or in another quantitative form, relative to some base figure.

market penetration A product-market growth strategy in which a company tries to sell more of its present products to its present markets.

market-penetration pricing See *penetration pricing*.

market potential   The total sales volume that all organizations selling a product during a stated time period in a specific market could expect to achieve under ideal conditions.

market segmentation   The process of dividing the total market for a product into several parts, each of which tends to be homogeneous in all significant aspects.

market share   The proportion of total sales of a product during a stated time period in a specific market that is captured by a single firm. Market share can refer to entire industries, narrow segments, or particular geographic areas and also can apply to past, present, or future time periods.

market-share analysis   A detailed analysis of the company's share of the market in total as well as by product line and market segment.

market-skimming pricing   See *skimming pricing*.

marketing   A total system of business activities designed to plan, price, promote, and distribute want-satisfying products to target markets in order to achieve organizational objectives.

marketing audit   A comprehensive review and evaluation of the marketing function in an organization — its philosophy, environment, goals, strategies, organizational structure, human and financial resources, and performance.

marketing concept   A philosophy of doing business that emphasizes customer orientation and coordination of marketing activities in order to achieve the organization's performance objectives.

marketing cost analysis   A detailed study of the ''operating expenses'' section of a company's profit and loss statement.

marketing information system   An on-going organized set of procedures and methods designed to generate, analyze, disseminate, store, and retrieve information for use in making marketing decisions.

marketing intermediary   An independent business organization that directly aids in the flow of products between a marketing organization and its markets.

marketing mix   A combination of the four elements — product, pricing structure, distribution system, and promotional activities—that comprise a company's marketing program.

marketing-orientation stage   The third stage in the evolution of marketing management, in which a company focuses on the needs of its customers and carries out a broad range of marketing activities.

marketing research   The process of specifying, assembling, and analyzing information used to identify and define marketing opportunities and problems; generate, refine, and evaluate marketing actions; monitor marketing performance; and improve understanding of marketing as a process.

markup   The dollar amount that is added to the acquisition cost of a product to determine the selling price.

Maslow's needs hierarchy   A needs structure consisting of five levels and organized according to the order in which people seek need gratification.

mass distribution   See *intensive distribution*.

merchant middleman   A firm that actually takes title to (i.e., owns) products that are being distributed.

merchant wholesaler   An independently owned firm that primarily engages in wholesaling and ordinarily takes title to the products being distributed. Same as *wholesaler*.

middleman   A firm that renders services directly related to the purchase and/or sale of a product as it flows from producer to consumer.

middleman's brand   A brand owned by a retailer or a wholesaler. Same as *private brand*.

missionary seller   A selling job in which the sales people are not expected to solicit orders but are expected to influence decision makers by building goodwill, performing promotional activites, and providing service to customers. In pharmaceuticals marketing, called detail sales person.

modified rebuy   In the business market, a purchasing situation between a new task and a straight rebuy in terms of time required, information needed, and alternatives considered.

motive   A need sufficiently stimulated that an individual is moved to seek satisfaction. Same as *drive*.

multiple buying influences   A situation in which a purchasing decision is influenced by more than one person in the buyer's organization.

multiple-segment strategy   A strategy that involves two or more groups of potential customers selected as target markets.

national brand   See *producer's brand*.

need recognition   The stage in the buying decision process in which the consumer is moved to action by a need.

neighbourhood shopping centre   A small group of stores situated around a supermarket and including other convenience-goods stores and specialty stores. Draws from a market located perhaps within 10 minutes by car.

new product   A vague term that may refer to (1) really innovative, truly unique products; (2) replacements for existing products that are significantly different from existing ones; or (3) imitative products that are new to the given firm.

new-product development process   Developmental stages that a new product goes through, starting with idea generation and continuing through idea screening, business analysis, limited production, test-marketing, and eventually commercialization (full-scale production and marketing.)

new-product strategy   A plan as to what role new products are to play in helping the company achieve its corporate and marketing goals.

new-task buying   In the business market, a purchasing situation in which a company for the first time considers buying a given item.

niche marketing   A strategy in which goods and services are tailored to meet the needs of small market segments.

noncumulative discount   A quantity discount based on the size of an individual order of products.

nonprice competition   A strategy in which a firm tries to compete based on some factor other than price—for example, promotion, product differentiation, or variety of services.

nonprofit organization   An organization in which profit is not an intended organizational goal.

nonstore retailing   Retailing activities resulting in transactions that occur away from a retail store.

objective   A desired outcome. Same as *goal*.

observational method   Gathering data by observing personally or mechanically the actions of a person.

odd pricing   A form of psychological pricing that consists of setting prices at odd amounts ($4.99 rather than $5.00, for example) in the belief that these seemingly low prices will result in larger sales volume.

off-price retailer   A type of retail institution, often found in the areas of apparel and shoes, that has a narrow and deep product assortment, emphasizes low prices, and offers few customer services.

off-price retailing   A strategy of selling well-known brands below the manufacturer's recommended retail price.

one-price strategy   A strategy under which a seller charges the same price to all customers of the same type who buy the same quantity of goods.

operating supplies   The "convenience goods" of the business market — short-lived, low-priced items purchased with a minimum of time and effort.

opinion leader   The member of a reference group who is the information source and who influences the decision making of others in the group.

organizational mission   The first step in strategic planning that defines the organization by asking the question, "What business are we in?"

organizational portfolio analysis   A key step in strategic planning that identifies the present status of each strategic business unit and determines its future role in the company.

organizational strategies   Broad, basic plans of action by which an organization intends to achieve its goals and fulfil its mission. These plans are for (1) the total organization in a small, single-product company or (2) each SBU in a large, multiproduct or multibusiness organization.

output performance measures   In sales force performance, indication of results produced.

outside order taker   A selling job in which sales people are primarily going to customers in the field.

packaging   The activities in product planning that involve designing and producing the container or wrapper for a product.

past-sales analysis   A method of sales forecasting that applies a flat percentage increase to the volume achieved last year, or to the average volume of the past few years, to predict future volume.

patronage buying motives   The reasons why a consumer chooses to shop at a certain store.

patterned interview   In sales force selection, an interviewing procedure in which the questions are planned in advance to ensure that all important issues are covered.

penetration pricing   A pricing strategy in which a low initial price is set to reach the mass market immediately. Same as *market-penetration pricing*.

percentage-of-sales method   A method of determining the promotional budget in which the amount is set as a certain percentage of past or forecasted future sales.

perception   Collecting and processing information from the environment in order to give meaning to the world around us.

perishability   A characteristic of a service indicating that it is highly perishable and cannot be stored.

personal interview   A face-to-face method of gathering data in a survey.

personal selling   The personal communication of information to persuade a prospective customer to buy a good, service, idea, or other product.

personality An individual's pattern of traits that influences behavioural responses.

physical distribution Activities involved in the flow of products as they move physically from producer to consumer or industrial user. Same as *logistics*.

physical distribution management The development and operation of efficient flow systems for products.

piggyback freight service The service of transporting loaded truck trailers on railroad flatcars.

pioneering advertising Primary-demand advertising in the introductory stage of the product life cycle.

place utility The utility created when a product is made readily accessible to potential customers.

planned obsolescence A product strategy designed to make an existing product out of date and thus to increase the market for replacement products. There are two forms: technological and style.

planning The process of deciding now what we are going to do later, including when and how we are going to do it.

positioning A company's strategies and actions related to favourably distinguishing itself and its products from competitors in the minds (and hearts) of selected groups of consumers.

possession utility The utility created when a customer buys the product — that is, ownership is transferred to the buyer.

postage-stamp pricing See *uniform delivered price*.

postpurchase behaviour Efforts by the consumer to reduce the anxiety often accompanying purchase decisions.

postpurchase service The final stage of the selling process, including delivery, financing, installation, routine maintenance, employee training, billing, and other areas important to customer statisfaction.

price The amount of money and/or products needed to acquire some combination of another product and its accompanying services.

price competition A strategy in which a firm regularly offers prices that are as low as possible, usually accompanied by a minimum of services.

price lining A retail pricing strategy whereby a store selects a limited number of prices and sells each item only at one of these selected prices.

pricing objective The goals that management tries to reach with its pricing structure and strategies.

primary data Original data gathered specifically for the project at hand.

primary demand The market demand for a general category of products (in contrast to the selective demand for a particular brand of the product).

primary-demand advertising Advertising designed to stimulate demand for a generic product.

private brand See *middleman's brand*.

private warehouse A warehouse that is owned and operated by the firm whose products are being stored and handled at the facility.

processing in transit A railroad in-transit shipping privilege under which a shipper can unload its product en route, have it processed, and then reload it to the final destination while being charged only the carload rate from the original shipping point to the final destination.

producer's brand A brand that is owned by a manufacturer or other producer. Same as *national brand*.

product A set of tangible attributes, including packaging, colour, price, quality, and brand, plus the services and reputation of the seller. A product may be a good, service, place, person, or idea.

product advertising Advertising intended to inform or stimulate the market about an organization's products.

product development A product-market growth strategy that calls for a company to develop new products to sell to its existing markets.

product differentiation The strategy in which one firm promotes the features of its product over competitors' brands offered to the same market.

product-liability claim A legal action alleging that an illness, accident, or death resulted from the named product because it was harmful, faulty, or inadequately labelled.

product life cycle The stages a product goes through from its introduction, to its growth and maturity, to its eventual decline and death (withdrawal from the market or deletion from the company's offerings).

product line A broad group of products, intended for essentially similar uses and possessing reasonably similar physical characteristics.

product manager An executive responsible for planning the marketing program for a given product or group of products. Same as *brand manager*.

product mix All products offered for sale by a company.

product positioning The decisions and activities involved in developing the intended image (in the customer's mind) for a product in relation to competitive products and to other products marketed by the same company.

product-related segmentation Market segmentation based on product usage rate or product benefits desired by consumers.

production-orientation stage The first stage in the evolution of marketing management, in which the basic assumption is that making a good product will ensure business success.

promotion The element in an organization's marketing mix that is used to inform, persuade, and remind the market regarding the organization and/or its products.

promotional allowance A price reduction granted by the seller as payment for promotional services rendered by the buyer.

promotional mix The combination of personal selling, advertising, sales promotion, publicity, and public relations that is intended to help an organization achieve its marketing objectives.

prospecting The stage in the personal selling process that involves developing a list of potential customers.

psychographic segmentation Market segmentation based on some aspect(s) of consumers' personality, life-style, or social class.

psychographics A concept in consumer behaviour that describes consumers in terms of a combination of psychological and sociological influences.

public relations A broad communications effort designed to build or maintain a favourable image for an organization with its various publics.

public-service advertising Advertising designed to improve the quality of life and indicate that the advertiser is a responsible member of the community.

public warehouse An independent firm that provides storage and handling facilities.

publicity A news presentation for a product or organization presented in any medium that is not paid for and has the credibility of editorial material.

''pull'' promotional strategy Promotional effort directed primarily at end users so they will ask middlemen for the product.

''push'' promotional strategy Promotional effort directed primarily at middlemen that are the next link forward in distribution channels.

qualifying The stage in the personal selling process in which the sales person determines if the prospect has both the willingness and capability to buy.

qualitative performance bases In sales force performance, judgmental indications of inputs and/or outputs.

quantitative performance bases In sales force performance, numerical measure of inputs and/or outputs.

quantity discount A reduction from list price when large quantities are purchased; offered to encourage buyers to purchase in large quantities.

questionnaire A data-gathering form used to collect the information in a personal, telephone, or mail survey.

rack jobber A merchant wholesaler that provides its customers with the display case or rack, stocks it, and price-marks the merchandise.

random sample A sample that is selected in such a way that every unit in the defined universe has an equal chance of being selected.

raw materials Business goods that have not been processed in any way and that will become part of another product.

recipient market See *client market*.

reciprocity The situation of ''I'll buy from you if you'll buy from me.''

reference group A group of people who influence a person's attitudes, values, and behaviour.

refusal to deal A situation in which a manufacturer desiring to select and perhaps control its channels may refuse to sell to some middlemen.

regional shopping centre The largest type of planned suburban shopping centre (sometimes large enough to be a mini-downtown). Usually includes two or more department stores and many limited-line stores, along with service institutions such as banks, theatres, restaurants, hotels, and office buildings.

reinforcement In learning theory, the satisfaction or dissatisfaction experienced as a result of behaviour.

repositioning The decision on the part of a business to alter the positioning of a brand or company so that it holds a different appeal or a different image for its target customers.

resale price maintenance A pricing policy whereby the manufacturer sets the retail price for a product.

reseller market Wholesaling and retailing middlemen that buy products for resale to other business users or to consumers. A segment of the business market.

resident buyer Independent agent located in central market who buys for wholesalers and retailers located in outlying areas.

responses In learning theory, the behavioural reactions to the drive and cues.

retail trade   See *retailing*.

retailer   A firm engaged primarily in retailing.

retailer cooperative   A type of contractual vertical marketing system that is formed by a group of small retailers who agree to establish and operate a whole-sale warehouse.

retailing   The sale, and all activities directly related to the sale, of goods and services to ultimate consumers for personal, nonbusiness use. Same as *retail trade*.

role ambiguity   Confusion among sales people about how much responsibility to assume in dealing with customers.

role conflict   The stress created for a sales person by the often contrary demands and expectations of his or her employer, customers, and family.

sales engineer   A selling job, often involving technically trained individuals selling some kind of sophisticated equipment, in which the emphasis is on the sales person's ability to explain the product to the prospect and perhaps to adapt it to the customer's particular needs.

sales-force composite   A method of forecasting sales that consists of collecting from all sales people and middlemen an estimate of sales in their territories during the forecasting period.

sales-force selection task   The three steps in assembling a sales force, consisting of (1) determining the number and type of people wanted by preparing a written job description, (2) recruiting an adequate number of applicants, and (3) selecting the most qualified persons from among the applicants.

sales forecast   An estimate of likely sales for one company's brand of a product during a stated time period in a specific market and assuming the use of a predetermined marketing plan.

sales-orientation stage   The second stage in the evolution of marketing management, in which the emphasis is on selling whatever the organization produces.

sales potential   The portion of market potential, applying only to one company's brand of a product, that a specific company could expect to achieve under ideal conditions.

sales promotion   Activities, including contests for sales people and consumers, trade shows, in-store displays, samples, premiums, and coupons, that are designed to supplement advertising and coordinate personal selling.

sales-volume analysis   A detailed study of the "net sales" section of a company's profit and loss statement.

satisfaction   The consumer condition when experience with a product equals or exceeds expectations.

scrambled merchandising   A strategy under which a middleman diversifies its assortment by adding product lines not traditionally carried by its type of business.

seasonal discount   A discount for placing an order during the seller's slow season.

secondary data   Information already gathered by somebody else for some other purpose.

selective attention   The process that limits our perceptions such that, of all the marketing stimuli our senses are exposed to, only those able to capture and hold our attention have the potential of being perceived.

selective demand   The market demand for an individual *brand* of a product, in contrast to the primary demand for the broad product category.

selective-demand advertising   Advertising that is intended to stimulate demand for individual brands.

selective distortion   The process of mentally altering information that is inconsistent with one's own beliefs or attitudes.

selective distribution   A strategy in which a producer sells its product through multiple, but not all, wholesalers and/or retailers in a market where a consumer might reasonably look for it.

selective retention   The process of retaining in memory some portion of what is perceived.

self-concept   A person's self-image.

self-image   The idea or image one has of oneself.

selling agent   A type of independent middleman that essentially takes the place of a manufacturer's marketing department, marketing the manufacturer's entire output and often influencing the design and/or pricing of the products.

service   An activity that is separately identifiable, intangible, and the main object of a transaction designed to provide want-satisfaction for customers.

service encounter   In services marketing, a customer's interaction with any service employee or with any tangible element, such as a service's physical surroundings.

service quality   The value that consumers perceive they are receiving from their purchase of services; generally very difficult to measure.

shopping centre   A planned grouping of retail stores in a multiunit structure, with the physical structure usually owned by a single organization.

shopping goods A class of consumer products that are purchased after the buyer has spent some time and effort comparing the price, quality, colour, and/or other attributes of alternative products.

shopping-mall intercept A method of gathering data by conducting personal interviews in central locations, typically regional shopping centres.

simulated test market A confidential variation of test marketing in which consumers are shown advertising for a product and then are allowed to "shop" in a test store in order to measure their reactions to the advertising, the product, or both.

single-segment concentration strategy The selection of one homogeneous segment from within a total market to be the target market.

single-source data A data-gathering method in which exposure to television advertising and product purchases can be traced to individual households.

singles Households that consist of just one person.

situation analysis The stage in a marketing research study that involves obtaining information about the company and its business environment by means of library research and extensive interviewing of company officials.

situational influences Temporary forces, associated with the immediate purchase environment, that affect behaviour.

skimming pricing A pricing strategy in which the initial price is set high in the range of expected prices. Same as *market-skimming pricing*.

social class A division of society based on education, occupation, and type of residential neighbourhood.

social environment Family, friends, and acquaintances who directly or indirectly provide information about products.

societal marketing concept A revised version of the marketing concept under which a company recognizes that it should be concerned about not only the buyers of a firm's product but also other people directly affected by the firm's operations and not only with tomorrow but also with the long term.

specialty goods A class of consumer products with perceived unique characteristics such that consumers are willing to expend special effort to buy them.

specialty store A type of retail institution concentrating on a specialized product line, or even part of a specialized product line.

stabilizing prices A pricing goal designed to achieve steady, nonvolatile prices in an industry.

Standard Industrial Classification (S.I.C.) system A coding system developed by the federal government that groups firms into similar types of businesses and thus enables a company to identify and analyze small segments of its market.

stimulus-response theory The theory that learning occurs as a person responds to some stimuli and is rewarded with need satisfaction for a correct response or penalized for an incorrect one.

storage An activity in physical distribution that creates time utility by holding and preserving products from the time of production until their sale.

straight commission compensation The method of sales force compensation in which payment is directly related to the tasks performed, usually the volume of the product(s) sold.

straight rebuy In the business market, a routine purchase with minimal information needs.

straight salary compensation The method of sales force compensation in which the sales person is paid a fixed amount, regardless of tasks performed or level of performance.

strategic business unit (SBU) A separate division for a major product or market in a multiproduct or multibusiness organization.

strategic company planning The level of planning that consists of (1) defining the organization's mission, (2) setting organizational objectives, (3) evaluating the firm's strategic business units, and (4) selecting appropriate strategies so as to achieve the organization's objectives.

strategic marketing planning The level of planning that consists of (1) conducting a situation analysis, (2) determining marketing objectives, (3) selecting target markets and measuring the market, and (4) designing a strategic marketing mix.

strategic planning The managerial process of matching a firm's resources with its market opportunities over the long run.

strategy A broad plan of action by which an organization intends to reach its objective(s).

style A distinctive presentation or construction in any art, product, or activity.

style obsolescence A product strategy in which superficial characteristics of a product are altered so that the new model is easily differentiated from the old one in order to make people dissatisfied with the old model. Same as *fashion obsolescence*.

subculture Groups that exhibit characteristic behaviour patterns sufficient to distinguish them from other groups within the same culture.

substitute products Two or more products that satisfy essentially the same need(s).

superego In Freudian psychology, the part of the mind that houses the conscience and directs instinctive drives into socially acceptable channels.

supermarket A type of retailing institution that has a moderately broad and moderately deep product assortment spanning groceries and some nonfood lines, that offers relatively few customer services, and that ordinarily emphasizes price in either an offensive or defensive way.

supermarket retailing A retailing method that features several related product lines, a high degree of self-service, largely centralized checkout, and competitive prices.

survey method A method of gathering data by interviewing a limited number of people (a sample) in person or by telephone or mail.

survey of buyer intentions A form of sales forecasting in which a firm asks a sample of current or potential customers how much of a particular product they would buy at a given price during a specified future time period.

syndicated data Research information that is purchased from a research supplier on a shared-cost basis by a number of clients.

tactic An operational means by which a strategy is to be implemented or activated.

target market A group of customers (people or organizations) at whom a seller aims its marketing effort.

target return A pricing goal that involves setting prices so as to achieve a certain percentage return on investment or on net sales.

task method A method of determining the promotional appropriation under which the organization first decides what is to be accomplished and then calculates how much it will cost to reach this goal. Same as buildup method.

telemarketing A form of nonstore retailing in which a sales person initiates contact with a shopper and also closes the sale over the telephone.

telephone survey A method of gathering data in a survey by interviewing people over the telephone.

territory manager A broadened concept of the sales job that includes identifying customers' needs, qualifying prospects, servicing customers, managing expenses, and collecting market intelligence.

test marketing A marketing research technique in which a firm markets its product in a limited geographic area, measures the sales, and then — from this sample — projects (a) the company's sales over a larger area and/or (b) consumers' response to a strategy before committing to a major marketing effort.

time utility The utility created when a product is available to customers when they want it.

total cost The sum of total fixed costs and total variable costs, or the full cost of a specific quantity produced or sold.

total cost concept In physical distribution, the optimization of the cost-profit relationship for the entire physical distribution system, rather than for individual activities.

trade discount A reduction from the list price, offered by a seller to buyers in payment for marketing activities that they will perform. Same as *functional discount*.

trademark A brand that is legally protected.

trademark licensing A business arrangement in which the owner of a trademark grants permission to other firms to use the owner's brand name, logotype, and/or character on the licensee's products in return for a royalty on sales of those products. Same as *brand licensing*.

trading down A product-line strategy wherein a company adds a lower-priced item to its line of prestige goods in order to reach a market that cannot afford the higher-priced items.

trading up A product-line strategy wherein a company adds a higher-priced, prestige product to its line in order to increase sales of the existing lower-priced products in that line and attract a higher-income market.

trend analysis A method of forecasting sales over the long term by using regression analysis, or over the short term by using a seasonal index of sales.

trial close The stage in the personal selling process when the sales person poses some ''either-or'' questions in such a way that the customer's answer is intended to close the sale.

trickle-across cycle In fashion adoption, a fashion cycle that moves horizontally within several social classes at the same time.

trickle-down cycle In fashion adoption, a fashion cycle that flows downward through several socioeconomic classes.

trickle-up cycle In fashion adoption, a fashion cycle by which a style becomes popular (fashionable) first with lower socioeconomic classes and then, later, with higher socioeconomic groups.

truck jobber A limited-function merchant wholesaler that carries a selected line of perishable products and delivers them by truck to retail stores.

tying contract A contract under which a manufacturer sells a product to a middleman only under the condition that this middleman also buys another (possibly unwanted) product from the manufacturer.

ultimate consumers People who buy products for their personal, nonbusiness use.

uniform delivered price A geographic pricing strategy whereby the same delivered price is quoted to all buyers regardless of their location. Same as *postage-stamp pricing*.

unit pricing A form of price reporting where the price is stated per kilogram, litre, or some other standard measure in order to aid consumers in comparison shopping.

unsought goods A type of consumer product that consists of new products the consumer is not yet aware of or products the consumer does not yet want.

unstructured interview In sales force selection, an interviewing procedure in which the interviewer is permitted the freedom to ask questions and explore issues as they develop in the flow of the interview.

users The people in a buying centre who actually use a particular product.

utility The attribute in an item that makes it capable of satisfying human wants.

valid test In selection, an employment test that accurately predicts job performance.

value The quantitative measure of the worth of a product to attract other products in exchange.

variable cost A cost that varies of changes directly in relation to the number of units produced or sold.

variable-price strategy See *flexible-price strategy*.

vertical business market A situation where a given product is usable by virtually all the firms in only one or two industries.

vertical conflict A form of channel conflict occurring between firms at different levels of the same channel, typically producer versus wholesaler or producer versus retailer.

vertical cooperative advertising Advertising in which firms at different levels of the distribution channel share the cost.

vertical marketing system (VMS) A tightly coordinated distribution channel designed to achieve operating efficiencies and marketing effectiveness.

voluntary chain A type of contractual vertical marketing system that is sponsored by a wholesaler who enters into a contract with interested retailers.

warehouse club A combined retailing and wholesaling institution that has a very broad but very shallow product assortment with very low prices and few customer services and is open only to members. Same as *wholesale club*.

warehousing A broad range of physical distribution activities that include storage, assembling, bulk breaking, and preparing products for shipping.

wheel of retailing The cyclical pattern of changes in retailing, whereby a new type of store enters the market as a low-cost, low-price store and over time takes business away from unchanging competitors; eventually, the successful new retailer trades up, incurring higher costs and higher prices and making the institution vulnerable to a new type of retailer.

wholesale club See *warehouse club*.

wholesaler See *merchant wholesaler*.

wholesaling All activities directly related to the sale of goods and services to parties for resale, use in producing other goods and services, or operating an organization.

wholesaling middleman A firm engaged primarily in wholesaling.

wholly owned subsidiary A business arrangement in foreign markets in which a company owns the foreign operation in order to gain maximum control over its marketing program and production operations.

zone-delivered price A geographic pricing strategy whereby the same delivered price is charged at any location within each geographic zone. Some as *parcel-post pricing*.

TOPICAL INDEX

COMPANY AND BRAND NAME INDEX

CREDITS

Page 348: Courtesy of The Maritime Life Assurance Company

Page 360: Courtesy of the Gillette Company

Page 361: Paul Margolies/Research Plus

Page 366: Tom Young/The Stock Market

Page 369: Courtesy of Merecedes-Benz Canada Inc.

Page 371: Courtesy of Toronto Transit Commission

Page 375: Courtesy of Petro-Canada

Page 381: Rick Bruner/Light Images

Page 408: Courtesy of Canadian Airlines International

Page 411: Charles Weckler, The Image Bank

Page 419: Catherine Gehm/Light Images

Page 421: Dan Kewley

Page 422: Bob Curtis

Page 426: Courtesy of Journey's End Corporation

Page 428: Courtesy of The National Ballet of Canada

Page 440: UTICA is a registered trademark of J.P. Stevens Enterprises, a Division of WestPoint Pepperell, Inc. By permission

Page 444: (top) William Johnson/Stock Market. (centre) Max Winter/Stock, Boston. (bottom) George Gardner/The Image Works

Page 452: Christos/Light Images

Page 454: Courtesy of Ports International and Ogilvy in Montreal

Page 458: Courtesy of United Colors of Benetton.

Page 460: Bob Curtis

Page 462: Gray Hofheimer

Page 470: Courtesy of Home Hardware

Page 478: Courtesy of G.N. Johnston Equipment Co. Ltd.

Page 482: Henley & Savage/The Stock Market

Page 485: Photo courtesy of Bull HN Info Systems, Inc.

Page 490: Courtesy of Midas Canada Inc.

Page 497: Photo courtesy of Viliam with special thanks, and Marketing Magazine

Page 499: (left) Courtesy of Eaton's, (right) Courtesy of North's Decorating Services Ltd. Coboconk, Ontario

Page 503: From top left, clockwise: Courtesy of Mr Submarine Limited; Courtesy of First Choice ® HairCutters; Courtesy of Ultramar Canada Inc.; Courtesy of Thrifty Car Rental; Courtesy of Kwik-Kopy Printing Canada Corporation; Courtesy of Midas Canada Inc.

Page 508: Courtesy of Consumers Distributing Co. Ltd.

Page 515: Courtesy of Canada Catering Co. Limited

Page 518: Courtesy of CMHC Granville Island

Page 546: Courtesy of General Tire

Page 553: Courtesy of Thomas J. Lipton

Page 554: (top) Courtesy of Volkswagen Canada Inc. (bottom) Courtesy of Levi Strauss & Co. (Canada) Inc.

Page 555: Gene Anthony/Research Plus

Page 564: Courtesy of Playtex Ltd.

Page 572: Courtesy of © Telegraph Colour Library/ Masterfile

Page 575: Jon Feingersh/Stock, Boston

Page 583: Pete Saloutos/The Stock Market

Page 588: Century 21 Real Estate Corporation

Page 589: Bob Kinmonth

Page 596: Courtesy of Everfresh Juice Co.

Page 599: Copyright of Joseph E. Seagram & Sons, Limited © 1990

Page 600: Courtesy of Canada Pork

Page 602: Courtesy of Marlin Travel

Page 605: Courtesy of Johnson & Johnson Inc.

Page 611: Courtesy of Evian

Page 615: Courtesy of Warner-Lambert Canada, Inc.

Page 620: Courtesy of Industrial Trade & Consumer Shows Inc.

Page 622: Courtesy of Trimark Investment Management Inc.

Page 638: Margot Granitsas/The Image Works

Page 642: Courtesy of Bombardier Inc.

Page 645: Benetton Services, Corp.

Page 649: Francie Manning/The Picture Cube

Page 655: Courtesy of Northern Telecom

Page 661: Robert Wallis/SIPA Press

Page 670: Courtesy of Procter & Gamble Inc.

Page 673: Courtesy of Hewlett Packard

Page 678: Light Images

Page 682: Courtesy of Panasonic

Page 694: Courtesy of Lever Brothers, Inc.

Page 697: Courtesy of Amex Bank of Canada

Page 698: Fred McConnaughey/Photo Researchers

Page 709: Herb Snitzer/Stock, Boston

Page 712: Courtesy of Imperial Oil

Page 714: Courtesy of the Environmental Choice Program

Page 716: Courtesy of Eveready

STUDENT REPLY CARD

In order to improve future editions, we are seeking your comments on *FUNDAMENTALS OF MARKETING*, Sixth Canadian Edition, by Sommers, Barnes, Stanton, Etzel & Walker.

After you have read this text, please answer the following questions and return this form via Business Reply Mail. *Thanks in advance for your feedback!*

1. Name of your college or university: _____

2. Major program of study: _____

3. Your instructor for this course: _____

4. Are there any sections of this text which were not assigned as course reading?
   If so, please specify those chapters or portions:

5. How would you rate the overall accessibility of the content? Please feel free to comment on reading level, writing style, terminology, layout and design features, and such learning aids as chapter objectives, summaries, and appendices.

6. What did you like *best* about this book?

7. What did you like *least*?

If you would like to say more, we'd love to hear from you. Please write to us at the address shown on the reverse of this card.

--------------------------------- CUT HERE ---------------------------------

CUT HERE

------------------------------ FOLD HERE ------------------------------

**BUSINESS
REPLY MAIL**

No Postage Stamp
Necessary if Mailed
in Canada

Postage will be paid by

7115

Attn: Sponsoring Editor, Business

The College Division
McGraw-Hill Ryerson Limited
300 Water Street
Whitby, Ontario
L1N 9Z9

TAPE SHUT